Adventures of Rabbah & Friends

Program in Judaic Studies
Brown University
Box 1826
Providence, RI 02912

BROWN JUDAIC STUDIES

Edited by

Katharina Galor
Jae Han
David C. Jacobson
Paul Nahme
Saul M. Olyan
Rachel Rojanski
Michael L. Satlow
Adam Teller

Number 374
ADVENTURES OF RABBAH & FRIENDS
by
James Adam Redfield

ADVENTURES OF RABBAH & FRIENDS

THE TALMUD'S STRANGE TALES AND THEIR READERS

by
James Adam Redfield

Brown Judaic Studies
Providence, Rhode Island

© 2025 Brown University. All rights reserved.

"Excerpts from Psalms." Copyright © 2007 by Robert Alter, from *The Hebrew Bible: A Translation with Commentary*, translated by Robert Alter. Used by permission of W. W. Norton & Company, Inc.

A previous version of chapter 5 has appeared as James Adam Redfield, "The Iridescence of Scripture: Inner-Talmudic Interpretation and Palestinian Midrash," in *Studies in Rabbinic Narratives*, vol. 1, ed. Jeffrey L. Rubenstein, BJS 367 (Providence, RI: Brown Judaic Studies, 2021), 115–75.

No part of this work may be reproduced or transmitted in any form or by any means, electronic or mechanical, including photocopying and recording, or by means of any information storage or retrieval system, except as may be expressly permitted by the 1976 Copyright Act or in writing from the publisher. Requests for permission should be addressed in writing to the Rights and Permissions Office, Program in Judaic Studies, Brown University, Box 1826, Providence, RI 02912, USA.

Library of Congress Control Number: 2025935734

For my father, who thinks with a sense of humor
σοφία ἀνθρώπου φωτιεῖ πρόσωπον αὐτοῦ

Signs are small measurable things, but interpretations are illimitable, and in girls of sweet, ardent nature, every sign is apt to conjure up wonder, hope, belief, vast as a sky, and coloured by a diffused thimbleful of matter in the shape of knowledge. They are not always too grossly deceived; for Sinbad himself may have fallen by good luck on a true description, and wrong reasoning sometimes lands poor mortals in right conclusions: starting a long way off the true point, and proceeding by loops and zigzags, we now and then arrive just where we ought to be.

— George Eliot, *Middlemarch*

Contents

Note on the Text	xi
Sources and Abbreviations	xiii
Complete Textual Witnesses	xiii
Partial Textual Witnesses	xiii
Medieval and Early Modern Talmud Commentators	xiii
Cited Editions of Rabbinic Works	xiv
Reference Works	xvi
Journals and Book Series	xvii
Other Abbreviations	xviii
Introduction: An Interpretive History of Nonsense	1
Meaning Is Reading	1
The Reader	14
The Tales	24
The Teller	27
Collection and Recollecting	38
The Telling	43
The Canon	47
The Constellation of Reading	50
1. Genre Trouble!	57
Tractate	58
Apocalyptic	62
Tall Tale	65
Myth as Cultural History	70
Myth as Narrative Cosmology	73
Exegesis	76
Genres for the Reader	81
2. The Sea Still Resists: Between Myth and *Midrash*	83
Midrash as Fugue: Excavating the Understory	87
The Storm as Framing Device	88
Order over Chaos	93

viii   *Contents*

YHWH's Arsenal	96
A White Shoot of Flame	96
The Priestly Crown	100
The Work of Re-revelation	103
Dramatizing Divine Ontology	105
A Man of War	105
Fires Strange and Familiar	108
Parting the Sea(s)	111
Point/Counterpoint	119
3. Genealogy and Birth of the Literary Collection	123
Placement	125
Boundaries	129
Structure	132
Voice	132
Setting	135
Attributions and Other Introductory Formulae	138
The Uses of Repetition	148
Poetry	154
Summary	164
Chronological Layers	166
4. A Wonderful World and the Romance of the East	177
Beyond Jewish Hellenization	180
How Greek is the Talmud?	184
The Genres of Wonder	186
History and Ethnography	186
Paradoxography	193
Parallel (Anti-)Heroes	197
From Wonder to Romance: Another Risky Swim	200
Believe It or Not: Fictionalizing Wonders in Late Antiquity	212
Two Seasons in Hell	213
Double Vision	216
5. The Iridescence of Scripture: Inner-Talmudic Interpretations	225
From Wonder to Eschatology	227
The Heavenly Banquet and the Eschatological Tabernacle	230
Doubting Thomas in the Study-House	236
Keywords, Catchphrases, and the Rebirth of a Theme	241
Beyond the *Sugya* and Back to the Sources	255
6. The Allegorical Canon	259
Twice Upon a Time: The Art of *Peshat*	265

The Breakdown of *Peshat*	269
Allegory as *Midrash*	275
Allegory Emancipated	284
The Plain Sense of Allegory	295
The Other Story (*Déjà Vu*)	307
Acknowledgments	311
Appendixes	
1. Translation (Part 1 & Part 2)	313
2. Edition of Part 1	341
3. Parallels to Part 2 in Pesiqta of Rab Kahana	367
4. Thieves in Heaven (?!) Heaven Forbid: A Geonic Apologetic	371
5. Commentary on Tale III by Elyaqum Getz	377
6. Commentary on Tale II by the Gra (Vilna Gaon)	383
Bibliography	387
Indexes	421
Sources	421
Subjects and Names	433

Note on the Text

This is a study of the interpretive history of a text that is best known as a thematically distinct section of the Babylonian Talmud in its tractate of civil law Baba Batra ("The Last Gate"), folia 73a–75b in the standard edition of reference (Vilna: Widow and Brothers Romm, 1880–1886). The text has two parts: strange tales, followed by interpretations of biblical verses—mostly from Isaiah and Job—about Leviathan and messianic visions of Jerusalem, as well as one rabbinic story. I will refer to this text as Part 1 ("the tales/stories") and Part 2; as one "collection" versus another; or as the whole "composition" of both. As most of the book (Introduction; chapters 2, 3, and 4) focuses on the history of Part 1, I also call it "our tales/stories" or "our collection."

An annotated translation may be found in an Appendix. The Translation of Part 1 is based on a manuscript (ms. H; see below), the Translation of Part 2 is based on the Vilna print. The Edition of Part 1, on which the text body and variant readings in its Translation are based, is also in an Appendix. The Edition and the Translation of Part 1 are referenced throughout the book by different numerals—Hebrew for the Edition; Roman and Arabic for the Translation—according to unit and line number. For example, Unit 15 Line 188 in the Edition is טו.קפ"ח; in the Translation, it is XV.188. A reference to Unit 15 alone is טו or XV; a reference to Unit 3a is IIIa or ג"א (depending, again, on which language is referenced). A cross-referenced section of any work, including this one, is preceded by §.

Unless otherwise noted, purely for stylistic reasons, the English translation used for the Hebrew Bible is the King James Version (KJV), with noted modifications if required by context, and reference to other translations. Masoretic verse numbers are added in parentheses if they differ from KJV.

All translations of sources and modern scholarship are mine if not otherwise noted.

I transliterate Hebrew, Aramaic/Syriac, and Greek according to the general-purpose conventions of the *Society of Biblical Literature Handbook of Style,* 2nd ed. (Atlanta: SBL Press, 2014), if transliteration can help readers to recognize a wordplay, etymology, or other poetic effect. (For the same reason, in chapter 3 §*Poetry*, I modify this transliteration system as noted there so that a reader has better access to the sounds of the original.) I transcribe these languages in their own scripts if transliteration has no such advantage.

Rather than appear in the Bibliography, all of my individual published and unpublished works cited in the notes are freely available via my website https://jamesadamredfield.omeka.net, including a supplement to this volume about the tales' textual history and their prior editions/translations, cited at n. 1 below.

Sources and Abbreviations

Complete Textual Witnesses
(see Appendix §*Edition*)

ה/H	Hamburg 19 (165)–*Thesaurus*, 7106	
פ/P	Paris 1337–*Thesaurus*, 8220	
ו/V	Vatican 115.II.2–*Thesaurus*, 7395	
ב/O	Oxford Bodleian Opp. 249 (369)– *Thesaurus*, 630	
מ/M	Munich 95–*Thesaurus*, 7204	
א/E	Escorial G-I-3 (1115)–*Thesaurus*, 8010	

The text body of the §*Edition* is based on ms. ה. In the notes, I list the reading of ms. פ; followed by full witnesses in estimated chronological order of completion (וו, ב, מ, א); then partial witnesses. To stress relationships among witnesses, I may list variants in another order.

Partial Textual Witnesses
(Appendix §*Edition*.
The range covered refers to Vilna by folio-side and line)

⁰פ/F Florence Biblioteca Nazionale Centrale II.1.9. Covers 73a.17 (אמ' רבא)-73a.27 (נאם ייי וגו')–*Thesaurus*, 468

⁰נ/N New York JTS Rab. 2308. Covers 73b.39 (לדוכתא פלנית)-74b.22 (גומרי דריתמא)–*Thesaurus*, 6075

⁰ב/B Bologna Archivio di Stato Fr. ebr. 420. Covers 74a.18 (הוא סבר)-74b.22 (דריתמא הוי)–*Thesaurus*, 288

⁰ק/C Cambridge T-S F 1(1).30. Covers 74b.18 (אמ' לי הונא בר נתן)-74b.22 (גומרי דריתמ')–*Thesaurus*, 2037

Medieval and Early Modern Talmud Commentators

Except the eleventh-century commentary misattributed in the Vilna print to Rabbenu Gershom of Mainz (960–1040); the lesser-known Polish authority Rabbi Elyaqum Getz (1643–1705); and authorities cited only once, I use traditional names, based on the Hebrew acronyms for their personal names (some dates are approximate):

Rif   Yitshaq ben Yaaqov ha-Kohen Alfasi (1013–1103), Fes
Rashi   Shlomo Yitshaqi (1040–1105), Troyes
Rashbam   Shmuel ben Meir (1085–1174), France
Ramban   Moses ben Nahman (1194–1270), Girona
Tosafot ("Supplements")
           The school of the Tosafists (mostly eleventh–thirteenth centuries), northern France and Rhineland
Rashba   Shlomo ben Avraham ibn Aderet (1235–1310), Barcelona
Ritva   Yom Tov Asevilli (fl. ca. 1320), Seville and Saragossa
Maharshal Shlomo Luria (1510–1573), Poland
Ari   Isaac ben Solomon Luria (1534–1572), Cairo and Safed
Maharal   Yehudah Loew (1525–1609), Prague. For the literature on his uncertain birth year, see Byron L. Sherwin, *Mystical Theology and Social Dissent: The Life and Works of Judah Loew of Prague,* (1982; repr., Oxford: Littman Library, 2006), 189.
Maharsha   Shmuel Eliezer Eidels (1555–1631), Poland
Gra (Vilna Gaon)
           Elijah ben Solomon Zalman (1720–1797), Lithuania

Cited Editions of Rabbinic Works

Ber. Rab.   Bereshit Rabbah
            Julius Theodor and Ch. Albeck, eds., *Midrash Bereschit Rabbah*, 3 vols., 2nd ed. (Jerusalem: Wahrmann, 1965).
Ex. Rab.   Exodus Rabbah
            Midrash Rabbah ha-mevo'ar (Jerusalem: Makhon Midrash ha-mevo'ar, 1983)
            Avigdor Shinan, ed., *Midrash Shemot Rabbah, Parashot 1–14* (Jerusalem: Dvir, 1984).
Kallah Rab. Kallah Rabbati, in *Massekhtot Kallah*, ed. Michael Higger (New York: Jewish Theological Seminary, 1936), 167–344.
Lam. Rab.   Lamentations Rabbah
            Solomon Buber, ed., *Midrash Eikhah Rabbah* (Vilna: Widow & Brothers Romm, 1899).
MdRSBY   Mekhilta of Rabbi Shimon bar Yohai
            W. David Nelson, ed. and trans., *Mekhilta de-Rabbi Shimon bar Yohai* (Philadelphia: Jewish Publication Society, 2006).
Midr. Ps.   Midrash on Psalms
            Solomon Buber, ed., *Midrash Tehillim ha-mekhuneh Shoher Tov* (Vilna: Widow & Brothers Romm, 1891; repr., Jerusalem: Hotsa'at Midrash, 1967).

Sources and Abbreviations   xv

Mishnah   Hanokh Albeck, ed., *Shishah Sidre Mishnah*, 6 vols. (Jerusalem: Mossad Bialik, 1955–1959).
Num. Rab.   Numbers Rabbah
              Midrash Rabbah ha-mevo'ar (Jerusalem: Makhon Midrash ha-mevo'ar, 1983).
Pesiq. Rab Kah.
              Pesiqta of Rab Kahana
              Bernard Mandelbaum, ed., *Pesiqta' de Rab Kahana*, 2 vols. (New York: Jewish Theological Seminary, 1962).
Pirqe R. El. Pirqe Rabbi Eliezer
              Dagmar Börner-Klein, ed. and trans., *Pirke de-Rabbi Elieser* (Berlin: de Gruyter, 2004).
Vay. Rab.   Vayyiqra Rabbah
              Mordecai Margulies, ed., *Midrash Wayyikra Rabbah: A Critical Edition Based on Manuscripts and Genizah Fragments with Variants and Notes*, 5 vols. (Jerusalem: American Academy for Jewish Research, 1953–1960).
Qoh. Rab.   Qohelet Rabbah
              Menahem Hirshman, ed., *Midrash Kohelet Rabbah 1–6* (Jerusalem: Schechter Institute, 2016); Reuven Kiperwasser, ed., *Midrishei Kohelet: Kohelet Rabbah 7–12, Kohelet Zuta 7–9* (Jerusalem: Schechter Institute, 2021).
Sifre Deut.   Sifre Deuteronomy
              Louis Finkelstein, ed., *Sifre on Deuteronomy* (New York: Jewish Theological Seminary of America, 1969).
Sifre Num.   Sifre Numbers
              H. S. Horovitz, ed., *Siphre d'Be Rab: Siphre ad Numeros adjecto Siphre Zutta* (Leipzig: Fock, 1917).
              Menahem Kahana, ed., *Sifre on Numbers: An Annotated Edition* [Hebrew], 4 vols. (Jerusalem: Magnes, 2015).
Sof.   Soferim
              Michael Higger, ed., *Masseket Soferim* (New York: Jewish Theological Seminary, 1937).
Tanh.   Tanhuma
              John T. Townsend, ed. and trans., *Midrash Tanḥuma*, 3 vols. (Hoboken, NJ; Jersey City: Ktav, 1989–2003).
              Solomon Buber, ed., *Midrash Tanhuma*, 2 vols. (Vilna; repr., Jerusalem: Ortsel, 1963).
Tan. Yel.   Tanhuma Yelammedenu
              Samuel A. Berman, ed. and trans., *Midrash Tanhuma-Yelammedenu* (Hoboken, NJ: Ktav, 1995).
Tg.   Targumim
              Cited from *CAL* unless otherwise noted.

Tosefta   Saul Lieberman, ed., *Tosefta*, 4 vols. (New York: Jewish Theological Seminary, 1955–1988)
y.   *Talmud Yerushalmi According to Ms. Or. 4720 (Scal. 3) of the Leiden University Library with Restorations and Corrections* (Jerusalem: Academy of the Hebrew Language, 2001) (cited as y., tractate, halakhah, folio and side in the standard edition of reference: Venice: Bomberg, 1523, per the margins of this edition).
Yal.   Yalqut Shimeoni
               Yitshaq Shiloni et al., eds., *Yalqut Shimeoni 'al ha-Torah*, 9 vols. (Jerusalem: Mossad ha-Rav Kook, 1973–1991).

Reference Works

CAL   The Comprehensive Aramaic Lexicon, Hebrew Union College–Jewish Institute of Religion. https://cal.huc.edu (accessed July 17, 2024).
DS   Raphael Nathan Neta Rabbinovicz, *Diqduqe Soferim Baba Batra* (Munich: Huber, 1881), 223–32.
FJMS   "Hachi Garsinan" database, Friedberg Jewish Manuscript Society. http://www.fjms.org (accessed July 17, 2024).
FTP   Fragment Targum, ms. Paris (Bibliothèque nationale 110; cited via *CAL*)
JBA   Michael Sokoloff, *A Dictionary of Jewish Babylonian Aramaic of the Talmudic and Geonic Periods* (Ramat-Gan: Bar Ilan University Press, 2002).
JPA   Michael Sokoloff, *A Dictionary of Jewish Palestinian Aramaic of the Byzantine Period.* (Ramat-Gan: Bar Ilan University Press, 1990).
LXX   The Septuagint (Greek Bible). Alfred Rahlfs and Robert Hanhart, *Septuaginta: Editio altera* (Stuttgart: Deutsche Bibelgesellschaft, 2006).
Ma'agarim   The Academy of the Hebrew Language. "Ma'agarim: The Historical Dictionary Project." https://maagarim.hebrew-academy.org.il (accessed July 17, 2024).
MT   Masoretic Text (Hebrew Bible). Karl Elliger and Wilhelm Rudolph, eds., *Biblia Hebraica Stuttgartensia*, 5th ed. (Stuttgart: Deutsche Bibelgesellschaft, 1997).
PGR   Alexander Giannini, ed., *Paradoxographorum Graecorum reliquiae* (Milan: Istituto editoriale italiano, 1966).
"the Talmud"
               Babylonian Talmud (cited as b., followed by tractate, followed by folio and side) unless Palestinian Talmud is noted.

Thesaurus   Yaakov Sussmann, in collaboration with Yoav Rosenthal and Aharon Shweka, *Thesaurus of Talmudic Manuscripts*, 3 vols. (Jerusalem: Yad Ben-Zvi, 2012), accessible via *FJMS* (accessed 17 July 2024 [Hebrew]).

Journals and Book Series

AB	Anchor Bible
AcOr	*Acta Orientalia*
AJEC	Ancient Judaism and Early Christianity
AJSR	*Association for Jewish Studies Review*
BJS	Brown Judaic Studies
BUFM	*Beiträge zur Ur- und Frühgeschichte Mitteleuropas*
BZAW	Beihefte zur Zeitschrift für die alttestamentliche Wissenschaft
CHANE	Culture and History of the Ancient Near East
ClAnt	*Classical Antiquity*
CP	*Classical Philology*
CRINT	Compendia Rerum Iudaicarum ad Novum Testamentum
DJD	Discoveries in the Judaean Desert
HSCP	*Harvard Studies in Classical Philology*
HTR	*Harvard Theological Review*
HUCA	*Hebrew Union College Annual*
ISBL	Indiana Studies in Biblical Literature
JAAR	*Journal of the American Academy of Religion*
JAJ	*Journal of Ancient Judaism*
JAJSup	Journal of Ancient Judaism Supplements
JHS	*Journal of Hellenic Studies*
JJS	*Journal of Jewish Studies*
JQR	*Jewish Quarterly Review*
JSJ	*Journal for the Study of Judaism*
JSJSup	Journal for the Study of Judaism Supplements
JSQ	*Jewish Studies Quarterly*
MGWJ	*Monatsschrift für Geschichte und Wissenschaft des Judenthums*
PAAJR	*Proceedings of the American Academy of Jewish Research*
REJ	*Revue des études juives*
RHR	*Revue de l'histoire des religions*
ScrHier	Scripta Hierosolymitana
SIr	*Studia Iranica*
SJ	Studia Judaica
SJLA	Studies in Judaism in Late Antiquity
STDJ	Studies on the Texts of the Desert of Judah
StPB	Studia Post-Biblica

TBN	Themes in Biblical Narrative
TSAJ	Texte und Studien zum antiken Judentum
VTSup	Supplements to Vetus Testamentum
WUNT	Wissenschaftliche Untersuchungen zum Neuen Testament
ZDMG	Zeitschrift der deutschen morganländischen Gesellschaft

Other Abbreviations

ms., mss.	manuscript, manuscripts
R.	Rabbi (an authority from Roman Palestine; Babylonian equivalent: "Rav")
s.v.	*sub verbo/sub verbum* (a citation of a medieval commentary on the following word/words)
Tg.	Targum

Introduction

An Interpretive History of Nonsense

Narishkayt iz narishkayt, nor di geshikhte fun narishkayt heyst visnshaft.
Nonsense is nonsense, but the history of nonsense is scholarship.
– Aphorism of Saul Lieberman
(retrojected into his Lithuanian Yiddish)

Meaning Is Reading

This is a book about stories that tells a story of its own. It works out a method over a series of interlocking arguments, arranged by chapters and by sections within chapters. The global integrity of those arguments depends on you, the reader. I will interrupt from time to time, prompting you to rearrange the pieces of each argument to keep them in line with the method. But what I say when I interfere in your reading process, let alone why I do so, will affect this book's meaning for you far less than whatever catches your attention and how you choose to read it yourself. Paradoxically, that might be the best demonstration of the method. In spite of what an author wants, a book has a life of its own (the better the book, the more so). The book creates its readers, who re-create the book. There is no stepping out of this circle. Nor is the reader static: each reader's selective, time-bound attention plays a vital role in recreating what "the" book is. And so, while they often say that there are as many books as there are readers, in reality there are many more, because no one can read a whole book at once. Readers gravitate to parts or aspects of a book and grow attached to them. They begin to see the book through those partial readings. Over time, for them, each act of their reading blurs with the book as they traverse its content over and over. In this way—gradually, not always intentionally—parts or aspects of stories take the place of entire stories; acts of reading turn into ways of reading; and each book joins a library that remains just as imaginary as the book as a whole.

On the other hand (there will be many other hands), no reader creates a book *ex nihilo*. We make our own books but not as we please. Peering through the lattices of other readers, following traces that they have left for us like marginalia or names on a library card, each of our acts of reading responds to theirs. Not only what we select in the book for our attention, but also how our reading will proceed thereafter, are both constrained and enabled by others' past selections. They have highlighted certain pages; drawn lines between others; cut, pasted, glossed, censored. Our book, full of their life, passes from mouth to mouth and hand to hand. In the process, its contents change. So does its canon: its library of potentially related books. Not even the act of placing this book by some, while distancing it from others, is ours alone. We pick up a book because it is there for us. We see it in light of others because they are nearby. We can access the book only as it was made legible for us, in a certain way, by other readers. Yet they and we are not the same. Each of us is always free to read the same book differently.

As a result, the meaning of any book, for you and me, is both less and more than what it says. Less, because we are never really reading the Book as such. The Book, in its totality, remains a horizon or background against which our selective acts of attention are configured. Yet any book is also more than itself, insofar as it preserves the real presence of other readers. As their selections guide our own, our book becomes a shared creation. We rediscover the book through its readers and they return to the book through us. Only in this sense can we — mere mortals of rational conscious mind — say that a book "has" a meaning. Even if it did have some original meaning that stood apart from encounters between readers — the author's intention, for instance — such meaning would be a tree falling in the forest, no one left to observe it. The myth that a transcendental meaning once existed, and must be recovered through our reading, surely changes the status of some Books as imaginary wholes. It expands their aura as sacred or "classic." For such Books, encounters between readers often stand in the shadow of this myth. Yet even in such exceptional cases, the myth becomes real and meaningful again only by means of an act of reading; by juxtaposing the real book as we remake it now — in our free and creative selectivity — with a book that past readers have thumbed over for us. One Book in many hands.

* * * * *

Regardless of whether all this is true in general, I do think it is true for a collection of tales in the Talmud. In our study of what they have meant to diverse readers over roughly fifteen centuries, I hope to develop this way of thinking about interpretation as a creative process; mediated but never determined by tradition and authorial, editorial, or academic conventions. Unlike most other methods arising from the study of rabbinic sources, ours is comparative by both necessity and design. It greets the challenge of interpreting interpreters across periods and cultures by framing their relationships with a constellation of interpretive dynamics that they all share at a higher level of analysis; rather than by applying a narrower literary theory, genre category, or historical-cultural context. Instead of analyzing readers' meanings as superficially different effects of such scholarly constructs, this constellation works in the reverse direction. By determining factors in interpretation that all readers shared, and showing why they reached different results anyway, we can find the differences that mattered to the readers themselves.

To begin with, by my definition, everyone we encounter will qualify as a "reader" of the tales. But defining "the" tales is itself a creative act that readers chose to perform in many ways. Consider variant versions of the text. In English, these tales are best known in translations based on the Talmud's standard print, easily found online. My translation, based not on that print but on a manuscript,[1] appears in our Appendix, with footnotes from other manuscripts and commentaries ("witnesses"), where each word of each tale was transmitted in variant forms ("readings"). At a glance, then, we can see that these tales have always existed not in one but in many slightly different versions, indicating different interpretations or performances (what I will call "tellings") of their content by scribes and other transmitters. That said, nowhere does their content vary so much from text to text as to yield distinct narratives; all witnesses transmit the same stories in a fixed order, with minimal exceptions.[2] I have divided them into twenty-one tales, some subdivided into two episodes.[3] Before you proceed, I would ask you to read the Translation in the Appendix carefully (Part 1 has the tales; leave aside Part 2 for now). Every reader whom we will get to know in the course of this book was familiar with at least some of these tales, so we should hold the whole collection in mind. Passages are quoted occasionally and (like every other reader) we will not pay equal attention to each tale. But all of the book's arguments, including the rest of this general Introduction, will bring us back to the tales on many levels—from a granular variant reading to the wider Jewish

---

1. For a discussion of each textual witness with bibliography, see Redfield, "Textual Witnesses, Editions, and Translations of the Tales of Rabbah bar bar Hanah & Friends," on my website (see §*Note on the Text*). On the "standard" Vilna print of the Talmud, see Michael Stanislawski, "The 'Vilna Shas' and East European Jewry," in *Printing the Talmud: From Bomberg to Schottenstein*, ed. Sharon Lieberman Mintz and Gabriel M. Goldstein (New York: Yeshiva University Press, 2005), 97–102.

2. On the order of I–III, see nn. 74, 154, and 489–490. On the disorder in XIX, see n. 408.

3. Even the numbering of tales was meaningful for Elyaqum Getz (see chapter 6 §*Allegory Emancipated*), who unusually divided them into twenty-four, because he read them as imparting practical life lessons (24 = וְחַי, "he shall live [in them," i.e., God's laws], Lev 18:5). Mushka Steinmetz, "To Strengthen the Words of the Sages: An Analysis of Rav Elyakum Getz's *Rappeduni Ba-Tappuḥim* and Its Consonance with Seventeenth-Century Polish Rabbinic Thought" (M.A. thesis, Touro University Graduate School of Jewish Studies, 2024), 42.

canon—and this book will be more accessible to a reader who has previewed the entire series.

* * * * *

What would you say these stories have in common, such that they belong together? Experience is not a bad place to begin: our capacity to understand other readers depends on it. What did you see in this story?

> VIIIa. And Rabbah bar bar Hanah said:
> Once I was traveling in a ship
> and the ship passed between one fin of a fish and the other
> three days and three nights
> it went upstream as we went downstream.

I see a moving picture of a ship and a huge fish, its internal instability held in place by tension. As the ship sails in one direction with the force of the current, the fish thrashes in the reverse direction against the current. Disaster seems imminent: logically, they should bypass one another or collide. Wondrously, eerily, they do not. Whether because the fish is so powerful that it counteracts the current/wind,[4] or because it is so big that the ship takes a long time to weave through its huge fins, or both, the bodies in contrary motion remain entangled. Humans and beast, fins and sails, metamorphose into a hybrid, a creature neither one nor two; neither swallowed whole nor spat out on dry land like Jonah in the whale. Only after "three days and three nights" (familiar from Jonah's story or, for that matter, Isaac's, as shorthand for a long mysterious journey),[5] does the ship exit the beast's foaming wake. The hybrid splits up; fish and ship go their separate ways without a scratch. Yet through it all, like Melville's Ishmael, only one seafaring narrator has "escaped alone to tell thee." As you and I have no other evidence—and, given his otherworldly setting, no way to get any—we cannot verify or nitpick what he says.[6] We believe it or not. And here's the rub: even if we do not, it's too late—we just saw it. Whether or not the events in the story happened, the story has happened to us.

The strongest evidence that what I myself have seen in this story—a wondrous display of motion held in tension; hybridity; a problem of nar-

---

4. Like the ἐχενηίς/*remora* of Hellenistic collections of wonders: a fish which holds and detains ships in the sea (Oppian, *Halieutica* I.180–190; see Immanuel Löw, *Fauna und Mineralien der Juden* [Hildesheim: Olms, 1969], 17). It is unclear whether wind or water is pushing them apart (Rashbam, b. B. Batra 73b s.v. איהו בזקיפא). Rashbam's commentary is cited from the margin of ed. Vilna, as variants in early prints (Pesaro, Venice) do not change his meaning. (They do shed some light on the tales' textual history, as discussed in my study: see n. 1.)

5. See n. 25.

6. On this conundrum, see Robert Foulke, *The Sea Voyage Narrative,* Studies in Literary Themes and Genres 14 (London: Routledge, 2002), 24–26, 32, 85.

rative reliability—was also visible to early readers is reflected in comments by voices that were appended to the tale by its editors:

> VIIIb. And perhaps you'd say:
> The ship wasn't moving much!
> When Rav Dimi arrived, he said:
> Like heating a kettle
> the ship moved six *parasang*.
>
> And there is one who says:
> A horseman shot an arrow
> but could not overcome it.

This detail by Rav Dimi is added as a retort to a rhetorical objection by a hypothetical reader of the tale. *Perhaps,* this reader says, *what you see as the tale's striking poetic feature*—the idea that ship and fish stick together, despite their rapid movement in opposite directions—*was a misunderstanding*. The objection seems sensible. Perhaps the fish was slow, or the ship was slow. Perhaps the ship spent all this time on its back, or winding through its fins along the current with slack sail. But no, Rav Dimi counters: the ship traveled six Persian miles (over a half-day's walk) in a flash,[7] no longer than it takes to boil water in a kettle (we say "mile per hour"; they say "*parasang* per kettle"). Multiply this speed by three days and the ship should have covered a vast span. Therefore, the fish must have been even stronger, or even larger, than in the original tale![8] The rhetorical objection backfires and heightens the narrator's hyperbole. By failing, it helps his storytelling to succeed. And perhaps that was the point of including it.

The following anonymous comment may seem to simply repeat Rav Dimi's counter-argument: the ship was moving fast, so fast that not even an arrow shot by a rider could catch up. Yet this is no mere repetition. It enhances, in its sheer incongruity, the tale's other striking creation: a hybrid being, ship/fish, with sails for fins or vice versa. A rider on horseback suddenly appears out of nowhere (in fact out of a prior tale in the collection, based in turn on a biblical verse).[9] Misplaced as he is in this sea-yarn (where would he stand?!) his appearance has the effect of leading our mind's eye

---

7. The Talmud defines a *parasang* as 1/10 of the distance that an average person can walk in a day (b. Pesah. 94a).

8. All other manuscripts read *"sixty parasang."* Exaggeration is contagious: it starts with the teller, transmits to a reader (Rav Dimi), and continues with the scribes of these manuscripts. It continues in another way in a medieval commentary: Ritva, b. B. Bat. 73a s.v. בין גלא לגלא ארבע מאה פרסי not only reads "four" *parasang* for "three," but also notes that a nautical parasang is twenty times the standard *parasang*—expanding tales I, VIIIb, and XVIIa twentyfold. *Hiddushe ha-Ritva 'al Massekhet Baba Batra*, ed. Yaaqov David Ilan (Jerusalem: Mossad Ha-Rav Kook, 2005), 592.

9. IIIa has the same formula: "a horseman (*parasha*) . . . but could not overcome him/it."

back to the strangeness of the first hybrid. By adding a horse/man to the original fish/ship (a hybrid in another domain of biblical cosmology: Dry Land rather than Sea), the second commentator sharpens one way to see the original strange image. Perhaps, like this misplaced centaur, the ship does seem to ride on the back of the fish, despite its rapid motion below the surface. And perhaps, like the famous "Parthian shot," in which the mounted archer would have been pictured according to an iconographic convention of the tale's time and place,[10] thrilling speed is dramatized by facing the "horse" (fish) and the "rider" (ship) in opposite directions, even as they simultaneously propel forward. In short, when each comment expands the tale, it is framed as an effort to compensate for a lone unreliable narrator by adding evidence; but, in effect, this intensifies his original artistry.

Figure 1. *Plate with Shapur II on a Lion Hunt*. Iran, 310–320s. Silver: forging, pierced ground, chasing, gilding, repousse work. Diameter: 22.9 cm. Inv.no.S-253. Used by permission of The State Hermitage Museum, St. Petersburg. Photograph © The State Hermitage Museum. Photo by Vladimir Terebenin.

In another tale, a similar way of making moving images, held by a tension, is at work:

In our big fish tale (VIII), the repetition aids oral performance, as it echoes *parasang* (*parsei*). For its basis in a verse, see n. 279.

10. Kaveh Farrokh et al., "Depictions of Archery in Sassanian Silver Plates and Their Relationship to Warfare," *Revista de Artes Marciales Asiáticas* 13.2 (2018): 82–113, at 96–101.

> VII. And Rabbah bar bar Ḥanah said:
> Once I was traveling in a ship
> and I saw a certain fish
> with sands settled upon its back
> and a thorn-plant had sprouted on it.
> We thought it was dry land
> and we went up, we kneaded, and we baked;
> The back of the fish got hot
> and it flipped over
> and if the ship hadn't been close to us
> it would have drowned us.

Whereas the other fish/ship hybrid was horizontal and dynamic, this one is vertical and seemingly static. The sailors mistake the fish for an island because it looks like one, covered in sand and sprouting vegetation. The primordial elements of Water and Dry Land are layered on top of one another in a mockup of biblical creation—paltry sands barely veiling the deep. Needless to say, this is not stable and will not last. Meanwhile, however, the storyteller uses time and perspective to maintain the hybrid's tension. By telling the audience in advance that it is *not* dry land, and by splitting the image into two levels (above and below "ground"), he creates irony and builds suspense. The sailors, as they come "ashore" and light their fire, have no clue where they are. We, the audience, do. By slowing down their actions ("we went up, we kneaded[11] and we baked; the back of the fish got hot ..."), the narrator exploits this gap between perspectives. Like the fish, our temperature rises as the pot heats up and breaks at the climax, when the beast submerges to put out the fire and the sailors swim for their lives.

This tale is no more inherently plausible than the tale of the journey along the back of the enormous fish. It does not help that again Rabbah bar bar Hanah is the only one to tell it, and this time, no one springs to his defense. The likelihood that his audience already knew a similar version told by someone else, due to its great age and wide diffusion,[12] may also

---

11. This seems to be the sense of the unique variant in ms. H (ופ.ב). If so, this is another of many readings where ms. H retains or mimics an oral-performative style (see, e.g., ln. ו"בע.ב where only ms. H lacks the subordinating conjunction; see chapter 3, §*Attributions and Other Introductory Formulae* and §*The Uses of Repetition*). Rather than distinct equivalent actions ("baked and cooked," "cooked and baked"), ms. H suspensefully stokes a single action (kneading, then baking), which sparks the story's crisis. Erich Auerbach noted a similar use of parataxis for suspense in the Hebrew Bible. See James I. Porter, "Old Testament Realism in the Writings of Erich Auerbach," in *Jews and the Ends of Theory*, ed. Shai Ginsburg, Martin Land, and Jonathan Boyarin (New York: Fordham University Press, 2018), 187–224, at 204–6.

12. This Tale Type is "Whale Thought to Be Object — Island" (J.1761.1) in Thompson's standard folklore index: Dov Neuman (Noy), "Motif-Index of Talmudic-Midrashic Litera-

Figure 2. Ms. Ludwig XV 3 (83.MR.173), folio 89v. Franco-Flemish bestiary, c. 1270. J. Paul Getty Museum, https://www.getty.edu/art/collection/object/103SAZ. CC0 licensed.

make it more likely that, in their eyes, it was a story plain and simple. Perhaps that is why his happy ending is not reframed as pious or miraculous by Rabbah himself or a peer like Rav Dimi. He says that he survived because his ship was parked nearby; if it hadn't been, he wouldn't have. By contrast, in a thirteenth-century Christian version, the mast is a cross and a sailor's hands are clasped in prayer: by now, the tale is an allegory with just one means of salvation.[13] For Rabbah, no such providence is at work. And yet, as no salvation is assured either, his markers of irony and fictionality do not break the story's spell. The audience relives each moment of his escape, lulled by his loquacity into forgetting that he has no

---

ture" (PhD diss., Indiana University, 1954), 549. Compare the Millennium Falcon's misadventure in a Space Slug's belly (Han Solo: "This is no cave …").

13. Already the Syriac poet Jacob of Serugh (d. 521 CE) declaims in a similar context, "May your cross, our Lord, be an oar that rescues me." See Robert Kitchen, "Jonah's Oar: Christian Typology in Jacob of Serug's Mēmrā 122 on Jonah," *Hugoye* 11.1 (2011): 29–62, at 33 (his trans.). Compare the sailors' poles engraven with divine names (II), see nn. 341–342.

proof and that, as soon as he opens his mouth, he should kill the suspense: he lived to tell the tale, didn't he?

At a glance, if we had to choose one word for our collection's narrative contents and techniques, you may share my feeling that it is a series of adventures—hence this book's title.[14] The tales of Rabbah and friends derive their adventurous quality from five features that they generally share.[15] First, the adventurer: a strong persona of a traveler-narrator who is spell-binding but not necessarily reliable as he speaks in his own voice about his own adventures.[16] Second, the settings of his adventures push or exceed the limits of normal experience: the sea, the desert, up in the air, down in the watery or fiery depths, the ends—or navel—of the earth.[17] Third and relatedly, many adventures conclude in narrow escapes from death or danger, cues that we can imagine performers amplifying with intonation and gesture: "had it lifted us any higher, we'd have been burnt by its heat" (I), "it was about to kill him" (XVIII), "it returned and was

---

14. For another subdivision–Adventure/Vision–because only the Adventure is a narrative, see chapter 3 §*Voice*.

15. The notion that early audiences perceived the commonalities of Rabbah's tales in terms of these five features gains traction if we observe that they are shared by a set of tales added at the end (XVI–XXI), as if storytellers/editors used these features to create new stories and harmonize old material with the collection (chapter 3 §*Chronological Layers*). In these additions we find two more Big Fish tales (XVI–XVII), similar to those told by Rabbah (VI–VIII) as well as related to one another (note the repetition of "two"). And we find a tale of the ultimate Big Fish: Leviathan (XX). In an inversion of the tale of sinners burned in hell beneath the desert (*as flesh in the caldron*, XIV), we hear another desert tale of flayed meat, *restored* to life by roasting on wondrous coals and herbs (XXI). We venture still farther into realms beyond: the sea deep (XVIII), the sky above a ship (XIX; compare II), where we see people battle monsters (XVIII) and monster battles (XIX). In sum, these added tales "dial up" Rabbah's earlier adventures by expanding; combining; or inverting them, thus revealing the durability of their basic narrative components. (Contrast XIIIa, where Rabbah sees monsters but does not approach; and IXa, where he cannot dive, unlike the brave diver in XVIII. On XVIII–XIX, see Reuven Kiperwasser and Serge Ruzer, "Aramaic Stories of Wandering in the High Seas of Late Antiquity," in *The Past through Narratology: New Approaches to Late Antiquity and the Early Middle Ages*, ed. Mateusz Fafinski and Jakob Riemenschneider (Heidelberg: Heidelberg University Publishing, 2022), 161–77; Kiperwasser and Ruzer, "Nautical Fiction of Late Antiquity: Jews and Christians Traveling by Sea," in *Jewish, Christian, and Muslim Travel Experiences: 3rd Century BCE–8th Century CE*, ed. Suzanne Luther, Pieter B. Hartog, and Clare E. Wilde, Judaism, Christianity, and Islam – Tension, Transmission, Transformation 16 (Berlin: de Gruyter, 2023).

16. In the first two tales (I–II) he only reports another narrator ("seafarers"), but they speak as similar adventurers. The problem of narrative reliability is, if anything, compounded by the exotic source of these stories; see n. 6.

17. As if to stress the cosmic journey as a frame for Rabbah's stories, the last place that he visits (XV) is generally interpreted as the most extreme of all: "where the firmament is overturned upon the earth" (ms. H); where the earth and firmament touch/kiss (all other mss.); the desert spot where the two meet (Rabbenu Gershom *ad loc.*); or the Land of Israel, the navel of Creation (Rashbam, b. B. Batra 74a s.v. היכא דנשקי ארעא ורקיעא). On this place, see nn. 401-402; Appendix §*Thieves in Heaven (?!)*.

swallowing the ship" (XIX). Other moments of crisis are more subtle but play an equally crucial role in the plot: sailors are nearly drowned in the sea (II), Rabbah nearly drowns (VIII; IXa) or is detained in the desert (XIIa), and only divine intervention or sage counsel prevents the heroes from being lost to the elements. Fourth, many adventures enhance their remote and dangerous settings by contrast with the opposite: a familiar setting for a Babylonian rabbinic audience. This polarity between Home and Away is created by comparing an adventure to a local sight (V, XVI) or by placing it there directly (IIIa, IIIb) and sometimes by adding a follow-up scene where it is reinterpreted by rabbis in a study-house (Xb, XIIb, XIIIb, XXIb). Either way, this polarity results in a paradox. On one hand, the adventure strains the limits of possibility. On the other, it should be perfectly accessible to local knowledge and experience. That tension would become a potent fuel for the meaning of these tales (see chapters 2, 4, 5). Finally, in content as well as structure, the tales are rife with the liminal or wondrous, that which defies common sense and knowledge: beings who conjoin opposed domains; travelers to East, West, and other extremes; actions that skirt or flaunt norms; life at the limit. Motifs include monsters or hybrids,[18] good versus evil, salvation and damnation, life and death. References to God and sacred texts abound but do not automatically "kosher" this transgressive energy. Sometimes God is a potent actor in the adventure (I, II, IIIb, IXa),[19] sometimes on the outside looking in (XIIIa). Bible verses are added as glosses of adventures (IXb, XIV, XVIIa, XX) but do not explain all of their contents; some seem only tangentially related. Each tale is a riddle with no solution,[20] a parable (*mashal*) without its lesson (*nimshal*). We will have to wait a long time for a more comprehensive answer to such paradoxes in the mode of allegory (chapter 6). In sum, these strange tales push the bounds of possibility in terms of both what is told and how. They cite cosmic extremes and liminal beings or experiences, raising questions of truth and lies, irony and fictionality. Yet some also circle back to an early listener's home: the study-house and other familiar locales. A constant motion between those primal domains of meaning—the known and the unknown, Kansas and Oz—will recur throughout their history.

* * * * *

Such are the collection's vague outlines, which suggest why it might be in the Talmud. But what do these stories mean? Rather than answer the ques-

---

18. For a survey of how commentators tried to reconcile some of these creatures with tradition, see Natan Slifkin, *Sacred Monsters* (Brooklyn, NY: Zoo Torah, 2007). I thank Ra'anan Boustan for giving me this charming book.
19. For the possibility of a theological interpretation of "authorities" in IIIb, see n. 282.
20. Galit Hasan-Rokem and David Shulman, "Afterword," in *Untying the Knot: On Riddles and Other Enigmatic Modes,* ed. Galit Hasan-Rokem and David Shulman (New York: Oxford University Press, 2006), 316–19.

tion, I develop a method for understanding other readers' answers that is broad enough to be useful across historical and cultural boundaries, yet consistent enough to render those cases comparable in its own terms; a set of complementary ideas that are also plastic and open to refinement by being applied to further cases, other worlds. In short, a hermeneutic. Below, I discuss the concept of meaning that supports this method and the constellation of analytic terms that emerge from it. In chapter 1, I will contrast this method with the methods of prior studies of our collection and exemplify the new kind of interpretation that it can offer. Then, in each analysis of each tale, each attribution of a tale's meaning to named or implied readers throughout the following five chapters, we will explore it together. The method's novelty, truth, or utility must rest on the sum of those cases. But first, a few foreshadowings of how I hope our adventure may nudge the discipline.

I would like us to venture even further beyond outmoded wars of "text" and "context" or rabbinic stories' "internal" (religious) versus "external" (historical) significance. While it is no longer the norm to take sides and, rhetorically at least, this way of thinking is in decline,[21] in practice, scholars still often impose a text/context distinction on rabbinic sources that is an artifact of the late twentieth century—rather than the "context," or *epistēmē*, of late antiquity.[22] I will not explain any story's meaning in terms of hermeneutics as opposed to the real world. The realia, events, and everyday interactions that these readers experienced were no less grist for their interpretive mill—no less part of their "text"—than Scripture or the Mishnah. On the other hand, in order to show how they read that "context" into their tradition–how they interpreted reality—of course we should consider how their world limited or guided them: for instance, conventional imagery that they used, or polemics in which they chose to engage. As long as we keep readers' agency front and center, and we emphasize how selective and creative they were in engaging their environment, rather than treating readers as passively reacting to dominant historical or cultural forces, we need not pit textual against contextual meaning.[23]

---

21. For this problem and key literature, see James Adam Redfield and Simcha Gross, "The Making of Rabbinic Pasts: Introduction," *JSQ* 30.4 (2023): 355–66.

22. Peter Burke, "Context in Context," *Common Knowledge* 8.1 (2002): 152–77. For valuable resistance to the text/context distinction by scholars of late ancient Judaism and Christianity, see C. M. Chin and Moulie Vidas, "Introduction," in *Late Ancient Knowing: Explorations in Intellectual History*, ed. C.M. Chin and Moulie Vidas (Berkeley: University of California Press, 2015), 1–13, at 7–8, on totalization; Blossom Stefaniw, "Knowledge in Late Antiquity: What Is It Made Of and What Does It Make?," *Studies in Late Antiquity* 2.3 (2018): 266–93, at 279–84, on *mimēsis*. Neither concept of relatedness is at all equivalent to "context."

23. For an application of a similar line of critique, see Shai Secunda, "Talmudic Text and Iranian Context: On the Development of Two Talmudic Narratives," *AJSR* 33.1 (2009): 45–69.

Instead, I hope to develop a method for comparing the known and unknown readers of these tales *across* historical contexts. As we will traverse a wide swathe of the tales' reception history, rather than only showing how one of their meanings was shaped by one set of con/textual factors, we must confront analytic challenges that other methods do not. Those challenges are chances to address new questions. How can we draw connections between the ways in which disparate readers found meaning in these tales—without proving direct influence or "overtheorizing" by flattening differences between readers with our own abstract concepts? What were *their* ways of making meaning from the tales? Can we compare and contrast those different ways without our own distorting projections? I approach this question by assuming that the tales' latent interpretive possibilities and their realization in any one interpretation are mediated by interpretive frameworks that competed and co-evolved in a nonlinear fashion. In other words, someone who was part of this tradition had access to a finite set of options for closing the gap between what the tale could mean and what—they concluded—it does mean. The tales' possible meanings and interpretive frameworks were not equally popular with all readers at all times. Nor, however, were they unique to one cultural context or the boundaries of one period. Interpretive frameworks zig-zagged over time, growing and becoming hegemonic, receding, then reviving in new hands even today. I try to describe those zig-zags.

Consider allegory. As I use the term in chapter 6, allegory is an interpretive framework that finds hidden meanings in a story in order to teach a moral—and sometimes a practical—lesson. From the high Middle Ages to early modernity, an internally consistent allegorical framework became available to the reader that did not exist before, based on a new role for the symbol. This new framework—what I will call its symbolic "grammar" and "syntax"—made it possible to read the tales' contents in a new way. It led readers to change the meaning of each tale; of all the tales in relation to each other; and the relations that constitute the entire Jewish canon. Yet, in a less systematic sense, allegory was an interpretive option from the start. Some of the first comments on the tales in the collection itself seem allegorical, and late ancient Jews were no strangers to allegory of a sort.[24] The tales themselves seem aware of allegory as an interpretive option, whether inviting it ("three days and three nights": a symbolic number),[25] or foreclosing it ("If the ship hadn't been close to us, it would have drowned us": a denial of hidden forces at work). Further, borders between allegorical and other modes of interpretation changed over time. A history of reading

---

24. Jonah Fränkel, *Darkhe ha-aggadah veha-midrash* (Masadah: Yad la-Talmud, 1991), 197–232; Jonathan Kaplan, *My Perfect One: Typology and Early Rabbinic Interpretation of Song of Songs* (Oxford: Oxford University Press, 2015), 25–30.

25. See Rachel Adelman, *The Return of the Repressed: Pirqe de-Rabbi Eliezer and the Pseudepigrapha*, JSJSup 140 (Leiden: Brill, 2009), 255–57.

must capture this internal continuity of the allegorical framework as well as gaps between how interpreters used it when others were also available. I do this by inventing a "constellation" to track abstract relationships within the interpretive history of our collection—a method informed by literary theories that I do not simply apply to rabbinic sources but select and tailor to fit their particular dynamics of text and reader.

By using this constellation, we can ask how the tales' interpretive possibilities were realized by specific interpreters, within their own interpretive frameworks, instead of using shorthand for types of meaning that may obscure their acts of reading. Rather than argue that "A is an allegorical interpreter [because they fit my definition]; B is not," we can compare A and B and wonder what is, or is not, or is differently "allegorical" about them. Is A allegorical because they treat the whole collection as the primary unit of meaning and fit all the tales into one mega-story, whereas B is not, because they proceed from tale to tale and are comfortable with discrepancies? Are both allegorists, but A is less, because they attend more to how the tales are told, whereas B is more, because they attend to their normative content? Questions like this become possible and meaningful across historical and cultural boundaries when we restore common denominators for comparison that are based on what all interpreters have to work with, somehow, more or less, rather than using terms with specialized meanings that vary widely across contexts and are not always crystal clear even among specialists. As those common denominators are grounded in a reception history of rabbinic literature that includes many nonrabbinic readers and could be adapted to study other oral-literary traditions in their own right, this method models a way of reading rabbinic literature as comparative literature.

The other way in which I hope to nudge the study of rabbinic literature in a comparative direction is to loosen the grip of genre and restore more creativity to the reader. Pursuing this comparative project and worried about the tendency of genre to impose a modern scholar's own interpretive framework on other readers (see chapter 1), I apply genre labels lightly only to stand for partial interpretive perspectives of specific readers at specific times. Rather than a type of text, its implied social setting, or its author/editor's compositional model, genre labels like Myth, Exegesis, and Wonder will join our large eclectic inventory of the interpretive expectations and frameworks that were available to other readers. Untethered from the search for a strict correspondence between the tales' genre and their meaning, I will try to use genres flexibly as a way to compare readers who shared an interpretive framework; those who did not; and those who did so only selectively. Rather than mold the reader to the genre, we see how readers used some genre conventions but suppressed others, or fused old and new genres to create meanings that no author, editor, or scholar could ever have foreseen.

Along the same lines, as I go on to parse the leading ideas of this comparative method, I hope you will read the rest of this book as a theory resting on the back of a history. Not the other way around. I do not aim to redefine these ideas as such; nor to claim that they relate, or apply, to all stories in one abstract way, nor that they are necessarily the best way to study our stories. What follows is merely a map or, in also apt nautical terms, constellation of ideas that we will use to track differences and continuities among how readers of the tales have re-created their meaning as each chapter travels forward in time and across cultures. Our waypoints are the readers' diverse minds; our end is this method of arriving at them, a method that will allow us to analyze and compare how readers of rabbinic stories created meaning across genres, periods, and cultures. To that end, these ideas have names that persist in each chapter; fixed as they are in the theoretical firmament, their arrangement shifts and some burn more or less brightly as our position and orientation change. Our constellation is the story or tale; storyteller or teller; collection and recollection; the telling; the canon; and, above all, the reader.

The Reader

If the first words of a book are Meaning Is Reading, its author owes you a definition of both terms and their relationship.[26] By "meaning," I mean the interpretation of a message by someone. This definition has three parts: the message (the "text"), someone who interprets it (the "reader"), and a concrete result (their "interpretation": both the product and the process of arriving at it). It may be easy for us to identify that result with certainty (e.g., a gloss in the form "X, that is Y"). It may be hard (e.g., a scribe silently changing a word while copying from a lost manuscript). But, having done so, we will trace connections and conflicts between our tales' readers by inferring their processes from their results. By piecing together the logic of their interpretations, we will reveal how they read and how their ways of reading relate: a story of the art of interpretation itself as it travels, grows, and changes in a Jewish tradition.

In this approach to reading, the main character is the reader, the star of our adventure. This brings me to what I mean by "reader" and where it sits in the field of rabbinic literature. No one would object to the premise that people are of diverse minds and do not necessarily interpret a text in the same way within a culture or period, let alone as their predecessors did. Few would dispute the commonplace that texts have no intrinsic

---

26. This approach to textual meaning is grounded in my six essays on Husserl; Auerbach; Alter, Sternberg, and Zornberg; Berdichevsky; Isaak Heinemann and Cassirer. It further reflects engagement between rabbinic texts, deconstruction, and interpretive anthropology in "Redacting Culture" (2016) and in my PhD dissertation (2017). See my website.

meaning and therefore no stable or universal meaning, which warns us against projecting our interpretation onto others. Yet, rather than accept the full implications of those assumptions and build a method on that basis, the study of rabbinic stories has favored the message—the text—as the driver of meaning. Each established method does imply some theory of the reader and their interpretive process. However, because scholars focus on the text, either the reader is conflated with the text itself, or the reader is equated to a general collective attitude (ideology and *Zeitgeist*), or the reader's agency is weakened by not distinguishing their role in meaning from that of the text's creators (composers and editors). Landmark studies illustrate these pitfalls over the past forty years.

The conflation of text and reader was a given for Jonah Fränkel, who transformed the field by making rabbinic stories legible as sophisticated literature.[27] His method went beyond close reading: it is closed reading, an effort to defend the artistic meaning of rabbinic stories from "reduction" to history by isolating each story from both historical and literary context.[28] Rabbinic stories are closed, for Fränkel, because each is an integrated, self-referential whole. Its elements are all complementary, and nothing is extraneous or lacking such that one would need to read outside the story in order to determine its meaning. On the contrary, the story's form carries its meaning.[29] Because the rabbinic story is so precisely structured and always has a didactic moral lesson,[30] Fränkel leaves little role for the reader but to get this message. While the story is being told, he allows for ambiguity, suspense, and other dynamics between the narrator and the

---

27. For his publications and an index of stories that he treated, see *Higayon L'Yonah: New Aspects in the Study of Midrash, Aggadah and Piyyut in Honor of Professor Yona Fraenkel* [Hebrew], ed. Joshua Levinson et al. (Jerusalem: Magnes, 2006), 569–80.

28. On "closure," see Fränkel, *Darkhe ha-aggadah*, 260–61; Fränkel, *The Aggadic Narrative: Harmony of Form and Content* [Hebrew] (Tel-Aviv: Ha-qibbuts ha-meuḥad, 2001), 32–39; Haim Weiss and Shira Stav, *The Return of the Absent Father: A New Reading of a Chain of Stories from the Babylonian Talmud*, trans. Batya Stein, Divinations (Philadelphia: University of Pennsylvania Press, 2022), 97 n. 4. For critique, see Hillel Newman, "Closing the Circle: Yonah Fraenkel, The Talmudic Story, and Rabbinic History," in *How Should Rabbinic Literature Be Read in the Modern World?*, ed. Matthew Kraus, Judaism in Context 4 (Piscataway, NJ: Gorgias, 2006), 105–35; and literature in Binyamin Katzoff, "A Story in Three Contexts: The Redaction of a Toseftan Pericope," *AJSR* 38 (2014): 109–27, at 110–11 nn. 3–4. See further n. 33. For both critique and development of Fränkel's "closure," see Itay Marienberg-Milikowsky, "'Beyond the Matter': Stories and Their Contexts in the Babylonian Talmud: Repeated Stories as a Test Case" [Hebrew] (PhD diss., Ben-Gurion University of the Negev, 2015), 28–58.

29. For instance, if the end mirrors the beginning, the middle is to be read in light of tension between beginning and end, thereby "closing" the story. Jonah Fränkel, "Chiasmus in Talmudic-Aggadic Narrative," in *Chiasmus in Antiquity: Structures, Analyses, Exegesis*, ed. John W. Welch (1981; repr., Eugene, OR: Wipf & Stock, 2020), 183–97.

30. This is a corollary of Fränkel's view that rabbinic stories are not "folklore" but by and for rabbis and their ilk. See Dina Stein, "Let the 'People' Go? The 'Folk' and Their 'Lore' as Tropes in the Reconstruction of Rabbinic Culture," *Prooftexts* 29.2 (2009): 206–41, at 219–21.

audience. In the end, however, the latter receives the meaning that was intended and implanted in the form.³¹

On one hand, Fränkel's New Criticism has been the most successful method in terms of sheer quantity of insights about techniques of rabbinic storytelling, as evidenced from its ongoing adoption by contributions to the study of how rabbis' stories convey ethical ideas.³² On the other, it has been criticized for neglecting two other factors in how readers create meaning: their cultural background and their use of texts beyond the story's closed borders.³³ Both of these are preconditions for the reader's interpretation and also catalysts for its results. Just as narrators rely on unspoken codes and norms as they convey messages to audiences, audiences refer to a larger archive of texts as they receive and interpret those messages. When audiences are hearing or reading a story, they create meaning from this matrix of expectations and associations in ways that cannot be foreseen by the author or deduced from the story's structure. Moving beyond closed reading, into that matrix, accords more agency to the reader.

A new method based on the concept of intertextuality was a leap in this direction.³⁴ It showed that early rabbis, like prior readers of the Hebrew Bible,³⁵ interpret its contents not as closed but as infinitely open, "gapped and dialogical."³⁶ Biblical texts hold contradictions and lacunae

---

31. Jonah Fränkel has a broader view of the social setting of rabbinic stories and a correspondingly more active role for the reader in his *'Iyyunim be'olamo ha-ruhani shel sippur ha-aggadah* (Tel-Aviv: Ha-qibbuts ha-meuḥad, 1981). He sometimes concludes with the interaction between narrator and audience (*'Iyyunim*, 15, 37), and each chapter is crafted around thematically linked stories that he connects in light of a social and theological theme.

32. Mira Beth Wasserman, *Jews, Gentiles, and Other Animals: The Talmud after the Humanities*, Divinations (Philadelphia: University of Pennsylvania Press, 2017), 18–19, 52–56, 145–49, 227–33; Jonathan Wyn Schofer, *The Making of a Sage: A Study in Rabbinic Ethics* (Madison: University of Wisconsin Press, 2005), 57–64, 111–15, 131–32.

33. Richard Kalmin, "The Modern Study of Ancient Rabbinic Literature: Yonah Fraenkel's Darkhei ha'aggada vehamidrash," *Prooftexts* 14.1 (1994): 189–204; Jeffrey L. Rubenstein, "Context and Genre: Elements of a Literary Approach to the Rabbinic Narrative," in *How Should Rabbinic Literature Be Read in the Modern World?*, ed. Matthew Kraus, Judaism in Context 4 (Piscataway, NJ: Gorgias, 2006), 137–65; Devora Steinmetz, "Agada Unbound: Inter-Agadic Characterization of Sages in the Talmud and Implications for Reading Agada," in *Creation and Composition: The Contribution of the Bavli Redactors (Stammaim) to the Aggadah*, ed. Jeffrey L. Rubenstein, TSAJ 114 (Tübingen: Mohr Siebeck, 2005), 293–337.

34. For invaluable recent surveys, see Christine Hayes, "Intertextuality and Tannaic Literature: A History," in *The Literature of the Sages: A Re-visioning*, ed. Christine Hayes, CRINT 16 (Leiden: Brill, 2022), 95–216; Alyssa M. Gray, "Intertextuality and Amoraic Literature," in Hayes, *Literature of the Sages*, 217–71.

35. Meir Sternberg, *The Poetics of Biblical Narrative: Ideological Literature and the Drama of Reading*, ISBL (Bloomington: Indiana University Press, 1985), 186–229.

36. Daniel Boyarin, *Intertextuality and the Reading of Midrash*, ISBL (Bloomington: Indiana University Press, 1990), 14.

that readers try to explain by putting them into dialogue with other biblical texts. The dialogue, however, also proliferates the contradictions, requiring more interpretation of more texts, until the only interpretive limit is the canon itself: as long as both qualify as Scripture, any verse can have meaning in light of any other verse. Analyses of how biblical intertextuality works helped scholars to show that rabbis are not abstruse or arbitrary readers. Their interpretation is always grounded in a relationship among intertexts, one which develops as each reading unfolds. By showing how rabbis' intertexts interact, one can show their interpretive creativity.

Against Isaak Heinemann, who attributed rabbis' creativity to their poetic originality, Daniel Boyarin combined a more traditionalist understanding of how rabbinic interpretation operates with the critical spirit of post-structuralist theory.[37] Boyarin added a major insight to Heinemann's inventory of rabbis' intertextual techniques: they are neither free nor original but have limits that, in turn, have their own logic. Those limits are not individual because this literature is a collective production. They are cultural codes and silent assumptions which regulate how meaning can be created: for instance, an assumption that texts can be intertexts *if* and *only if* they are canonical. All such limits to interpretation reflect the shared ideology of interpreters and audiences. By the same token, if limits are contested, this is a symptom of ideological conflict and change. By defining ideologies that limited the intertextual creation of meaning, hence the "border lines" dividing groups of readers, scholars began to mine their texts for histories of debate on categories of human difference: gender, sexuality, ethnicity, religion, and so on. The cultural and intertextual factors that Fränkel had repressed sprang back in full force.

Yet, as this leap was overextended to all of rabbinic literature, even literature per se,[38] it took two steps backward from a theory of the reader's creativity. First, because the original model for intertextuality was rabbinic exegesis of the biblical text, it carried assumptions that do not necessarily apply to all rabbinic sources. If Scripture is "omnisignificant" such that every verse potentially relates to every other verse and its received interpretations,[39] the tales in our collection are practically the opposite—rich in interpretive possibilites, yes, but poor in received meanings. No

---

37. See Boyarin's List of Publications, e.g., items ##74, 78–80, and 111, in James Adam Redfield, "Crossing Border Lines: Daniel Boyarin's Life/Work," *Talmudic Transgressions: Engaging the Work of Daniel Boyarin*, ed. Charlotte Elisheva Fonrobert et al., JSJSup 181 (Leiden: Brill, 2017), 541–65.

38. See Ishay Rosen-Zvi, "What Else Is Left to Interpret?: Reflections on Boyarin and What Comes Next," in *Midrash Tannaim: Intertextuality and the Reading of* Mekhilta [Hebrew], ed. Elhanan Reiner, trans. David Louvish and Ruthi Bar-Ilan (Jerusalem: Hartman Institute, 2011), 273–86, at 279–80; Samuel P. Catlin, "The Rest Is Literature: *Midrash* and the Institution of 'Theory' in America" (PhD diss., University of Chicago, 2022), 60–65.

39. Yaakov Elman, "Striving for Meaning: A Short History of Rabbinic Omnisignifi-

lists of rules or culturally approved interpretive practices provide for their decipherment. They are strange to the point of nonsense, spurring readers to exercise maximum creativity as they canvass intertexts and frameworks through which to make some sense of their contents. A Scripture-like intertextuality did sometimes extend to this collection (see chapters 2, 5, 6). But other options were open: readers used a wider range of interpretive frames and intertexts, partly out of deference to the strange or transgressive contents of the tales and partly out of desperation.

Second, for all its success in relating readers, their sacred text, and their tradition, the intertextuality model has suffered from conceptualizing "culture" as a synonym for ideology or as a surrogate for religion. This has fostered a way of thinking about rabbinic interpretive communities that lacks individual agency and internal diversity.[40] In its model, rabbinic "culture" (ideology/religion) is the creative force that each individual reader either reproduces or resists. Instead, I argue for a return to Heinemann (if only in the sense of Lacan's return to Freud): we should allow room for readers to use texts to engage *with* their culture in more creative ways. Beyond closed readings of single texts, or critiques of the ideological norms of intertextuality, I aim to develop a third way—a poetics of reading rabbinic texts as they transform over time.[41]

In this effort to reveal chronological differences and diversity among readers, I rely on tools of source criticism forged by David Weiss Halivni and Shamma Friedman: criteria for distinguishing editorial layers and voices beneath the Talmud's smooth stream of discourse. Such criteria have already been tested, refined, and applied to historical reconstructions of the institutions and lived realities reflected in later layers by the editors of the Talmud's anonymous voice ("Stam"), or the "Stammaim."[42] These are potent tools for showing how and why editors interpreted and transformed their sources, distinguishing how they read their inherited texts

---

cance," in *World Philology*, ed. Sheldon Pollock et al. (Cambridge, MA: Harvard University Press, 2015), 63–91.

40. See Charlotte Elisheva Fonrobert, "On 'Carnal Israel' and the Consequences: Talmudic Studies since Foucault," *JQR* 95.3 (2005): 462–69. For this critique of the implicit culture concept in 1990s–2000s studies of "rabbinic culture," see my dissertation (Redfield, "Sages and the World," 44–55).

41. On critics who developed this approach to (mostly modern) literature, see Robert Holub, "Reception Theory: School of Constance," in *The Cambridge History of Literary Criticism*, vol. 8, *From Formalism to Poststructuralism*, ed. Raman Selden (Cambridge: Cambridge University Press, 1995), 319–46. See, e.g., Wolfgang Iser, "The Reading Process: A Phenomenological Approach," *New Literary History* 3.2 (1972): 279–99; Inge Crosman Wimmers, *Poetics of Reading: Approaches to the Novel* (Princeton, NJ: Princeton University Press, 1988). On adaptations of this theory to rabbinic literature by Barry Wimpfheimer and Zvi Septimus, see below.

42. On contributions by Jeffrey L. Rubenstein and Moulie Vidas in this regard, see Redfield, "Redacting Culture."

from how this was done by earlier named authorities: the "Amoraim," or speakers. Amoraim, too, have been distinguished by their rulings, interests, and general interpretive approaches.[43] These left their mark on earlier layers in the Talmud: Amoraic ways of reading were not fully erased by the Stammaim. Further, within the Stam itself, one can detect diverse stances and ways of reading.[44] Whether those differences are due to time (preservation of heterogeneous material) or due to live debate among Stammaim themselves, neither textual layer is cut from whole cloth: anonymous and attributed material co-evolved in the academies for generations.[45]

It stands to reason that the text's gradual and fluid transmission should open our eyes to a wider range of readers who gave it different meanings over time. However, applications of source criticism freeze that dynamic history when they split two layers and social groups: later Stammaim versus earlier Amoraim. That way of framing readers' differences tends to grant more agency to the Stammaim, as they are the ones who shaped the text's (more or less) final form.[46] In this model, thinking about redactors-as-authors and their intentional design of the so-called final textual unit takes precedence over thinking about redactors-as-readers, who received and transmitted just one interpretation in dialogue with predecessors or peers.[47] Further, because similarity, rather than conflict,

---

43. See Tzvi Moshe Dor, *Torat 'erets-yisrael be-bavel* (Tel Aviv: Dvir, 1970; for a critique, see Redfield, "'When X Arrived,'" 8–32); the work of Yaakov Elman (cited and developed in Barak S. Cohen, *The Legal Methodology of Late Nehardean Sages in Sasanian Babylonia*, Brill Reference Library of Judaism 30 (Leiden: Brill, 2011), 7–8, n. 34; and Elman's students, e.g., Shana Strauch Schick, *Intention in Talmudic Law: Between Thought and Deed*, Brill Reference Library of Judaism 65 (Leiden: Brill, 2021); and the work of Richard Kalmin and his students, e.g., Noah Benjamin Bickart, *The Scholastic Culture of the Babylonian Talmud*, Judaism in Context 31 (Piscataway, NJ: Gorgias, 2022), 96–153; Marcus Mordecai Schwartz, *Rewriting the Talmud: The Fourth Century Origins of Bavli Rosh Hashanah*, TSAJ 175 (Tübingen: Mohr Siebeck, 2019).

44. Daniel Boyarin, *Socrates and the Fat Rabbis* (Chicago: University of Chicago Press, 2009); Moulie Vidas, *Tradition and the Formation of the Talmud* (Princeton, NJ: Princeton University Press, 2014). On why this diversity within the Stam can be hard for readers to detect, see Ron Naiweld, "There Is Only One Other: The Fabrication of Antoninus in a Multilayered Talmudic Dialogue," *JQR* 104.1 (2014): 81–104.

45. See the classic statement of Yaakov Sussmann, "Ve-shuv li-yerushalmi neziqin," in *Talmudic Studies I*, [Hebrew] ed. Yaakov Sussmann and David Rosenthal (Jerusalem: Magnes, 1990), 55–133, at 100–101 n. 186.

46. E.g., Shamma Friedman, "Regarding Historical aggadah in the Babylonian Talmud," in his *Talmudic Studies: Investigating the Sugya, Variant Readings, and Aggada* [Hebrew] (New York: Jewish Theological Seminary of America, 2010), 389–432, at 413 n. 152: Amoraim themselves transmitted stories about certain Tannaim, which were later bundled together with stories about those same Amoraim, until eventually they came to rest in the Gemara. Alternatively, a Gemara's composer himself compiled material about named rabbis into collections (401–2, 413); or a talmudic text is based on a specific text elsewhere in the Talmud, rather than both deriving from a common source (422).

47. Friedman often attributes the Talmud's innovations with respect to Palestinian

is a more common way of thinking about the editors' relation to their immediate audience, their readers are assumed to mirror their intent.[48] Much is left to the imagination about how each edited unit (*sugya*) or rarer "story-cycles" like ours—even after they were edited—continued to be received, contested, and altered in relation to intertexts: earlier and later, Palestinian and Babylonian, in the Talmud itself and beyond.[49]

Centering the Talmud's readers and how they create meaning, beyond its editors, is thus a relatively new line of inquiry. Three avenues for redefining the reader and reimagining their role are emerging. First, critiques of the default affinity between the editors (Stammaim) and audience have opened up a space in which to foreground those who received and circulated rabbinic texts as agents who read and used shared stories in their own ways. Sarit Kattan Gribetz, for instance, points to scenes in which a metaphorical and literal association with the "consumption" of rabbinic texts shifts our focus to women and their interpretations, even within male-dominated learning and transmission.[50] This move to expand who

---

sources to the agency of the "composer(s) of the Gemara" (Friedman, "Historical *aggadah*," 390, 392), whom he sometimes sees as composing directly from earlier sources like those preserved in Palestinian works or other parts of the Talmud (408, 412). For him, many such changes came to an end in the Talmud as we have it. In his model, most of the reader's creativity is located in the redacted text, with its internal "layers." On the other hand, he also identifies phenomena that I will use in chapter 5 to track interaction among units *within* the Talmud: distinctive ways of reworking Amoraic sources, shared with Palestinian midrash ("Historical *aggadah*," 397); stylistic flourishes like repetitions of rare words/phrases, which he agrees point to ongoing integration of talmudic texts (412–13). Similarly, Friedman, cautions against speaking of variant "traditions" ("On the Historical Character of Dama ben Netinah: A Study in Talmudic *aggadah*" [Hebrew], in his *Talmudic Studies*, 433–74; see 455 n. 102; and "Historical *aggadah*," 429–30). Instead, he favors a linear model of literary development, e.g., three chronological layers (history, halakha, and pure fiction) redacted into one literary unit ("Dama ben Netinah," 468–69). On the other hand, Friedman shows editorial devices for reworking Palestinian sources (transition words: "Dama ben Netinah," 440 n. 121; changes of names and doubling/collapsing of characters: "Dama ben Netinah," 446) that I will use in chapter 5 to track the coevolution of sources *within* the Babylonian talmudic canon, even *after* it was heavily edited: a model of literary development that is "layered" in a less linear and controlled way. In sum, we can read Friedman to go beyond the governing assumptions of his own method.

48. Note the passive verbs in Jeffrey L. Rubenstein, *Talmudic Stories: Narrative Art, Composition, and Culture* (Baltimore: Johns Hopkins University Press, 1999), 21: "[The] implied audience of the Stammaim were like-minded sages in the rabbinic academy who could be expected to be persuaded by the rhetoric, to decode the structures and literary features, and to understand the conventions and cultural tensions of the stories." See other examples of this tendency in Vidas, *Tradition and the Formation*, 46–47.

49. In this direction, see Jeffrey L. Rubenstein, "The Story-Cycles of the Bavli: Part 1," in *Studies in Rabbinic Narratives*, ed. Jeffrey L. Rubenstein, BJS 367 (Providence, RI: Brown Judaic Studies, 2021), 227–80, at 238–40, 277–79.

50. Sarit Kattan Gribetz, "Consuming Texts: Women as Recipients and Transmitters of Ancient Texts," in *Rethinking 'Authority' in Late Antiquity: Authorship, Law, and Transmission in Jewish and Christian Tradition*, ed. A. J. Berkovitz and Mark Letteny, Routledge Monographs in

counts as an implied "reader" of rabbinic texts is wide-ranging; queer and trans readers and readings now operate *within* the rabbinic horizon.[51] Second, as the rabbinic reader is being redefined, work on material practices in rabbinic and surrounding cultures is also beginning to shift our view of what "reading" itself means. Recent studies go beyond the orality/literacy distinction, introducing more complex models for how readers engaged texts and generated meaning.[52] Rebecca Wollenberg, among others,[53] has emphasized that reading in rabbinic culture was not limited to the interpretation of a critic who assigns an abstract meaning to an abstract text. Rather, reading included diverse practices for various purposes with an ideological hierarchy. Informational, practical, and recitational modes of reading, for instance, were not equivalent, nor did they result in kinds of meaning with a uniform ideological status or function.[54] Texts were used as sources, scripts, objects, and so on, each with its own role at each stage of the culture. Meaning, in the literary-interpretive or hermeneutic sense, is not all that rabbinic readers did.

Yet no one denies that rabbinic readers have also engaged in advanced hermeneutics. The third set of methods—of which ours is a new iteration, designed for comparative analysis—considers how they did so and how we can access their own theories by way of contemporary literary theory. These methods use combinations of four broadly shared concepts: the implied reader, dialogue, performance, and narrativity. By identifying how rabbinic texts create recurrent interpretive puzzles and direct atten-

---

Classical Studies (New York: Routledge, 2018), 178–206, at 182–85. For a similar extension of the concept of authorship to Jewish Babylonian women, see Mika Ahuvia, "Reimagining the Gender and Class Dynamics of Premodern Composition," *JAJ* 14 (2023): 321–54, at 333–45.

51. Max K. Strassfeld, *Trans Talmud: Androgynes and Eunuchs in Rabbinic Literature* (Oakland: University of California Press, 2022), 13–25, 154–81; Sarra Lev, *And the Sages Did Not Know: Early Rabbinic Approaches to Intersex* (Philadelphia: University of Pennsylvania Press, 2024), 69–72, 143–45, 238–51.

52. For helpful concepts, see Elizabeth Shanks Alexander, *Transmitting Mishnah: The Shaping Influence of Oral Tradition* (Cambridge: Cambridge University Press, 2006), 41–55 (on oral structures), 84–103 (on excerpting).

53. On rabbinic practices of using psalms materially as liturgy and magic, see A. J. Berkovitz, *A Life of Psalms in Jewish Late Antiquity*, Jewish Culture and Contexts (Philadelphia: University of Pennsylvania Press, 2023), 106–10, 118–48. On how the Talmud develops and adds new social functions for traditional rabbinic reading practices of excerpting, repetition, and text criticism, see Daniel Max Picus, "Ink Sea, Parchment Sky: Rabbinic Reading Practices in Late Antiquity" (PhD diss., Brown University, 2017), 62–65, 91–105, 199–205. On Monika Amsler, *The Babylonian Talmud and Late Antique Book Culture* (Cambridge: Cambridge University Press, 2023), see Redfield, "What Difference Does the 'Writtenness' of the Talmud Make for the Interpretation of the Talmud?"

54. Rebecca Scharbach Wollenberg, *The Closed Book: How the Rabbis Taught the Jews (Not) to Read the Bible* (Princeton, NJ: Princeton University Press, 2023), 101–12; Wollenberg, "The Dangers of Reading As We Know It: Sight Reading As a Source of Heresy in Early Rabbinic Traditions," *JAAR* 85.3 (2017): 709–45.

tion along fixed pathways as one's reading unfolds over time, scholars show how they imply an ideal or typical reader, who may vary among works or genres.⁵⁵ By distinguishing forms of rabbinic discourse like subtypes of law, exegesis, and narrative, and then showing how readers interpreted one in light of the other, scholars reveal how dialogue rather than one dominant editorial intention creates meaning.⁵⁶ Conversely, these critics show how a hegemonic monologue is scripted by some of the text's voices or agents, especially the Stam(maim).⁵⁷ By rethinking literary features like repetition, textual variance, transposition, and assonance, not as accidents of the text's oral transmission but as props for multiple possible renditions, we have new ways to view the Talmud's reader as participating in traditions of performance.⁵⁸ By analyzing how narrative frames on which rabbinic traditions were woven mediate the interaction between reader and text, we can see how not only the author and narrator, but also the reader and their ways of engaging the text, are shaped by cultural norms and rhetorical patterns that define what a story is and does.⁵⁹ New

---

55. David Kraemer, "The Intended Reader as a Key to Interpreting the Bavli," *Prooftexts* 13.2 (1993): 125–40; Kraemer, *Reading the Rabbis: The Talmud as Literature* (Oxford: Oxford University Press, 1996), 146–49; Aryeh Cohen, *Rereading Talmud: Gender, Law and the Poetics of Sugyot*, BJS 318 (Atlanta: Scholars Press, 1998), 131–51; David Stern, *Parables in Midrash: Narrative and Exegesis in Rabbinic Literature* (Cambridge, MA: Harvard University Press, 1994), 86–93; Zvi Septimus, "The Poetic Superstructure of the Babylonian Talmud and the Reader It Fashions" (PhD diss., University of California, Berkeley, 2011); Barry Scott Wimpfheimer, "The Mishnah's Reader: Reconsidering Literary Meaning," *JQR* 113.3 (2023): 335–67.

56. Joshua Levinson, "Dialogic Reading in the Rabbinic Exegetical Narrative," *Poetics Today* 25.3 (2004): 497–528; Levinson, *The Twice Told Tale: A Poetics of the Exegetical Narrative in Rabbinic Midrash* [Hebrew] (Jerusalem: Magnes, 2005), 192–238; Galit Hasan-Rokem, *Tales of the Neighborhood: Jewish Narrative Dialogues in Late Antiquity*, Taubman Lectures in Jewish Studies 4 (Berkeley: University of California Press, 2005).

57. Boyarin, *Fat Rabbis*; Vidas, *Tradition and the Formation*; Barry Scott Wimpfheimer, *Narrating the Law: A Poetics of Talmudic Legal Stories*, Divinations (Philadelphia: University of Pennsylvania Press, 2011), 147–160.

58. A Cornell conference, "Talmud: Process and Performance" (17–18 May 2016) was devoted to this direction: see Christine Hayes's keynote ("'The Play's the Thing': Performance and Performativity in Rabbinic Literature") at https://www.cornell.edu/video/performance-performativity-rabbinic-literature-christine-hayes (accessed 3/28/24). See Sergey Dolgopolski, *The Open Past: Subjectivity and Remembering in the Talmud* (New York: Fordham University Press, 2013), 158–78; Zvi Septimus, "Trigger Words and Simultexts: The Experience of Reading the Bavli," in *Wisdom of Bat Sheva: In Memory of Beth Samuels*, ed. Barry S. Wimpfheimer (Jersey City, NJ: Ktav, 2009), 163–86. Orality (see §*The Teller* and chapter 3 §*Poetry*) is the other major area in which a performance lens has already been productively applied. On how the Talmud's (oral) readers enacted meaning via textual or ideological cruxes, respectively, see David Rosenthal, "'Al ha-qitsur ve-hashlamato: Pereq be-'arikhat ha-talmud ha-bavli," in *Talmudic Studies*, ed. Yaakov Sussmann and David Rosenthal (Jerusalem: Magnes, 2005), 3.2:791–863, at 856–61; Yoav Rosenthal, "Transpositions: Text and Reality," *AJSR* 41.2 (2017): 333–73, at 358–60.

59. Moshe Simon-Shoshan, *Stories of the Law: Narrative Discourse and the Construction of Authority in the Mishnah* (Oxford: Oxford University Press, 2012), 16–22, 83–91, 220–31.

readings of rabbinic sources that thoroughly integrate structuralist theory and related fields show how they recreate an ideal reader in their image, using narratives to internalize their particular culture's way of thinking through universal tensions in human experience.[60] Taken together, these new approaches to dialogue, performance, and narrativity make it easier than ever to glimpse the creativity and diversity of readers behind the text of a talmudic story apart from its anonymous editors—whether those readers are named or only hypothesized, late ancient or more recent. By synthesizing parts of these methods in a wider comparative study, I aim to trace connections across readers' interpretive frameworks without assimilating the reader to familiar constructs like textual layers, historical periods, cultural contexts, or literary genres.

* * * * *

Having covered a few key divergences and overlaps between this book's constellation and other methods in the field, let me reiterate that my choice to prioritize the reader follows from the concept of textual meaning as understanding: not meaning in general, but meaning to someone in particular, such that the meaning of our collection shifts from reader to reader and is never more or less than a specific reader's understanding at a time. In seeking a way to compare readers' understandings of the text without privileging my own axis of comparison, my role is as a meta-reader or "reader of readers": a participant in the "fusion of horizons."[61] My task is to integrate others' points of view on these texts into a still-partial view of their whole range of meaning that is richer in perspective: to shine light on potentially meaningful aspects of each text that I myself can no longer see directly but can at least see that others have seen. In this hermeneutic approach to hermeneutics, gaps among readers' understandings are not obstacles to be overcome by more accurate knowledge but are integral to understanding as such. A proverbial elephant in the dark, one reader grasping its trunk and the other its tail, our strange text is essentially unknowable in itself. But we can know parts of it via our own horizon, our own culture's interpretive framework. By piecing together those parts with what we infer from other readers' remote horizons, we may begin to sense the text's shape; how it moves in space and time; its consistent effects in the form of problems that it raises for diverse readers. In that

---

See the groundbreaking dissertation of Itay Marienberg-Milikowsky, "'Beyond the Matter'" [Hebrew], 80–82, 288–305, 320–29 (cited in n. 28 above).

60. Weiss and Stav, *Return of the Absent Father*; Mira Balberg and Haim Weiss, *When Near Becomes Far: Old Age in Rabbinic Literature* (Oxford: Oxford University Press, 2021).

61. On this fundamental hermeneutic concept, see Hans Robert Jauss, "Literary History as a Challenge to Literary Theory," *New Literary History* 2.1 (1970): 7–37, at 19–23; Redfield, "Rabbinic Historical Horizons."

process, we should trust our intuitive responses to the text as a starting point for going beyond them. To the extent that we can know our minds, we become the basis for comparison.

Again, however, no reader, however creative, interprets any text *ex nihilo*. The literary form of the tales; their tellers; the process of collection which puts them together with each other and other texts; their telling, i.e., how they are told; and the canon where they circulate also play a role in meaning. The key here is to redefine those ideas in terms of the understanding of a specific reader—named or implied, known or unknown—at each historical conjuncture which forms each chapter of this book. Focusing on a specific reader's perspective helps us to assess how relatively creative each idea within our constellation was over time—in theory, all are equally meaningful, but some were more so than others, for some people. To get acquainted with our supporting actors vis-à-vis the reader, in our story of these stories, let's begin at the beginning . . .

The Tales

Today, like us, most readers access these tales in some kind of anthology, especially the Talmud itself. Picture the earliest readers of the tales, who had no such thing; strictly speaking, they probably did not "read" them at all. What were the tales, the message, for them? One way to answer this is as a folklorist: typologically. By comparing these tales with types that are so common and ancient as to be well known, one can isolate their parts and structure; profile their types of readers; and imagine what they meant to such readers, based on how our versions compare to others. In our case, typology may have borne the fruit that it can bear (see chapter 1). Cataloguing the tales' forms and deducing what they meant, as if oral-literary forms carried intrinsic meanings, elides the reader's creativity even more than other methods.

Against typology and formalism, I define our tales as the inventory, shape, and content of actual texts whereby a specific reader would have accessed their content, whether this content was neatly packaged as a set of discrete stories or whether it was a looser set of textual fragments. By this definition, the tales change a great deal over time and the reader changes with them. Early on, "the" tales were very far removed from what we can now easily access in this book: twenty-one stories, attributed to six or seven Amoraim, and one to anonymous predecessors (Tannaim), plus attributed and anonymous comments, in one continuous unit of the Talmud.

As even that brief summary indicates, our talmudic collection has an elaborate form that is, we will see, a layered accumulation and reworking of eclectic material with a unified design. Perhaps this material reached its retellers/composers intact, and their main creative work was to arrange it, adding only connections or minor changes. Chapter 3 allows for such a model, analyzing the collection accordingly. On the other hand, as there are no definitively earlier direct parallels to these tales (as opposed to their oral raw material, which is undatable), we also have to consider an alternative: most if not all of these tales were first told by the editor/composers themselves or closer to their own time. In that case, their "early" reader would be much later, inhabiting a new phase of rabbinic culture, with access to a wider range of more recent intertexts for interpreting them. Chapter 5 explores such a model in its scholastic setting. For now, the key point is that, because meaning is a function not only of what readers can access, but also of how they read texts together—the archive at their disposal and its organization—in order to say where and when our story starts, we must make an educated guess about the minimal tale-content and some other texts to which their first readers had access. Let us adopt the safest assumption that readers knew *some* of some of the tales, before today's version in the Talmud, even though we cannot be certain what they knew. If we reject the typological approach of breaking down the tales into abstract bits (disappearing message and reader in so doing), what is left? What, in our text, was most likely interpretable for them?

In transmission of oral literature, the Talmud included,[62] stability is an index of antiquity.[63] Oral traditions are highly fluid in content and composition, yet markers of traditions that allow them to be memorized and transmitted tend to be more conservative.[64] Much as the text of Homer offers us "embedded genres" of hexameter, whose contents and even ritual *Sitz im Leben* we may be able to reconstruct apart from his poems,[65] rabbinic

---

62. Robert (Yerahmiel) Brody, "Sifrut ha-geonim veha-teqst ha-talmudi," in *Talmudic Studies*, ed. Yaaqov Sussmann and David Rosenthal, 4 vols. in 6 (Jerusalem: Magnes, 1990–2024) 1:237–303. On the scant direct evidence of written classical rabbinic literature (apart from a few chronographical works from Roman Palestine), see Yaaqov Sussmann, " 'Torah shebe-ʿal peh' peshutah ke-mashmaʿah – koho shel qotso shel yod," in Sussmann and Rosenthal, *Talmudic Studies*, 3.1:209–384, at 214–19.

63. A standard working assumption for oral literatures. See, e.g., Umberto Cassuto, *Biblical and Oriental Studies: Bible and Ancient Oriental Texts*, 2 vols., trans. Israel Abrahams (Jerusalem: Magnes, 1975), 2:80. See generally John Miles Foley, *How to Read an Oral Poem* (Urbana: University of Illinois Press, 2002), 137–38.

64. I would distinguish the focus of my inquiry here from the *communis opinio*, summarized by Günter Stemberger ("Dating Rabbinic Traditions," in *The New Testament and Rabbinic Literature*, ed. Reimund Bieringer et al., JSJSup 136 [Leiden: Brill, 2010], 79–96), that earlier rabbinic traditions' *content* tends to be well preserved (if not its precise wording). Regardless of how accurately Rabbah's tales' content was transmitted, the set of formulae under which they were collected itself became an oral tradition: a way to associate or "cross-index" his name with a strange kind of story. This kind of storytelling, his name, and his tales arose—and continued to circulate!—independently. But his reader, our first reader, becomes identifiable in history only when all three were interpretable at one time.

65. Christopher Athanasious Faraone, *Hexametrical Genres from Homer to Theocritus* (Oxford: Oxford University Press, 2021).

texts offer us citation formulae, attributions, and parallels.[66] Any of those units may have been corrupted, falsified, or conflated with another as it was filtered through a matrix of "microforms" and "macroforms," parts and wholes of the oral tradition.[67] But, as a general rule, the memory of who recited a tradition, or another memory of a parallel, is unlikely to have been invented or harmonized systematically by a few rogue rabbis. Even in the large and long-lived canon of the Talmud, generations of otherwise highly creative editors preferred to leave their mark, not on those features of their oral traditions, but by adjusting their content and order;[68] adding citation formulae;[69] expanding a tradition by refashioning an older version;[70] swapping attributions between fixed pairs of authorities;[71] or, rarely and selectively, intentionally deleting an attribution (but leaving behind contradictory parallels).[72] Willful pseudepigraphy does exist, especially if it was deemed to be useful *for* the tradition.[73] But we can treat paralleled attributed traditions cited under stable formulae as relatively early.

---

66. See Martin Jaffee, "What Difference Does the 'Orality' of Rabbinic Writings Make for the Interpretation of Rabbinic Writings?," in *How Should Rabbinic Literature Be Read in the Modern World?* ed. Matthew Kraus, Judaism in Context 4 (Piscataway, NJ: Gorgias, 2006), 11–34, at 31, documenting "core oral-compositional elements analogous to the epithets so often noticed by students of oral-epic composition or *topoi* employed by rhetoricians and public speakers in Greco-Roman antiquity." For example, uses of the *chreia* form—a short biographical datum about the life and teaching of a named sage—have been extensively compared between these oral-performative traditions; see Richard Hidary, *Rabbis and Classical Rhetoric: Sophistic Education and Oratory in the Talmud and Midrash* (Cambridge: Cambridge University Press, 2018), 133–34.

67. For an influential model emphasizing the fluidity between fixed kernels of tradition and compositional forms, see Peter Schäfer, "Handschriften zur Hekhalot-Literatur," in his *Hekhalot-Studien*, TSAJ 19 (Tübingen: Mohr Siebeck, 1988), 154–232, at 215–17.

68. Friedman, "Historical *Aggadah*"; Friedman, "Literary Structure in Bavli *Sugyot*" [Hebrew], in his *Talmudic Studies*, 136–48, at 143–48; Friedman, "The *Sugya* and Its Boundaries" [Hebrew], in his *Talmudic Studies*, 37–56, at 48–54.

69. Richard Kalmin, "Quotation Forms in the Babylonian Talmud: Authentically Amoraic, or a Later Editorial Construct?," *HUCA* 59 (1988): 167–81; Barak S. Cohen, "Citation Formulae in the Babylonian Talmud: From Transmission to Authoritative Traditions," *JJS* 70.1 (2019): 24–44; Shamma Friedman, "Uncovering Literary Dependencies in the Talmudic Corpus," in *The Synoptic Problem in Rabbinic Literature*, ed. Shaye J. D. Cohen, BJS 326 (Providence, RI: Brown Judaic Studies, 2000), 35–57, at 39.

70. Devora Steinmetz, "A Portrait of Miriam in Rabbinic Midrash," *Prooftexts* 8.1 (1988): 35–65, at 47–48.

71. Chanan Gafni, "Orthodoxy and Talmudic Criticism? On Misleading Attributions in the Talmud," *Zutot* 13 (2016): 70–80. On retroactive attributions to famous sages, especially Rabbi Yohanan, see Friedman, "'Wonder Not at an Addition Recorded in the Name of an Amora': The Dicta of the Amoraim and the Anonymous Talmud in Bavli *Sugyot* Revisited" [Hebrew], in his *Talmudic Studies*, 57–135, at 66–68.

72. Vidas, *Tradition and the Formation*, 64–67.

73. Marc Bregman, "Pseudepigraphy in Rabbinic Literature," in *Pseudepigraphic Perspectives: The Apocrypha & Pseudepigrapha in Light of the Dead Sea Scrolls; Proceedings of the International Symposium of the Orion Center for the Study of the Dead Sea Scrolls and Associated*

On that basis, it is not hopeless to imagine our tales for someone who heard them long before they were collected as they are now, even though we cannot know their scope and content at that time. Their most stable feature is the first as well as the most consistent. Indeed, the whole collection is very often called by its name: "the tales of Rabbah bar bar Hanah," their teller, remembered as the one to transmit eleven, or fourteen,[74] of these stories in the Talmud today. Most probably, then, a bare innocuous citation formula linking teller to tales ("Rabbah bar bar Hanah said") is our first clue to how these tales were initially received.

The Teller

What's in a name? For historians of rabbinic literature, less than there used to be.[75] Yet for early readers, who accorded great power and many kinds of meaning to names,[76] the teller and his tales went hand in glove.

Literature, 12–14 January, 1997, ed. Esther G. Chazon and Michael E. Stone, STDJ 31 (Leiden: Brill, 1999) 27–41, with essential literature at 32 n. 24.

74. The first section (I–III) is transmitted in the name of "Rabbah" in some manuscripts, "Rava" in others. In ms. E, II is attributed to "Rabbah bar Hanah." Neither "Rabbah" nor "Rava" by itself is Rabbah bar bar Hanah for us today. As shown by Shamma Friedman, however, Geonic sources invent rules to make sense of the names Rabba(h)/Rava (Rav/Rabbi, "[my] master" + Abba, "father"), and to identify these names with individuals ("On the Orthography of the Names 'Rabbah' and 'Rava,'" [Hebrew], *Sinai* 110 [1992]: 140–64, esp. 151–52; and see Schwartz, *Rewriting the Talmud,* 65–66). Those rules are much later: based on orthography, not on the oral tradition which interests us here. As evidence for *which* rabbi an early reader would have identified as its teller, "Rabbah/Rava" is a distinction without a difference. Indeed, Friedman cites our collection to show that Rabbah bar bar Hanah was called by the same cognomen as *both* (unrelated) figures whom the manuscripts of I–III appear to name, *Abba* (see XIIb and XIIIb). Therefore, the fact that "[bar] bar Hanah" is missing from most manuscripts of I–III is evidence only that *scribes* distinguished the attribution of I–III from that of other tales. This supports further evidence that, as I argue throughout chapter 2, I–III was received as a literary unit. It points to the tales' transmission, not their teller.

75. W. S. Green, "What's in a Name? The Problematic of Rabbinic 'Biography,'" in *Approaches to Ancient Judaism,* vol. 1, ed. William Scott Green, BJS 1 (Missoula, MT: Scholars Press, 1978), 77–96; Jacob Neusner, *Development of a Legend: Studies in the Traditions Concerning Yoḥanan ben Zakkai,* StPB 16 (Leiden: Brill, 1970), 104, 133–34, 190, 273–74; and further literature in Martin S. Jaffee, *Torah in the Mouth: Writing and Oral Tradition in Palestinian Judaism 200 BCE–400 CE* (Oxford: Oxford University Press, 2001), 186 n. 25. These studies are better known for criticizing the historical biography of a rabbi as methodologically indefensible. Yet they also generated valuable models for my subject here: the history of how a figure was read and portrayed, across rabbinic documents, periods, and cultures. For full expositions of this approach, see Alon Goshen-Gottstein, *The Sinner and the Amnesiac: The Rabbinic Invention of Elisha ben Abuya and Eleazer ben Arach,* Contraversions (Stanford, CA: Stanford University Press, 2000), 16–17, 34–36, 73, 199–200, 223–24, 225–29, 258–65; Azzan Yadin, *Scripture and Tradition: Rabbi Akiva and the Triumph of Midrash,* Divinations (Philadelphia: University of Pennsylvania Press, 2015), 103–57.

76. See Redfield, "Names (Rabbinic Judaism)."

One early perspective on their relationship is documented in the tales themselves. After he told two of the tales to Babylonian rabbis, Rabbah bar bar Hanah (Rabbah, for short) reports their reply: "Every Abba is an ass, every bar Hanah is a jackass!" Whatever they were saying exactly,⁷⁷ to them, his name was somehow related to the character of his tales. Neither was good. Perhaps his tales were not taken seriously because he was not; perhaps vice versa or both. "Hanah," the only element of his name that is not generic, connotes "favor"; a "bar Hanah" is not literally a jackass but a son or man of favor (with a feminine ending).⁷⁸ Was he seen not just as an ass but also as wine (homophone of "ass"), intoxicated by his own supply of tales?⁷⁹ Did he play the popular role of entertaining, erudite but unreliable narrator? Those questions will find somewhat firmer historical footing in chapter 4. For early readers, this abuse of the teller's name shows at least that they were not shy about *ad nomen* interpretation—an expedient shortcut if they had no clue what he meant.⁸⁰

Some of Rabbah's tales, also attributed to him, are paralleled elsewhere in the Talmud. This could offer precious evidence for how they were read prior to the stage of the collection. Unfortunately, as the parallels are verbatim and do not fit their other contexts more naturally, they are not necessarily earlier. They could be sources for the collection or extracts from it. Even if we do assume that they are earlier, because our collection seems at first glance like a swollen sore thumb in its own context (see, however,

---

77. The insults are essentially parallel in this context. Babylonian rabbis use "ass" as an insult including for rabbis (b. B. Qam. 92b, b. Ned. 81a). As for "jackass" (סיכסא), its rhetorical function is clarified by a similar string of insults in a fragment of Ben Sira cited by Abbaye at b. Sanh. 100b ("a thick-bearded man is a jackass"). There, too, Amoraim use the word to malign an author's "extreme silliness" (Jenny R. Labendz, "The Book of Ben Sira in Rabbinic Literature," *AJSR* 30.2 [2006]: 347–92, at 366).

78. A man's name, however. Wilhelm Bacher sees Rabbah bar bar Hanah as the son of Rabbah bar Hanah, named after his uncle Hanah, the brother of Hiyya (he is just parroting Tosafot b. Sanh. 5a s.v. רבה בר חנה) (*Die agada der babylonischen Amoräer* [Budapest: Royal University Press, 1878], 87). The evidence for this genealogy is soft.

79. By that logic, the insult is not a repetition but a cause-and-consequence: "[If] every Abba is wine [then] every bar Hanah is a 'son of wine,' " e.g., a man "who blusters about his virtues" (Geonic gloss of סיכסא: *JBA*, 803). Compare the insult "Vinegar, son of wine" (y. Ma'as 3:8, 50d = Pesiq. Rab Kah. 11:19; b. Hul. 105a). Maharshal (*Hokhmat Shlomo* [Brno: Neumann, 1796]), b. B. Bat. 73a s.v. כל אבא חמרא, following Tosafot (see n. 78), similarly analyzes the insults as referring to son and father. "Wine" is not what the text says, but it could have occurred to a reader. Note that ms. H uniquely writes "ass" in Hebrew, nullifying the ambiguity (יב״ב.ק.קנ״ח) and יג״ב.ק״ע).

80. "The play upon equivocal words is particularly clever and depends on language, not on facts, but it seldom raises any considerable laughter, being chiefly praised as evidence of excellent scholarship" (Cicero, *De Oratore* 2.253, quoted in Christopher Rollston, "Ad Nomen Argumenta: Personal Names as Pejorative Puns in Ancient Texts," in *In the Shadow of Bezalel. Ancient, Biblical, and Near Eastern Studies in Honor of Bezalel Porten*, ed. Alejandro F. Botta, CHANE 60 (Leiden: Brill, 2013), 367–86, at 383.

chapter 3), these parallels provide little information about how the teller or his tales were received. If anything, they confirm our impression from the *ad nomen* reactions to Rabbah: he seems both well known and poorly understood. In one parallel, his vision of a giant mythological creature is cited to prove its size in a debate about whether a specimen could have fit in Noah's ark.[81] In another, his encounter with the camp of Qorah, who were swallowed up by the earth, is cited to support a similar tradition that they "did not die" (Num 26:11), but survived to acknowledge God from their infernal resting-place.[82] That is, both parallels absorb Rabbah's tales into a collection of biblical legends, whereas, in our collection, they are filed under his name. Yet the parallels do not explain or expand his tales themselves. Alas, scholarly citation is not always evidence of meaningful understanding. Perhaps just the opposite: perhaps these quotations or other tellings of Rabbah's tales mine them for "data" because no other interpretive tradition yet existed.

Nevertheless, three lines of indirect parallels help to flesh out the sort of teller that an early reader would likely have recognized in Rabbah. The first is a formula, "I myself have seen," by which he introduces many tales, both in our collection and elsewhere. This unusual appeal to the evidence of the eyes is characteristic of Rabbah.[83] I will return to it often, as no reader could ignore it, although the meaning of "vision" would change radically over time. Minimally, an early reader likely interpreted Rabbah's claims to have "seen" strange happenings and sites in the Land of Israel in terms of his common presentation as a sojourner in the West.

A Wild West setting also relates to Rabbah's second characteristic: travels with Arabs, associated with the exotic sort of phenomena that he claimed to have "seen."[84] He says that he saw one Arab woman nursing her infant with her breasts over her shoulders;[85] another who spun

---

81. B. Zevah. 113b. Just as the beast's size ("forty *parasang*") is added in a remark by the anonymous Talmud on the parallel in our tale (IV; chapter 3 §*Chronological Layers*), here too the Talmud is interested only in the beast's size. This suggests that, like their insulting plays on Rabbah's name, "objective" data peripheral to the tales became a safe target when readers had no tradition about what they were about—just as any ill-informed reader tends to judge a book by its cover or publisher, attack *ad hominem*, or substitute classification for interpretation.

82. XIV (= b. Sanh. 110a–b) = Tan. §*Qorah* 27 (= Num. Rab. 18:20).

83. Reuven Kiperwasser, "The Travels of Rabbah bar bar Hanah" [Hebrew], *Jerusalem Studies in Hebrew Folklore* 20 (2008): 215–41, at 224–25.

84. On the term for "Arab" in Rabbah's stories and its connotations, see Sara Ronis, "Imagining the Other: The Magical Arab in Rabbinic Literature," *Prooftexts* 39.1 (2021): 1–28.

85. B. Ketub. 75a. Again, the Talmud cites Rabbah's story to prove how large X (here, a woman's anatomy) could be. The same trope is found in Hellenistic ethnographers: Jennifer L. Morgan, "'Some Could Suckle over Their Shoulder': Male Travelers, Female Bodies, and the Gendering of Racial Ideology, 1500–1770," *William & Mary Quarterly* 54.1 (1997): 167–92, at 170 n. 9.

rose-colored thread and beckoned to him licentiously in the marketplace.[86] He saw an Arab man slice through his camel's arteries with a sword;[87] another who, holding a spear, rode his camel under the towering "Horn of Darkness";[88] and yet another from whom he gleaned the gloss of a rare word in the Bible simply by listening to him talk about his camel.[89] Beyond Arabs with camels and spears in remote locales, who will also appear in our tales, this image of the teller as a rabbi who has learned rare things from them is equally consistent.[90]

Combinations of other Arab motifs, in other Rabbah stories, confirm that our Rabbah was not an unknown figure but, on the contrary, a traditional storyteller with a special profile. He tells a tale of using the excuse that he "forgot a golden dove" for his caravan in the desert, leaving them stranded as he returns to pray in the proper place. His reward is a golden dove.[91] Similarly, in one of our tales (XV), he travels with an Arab to a

---

86. B. Ketub. 72b. This version of the story is marked by the keyword "Arabess" (*'arvaya'*), who sounds like—and trades places with—the biblical woman *'Orpah* in a parallel, interpreting, in turn, "giant" (*harafah*, 2 Sam 21:16). See Geoffrey Herman, "'One Day David Went Out for the Hunt of the Falconers': Persian Themes in the Babylonian Talmud," in *Shoshannat Yaakov: Jewish and Iranian Studies in Honor of Yaakov Elman*, ed. Shai Secunda and Steven Fine, Brill Reference Library of Judaism 35 (Leiden: Brill, 2012), 111–36, at 104 n. 10; 117–18 n. 29. Unusually, Rabbah speaks Hebrew here, but, due to his association with Arabs, he would have been readily cast as a suitable narrator, once the tale was retold about an Arabess. (In mss. Munich 95 and Vatican 113, *FJMS*, he attributes it to his Palestinian teacher Rabbi Yohanan; see n. 71. That could explain the Hebrew—but not why Rabbah retells it, of all people.)

87. B. Yevam. 120b. In b. Sanh. 67b (all mss.), Rav tells the same first-person story. Both tellings are cited to prove similar claims: that the camel died quickly (Rabbah) or was truly dead (Rav). Each teller adds to the report as he predicates his claim, a claim that is immediately challenged by others. This shows that "I myself saw an Arab slice a camel" was a rhetorical topos not unique to Rabbah. But, like other Arab-related topoi, it suited him well.

88. B. Ta'an. 22b. Here again the Talmud uses Rabbah's story just to prove how big something was. Rabbah cites the height of an Arab's spear to show how big something was in our collection as well (XIIa). "Height of a spear length" is also a figure for great size in the Avesta; see Helmut Humbach and Pallan R. Ichaporia, *Zamyād Yasht: Yasht 19 of the Younger Avesta; Text, Translation, Commentary* (Wiesbaden: Harrassowitz, 1998), 40, 118.

89. B. Rosh Hash. 26b = b. Meg. 18a (compare y. Meg 2:2, 73a). See also Ber. Rab. 79:7 (ed. Theodor-Albeck, 945–49); and Arthur Cohen, "Arabisms in Rabbinic Literature," *JQR* 3.2 (1912): 221–33, at 232. These sources contain similar material about learning rare words from colloquial Arabic speech, featuring different rabbis.

90. In our collection (XI), the same verb that Rabbah says he learned from an Arab (י.ה.ב) is repeated in the mouth of an Arab in all manuscripts except H, P. This could be anything from a faint memory to a direct allusion to the sources in n. 89. Compare the fourfold conjunction with Rabbah of ש.ע.י (b. Yoma 9b), a verb that was also used to expand the collection of his tales (see nn. 133–134). Repeated words linked to a particular character may signal a reading tradition about him.

91. B. Ber. 53b. Mira Balberg shows that this story is the exemplification of a legal rule: the view of the House of Shammai (vs. House of Hillel) that one should return to pray in a place where one forgot to do so (*Fractured Tablets: Forgetfulness and Fallibility in Late Ancient*

holy place where, as he is praying, his basket (or skullcap under his turban, in an old Sephardi reading),[92] goes missing. If he stays in place, the Arab assures him, he will get it back.[93] In another tale, he finds a dried ram's lung in the desert and, returning to Babylonia, consults the sages about its legal status. While it is told *about* Rabbah, rather than by him, its teller uses one of his introductory formulae in our tales; the two tellers may be on intimate terms, if not one and the same.[94] And one of our tales (XIII) fuses the above motifs, resulting in a somewhat disjointed structure. Rabbah is again "traveling in the desert" and takes a special item. His Arab guide tells him that he must return it before his camel can go on; but when he tells this story to the sages, they comment only on its legal status. It looks as if two Rabbah story-types (Western Travels; Reports to the Academy) were stuck together as a diptych: his Arab guide represents knowledge of the exotic landscape,[95] whereas the Babylonian study-house stays in its own world. From this rough draft, the diptych form—East and West, Home and Away, Scholars and Exotica—would become part of the

---

Rabbinic Culture [Oakland: University of California Press, 2023], 154–55). It is noteworthy that one of our tales (XIIa) has the same structure: Rabbah is again told to turn back, from his caravan, to return to his place; and again, his peers interpret his actions in light of *another* legal dispute between the Houses of Shammai and Hillel—this time explicitly. Making sense of his stories using this legal framework already seems popular among Amoraim. It develops in the anonymous Talmud: in mss. H, P, M, E (יב״א.קנ״ד), the instruction to Rabbah to turn back is in the Arab's voice but uses a formula (גמירי) that makes the Arab sound like a legal scholar, suggesting a scholastic reading tradition of the tales by anonymous readers. On this formula, see Emanuel Fiano, *Three Powers in Heaven: The Emergence of Theology and the Parting of the Ways*, Synkrisis (New Haven: Yale University Press, 2023), 200–202 nn. 16–19; Vidas, *Tradition and the Formation*, 57 n. 28; Wilhelm Bacher, *Die exegetische Terminologie der jüdischen Traditionsliteratur*, 2 vols. (Leipzig: Hinrichs, 1905), 2:30–31, and see n. 400.

92. The Rif, cited by Joseph Ibn Migash, in Betsalel Ashkenazi, *Shitta Mequbbetset*, 2nd ed., 8 vols. (Tel-Aviv: Tsiyoni, 1955), 7:340, b. B. Bat. 73b s.v. עתידין ישראל ליתן עליהם את הדין (reading לכומתא for לסילתא, ln. טו.קפ״ט).

93. For a similar cosmology, see t. Qidd. 5:17. Saul Lieberman, *Tosefta Ki-feshutah: A Comprehensive Commentary on the Tosefta* [Hebrew], 10 vols. (New York: Jewish Theological Seminary, 1955–2001), 8:986 notes b. B. Bat. 16b, where some manuscripts trace this motif of solar "wheels" or "wings" to Mal 3:20. Similarly, note that in b. Pesah. 94b, gentile astronomers hold that the earth turns, whereas Jewish astronomers hold that the stars turn around the earth. Similarly here, our speaker is an Arab, but his astronomy reflects the Jewish view. Compare his effortless quotation of Micah 3:3, XIV.186, which further undercuts his stereotype as an exotic Other. See also n. 402.

94. B. Hul. 55b; "I/we was/were traveling in the desert" appears at Xa; XI; XIV (mss. N, B). See also XXI, where the formula is picked up by a later teller in his addition to Rabbah's tales.

95. Compare b. Shabb. 85a: biblical Horites are so called because, like the Arab, they "smell [*merihim*] the earth." Similarly, in a Geonic midrash, "children of the east" (1 Kgs 4:30 [1 Kgs 5:10]) become "the Arabs, who know what the birds of the deserts are, who sniff the dust and are familiar with everywhere they go" (*Sefer Pitron Torah: A Collection of Midrashim and Interpretations* [Hebrew], ed. E. E. Urbach [Jerusalem: Magnes, 1978], 172).

pattern for recollecting Rabbah's tales (see chapter 3 §*Chronological Layers*). Editors of his tales thus show awareness of how they had been read.

By the same token, beyond our tales or similar ones that he told, Rabbah had his own niche in the sages' institutional memory. One did not have to know any of his stories well to recognize a familiar face. He was remembered as a traveler to the study centers of Roman Palestine, where he learned legal dicta from major third-century rabbis.[96] Yet he seems to have been a perpetual outsider—a Babylonian to the Palestinians, a Palestinian to the Babylonians. A Palestinian tells Rabbah, "God, I hate you people!" (i.e., Babylonians in Palestine),[97] and he is a reluctant visitor to a lecture in Pumbedita, where he chimes in, citing a Baghdadi authority.[98] Yet he is also remembered as a student of the foremost Palestinian Amora, Rabbi Yohanan,[99] to the extent that some of their dicta would become confused.[100] He even reportedly said that he would have preferred to live under Roman rather than Persian rule.[101] Later Babylonians imagined that

---

96. Hanokh Albeck, *Introduction to the Talmud, Bavli and Yerushalmi* [Hebrew] (Tel-Aviv: Dvir, 1969), 305–6. Using this and other reference-works, I reexamined all of the sources on Rabbah and drew up his character sketch in an early reader's mind. This is evidence for the afterlife of a fictional persona, not the life of a person. Contrast Tziona Grossmark, *Travel Narratives in Rabbinic Literature: Voyages to Imaginary Realms* (Lewiston: Mellen, 2010), which, by trying to harmonize the same data-set into a realistic biography, misreads a stock polemic as a personal anecdote (40) and underplays gaps between Babylonian and Palestinian sources (41–42).

97. B. Yoma 9b. On this famous story and its cultural dynamic, see Reuven Kiperwasser, *Going West: Migrating Personae and Construction of the Self in Rabbinic Culture*, BJS 369 (Providence, RI: Brown Judaic Studies, 2021), 127–32. Yonatan Feintuch argues convincingly that the Babylonian version is a subtle polemic against Palestinian rabbis' chauvinism ("The Story of the Encounter between Resh Lakish and Rabbah bar bar Hannah [bYoma 9b] in Its Broader Talmudic Context" [Hebrew], *Jewish Studies, an Internet Journal* 12 [2013]: 1–23).

98. B. Shabb. 148a. In this story, Rabbah is an outsider. Unlike the Baghdadi, the lecturer does not call him "one of ours." Rather, he dragged Rabbah to attend the talk (after he "happened to come" to town). On this story formula, see Judith Hauptman, *The Stories They Tell: Halakhic Anecdotes in the Babylonian Talmud*, Judaism in Context 32 (Piscatawy, NJ: Gorgias, 2022), 45–88. Yet nor is Rabbah identified as Palestinian. He is merely an outsider to this local center, and the point—as the story concludes—is that his visit actually helps that place to *preserve* its own legal traditions. A similar implicit point is made by the surrounding passage (b. Shabb. 147a–148a), where Rabbah is the conduit for legal traditions from both regions that the Talmud cites solely on their merits without placing him anywhere. The effect is to delocalize Rabbah, making him a traveler across time and space rather than a *homo academicus*.

99. B. Shabb. 60b. Here, Rabbah's encounter with a Babylonian sage again puts him "out of place" and Rabbah's view is explained by his Palestinian teacher's practice, as opposed to that of Babylonians (again, in Pumbedita).

100. See b. Yoma 20b = b. Yoma 39b. In the latter, ms. British Library 400 and prints (*FJMS*) "forget" that R. Yohanan was Rabbah's source. The reverse confusion occurs in prints of b. Eruv. 55b and, in b. Meg. 6a, in prints and mss. British Library 400, Munich 95, and the Geniza fragment Cambridge T-S F1(2) 120 [ב]. See nn. 71 and 86.

101. B. Git. 17a. See Isaiah M. Gafni, "Babylonian Rabbinic Culture," in his *Jews and*

he planned to return to the Land of Israel, when they recalled him telling his own son that he could not transmit Rabbi Yohanan's legal custom, because it was invalid outside the master's presence.[102] Was Rabbah nostalgic for the West?[103] Perhaps. Yet his bond to the Palestinian master was useful in Babylonia, rendering old glosses for flora native to Palestine.[104]

Like John Wayne and the Wild West, Rabbah and the landscape of the Land of Israel ran together in his early readers' minds, even if not one of his tales was shot on location. He seemed to have been everywhere: measuring distances from Jerusalem to Jericho,[105] across the Plains of Moab,[106] from the village of Ludim to the city of Lod beyond the Land's borders.[107] He was irrepressibly vivid in recounting not only distances but quantities and wonders of all kinds. Of course he added to a utopian composition about the bounties of the Land of Israel, claiming to have seen this "land flowing with milk and honey," and evoking its vast scale in a way that made it easy for his audience to picture—by comparison with real Babylonian places.[108] Similarly, Rabbah reported that he had personally wit-

---

Judaism in the Rabbinic Era: Image and Reality—History and Historiography, TSAJ 173 (Tübingen: Mohr Siebeck, 2019), 219–45, at 221–22.

102. B. Pesah. 51a. Here, Rabbah figures in a debate on a similar topic as b. Shabb. 60b (see n. 99): the authority and transmissibility of a local teacher's legal practice given differences in this law between Palestine and Babylonia. Again we see that Rabbah was useful as a figure for the interloper to both Amoraim and anonymous readers.

103. His statement in b. Git. 17a is interpreted as such *ad loc*. B. B. Bat. 52a quotes Rabbah's wife but, due to generic names, textual instability, and vague chronology, it is unclear where this storyteller thought they lived.

104. B. Ber. 40b (on m. Demai 1:1).

105. B. Yoma 20b = b. Yoma 39b (on the attribution, see n. 100).

106. B. Yoma 75b = b. Eruv. 55b. Rabbah, or his source R. Yohanan (see n. 100), claims, "I have seen that place myself." The same measure reappears in b. Ber. 54b as an anonymous later tradition. Contrast Tg. Ps. Jon. Num 21:35: a related, even bigger version, with the measure doubled. Exaggeration is contagious! (See n. 8).

107. B. Git. 4a. For an explanation of these locations in the context of this passage, see Gottfried Reeg, *Die Ortsnamen Israels nach der rabbinischen Literatur*, Beihefte zum Tübinger Atlas des Vorderen Orients B.51 (Wiesbaden: Reichert, 1989), 349 [read 4a, not 6a]; 381–84.

108. B. Ketub. 111b = b. Meg. 6a (see b. Git. 4a). Hyperbolic natural bounty is also a stock feature of Greek exoticism: "Somehow the edges of the inhabited world have been endowed with the best and finest resources" (Herodotus, *Histories* 3.106; in *The Landmark Herodotus: The Histories*, ed. Robert B. Strassler, trans. Andrea L. Purvis (New York: Pantheon, 2007), 258. On this utopian source, see Jeffrey L. Rubenstein, "Coping with the Virtues of the Land of Israel: An Analysis of Bavli Ketubbot 110a–112b" [Hebrew], in *Center and Diaspora: The Land of Israel and the Diaspora in the Second Temple, Mishna, and Talmud Periods*, ed. Isaiah Gafni (Jerusalem: Shazar Center, 2004), 159–89. This source uses editorial techniques and anonymous traditions that overlap closely with both parts 1 and 2 of our composition. Such overlaps include rhetorical patterns (Two introductory formulae: "Once ..." [פעם אחת/זמנא אחד]; "But perhaps you'll say, it hurts ...? The statement teaches ..."). Both sources also share a tale about "X *as large as* Y" followed by a formulaic question-and-answer sequence, and motifs (hyperboles: "up to the ankles" for depth, "sixty" for size; the phrase "X [standing] as big as Y," where X or Y is an animal—compare b. B. Ketub. 112a/ה"סק.א"יג). They even share

nessed the shade cast by the miraculous castor plant in the book of Jonah, which heals "the invalids of the West" to the present day.[109] Naturally, this sort of claim left Rabbah open to charges of hyperbole. One of his reports was received as an exaggeration—possibly in the face of evidence that its source, Rabbi Yohanan, had meant something else entirely.[110] When Rabbah recited his teacher's view on the extreme case of a placenta that stayed in the womb for twenty-three days, a colleague queried his high figures as self-contradictory and therefore inaccurately reported: "You had told us twenty-four."[111] Already in his time, it seems, Rabbah was acquiring a reputation.

But a reputation to whom? Where and when were these early readers of Rabbah? The patterns that we have just identified come almost entirely from the Talmud (of Babylonia) because only there did Rabbah ("our" Rabbah, the collection's main and original teller) flourish.[112] In Palestinian sources, the man whose name he bears, (R.) Abba bar bar Hanah, has none of his characteristic features. True, Abba's pedigree is no better than

---

type-scenes like playful competition with an autochthonous "local" over the literal land of Israel [Amorite, b. Ketub. 112a; nomadic Arab, XI]. The extent, variety, and depth of these overlaps reveals a similar signature for the composers of both complex literary units. This supports the proposal that comparison of story cycles, and perhaps other extended compositions in the Talmud, can reveal the "methods of reworking, composition, and even narrative art of the redactors" (Rubenstein, "Story-Cycles," 279).

109. B. Shabb. 21a (my translation follows Rashi, who will be cited from the margin of ed. Vilna throughout the book. Compare the idea that infirm Jews who live in the Land of Israel are forgiven their sins: b. Ketub. 111a. Most manuscripts attribute the latter idea to Rabbah's namesake "R. Abba," reinforcing the link between traditions. See n. 74).

110. In b. Ber. 44a (= b. Erub. 30a), one of Rabbah's exotic tales is appended to a legal debate. His master, Rabbi Yohanan, ate a thousand of the sweetest fruits from the Land of Israel, but "swore that he had never tasted food." The Talmud then attacks Rabbah's wording: Rabbi Yohanan did not mean "food" literally! This objection likely alludes to another of Rabbah's stories about when he brought fruit to Palestinian rabbis and they, too, did not act as if fruit counts as a meal (b. Hul. 106a; see Rashi, b. Ber. 44a s.v. זיינא and s.v. מזונא). That is, the attack on Rabbah's tale by the anonymous Talmud is a voice of a reader who holds that he misunderstood his own teacher—a valid critique if this reader knows that Rabbah had *already* told a contradictory story about other Palestinians. The net effect is to lower his credibility as a teller by reading the language of his tales through a narrow legal logic, assuming that they were told to exemplify a single legal idea and must be mutually consistent in that light. Compare the reading tradition in n. 91.

111. B. Nid. 27a. In the next source cited there (mss. Vatican 113, Bologna AS Fr. ebr. 195, Cambridge T-S NS 329.73; *FJMS*), Rav Yosef attacks another report of Rabbi Yohanan's view, about the same question, in the same way. It seems, lacking another tradition or rationale, he likes to use self-contradiction against opponents.

112. The exceptional variety and quantity of Palestinian traditions that Rabbah cites in the Babylonian Talmud may show that he was "a critical link in moving traditions" from West to East (Michael Satlow and Michael Sperling, "The Rabbinic Citation Network," *AJSR* 46.2 (2022): 291–319, at 314). Conversely, lack of uptake of his traditions by other rabbis, and his lower profile in the Palestinian tradition, may indicate that he was not influential or authoritative in his own right—a conduit, not a generator.

Rabbah's; one colleague attacks him for acting above his station.[113] Like Rabbah, Abba is tied to Rabbi Yohanan; in fact, he is cited almost only as a transmitter of his teacher's legal dicta.[114] But Rabbi Yohanan had many students; there is nothing special about what this Abba learned from him.

Only one Palestinian story has closer parallels to the Babylonian Rabbah tradition. The Mishnah holds that, if someone who was transporting a bill of divorce (*get*) misplaces it, it must be found "on the spot" or becomes invalid lest it have been tampered with meanwhile. Rabbi Yohanan defines "on the spot" as "anywhere that no creature has passed through [meanwhile]." The Palestinian Talmud asks about a *get* that was misplaced where a gentile (*goy*) passed through. Is this valid? To prove that it is, a story follows of Abba bar bar Hanah, who was delivering a *get* that he misplaced. An Arab ("Saracen") returned it to him and Rabbi Yohanan himself validated it.[115] This story could be a Palestinian rendition, also in legalese, of motifs from Rabbah's adventures with a golden dove and a basket at the end of the earth.[116] In all three stories, our hero misplaces a special item on the road with Arab travelers.[117] Like a treasure hunt, the key to getting it back is to stay in, return to, or mark the true "spot"/"place." A legal reading tradition for making sense of these exotic motifs already seems in effect here.

This relationship between one Palestinian and two Babylonian stories shows that we might be able to draw a line from Abba bar bar Hanah to Rabbah in an early reader's mind. But the line is paper-thin: a few of the legal problems that a few of his stories raised were interpreted along generally similar lines. Unlike past efforts to create a unified biography of the Palestinian and Babylonian figures because they have the same name and

---

113. Y. Ber. 8:5, 12b. Abba bar bar Hanah is rude, witty, maybe tipsy here—a similar *raconteur* but not the same.

114. Albeck, *Introduction to the Talmud*, 305.

115. Y. Git. 3:3, 44d = y. Yebam. 16:6, 15d. This is also consistent with Rabbi Yohanan's position reported by Abba bar bar Hanah in y. Eruv. 2:1, 20a. For early readers, this may bring Abba bar bar Hanah closer to R. Yohanan, but it does not make him the same as Rabbah bar bar Hanah.

116. B. Ber. 53b. See n. 91. Rabbah bar bar Hanah also transmits Rabbi Yohanan's view on a *get* in b. Git. 21b.

117. In b. Ber. 53b, Arabs are not mentioned, but they may be in Rabbah's "caravan," as his caravan does not seem to accept Jewish prayer customs (which is why he has to lie to them about the "golden dove" in the first place). The "caravan" also speaks of God differently, in a florid, perhaps deliberately foreign idiom: "Pray–wherever you pray, you pray to the Merciful One [*Rahmana*]." This became a predominant name for God in Judaizing late ancient southern Arabia. See Sigrid K. Kjær, " 'Rahman' Before Muhammad: A Pre-history of the First Peace (*Sulh*) in Islam," *Modern Asian Studies* 56 (2022):775–96; Christian Robin, "The Judaism of the Ancient Kingdom of Himyar in Arabia: A Discreet Conversion," in *Diversity and Rabbinization: Jewish Texts and Societies between 400 and 1,000 CE*, ed. G. McDowell et al., Cambridge Semitic Languages and Cultures 8 (Cambridge: Open Book, 2022), 165–269, at 176–81.

same (prolific) teacher, once we focus on an early reader's perspective, the two figures have little in common. If they knew this story, perhaps a reader in Palestine was aware that Abba not only studied with Rabbi Yohanan but also traveled with Arabs and was cast as absent-minded but lucky. So this reader might not have been surprised that Abba led a double life as a wild storyteller in the East. But most, if not all, would have found Rabbah unrecognizable, because he did not resemble their Abba. And vice versa: Rabbah's tales are not linked to Abba, and we have no evidence that either rabbi told them in Palestine (even if they returned there later) before they were told in Babylonia. Early Palestinian traces of either the teller or his tales do not a tradition make.

No better evidence is offered by Palestinian works of biblical exegesis (*midrash*), where we might expect to find Rabbah's stories in some form. Either they are not paralleled very closely,[118] or they are not attributed to Abba bar bar Hanah.[119] One version has signs of accommodation to the Babylonian tradition and may show transmission from East to West.[120] Rabbah himself addresses his audience as Babylonians: he measures distances in Palestine in Babylonian terms[121] and speaks pointedly of "the West."[122] Although most of his tales are set in the Wild West of the Land of Israel, his first reader was more likely in the eastern diaspora. And far before they were collected in the Talmud as a literary whole, some of his

---

118. Ber. Rab. 19:4 and Vay. Rab. 22:10 describe a mythological bird (*ziz*); the latter's prooftext is also Rav Ashi's (IXb). They also contain midrashim like those in part 2. Those sources are not direct parallels to Rabbah's own tales but later compositions from a common pool of traditions (see chapter 5 and Appendix §*Parallels to Part 2 in Pesiqta of Rab Kahana*). Similarly, Qoh. Rab. 10.1.2 has a midrash that builds on Rabbah's tale (XIV, see n. 120; and see ed. Kiperwasser, 255). Midr. Ps. 120:4 (see Ber. Rab. 98:19 / y. Peah 1:1, 16a) has content attributed to Huna bar Natan and Amemar in XXIa (itself an addition to Rabbah's core collection; see chapter 3 §*Chronological Layers*).

119. Even where the content is fully parallel: Ber. Rab. 79:7 (= b. Rosh Hash. 26b = b. Meg. 18a. See nn. 89-90).

120. Tan. §*Qorah* 27 (= Num. Rab. 18:20, a later work). In this expanded version, Rabbah appears to end his nasty tale in the Talmud (XIV) on a note of consolation, which is a basic convention of rabbinic preaching: "And in time to come, the Holy One, Blessed Be He, shall bring [the followers of Qorah] out [of Gehenna]. And of them says Hannah, *The Lord deals death and grants life, brings down to Sheol and lifts up* [1 Sam. 2:6]" [trans. Alter]. This looks like an apologetic for his original story, constructed by editors who recycled an identical comment about Qorah (b. Sanh. 109b) and connected the sources by similar-sounding names (Rabbah bar bar Hanah and the biblical Hannah). For similar examples, see Shamma Friedman, "*Nomen est Omen*: Dicta of the Talmudic Sages which Echo the Author's Name" [Hebrew], in *These Are the Names: Studies in Jewish Onomastics*, vol. 2, ed. A. Demsky et al.; Ramat-Gan: Bar-Ilan University Press, 1999), 51–77, at 66–67.

121. B. Ketub. 111b–112a; in b. Git. 4a, Rabbah eyewitnesses Palestinian places and measures them by Babylonian ones.

122. B. Shabb. 21a (in b. Shabb. 145b, "sick men of the West" may be polemical; compare "pampered," and see n. 831).

Introduction 37

adventures were already studio productions: staged and scripted for Rabbah by anonymous Babylonian storytellers who left little trace of their motives, obliging us to ask an equally bemused crowd of readers what his stories meant.

* * * * *

Such bemusement is itself a salient factor in the tales' history. Our survey of a reader's associations with the most prominent and stable feature of Rabbah's tales—the teller himself—has given us a feel for this strange quality of their early reception more broadly. In a word, it was mixed. "Rabbi Father, Grandson of Favor" didn't have much of a pedigree.[123] His name's uses or abuses show that he was not always taken seriously. He claimed to have seen more things firsthand than anyone else, but his audience tended to look at them through the other end of their scholastic telescope. "Well …," they replied, again and again, "just how big was it?" Or: "Yesterday, you said it was a bit smaller…" His claims to travel in the desert with Arabs and caravans yielded new information in many areas (comparative Semitics;[124] biology; exotic locales of all kinds), and other data that he imported was useful for rabbinic botany and zoology. Still, early readers' favorite solution to the interpretive challenge that his tales posed was to under-read them. They valued his transmission of laws and rare words from the West, especially from Rabbi Yohanan. But, as a marginal Babylonian abroad, he was also a useful target (or agent) for rabbinic self-criticism. Back home, all the more so. An Arabic word or tale of fantastic flora and fauna helped some colleagues to interpret the Bible. Others insulted him outright. Many opted for a devastating No Comment. The fact that his tales survived proves they were more popular than his first readers let on—but not that they understood him. One can enjoy a tale without knowing what it means. In some, not knowing is part of the fun.

This brings to hand a better word for the teller and his tales in their first documented context, that is, rabbinic centers of Babylonia in the late third and fourth centuries. Above and beyond this mixed bag of praise, blame, misapprehension, or indifference, both were received as simply very *strange*. That strangeness is the true hero of our own adventure in this book. It is the strongest, most predictable reaction of Rabbah's readers as far as the eye can see, from the very beginning to the present day. Show

---

123. On the name's etymology and distribution, see Tal Ilan, *Lexicon of Jewish Names in Late Antiquity*, 4 vols. (Tübingen: Mohr Siebeck, 2002–2009), 4:365–66.

124. See nn. 89–90, n. 119. Note that the Arab woman, in a story told by Rabbah (b. Ketub. 72b), addresses him with the coquettish Arabism עולם ("young man") and the same verb as his other story about Arabic (ב.ה.י). Rabbah not only travels with Arabs but has an ear for Arabic (like the Palestinian Rabbi Levi, who collects other words in this semantic field). See editors' notes to Ber. Rab. 36:1 (ed. Theodor-Albeck, 335); see Ber. Rab. 87:1.

me a reader who fully, truly understands these stories and—as they say of the reader of Augustine's complete works—I'll show you a liar.[125] Rabbah was received as a stranger in a strange land, estranged from his own colleagues and readers, telling strange stories that passed without comment (including his own) or were soon reduced to mundane academic exercises: ridicule, biblical glosses, footnotes to legal debates. Readers resorted to criticizing his name, numbers, and logical inconsistencies. Or they simply changed the subject. Yet no one said that they had thereby exhausted the meaning of his tales. On the contrary, even in their mockery, pedantry, incomprehension, apologetics or polemics with respect to Rabbah himself, his readers marked a persistent gap between what he said and the sense that they could make of it. In spite of their varied efforts at interpretation, the sheer strangeness of his tales defied any clear resolution, even as his gift of gab brought them back begging for more. For the next fifteen centuries, the story of Rabbah's adventures is a perfect model for a "history of nonsense" at the heart of traditional Judaism;[126] a search for lines of dis/continuity in how readers tried to grasp something that they never truly could. The end of such a story, then, cannot be to return to the tales' pure original meaning, which never existed for anyone we know. However, by taking up links in a chain of specific readers' irrepressibly creative ways to make sense of Rabbah's nonsense, we can reconstruct the unity and diversity of their own approaches to the art of reading, and thereby find our way back to each of them.

Collection and Recollecting

By repeatedly underlining the difference between the talmudic collection of Rabbah's stories, on one hand, and early responses to the individual stories and storyteller, on the other, collecting has come into view as a potent vehicle for interpretation in its own right. Readers interpreted much of the content in the collection without being aware of the collection itself. There is no proof that verbatim parallels in other rabbinic texts are taken from the collection, or vice versa. A parallel collection in the Zoroastrian *Bundahišn* resembles it, but no one has proven that one is a direct

---

125. *Mentitur qui te totum legisse fatetur / Aut quis cuncta tua lector habere potest?* ("He lies who says he's read all of you / or which reader is able to?"). *Graffito* above the cupboard where Isidore of Seville kept his copies of Augustine, in Peter Brown, "Saint Augustine," in *Trends in Medieval Political Thought*, ed. Beryl Smalley (Oxford: Clarendon), 1965, 1–21, at 18 n. 1.

126. On the epigraph of this introduction, see Abe Socher, "The History of Nonsense," *AJSR Perspectives* (Fall 2006): 32–33; Yaacob Dweck, *The Scandal of Kabbalah: Leon Modena, Jewish Mysticism, Early Modern Venice* (Princeton: Princeton University Press, 2011), 1.

source for the other or that verbatim content was exchanged.[127] The facts that our collection is unique to Babylonia, and that it seems to interrupt its context, may indicate that it is a late interpolation. Even if so, this would not prove that it is a late collection: it could have been collected earlier and simply transmitted there.[128] All this goes to show that we need to carefully establish, rather than assume, that a reader had access to something like our collection and interpreted the stories in that light, rather than as single motifs or episodes.

As we saw by studying the teller of the tales and some of their widely cited early content, before Rabbah's tales were collected as a whole, some readers seem to have interpreted them not as narratives at all but more as a data-set. Honing in on "objective" content like names, numbers, or rare words, readers raised and resolved problems about laws, large phenomena, and the teller's reputation—not about narrative structure or content. By contrast, revisit, for a moment, my translation of the entire collection of Rabbah's tales (I–XV). On the page alone, you have rich resources for creating the tales' narrative meaning. This collection spurs you to form connections among its parts along a spiderweb of lines, activating many dimensions of intellect, affect, or devotion. Taking the collection as a literary unity, how can we describe those potential intersections between collection, text, and reader?

Some are lines of connection along which our culture teaches us to interpret any story. We simply read a group of stories in the same way. If, in my culture, a story has three parts—beginning, middle, end—that are related causally, in linear time, with tension in the middle and an upward or downward arc,[129] I can read texts together as if they had a story structure. In our collection, I might, for instance, read unit I (Sailors on a Stormy Sea) as the beginning; II (Sailors Subdue Waves with God's Name) as the middle; and III (Hormiz Leaps/Is Killed) as the end. Regardless of whether

---

127. Bnd. 24.II.8–9. See *The Bundahišn: The Zoroastrian Book of Creation*, ed. and trans. Domenico Agostini and Samuel Thrope (Oxford: Oxford University Press, 2020), 119–24. The source is layered, "heterogeneous and composed of fragments of earlier textual traditions," (Reuven Kiperwasser and Dan D. Y. Shapira, "Irano-Talmudica III: Giant Mythological Creatures in Transition from the Avesta to the Babylonian Talmud," in *Orality and Textuality in the Iranian World: Patterns of Interaction across the Centuries*, ed. Julia Rubanovich, Jerusalem Studies in Religion and Culture [Leiden: Brill, 2015], 65–92, at 66–70) and lacks well-documented intermediate stages, making any chronology of motifs or narrative structures speculative.

128. The paucity of anonymous material and relatively straightforward chronological organization by attribution might point to a gradual but still relatively earlier dating. See chapter 3 §*Chronological Layers*.

129. These ingredients are prescribed in Aristotle, *Poetics* 7.1450b; 10.1452a; 13.1453a; 18.1455b. See the new translation: Aristotle, *How to Tell a Story: An Ancient Guide to the Art of Storytelling for Writers and Readers*, trans. Philip Freeman (Princeton, NJ: Princeton University Press, 2022).

I am aware of this, once I have collected the text's parts as a story, further story structures in my culture will snap into place and affect how I read the collection. I might start to think that Waves mark themes and build tension; God's Name is the climax; and Death is the moral. I might incorporate more stories in the collection into this reading, creating a four-part story. I might even read units I–III as a "drama" or a "tragedy," applying a genre label for its features that would help me to derive further meaning from it by comparing it to others in the same genre, or vice versa. I might, and another reader might not: "myth" seems closer than "drama" to how early readers did so, and we will revisit this hypothesis in chapters 1–2.

Here, the general point is that, for a reader, collection is both an activity and the result of such activity. That result, in turn, limits and redirects the activity itself—a recursive process of traditional interpretive creation. By connecting texts (reading-together), readers form new collections. Yet new collections are patterned on old—not only at the level of form or content, but also in the lines along which readers engage them. Hence, the idea of collection contains two analytically separable processes. First, collecting texts to form new links between them. Second, identifying and reworking those inherited links, as one reader in dialogue with other readers, who are all actively recollecting a group of texts along interpretive lines nowhere "in" the texts themselves. Both aspects of the reading process—collection and recollecting—develop within a tradition and may leave traces on its texts. But they are driven by the development of the tradition—not by the texts' actual content. Each tradition has its norms for how collections can be made, what constitutes a valid link between texts, and how readers can recollect its collections.

Returning to our hypothetical example of a three-part story (I–III), units I–II have no narrative connection with III. The characters never interact. The settings differ. The sole link between them is the name of a teller, "Rabbah" (itself unstable in manuscripts). Yet, unless we prove that another specific reader *also* read I, II, or III separately, how do we know that the earliest reader did *not* see I–III as a three-part story that features a change of scene and characters? Short, simple tales are neither primordial nor universal; if anything, ancient oral sagas suggest the opposite. Indeed, chapter 2 will show how a reader may have created the meaning of I–III by way of other narratives that they knew (e.g., a story embedded *within* it, based on Ps 107), or via fluid connections to a treasury of mythic imagery and exegesis that they had received. Again, the general point here is that we can never take for granted even the basic message, "the" text, that a specific reader was perceiving, let alone interpreting. The elementary units of meaning are in the eye of a reader, whose gaze is guided by the collector and other readers, along the lines of a shared interpretive tradition. As collectors connect stories, even borders between stories that were once independent can blur. In the process, stories can disappear into a series of stories, and a collection itself can become interpretable as a single larger story.

Nor, again, did readers necessarily interpret our collection as a narrative. Collections in the Talmuds and the Midrashim reflect a large cultural inventory of compositional patterns. A reader may have engaged our collection as a story, as another sort of pattern, or as both. By way of example, glance back at my translation of Part 1. It is harder to capture in English, but the numbered units that I am calling "stories" or "tales" also connect along non-narrative lines. The connections that you notice and, thus, the very kind of recollection that you create by reading-together texts in the collection, depend on what grabs your attention. If you focus on repeated introductory formulae about traveling, or cosmic extremes like Sea and Desert, you may recollect this collection as a narrative—even a swashbuckling subtype of narrative, an Adventure. On that basis, you may assimilate other textual content into your interpretation. If, on the other hand, you attend to refrains, meter, and sound, you may turn at least parts of this collection into a poem. In a poem, links between some parts are better foregrounded or marked—more full of potential meaning—than others. A reader/hearer does not have to, indeed cannot, attend to every element equally. When one listens to a poem rather than analyzing a narrative, the most vivid images, the most singular words against the background of repeated sounds and rhythms, draw attention to elevated moments. Merely stereotypical and stale repetitions fade from view; other repetitions can become an incantatory litany. A hearer's interpretation of a poem, their dynamic response—not only rational but also affective, devotional, etc.—recollects select elements of its language in sequences of images, sounds, and rhythms that need not dovetail with plot. A reader of a poem may notice different aspects of the text than its climax, for instance. To show this, I will ask how subtle shifts in attention led audiences to perceive the tales in one way or another (chapter 3 §*Structure* and §*Poetry*).

By highlighting how these competing construals of "the" text can arise from interplay between a collection and its readers, I am not saying that all texts are Rorschach blots, where readers merely project their own desires and interests. In a trivial sense, we all know that is true: who has not toiled over writing only to have a superficial or hostile hermeneut perceive something else entirely? The story of our collection is worth telling, however, as a rarer case of the reverse dynamic. Rather than a know-it-all reader who manipulates a plastic text, these tales bewildered anyone who paid attention. No one really knew what they meant. And many admitted that they did not know. The tales were strange to them and should stay strange to us. Our story is about how they came to mean so much, not despite but because of this; why readers were moved to make sense of their strangeness; what their results were; and how their methods circulated and changed. Readers' experiments were so inventive and diverse that, over time, the tales became a bustling hermeneutic laboratory. Faced with their strangeness, yet unwilling to write off anything in their tradition as total nonsense, readers sought interpretive resources in every corner. What they came up with is as incredible as the tales themselves.

＊＊＊＊

So far I have introduced three supporting roles in our story (tale, teller, and collection) in relation to the main character, the reader. My aim in doing so is to free their creativity from models of text-centrism, on one hand, and ideological ("cultural") homogeneity, on the other. Rather than dub a parallel the best intertext for imagining how readers interpreted these tales, I aim to compare how different readers used different texts or used the same texts differently. Rather than choose one historical context or set of norms in which to critique the reader, we need ideas flexible enough to track the interaction between text and reader across contexts. Thus, I have not claimed (and will try not to claim) anything about the meaning of these tales per se, apart from the core premise of this book—namely, that in this case such claims are especially iffy. I have only exemplified how, if we define our constellation of ideas in relation to the reader, and use those ideas to describe how the reading process works for specific readers, we can say meaningful things about the history of these tales without knowing what they mean.

For the same reason, the inescapable circularity of this interaction between the reader and the collection will shape the adventure before us. Collecting was a vital instrument in the readers' laboratory. They used whatever form of the collection they had–if any–to interpret its content, and vice versa: their ways of connecting and recollecting its contents continually redefined the collection. It would be comforting to assume that we are unclear only about what a reader was reading *before* this collection of twenty-one stories was "closed" (if we can use such a term for a text whose content fluctuates in each rendition and each witness). Yet the instability (better, dynamism) of their relationship runs deeper, as collection is both a thing and a process. Rather than decide what the reader knew based on our reconstruction of the text at each stage or layer of its evolution, as is usual in talmudic philology, I generally take a dialectical approach to this question (already tested in §*The Teller*). I identify one or more actual texts that a reader in a specific period could have accessed in order to interpret the form of the tales that they likely had. That is, I start by tracing an intertextual network—in the collection, or between the collection and other texts—and put us in the mindset of a reader who could have traveled that specific network. I ask how, along the network, the reader might have experimented with new forms—recollections or "reading-together"—of at least part of our collection. I ask how their experiments would have informed their interpretation of it, in a broad sense: not only how they rationally explained its strangeness but how, even at a loss for explanations, they disclosed and experienced new meaning by relating the tales to intertexts.

In the case of our paradigmatically strange tales, focusing on this intertextual reading process is both more reliable and more revealing than treating the tales as a single dated and layered artifact that we assume was always read as an integral whole, even if it grew with time. Certainly, the gradual composition of a collection of similar tales, within the talmudic canon, did change their interpretation (chapter 3). It both arose from and yielded new interpretations (chapters 4–5). Yet that era, around the end of late antiquity, was no Rubicon that blocked new interpretations and recollections of the tales. Anthologies based on the Talmud's collection, and poems based on those anthologies, are illustrations of the principle that the intertextual reading process never ends.[130] A text's meaning is never inherent in the text, not even after its content is "fixed." Meaning is created by constant intertextual collecting and recollecting; by reading.

The Telling

Luckily, our clues to the tales' reception are not exhausted—not even at this first stage. Beyond their content (strange tales and a strange teller, claiming to have seen some himself), we find traces of their telling: how the tales were told. Unlike stylistic conventions shared by storytellers (what I call their *literary language*), the *telling* refers to more evanescent and flexible ways that a teller interacts directly with a reader. This interaction can occur in writing, live performance, or both. Cues for intonation and emphasis, gesture, rewordings and improvisations on a written source or other "scripted" content all contribute to the telling. Gaps in the narrative or other structural features such as introductions and conclusions are often occasions for tellers and readers to train their attention on the telling and its subtleties. As a story is retold in new ways and settings, these traces of its telling are passed on with it. We can speculate about the telling by analyzing a single tale in one context. In that case, there is no clear distinction between the tale and the telling: narrative content and form are often indissociable. But we can contrast, for instance, how a simple summary of the basic story was "emplotted" by a teller into event sequences, arcs and crescendos, pacing, suspense, and so on. We can also distinguish the telling from the tale by comparing versions of one tale or

---

130. Haim Weiss, "Ha-tsitsit shel Rabbah bar bar Hanah: ben ha-Talmud le-Sefer ha-aggadah," *'Odot* (9/4/17). Available at https://odotmag.wixsite.com/odot/5 (accessed 29 January 2025).

parallels that share unusual stylistic tics or were transmitted with unusual flourishes, signs that their content was embellished by specific tellers and received by specific readers in shared ways.

One such tic surfaced between our collection (Appendix, Part 1) and its literary core, the tales attributed to "Rabbah bar bar Hanah" (IV–XV). In this interval, I will show, new tales were added to the end of the collection as well as the beginning.[131] If so, we might ask, "What, in these additions, was inspired by how the earlier tales had been told?"[132] Consider the new formula that introduces the additions: "recounted." The tales added at the end begin "Rav X *recounts*"; at the beginning, "X said: Sailors *recounted* to me." In the dictionary, this verb means nothing special; to say, tell such-and-such, converse with so-and-so. But in other Jewish Aramaics,[133] as in Syriac,[134] its root can connote speech that is implausible, jesting, or deceitful. As we saw, such connotations had already accrued to the original teller, Rabbah, in the Talmud's tradition. When new tellers "recount" similarly fantastic stories, the taste of his telling may have lingered. For readers of their newly expanded collection, this new introduction may have meant more than it denoted, its interdialectal connotations—fantasy, jest, deceit—spilling over. For such a reader, at such a time, these additions may have been a new spool of old yarns: guilty pleasures, not to be taken seriously, and perhaps not to be associated with too openly.

Our question here is not this verb's semantics nor its standard usage. Our question is how, within the reading process during a specific period, its root meaning shaped *how* the new tales were told by bringing something to a reader's attention; by making an aspect of a new telling, based on older tellings, interpretable. By focusing on a historically specific reader's structures of attention—choices that a reader was led to make about what counts as *possibly* interpretable in a tale, based on how it was told—we see how a telling sets foreground/background relations

---

131. This is argued in chapter 3 §*Chronological Layers*, where I also account for further anomalies in XX and III.

132. For this question, applied to the additions' narrative *content* (the idea of the *tale*, not the *telling*), see n. 15.

133. See *JPA*, 562: *pa'el* ש.ע.י (= Hebr. ח.ל.ק) means "to make smooth," from which derive the noun "smooth talk" (שעועא or שעיעותה, Tg. Prov. 6:24) and adjectival forms (Tg. Prov. 5:3 and 7:5; Tg. Ps. Jon. Lev. 19:17). This pejorative sense of ח.ל.ק was alive and well in CD I, 18, alluding to Isa 30:10. See Harry Fox, "A New Understanding of the Sobriquet דורשי החלקות: Why Qumranites Rejected Pharisaic Traditions," in *Law, Literature, and Society in Legal Texts from Qumran: Papers from the Ninth Meeting of the International Organization for Qumran Studies, Leuven 2016*, ed. Jutta Jokiranta and Molly Zahn, STDJ 128 (Leiden: Brill, 2019), 65–98, at 69–70.

134. The Syriac equivalent of "recount" in our tales means both "to tell" and "to play," from which are derived "jest, wit" (*she'aya'*) and "deceit, mockery" (*sha'ayutha'*). See Michael Sokoloff, *A Syriac Lexicon: A Translation from the Latin: Correction, Expansion, and Update of C. Brockelmann's Lexicon Syriacum* (Winona Lake, IN: Eisenbrauns, 1999), 1582–83.

that shift over time.¹³⁵ For any reader, some parts of a tale will be marked as more potentially meaningful than others. As a result, others must stay in the background, no matter how self-evidently significant they seem to you or me. Nor is this foreground/background structure static in any one tale. As a reader's attention shifts throughout its unfolding, the language of its telling calls their attention to selected aspects, activating clues that bring to mind related parts of other texts. The tale becomes newly interpretable via such activated intertexts; part of new, often highly transient, collections and recollections. These foreground/background structures are not in the language,¹³⁶ but only in the minds of historically specific readers.¹³⁷ One retelling rearranges the cues for a reader's attention that an earlier telling has left behind.

Again, no one interprets a tale *ex nihilo*. Its telling leads readers to make connections: within a tale itself, as well as between a tale and intertexts. Such connections may be genetic, to sources; contextual, to adjacent texts; generic, to texts of the same type; purely analogical or loosely associative, sparked by whatever the language of a tale brings to mind. Or, readers can make such connections via *how* a tale is told: a teller's stress on vision may cue a reader to look for the theme of visual evidence, for example. There are no absolute rules for what counts as a more meaningful connection—only conventions in each reading tradition. Yet there is a phenomenological threshold. Readers cannot read what they cannot perceive and cannot notice what is not brought to their attention. In that narrower sense, no reader interprets a tale for the first time. Readers rely on what they are told and what they know, led by foreground/background structures of attention in an unfolding tale, to create legible and meaningful connections. For the reader, each tale rests on another tale, and every telling is half retelling.

Telling thus touches both the tale—its form and content—and the collection, its links to other texts. As for the former, the telling is how the tale

---

135. Iser, "Reading Process"; Sternberg, *Biblical Narrative*, 186–222; Redfield, "Auerbach's 'Background.'"

136. Per the "Proteus Principle," that is, no fixed literary "functions" correspond to those of language; see Meir Sternberg, *Hebrews between Cultures: Group Portraits and National Literature*, ISBL (Bloomington: Indiana University Press, 1988), 58–59.

137. For example, consider the following sentence: "Say, if you've got a tell in a speakeasy, you'll get a talking-to from the missus." The related verbs ("to say," "to tell," "to speak," "to talk") are just as broad and neutral in their dictionary meaning and usage as "recount" in our tales. However, a reader who knows, say, 1920s American English, including gambling jargon like "tell" and "speakeasy," immediately interprets the introductory formula ("Say"), not as an imperative, but as the marker of a precise intonation in dialogue. This canny intonation cues the reader to interpret the rest of the sentence to the same effect—less as a threat than as a friendly warning. I am illustrating that a reader of the original tales needed no more than the same minimal familiarity with their own literary language for the addition of ס.פ.ר to shape a reading tradition of the added tales in an equally precise way.

unfolds in time. Whether its medium is written, oral, or both, how readers engage its content has a temporal structure. By using the term "reader" for any medium (although I consider oral/written differences in many cases),[138] I aim to refocus our attention on how the telling leads its audience to create meaning in time. As readers perceive its form and content, they interpret a tale by selecting from its own cues and clues: gaps in the plot to close; logical contradictions to solve; characters to characterize based on how they talk or interact; their descriptions, names, genealogies, and so on. Readers notice repetitions—plumb echoes of language that help them to winnow the infinite possible relations between form and content so as to create the tale's meaning, to interpret its message for them. In this sense, the telling is a structure for readers' attention that guides them through a tale along one interpretive route or another. By the way in which a tale is told, the reader is led to notice what is salient and interrelated, what may be interpretable. At the same time, their attention is finite. They cannot read everything at once. The telling sets some signs in the foreground, others in the background, others in the dark: perceptible, perhaps, but senseless.

As every telling is half retelling, readers interpret those interpretive cues accordingly. As soon as a tale begins, readers' structures of attention are not only shaped by the tale's own form and content, nor only by its teller's persona. The reader also leans on other texts that a tale brings to hand and to mind. I am calling those received intertextual connections a *reading tradition*. A reading tradition throttles infinite possible intertexts down to more familiar ones, from clichés to faint allusions. Beyond the tale itself, within a reading tradition, other texts and other tellings guide the reader's intuitions about what to expect in the plot and what is most salient in this telling of an older story—that is, what in a text might be most meaningful.

Literary languages rely heavily on unmarked repetitions in the background in order to bring a few marked or stylized features to the foreground of a reader's attention. They play across the gap between what-a-teller-knows-that-a-reader-knows and what a reader perceives. They hone readers' intuitions for new and old; important and irrelevant; a teller's distinctive voice versus the form and content that she uses. In so doing, storytellers adopt and adapt each other's techniques for communicating with their readers.

Reading traditions reverse the direction of this communication. In a reading tradition, the reader apprehends a tale in relation to other texts, notices shared and different features, and interprets the tale partly on that basis. This can include not only philological comparison—such as explaining obscure words in a tale by their prior uses—but also the sort of com-

---

138. See nn. 154, 157, 230–33, 242, 251, 265, 273, 277, and chapter 3 §*Structure and Poetry*, for examples from the first three chapters.

parison favored by literary critics, such as interpreting a storyteller's voice and tone in terms of a familiar teller or everyday register of social speech. A reading tradition can be more or less attuned to a literary language. A reading tradition can be small and fragile—minimally, two intertexts for a short time—or large and durable, like the tradition of reading our tales as "dreams" (see chapter 6 §*Allegory as* Midrash). We cannot know which reading tradition a reader will use based on their culture alone. We can only infer it from the evidence for their actual reading process—for example, which texts they read together—and the structure and logic of their recollections.

Nor does the form of a collection dictate what a given reader can do with its contents. Yet we should not discount the impact of a collection's very existence on the reading process. How texts were already collected exerts *inertia* on how new intertexts can be recollected. As we have seen, the original core collection of tales attributed to Rabbah influenced new tales that were added at the end and the beginning of Part 1. Even my decision to collect (edit/redact) some material as two episodes of a single tale (e.g., IIIa–IIIb) obliges you to do some mental work to read both episodes as a single story, or, by contrast, to read them apart again. Creative as readers are at reading collections in multiple ways, or recollecting their contents with intertexts, we cannot ignore contrary evidence that the inertia of a given collection has limited what readers could do with the tales. On the other hand, the opposite is equally true: inertia fuels ways to read together each collection with intertexts, both in and out of the Talmud.

The Canon

This idea of inertia leads us to the outer rung of meaning, the idea of a canon. Approaching the canon from inside the hermeneutic circle, from the side of the collection, we can define a canon as an extension of the same process over time: a collection of collections. As the inertia of one collection takes hold on the reading process, readers begin to interpret it as a whole in relation to itself. They read collections in relation to each other along various lines, forming recollections that are themselves edited and transmitted according to changing literary languages and other conventions. For example, whatever the Mishnah was for its framer,[139] the Talmud often reads it as a canon in this sense: a collection of (advanced) study texts, not a systematic law code. Interpreting the Mishnah's heterogeneous textual units, the Talmud assumes that they are porous or par-

---

139. David Weiss Halivni, "The Reception Accorded to Rabbi Judah's Mishnah," in *Jewish and Christian Self-Definition*, ed. E. P. Sanders et al., 3 vols. (Philadelphia: Fortress, 1981), 2:204–12, 379–82, at 379–80 n. 3.

tial, leaving them intact but probing their logical contradictions and gaps.¹⁴⁰ The Talmud does not always read the Mishnah as a loose "anthology" of traditions on which it draws for recollections that it arranges on entirely *sui generis* principles. Often, the contrary paradox shapes its hermeneutic: the Mishnah is perfect yet incomplete. This paradox licenses the Talmud to challenge, depart from, or reconcile collected Mishnah units with other texts—nearly anything goes, if the Mishnah reemerges from those acts of recollection restored to greater coherence. By holding itself accountable to the Mishnah's exact language *and* full meaning, the Talmud reads the Mishnah figurally, as a text that must go beyond itself to be meaningful. Thus, the Talmud/Gemara "completes" the Mishnah. Its canonicity is nominally driven by the Mishnah's inertia and strives to fulfill it.¹⁴¹

Yet, if we define a canon from the outside in, with its face toward the other two circles, this idea shifts. Rather than a collection of collections that emerges from their own inertia—let alone a superficially uniform library of eclectic content, an anthology or "encyclopedia"—the mere fact that a tale is included within a canon is the starting point to create its meaning. Changing interpretive norms surrounding each canon *qua* canon also impact how its sources, from a tale to an entire collection, can be read—indeed, even how they are preserved—to the extent that precanonical forms may become irretrievable. Every source in the Talmud—and Scripture most of all—has been "Talmudized," transformed by acts of study and transmission, a process that we are only starting to understand as the Talmud's intentional design becomes more clear.¹⁴² Due to Talmudization,

---

140. For example, consider how the Babylonian Talmud exploits its premise of a "contradictory case" (מעשה לסתור) in a unit of Mishnah in order to argue that "[the Mishnah] is surely lacking [here], but this is how it is to be recited" (חסורי מחסרא והכי קתני). Rather than simply solve the contradiction, this premise creates new contradictions, which, in turn, create new collections (e.g., b. Sukkah 26b–27a). Unlike the Palestinian Talmud's similar formula, "thus is the Tannaitic source" (כיני מתניתא)—which does amend, explain, or add to the Mishnah—the Babylonian Talmud uses its premise of a gap in the Mishnah to recollect, and thereby expand, the Mishnah's "own" collections of contradictions. The mishnaic canon is a collection that makes new collections necessary, and a new canonicity emerges from it. See Y. N. Epstein, *Introduction to the Mishnaic Text* [Hebrew] (Jerusalem: Magnes, 1948), 595–606; Hanokh Albeck, *Introduction to the Mishna* [Hebrew] (Jerusalem: Mossad Bialik, 1959), 121–22; Abraham Goldberg, "The Mishna: A Study Book of Halakhah," in *The Literature of the Sages*, ed. Shmuel Safrai et al., 2 vols., CRINT 2.3 (Assen: Van Gorcum; Minneapolis: Fortress, 2006), 1:211–51, at 243–44; Leib Moscovitz, *The Terminology of the Yerushalmi: The Principal Terms* [Hebrew] (Jerusalem: Magnes, 2009), 276–80; Ishay Rosen-Zvi, "Introduction to the Mishnah" [Hebrew], in *Palestinian Rabbinic Literature: Introductions and Studies*, ed. Menahem Kahana et al. (Jerusalem: Yad Ben-Zvi, 2018), 1–64, at 52–55.

141. See Christine Elizabeth Hayes, *Between the Babylonian and Palestinian Talmuds: Accounting for Halakhic Difference in Selected Sugyot from Tractate Avodah Zarah* (Oxford: Oxford University Press, 1997), 105–21.

142. Barry Scott Wimpfheimer, *The Talmud: A Biography* (Princeton, NJ: Princeton University Press, 2018), 32–40. On diverse concepts of canon and their ir/relevance to the Tal-

collections in this canon—as well as tales, their tellings, and tellers—lose some of their discrepancies and are gradually harmonized along certain lines. This process feeds on itself, both reinforcing and developing the canon's interpretive norms. Thus, the Talmudized or canonical form of our collection became more than the sum of its parts, more than a collection of collections. With each successive version, composers and readers developed it by applying interpretive tools to its special features, inspired by their common education and shared interpretive assumptions. These rearrangements, expansions, and readings preserved the strangeness of the tales and their teller. Yet, at the same time, they domesticated the strangeness by Talmudizing it. Readers created meaning from our collection by interweaving allusions or homilies to the same biblical verses; correlating rare motifs; glossing rare words; interpolating technical debates; absorbing covert external sources; and many more typically Talmudizing (canonical) maneuvers that shed light on the meaning of these tales by linking them to other texts in the canon, both legal and nonlegal. In this way, a canon operates like a culture: it is the process of creating meaning (from texts) mediated by shared meanings (which span intertexts and collections). A canon is a horizon of reading, both a collection of collections–through inertia–and a model for generating new collections.

For any reader, then, the canon both expands and constrains the creation of meaning. On one hand, it grows through inertia as a collection of collections and individual texts that have their own meanings, some of which are revived by even much later readers. On the other hand, to the extent that the form, teller, and style ("telling") of a tale remain accessible to readers, they can create meaning from the tale *without* recourse to its precanonized layers of meaning. For both reasons, a canon cannot be said to autonomously determine the meaning of its texts. It does, however, regulate their meaning according to its own recursive interpretive norms. In that sense, a canon is a cultural product that becomes naturalized in the mind of its reader. It constrains their avenues of interpretation, their valid and invalid ways of creating meaning. Through education, readers internalize and refine this model to the exclusion of alternatives. The higher the prestige and diffusion of a canon among a given readership, the more likely it is that any text's canonicity (or lack thereof) will constrain its transmission and interpretation.

Such tension between the reader's irreducible freedom and the specializing tendencies of an elite scholastic canon like the Talmud is further complicated by the fact that, in rabbinic culture, there is never just one canon, nor just one type of canonicity, in effect at a given time. The canon of Scripture and the rabbinic canon, each of which has internal shades

---

mud, see Robert Timothy DeBold, "The Hermeneutics of Textual Hierarchies in the Babylonian Talmud" (PhD diss., Stanford University, 2015), 71–118, esp. 89–91 and 102–3.

of canonicity,[143] are very often formally distinguished and related in the reading process to complex effect. A rabbinic reader hardly ever loses sight of the Bible, even if it is not explicitly cited. Nor can we ignore it when we ask how readers made sense of our nonscriptural, nonsensical tales. Scripture is Talmudized but not Talmud; that distinction can be as meaningful as its elision.

For us, the dialectic between two canons within the talmudic canon is doubly critical. We cannot recover a pure precanonical ("folkloric" or "legendary") origin for these tales. Even in chapter 2, for example, long before there was such a thing as the Talmud, I will argue that readers recollected and interpreted some of our tales (I–III) via the Bible and its early history of reception in midrash. Some relation between readers' creativity and their reading tradition of the Bible is attested from the very beginning as readers peppered the tales with images of parabiblical myth. All the more so by the tail end of late antiquity in chapter 5, where we explore how reading traditions of Scripture shaped interaction between the Talmud's editors and readers, and chapter 6, where we will encounter an early modern commentator, Maharsha, who used scriptural and rabbinic texts to create a Janus-faced argument for different implied readers. A plural canonicity of Scripture and Talmud is generative for readers' interpretive frameworks, and there is no "before" or "after" canonization in this regard: both canons as such are always potentially meaningful.

The Constellation of Reading

To summarize the method that our story will unfold over time and thereby develop so as to reconstruct and compare how readers made creative sense of traditionally nonsensical tales, I have introduced five main ideas from the standpoint of the reader, that is, interpreter: tale, teller, collection, telling, and canon. I have also described interpretive dynamics whereby we can interrelate these ideas: strangeness, recollecting and inertia, literary language and reading tradition, plural canonicity and Talmudization. Finally, I have stressed a reader's selectivity—the movement between textual foreground and background, expectation and fulfillment—as they create meaning. I will use this constellation to connect dots between local arguments about the tales' interpretive history that are advanced by each section and chapter. The constellation is both interwoven throughout each argument and reappears to frame each chapter, updating how its ideas have been tested, have been reconfigured, and have come into clearer view by being used to reconstruct and relate specific readers over time.

---

143. On the terminology/hermeneutics of these dynamics, see Azzan Yadin, *Scripture as Logos: Rabbi Ishmael and the Origins of Midrash,* Divinations (Philadelphia: University of Pennsylvania Press, 2004); Yadin, *Scripture and Tradition.*

Definitions are not the end of this adventure, because each idea's scope and utility will shift as it is applied across periods/contexts. But a pet lexicon may be a useful reference point. Condensing the discussion so far:

A **tale** is the form and content of a meaningfully bounded text that a reader perceives in some medium and interprets, whether by reference to itself or by reading it together with other texts (intertexts). This idea does not imply that all readers interpreted the tales as prose narratives rather than, for example, epic poems or allegorical symbols. Our confidence about how readers grasped the tales—parsed and classified their meaningful units—will grow over time. So far, we have allowed only the possibility that the identity of the **teller** was their most stable and familiar early traditional element, serving both to connect the tales and to identify them for the reader. In that reading tradition, the teller is Rabbah bar bar Hanah, who had a dubious reputation and was well known as a teller of broadly similar tales. (This image of the teller will change over time into, for example, a sage recounting parables.) Furthermore, this teller of an individual tale or cluster of tales—tagged by attribution formulae—is not the only teller in our collection. Some tales also feature auxiliary tellers ("sailors" or others, mostly later Babylonian rabbis). Furthermore, all of the tales have an implied teller: whoever *said* "Rabbah bar bar Hanah said" in the first place. Some readers will simply ignore all of those tellers in favor of a meta-teller who stands in for the canon, "The Talmud" (for instance, medieval anti-Jewish polemics, which begin "Your Talmud says that . . ."). As when we define the tale, then, we must take care to define the teller or tellers that each specific reader selected. Common as it is to read this as a cycle of stories by a storyteller, it is not natural or universal.

The **telling** has two aspects: first, the tale's internal structure as it unfolds in sequence; second, the ways that a tale is linked, by how it is told, with familiar ways that others are told. Both aspects operate on a reader's attention, which has a structured *selectivity*. Granted that identifying and closing problems or "gaps" in a text often guides an interpretation, we cannot presume a generic or passive reader who simply follows the cues of the text and its author. Our study of each telling must be informed by our own degree of distance from other readers; by an awareness that not every gap *we* select was a gap for them, and vice versa.[144] To gauge that gap between our gaps, we must also examine other aspects of telling: *literary language* and *reading tradition*. Those ideas describe—from teller's

---

144. This gap/blank distinction is central to a debate on *midrash* in the pages of *Prooftexts* and other venues for literary theory in the 1980s–1990s. See Catlin, " Rest Is Literature," 196–99, 225–26, 233–34, 334–40. It is also the crux of a debate between American reader-response criticism and the Constance school of reception history. See Holub, "Reception Theory," 337–39; Stanley Fish, *Is There a Text in This Class? The Authority of Interpretive Communities* (Cambridge, MA: Harvard University Press, 1980), 44–51, 49–65, 86–87, 93–96, 103–4, 259, 322–37.

and reader's vantages, respectively—how the way in which a tale is told guides a reader to select signs as meaningful and to assign them meaning. Both hold a history that, depending on our distance from each specific reader, may be more or less accessible to us today—not only an archive of texts that reader and teller both knew but also more diffuse literary idioms or conventions bearing intricate connotations, as well as their social background in spoken languages, voices of stock character types, and so on.

The duality of **collection**—a literary whole—and **recollecting**—an interpretive process—reflects two different ways in which one can operate on the tale and the telling. In one sense, it is a quantitative operation: a collection puts together multiple texts according to a conventional pattern.[145] Different collectors do this in different ways. A teller may extract a feature from the telling of a tale, such as a narrative sequence, and reapply that feature to adjacent tales. A reader may perform the same operation in reverse, reinterpreting discrete tales as a sequence in light of shared features of their literary language, thereby recollecting them. Inversely, a collection can impose a new logic on tales that is emergent from neither them nor a conventional collection template. Regardless, collections never spring full-blown from the head of a collector. They result from dialogue with the reader, by joint attention to select aspects of the telling, further mediated by a literary language anchored in the society and education that they share—their interpretive community. By the same token, the reader's selective, motivated recollection of tales into a new unity or group of intertexts may focus on the same features of a text that interested its collector.

Yet readers also in another, qualified sense, have their own way to operate on the tales and telling: established reading traditions, which structure their intuitions for what to select from the telling beyond an accretion of new material for attention. These traditions inform readers that some signs are more significant than others or that certain signs are already significant in certain ways. Reading traditions guide readers not only to recollect texts but also to forget them. Our collection is useful for tracing the formation and transmission of diverse reading traditions because of its *strangeness*—the documented lack of any dominant reading tradition that taught readers what it was, what to select, or how to connect its parts. New reading traditions grew in and around it because readers had no strong fallback position.

The same oscillation between quantitative and qualitative, linear and dialectical literary creativity describes the idea of a **canon**. As a collection of collections that emerges, in part, through the sheer *inertia* of texts being assembled and interpreted in the same ways that other texts had been, a

---

145. On principles for collecting sources in the Talmud, see Alexander Samely, *Forms of Rabbinic Literature and Thought: An Introduction* (Oxford: Oxford University Press, 2007), 33–38, 161–77.

canon could be simply called a mega-collection born of other collections. Each collection in a canon has, by definition, its own principles of composition (some are simple and stereotypical for ease of transmission, hence relatively easy to detect), as well as its own intertextual history: layers of readers who recollected its collected texts. Some principles of composition and some intertextual reading strategies generate larger units, as when the core of tales attributed to Rabbah bar bar Hanah was collected with other tales, and that larger, later collection was then gradually recollected with the adjacent section of midrash by rabbinic reading traditions that were, themselves, inspired by midrash (chapters 2 and 5). This is a linear way in which a canon can emerge from the reception of its sources. Their inertia—the way in which they had been put together—informs how a canon is assembled.

On the other hand, a canon tends to attract new notions about how its sources should make sense and fit together. Those notions may or may not be well founded in the principles whereby the collections on which it is based were once collected. To the extent that they are not, tension arises within a canon composed of nested collections. We can call this a tension between the "first-degree" logic of earlier collections and "second-degree" logic of the canon. The talmudic canon reflects second-degree logic when it, for example, juxtaposes collections in a new argument on a topic/problem, or harmonizes traditions across multiple collections by paraphrasing and/or anonymizing them. Depending on its level of creativity (or, if you dislike its results, "violence") vis-à-vis its collections' first-degree logic, the canon may display a more or less second-degree logic. At one end of this spectrum, we see arguments resembling direct responses to problems raised by Amoraim, with relatively little abstraction or anonymous punctuation.[146] At the other end, we see arguments that are anonymous, abstract, and concerned with problems that arguably made more sense in a later cultural milieu.[147] The first-degree inertia of collections of traditions from Amoraim did help to build the canon. But so did the new second-de-

---

146. For an example from tractate Ketubbot, see Robert Brody, "The Contribution of the Yerushalmi to Dating 'The Anonymous Talmud'" [Hebrew], in *Melekhet Mahshevet: Studies in the Redaction and Development of Talmudic Literature*, ed. Aaron Amit and Aharon Shemesh (Ramat-Gan: Bar Ilan University Press, 2011), 27–37, at 31–32. Rather than merely sharing a common source, Brody argues that the two Talmuds are interdependent when their solutions to a problem in the Mishnah are both similar *and* logically "difficult." In our terms, in such a case, the talmudic canons' second-degree logic peels apart from the first-degree logic of the mishnaic canon.

147. See Yaakov Elman, "The World of the 'Sabboraim': Cultural Aspects of Post-Redactional Additions to the Talmud," in Rubenstein, *Creation and Composition*, 383–415. In this case (versus the previous note), the Babylonian Talmudic canon breaks from the Palestinian one. That break is not only a matter of earlier versus later sources but also of different hermeneutic orientations to different problems already among the Amoraim.

gree logic of Stammaim who edited it, creating a canon that sometimes undermined the logic of the original collections or at least engaged it at a distance.

More generally, this is common in the evolution of canons: the quantitative variety of voices *within* a canon (and the related tension between first- and second-degree collections) develops into a qualitative distinction *between* understandings of what the canon should be. From that time on, a collection of collections yields to a unified canon, which acquires, so to speak, self-consciousness. Tellers and readers more routinely—and less apologetically—use the canon's second-degree logic to give meaning to its sources. In the case of the Talmud, I called this process Talmudization (in chapter 6, we will see how allegorization can work similarly). Even Scripture is "Talmudized," as its received meanings in midrash reenter the canon and are applied to intertexts in new ways. This process, however, is neither total nor teleological. Alongside its Talmudized Bible, the Talmud preserves and explicitly theorizes interpretive distinctions between itself and other canons—the Bible most of all—and uses those distinctions to both bolster and question its hermeneutic autonomy. In that sense, a pervasive condition of *plural canonicity*, wherein a reader's interpretive framework contains distinct canons, even as all of their content is canonized, offers the reader multiple ways to create meaning from the parts with reference to the whole.

To summarize this constellation and its internal dynamics:

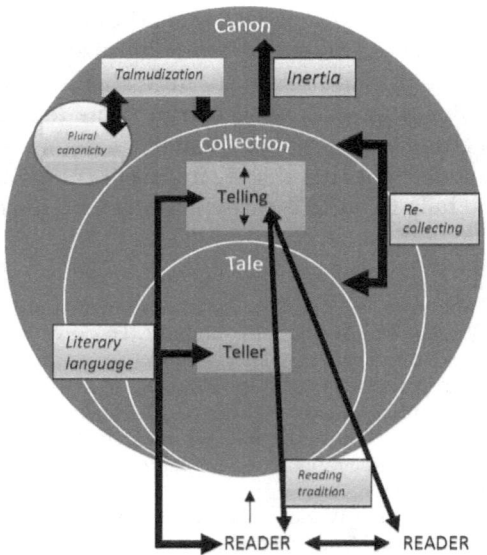

Figure 3. The Constellation of Reading

Each chapter refines this methodological schema both analytically and comparatively, synchronically and diachronically, over successive periods of the tales' interpretive history. I hope scholars of other literatures find the method useful and adapt it to their own purposes. On the other hand, none of my analyses of rabbinic texts depends on the method. They do not rely on it but the reverse: the method came from studying, then abstracting, the structure and dynamics of our sources' interpretive history. Specialists in rabbinic texts should therefore be able to find something useful in my arguments, even if they do not find the method itself useful. And vice versa: the method alone may be of use to scholars of premodern oral-literary traditions beyond the Talmud, given that most available related theories were modeled on modern texts.

* * * * *

The first chapter encapsulates both critical and constructive implications of this return to the reader by evaluating previous studies of our tales accordingly. Within each study's own theoretical model, what can the reader do or not do? What is the reader's role in creating meaning? In the critique that opens the first chapter, the foil for our constellation is the hegemony of genre—more specifically, a way of thinking about the genre of the text that limits the reader's role. Whether by presenting our composition as estranged from its legal canon rather than as an associative digression within it; by positing an interpretive hierarchy of one of its collections over the other; or in bypassing their literary structure altogether by presuming that a universal type of storytelling was transparently meaningful to everyone, those studies sacrifice readers' diversity and agency for a deterministic theory of the genre of the text.

A more constructive use of the categories Myth and Exegesis, I go on to argue, is to reconstruct genres for the reader. "Myth" indexes a cross-cultural story outline and motif archive preserved in the Bible and shows how the Talmud's editors renewed it in a dynamic story—a narrative cosmology that sharpens certain divine attributes and arcs toward messianic fulfillment. This use of myth as what I call a "genre for the reader" shows how editors' retelling selects those meanings for readers' attention. It also allows readers and editors to engage in dialogue between the lines of the new/old story by adding and reacting to interpretive cues ("flourishes") peripheral to its exegetical frame. Conversely, by examining how Amoraim in the Talmud used exegesis to read our entire composition—not only the myth but also the tales—back into biblical verses and the latter's reading tradition, I show how they enlarged their canon's frame to contain and make new sense of its contents. Both ways of Talmudizing—reading the tales out of, or back into, a canon of midrashim—will recur throughout our story. But in this case, following Michael Fishbane and Dina Stein, I stress that they never defeated the myth beneath the canons of Scripture, midrash, and Talmud. Early readers knew the difference between those genres yet made meaning from their tension.

In chapter 2, I offer a model for how readers may have used these genres in their interpretation of an integral unit (I–III), before our collection of strange tales (let alone full two-part composition) was put together. This begins a dual structure for the argument that runs through the book. Each chapter moves forward in time—from early Palestinian and Babylonian tradition through the Talmud's editing, to its high medieval and early modern commentary—as well as outward in the constellation of reading. I study the tale and its telling in light of midrash (chapter 2); collection and recollecting, in terms of how its editors read their sources and how their poetry affected their listeners (chapter 3); and how the whole composition was read in and out of an emergent talmudic canon with intertextual devices derived from the study of the canon of Scripture (chapter 5). Chapter 4 detours into cultural history. It has the same late ancient Babylonian rabbinic setting as chapter 5 (after the tales were collected but before the Talmud was edited) and complements it, showing how both tellers and readers also engaged Hellenistic literary forms. It pushes outward in the constellation of reading, on the hinges between collection and canon, and explores how our collection of strange tales recollected Greek wonder books according to their Greek conventions but also made new sense of those conventions with talmudic logic. Once the talmudic canon was edited, and frameworks for its interpretation well established (plain sense, *midrash*, and allegory), I show how those frameworks interacted among the tales' high medieval to early modern commentators (chapter 6). In seventeenth-century Poland, Rabbah and friends were used to teach moral allegories including a strict sexual ethics based on *kabbalah*, then read back into the full scope of their own interpretive history in Enlightenment Vilnius, where our story rests.

1

Genre Trouble!

In this search for a method to understand and compare what these tales have meant to a diverse sample of readers in the past, the literary historian faces the anthropologist's problem. Past readers, by definition, do not share our interpretive categories, conundrums, or priorities. Yet we cannot interpret their interpretations otherwise. When we think about them in our own terms, the question is not whether to betray them, but which betrayal/translation of their terms draws them nearer and in which respect (knowing that it will also push them away in others).[148] Modern scholars of these tales have often used genre labels as such a translation. Given that the tales were collected because they have something in common, and given that they share content and themes with the following collection in the talmudic canon (Part 2), a tacit consensus has been that applying a genre label is the best way to interpret how readers made sense of those relationships within and between collections. I submit that, except for cautious uses of the genres Myth and Exegesis, genre has been more trouble than it is worth.

I came to this position the hard way. I, too, began a concise (!) conference paper on these tales seven years ago with the illusion that, because "to mistake the genre of a literary work inevitably produces misinterpretation,"[149] getting their genre right would restore their meaning. If I decided that the tales were fables, I would interpret them as fables; a genre with formal and thematic conventions that I would decode to access its meaning. I would support my interpretation by comparing this classical rabbinic form of the fable with fables from other cultures bearing parallels in form or content. I would mine clues to the fable's changing uses and conventions from its transmission-history and direct responses by ancient audiences. I would then be able to tell a story about how the rabbinic fable—or whatever genre I chose—assimilated and expressed, but also

---

148. Galit Hasan-Rokem, "Did Rabbinic Culture Conceive of the Category of Folk Narrative?," *European Journal of Jewish Studies* 3.1 (2009): 19–55; Joshua Levinson, "From Parable to Invention: The Rise of Fiction as a Cultural Category" [Hebrew], in Levinson et al., eds., *Higayon L'Yonah*, 1–32.

149. Rubenstein, *Talmudic Stories*, 5.

transformed, the narrative conventions of other cultures. I would show how the tales had been interpreted by rabbis and other readers in line with those genre conventions. No longer mistaken about their genre, I would interpret the tales correctly.

The trouble with genre ("armchair philology," to extend the anthropological analogy) is twofold. Genres do not capture the process of reading a story at a given time, and they tend to obscure differences between readers' own interpretive frameworks over time. For readers—more than for authors/editors, who do use conventional forms—genre is not essential, as the act of interpretation mobilizes either too many genres or too few. On one hand, genres are so fluid and ubiquitous in speech and society that every text is a dialogue of genres—never "in" a genre.[150] On the other, a reader need not control any genre to create a text's meaning; strong misreadings of genre abound.[151] Readers toggle genres; flout or parody their rules; blend, blur, scrap; and invent genres as they read. Their interpretive process is an adventure with a chaotic internal structure that we can analyze in retrospect but not predict. Our uses of genre should at least reflect readers' own uses of genres: as flexible and nonexclusive ways to create meaning. After critiquing how several genres have been applied to our tales, I show how Myth and Exegesis have been useful in precisely this respect: a shift from the genre of the text to what I call genres for the reader. Chapter 2 will focus on how genres for the reader interact in I–III.

Tractate

For form and source critics, applying genre labels has helped to isolate our tales' distinctive features and to compare them with the following collection (Part 2). This has come at the cost of defining both collections as overly self-contained units. Meaningful links between them, not to mention other collections in the canon, fade from view: both from the standpoint of late editors (who put together Parts 1 and 2) and especially from our standpoint, that of the reader. In terms of our constellation, this use of genre ignores how the tales were Talmudized–constantly reintegrated into the canon through interpretation.

---

150. For this Bakhtinian point, see Joshua Levinson, "Dialogic Reading"; Moshe Simon-Shoshan, "Talmud as Novel: Dialogic Discourse and the Feminine Voice in the Babylonian Talmud," *Poetics Today* 40.1 (2019) 105–34. For counterpoints, see Boyarin, *Fat Rabbis*; Fiano, *Three Powers in Heaven*; and the survey of the limits of "dialogue" in Bakhtin's œuvre itself in Redfield, "Redacting Culture," 71–72 n. 75.

151. Harold Bloom, *A Map of Misreading* (Oxford: Oxford University Press, 1975). See, e.g., Kaplan, *My Perfect One*, 79–82, on the rabbis' creative misreading of the Song of Songs as "epic."

Genre Trouble! 59

A concise case of this pitfall can be found in the pioneering work of Avraham Weiss.[152] By identifying compositions and editorial techniques in the Talmud that he assigned to the Amoraim, before its "final" redaction by the generations now known as Stammaim, Weiss contributed to distinguishing early from late, named from anonymous creators in the canon. This search for diversity, however, led him to impose a generic schema on Amoraic sources that he found inside the Talmud and to set our collection among them. He chose the genre Tractate (*massekhet*) for the larger, self-contained Amoraic sources, implying that, just as the Talmud's final redaction comments on tractates of the Mishnah in linear order, Amoraim had also left behind independent "tractates" arranged by non-Mishnaic content and themes.[153] Specifically, based on its unusual content, Weiss titled our composition "The Tractate of Wonders and Visions"—a genre whereby he included not only the wonders in Part 1 (the collection of tales starring Amoraim like Rabbah) but also the midrashim in Part 2, devoted to eschatological visions like Leviathan. Because of their strange content, first and foremost, as well as their apparent disconnection from the legal discussion which begins before and continues after them, Weiss assumed that these two collections were in fact one independent collection.

Weiss's compartmentalization of both collections as a generic "tractate" on those topics led him to miss two signs of intertextuality with their immediate legal context as well as with one another. One is a rare word, the last in the Talmud's commentary on the Mishnah which transitions into our collection. This word "boat" (ביצית, *bitsit*), especially the plural (בוציתא, *butsiyya'ta'*), which the Talmud cites in its gloss, sounds like the *first* rare word in our collection:[154] "shoot" (צוציתא, *tsutsita'*).[155] Hence Part 1

---

152. See Meyer S. Feldblum, "Prof. Abraham Weiss: His Approach and Contributions to Talmudic Scholarship," in *The Abraham Weiss Jubilee Volume*, ed. Samuel Belkin et al. (New York: Jubilee, 1964), 7–80, at 50.
153. Avraham Weiss distinguishes subtypes of these "tractates" of non-legal tradition or *aggadah* (*Studies in the Literature of the Amoraim* [Hebrew] [New York: Yeshiva University Press, 1962], 273). He notes that some of the collections' content is presented at multiple places in the Talmud "for some reason," whereas other collections were fused in order to expand the presentation of a single topic. This shows that Weiss did allow for Talmudization, that is, for the process whereby traditions were harmonized into the canon's contexts and conventions. However, he sees our collection as the least Talmudized "Tractate" of all: one that "completely breaks from the Talmud's standard framework."
154. According to all of the manuscripts and indirect witnesses except ms. H, where the unit that "should" form this verbal transition appears second (in ms. P it is also second but added in the margin and is less connected to the previous unit insofar as it does not begin with ו ["and"] as in ms. H). This could indicate that the "flipped" order of ms. H is not original. Perhaps a scribe dropped the first unit, due to eye-skip between similar words (אמר רבא ביצית . . . בוציתא . . . אמר רבא . . . כיצוציתא), so then the missing unit was inserted in reversed order when restored to the *Vorlagen* of ms. H and of ms. P's corrector.
155. See chapter 2 §*A White Shoot of Flame*.

does not start "in an unmediated fashion."[156] It is linked to its legal context by an echo of rare words: "boats/shoot." Further, both words are marked as Babylonian by their tellers, Rabbah and Rabbi Natan ("who was a Babylonian," the Talmud adds—contrasting his gloss with a Palestinian synonym). And both are situated in "folk"—collective, anonymous, non-rabbinic—registers: sailors' yarns or everyday talk.[157]

In sum, there is in fact a transition from legal comments on a Palestinian *mishnah*, on one hand, to Babylonian reports of sailors' tales, on the other. That transition, combined with a structural parallel (sailors' *tales* take the place of a commentary on the *word* "sailors" in the *mishnah*),[158] partly bridges legal with nonlegal content. A gap between the two remains, and readers had to make sense of that gap; including Amoraim like readers in our collection itself, who seem to inform Rabbah that only the legal content of his tales is meaningful (XIIb–XIIIb). Yet this more gradual transition from the Mishnah to Part 1 makes it less likely that the Amoraim read Parts 1 and 2 as a discrete "tractate." More likely, they read them as another literary form: a digression.[159] They had heard of a boat, Babylonians, and sailors. Now a Babylonian was telling them about sailors and a "shoot" that sounds like "boat." Rather than turn the page on a new text, this would have led readers to track the accumulation and variation of those words and associations—a process of reading that is not too radically different from digressions among its legal traditions with which they were intimately familiar.

Weiss again compartmentalizes and limits the reader's creativity when he analyzes the relation between Part 1 of our Appendix (what he calls "Wonders") and Part 2 ("Visions"). He points to the passage between the two as the point of transition: an exegesis of Gen 1:21, "*and God created the great sea-serpents.*" With this claim, Weiss is using a genre category to revive a medieval reading tradition: that of Rashbam, who also interpreted these two collections as a diptych about God's works of Wonder and eschatological Visions such as Leviathan.[160] In other words, Weiss argues not only that his two-part tractate is isolated from literary context due to subject matter, but also that its two parts were collected because Amoraim equated an item in Part 1 with an item in Part 2. The term "sea-serpents," which Rabbi Yohanan immediately glosses as *two* Leviathans (Isa 27:1), moves mechanically from tales of Wonders to messianic Visions.

---

156. Weiss, *Studies in the Literature*, 273.
157. Weiss sees attribution as the only real connecting link (*Studies in the Literature*, 275). On this word "boats" (*butsiyya'ta'*) as stylized Babylonian folk speech, see Jonathan Aaron Pomeranz, "Ordinary Jews in the Babylonian Talmud: Rabbinic Representations and Historical Interpretation" (PhD diss., Yale University, 2016), 293–328, at 313.
158. See chapter 3 §*Placement*.
159. Again, see chapter 3 §*Placement*.
160. See chapter 6 §*Twice upon a Time: The Art of Peshat*.

For an Amoraic reader, that relation between collections need not be a linear progress from one to the other due to shared content. It could be a recursive and associative process. This is the main argument of chapter 5; here I illustrate only how it differs from Weiss's view. Before the gloss about "sea-serpents" that he sees as the transition from Wonders to Visions,[161] another gloss, which Weiss ignores, gives a Babylonian translation (*targum*) of "sea-serpents": "Here, they rendered: *gazelles of the sea*." Like the Babylonian gloss of the Palestinian word "boat" at the beginning of Part 1, this does more than define a word. It relocates the entire discourse—from "there" (the West, Palestine) to "here" (the East, Babylonia).[162] This transition picks up the role of the previous digression on the word "boat." Having heard of biblical "sea-serpents," readers are reminded that "here" in Babylonia—where "we" are—we call them another name. Again, folk speech anchors the text in a reader's world. Further, this local name ("gazelle of the sea," *'urzila' deyama'*) is strikingly similar to a name for a Wonder in Part 1 (IV): a "day-old gazelle" (*'urzila' bar yoma'/yome*; or, another reading, "aurochs gazelle," *'urzila' derema'*).[163] An effect of that gloss, for a Babylonian reader of Part 2 who knows Part 1, is to associate the content of the two parts as well (sea-monster/land-monster, Leviathan/Behemoth). Thus the transition to Part 2 makes it interpretable in light of Part 1. In Weiss's analysis, the implied reader must look forward, from the Wonders to the Visions. Yet, if a reader also attended to this other point of transition, they could also look back and forth. Whereas Weiss makes the two collections seem disjunctive, and seeks their bond in a genre, a new focus on the reading process allows ambiguous and partial associations between both collections—recollections whereby they were read back together.[164] Such associations would have sparked new questions.

---

161. Note, furthermore, that Leviathan also features prominently within Part 1 (XVIIa; XX). Hence, Weiss's proposed transition, based on subject matter, cannot be divided precisely between his two subgenres.

162. "Here, they rendered ..." is typically used to contrast Babylonian with Palestinian *targumim*. In this case, it contrasts a Babylonian targum to a Palestinian midrash (by R. Yohanan, which follows). See Willem F. Smelik, *Rabbis, Language and Translation in Late Antiquity* (Cambridge: Cambridge University Press, 2013), 399–405.

163. Rashi (b. Zev. 113b s.v. אורזילא and s.v. בר יומא) knows all three epithets of this gazelle in the manuscripts (ד.מ."א): "day-old" (בר יומא); "of the Re'em [mythical land-beast, see Job 39:9]" (דרימא); "of the sea" (דימא). His glosses harmonize: "A gazelle"—*that is the Re'em of the sea, who is on the seashore*; "day-old"—*on the day he was born*. Tosafot b. B. Bat. 73b s.v. הכי גרסי' אורזילא בר ראימא דהוי כי הר תבור address the variants in the opposite way, arguing first for the land-gazelle and second for the sea-gazelle. In both cases they defend the view that the beast could have survived the flood (b. Zev. 113b; b. Qidd. 13a), and therefore that Rabbah did not lie about seeing it. Tosafot is cited from the margin of ed. Vilna throughout the book.

164. I also show (chapter 3 §*Chronological Layers*) that XX is a later Babylonian tradition in Palestinian style inserted as a transition to Part 2. This weakens Weiss's simple "Wonders and Visions" structure for the two parts.

For example, *Why do we* ("here" in Babylonia) *call sea-serpents "gazelles"?
Are the species related?*[165] *If so, is Leviathan's fetid odor, which poisons the sea in
Part 2,*[166] *like the huge ball of dung of a "gazelle" which dams the Jordan in Part
1?* I cannot prove how Amoraic readers answered such questions, but we
have reason to suspect that they asked them. The way in which our collection begins, as well the transition points between its parts, prompted them
to move more freely between Wonders and Visions in a nonlinear way.

Apocalyptic

In Günter Stemberger's far longer and more nuanced study of Parts 1 and
2, integrating form criticism with literary analysis, he makes a better case
than Weiss that the entire composition is an integrated whole—one where
the Talmud engages critically with apocalyptic literature.[167] I develop an
alternative to his approach throughout chapter 5. Here I illustrate only
how I think he goes wrong in using a genre label to give an overly linear
and formal analysis of the structure of these two collections, which again
restricts the reader's creativity. He says, "We must attempt a definition of
the genre of the entire unit which sensibly connects and forms a whole
of the Aramaic section's sailor and desert tales [Part 1], on one hand,
and the Hebrew section's dicta about Leviathan and the eschaton [Part
2], on the other."[168] Must we? Speculating that our two-part composition
mimics Daniel (a two-part Hebrew/Aramaic text), Stemberger nominates
Apocalyptic—with its blend of wonders and visions, travels and eschatological expectations—as the genre that the Talmud's editors must have
used. However, he does not see both parts of this composition as equally
meaningful. Rather, in his account, Part 2 "domesticates" and delimits the
meaning of Part 1.[169] For him, the tales in Part 1 were too strange to stand
on their own in the Talmud (a "religious" canon), and only the tales' "religious" meaning could have mattered to the rabbis.[170] Therefore, if Part 2

---

165. For example, the gazelle/unicorn/aurochs (ראם, רימא) is said in *aggadah* to have survived the flood (see Tosafot at n. 163) by lodging its horns in the ark (Louis Ginzberg, *Legends of the Jews*, 2nd ed., 2 vols., JPS Classic Reissues (Philadelphia: Jewish Publication Society, 2003), 1:146 n. 34), just as Leviathan clearly survived the battle with the waters at Creation.

166. This motif of "stinking evil sea-monster" links Leviathan to the Stinking Ghost who resists the good deity Ahura Mazda in the Iranian parallel (Kiperwasser and Shapira, "Irano-Talmudica III," 88-90, and see n. 278).

167. Günter Stemberger, "Münchhausen und die Apokalyptik: Baba Batra 73a–75b als literarische Einheit," *JSJ* 20.1 (1989): 61–83.

168. Stemberger, "Münchhausen und die Apokalyptik," 71.

169. Stemberger, "Münchhausen und die Apokalyptik," 83: "Apocalyptic is domesticated within the sphere of control of the rabbis."

170. Stemberger, "Münchhausen und die Apokalyptik," 61–62: "Of course the Talmud

parodies or attacks Part 1, the editors must be attacking apocalyptic with their own exegetically based authority. For Stemberger, the very existence of Part 1 was the problem that Part 2 resolved.

Like Dina Stein's important work that I develop in chapters 2, 4, and 5,[171] Stemberger spotlights a central tension in this composition between apocalyptic sources of authority (wonders, travels, visions) and rabbinic textual expertise. However, his use of a genre to claim that the Talmud sets up a hierarchy between them and, therefore, that Part 2 controls the meaning of Part 1, shackles the reader, who could have taken up Part 1 on its own terms or related it more dynamically with Part 2. In fact, there are signs of both alternative approaches in the Talmud.

For example, Stemberger interprets Rabbah's desert wanderings as the expression of an apocalyptic philosophy of history: the present age is a state of decline that is passing away; one can only hope for the End. Therefore, when Rabbah sees giant bones of "the dead of the desert" (XIIa), and then he is blocked from Mount Sinai by giant scorpions as he hears a divine voice lamenting, "Woe is me for having sworn, and now that I have sworn, who will annul it for me?" (XIIIa), Stemberger interprets those bones as relics of a lost "golden age" in Israel's past, and the "vow" as a sign of the perennially exilic quality of the Jewish present.[172]

We have direct evidence, however, that early rabbinic readers did not look at either image in such a lachrymose light. As for the divine vow, while it is associated with exile,[173] when Rabbah tells his colleagues about it, they entertain the idea that he could have released God from God's vow, had he only applied the proper formula![174] Rabbah retorts that he had read the vow differently: as God's vow never again to destroy the

---

contains plenty of texts that are primarily interested in narration. But we should hesitate at such a rather superficial evaluation of a text; for, as a whole, the Talmud is certainly interested in being religious literature, even if taken in the widest sense of the term." In other words, in his view of Talmudization, the merely strange tales must be subordinated to a dogmatic message. We should interrogate the work that the word "religious" is doing in this argument as a possible symptom of the well-studied tendency for secular literary philology to mask a culturally Protestant hermeneutic, such that only a text's "religious" content is enough to justify its literary form. See Catlin, " Rest is Literature," 92, 133–36.

171. Dina Stein, "Believing Is Seeing: A Reading of Baba Batra 73a–75b" [Hebrew], *Jerusalem Studies in Hebrew Literature* 17 (1999): 1–24, at 14–17; Stein, *Textual Mirrors: Reflexivity, Midrash, and the Rabbinic Self*, Divinations (Philadelphia: University of Pennsylvania Press, 2012), 58–63.

172. Stemberger, "Münchhausen und die Apokalyptik," 75–76.

173. The divine cry is associated with Israel's exile and Jerusalem's destruction in a structurally similar story at b. Ber. 3a and the withdrawal of the Divine Presence at b. Sotah 47b. Both can be read into XIIIa; see n. 666.

174. XIIIb: "You should have said, 'It's annulled for you, it's annulled for you!' " This formula's repetition corresponds to God's repetition in ms. P (יג"א.קס"י):"'Who will release me? Who will annul it for me?'"

world after the flood, a vow that no one would want to revoke.[175] Perhaps this debate is already a parody of Rabbah's tale, anticipating in some sense the deconstruction of apocalyptic that Stemberger finds in Part 2. Yet it is deeply embedded *within* Part 1 itself: its interpretation is not controlled by Part 2. It thus shows that this tale and its genre were interpreted by early readers in their own ways.

Nor did every reader take these giant bones of their ancestors as relics of a "golden age" from which they had fallen. Rather than the wilderness generation, as Stemberger and several others assume,[176] rabbinic lore links the bones more directly to Ephraim—the tribe who attempted a premature exodus and were killed by the Philistines as divine punishment.[177] Their size reflects exegesis identifying them as "mighty men of valor."[178] Rabbah's comment that they were "reposing, like one who is intoxicated," echoes the epithet "drunkards of Ephraim" (Isa 28:1, 3). So his vision of their bones was not necessarily read as the sign of a generation in decline. For Babylonian Amoraim, it may have been the revelation of a lost mystery: according to *midrash*, God did not let Israel see Ephraim's bones, lest they lose heart,[179] but now they were visible. Babylonian interest in those bones was rising, sincere, and ambivalent about their meaning. Rav ventured an apocalyptic gloss, but just the opposite of Stemberger's: mes-

---

175. The sages' counterargument ("One doesn't say 'Woe' to that!") is based on an inference from the vow's language. By contrast, Rabbah's argument points back to the collection itself, which starts with a primordial war between Sand and Sea (I; see the full prooftext, Jer 5:22). It is as if Rabbah reads holistically, whereas the sages read literally. Both serve as competing figures, of course, for different kinds of readers that a reader of this story could become.

176. Bacher, Die Agada, 91; Shraga Abramson ed., *Talmud Bavli Massekhet Baba Batra* (Tel-Aviv: Dvir, 1958), 90 n. 72; Stemberger, "Münchhausen und die Apokalyptik," 76–77; Dan Ben-Amos, "Talmudic Tall Tales," in *Folklore Today: A Festschrift for Richard M. Dorson*, ed. Linda Dégh, Henry Glassie, and Felix J. Oinas (Bloomington: Indiana University Press, 1976), 25–43, at 31–32; Stein, "Believing Is Seeing," 12. Haim Weiss cites Lam. Rab. 33 (ed. Buber, 36–37) in support of this but it is inconclusive ("Ha-tsitsit shel Rabbah"). After all, a verse says that the wilderness generation's remains did *not* survive (Num 14:35). As Tosafot recall (b. B. Batra 73b s.v. ודמו כמאן דמיבסמי) with b. Sanh. 110b), this was a dispute between Tannaim and Amoraim.

177. Avigdor Shinan and Yair Zakovitch, *From Gods to God: How the Bible Debunked, Suppressed, or Changed Ancient Myths and Legends*, trans. Valerie Zakovitch (Lincoln: University of Nebraska Press, 2012), 162–63. On the broader cultural interest in giant bones, see Elisha Fine and Steven Fine, "Rabbinic Paleontology: Jewish Encounters with Fossil Giants in Roman Antiquity," in *Land and Spirituality in Rabbinic Literature: A Memorial Volume for Yaakov Elman*, ed. Shana Strauch Schick, Brill Reference Library of Judaism 71 (Leiden: Brill, 2022), 3–37.

178. Joseph Heinemann, "The Messiah of Ephraim and the Premature Exodus of the Tribe of Ephraim," HTR 68.1 (1975): 1-15, at 12.

179. That is why Israel did not pass from Egypt to Canaan "by way of the land of the Philistines, although that was nearer, for God thought, 'If the people face war, they may change their minds and return to Egypt'" (Exod 13:17 NRSV, as exposited in Pesiq. Rab Kah. 11:10, ed. Mandelbaum, 1:186).

sianic hope, interpreting them as Ezekiel's "dry bones."[180] In taking up this line of thought, Bialik's national epic poems revive early ambivalence about their apocalyptic message.[181] Rather than "control" what this motif meant in Part 1 through parody, the apocalyptic genre captures, at most, a serious conversation that only some readers were having about what it might mean.

Tall Tale

Where form and source criticism have used abstract genre labels to impose structure on our strange collection—defining its introduction, transitions, ending, parts, and whole with labels that suppress its readers' creativity and historical diversity—folklore uses a stable construct of genre to create a psychological profile of its idealized reader. This reader is identified with "the people": a collective, anonymous, and universal subject.[182] By speaking in the name of such a subject and asking their reader to identify with it as well, folklorists project their idiosyncratic intuitions about the text onto the "function" of popular genres. This projection suppresses the role of the reader as well as diversity among readers when it ignores contrary evidence for how the tales were read; when it, so to speak, "essentializes away" other possible (and actual) readings because meaning is fixed by the scholar's construct of how a genre works. A genre autonomously transmits meanings that everyone innately knows.

The founding study of this approach, based on part of his dissertation, is Dan Ben-Amos's "Talmudic Tall Tales."[183] As the title indicates, Ben-Amos defines a folk genre, the "tall tale," and classifies most of Part 1 as such. For him, "historical and literary" interpretations of these tales are misguided, because the tellers, as well as their original audience, already had their own indigenous genre. That "tall tale" genre determined their telling, collection, and interpretation. Once we recognize this genre, we

---

180. B. Sanh. 92b; see also Heinemann, "Premature Exodus," 10–11. Rav's argument is based on his prooftext about the death of Ephraim's tribe, which concludes, "and his brethren came to comfort him" (1 Chr 7:22). He interprets this "comfort" as the messianic gathering of "dry bones" in Ezek 37 because dry bones are followed by another prophecy: the gathering of the "sticks" of the tribes ("brethren"): Joseph, Israel, Judah, and Ephraim (Ezek 37:16). Both prophecies thus point to Ephraim.

181. Weiss, "Ha-tsitsit shel Rabbah." See Gershon Shaked, "Ha-yesodot ha-mitiyim be-'Mete Midbar'" [Hebrew], in On 'The Dead of the Wilderness' (Metey Midbar): Essays on Bialik's Poem, ed. Zvi Luz (Ramat-Gan: Bar-Ilan University Press, 1988), 43–54, at 44–45.

182. For a debate about this, see Stein, "Let the 'People' Go?"; Hasan-Rokem, "Did Rabbinic Culture Conceive."

183. Ben-Amos, "Talmudic Tall Tales," 25–43; Ben-Amos, "Narrative Forms in the Aggadah: Structural Analysis" (PhD diss., Indiana University, 1966), 114–33.

can forgo historical and literary analysis, empathizing directly with the mindset that produced these tales and governed their reception. Furthermore, this genre is universal: it is found in American frontier lore like Davy Crockett just as it is in the Talmud. (By Ben-Amos's logic, when I read my own nation's tall tales, I should feel just like Rabbah's first listeners. Therefore, his analysis should apply in the other direction: I should be able to understand my own culture's tall tales by reading Rabbah's.[184])

Ben-Amos defines his universal tall tale genre by a psychological tension of extremes. In one sense, a tall tale is plainly incredible. In another, it is realistic: its telling adorns the unbelievable subject matter with culturally authenticated tokens of verisimilitude. Hence, the tale is believed and disbelieved at once, amusing readers and holding their attention by vacillating between the extremes. Recognizing that the rabbis had no name for this genre, and proposing no formal criteria for distinguishing it among the forms of *aggadah*,[185] Ben-Amos still holds that it was self-consciously used and clearly recognized by the rabbinic audience.

Because he defines the genre by a psychological tension, without clearly documenting how specific readers marked or reflected upon it, Ben-Amos projects his own intuitions about the tension onto tales that evidence suggests actual readers would have taken differently. Let us

---

184. Even as a small child, I felt no such thing about the tall tales in a picture book featuring Paul Bunyan and his giant blue ox, Babe. I recognized the story of the furrows that his axe and plough left in the earth as a poetic etiology of the western landscape and remembered this story on a family trip to the edge of the Grand Canyon. Yet I felt none of the ambiguity of reality and fantasy, truth and exaggeration, whereby Ben-Amos defines this universal folk genre. Nor, as I gazed out at the nation's legendary frontier, did this tall tale stir patriotic feeling in me by association with its larger-than-life hero. Perhaps this is because I was a dull boy, but I think it is due to historical or cultural differences among readers that Ben-Amos's genre, unlike our constellation, aims to minimize.

185. Ben-Amos contrasts the tall tale to "a clear generic term meaning, literally, false and imaginary words" ("Talmudic Tall Tales," 28). This is based entirely on his misreading of a word in the Talmud (מילי דבדיאי, b. Bekh. 8b), a *hapax* like its Syriac cognate, which does have such a meaning. (His misreading, like many of his ideas about this tall tale genre, is repeated by Eli Yassif, "Humorous Stories in *Aggadah*: Typology, Theme, Meaning" [Hebrew], in *Talmudic Studies*, ed. Yaakov Sussmann and David Rosenthal, 3 vols. [Jerusalem: Magnes, 2005], 3.1:403–37, at 424.) The better reading, in manuscripts of b. Bekh. 8b, is מילי דכדיב ("false matters"), with an apocopated form at b. Sanh. 29b, מילי דכדי, "matters of nothing" (that which is "indefinite," שלא בודאי: Geonic explanation in *JBA*, 553). The distinction is not possible versus impossible, but something versus nothing! Nor does Ben-Amos explore related speech genres in the Talmud such as "jesting words" (מילי דבדיחותא). This is a weapon for scholars aiming to deflate their opponents' legal arguments without responding (b. B. Bat. 9b; b. B. Qam. 17b). It may preface a legal teaching, much as lecturers conventionally start with a joke (b. Shabb. 30b = b. Pesah. 117a). Apparently, then, "jesting words" punctuated or began a Talmudic legal discussion, and they were both opposed and related to law. Might such a telling be better compared, in both form and function, to ours: a well-structured digression *within* a legal discussion? (See chapter 3 §*Placement*). In any case, Ben-Amos is plainly incorrect when he claims that rabbis were self-conscious and yet silent about their own speech genres.

return to Rabbah's encounter with "the dead of the desert" (XIIa). Like Stemberger, Ben-Amos says that this motif alludes to the corpses of the wilderness generation (Num 14:32–37).[186] He interprets this allusion as a way to "validate" the tall tale by citing the text of Scripture. Yet, as we saw above, it is more likely an allusion to a rabbinic legend about the Ephraimites. There is no reason to think that Rabbah's audience would have heard some of this tale as true, whereas the bodies' "intoxicated" state and huge limbs would have sounded exaggerated or unbelievable. For them, the whole tale probably sounded like a variation on tales that they already knew, and they likely read all of its details as some form of imaginative recollection of such tales. Ben-Amos's distinction between the Bible's true witness and rabbis' tall tales meant nothing to them. Similarly, in Rabbah's tale of giant birds (IXa) that a reader, Rav Ashi, ties to a biblical verse (IXb/Ps 50:11), Ben-Amos uses Rav Ashi's gloss ("That was *ziz saday*") as further proof that the "tall tale" genre cites Scripture to maintain its tension between truth and lies. Here again, he conflates the Bible with another rabbinic tradition: one that may be based on this very tale![187] Ashi's gloss makes sense only in light of the rabbinic motif of the *ziz* as a bird so big its wings cover the sun, a rabbinic reading tradition of Ps 50:11 that also was current elsewhere.[188] Here, too, there is no distinction, thus no generic tension, between a verse and a tall tale. Both intertexts are Talmudized: integrated into a reading tradition where readers create their meaning without being bothered by this tension between truth and fiction.

I do not mean that such tension never existed for some readers of these strange tales, only that "genre" should not be a substitute for examining their specific acts of interpretation. Yet it has continued to function as such a substitute in folklore studies following Ben-Amos. By classifying our stories not only as "tall tales" but also as "humorous," for example, Yassif added a genre that enlarges Ben-Amos's psychological profile

---

186. This would not explain the bones' size: the wilderness generation were *not* giants (Num 13:33; Deut 1:28). If not for their ritual fringes, a more plausible source for this legend would be giant Philistines with six fingers and toes, whose giant *spears* (see n. 88) are cited in 2 Sam 21:19 = 1 Chr. 20:5, and who were slain by David's warriors. See Josephus, *Ant.* 7.12.2, in Flavius Josephus, *Judean Antiquities 5–7*, trans. Christopher T. Begg, ed. Steve Mason, Flavius Josephus, Translation and Commentary 4 (Leiden: Brill, 2005), 287–88.
187. A distinction noted already in Ginzberg, *Legends*, 1:32 n. 131.
188. Ber. Rab. 19:4 = Vay. Rab. 22:10 (only the latter cites Pss 50:11 and 50:10). The same is said of the *ziz*'s wings and Leviathan's fins—one of many correspondences among this composition's cosmic creature-types (bird, beast, fish). See Irving Jacobs, *The Midrashic Process: Tradition and Interpretation in Rabbinic Judaism* (Cambridge: Cambridge University Press, 1995), 161 n. 34; Jefim Schirmann, *The Battle between Behemoth and Leviathan according to an Ancient Hebrew Piyyut* [Hebrew] (Jerusalem: Israel Academy of Sciences and Humanities, 1970); Laura Lieber, "Theater of the Holy: Performative Elements of Late Ancient Hymnography," *HTR* 108.3 (2015): 327–55, at 339–41, 351–55.

of the universal "folk" reader. Not only do these tales express a tension between truth and fiction; that tension, in turn, fits Yassif's vague definition of humor as a sense of "incongruity" between narrative elements.[189] Wherever Yassif himself feels incongruity, he projects his new subgenre onto the reader's mind.

This "humorous tall tale" genre becomes a substitute for analysis when, for example, Yassif conflates Rav Pappa's comment *about* the story of a giant frog, serpent, bird, and tree (V) with Rabbah's telling of the story itself. Rabbah began his tale "I myself have seen . . ." and in conclusion, Rav Pappa comments: "If I hadn't been there,[190] I wouldn't have believed it." For Yassif, both claims have the same function: they strengthen one side of the tension in the tall tale genre by enhancing the fiction's verisimilitude. Further, Yassif says, because Rav Pappa was a familiar authority to Babylonian readers, his comment has the same role as other local details like "the fort of Hagrunya." That is, Rav Pappa makes this incredible tale more credible by clothing it in a well-known, trustworthy garb.

Again, I am not arguing that readers ignored the tension between this strange tale and its familiar telling; I agree it was important for how some readers read some tales (chapter 2). But by reducing Rav Pappa's remark to the "amusing testimony of another well-known sage," Yassif puts his generic cart before the textual horse. Rav Pappa is not saying the same thing as Rabbah: his comment supports both sides of the tension between credible and incredible, both the teller ("I saw it [too]") and his skeptical audience ("or I wouldn't have believed it [either]"). Those clashing readings, in one concluding comment, do stress an "incongruity." Yet there is no reason to assume that it was humorous. What if it was self-critical? As we know, Rabbah was famous in his day as an unreliable *raconteur*.[191] Maybe the figure of Rav Pappa is saying that, despite Rabbah's reputation, here he was telling the truth. Might such a claim have led the story's readers to doubt their own prejudices against Rabbah-as-teller? And thus to rethink, even to attack, the binary of credibility and incredibility in this collection that—for these folklorists—should define any generic reader's feeling about tall tales? If we reject stable and deterministic notions of genre, in favor of specific readers and their interpretive horizons, we find that readers could create meanings different from those dreamt of in folk psychology.

---

189. Yassif, "Humorous Stories." Yassif neglects Henri Bergson, *Le rire: Essai sur la signification du comique* (1900 repr., Paris: Presses Universitaires de France, 1954), which argued strongly against his definition of humor and advanced a new approach.

190. V.61, mss. V, O: "seen it." This could already be an interpretation of the comment that harmonizes the voices and authenticating strategies of both tellers—Rav Pappa and Rabbah, see V.52—just as Yassif himself does here.

191. See Introduction §*The Teller*.

Genre Trouble! 69

The final application of the tall tale genre to our collection, Daniel Frim's more recent study, takes the discussion in a more comparative direction.[192] Frim invents yet another subgenre of the tall tale, "maritime" or "nautical," arguing that this genre influenced the meaning of Parts 1 and 2 for the Talmud's readers. To its credit, his analysis is based not just on a psychological tension of truth and fiction but also on comparing how parallel motifs function in other cultures' tales with some tales in Part 1 (VIa-b; VII; XIX).[193] Further, by showing how rare words direct a reader's attention to intertexts within the two-part composition, Frim sheds new light on one of our questions (chapter 5): How did meanings transfer between Parts 1 and 2 as they were recollected and Talmudized? Finally, he offers insights about comparable sources in the Zohar and magic bowls.[194] Frim's uses of genre, however, perpetuate the flaws of folklore's "tall tale" label. This mental construct of genre continues to substitute for or even contradict what past readers actually did. Rather than expand our access to their minds, genre minimizes how meaning was created by readers and reading traditions where the "nautical tall tale" had no clear effect.

For example, addressing the relation between Part 1 ("tall tales") and Part 2 ("myth"), Frim argues that the former's genre affected how the latter was interpreted in general. Myth is true, cosmic, believable.[195] Tall tales are the opposite: false, homespun, incredible. So, he asks, how did readers respond to seeing their sacred myths set side by side with these tall tales? Frim's question presumes that his genre labels will explain how readers navigated this relation between the collections—that "the folk" carried around his categories in their heads. It argues against this that

---

192. Daniel J. Frim, "'Those Who Descend upon the Sea Told Me …': Myth and Tall Tale in *Baba Batra* 73a–74b," *JQR* 107.1 (2017): 1–37.

193. Beyond the few parallel motifs that Frim discusses, we might note that many are the same tale, the same basic narrative content: the two-horned lobster (XVIIIa; Ramhormuz V); the ship held in place by a giant fish/lobster (VIIIa-b; Ramhormuz VI); the beached whale, oil from whose eyes is extracted and sold in vast quantity/to vast profit (VIa; Ramhormuz IX. This tale is already in the second-century CE: Arrian, *Indika*, XXIX; see n. 550); the height of a whale/wave that tries to sink a ship, and how sailors use slats of wood to ward it off (II; Ramhormuz IX); a fish/turtle mistaken for an island, heated by a cooking fire and almost drowning sailors (VII; Ramhormuz XVIII); and looser collocations of motifs, such as the circulation between a bird, a piece of meat, and a precious stone (XIX; Ramhormuz LXXXII). I cite the units of the edition of Captain Buzurg ibn Shahriyār of Ramhormuz, *The Book of the Wonders of India: Mainland, Sea, and Islands*, ed. and trans. G. S. P. Freeman-Grenville (London: East-West, 1981).

194. On Zoharic expansions, see n. 756. On magic bowls, see Jacobs, *Midrashic Process*, 156 n. 7.

195. Paraphrasing the definition by Frim, "'Those Who Descend,'" 10. On whether "belief" belongs here, see Paul Veyne, *Did the Greeks Believe in Their Myths? An Essay on the Constitutive Imagination*, trans. Paula Wissig (Chicago: University of Chicago Press, 1988 [1983]), 14–15. The same should be asked of ancient Jews.

readers actually identified the mythic Leviathan *in* a "tall tale,"[196] and even in a tale that was crafted and inserted precisely in order to connect Part 1 with Part 2.[197] In that case, at least, Frim's genre boundary had no effect on either the editor of the two parts or on a reader of XX *within* XX who interprets what he just heard as literally seeing Leviathan. Those readers did not try to "[shield] the Leviathan from direct association" with tall tales—on the contrary, they used Leviathan to recollect tall tales with deep myths.[198] If Frim's genre boundary did not restrict their activity, we can also question whether it existed for their peers. Perhaps mixing tall tales with Leviathan myths did, as he argues, make readers "delegitimize" the latter, doubting that Leviathan was "'real,' tangible, visible."[199] But the tradition points the other way: tale XX, and especially Part 2, make Leviathan more tangible, more visible. Without Frim's genres in mind, why would readers have doubted Leviathan's reality *more* after they read both collections than before? If a genre distinction has no effect, does it exist?

Myth as Cultural History

If the genres "Tractate," "Apocalyptic," and "Tall Tale" have caused trouble insofar as they did not constrain how real readers created meaning, yet do limit their creativity in theory, a fourth genre label, Myth, is a better translation of what readers did and might have done. We can see its value by asking the same questions about Myth as we did of the other genres. Can we document that readers were aware of something like this category? What were its effects on how they interpreted Part 1, Part 2, or both together? Myth stands up better to such questions because scholarly applications of this genre correspond more closely to how some readers seem to have interpreted both collections and help to explain the logic of their results.

One valuable use of this genre has been in cultural history. Here, myth helps to contextualize talmudic tellings of the tales in rabbis' own Sasanian, Zoroastrian environment. By contrasting Rabbah's telling of a common "whale mistaken for an island" story (VII) with Zoroastrian tellings and their reception, for instance, Samuel Thrope sees his Zoroastrian counterpart, Keresaspa, as received very differently. Keresaspa seems to

---

196. Frim, "'Those Who Descend,'" 160 n. 37: "no character or narrator … explicitly claims to have seen or encountered the Leviathan." R. Eliezer glosses what his shipmate has just seen as Leviathan (XX). This is *more* of an explicit encounter than, e.g., Rav Ashi glossing a bird as the *ziz* in a story from four generations ago (IXb).

197. See nn. 493–496 and §*Exegesis* below.

198. Frim, "'Those Who Descend,'" 37.

199. Frim, "'Those Who Descend,'" 37.

have been punished for what was (for Jews) a "meaningless" side motif: when the monster awakens and he flees, he puts out the flame under his cooking pot—a cosmic element of fire that is sacred in Zoroastrianism.[200] Thrope thus shows how Persians read their own cultural norms into their telling of the myth. He is less effective at turning the gaze back on rabbinic readers,[201] but Reuven Kiperwasser and his collaborators have made progress in that direction in an important series of essays.[202] By analyzing substantial parallels and differences between our tales and Mesopotamian myths, especially a section of the Zoroastrian cosmology *Bundahišn*—not only in content but also in structure and form—they suggest how rabbis' tellings of myth may reveal Jewish ideologies.

Three of their analyses are novel, well-supported examples of the kind of ideological tendency for which their studies argue in general. First, when Rabbah turns motifs that are all sacred in foreign cultures into a narrative sequence of one swallowing the other (V), reminiscent of folk songs like "Had Gadya," Kiperwasser sees this as a "sarcastic" Jewish use of foreign cultures. Similarly, he notes a gap between the mythic content of the tales and the profile of their teller, who is more an inept "anti-hero" than a hero.[203] Rabbah travels to distant lands; undergoes trials similar to those of heroes of other Mesopotamian myth;[204] and returns home—a classic "hero's journey" pattern.[205] Yet his behavior and reception back "home," in the talmudic study-house, are hardly heroic. Like Thrope, Kiperwasser concludes that our tales were received as a "parody" of other

---

200. Samuel Thrope, "The Alarming Lunch: Judaism, Zoroastrianism and Colonialism in Sassanian Iran," *Journal of the Associated Graduates in Near Eastern Studies* 12.1 (2006): 23–44, at 28. For similar arguments about water and urine in III–IV, see n. 241.

201. Thrope contends that the Talmudic version of the tale engages in "mimicry" of the Zoroastrian version by reiterating the same motifs *without* their accompanying cultural themes ("Alarming Lunch," 36–38). Yet he cites no evidence of such "mimicry" nor analysis of how it works in the tale: this is a circular argument from silence.

202. Kiperwasser, "Travels of Rabbah"; Kiperwasser and Dan D. Y. Shapira, "Irano-Talmudica I: The Three-Legged Ass and Ridyā in B. Ta'anith: Some Observations about Mythic Hydrology in the Babylonian Talmud and in Ancient Iran," *AJSR* 32.1 (2008): 101–16; Kiperwasser and Shapira, "Irano-Talmudica II: Leviathan, Behemoth, and the 'Domestication' of Iranian Mythological Creatures in Eschatological Narratives in the Babylonian Talmud," in *Shoshannat Yaakov: Jewish and Iranian Studies in Honor of Yaakov Elman*, ed. Shai Secunda and Steven Fine, Brill Reference Library of Judaism 35 (Leiden: Brill, 2012), 203–36; Kiperwasser and Shapira, "Irano-Talmudica III," 65–92; Kiperwasser and Ruzer, "Aramaic Stories," 161–77; Kiperwasser and Ruzer, "Nautical Fiction," 295–311.

203. See Joshua Levinson, "The Rabbinic Anti-Hero in the Exegetical Narrative" [Hebrew], in *Studies in Talmudic and Midrashic Literature*, ed. Mosheh Bar-Asher, Joshua Levinson, and Berachyahu Lifshitz (Jerusalem: Mossad Bialik, 2005), 217–30.

204. For another pan-Mesopotamian motif in XIIIa that I happened to notice in Gilgamesh, see n. 588.

205. Joseph Campbell, *The Hero with a Thousand Faces*, Bollingen Series 17 (1949; repr., Princeton, NJ: Princeton University Press, 2004).

cultures' heroes.[206] His genre categories (Satire, Parody) may be right or wrong, but methodologically they are better-founded than "tall tale," for instance. They are not imposed on all readers as psychological universals but reflect his view, by comparing one tale with another, of how some Jews may have read these tales in light of others. These genres emerge from a *contrast* between a common-denominator genre, Myth, and interpretive frameworks of historically specific Jewish readers.

Similarly, in the case of "Hormiz," who leaps in the air while juggling goblets of water and is named after a Zoroastrian demon or deity (III), Kiperwasser and Shapira reconstruct an intricate three-stage process — linguistic, mythological, exegetical — which generated that figure. As they say, this figure was not cut-and-pasted into the rabbinic tale from Iranian sources, but was subjected to "mechanisms of absorption and reworking of Iranian concepts, with names and functions adapted to the existing Jewish ones."[207] Specifically, they argue that his mythic role, to mediate between "upper" and "lower" waters, reflects local Babylonian Jewish cosmology based primarily on the Bible. By contrast, the very existence of that mythological mediator was rejected in Palestinian rabbinic sources.[208] Hence, as the authors say in another context, the Babylonian Talmud "elaborates the margins of its own culture using the materials of the surrounding culture."[209] By subtly modifying and assimilating an Iranian myth into their own cosmological debate, Babylonian rabbis set themselves apart from Palestinian peers. Rather than satirize or parody Zoroastrianism, here, readers brought its myth into their local Judaism.

A final example of this promising new direction in cultural history is Kiperwasser and Ruzer's interpretation of the tale of the precious stone in the depths of the sea and the battle of sea-serpents with a wondrous bird (XIX). Here, again, they note that a unique teller ("Rabbi Judah the Indian") parallels the hero of a Syriac Christian version, the apostle Thomas, a traveler to India. In the Syriac version — the Song of the Pearl embedded in the Acts of Thomas — this motif of retrieving a pearl in the depths, encircled by a sea-serpent, was, the authors hold, originally a "Babylonian fairy tale" with a "sailor story prototype."[210] The Talmud loaded it with more explicit wondrous properties and eschatological symbolism. By arguing that Jewish and Christian tellers in Iran used the same hypothetical source

---

206. Kiperwasser, "Travels of Rabbah," 234–35.
207. Kiperwasser and Shapira, "Irano-Talmudica I," 112, and esp. 112–14.
208. Kiperwasser and Shapira, "Irano-Talmudica I," 107–9.
209. Kiperwasser and Shapira, "Irano-Talmudica III," 83.
210. Kiperwasser and Ruzer, "Aramaic Stories," 172. Somewhat awkwardly, their hypothesis of this "sailor story prototype" leads them to treat the Gnostic allegorization of the Song of the Pearl, and its inclusion in the Acts of Thomas, as a later independent development. As their notes indicate *ad loc.*, however, that view is debated. Contrast a more recent and cautious phrasing of the argument in Kiperwasser and Ruzer, "Nautical Fiction," 303.

in their own ways, they help us to picture how Jewish *readers* might have assigned specific meanings to this tale: for instance, by deferring salvation to the eschaton, and by pinning salvation on one key item—the thread of the prayershawl (*tekhelet*), which is a leitmotif in both the prior pearl tale (XVIII) and another tale in the first collection (XII). In this instance, too, it seems that Jewish cultural appropriation was selective and ideologically motivated. These essays suggest how some Jewish composers and readers in Sasanian Iran were motivated by certain mythic elements and why they selected those as culturally marked. Storytelling and retelling thus contribute to an understanding of how Jewish identity was articulated and developed in its cultural context. These reception dynamics may explain some of the interests of Sasanian Jewish readers whom we will meet below.

Myth as Narrative Cosmology

Another helpful use of the genre Myth is classically structuralist. This approach focuses on how the Talmud transforms cross-cultural patterns of mythic meaning, rather than on historical reasons for why it made the precise changes that it did. The pioneering work in this mode on our material as Myth, despite its already obsolete usage of the term *myth* itself,[211] was Umberto Cassuto's comparison of Part 2 with ancient Near Eastern sources. He was the first to recognize Part 2 as a talmudic archive for "echoes" of a widespread myth.[212] This is a creation-and-battle myth: on one side, primordial waters, dragons, and so on; on the other, a victorious deity. Based on a catalogue of cross-cultural motifs, Cassuto sketched its narrative outline, noting that, uniquely among Jewish sources, these motifs cluster in Part 2. Further studies of Part 2 illuminated with more precision how this retelling of the myth develops a new cosmology that reconfigures relations of power, origins, and endings as the Talmud plucks symbols from its archive and joins them in a dynamic narrative.

Building on this approach, Irving Jacobs showed how the biblical

---

211. In *Biblical and Oriental Studies*, Cassuto uses the actual term *myth* polemically as the religion of Others. This is not in dialogue with the anthropology of his day (1942). For example, Isaak Heinemann based his 1949 theory of *aggadah*-as-myth on Ernst Cassirer, who had already published the Myth volume of his *Philosophy of Symbolic Forms* in 1925 against Cassuto's definition. See Redfield, "Creative Historiography Today," 412 nn. 62–66.

212. Cassuto, *Biblical and Oriental Studies*, 2:82 and 101: "Not merely allusions, but actual narratives, even though they are of extreme brevity and lacking in detail.... This tradition continued to live in the people's memory, and was given renewed expression in rabbinic teaching ... even some typical expressions of the ancient poem, having become literary conventions, succeeded in surviving and reappearing here and there in later books." For this myth's retelling in the story of Jonah in Pirqe R. El., see Adelman, *Return of the Repressed*, 226–28.

repressed returns in rabbinic myth by reactivating tropes of power that the Bible had half-garbed in monotheism. For instance, in a Palestinian midrash related to Part 2,[213] Jacobs pointed to a rabbinic reading of a difficult verse on Leviathan: "His scales are his pride" (גַּאֲוָה אֲפִיקֵי מָגִנִּים, Job 41:15a [41:7a]).[214] This reading derives the Hebrew noun "furrow" (*'afiq*) as a causative of the Aramaic verb, "to go out" (*n.f.q*.). Rather than describe "furrows" in Leviathan's hide (or "scales": t. Hul. 4:13, Ma'agarim), that new reading creates a new story from the verse: "[Because] of his [Leviathan's] Glory, He [God] brings out defenders."[215] Leviathan thus regains a mythic trope: his Glory ("pride"), a divine light that haloed and clothed "dragons" in the myth. This Glory causes God to marshal *His* own troops in the battle. Similarly, in this Palestinian telling of the myth, God's "defenders" are angels, just as, in our Babylonian telling, the angel Gabriel "hunts" Leviathan (Appendix §*Translation* Part 2.A).[216] Rabbinic retellers culled this mythic archive from verses of Job and expanded its motifs to strengthen God's side. Part 2 contains other retellings of the myth to just that effect.[217]

Jacobs also correctly emphasized how Part 2 reorients the temporality of the myth: from one pole of time to the other, from primordial *Urzeit* to eschatological *Endzeit*. Whereas a reader of the biblical Job is not wrong to feel that God rehearses this old myth of how God subdued Leviathan and other rivals at creation in order to display dominion over the cosmos and silence Job's complaint,[218] in Part 2's talmudic retelling of this myth

---

213. Pesiq. Rab Kah. Supplement 2 (ed. Mandelbaum, 455–56). This is also in ms. Oxford of Tanh. §*Nitsavim* 4, from which it was added to the 1563 Mantua print; see ed. Buber, 2:50 n. 16. I thank Dov Weiss for help with this reference.

214. See Jacobs, *Midrashic Process*, 159–60.

215. The same interpretive move is made in Part 2.A and Pesiq. Rab Kah. (n. 213), which read "barbed irons" (*śukkot*) of Leviathan's skin in Job 41:7a [40:31a] as "canopies" (*sukkot*) that God will make for the righteous. For their shared source, see n. 226.

216. For a vision of this messianic "hunt" (a Greco-Roman term), in strongly Greco-Roman terms, see Lev. Rab. 13:3 (ed. Margulies, 277–80). There, Jews who were righteous enough *not* to attend Roman gladiatorial games in this life become gladiators in the hereafter, with Gabriel as ringmaster (reflecting his traditional role as angel of war [Ginzberg, *Legends*, 1:53 n. 13; 2:1047 n. 55] and his name's etymology ג.ב.ר = *vir, virtus*).

217. For example, instead of one Leviathan with two names (Isa 27:1), there are now two Leviathans: "bent" and "straight," male and female, one castrated and one preserved in salt by God at Creation (2.A. Compare the debate on whether Leviathan has a partner: Ber. Rab. 7:4, ed. Theodor-Albeck, 52–54). Instead of "sea-serpents" or dragons, themselves gods in the original myth (Cassuto, *Biblical and Oriental Studies* 2:95), Part 2 begins by identifying *both* Leviathans as God's creations ("And God *created* the great sea-serpents," Gen 1:21. Tg. Jon. Gen 1:21 reads *midrash* like Part 2 back into this verse: both are "destined for the day of consolation").

218. "Where wast thou when I laid the foundations of the earth?" (Job 38:4) also recalls the alternate narrative logic of Gen 1. In that monotheistic retelling of the myth, it is all creation, no battle. No gods resist God. No divine hypostasis (Wisdom/Logos/Memra/Torah)

(following Isaiah), the battle is not over. It will be finished only at the end of time. For example, as Jacobs notes, its trope of the Glory resurfaces not only in Part 2 but also in Part 1.[219] In that strange tale, the Glory is a wonder ("great light in the sea") that one rabbi glosses as the "eyes" of Leviathan. Then, in Part 2 (2.B), the Glory is alluded to again: in the eschaton, God will make a canopy for the righteous of Leviathan's skin and stretch its skin over Jerusalem such that its "radiance will shine from one end of the universe to the other." Taking these images in isolation, we may think that the Talmud repeats the mythic archive of the Glory only to reiterate the same dogmatic point as Job: this foe is radiant with power, yes, but it merely heightens God's own.

However, once we realize that Part 2 adds an entire eschatological frame to the myth, its use of the Glory can generate a sharper reading with a more pointed narrative cosmology. "Why"—the Talmud's reader is asked to ask—"do the righteous *need* a canopy in the eschaton?" Later in Part 2 (2.C), the Talmud answers: this canopy will be made of Leviathan's skin, but its skin is now the Glory of God and Israel. With it, God will reward the righteous for their own minor "glory" (*kavod*: honor) in life. With it, God will shelter Israel from another Glory: God's heat/wrath, blazing on the wicked and less wicked alike,[220] covering Zion in "cloud and smoke" by day and a "flaming fire" by night (a messianic fulfillment of the "pillar of cloud" and "pillar of fire" that sheltered Israel's ancestors).[221] In this talmudic retelling, the Glory shifts from God's rival back to God again, an intercultural reappropriation. The rabbinic myth thus develops another stage in the narrative: God's judgment is the true end of the original battle for creation. In this light, rather than

---

is invoked. God is present as speech and vision alone, which the Voice from the Whirlwind re-reveals to humanity: "I have heard of thee by the hearing of the ear / but now mine eye seeth thee" (Job 42:5).

219. Rabbinic awareness of this original mythic sense of "glory" in the parallelism of Zech 2:5 [2:9]—"a wall of fire round about / the glory in the midst of her"—is missing in Ira Chernus, "'A Wall of Fire Round About': The Development of a Theme in Rabbinic Midrash," *JJS* 30.1 (1979): 68–84.

220. Sitting in a *sukkah* is the paradigm for a "minimal commandment" (*mitsvah qalah*) in the opening *sugya* of Talmud Avodah Zarah, which has a few parallels to the first part of this section (see notes in Pesiq. Rab Kah. Supplement 2, ed. Mandelbaum, 452–53). In that source, because non-Jews fail even that "minimal commandment" in the eschaton, God does not give them shade (as God does with the "canopy" of the Leviathan's skin for the righteous in the eschaton in 2.B). Rather, God "makes the sun blaze upon them" (trans. Jeffrey L. Rubenstein, "An Eschatological Drama: Talmud Avodah Zarah 2a–3b," *AJSR* 21 [1996]: 1–37, at 6; see also 24–26). Compare the descending scale of rewards for declining levels of good deeds/commandments in 2.B (cover → shade → chains → amulet) ending with yet another divine reappropriation of Leviathan's power (light/"Glory").

221. For sources of this motif of the Pristine Light, see Adelman, *Return of the Repressed*, 152 n. 3 and Isa 30:26.

76   *Adventures of Rabbah & Friends*

either a loose mixture of oral traditions or a purely preserved archive, as Jacobs clearly assumes,[222] Part 2 is a rhetorical Talmudization and crafted retelling. For its reader, it is no longer enough to extol the Glory of the Leviathan and its past defeat. It is no longer enough to recall the start of the battle, when God marshaled the angels. One must now read the myth to the very End—the final triumph of God, Jerusalem, and the righteous among Israel.

Such intricate variations on motifs and narrative structures show how the Talmud restaged this myth from a biblical script. As it made a picture *of* Leviathan into a story about God's war *against* Leviathan, it reintroduced intermediaries (angels, Glory) and heightened God's power. Its casting intensified the cosmic battle, raising tension between the two sides. The Talmud gave the story a new arc, reviving mythic struggle to be resolved in the eschaton. This is typical of rabbinic myth,[223] which, in dramatizing how God's power manifests in the world, makes God more concrete, even anthropomorphic.[224] In Part 2, that new vision of God is both cause and effect of how the mythic archive was Talmudized: read out of Scripture's dialogue with Job—where God is omnipotent, *nothing but a voice*—into a more vivid narrative.

Exegesis

What were the effects, for a reader, of this structure's conversion into narrative? I have noted a few ways that Part 2's retelling of the myth intensified aspects of God and sharpened its messianic vision as it reappropriated tropes of power from a cross-cultural mythic archive. But we must take care not to derive the text's meaning directly from how it transforms myth. That would put all interpretive creativity back in editorial hands and reduce the reader's role. Michael Fishbane's studies of Part 2 allow for both perspectives.[225] On one hand, he showed that Part 2 has a

---

222. Jacobs, *Midrashic Process*, 157–58.

223. Part 2's process of narrativizing a cluster of mythic motifs around a theme was examined in later works by Jeffrey L. Rubenstein, "From Mythic Motifs to Sustained Myth: The Revision of Rabbinic Traditions in Medieval Midrashim," *HTR* 89 (1996): 131–59. Nor is the Talmud's way of doing this *de novo*: it builds on earlier expansions of these motifs in apocalyptic literature, e.g., Gabriel the serpent-tamer in 2.A = 1 Enoch 20:7. (See further Kiperwasser and Shapira, "Irano-Talmudica II," 221–22, 223 n. 76).

224. See Redfield, "Myth, Rabbinic Judaism."

225. Michael Fishbane, "The Great Dragon Battle and Talmudic Redaction," in Fishbane, *The Exegetical Imagination: On Jewish Thought and Theology* (Cambridge: Harvard University Press, 1998), 41–55. This study has the same basic analysis as Fishbane, *Biblical Myth and Rabbinic Mythmaking* (Oxford: Oxford University Press, 2003), 120–24; Fishbane, "Rabbinic Mythmaking and Tradition: The Great Dragon Drama in b. Baba Batra 74b–75a," in

well-edited chiastic structure and narrative arc: it starts with the primordial and focuses a reader's attention on its fulfillment in the eschaton. Yet he also gave due weight to this new story's exegetical form. He showed how it is based on a point-by-point exposition of a verse on Leviathan (Isa 27:1), followed by a collection of glosses and solutions to interpretive gaps in consecutive verses about Leviathan/Behemoth in Job (40–41).[226] Fishbane usually treated the editor ("mythmaker") as primarily in charge of Part 2's meaning.[227] But his attention to its exegetical form also suggests other ways that it may have spoken to readers.

For instance, Fishbane notes that three times, in editorial expansions of named rabbis' comments on verses, the Talmud uses a formula including "If not …" (אלמלא)[228] and the verb "to be able to" (י.כ.ל, meaning here "withstand, resist, overcome so-and-so").[229] This flourish goes beyond the content of the exegesis; at first glance it seems merely stylistic. Yet Fishbane asks why the Talmud's "editorial hand" added those repetitions. He concludes that it aimed to "balance" the two poles of its new myth, Creation and End Time, strengthening the editor's narrative arc. Yet Fishbane also notes, only in passing, that one part of this formula ("If not …") appears twice more in Part 2, just as we may further note that the other part of the formula ("[could not] overcome him") appears in two tales within Part 1 as well (IIIa; VIIIb).[230] What if a reader paid attention to those repeated

---

Tehillah le-Moshe: Biblical and Judaic Studies in Honor of Moshe Greenberg, ed. Mordechai Cogan, Barry L. Eichler, and Jeffrey H. Tigay Winona Lake, IN: Eisenbrauns, 1997), 273–83.

226. Fishbane, "Great Dragon Battle," 52: "Evidently we have before us part of a lost *midrash* on Job 40–41, reworked into a myth spanning Urzeit and Endzeit." Rashbam, b. B. Bat. 73a s.v. אמר רבא אשתעו already noted that "all these matters may be accounted for in terms of … interpreting verses that are pronounced in the book of Job, which speak of giant birds, beasts, and fish"; see chapter 6 §*Twice Upon a Time: The Art of Peshat*). Jacobs (*Midrashic Process*, 158 n. 17) suggested that Part 2 preserves part of a lost esoteric work, "The secrets/chambers [חדרים] of Behemoth and Leviathan" (Song of Songs Rabbah 1:4, 6), perhaps such a Job commentary. Kiperwasser and Shapira dispute that חדרים there is a source ("Irano-Talmudica II," 222–23 n. 73).

227. E.g., Fishbane, "Great Dragon Battle," 54–55: "His voice is the continuous coordinator of the complex Talmudic chorus … such that the (local) debates are subordinated to the (larger) narrative development."

228. This word, which can mean either "If" or the opposite, "If not," has long drawn the attention of commentators, e.g., Tosafot b. Meg. 21a s.v. אלמלא (attributed to Rabbenu Tam. I thank Elitzur Bar-Asher Siegal [personal communication, 14 November 2023] for explaining the flaws in his analysis).

229. Fishbane, "Great Dragon Battle," 52, describing Leviathan and its battle with Gabriel in 2.A: "If waters were not covering him, no creature could remain due to his stench …"; "If [God] does not help [Gabriel], he will not be able to overcome him …"; "If he did not put his head into the Garden of Eden, no creature could resist his stench.…"

230. Both instances in those tales "recycle" the uncited end of a verse from a previous story (I): see n. 279. We can imagine a three-stage process: first a teller of IIIb recycled the uncited conclusion of a prooftext as the conclusion to his story; then a reteller of VIIIb did

words in both parts—not only to the editors' intent? How might readers have drawn connections within or between Parts 1 and 2 on that basis? Is a giant fish—whom a horseman "could not overcome" with his arrow (VIIIb)—like Leviathan, whom Gabriel will "overcome" with his sword *only* if God wills it (2.A)? If that tale is indeed like that myth, how would the meaning of both change? In chapter 5, we will test a model for how readers interacted with editors via such repeated flourishes (keywords and catchphrases). In terms of how genre can get us closer to the reader's creativity, the point here is that tracing Part 2's exegetical structure also helps us to see the editorial interventions beyond it, and to ask how those decisions guided the editors' readers. Insofar as both tales (Part 1) and myths (Part 2) were gradually reshaped by one "editorial hand," readers at a relatively late stage of the composition may have noticed this hand and used its flourishes to recollect both parts. Their reading process need not have been bound by any genre dichotomy between the two parts.

Readers could have made those connections on the basis of narrative content as well. Although Part 2 is grander and more openly messianic than the tales in Part 1, some stories in both parts are strikingly similar. Consider the giant fish who destroys towns from whose bones the towns are rebuilt a year later (VIb). Is this really so unlike Leviathan, the ultimate big fish, whose skin will bedeck Jerusalem and shelter the righteous (2.A)?[231] Granted, that retelling of Leviathan as the Glory of God and Israel is drawn from a deep mythic archive and tied to a verse from Isaiah, whereas the other big fish story looks like humble folklore. But their narrative content survives any genre gap; readers might still have put them together. Conversely, readers also applied the interpretive framework of exegesis in Part 2 back to the so-called tall tales in Part 1. Consider a story that, as I have said and will show,[232] was built to look like an early tradition and inserted near the end of Part 1 as a transition to Part 2 on Leviathan. In this story, one rabbi has a strange vision that another interprets as Leviathan.

---

the same thing, using the same phrase as his new conclusion; then an editor, noting their usage, again recycled the phrase in a formula that gives section 2.A thematic unity. Those three hypothetical retellers/editors could be one person or many generations, early or late; we cannot say.

231. All manuscripts contain readings that strengthen this connection between the town rebuilt from the big fish (VIb) and the rebuilt Heavenly Jerusalem in Part 2.C. Some recycle a formula: "He **saw** the ministering angels, who were **chiseling** (מינסרי ... חזא) precious stones and pearls" (2.C); "We **saw** ... they were **hewing** from its bones" (מנסרי ... חזינן, VIb, mss. P, M, E, O, V). Only ms. H and Rashbam (Pesaro) lack that formula, which may have arisen due to a later harmonization. But even ms. H reads, "When we returned the next year ..." (VIb) echoing 3.B, "A year later, he returned ...") For another good example in ms. M, see Frim "'Those Who Descend,'" 13.

232. See n. 197 and nn. 493–496.

XX. Our rabbis taught:
A story about Rabbi Eliezer and Rabbi Yehoshua,
who were traveling in a ship,
and Rabbi Eliezer was sleeping,
and Rabbi Yehoshua was awake.
Rabbi Yehoshua gave a start and Rabbi Eliezer woke up.
He asked him: "What is it, Yehoshua?"
He replied: "Rabbi, I have seen a great light in the sea."
"Perhaps it was the eyes of Leviathan you saw," he said.
As it is written of him: *and his eyes are like the eyelids of the morning* (Job 41:18 [41:10]).

The pivot of this story is the word "Perhaps." The interpreter has not seen this sight. Nevertheless, he ventures to interpret it on the basis of what he was told and what he knows: the Bible (specifically, the same verses in Job on which Part 2.A is based), where Leviathan matches the story's description. Yet with his "perhaps," this interpreter admits that he is going out on a limb.[233] In mediating these two domains of meaning, the vision and the verse, he is imagining a way to link Part 1 and Part 2 (in that respect, he presages the editorial hand). Will his strategy work? We do not hear Rabbi Yehoshua's reply: the Talmud leaves a silence for its reader to fill, and counterarguments are not hard to imagine. But his tentative exegetical approach to the tales is significant. It shows how some readers, as soon as the tales were told, tried to contain their strangeness by Talmudizing them — reading them into a familiar canon.

This exegetical framework was in vogue even before the editorial hand came on the scene and put the tales in Part 1 together with Part 2. There are already signs of it in Part 1. An important example is Rav Ashi glossing a giant bird — a beast that, again, he did not see — as a rabbinic legend based on a biblical verse (IX).[234] For now, note how confident Rav Ashi is. He says, "That is X," not "Perhaps it was...." His confidence is warranted: as I will show, two details within the telling, as well as another exegesis of his prooftext, support his gloss. It is not just based on someone else's report of a vision that he missed while he was snoozing. On the other hand, Rav Ashi is centuries apart from the original story told by Rabbah. But that may also be a confidence booster: it is easier to interpret something that you didn't see when no one else did either. A similar example of growing confidence in exegesis as a way to tame the strange beasts in these tales is one of the additions to Rabbah's collection by a later teller:

---

233. The corrector of ms. O is more confident: "Understand [reading *shma'* for *shema'*] — it was the eyes of Leviathan you saw...."
234. See chapter 4 §*History and Ethnography* and n. 188, n. 619.

XVIIa. Rav Safra recounts:
   Once I was traveling in a ship
   and a certain fish lifted up its head
   and it had two horns
   and upon them was engraven: *I am a minor creature of the sea,*
   　　　　　　　　　　　　　　　　and I am three hundred parasang,
   　　　　　　　　　　　　　　　　and prepared for the mouth of Leviathan.
XVIIb. Rav Ashi said:
   That one is the goat of the sea, and it is lean.

This teller himself seems to interpret his vision in light of the Bible and rabbinic lore. It is written onto the strange feature of the fish's horns: the telling advertises that this is not just a paranormal phenomenon. The wonder makes itself exegetically legible. Not only does it allude directly to a Psalm,[235] but in this telling of the tale where it is "prepared for" Leviathan's mouth, it also alludes to a not-so-small fish that God "prepared" to swallow Jonah.[236] That is the same fish who, in a midrash on Jonah, tries but fails to flee Leviathan and is swallowed by it.[237] One reader's "perhaps" has become another's certainty: the meaning of strange beasts seen in the tales is already explained by tradition. The Talmudization of the strange continues.

Here again, Rav Ashi proves himself adept at this exegetical framework.

---

235. Of the sea's "small and great beasts" this is the former, mentioned just before Leviathan (Ps 104:25–26). See also VIa: just as our "goatfish" enters Leviathan's mouth, this "mud-eater" (a common earthworm: *JBA*, 131), who enters the nostril of a big fish and kills it, is glossed as כילבית by Rashbam (b. B. Bat. 73b s.v. באוסייה). He is following Rashi b. Shabb. 77b s.v. כילבית: a *small fish* whom *Leviathan* fears, as it enters *Leviathan's* nostril. That gloss, linking the tall tale to the Leviathan myth, reappears in ms. O (ו'ס.א"ג). But it is a correction of the first reading "mud-eater": a corrector interpolated Rashbam's gloss. It does not show an older "allusive link" to Part 2; *pace* Frim, "'Those Who Descend,'" 12–13.

236. Tg. Jonah 2:1: ודזמין יי נונא רבא למבלע ית יונה; XVIIa: דלויתן לפומיה וזמין; (ms. H). Other manuscripts read "going into the mouth of Leviathan," ending the story by repeating the introductory formula ("going in a ship") in an envelope structure. This is more formulaic and uses a stock introduction in Part 1 (see chapter 3 §*Attributions and Other Introductory Formulae*). By contrast, ms. H seems like a deliberate allusion to Jonah, akin to Pirqe R. El. 10 (text in Adelman, *Return of the Repressed*, 301). "Rabbi Tarfon says: 'That fish was prepared [ממונה] to swallow Jonah since the six days of Creation … and the two eyes of the fish were like shining shuttered windows, and he saw all that was in the sea, and in the deep.' Rabbi Meir says: 'There was a pearl hanging in the fish's stomach and it illuminated for him all that was in the seas and in the depths.'" (Compare XVIII–XX and 2.C). On this rare keyword ("prepared," Hebrew ממונה = Aramaic מזמן), see Adelman, *Return of the Repressed*, 241 n. 90. The translation "shuttered windows" follows Adelman, *Return of the Repressed*, 277 n. 77.

237. Like an aquatic game of cat and mouse. Pirqe R. El. 9 (ed. Börner-Klein, 89): "And he opens his mouth and the great sea-serpent, whose day has come to be eaten, eludes and flees but enters the Leviathan's mouth [anyway]. And the Holy One, Blessed Be He, plays with it, as it is said: *There is that Leviathan, whom thou hast made to play therein*" (Ps 104:26). In Pirqe R. El. 10, Jonah helps the fish escape and prepares Leviathan for the messianic banquet — winning the mythic battle again.

He glosses the two-horned fish as a goatfish: a Mesopotamian supernatural entity related to Capricorn.[238] Yet rather than only affirm the strange and foreign beast's existence, he keeps it in proportion and reconciles it with Jewish tradition. "It is lean," he says, because, as the teller said, it is a "*minor creature of the sea*" (in biblical terms, "*small* beast" of the sea). And "it is lean" because Rav Ashi seems to know that one of his predecessors used the very same gloss to curtail the meaning of an earlier strange tale—a tale of our very own Rabbah bar bar Hanah.[239] In a few words, he Talmudizes the new strange tale, reading it into both of these frameworks.

In sum, the sources of this story are diverse and could be assigned to five "genres": a strange tale of a giant fish; exegesis linking the fish to a verse where it is small (as compared to Leviathan!); allusions to other rabbinic tales about Leviathan swallowing another small or not-so-small fish; a cross-cultural "goatfish" entity related to Capricorn; and a scholastic formula for limiting the size and thus the significance *of* a strange tale like these. At some point–I think we have passed it—labeling texts by genre in this manner reveals nothing about their meaning. If this short tale has five genres, how many genres are in Parts 1 and 2? Do we suppose that readers made sense of the texts by labeling each fragment's genre one by one? I argue instead that, as we saw in Rav Ashi's synthesis of three genres in one terse comment that balances them, only the interpretive framework or approach of a specific reader can produce a result—a meaning—from all of those possible generic interpretations. A story does not mean anything to someone merely due to its origin or the type of story that it was originally. A reader makes its meaning by reading it and reading it with intertexts: into one genre, out of another, or back and forth between them. A genre becomes meaningful, if it does, through the reading process.

Genres for the Reader

I began this critique and cautious recovery of the concept of genre by showing how three genres had been used to shift the creation of meaning onto the text instead of the reader. Whether by isolating the text from its literary context, by positing that one part of the text controls the meaning of the other, or by assuming that a universal psychological conflict determined how it was received, these misuses of genre all tried to deduce meaning from the text. In each case, a genre label served to identify a general kind of text with a general kind of meaning and limited readers' interpretive options. I then examined how the genres of Myth and Exegesis have been

---

238. *JBA*, 852. For the humble goatfish of the Peripatetics, see Ephraim Lytle, "The Red Sea Aristotle," *JHS* 142 (2022): 100–143, at 127.
239. B. Yevam. 120b, attributed to Rav Ashi's predecessor Abbaye. See n. 87, n. 458.

used to compare texts within each genre and to trace evolution of tropes and motifs across genres. Genres, in that sense, are flexible frameworks through which different readers interpret a text or read together intertexts in order to create meaning. As opposed to the genre of the text, this invited a way of thinking about genres for the reader.

In retrospect, the constellation of reading is already helping to lead us on this journey. The outlines of similar tales in both parts of the composition—not only the strange creatures in Part 1 but also their messianic fulfillments in Part 2—are one way, I suggested, that readers may have ignored any genre division between the parts and read them together. The idea of telling helped us to distinguish the raw stock of tropes and motifs ("mythic archive") underlying Part 2 from its vivid narrative retelling in the Talmud, and to appreciate how the narrative arc of this new story brings its primordial battle to a messianic conclusion. Rather than treat Parts 1 and 2 as static collections in distinct genres, we saw how one story was added as a transition between them; how a reader may have interpreted the beginning of Part 1 as a digression rather than a break from its legal context; and how readers' recollections of Parts 1 and 2 may have been cued by flourishes left behind by their editorial hand. In showing how readers used an exegetical framework even for the so-called tall tales in Part 1, we saw how they used the biblical canon and its reading tradition (midrash) to make sense of stories' strangeness by Talmudizing them—by reading them just like any other canonical text. By showing how these dynamics of the reading process were catalyzed by genres and, conversely, reactivated selective aspects of genres, we considered how genres guide readers' attention and help them to create new meanings from the text instead of affixing it with one abstract kind of meaning.

As we begin our story about these stories, chapter 2 will show how this shift in focus—from genres of the text to genres for the reader—captures the interpretive history of what is now the beginning of the composition. Even before Part 1 (let alone the whole two-part composition) was edited in its current form, its language and structure led readers to create its meaning by navigating Myth and Exegesis, by locating Rabbah's tales between genres, not "in" one. As Dina Stein argues in her important studies of our composition, "The embedding of midrash into these stories stresses precisely the possibility of *duality* between the genres, as well as their *individual* functions, *and* the tension constructed between them in the cultural discourse."[240] Rather than abandon the concept of genre, studying how Myth and Exegesis interact reveals readers' interpretive creativity as they intensified one over the other, blended both, and tried to make sense of the tension between genres as a message of its own.

---

240. Stein, "Believing Is Seeing," 25 (emphasis added).

2

The Sea Still Resists: Between Myth and Midrash

Iranian elements are prominent in the first four tales (Part 1, I–IIIa/b), and the way in which the telling uses those elements brings the tales closer to the world of Jews—and especially rabbis—in Sasanian Iran. The star of the show is a Zoroastrian deity, "Hormiz," but he makes a solo appearance on a well-trodden stage. He is not a member of a pantheon, nor does he portray cosmic dualism.[241] This Hormiz is mortal (he even has a quasi-genealogy),[242] and he is hardly all-powerful. It is unclear what is so transgressive about his juggling act,[243] but it does not prevent his

---

241. The Talmud is well aware of those Zoroastrian ideas (*Arukh Completum,* ed. Kohut [Vienna: Brog, 1882], 3:245). It cites them at b. Sanh. 39a (Shai Secunda, "Reading the Talmud in Iran," *JQR* 100.2 [2010]: 310–42). Both there and in our tales (IIIb), the Talmud may parody the Zoroastrian deity by alluding to urination ("passing water"), purity of water (Kiperwasser, "Travels of Rabbah," 231), or its purification *by* urine (Kiperwasser and Shapira, "Irano-Talmudica I," 110–13). In that sense, these texts may reflect a "strikingly similar" Jewish polemic against Zoroastrian tenets (Yaakov Elman and Shai Secunda, "Judaism," in *The Wiley Blackwell Companion to Zoroastrianism,* ed. Michael Stausberg and Yuhan Vevaina [London: Wiley, 2015], 423–35, at 429). Yet in the actual telling of our tale as such, Hormiz is no god, and there is no theology.

242. By naming him "son of [a] Lilith" (*bar Lelawata',* "Liliths"—rhyming with "poles," *'ilwata,* in II; ט"י.ב), the Talmudic telling domesticates Hormiz, even as it demonizes him. His mother had wings (b. Nid. 24b; see n. 824), but he can only jump high and soon will fall. Hence, he is only half-demonic. (Logically, then, his father was a human: see n. 815. On how late ancient Jews imagined such demonic half-breeds were conceived, see n. 820.)

243. Kiperwasser and Shapira explain the mythical figure of Ridya ("the Pourer"), in another tale by Rabbah bar bar Hanah, in light of Zoroastrian and rabbinic cosmology ("Irano-Talmudica I," 103–16). Our Hormiz is a "pourer" as well: in fact, a similar story is told about a Palestinian rabbi enacting a similar cosmological ritual (b. Sukkah 53a). Hormiz, however, "did not spill a single drop," whereas Ridya's role is to bring rain and groundwater. Is that why "the [divine] Kingdom" punished Hormiz with death? Or—more in Roman Palestine's cultural context—we might consider the allegory of God sustaining Creation by mixing wine (justice) with water (mercy) in two cups (Shlomo Naeh, "ποτήριον ἐνχειρὶ κυρίου: Philo and the Rabbis on the Powers of God and the Mixture in the Cup," *Scripta Classica Israelica* 16 [1997], 91–101). Hormiz has only one fluid: water (ms. H) *or* wine (all other mss.). Does he represent a chaotic antithesis to that Hellenistic cosmology? Early readers likely asked such questions, and one can indicate how they might have varied from East to West, but in this case the answers are lost.

84 *Adventures of Rabbah & Friends*

death at the hands of "the authorities," divine or human. The tale is set at a prominent port,[244] by a famous river,[245] in the Persian capital with special architectural details.[246] This was also a cultural capital for Jews in the teller's time, as a rabbinic academy flourished there under the aegis of Rava,[247] whose name resembles Rabbah's and alternates with it in the manuscripts.[248] With all of this in mind, for an early reader, the teller's claim that "I myself have seen" Hormiz is as close as possible to the setting of the tale; which is, in turn, as close as possible to the reader. Its content may be self-consciously incredible or hyperbolic,[249] but its telling enhances just the opposite conceit: it could all have happened right here.

Further dashes of local color suffuse not only the tale of Hormiz but this section as a whole. Imagery, phrasing, and geography are markedly regional: units of area and distance;[250] rhetorical markers;[251] and the natural world[252]). Even the waves talk like a Babylonian rabbi, praising YHWH's

---

244. Mahoza, the rabbinic name of Ktēsiphōn-Seleucia: "town" or "port"—it was indeed a river port with a bridge. See Aharon Oppenheimer, *Babylonia Judaica in the Talmudic Period*, Beihefte zum Tübinger Atlas des Vorderen Orients B.47 (Wiesbaden: Reichert, 1983), 186, 203–4.

245. See n. 550.

246. In addition to its wall and bridge, in ms. H it has a "dome" (קובנאה, Middle Persian *gumbad*) or, in other mss. (P, O, M, E), "turrets of the wall" (קופי/קוקפי דשורא) of Mahoza. The walls of the citadel at this conurbation did have "elongated semi-circular or projecting towers separating straight sections" (see diagram, St. John Simpson, "The Land behind Ctesiphon: The Archaeology of Babylonia during the Period of the Babylonian Talmud," in *The Archaeology and Material Culture of the Babylonian Talmud*, ed. Markham J. Geller, IJS Studies in Judaica 16 [Leiden: Brill, 2015], 6–38, at 10). These manuscripts may picture Hormiz bounding from one to the other. How he could have done so on a single dome (ms. H) is unclear. I thank Simcha Gross for discussing this with me.

247. See Yaakov Elman's studies, cited and developed in B. S. Cohen, *Legal Methodology*, 7–8 n. 34.

248. Rabbah bar bar Hanah is never located in Mahoza (Albeck, *Introduction to the Talmud*, 305–6; Bacher, *Die agada*, 87–93), which is another possible reason that scribal transmitters of this story read "Rava" here. Again, however, their medieval spelling of the name does not indicate how earlier listeners would have identified the teller; see n. 74.

249. The formula introducing IIIa, IV, V ("I myself have seen") has been analyzed as a marker of fantasy or hyperbole (Kiperwasser, "Travels of Rabbah," 225 n. 41; Ben-Amos, "Talmudic Tall Tales," 39). But see chapter 4 §*Double Vision*.

250. *Griv* (I); *parasang* (I, IV, VIIIb, XI, XVIIa). If the Geonic explanation applies (*JBA*, 782), a *griv* equals a *se'ah*, so this teller chose a Babylonian term over a Palestinian term that the Talmud also uses. On *parasang* or "Persian mile"—another local feature—as a structural device in our collection, see n. 9, n. 379, and chapter 3 §*Poetry*.

251. See א.מ: *Mi* ("Is it [not] so?"): mss. H, P, O; *Mide* ("anything," all mss.). See n. 423, n. 460 for other markers of orality in those manuscripts.

252. A wave's crest like "a white shoot of flame" (see Reuven Kiperwasser, "Narrative Bricolage and Cultural Hybrids in Rabbinic Babylonia: On the Narratives of Seduction and the *Topos* of Light," in *The Aggada of the Bavli and Its Cultural World* ed. Geoffrey Herman and Jeffrey L. Rubenstein, BJS 362 [Providence, RI: Brown Judaic Studies, 2018], 23–45, at 33 n. 33); the "cradle" of a star in the heavens (I) or of an animal's head (IV). On these terms,

power in a talmudic idiom for citing evidence (I: "Come see!" See also V). Hormiz "bounds" from tower to tower of the walled capital's turrets, pursued by a horseman who races alongside him on the ground. If this story had had an illustrated edition in the Sasanian era, horse and rider would have posed in the iconographic convention of a "flying gallop"—all four hooves off the ground, the horse itself bounding in flight.[253] Not only the verbal imagery in this text but even its poetic and visual style are adapted to the aesthetics of Babylonian rabbis. Exotic as the tales are for them, the telling was closer to home.[254]

Figure 4. P. 58777/N. 38584: Iran, Naqsh-i-Rustam, relief depicting equestrian combat of King Hormizd II (P-980a). Courtesy of the Institute for the Study of Ancient Cultures of the University of Chicago.

---

see Daniel Boyarin, "Towards the Talmudic Lexicon II" [Hebrew], in *Teudah*, ed. Mordecai Akiva Friedman et al. (Ramat-Gan: Bar-Ilan University Press, 1983), 3:113–19. Building on Boyarin's proof that ב.ז.ר means "to sow seed," Shamma Friedman (*Talmud Arukh: BT Bava Metzia VI. Critical Edition with Comprehensive Commentary*, 2 vols. [New York: Jewish Theological Seminary, 1996], 1:147) connects this imagery to the scattering of light, proposing that the corona or "cradle [בי מרבעא]" of the star, its lying-down place and dwelling-place, is precisely the radiance and lightning [ברק = בזק; see א.ז, mss. H, M, E] appearing around a star as it gives off light, like a diamond in its setting."

253. Around the period of this composition, this motif became characteristic of Iranian art. See Irma B. Jaffee and Gernando Colombardo, "The Flying Gallop: East and West," *Art Bulletin* 65.2 (1983): 183–201, at 187.

254. Stein captures this tension between the collection's narrating/narrated worlds (*Textual Mirrors*, 69–70).

With all this in view, we should question why scholars routinely use "myth" to designate how this unit would have sounded to early audiences. Myth, by any definition, lies a marked distance from the everyday, where these tales are firmly set. Storytellers may collapse that distance between the *Urzeit/Endzeit* of myth and familiar here-and-now of a narrative. They may derive powerful effects from doing so. But in theory, the distance as such is crucial to what myth is.[255] Indeed, when scholars use "myth" in order to picture how this sub-collection of four tales was received by its audience, they tend to exaggerate the reader's distance from the content: pointing to its vast proportions; cosmic structure; and ancient, abiding meanings.[256]

What has not been fully deciphered, by contrast, is an integral layer of midrash in these very tales: between the depths of myth and surface of the Talmud's everyday world.[257] I suggest that this layer of midrash mediates the mythic subject matter of these tales, on the one hand, with the here-and-now of their retelling, on the other. While the original myth of YHWH's Battle with the Sea that we studied in chapter 1 is still very much alive in the tales, it was not just transposed to their contemporary Sasanian Jewish setting in a crude "remake." Rather, by adding Bible verses and allusions to the rabbinic reception *of* those verses (among other Talmudizing moves), its tellers made the mythic archive newly relevant for their reader. Contemporary details are not merely a fresh coat of paint but a sign of this ongoing dialogue with the mythic past. "Given that we are here now—with our canons of Scripture and exegesis in our hands—what does this old myth of creation-and-battle still mean to us?" That implicit question, and the audience's answers, determine the finer points of interaction between these tales and their telling.

As a result of this retelling of myth through midrash, I suggest, early readers likely interpreted this set of stories as a contemporary rendition of rabbinic themes, along lines not unfamiliar to them—not only as a reprise of perennial cross-cultural symbols and binaries. In other words, the meaning of this retelling of the myth was re-created by an active well-informed rabbinic reader, not only by its composers. Thus, beyond rediscovering the originality of tellers and editors who made present the mythic past, we should also try to hear how they spoke to tastes and expectations of a specific implied reader who already knew similar rabbinic riffs on mythic themes. Turning to such a reader, tellers and editors crafted a rendition of the mythic archive, integrating local color and lively details. We will excavate this dialogue between the creators and the reader by excavating the literary form of this unit. As we saw, its characters, dialogue, settings,

---

255. See Redfield, "Myth, Rabbinic Judaism."
256. See chapter 1 §*Myth*.
257. As first noted by Fränkel, *Darkhe ha-aggadah*, 1:259.

and *realia* are adapted to the here-and-now. Its themes and contents are mythic. Yet the model for this unit's composition arises not from myth but from midrash: an oral-poetic art of mediation between near and far, primordial and contemporary forms of meaning.

Midrash as Fugue: Excavating the Understory

This compositional form is what I call an "understory," attached to the cited biblical intertexts (Ps 107, Jer 5, Exod 3) and running throughout the section, from first line to last. Like a fugue, this midrashic understory is a point/counterpoint hermeneutic structure, a systematic interweaving of spoken text with unspoken subtext.[258] For each dramatic tension and critical event in the tales, biblical verses—in their received meanings, their reading tradition—are added to supply correlative narrative tensions and event sequences in the subtext. A reader who is fluent in the verses' received meanings (early Palestinian and Babylonian midrash), hearing these tales, also hears new meanings in counterpoint with the subtext. What they hear is neither redundant with the tales nor a scattershot of mere allusions. This understory itself has a degree of thematic coherence. It guides a reader's attention to select verses—unconjugated in any other source—and strings those verses together into a narrative arc that parallels the story. As each voice of a fugue reiterates one subject in asynchronous harmonies, the understory has its own beginning and end; its own protagonist; its own theme, dynamics, and development. Yet it never quite rises to the level of a single explicit textual interpretation. The listener perceives it as a background of affects, images, structures, and arcs, which undulate and modulate beneath the telling. The story and the understory thus resonate stereophonically.

The theme of both stories and understory is a mythic archive, as we saw in chapter 1: YHWH's Battle with the Sea. This subject left only faint traces in Gen 1, like the motifs of subduing the primordial waters or the goddess Tiamat (a.k.a. "The Deep," *ha-tehom*). But it recurs throughout the

---

258. Compare Kiperwasser, "Travels of Rabbah," 231–32; Kiperwasser and Shapira, "Irano-Talmudica III," 74: "This 'tractate [...]' is loosely structured around Psalms 104 and 107, which serve as a kind of counterpoint to the sailors' yarns [...] the Talmudic source actually constitutes an exegetical structure of sorts." I use the same metaphor for the same idea, yet my approach is different. For them, exegesis is how the *composer* related these tales to verses. For example, they suggest, the setting of III (*Mahoza*) was inspired by a phrase in Ps 107:30 (*mehoz heftsam*). They show other such likely associations between continuous verses of Psalms and adjacent motifs in the tales. However, they do not examine how associations between verses and motifs may have been created by readers, nor how readers may have used those exegetical links to draw a wider network of sources into their meaning.

Tanakh—and this unit of tales evokes a more full-throated version.[259] I and III retell the drama of a storm at sea (Ps 107:23–30), setting up the stakes of the understory along the same broad lines as other midrashim that use similar battle imagery. Tale II indexes the Burning Bush and midrashim on the parting of the Red Sea. As a whole, I–III fuses motifs from Bible, Targum, and midrash into a set of narrative subtexts—an understory—with its own dramatic movement. After reconstructing this understory's framing and development, we will be better positioned to imagine how, for an early reader of this fugue, it could have harmonized with, complicated, and thereby enriched the meaning of the stories in I–III—specifically, by mediating between their deep mythic archive and its proximal telling.

The Storm as Framing Device

Both the stories and the understory are framed by an envelope structure: a pair of citations of Ps 107. The first citation is not obvious and is often overlooked, because it doubles as an attribution: *"Those who go down to the sea in ships* recounted to me ..." (Tg. Ps. 107:23/I–II). The second citation falls at the conclusion of this section of tales: "they mount up to the heaven, they go down again to the depths" (Ps 107:26/III). Strikingly, these citations not only frame our section in the Talmud but also—as we will see—come from verses that were read, elsewhere in the Talmud, as a discrete subunit within Ps 107. Some intertextual relationship between this psalm unit and these stories is, so to speak, part of their literary DNA.[260] By comparison to early midrashim on this subunit of the psalm, then, we can begin to recover our understory: how our tales could have been read through their intertexts' reading tradition.

Both of these midrashim employ the phases of the storm in Ps 107 as a way to frame their own ideas about a divine "sentence"—a term whose polysemy in English is useful, as it conveys both the finality of judgment and the meaning enacted by a textual pause. They break up the storm into parts, reading each part as representing a decisive moment in the drama between God and the "sailors" (who figure the psalm's audience within the psalm, just as they will for readers of midrash and our tales). By choosing to cut off their renditions of the storm at distinct moments, readers turn its conclusion to precisely opposite ends. Regardless, they pose the

---

259. For the classic literature on this biblical myth, see Scott Noegel, "Jonah and Leviathan: Inner-Biblical Allusions and the Problem with Dragons," *Henoch* 37.2 (2015): 236–60, at 245 n. 46.

260. See Bezalel Naor, *Rabbi Abraham Isaac Hakohen Kook: Commentary to the Legends of Rabbah bar bar Ḥannah* (New York: Kodesh, 2019), 240–43. For the Vilna Gaon's interpretations of these signs, see n. 856.

The Sea Still Resists   89

same exegetical question to the storm. Their different ways of giving a sense to their opposite endings, by parsing the storm's phases and turning points (*kairoi*),[261] are mutually illuminating—and will help us to clarify nagging oddities in the death scene of Hormiz.

Their shared unit of Ps 107 reads as follows (lines in **bold** frame I–III, in all mss.):

> 21. Let them acclaim to YHWH His kindness,
>   and His wonders to humankind,
> and offer thanksgiving sacrifices
>   and recount His deeds in glad song.
> **23. Those who go down to the sea in ships,**
>   who do tasks in the mighty waters,
> it is they who have seen the deeds of YHWH,
>   and His wonders in the deep.
> He speaks and raises the storm wind
>   and it makes the waves loom high.
> **26. They go up to the heavens, come down to the depths,**
>   their life-breath in hardship grows faint.
> They reel and sway like a drunkard,
>   all their wisdom is swallowed up.
> 28. And they cry to YHWH from their straits
>   from their distress He brings them out.
> He turns the storm into silence,
>   and its waves are stilled,
> and they rejoice that these have grown quiet,
>   and he leads them to their bourn.
> 31. Let them acclaim to YHWH His kindness
>   and His wonders to humankind ...
>   (Trans. Alter)

Two questions stand behind the midrashic reception of this subunit of the psalm: Where does it end? Why does that matter? Those questions are also reflected in its text tradition, both scribal and oral. In the Leningrad codex, this subunit spans vv. 21–26, ending in the middle of the storm ("their life-breath in hardship grows faint"). In the rabbinic Bible,[262] it falls two verses later (vv. 23–28), ending with the "cry to YHWH" and salvation.[263]

---

261. On "falsification of simple expectations as to the structure of a future" (*peripeteia*), and the "turning-point" (*kairos*), which interrupts, subdivides, and rearranges narrative structures, see Frank Kermode, *The Sense of an Ending: Studies in the Theory of Fiction, with a New Epilogue*, 2nd ed. (Oxford: Oxford University Press, 2000), 23, 44–51, 192–95.

262. *Biblia Rabbinica: A Reprint of the 1525 Venice Edition*, ed. Jacob ben Hayim ibn Adoniya (Jerusalem: Makor, 1972), 100.

263. The subunit is marked by the so-called "inverted" or "separated" *nun* (or, rarely,

The rabbinic Bible's division of verses is reflected at—in fact, may derive from—a long discussion in the Talmud (b. Rosh Hash. 16a–17b). Here, Amoraim debate Rabbi Yitshaq's claim that "four things tear up," or annul, God's "sentence [*gezar din*]" (16b). One, as R. Yitshaq says, is a "cry" for mercy. To prove it, he cites the end of this unit, as it appears in the rabbinic Bible: "And they cry to YHWH from their straits" (v. 28). Again he is cited (b. Rosh Hash. 16a, 18a) to the effect that a "cry" for mercy is "beneficial to a person": not only before God's "sentence" is issued, but also after. As R. Yohanan says of repentance (b. Rosh Hash. 17b), a "cry" not only prevents God's "sentence"—it can repeal *ex post facto*.

Babylonian Amoraim there, however, are uncomfortable with R. Yohanan's broader view of the saving power of repentance. They debate whether repentance is effective after God's sentence has been issued (Abbaye: Yes; Rav Pappa: No). As the anonymous voice of the Talmud builds upon their debate, it applies Rav Pappa's narrower view (no *ex post facto* salvation) back to a corollary of R. Yohanan's view, that is, R. Yitshaq's claim about the sailors' "cry." Here, at this anonymous and more involved stage of that debate, the Talmud supports Rav Pappa's objection to Abbaye/R. Yohanan with the section markers of our unit.[264]

Come and hear:

"Those who go down to the sea in ships, who do tasks in the mighty waters, it is they who have seen the deeds of YHWH," [v. 23], etc.
"He speaks and raises the storm wind and it makes the waves loom high.... They reel and sway like a drunkard," etc. [vv. 25–27].
"And they cry to YHWH from their straits," etc [v. 28].
"Let them acclaim to YHWH His kindness," etc. [v. 31].

---

kaf): a scribal sign that evolved from the use of *sigma* in Greek manuscripts [the equivalent of modern brackets]. It is now generally agreed that this sign marks a passage as being out of place. An anonymous Tanna (R. Simeon ben Gamliel, per b. Shabb. 116a) foreshadows the modern scholarly view. According to R. Judah the Patriarch and other authorities (see Sifre Num., ed. Kahana, 3:573), the sign marks an independent textual unit (see Sifre Num. 84, ed. Horovitz, 80 and parallels in ed. Kahana, 1:204; b. Shabb. 115b–116a; Sof. 6:1). The views need not be incompatible: both are supported by Greco-Roman scribal practice. See Saul Lieberman, *Hellenism in Jewish Palestine: Studies in the Literary Transmission, Beliefs and Manners of Palestine in the I Century B.C.E.–IV Century C.E.*, 2nd ed., Texts and Studies of the Jewish Theological Seminary of America 18 (New York: Jewish Theological Seminary of America, 1962), 38–43; Emanuel Tov, *Textual Criticism of the Hebrew Bible*, 2nd ed. (Minneapolis: Fortress, 2001), 54–55. No similar scribal signs are found in the text of Ps 107:22–30 in 4QPs^f (4Q88) in *Qumran Cave 4.XI: Psalms to Chronicles*, ed. Eugene Ulrich et al., DJD XVI (Oxford: Clarendon, 2000), 91–93. The opening refrain (v. 21) is likely missing; after the storm (v. 29), the text is confused. But this early evidence does at least indicate that the storm was transmitted as a unit.

264. B. Rosh Hash. 17b (Vilna). As usual, manuscripts vary in how they cite the Bible, but all focus on this subunit.

He[265] made signs for them like the "onlys" and "solelys" [*'akhin ve-raqin*] in the Torah,[266] to inform you: [If] "they cry out" *before* the sentence, they are answered. If "they cry out" *after* the sentence, they are not answered.

Already from Rabbi Yitshaq's dicta, it is clear that he saw the moment of the sailor's "cry" (v. 28) as the turning point in the psalm.[267] The cry is a means of salvation from the storm, which he interpreted as God's "sentence." Probably, then, the question of whether the "cry" must come *before* the "sentence" had already been raised—provoking him to argue that a cry is salvific ("beneficial for a person")—whether before *or* after, just as R. Yohanan had said of repentance. For the sake of counter-argument,[268] the Talmud now cites these scribal "signs" in Ps 107. Perhaps, the Talmud ventures, God ended this unit at v. 28 ("And they cry to YHWH") in order to indicate that the "sentence" was not sealed. The storm is still raging! Only in the next verse ("He turns the storm into silence") does it end. Here, the Talmud's way of parsing the phases of the storm supports Rav Pappa's pessimistic view of salvation.[269] The "cry" of the sailors (repentance) is a means of salvation "*only* and *solely*" when the storm (sentence) is ongoing. If God's wrath were spent, the cry would come too late.

By contrast to the sailors, for Hormiz (IIIb), the storm is cut off abruptly—and so is he.

---

265. Several manuscripts add the abbreviation הקב"ה, clarifying that God inserted these paratextual signs. Ludwig Blau rejects this as a corruption by dittography: עשה לה was misread as עשה לה ה' and "clarified" as עשה לה הקב"ה (*Masoretische Untersuchungen* [Strasbourg: Trübner, 1891], 42). Perhaps it is scribal error, or perhaps scribal hubris: the notion that God did add these signs is consistent with b. Menah. 29b, מצאו להקב"ה שיושב וקושר כתרים לאותיות.

266. Rabbenu Hananel *ad loc.* (cited from the margin to ed. Vilna) cites Num 18:15, Deut 12:26: laws where "only" or "solely" have a restrictive function, excluding certain types of animal from sacrifice. In our context, we might more aptly compare verses where "only" stresses God's punishment (Deut 28:29/28:33) and qualifies a plea for God's mercy (Exod 10:17).

267. For a similar example in the Palestinian tradition, see Sarit Kattan Gribetz, " 'Lead Me Forth in Peace': The Origins of the Wayfarer's Prayer and Rabbinic Rituals of Travel in the Roman World," in *Journeys in the Roman East: Imagined and Real*, ed. Maren Niehoff, Culture, Religion, and Politics in the Greco-Roman World 1 (Tübingen: Mohr Siebeck, 2017), 297–327, at 309–10.

268. On the other hand, the Talmud's conclusion of this debate ("They [the sailors] are like individuals," b. Rosh Hash. 17b) returns to R. Yitshaq's more optimistic view, and in fact it is derived from his own language: "A cry is beneficial for *a* person [*'adam*]" (emphasis added). There, the Talmud argues that each sailor cries out for salvation as an *individual*; therefore, his cry is salvific *ex post facto*. If we view them as crying out as a *group* ("*They* cry to YHWH from *their* straits," v. 28), however, their cry is effective only *before* the sentence (which is why God added the "signs" to this unit of the Psalm). Thus, the Talmud can maintain both competing opinions.

269. By that logic, the Leningrad codex, which breaks off the unit before the "cry," reflects Abbaye's position. The logic of its textual division may be entirely unrelated.

Once
> two mules were saddled for him
> on two bridges of the Ravnag,
> and he bounded from one to the other and back again
> and he held two goblets of wine [ms. H: water] in his hands
> and he poured from one to the other and back again
>> but did not spill a single drop.

And upon that day,
> *They mount up to the heaven, they go down again to the depths*
> The authorities heard of it and brought him to an end.

This poetic parallel, between Hormiz in the Talmud and the sailors in the psalm, prompts early readers to superimpose one text upon the other and invert their narrative logics. As the sailors "go up to the heavens" and back down into the waves, Hormiz "bounds" along the city walls and across the river. As they "sway like a drunkard," as they "circle"/"reel"[270] on the heaving deck of a ship, Hormiz leaps back and forth across two bridges juggling goblets of wine.[271] Yet they cry for God's mercy, whereas "all of his wisdom/craftiness"[272] is to no avail. They fear for their lives, cry, repent, and are saved. But Hormiz is taken down and killed.

Yet even those indirect allusions to Ps 107 do not account for the full language of Hormiz's demise. For this, we must turn from intertextuality to the understory: the deeper, transformative narrative relation created by a reader who constantly relays new questions from one text to the other (rather than a composer who used one text to create the other). Why does our tale say "the authorities [literally: the kingdom] *heard of*" (š.m.ʿ ʿal) Hormiz, when all of his actions are spectacularly visual, not aural? Why

---

270. This vocalization (MT יָחֹגּוּ) connotes a breakdown or "breach" (שבר: Rashi to Gen 21:16, Isa 19:17, Song 2:4). That idea could link Hormiz's transgression (III) to the waves (I), which strive to breach the shoreline's "eternal ordinance" (חוק עולם), yet are broken upon it. (For חוג = חוק, "ordinance," see Lev. Rab. 35:4). An early reader may thus have linked Hormiz in III to the waves in I as rebellious figures subdued by a wrathful God. If we read יָחֻגּוּ ("they circled," as emended by Mitchell J. Dahood, *Psalms: Introduction, Translation, and Notes*, 3 vols., AB 16, 17, 17A [Garden City, NY: Doubleday, 1966–1970], 3:88), then a reader would have linked Hormiz to the sailors rather than the waves.

271. Only ms. H reads "water," more consistent with the Iranian mythological parallels (see n. 243). But the "drunken man" of the next verse (Ps 107:27), and especially Targum Jonathan's addition ("drunk *on wine*") make it equally likely that the imagery about Hormiz is based directly on the Psalm, rather than on mythology—hence, "wine" is an alternative reading because it characterizes him, like the Targum's sailors, as drunken.

272. In Ps 107:27, "their wisdom" is the sailors' ship ("craft," as we still say) that sinks in the sea. A pejorative connotation is also attested ("crafty," e.g., Job 5:13), and this would apply better to Hormiz's clever juggling act. Alternatively, this tale's relationship to Ps 107 may end with "sway like a drunkard" (Fränkel, *Darkhe ha-aggadah*, 1:259). The next words of the Psalm ("all their wisdom is *swallowed up*") could be the frog who is "swallowed" two tales later (V). That, in turn, would make the "frog" an allegory for "wisdom"; see n. 752.

does it say he was killed by this "k/Kingdom"—ambiguously referring to a foreign or a divine King? Why did it "end him" or "cut him off" (*q.t.ʿ*), rather than the prosaic "killed" (*q.t.l*)?[273] Such oddities make sense neither as renditions of an old myth nor as direct intertextual variations on verses in Ps 107, but for an early reader who already had in mind a theological debate along the lines of what we saw in the Talmudic discussion of these verses.

For such a reader, the death of Hormiz in our tale functions, not simply as the opposite of the sailors' salvation, but as the opposite of how R. Yitshaq *interpreted* their salvation. The sailors "cry to YHWH" at the end of the storm; God hears their cry, and repeals the "sentence" (*gezar din*). In our story, Hormiz says nothing. He does not repent. Hence, fittingly, the divine or earthly "K/kingdom" (*malkhuta*) "heard" him and "cut him off" (*q.t.ʿ* synonym of *g.z.r.*).[274] The redemptive understory stops the storm as it subsides, before the calm. The condemnatory story interrupts the storm at its lowest ebb—as Hormiz "come[s] down to the depths." He does not repent and the artificially stable ("saddled") *terra firma* beneath him fails.

Rather than using such correspondences to argue for point-to-point influence between these two talmudic sources, I would argue that both a reader of our tale and this collection of *midrashim* in tractate Rosh Hashanah derived the same literary structure, and the same interpretive problem, from the storm in Ps 107: a protagonist, going up and down in precarious balance; a critical moment of God's judgment; and the question of *when* that crisis occurs so as to bring the story to a life-or-death ending. This reconstruction of an early reader's interpretive background gains even more texture when we see that the entirety of this subunit of our tales (I–III) is legible in terms of the same early debate, which, furthermore, turned around the same subunit of Ps 107. What is the sense of its ending? Repentance and salvation, or transgression and death?

Order over Chaos

As we saw in I/IIIb, the frame for the understory generated by Ps. 107 is the theme of chaos, that is, transgressing the cosmic limits and order that God has established and maintains. The middle of the section (II–IIIa) develops this understory in two ways. First, it saturates the theme of chaos/transgression by exploring the actual boundaries that are transgressed: the ver-

---

273. Mss. P, O, E, and the Venice print do reflect the reading *q.t.l*, but ms. O is corrupt, and "וקטלוה" (ms. P, *sic*) may be a corruption of וקטעתיה (H). This is another case (see n. 251) where I see a group of witnesses aligned with ms. H as closer to the oral-poetic logic of the text—"better" in this sense, but not necessarily more original.

274. Ber. Rab. 80:8 (synonyms for circumcision).

tical and horizontal borders of antithetical cosmic domains. Against this understory's backdrop, each tale's spatial organization indexes a cosmic order patterned on the biblical order of creation. Each spatial limit, each cosmic element, accumulates lines of conflict between elements that proliferate as the text unfolds. The second development in the middle two tales is that, alongside Hormiz, the understory builds up another transgressive protagonist: the Sea. As a primordial antithesis to YHWH's dominion, as a figure for chaos, the Sea seems to pose a threat. Thus, the Sea's suppression by divine Names deepens the underlying theme of divine salvation. This midrashic understory about the perpetual threat of chaos, oscillating with cosmic order and God's saving power, is mirrored poetically by each tale's rising/falling motion.

This vertical axis of the understory recurs in nearly every line. It begins with the first verb ("*go down* to the sea"), immediately changing the verb's literal meaning to a description of sailors plunging into the waves; just as it transforms the last verse ("go *up* to the heavens, come *down* to the depths") into a vivid restatement of the rise and fall of Hormiz. In the first story (I), waves lift the ship from the depths to the firmament, breaching the limit between cosmic domains that was established at creation.[275] As the waves roar, each "casts" its voice to another, and sailors tremble in the "deep" between their peaks.[276] The middle story (II) moves in the reverse direction: waves crash down upon the ship, threatening to sink it, then are flattened back down as they are struck by the divine Name. The third/fourth stories (IIIa/IIIb) reverse direction yet again, from sea to air. The juxtaposition of "bounding" Hormiz to the horseman, who races along the ground but cannot "overcome him," mirrors the power of the waves over the sailors, just as Hormiz's leaping and juggling of liquid "from side to side" echoes the waves' free and wild chorus.[277] Each of these vertical zones reflects the biblical cosmos—sea, land, air, firmament, heavens. But the Sea and Hormiz mix and transgress those elements: raising liquid into air, threatening to "destroy" the earth.

Yet the horizontal plane, represented by the element of earth ("dry

---

275. *Pirqe R. El.* 4: "If not for the firmament, the world would be *swallowed up* by the waters above it and below it." Compare Ps 107:27 (at IIIb, referring to Hormiz): *all their wisdom is swallowed up.*

276. This image of waves "casting" their voices to each other inverts the verse "depths calls unto depths" (Ps 42:8, trans. modified). In midrash, the "deep" (*metsulah*, Ps 107:24) is not the lowest primordial "depths" (*tehomot*), but the midst of the waves: "The 'deep' is only [where] the waters are fierce ['*azim*], as it is said, 'You flung me into the deep, in the heart of the sea' [Jonah 2:1], and it is written, 'Their pursuers You flung into the deep like a stone in fierce waters' [Neh 9:11]." Mekhilta §*Shirata* V to Exod 15:5, ed. Lauterbach, 193. Compare Rashi to Exod 15:10; *pace* Cassuto, *Biblical and Oriental Studies*, 83.

277. The two lines are not verbatim, but poetically resonant: מהאי להאי ומהאי להאי (ג״ב.ל״ב) / רמא לי גלא קלא לחבריה (א.ט).

land"), stands firm. As the waves approach the seashore, their power disappears.[278] Now that the sand has formed a "bound of the sea / by a perpetual decree, that it cannot pass," the waves "could not prevail" over it,[279] however much they may have "raged" (Jer 5:22).[280] Just as YHWH "broke" the sea with the sand of the shore,[281] the earthly authorities put an "end" to Hormiz's "bounding" by "cutting off" his life.[282] Each story (I, II, IIIa, IIIb) ends by reimposing order over chaos. Yet their poetic energy springs from protagonists—the waves and Hormiz—who personify and push chaos both beyond its preordained limits and, in its telling, closer to the world of the reader.

If the central conflict is between the elements of Sea and Land, the middle story (II), by citing Exod 3:14, alludes to the divine Names YHWH / *Ehyeh Asher Ehyeh* at the burning bush. These Names subdue the Sea not horizontally but vertically, beating down the waves by being engraven on the sailors' poles.[283] Those "poles," in turn, recall Moses's staff at the part-

---

278. The same image of subduing the Sea with sand repeats, on a vertical axis, at the end of our collection of tales: "He surfaced, held *a skin-bottle of sand* [זיקא דחלא] over it, and it went down" (XVIII). See the gloss of Rabbenu Gershom to XVIII (b. B. Bat. 74b, ed. Vilna; compare ms. V ln. יח.רכ״ב): "*he threw sand at it, from the sand of the seashore, and it fled.*" That story of defeating a sea-monster fuses, first, another motif (Tg. Neofiti; FTP; Tg. Jon. to Exod 15:8; Tg. Ps 33:7; Tg. Ps 78:13; Mekhilta §*Beshallah* 5 (ed. Lauterbach, 148), Ber. Rab. 5:2), that God binds and raises the waters at the Parting of the Red Sea "like a *skin-bottle* [MT: *heap*, נד]") with this motif of *sand* as the sea's "breaker" or limit (Jer 5:22; Job 38:8–11; Rashi to Exod 15:8 contra Tg. Onq. *ad loc.*). The competing gloss of XVIII.220 (*vinegar*; Rashbam; also cited by Rabbenu Gershom) posits that the sea-monster "*fled* from its odor"—echoing an exegesis of Job 41:31 (41:23), Part 2 (2.A) about countering the Leviathan's deadly stench. Manuscripts and commentaries thus reiterate the Battle with the Sea by drawing out and recombining its motifs and, in doing so, recollect our composition differently.

279. This phrase in Jer 5:22 (ולא יוכלין) and Tg. Jon. *ad loc.* (ולא יכלין) transfers from the end of I to the end of IIIa ("but could not overcome him," ולא יכיל ליה). That is, our section (I–III) has recycled the uncited part of one prooftext as a conclusion for an adjacent story. See similarly V.55–56/Ps 107:27b (n. 272) and "minor creature of the sea" in XVIIa/Tg. Ps. 104:25–27 (chapter 1 §*Exegesis*). See also n. 9.

280. I render *va-yyitga'ashu* in Jer 5:22 as "raged" (KJV: "roar"; Alter: "the waves tossed"), in line with b. Shabb. 105b: "This [i.e., the name *Mount Ga'ash*] teaches that the mountain *raged against them* [*ragash 'alehen*], to kill them." This midrash on Josh 24:30 portrays the Mountain just as our midrash on Jer 5:22 does the Sea, using the same verb. Nothing in Josh 24:30 prompts this (nonetymological) gloss; they are light variations of a single exegesis.

281. "Breakers of the sea": Job 38:10; Sifre Deut. 306 (ed. Finkelstein, 332).

282. Tg. Neof. Exod 15:18: "The Children of Israel said: How becoming is the crown of Kingship to you, YHWH! When your children saw the wonders of your miracles at the sea, and your Might between the waves, at that moment, their mouths opened as one and said, '*YHWH's is the Kingdom, from the beginning of the world unto eternity.*'" On such a basis, a link between I–II and III was not hard for early readers to draw: viewing YHWH as agent of the "Kingship," praising YHWH's "Might" over the waves, and the divine Kingdom's power over Hormiz, rather than the Persian authorities'.

283. A similar incantation, on hyena skin, is a remedy for the bite of a mad dog (b.

ing of the Red Sea. Thus, II adds a new cosmic element, Fire, and intertexts to the understory.

Like the framing prooftexts (I, III) and demise of Hormiz (IIIb), both of those additions in II make less sense as free variations on myth than as elaborations of stock midrashic motifs. Such motifs are tailored to I–III so as to develop its war between transgression/chaos, on one hand, and salvation/order, on the other, as well as its wavelike, undulating poetics. To track this even closer point/counterpoint integration between the psalm's understory and our previous three tales, let us proceed by asking how it may have worked for a reader who knew related early midrashim. I begin this analysis by examining the symbolism of Fire as a token of YHWH's militant dominion in the tradition that such a reader would have occupied. I proceed to examine assocations and potential links between our tale (II) and the understory of the Battle with the Sea. As we will glimpse periodically, this tale's core "rising-and-falling" poetics resurfaces in early midrashim with parallel motifs. As a result, this analysis of II adds to my central argument that not only raw materials of the unit I–III, but also its literary form, were likely received by early listeners as a midrash about the war between order and chaos, and that they would have interpreted this section in those specific terms, not only as a myth.

YHWH's Arsenal

A White Shoot of Flame

In the next story (II), the sailors are menaced by a potent image and respond in kind:

> That wave that sinks the ship
> has a white shoot of flame upon its crest,
> but we have poles upon which is engraven:
> "*I am that I am*," God, the LORD of Hosts,
>   Amen, Amen, Amen, Selah, Selah, Selah
> and we strike it,
> and it subsides

As Daniel Boyarin has shown, "shoot" (*tsutsita'*) and related words are botanical in origin: branchlike protrusions or patterns, in this case a flame ("tongue of flame," we say).[284] Genre-based analysis would treat

---

Yoma 84a). Another verse on the Burning Bush (Exod 3:2) fights fire/fever by the principle of sympathetic magic (b. Shabb. 67a). See Kiperwasser and Ruzer, "Aramaic Stories," 166 n. 16; Kiperwasser, "Facing Omnipotence and Shaping the Sceptical Topos," in *Expressions of Sceptical Topoi in (Late) Antique Judaism*, ed. Reuven Kiperwasser and Geoffrey Herman, Studies and Texts in Scepticism 12 (Berlin: de Gruyter, 2021), 101–23, at 118 n. 60.

284. See Isa 5:24. Daniel Boyarin notes that in Galilean Aramaic (Ber. Rab. 59:4, ed.

it as a "mythic" motif or even as rabbinic counter-"myth."[285] Poseidon/Neptune's trident, for example, was often depicted as a lotus, or alongside a lotus,[286] similarly fusing a naval projectile weapon with a botanical motif. Naval rams, which were literally used to "overwhelm" a ship by striking its hull, were also adorned with tridents of fire: a branched ("Ptolemaic") thunderbolt.[287] Similarly, the "poles" that the sailors use against the wave resemble other weapons that subdue the waters in Greek and Iranian mythologies.[288]

Via the actual word *tsutsita'*, however, we can reconstruct a different inner-rabbinic, post-mythical interpretive background for this image. A cluster of associations with the word, as well as etymologically related words and related symbols, belong to YHWH's special arsenal. YHWH's use of these weapons of course reflects cross-culturally shared aspects of myth and magic, yet employs a divine Name, the Tetragrammaton, which was a highly marked and more specific symbol for early readers of our tale, especially given its allusion to Exod 3:14.[289] In midrash, some weapons in this arsenal, like Moses's staff at the parting of the Red Sea, function like the sailor's poles engraven with YHWH. Therefore, early readers' associations with this "white shoot of flame" made the image legible for them, not as a mythic or magical item that was simply added to our tale

---

Theodor Albeck, 632–33), we have שבשה דנור, i.e., ענף של אש: a flame that "was made [to look] like a myrtle branch" ("Towards the Talmudic Lexicon" [Hebrew], *Tarbiz* 50 [1980]: 164–91, at 170).

285. Cassuto classifies the Bible's divine arsenal as a fragment of this cross-cultural Battle with the Sea myth: "sword, spear, rod, bow, and arrows (an allusion to flashes of lightning)" (*Biblical and Oriental Studies*, 91).

286. Gold octodrachms minted by Ptolemy IV (222–205 BCE) have a trident with lotus finial protruding from the center (Bernhard Woytek, "Heads and Busts on Roman Coins: Some Remarks on the Morphology of Numismatic Portraiture," *Revue numismatique* 171.6 [2014]: 45–71, at 66 fig. 2). A trident superimposed on a lotus appears on, e.g., fifth-century CE Bactrian coins with a fire altar on the reverse (Klaus Vondrovec, "Numismatic Evidence of the Alchon Huns Reconsidered," *BUFM* 50 (2008): 25–56, at 50, Type 102).

287. I thank Stephen DeCasien (personal correspondence, 11 May 2021) for sharing his copious expertise on naval rams. For this iconography, see the Bremerhaven Ram on his site at https://shiplib.org/index.php/rams-2, accessed 29 October 2024. See Jeffrey G. Royal, "Iconographic Elements on the Warship Rams," in *The Site of the Battle of the Aegates Islands at the End of the First Punic War: Fieldwork, Analyses and Perspectives 2005–2015*, ed. Jeffrey G. Royal and Sebastiano Tusa, Bibliotheca archaeologica 60 (Rome: "L'Erma" di Bretschneider, 2020), 137–46.

288. Wand and Horn of Sleep: Valerius Flaccus, *Argonautica* 8.67; Whip, Shackles and Branding Iron: Herodotus, *Hist.* 7.34 (Strassler, *Landmark Herodotus*, 512; see further Jon D. Mikalson, *Herodotus and Religion in the Persian Wars* [Chapel Hill: University of North Carolina Press, 2003], 44–49). See Kiperwasser and Ruzer, "Aramaic Stories," 166–68; Noegel, "Jonah and Leviathan," 253.

289. Allusions to this verse are ubiquitous in magic bowls in the Talmud's cultural environment. See James Daniel Waller and Dorota Molin, *The Bible in the Bowls: A Catalogue of Biblical Quotations in Published Jewish Babylonian Aramaic Magic Bowls*, Cambridge Semitic Languages and Cultures (Cambridge: Open Book, 2022), 11–12.

(II), but as the direct symbolic proxy for YHWH's role. It performs, here, the same polarity between YHWH and the forces of Chaos that we saw in I and III. Early readers could have linked it to the understory of I–III according to a similar logic. To reconstruct how, precisely, they might have done so, we must inventory their associations.

YHWH's arsenal contains an array of weapons: arrows, fire, God's "finger" and "hand," tablets, poles, and staves. Several of these weapons appear in a story in b. Taʿan. 25a, the only other instance of the "white shoot of flame" in the Talmud. Rabbi Elʿazar ben Pedat faints, after a bout of bloodletting. In a sort of trance,[290] he seems to outwit God for forgetting about God's own omnipotence. God admits defeat by striking him on the forehead "with the finger-bone" (*beisqutla*'), saying wryly, "Elʿazar, my son, my arrows are [shot] at [literally, *in*] you,[291] my arrows." The outward sign of this action—visible to his colleagues as he sleeps—is the "white shoot of flame," which projects from Rabbi Elʿazar ben Pedat's forehead.[292]

In that story, this "white shoot of flame" is linked to other items in YHWH's arsenal: "arrows" and "finger-bone." Both might have been associated with role of the "white shoot of flame" in our tale as well. YHWH's "arrow" appears as lightning in storm theophanies such as Zech 9:14 ("And his arrow shall go forth as the lightning"), extolling YHWH's triumph over enemies like the rebellious primordial waters (Ps 77:18–19). Targum Neofiti develops this imagery by depicting YHWH shooting *arrows of fire* during the parting of the Red Sea.[293] In a midrashic light, then, our "white shoot of flame" is easy to connect with the flaming "arrows" of YHWH: not only part of the Sea but also potentially aimed against it.

---

290. Glossing "his mind went into a trance *and* he fell asleep" (*halash libbei ve-nim*) with Rashi to b. Pesah. 50a (= b. B. Bat. 10b) s.v. ואיתנגיד. First a rabbi loses consciousness (*halash*), then he enters a new liminal state. Here, the second verb is found only in the prints. But the same two stages (compare Job 3:13) appear in the earlier Palestinian version. See Kiperwasser, "Facing Omnipotence," 101–23, at 106, for a fascinating reading of the theological themes in this story.

291. See Ps 38:2 (38:3), "Your *arrows* are *gone into* me, your *hand* is come down upon me" (emphasis added). Several manuscripts (*FJMS*) have a correction ("*Let* my arrows *be loosed* upon you"). The others stick closely to this biblical allusion.

292. Compare b. Nid. 30b. When a fetus is in the womb, "a candle is lit for it above its head," where it learns the whole Torah. Before it is born, an angel "slaps it on the mouth" and it forgets. Like clicking ruby slippers, a divine gesture punctures liminality, leaving its trace in "reality" (a cleft under the nose, a wrinkle on the brow).

293. Tg. Neof. Exod 15:4 (קשת עליהון גירין דאשא); MT has simply ירה (which the Targum reinterprets as "shot"). Compare Tg. Neof. Exod 19:13, also reading ירה as shooting *arrows of fire*; see also Tan. §*Shemot* 18 (ed. Buber, 10). The battle at the Red Sea often features "arrows" of "lightning" from Ps 18:14 (18:15) (Mekhilta §*Beshallah* 3, ed. Lauterbach, 1:141); "arrows ... stones of hail, of fire and brimstone" (Mekhilta §*Beshallah* 7, ed. Lauterbach, 163); "fire from above" and "thunder from above" (Mekhilta §*Beshallah* 6, ed. Lauterbach, 160 = MdRSBY XXV.3 to Exod 14:25, ed. Nelson, 111).

Another sign that our tale draws from the same stock of motifs is this flame's location on the wave's crest ("head"), just as it shoots from R. El'azar b. Pedat's "forehead." As for the rare word "finger-bone" (*isqutla'*), its cognate, σκυτάλη, did acquire that manual sense in Byzantine Greek,[294] but earlier, and more normally, it is a "stick" or "staff."[295] That common sense of the loanword recalls the sailor's "poles" in our tale; which are, as we will see, closely linked with Moses's staff at the parting of the Red Sea.

In sum, if we read tale II in isolation, this "white shoot of flame" belongs to YHWH's primordial nemesis, the Sea. However, it is also joined elsewhere to YHWH's arsenal, like the "arrows" or "lightning" that YHWH wields *against* the Sea. Even if we were to read narrowly and ignore these assocations with the image in Targum/midrash, much is shared between the two instances of the "white shoot of flame" in the Talmud itself: a demonstration of YHWH's power, by striking on the "head," with a rare loanword, which also literally means the kind of weapon that is used in our story. The fact that, in our story, this weapon *opposes* YHWH, whereas in the other instance it is identified *with* YHWH's arsenal, does not undermine its link with YHWH for a reader. On the contrary, it sharpens the motif as a symbol of YHWH's power. In the sources that we just traced, it is part of YHWH's larger arsenal (finger-bone, arrow, staff) and is activated by the gesture of striking on the "head"—a symbolic act of dominion. In that light, the Sea is an agent of YHWH's punishment of those "sailors" who do not repent in time, which does not contradict their claim that they can repel their fate by wielding YHWH's Name. Both sides of the superficial conflict are unified, symbolically, in light of a single deity.

Lest we suppose that this collection of weapons and gestures is isolated, we may seek further evidence of its widely diffused, and therefore—to an early rabbinic reader—plastic and accessible symbolism, in variations surfacing in midrashim with a cluster of intertextual, etymological, and symbolic correspondences. Again, the interpretive key to such correspondences is not one universal mythic pattern, but specific words, whose connotations allow for both the efflorescence of interpretation among early rabbinic readers and associations to other early sources. Later interpretive inversions or recollections of this arsenal—for example, displacing it *from* the Sea *to* YHWH—were available to any early reader

---

294. As a synonym for "phalanx" (φάλαγγος): the flat bones, as opposed to the joints (Paulus Aegineta, *The Medical Works*, vol. 1, trans. Francis Adams [London: Welsh, Treuttel, Würtz, 1834], 329). Both are generic words for a flat surface ("log" and "staff"), extended into anatomical and military domains.

295. One Syriac lexicographer glosses it as "a head of iron" (hammer or mace?) *Lexicon Syriacum Auctore Hassano Bar Bahlule*, vol. 1, ed. Rubens Duval (Paris: Leroux, 1901), 240.

who had these assocations and who could, therefore, have interpreted II in many ways — not just as a repetition of the myth of the Battle with the Sea.

For example, while there is, at most, an indirect etymological link between YHWH's "arrows" (*gere*) and the white "shoot" of flame (*tsutsita'*),[296] the *tsutsita'* shares the root of the priestly "crown" (*tsits*) in the Bible. Further, like both *tsutsita'* and *isqutla'*, the *tsits* is located on the head, where it has the power to repel YHWH's foes.[297] As the Name YHWH is engraven on the *tsits* when it is thus wielded, this weapon also resembles the sailor's "poles." From an early reader's perspective, then, an unusually high density and diversity of functional overlaps between the *tsutsita'* and other weapons in YHWH's arsenal licensed one to read this tale (II) as a re-enactment of other rabbinic battle scenes; e.g., to read *tsutsita'* in light of *tsits*.

The Priestly Crown

In midrash, the *tsits* figures centrally in Israel's battle with the five kings of Midian:[298]

> *And he shall drink the blood of the slain* [Num 23:24, modified]. Those are the five kings of Midian. And *the vessels* [Num 31:6, modified] — that is the *tsits*, on which the Name of the Holy One, Blessed be He, is engraven, as it is said: *and the trumpets to blow in his hand* [Num 31:6].[299]

> Moses said to Israel: "Balaam the Wicked has performed enchantments for them. He has set fly the five kings; he is flying and he sets fly. Show him the *tsits*, on which is engraven the Name of the Holy One, Blessed be He, and they shall fall before you."

Here, an old exegetical problem ("Why was Balaam slain together with the five kings of Midian during their battle against Israel in Num. 31:8, if he went home in Num. 24:25?")[300] is exploited by a midrash in

---

296. Just as "shoot" (*tsutsita'*) has a botanical metaphor at its root, so does its counterpart, "arrow" (*gera'*), e.g., "shoots of fenugreek" (*gere de-ruvya'*, b. Shabb. 109b).

297. In fact, R. Yehudah (b. Sanh. 12b = b. Yoma 7b) holds that the *tsits* lacks power if it is *not* worn on the head. Rabbenu Gershom comments on our *tsutsita'* b. B. Bat. 73a ad loc: "like a crest [*tsitsit ha-rosh*]."

298. Tan. §*Balaq* 23 (ed. Buber, 2:ג״ע) = Num. Rab. 20:20.

299. The verse did not state which "holy vessels" go into battle. But <u>Holy</u> to YHWH (Exod 28:36) is on the *tsits*, and "trumpets" (*hatsotsrot*) has the same doubled letter, so the midrash infers that the *tsits* was specifically implied.

300. See Tan. §*Mattot* 4; b. Sanh. 106a. Mar bar Ravina's dictum suggests in the latter source that these polemics against Balaam were fueled by his role as a sort of exegetical pin-the-tail-on-the-donkey: "Do not exert yourself to expound verses [derogatorily: Rashi

order to portray the *tsits* as a priestly foil for Balaam's sorcery. The midrash pictures Balaam as holding up the Midianite army with his spells ("he is flying and he sets fly"). Moses directs Pinehas to hold up the *tsits* with the Name YHWH engraven upon it.[301] This weapon makes the Midianites "fall,"[302] both literally and figuratively—in an ironic twist, fulfilling Balaam's very own prophecy that, like a "lion" or "lioness," Israel will "*rise up ... lift himself up ...* and drink the blood of the slain" (Num 23:24, emphasis added).[303]

In other words, in light of this midrash, the *tsits* and *tsutsita'* share more than a root. As the *tsutsita'* reared up on the wave's crest, only to be struck down by the engraven Name, so did Balaam and his minions "fly" and "fall" under the engraven Name on the *tsits*—and this miracle was performed *so that* Israel could "rise." That is, the rising-and-falling poetics of our Battle with the Sea also shapes another battle scene.[304] Further, the motif of the "head," as site of YHWH's dominion, is also implicit in the *tsits*. In addition to these rabbinic associations with the *tsits*, which may be active in *tsutsita'*, the images' role in both tales further mirrors nonrabbinic magical uses of the Tetragrammaton (including in Greek—and not only

---

ad loc.], except for Balaam the Wicked. Anything that you find about him, expound against him." On the other hand, as here, some rabbis make Balaam into the gentile foil for Moses. See Isaak Heinemann, *The Methods of Aggadah* [Hebrew], 2nd ed. (Jerusalem: Magnes, 1954), 98.

301. Compare Tg. 2 Chr 23:11, where David's crown has "the Great Name engraven and spelled out upon it."

302. There is a Babylonian allusion to this Palestinian midrash in a dispute in b. Yevam. 60b: "Rav Ashi said: [*and it* [the *tsits*] *shall be always upon his* [Aaron's] *forehead, that*] *they* [*may be accepted before YHWH,* Exod 28:38] is written. *They* [the Jews, use the *tsits*] for acceptance and not for retribution. But, for the *goyim*, it is even for retribution." It is no coincidence that "the *goyim*" named here are the Midianites.

303. Compare the blessing of Judah (Gen 49:9): "Judah is a lion's whelp: from the prey, my son, thou art gone up: he stooped *down*, he *couched as a lion*, and as an old lion; who shall *rouse him up?*" (emphasis added).

304. One might object that "rising" and "falling" are generic, dead metaphors for victory and defeat. This ignores their marked poetic use in both stories (as emphatically theorized in a similar manner in m. Rosh Hash. 3:8), which thereby form a potential reading tradition. As we saw, "rising and falling" is a dominant oral-poetic trope of section I–III. And, the implied words of the prooftext ("rise up ... lift himself up") contain the precise wording of Balaam's prophecy that the midrash fulfills by way of his—so to speak—takedown. Here, the reading tradition revives an arguably dead metaphor. Another midrash (cited from Rashi to Num 31:8; see y. Sanh. 10:2, 29a, and the addition to Tan. §*Mattot* 4; see n. פ in ed. Buber, 2:33) uses the same trope: "*Upon* those slain by them [על חלליהם]: because they [i.e., Balaam and the kings of Midian] fell upon the slain from the air. And so is it written of Balaam, in the book of Joshua, *did the children of Israel slay ... upon those pierced.*" [Josh 13:22; where MT reads אל, *unto* those pierced]. The midrash exploits a contamination of these parallel clauses in MT Num 31:8/Josh 13:22.

by Jews),[305] which hung in gold on the Temple wall.[306] In other midrashim, like the sailors and their poles, Moses uses the Name, engraven on a gold tablet or shard, against another body of water:[307] the Nile, which, like the Sea of our understory, midrash knows to be a foreign deity.[308]

My point is not that *tsits* and *tsutsita'* were interchangeable images for an early reader. One is a weapon with the engraven Name; the other is vanquished by it. Nor would I propose that we draw a direct line from midrash about the *tsits* and Tetragrammaton to our story about the *tsutsita'*. Rather, these symbols intersected at a deeper cultural level as a nexus of tropes and inventory of potential associations. On that level, we can access the standpoint from which we approach all of the sources in this chapter: the poetic sensibility and interpretive reflexes of an early reader of I–III, who was primed to perceive this "white shoot of flame" as part of a larger mythic drama, or understory, about YHWH's militant dominion. In that light, we now appreciate how this reader would have identified with the sailors, wielding YHWH's engraven Name against a common foe, in a battle scene featuring a gesture (striking), a location (head), a divine arsenal (*tsits/tsutsita'*/arrow/pole), and recurrent analogical structure or poetic trope (rising : victory :: falling : defeat). Like these sailors, like Moses, like Pinehas—but markedly *un*like the sailors in Ps 107, who "cry" for salvation—a reader would have seen the understory of the Battle with the Sea in terms of YHWH's dominion over forces of chaos/transgression. Their associations with those images would have redoubled the surface meaning of this war with the waves: salvation comes not through a "cry" but by forcing order on agents of chaos.[309]

---

305. A Persian mother or father, for instance (y. Yoma 3:8, 40d = Qoh. Rab. 3:11). See parallels/bibliography at Qoh. Rab. ed. Hirshman, 201; Gideon Bohak, *Ancient Jewish Magic: A History* (Cambridge: Cambridge University Press, 2008), 117–19.

306. M. Yoma 3:10: Queen Helena engraved the passage of the *sotah* (the whole text verbatim, some insist–y. Yoma 3:10, 41a) on a golden placard, where YHWH appears twice in a potent adjuration or spell (Num 5:21).

307. Mekhilta §*Beshallah* 1, ed. Lauterbach, 120; Pesiq. Rab Kah. 11:12 (ed. Mandelbaum).

308. See Rivka Ulmer, *Egyptian Cultural Icons in Midrash* SJ 52 (Berlin: de Gruyter, 2009), 70–74. See also Philo, *Life of Moses* 2.36: "They speak of the Nile as of some imitation of Heaven; forming it, as it were, into a god."

309. This dialectic in the understory of I–III, which is implicitly built on Ps 107, reflects a dialectic in the psalm itself, praising a militant God (vv. 16, 25, 40) but stressing a merciful God in refrain/conclusion (vv. 8, 15, 21, 31, 43). Those two aspects of God are also opposed in other rabbinic renditions of the same sea-battle myth, e.g., R. Yitshaq's view in b. Rosh Hash. 16a = 18a (§*The Storm as Framing Device*). Even more aptly, consider Pesiq. Rab Kah. 8:2, which cites God's instruction to Moses at the Red Sea ("Why do you cry [תצעק] to me? ... But *you*, lift up *your* staff]," Exod 14:15–16; trans. modified, emphasis added) to prove the opposite of what it says: Israel's victory came "*not* by sword and *not* by shield, *but* by prayer and words of supplication." See already m. Rosh Hash. 2:8 and the homily to וייראו מאוד ויצעקו, Exod 14:10 (Mekhilta §*Beshallah* 3, ed. Lauterbach, 137–39), with Ishay Rosen-Zvi, "Can the

The Work of Re-revelation

By now, in our reconstruction of the understory, we may seem to be playing with fire. To argue that, for an early reader, this section was subtextually about YHWH's triumphant dominion over chaos, personified as the Sea and foreign nations, may be taken to imply that it is really an *apologia* for Jewish zealotry: "Rabbah & Friends" typecast as Pinehas. Nothing could be farther from my aim than to give our tales one subliminal meaning.[310] Rather than project our problems onto the readers, my goal is to uncovers theirs. As our definition of "the reader" and their stake in the tales shifts, so will the tales' meaning—and readers at any one time disagree with each other.[311]

A better formulation of our question is not *whether* but *how* an early rabbinic reader would have engaged the conflict in this section; how its theme, of YHWH violently reestablishing the order of creation, would have spoken to them. How they would have identified: as militant agents of YHWH's dominion, or as repentant sailors on the corrupting sea? Refocusing on the reader's self-identification in the text brings to light another flaw in using "myth" to describe how these tales were received. Rather than an internal force in Jewish tradition, myth has often been implicitly opposed to Jewish religion and identity: "myth" as a synonym for deities and cults of non-Jews.[312] By that logic, one assumes anything in these tales that is paralleled in Zoroastrian or Mesopotamian texts, for instance, to

---

Homilists Cross the Sea Again? Revelation in *Mekilta Shirata*," in *The Significance of Sinai: Traditions about Sinai and Divine Revelation in Judaism and Christianity*, ed. George J. Brooke, Hindy Najman, and Loren T. Stuckenbruck, TBN 12 (Leiden: Brill, 2008), 217–45, at 220 n. 14, 224 n. 32, 228 n. 50, 229 n. 52. See generally E. E. Urbach, *The Sages: Their Concepts and Beliefs*, trans. I. Abrahams, 2nd ed. (Jerusalem: Magnes, 1979), 448–61.

310. For such an allegorical-nationalist approach in the High Middle Ages, see Ritva at n. 793.

311. Similarly, Rosen-Zvi ("Can the Homilists Cross," 234–35, nn. 64–65) notes that, previously, scholars had read some homilies in Mekhilta §*Shirata* as political polemic even as they ignored the text's opposite and adjacent ideologies. In order to contextualize midrash historically, one must first treat the source as a whole, in all its contradictions.

312. Frim, "'Those Who Descend,'" 2: "Mythologically oriented readings argue ... that the first-person narratives in bBB 73a–74b appropriate and recast mythological motifs as symbols of rejected cultural alterity." This trend goes back at least as far as Cassuto, whose interpretation of the evidence sounds quite nationalist in its own right when he opposes "national" and "ethical" revisions of "pagan" myths, for example: "Although these legends had cast off, among the Israelites, their original mythological garb, and had assumed a form more in keeping with the national ethos, there nevertheless remained certain elements that were still redolent of an alien origin; hence the Torah's attitude towards them was not sympathetic"(*Biblical and Oriental Studies*, 101). On myth as a scholarly and modern Christian category for "the religion of the Other," see Bruce Lincoln, *Theorizing Myth: Narrative, Ideology, and Scholarship* (Chicago: University of Chicago Press, 1999), 52–54, 67–68, 205–6; Jonathan Z. Smith, *Drudgery Divine: On the Comparison of Early Christianities and the Religions of*

have been already interpreted by a Jewish reader in light of the latter—as intrinsically foreign myth. By that logic, Jewish retellings of "alien" mythic content must have been meant to resist/subvert other religions. By ignoring the actual telling of these tales for early Sasanian readers—which, as we saw, moves back and forth between the deep past and the present, culturally remote and familiar, not between the Other and the self—one is led to believe that Jewish readers took sides in a culture war. But what are the stakes of this Battle with the Sea? Is an Other the actual enemy?

In light of our final set of midrashic intertexts, I would suggest that the nature of early Jewish readers' engagement with this section was more speculative and ontological than polemical. Perhaps some did connect chaos to a specific nemesis of the people of Israel—from the Mesopotamian *Yam* (Sea) to Zoroastrian Ahriman—but YHWH's role as agent of cosmic order goes beyond national zealotry.[313] Nor do YHWH's foes *cause* chaos or transgression. They personify one pole of a struggle between YHWH, in his creative role as "man of War," and the elements to which YHWH must give form: the raw, unordered materials of creation itself. Yet this struggle is not between equals; on a deeper reading, both the Sea and its antitheses are aspects of divine being.

When we examine how the understory and tales amplify this theme, in point/counterpoint with one another, we will see that their effect on a reader would have been much like an early commentary on Exodus, Mekhilta §*Shirata* (as analyzed by Daniel Boyarin and Ishay Rosen-Zvi, whose readings I aim to amplify and develop). As *Shirata* reenacts the revelation of the Parting of the Red Sea in midrash, transforming a one-time event into a pattern,[314] so were early readers of these tales and their mythic understory called to witness how YHWH founds and upholds, in precarious balance, the order of their temporal existence and salvation. Hence it is no accident that the mythic theme of the Battle with the Sea was, as we have seen, conjugated with imagery from other theophanies in the midrashic imagination: the Burning Bush and Parting of the Sea. In all of those intertexts' early rabbinic readings, the *mediation* of revelation is the core ontological problem. YHWH's arsenal is no mere tool of domi-

---

Late Antiquity, Jordan Lectures in Comparative Religion 14 (Chicago: University of Chicago Press, 1990), 87–115.

313. On Ahriman, see n. 815. Contrast Mekhilta § *Beshallah* 4 (ed. Lauterbach, 143–48), which develops a nationalistic view of the Parting of the Red Sea by embedding it in the whole history of Israel. Contrast especially its use of Jer 31 to the prooftext from Jer 5 in II. There, when waves roar "The Lord of Hosts is his Name," it proves that "the seed of Israel" *is* "a nation forever and ever"—due to the commandments and the merit of the Jews' ancestors. II makes no such nationalist equation.

314. Rosen-Zvi ("Can the Homilists Cross") shows three techniques whereby midrash does what I call re-revelation: (a) scrambling tenses; (b) exploiting multivalent symbols; (c) constructing complementary temporal paradigms. My analysis of I–III, in light of early midrash, focuses on (b): a rhetoric of multivalent symbols of divine power.

nation/triumph over enemies (whether the Babylonian Sea, Egyptian Nile, or Hormiz). YHWH's arsenal is a means to reveal to Israel the process of revelation itself. By repurposing images and phrases whereby early midrash reenacts or, in my terms, "re-reveals" divine being, readers learned to see an apparently dualistic war between God and the cosmos as less than meets the eye: God *is* the order underlying the chaos on the surface. Poetic re-revelation, via midrash, dramatized YHWH's cosmic order/ontology by focalizing these tales through the opposite rhetorical figure: the fearful sailors on a violent sea and, through their eyes, a suspense-ridden reader.

Dramatizing Divine Ontology

A Man of War

From the vantage of the sailors on the ship, the cosmic order seems far from stable. In the first tale (I), they rise to its upper limit: "had it lifted us any higher, we'd have been burnt."[315] In the second (II), they teeter on the edge of an abyss: "that wave that sinks the ship," armed with a "white shoot of flame," must be beaten back down by the divine Name. One possible meaning of this conclusion for an early reader, identifying with the sailors, is simple. *The mythic Sea has its arsenal, "but we have" the divine arsenal—and ours is more powerful.* Given common magical uses of the divine Name (not only in magical sources proper but also in midrashic battles, as we saw above), and given that sailors do physically strike the wave,[316] as if the Name had a direct effect on the enemy, one might suppose that an early reader took this tale as just a vivid demonstration that YHWH and his chosen people are more powerful. Such a reading furthers a nationalistic thesis that the tales aim to vanquish their mythic origins.

Such an interpretation, however, obliges us to assume that a rabbinic reader would have held a dualistic, mechanical notion of how God works in the world. This is refuted by a series of midrashim in Mekhilta §*Shirata*, which closely parallels our tale. This source argues against the idea that YHWH "needs" his arsenal at the Parting of the Red Sea whatsoever.

> *YHWH is a man of war, YHWH is His Name* (Exod 15:3): Rabbi Judah says, "This is indeed a verse enriched by many sources: it informs [us] that He is revealed *to them* with all the weapons of war" [emphasis added].

After adding verses to bolster the divine arsenal that we have seen, the midrash ends:

---

315. By the corona or "cradle" of the star; see n. 252.
316. Missing in ms. F. Perhaps the "poles" are held over the waters in this telling instead, like Moses's staff.

[Yet lest] I take it that He needs any of these means [*middot*], the statement teaches, *The Lord is a man of war, the Lord is His Name*: He wages war with His *Name*, and He does not need any of these means.

If so, then why did Scripture need to detail each of them, one by one? Only because, if they are needed *by Israel*, then the Lord will wage war *for them*. And woe to the nations of the world: what do they hear with their ears? That, indeed, the One who Spoke and the World Came to Be will, in future, wage war upon them.[317]

Rejecting magical mechanism as it reprises the same theme of the Battle with the Sea, this midrash makes two points. First, the Tetragrammaton, and it alone, is YHWH's weapon. The rest of the divine arsenal is meaningful, however, in terms of God's relationship to Israel. And the sense of that arsenal for Israel (*"for them"*) is the reverse of what it is to the nations: not proof of YHWH's sheer power—none is needed—but of love, in a well-established theological sense. A double-meaning of *middah* drives this point home: a "means" or weapon of war, and the quality or "measure" of love, associated with the name YHWH. What to the nations is only a weapon/means of war (the divine "measure of judgment," *middat ha-din*), Israel knows as the "measure of compassion" (*middat ha-rakahamim*). Phenomenologically, to the nations, God *is revealed as* a "man of war." Ontologically, for Israel, YHWH is love.[318] That is, only Israel has access to the inward ontology that YHWH's arsenal reveals outwardly.

With this well-worn theology in mind, an early reader of Rabbah's tales would have heard the sailors' voice differently: "But *we* have ... YHWH ... and *we* strike [the wave] ... and it subsides."[319] This is no simple battle between the Sea, with its weapon, and Israel, with theirs. Rather,

---

317. Mekhilta §*Shirata* 4, ed. Lauterbach, 188 (emphasis added). My understanding of this midrash follows closely Rosen-Zvi, "Can the Homilists Cross," 235–41; Boyarin, *Intertextuality*, 27.

318. See another homily in this series: "*YHWH is a man of war* in that he wages war against the Egyptians, [but] *YHWH is His Name* in that he has compassion for his creatures, as it is said *YHWH, YHWH who is merciful and gracious* [Exod 34:6]." Mekhilta §*Shirata* 4, ed. Lauterbach, 190. (This is an argument by analogy and superfluity, glossing each "YHWH" in Exod 34:6 as the measure of judgment and the measure of compassion within Exod 15:3). The parable that follows is clear that, despite universal-sounding language ("creatures"), Israel has a unique status regarding YHWH's "measures": when Israel receives love, the nations receive judgment (God's "sword").

319. As noted by Rubenstein (*Talmudic Stories*, 321 n. 78), similar stories end with phrases like נח הים מזעפו, "And the sea rested from its raging," alluding to Jonah 1:15 (b. B. Metz. 59b and 86a; b. Yoma 38a). This is added to II by Rashbam, b. B. Bat. 73a s.v. וניהי but absent in all manuscripts. The latter tellings stress how YHWH lays the Sea to rest, rather than its rebellious swell. A more dualistic retelling of I and II, which links them, is in a medieval commentary: "When the Holy One *quiets the roar* of the sea that He created, the world sees His might [see Ps 65:7 (65:8), trans. modified], as the sea fears him; just as one wave attests when it calls out to another, and the other wave replies, *Fear ye not me?* And this

it opens up a gap between those to whom YHWH is revealed in his full dual ontology (inner and outer; compassion and judgment), and those to whom he is *only* a "man of war."[320] Accordingly, YHWH's Battle with the Sea is Janus-faced. To the nations, it is a finite event.[321] To Israel alone, YHWH is re-revealed as an ontological structure of the cosmos across apparently discrete mediations from *Urzeit* to *Endzeit*. What Other readers of the signs of God's power see only as their suspended fate in an eschatological future—a rabbinic Sword of Damocles—Israel alone can see as God's perennial twofold nature: a *man of war* (the measure of judgment) and YHWH of love (the measure of compassion).

This gap between insider/outsider readings does not require immersion in an esoteric doctrine. But it primes readers conversant in midrash to see that a dualistic, mechanical interpretation of II, along the lines of an action movie, is not the whole story. YHWH is not merely a superior power but the ontology of power, a being-who-will-be. The Sea, striving to overwhelm that power, is not merely defeated but restored to its place in the encompassing ontology of the divine which defines creation: "But we have poles/on which is engraven/*I am that I am*/and we strike it/and it subsides."

Both points are reiterated in the midrash on the Song at the Sea in Mekhilta §*Shirata* 4. Here, as in II, the power of the Tetragrammaton is tied to the Name, *I am that I am* (Exod 3:14), which this midrash reads as God's ability to span the gap between past, present, and future.[322]

> *YHWH is a man of war, YHWH is His Name*: Why is this said?
>
> Just as He is revealed at the sea as a hero waging battles—as it is said, *YHWH is a man of war*—so is He revealed on Sinai as an old man full of

---

is based on a *haggadah*: 'The waves cast their voices in chorus,' etc." (Abraham ben Azriel, *Arugat ha-Bosem*, ed. E. E. Urbach, 4 vols. [Jerusalem: Mekize Nirdamim, 1939–1963], 1:239).

320. Mekhilta §*Shirata* 4, ed. Lauterbach, 190. YHWH is called a *"man* of war." Yet he is not anthropomorphic. How can this be? Israel sanctify his Name by their acts of holiness, just as he is sanctified through them, in his aspect as the God of love. Therefore, "though I am God, and not man, [I am] holy in your breast" (Hos 11:9, trans. modified). For an inversion of the same logic, see Sifre Num. 42 (ed. Horovitz, 48; see also ed. Kahana, 1:125). Here the argument is that, in theory, the impersonal and merciless Sea should have no virtues (*middot*), as it has no children to care for. Still, it fears YHWH. All the more so should the nations, who *do* have children to care for, fear God—but do not.

321. Even if, as Rosen-Zvi notes ("Can the Homilists Cross," 238 n. 31, 241), the nations do share (some of) Israel's ability to read it as an omen of YHWH's judgment upon them: *the nations have heard, they tremble* (Exod 15:14; trans. modified).

322. This is a good case of "scrambling tenses," bridging a gap between Rosen-Zvi's temporal structures of re-revelation (the perennial and the prophetic). The midrash shows that YHWH *is*, what YHWH *was* and *will be*: "a discursive practice, which makes the revelation present here and now" (Rosen-Zvi, "Can the Homilists Cross," 219).

mercy, as it is said, *And they saw the God of Israel [but upon the nobles of the children of Israel, he did not stretch out his hand*, Exod 24:10–11]."[323] And after they were redeemed, what does it say? *And the like of the very heaven for clearness* [Exod 24:10], and it says, *I beheld until thrones were placed [and the Ancient of Days did sit]* and it says, *a fiery stream issued [and came forth from him;* Dan 7:9–10].

So as not to allow an opening for the nations of the world to say that there are two powers. Rather, YHWH *is a man of war* **[and]** YHWH *is His Name*: He is in Egypt, He is at the sea, He is in the past, He is in the future, He is in this world, He is in the world to come, as it is said, *See now that I, even I, am He* (Deut 32:39), and it says, *Who hath wrought and done it? He that called the generations from the beginning. I, the Lord, who am the first, and with the last, I am He* (Isa 41:4).[324]

Again a doubled YHWH stands for both of God's "measures," judgment and compassion. The human warrior and heavenly old man are one, complementary revelations of the same.[325] There are not "two powers" in heaven—both are bound to God as an ontological whole, a Name which does not name any one thing.[326] By the same token, a twice-doubled "I" proves that YHWH's ontology subsists across and beyond time and space.[327] YHWH is at once "now" and "the first and the last," simultaneously "I am" and "I will be." By heresy or error, the nations perceive only half of what is inwardly, for Israel, one ontology: the unity of God's opposite "measures," and of God's power, which stabilizes the outwardly rebellious cosmos.

Fires Strange and Familiar

A reader would have experienced the same modulation in this Battle with the Sea's meaning—from outer signs of YHWH's arsenal to their inner

---

323. Unlike the biblical verses (Exod 14:8, 16, 21–22, 26–27, 29–30), where God's "hand" parts the Sea and strikes the Egyptians. See Michael Fishbane, "The Arm of the Lord: Mythic Creativity and Exegetical Form in the *Midrash*," in *Language, Theology, and the Bible: Essays in Honour of James Barr*, ed. Samuel E. Balentine and John Barton (Oxford: Clarendon, 1994), 271–92.

324. Mekhilta §*Shirata* 4, ed. Lauterbach, 188–89. The concept **[and]** is the essence of this midrash, added here for clarification.

325. Scholars debate whether this discourse on God's many forms implies that they are merely apparent, not real. See Dov Weiss, *Pious Irreverence: Confronting God in Rabbinic Judaism*, Divinations (Philadelphia: University of Pennsylvania Press, 2017), 241–42 n. 18.

326. B. Ber. 9b phrases this idea in temporal terms by way of Exod 3:14: "*I was* with you in this enslavement, and *I will be* with you in the enslavement of the [foreign] kingdoms."

327. This idea is drawn from the infinitive absolute, פקוד יפקוד, in Mekhilta §*Beshallah* 1 (ed. Lauterbach, 122): just as God "remembered" Israel during the exodus, so will God "remember" Israel in this world and the next.

ontology—by interpreting its element of Fire through an early midrashic lens. This weapon, like others in the divine arsenal, could be viewed as a "special effect" with sheer magical mechanics: a "white shoot of flame" on a wave's crest is subdued by an allusion to the Burning Bush. This is sympathetic magic,[328] fighting fire with fire; amulets using Exod 3:2 against fever show that people did believe this.[329] By that naïvely dualistic interpretation, the sailors are nearly burnt by the star's heat,[330] then menaced by the wave's flame, but ultimately rescued by an equal and opposite divine potency—the Burning Bush. Similarly, their poles work like a rod: a ruler's sign,[331] heralding YHWH's power. One might gloss both weapons, again, as tokens of YHWH's dominion over the Sea.

However, early midrashim explore the very symbolic oppositions that would support such an interpretation as representations of competing forces *within* a unified divine ontology. On that basis, one would better read this moment in the Battle with the Sea as an ontological continuum that is internal to divinity, rather than as a war between YHWH and the elements.

To begin with, distinctive features of the "white shoot of flame," in this context, are equally marked as signs of the divine presence in others. The "white" flame recalls not only a widely diffused midrash about the inscription of the Torah "in black fire upon white fire,"[332] but also one where God gives Moses four-colored heavenly fire (white, black, green, and red) with the divine template [*tavnit*] for the Tabernacle.[333] As we saw, botanical imagery for fire is common. Yet here, its link with the divine presence is highly marked. So, too, in a midrash on why "the bush was not consumed" in a late work (citing and resembling earlier traditions):

---

328. Meir Bar-Ilan, "Between Magic and Religion: Sympathetic Magic in the World of the Sages of the Mishnah and Talmud," *Review of Rabbinic Judaism* 5.3 (2002): 383–99.

329. Dorothea M. Salzer, *Die Magie der Anspielung: Form und Funktion der biblischen Anspielung in den magischen Texten der Kairoer Geniza*, TSAJ 134 (Tübingen: Mohr Siebeck, 2010) 152–53. Fever is defined in the Talmud as a type of fire (b. Yoma 21b). See n. 283 and m. Sanh. 10:1 (the Name in Exod 15:26 was also used to heal).

330. For the unique reading in ms. H ("damage of the fire" as opposed to " heat of the fire"), see b. Sanh. 93b.

331. E.g., Aaron's rod, which, like the "white shoot of flame," is botanical, and, like the "poles," was "often confused [in midrash] with the rod of Moses," which bore the Name (Ginzberg, *Legends*, 496 n. 88; 730 n. 600).

332. Y. Sotah. 8:1, 22d = y. Sheqal. 6:2, 49d; Tan. Yel. §*Bereshit* 1:1. Mekhilta §*Bahodesh* 4 (ed. Lauterbach, 308): "The Torah is fire, given from fire, and likened to fire."

333. Pesiq. Rab Kah. 1:3. Rav Yosef cites Bet Hillel (b. Ber. 52b): "There are many lights"—i.e., colors—"in a fire" (hence the *havdalah* blessing, "He who creates the lights of the fire"). See further Zvi Meir Rabinovitz, ed., *The Liturgical Poems of Rabbi Yannai according to the Triennial Cycle of the Pentateuch and the Holidays* [Hebrew] (Jerusalem: Mossad Bialik, 1985), 1:271 n. 78.

And he saw, and behold, the bush burned with fire [and the bush was not consumed, Exod 3:2]:
> On that basis they said: 'Upper fire sprouts branches [*ha-'esh shel ma'elah ma'alah lulavin*] and blooms,³³⁴ but does not devour, and it is black.'"³³⁵

This divine "upper fire," with the miraculous property to put forth "branches" around fuel without consuming it,³³⁶ is related to the typology of fires in the Talmud (b. Yoma 21b):

Our Sages taught: There are six fires:
> fire which devours and does not drink,
> which drinks but does not devour,
> which both devours and drinks,
> which devours wet and dry alike,
> and there is fire which repels other fire,
> and there is fire which devours fire.

Commenting on the last item in this list, the anonymous Talmud adds:

"And there is fire which devours fire": Of the divine Presence
> [*shekhinah*], as the Master said:³³⁷
> "He stretched out His finger between them and burned them."

While other traditions indirectly associate the divine presence with the "white shoot of flame"—via the images of "white" fire, or the bush with its "branches" and "blooms" of flame—this tradition directly links the "fire which devours fire" to the presence ("finger") of YHWH. And in another talmudic story, as we saw, the "white shoot of flame" *is* God's "arrow" or "finger-bone." Thus, an early reader of II could have not simply associated, but even gone so far as to *identify*, the "white shoot of flame" with the Presence of YHWH. As Shinan says, this "seems con-

---

334. As shown by Saul Lieberman, the better reading is צורפת ("blooms"; perhaps a corruption for טורפת, "grows leaves"), not שורפת ("burns") ("Torah Shelemah," *JQR* 36.3 [1946]: 317–24, at 317–18). See also Rabinovitz, *Liturgical Poems of Rabbi Yannai*, 1:272 n. 82.

335. Exod. Rab. II:5.8 (ed. Shinan, 115).

336. This stunning image reads the odd phrase *labbat-'esh* (Exod 3:2) as "a branch [*lulav*] of flame." See n. 284.

337. b. Yoma 21b = Tan. Yel. §*Shemot* 15:1 = b. Sanh. 38b. In the latter parallel to this individual tradition, the "fire" devoured by divine fire is a group of angels. Compare Ber. Rab. 77:2: "He [the angel] stuck his finger into the earth, the earth began to brim with fire. Jacob said to him: 'You'd frighten me with that?! I am wholly of it, as it is written: *And the house of Jacob shall be a fire*' (Ovadya 1:18)." Consider Lev 10:2: God's fire "devours" Nadav and Avihu, because they offered "strange fire" to YHWH; yet, miraculously, it does not devour their "tunics" (Lev 10:5). Divine fire is nothing like ordinary fire. (And that is the entire theme of the homily in Tan. Yel. §*Terumah* 11).

nected to the world of esotericism":[338] without being able to trace one line of influence between a single source and our "white shoot of flame," we can say that, due to the density and volume of symbols that this image shares with other midrashim about divine fire, early readers would likely have connected the two. That connection, in turn, would have led them to read the sea and the divine presence, the menacing "white shoot of flame" and God's own power to strike those who do not repent, as complementary symbols within one ontology—rather than setting them in dualistic or mechanistic opposition. By the same logic whereby YHWH is revealed to the nations at the sea as a "man of war," even as he reveals his other side to Israel as well—the "measure of compassion"—so does this arsenal manifest God's Presence, even as it resists itself. *Yet the bush was not consumed*: readers may have experienced the sailors' poles and the wave's "white shoot of flame" as a conjuncture of binary aspects of divine being. Not an alien Other versus YHWH, but one divine fire devouring another: black fire and white fire again.

Parting the Sea(s)

If the Burning Bush and its antithesis in II, the Sea, could have been turned, via midrash, into a re-revelation of divine ontology, even a less attentive audience would likely have heard the sailor's "poles" in the same way. Not only does this weapon resemble Moses's staff in both form and function, but another telling of the Battle with the Sea, where Moses wields the staff, had long been read as a retelling of God's primordial division of the waters:[339] a re-revelation of creation as national sal-

---

338. In *The Zohar*, Pritzker edition, ed. and trans. Daniel C. Matt (12 vols. Stanford, CA: Stanford University Press, 2004–2018), 4:473, this "black fire on white fire" represents the intertwining of apparently opposed aspects of being, "the left contained in the right." I thank Daniel Matt for teaching this text in his Zohar course. See Moshe Idel, *Absorbing Perfections: Kabbalah and Interpretation* (New Haven: Yale University Press, 2002), 45–79; Gershom Scholem, "Colours and Their Symbolism in Jewish Tradition and Mysticism," in Scholem, *On the Kabbalah and Its Symbolism*, trans. Ralph Manheim (New York: Schocken, 1965), 64–76.

339. See Exod 14. Already there, the restaging of creation is not a monotonous repetition but a poetic transposition from upper to lower planes. Moses's "splitting" (ב.ק.ע.) of the sea (Exod 14:16, 22) mirrors God's "division" (ב.ד.ל.) of upper from lower waters; the firmament "in the midst" (בְּתוֹךְ) of the upper/lower waters (Gen 1:6) parallels the "dry land" between the wall of waters, "in the midst" of which the Israelites can cross (Exod 14:16, 27, 29; contrast Exod 14:23). For a similar transposition, see a "seafarer's prayer" recorded at y. Taʿan. 4:3, 68b: "Let there be a firmament in the midst of the waters." Conversely, when the Egyptians are drowned (Exod 14:27), "the sea returned *around morning* to its *strong-perpetual state [leʾetano,* trans. modified]" in a partial apocalypse of creation: re-covering the dry land with the waters as first light breaks again. (For my translation of *ʾetan* as "perpetual *and* strong," see Mekhilta §*Beshallah* 7, ed. Lauterbach 162). Compare a more balanced rendition

vation history.³⁴⁰ Such a reader may have taken a similar interpretive cue from the frame of our tale's understory. The refrain of Ps 107 ("and they *cry out* to YHWH from their straits")—to which the response is YHWH's silencing of the waves—could have made sense to early readers in light of God's seemingly unprovoked question to Moses ("Why do you [sg.] *cry out* to me?" Exod 14:15): a "cry" that is, as in our story, followed by the command to part the sea with the staff.³⁴¹ An early audience was thus primed by intertexts to associate the sailors' poles engraven with divine Names, on one hand, and Moses's staff,³⁴² on the other—especially as both symbols had the same role in a shared understory, the myth of restoring the order of creation and saving Israel by subduing the Sea again.

A few closely related and relatively early sources suggest how those intertextual links could have shaped the early reception of this symbol in our tale. Consider a common type of dispute about what, precisely, caused the sea to part:³⁴³

> *But I am the Lord thy God, that divided the sea, whose waves roared: YHWH of Hosts is His Name.* (Isa 51:15, trans. modified)

> But what was it that the sea saw and fled? R. Judah vs. R. Nehemiah. R. Judah said: It saw Moses' staff and fled. R. Nehemiah said: It saw the Tetragrammaton engraven upon it–*YHWH of Hosts is His Name*–it saw and fled.³⁴⁴

Notably, the teller of II not only shares R. Nehemiah's opinion—switching Moses's staff for the sailors' poles—but also takes a divine Name from his prooftext ("YHWH *of Hosts*")³⁴⁵ and stages a similar scene: a dialogue between the waves, roaring as they see YHWH's power ("The

---

of the same theme in Ps 74:15–16: *You, You split fountain and stream / You dried up strong-perpetual rivers / Yours is the day, Yours, too, is the night / You have appointed radiance and sun* (trans. modified).

340. See Isa. 51:9–16 with Joseph Blenkinsopp, *Isaiah 40–55: A New Translation with Introduction and Commentary*, AB 19A (New York: Doubleday, 2000), 331–35.

341. If God's question is addressed not to Moses but to Israel, who do "cry out" to God in Exod 14:10, per ibn Ezra to Exod 14:15 (contra Rashi *ad loc.* = Mekhilta §*Beshallah* 4, ed. Lauterbach 147), then our intertexts (Ps 107/Exod 14) are even more tightly linked. The sailors, i.e., Israel, "cry out" to God, but are saved by the poles/staff.

342. The word "poles" (אלוותא, אלוותא) itself invokes the "God of Hosts" (אלהי צבאות) whose Name it bears.

343. In Lev. Rab. 32:4 (ed. Margulies, 744–45), replying to the same prompt (מה ראה), these rabbis dispute whether Moses also used the Name in a different verse of Exodus; decisive evidence that this was a stock topos.

344. Pesiq. Rab Kah. 19:6 (ed. Mandelbaum, 308). See also Jer 31:35 (31:34).

345. In all manuscripts (even the fragment in ms. F, whose scribe seems to have suffered from a severely defective copy; see my supplement to this volume cited at n. 1). This divine Name is not in Exod 3.

waves cast their voices in chorus"; literally, "One wave cast its voice to its fellow"). Both the *midrash* and the tale, then, focus on a key moment in the battle when the Sea recognizes God: "Come see the might of your Master!" Here again, comparison to early midrash shows us that, rather than attacking the forces of chaos in a direct, magical,[346] dualistic way—which would be closer to R. Judah's staging of the scene—early readers could have interpreted II as a critical moment of re-revelation: the recognition of their God by another god, the Sea.

A second early midrash shows the difference that this difference would have made for how II was received. Again, the interpretive background is the same: an old rabbinic debate about how, exactly, to stage the moment in Exodus when the sea parted. By tracing striking poetic connections to our understory, we will find that a reader could have interpreted II as a reflection on divine ontology, in relation to both the sea and the figure of the sailors/Moses.

Focusing on the moment when the sea parts, midrash stages a multilayered dialogue:

And Moses stretched out his hand over the sea [*'al ha-yam*; Exod 14:21]:

The Sea began to withstand him [*'omed ke-negdo*]. Moses spoke to it in the Name of the Holy One, Blessed Be He, that it might part, but it did not submit to him. He showed it the staff, but it did not submit.

To what may the matter be compared? To a king who had two gardens, one within [*lifnim*] the other. He sold the inner one and the buyer went to enter the inner garden, but the watchman would not let him. The buyer spoke to him in the name of the king, but he did not submit to him. He showed him the signet of the king, but he did not submit to him, until the buyer brought the king himself, and he arrived. As soon as he had brought the king and he arrived, the watchman began to flee. He said to [the watchman]: "All day long, I've been speaking to you in the name of the king, but you would not submit to me! So now, why [*mi-penei mah*] do you flee?" He replied: "Not from you [*me-faneikhah*] am I fleeing, but from [*mi-penei*] the king!"

So did Moses come and stand at the sea. He spoke to it in the Name of the Holy One, Blessed Be He, but it did not submit to him. He showed it

---

346. That view appears in Amulet 27 in Joseph Naveh and Shaul Shaked, eds., *Magical Spells and Formulae: Aramaic Incantations of Late Antiquity* (Jerusalem: Magnes, 1993), 93–94: "By the name of He who rebukes the sea, *and its waves roared YYYY of Hosts is His Name* (Isa 51:15/Jer 31:35 [31:34]) may he rebuke from Marian daughter of Sarah and from her foetus this evil spirit." As the editors note, the biblical intertexts play on two verbs: "to roar" (רגע) and "rebuke" (געׂ, "to exorcise"). God's battle with the sea is itself a magic rite, not only a source for one.

the staff, but it did not submit to him—not until the Holy One, Blessed Be He, was revealed to it in His glory. But once the Holy One, Blessed Be He, was revealed in his might and his glory, the sea began to flee, as it is said: *The sea saw it, and fled* [Ps 114:3].

Moses said to it, "All day I have been speaking to you in the Name of the Holy One, Blessed Be He, and you would not submit to me. But now, why are you fleeing? *What ails you [mah lekhah], O Sea, that you fled?* [Ps 114:5, trans. modified]." It replied: "Not from you [*me-faneikhah*], Moses; not from you, Ben Amram, but from the presence of [*mi-lifnei*] the Lord: *Tremble, earth / from the presence of the God of Jacob / who turned the rock into a pool of water, the flint into a fountain of waters* [Ps 114:7–8, KJV trans. modified]."[347]

This version of the Parting of the Sea answers the same question as the previous midrash: When *the sea saw it, and fled* (Ps 114:3), what exactly did it see (*mah ra'ah ha-yam*)? In other words, "*what ails* [literally, "*is toward*"] *you, O sea, that you take flight?*" (Ps 114:5). The answer hinges on double meanings of prepositions: "toward" and "before," also meaning "in the face/presence of." Psalm 114 says that the sea fled "from the presence of (*mi-lifnei*) the Lord." The midrash parses *mi-lifnei* in both senses and exploits each to develop distinct ideas. First, it is the "presence" of God, not Moses, who parts the sea.[348] Moses is not the cause. Not his staff, nor even God's Name, is enough. God must be "revealed in his might and his glory."

This leads to the second argument of the midrash. What exactly was revealed? What is the true distinction between YHWH's "presence" and mere signs thereof? The midrash names two aspects of God's revelation ("might" and "glory"), to which we will return. It also shows its paradoxical answer in the form of the parable. God's "presence/face" (*panim*) is like the garden within (*lifnim*). It is not seen gradually or indirectly by signs— it is revealed in total. As soon as it arrives, apocalypse occurs.[349] Cosmic elements become their opposites: mountains skip like rams, rivers turn back; earth trembles, flint becomes water, roaring waves rest. And yet, the parable insists, this presence is an irreducible enigma. *What* did the sea flee from? What ailed (literally, what was "toward") the sea? Not any thing (staff, signet, Name), nor anyone (the "buyer," Moses). The sea fled

---

347. Mekhilta §*Beshallah* 5, ed. Lauterbach, 151–52. I build here on the reading of Boyarin, *Intertextuality*, 95–100. The text appears at Mekhilta §*Beshallah* 4, ed. Horovitz, 102–3.

348. This addresses an interpretive problem or "gap" (Exod 14:21): Moses stretches his hand over the sea, yet God is the one who splits it, unlike other verses where Moses appears to do it himself (Boyarin, *Intertextuality*, 96).

349. Enclosed gardens (some did have royal watchmen) were already an old metaphor for dominion over nature. See Elaine T. James, *Landscapes of the Song of Songs: Poetry and Place* (Oxford: Oxford University Press, 2017), 68.

"From What [*mi-penei mah*]"—from the presence of the divine enigma.[350] The parable is a riddle whose question becomes its answer. "*What* did the Sea see and flee?" — "From *What*," from the presence of God. God, in God's essence as *What*, is radically unmediated. Like the king, God's presence is no staff, servant, or Name. Its revelation brooks no resistance; when it arrives, the sea retreats, the battle ends.

This parable's Escher-like structure enhances the riddle and thereby the midrashic solution to the original question of *what* the sea saw and fled. Why, after all, are there two gardens here, inner and outer? If there were only one garden, the parable could draw the same distinction between the king's presence and the buyer, between the moment of revelation and mere signs of God, which are not effective in themselves. (Try interpreting the parable without the second garden: that point is no less clear.)[351] It is not a fully satisfactory solution that this unit's teller "needs" two gardens ("one within the other," *zo' lifnim zo'*) in order to connect the parable's form with the double meaning of *mi-lifnei* in the verse that it interprets. I suggest that, rather than simply wedge both parts of the unit together, this geometry develops a poetic interaction between the parable and the midrash so as to sharpen and heighten their combined effect.

On one hand, the midrash mirrors R. Nehemiah's view that Moses's staff has no power of its own. He raises his hand "over" the sea but it does just the opposite, rising up "against him."[352] On the other hand, the parable shows why Moses would *think* that his staff *does* have power over the sea. Just as the king enters the inner garden *behind* the buyer (the buyer cannot see him—that is why he asks the watchman "So now, why do you flee?"), so is God standing behind Moses. This precise geometry of two gardens, two rings of power facing the sea behind Moses, was clearly established by the verse just before this one: "And the angel of God, who went before the camp of Israel, removed and went *behind* them; and the pillar of cloud removed from before [*mi-lifnei*] them, and stood *behind* them" (Exod 14:19; emphasis added). God's Presence is thus located not only "*between* the camp of the Egyptians and the camp of Israel" (Exod 14:20) but also at Moses's back as Moses faces the sea. From the sea's perspective, then, the midrash rightly concludes that, when Moses "lifted his hand over the

---

350. Compare Exod 16:15–16:31 (the Israelites' question, "What is it?," *mah hu*, becomes "manna," *man*: literally, "Who?").

351. I develop Boyarin citing his conversation with Uriel Simon (*Intertextuality*, 99, 153 n. 19), who suggests that the two gardens represent a contradiction between the eternal cosmic order and its subversion by the apocalypse of the sea's parting.

352. In a later expansion of this tradition, Job 38:8 and other verses are cited in a debate on the Parting of the Sea. There, rabbis take the sea's perspective: on what condition would God turn the sea into dry land, if the latter is supposed to be the limit and antithesis of the former? Exod. Rab. 21.6, in ed. *Midrash Rabbah ha-mevo'ar*, 557; *Midrash Rabbah: Exodus*, trans. S. M. Lehrman (London: Soncino, 1939), 267–68.

sea," it saw what Moses could not: God's presence.[353] Moses and the presence are like a body that cannot see its own shadow. The space of this parable, based on a reading of the geometry of Exod 14, evokes what only the sea saw and what the reader, like Moses, is unable to see. Its whatness can be re-revealed only in the sea's response; a *prosōpopoeia* of the divine *prosōpon*.[354] Like a closeup of an actor's face as she reacts to an event offscreen, the sea's speech (*Tremble . . . from the presence*) helps its reader to visualize God by displaying God's effects in the world.

Now that we appreciate how this midrash is grounded in a very close reading of Exod 14, we also understand why it names the two specific aspects of God that are revealed to the sea: Glory (*kavod*) and Might (*gevurah*).[355] Like the buyer (Moses) with his back turned, those terms are inspired by the verse just before the parting of the sea. The Glory is the "pillar of cloud," the Might is the "angel of God," which take up their positions *behind* Moses (Exod 14:19).[356] As the watchman heralds the arrival of the king behind him "in his might and in his glory," so does Moses's staff beckon not only YHWH but also his retinue, like courtiers flanking the king. From Moses's view, God is invisible. Yet the two courtiers heighten God's visual impact on the sea even more. No wonder it "saw and fled" so quickly!

In sum, motifs and their uses that are shared between midrashim on parting the sea and an episode in our Battle with the Sea (II) would have led an early reader of the latter to interpret it as a re-revelation of divine ontology at the moment of the sea's retreat. This reader would have had ample resources to interpret it as a dramatization of YHWH's power, which is not an act of physical/magical mastery over the sea's chaos and cosmic transgression, but a visual demonstration of an invisible enigma who can violate yet equally restore cosmic order. The sailor's poles striking down the waves—like Moses's staff, which only seems to part the sea—are not the cause of this apocalypse; they are symbols of the king,

---

353. Exod 33:23, trans. modified: *And I will <u>take away</u> your hand, and you will <u>see my back</u>; but my face/presence will not be seen* (precisely the inverse configuration of God and Moses).

354. I build explicitly upon Boyarin, *Intertextuality*, 97–98, who noted generally that the sea "saw God," and drew a comparison to the technique of telling-by-showing (*prosōpopoeia*), but did not mention these specific exegetical cues.

355. Mss. Oxford and Vienna refer only to the "glory," as they do not include the longer and somewhat redundant phrase "But once the Holy One, Blessed Be He, was revealed in his might and in his glory...." See Mekhilta §*Beshallah* 4 (ed. Horovitz-Rabin), 103 n. 1. It seems that this phrase was added to balance the "signs" and "Name" of the king in the *mashal* with God's "might" and "glory" in the *nimshal*, both based upon the verse.

356. On Glory as the "pillar of cloud", see Mekhilta §*Pisha* 14, ed. Lauterbach, 74; Mekhilta §*Beshallah* 1, 124–26. On Might as "angel of God" (or "fire"), see Urbach, *Sages*, 93–94; Michael Zank, "The Rabbinic Epithet *Gevurah*," in *Approaches to Ancient Judaism*, ed. Jacob Neusner (Atlanta: Scholars Press, 1998), 14:83–169, at 114. Zank calls Glory and Might "the most striking feature of this *midrash*" (157) but ignores their basis in the verse.

who remains mysterious. Tale II is a simpler rendition of this re-revelation but preserves the same poetic structure. The same is true for I, where the sea shrinks from God's "might" just as it did in the parable:

> I. The waves cast their voices in chorus:
> "So, is there anything in the world you've left alone and not destroyed?
> Let us go, you and I, and destroy it."
> And replied:
> "Come see the might [*gevurta'*] of your Master!
> I cannot pass so much as a grain of sand the width of a thread,"
> as it is said:
> *Fear ye not me? saith the Lord. Will ye not tremble at my presence* [mi-panay]? [*Which have placed the sand for the bound of the sea, by a perpetual decree, that it cannot pass it; and though the waves thereof toss themselves, yet can they not prevail; though they roar, yet can they not pass over it* (Jer 5:22)].

As in our midrash on Exod 14/Ps 114 (where earth "trembles" before the "presence" of God, who turns rock into water), in Jer 5, the sea "trembles" before the "presence," who "bars" it with the shore—the antithetical cosmic element of dry land. This parallel imagery, a mighty cosmic element humbled by the smallest iota of its opposite element, develops the core theme of divine dominion. If God delimits the primal forces of nature and marshals them against each other, then God must be a power of a higher order. From the perspective of the waves, that is the lesson. To them, what is re-revealed is God's power ("Come see the might of your Master!"), which they answer with fear and trembling like the sea in the parable. For the reader, however, our tale takes a further and more delicate step. It portrays not only power but divine being: the paradoxical question of *what* God is, such that one can see or know God as revealed by its ripples in the cosmos, without reducing it to the visible realm.

This tale (I) melds that imagery from midrash into ontological reflection by exploiting the very same double meaning (Jer 5:22): *mi-panay*, "away from" and "from my face/presence." This double meaning sets up a structure in the tale that is just like the two walled gardens of the parable on the Parting of the Sea. Just as there are two gardens, two figures facing the sea (Moses and the divine presence behind him; the buyer and the king), so are there two waves, forming concentric rings as they hit the shoreline. The waves thus encounter and re-reveal God's presence in the same way as the parable of the buyer and the watchman. Just as the sea "stood against" Moses until it "saw" the "presence"—when it shrank "away from" Israel to form a protective "wall" against the Egyptians—so did the watchman resist the buyer, within the inner garden, until he saw that the king arrived, when he immediately fled. In the very same manner, the inner wave—the wave that has not yet reached the shoreline—

stands at a towering height, roaring to the outer wave of its intention to drown the whole world. But, as soon as the outer wave sees God's Might (*gevurah/gevurta'*)–here, in the form of dry land–it also sees the limit of its power. It crashes from its height and recedes from the shore, roaring God's supremacy to the inner wave as it ebbs into the current. This precise poetic form and its effect resurface in one of the tale's first commentaries, attributed to Rabbenu Gershom (ed. Vilna, *ad loc.*):

> Because one wave saw the other rise so high, it seemed to one—the inner wave—that the other, outer wave would drown the whole world. [So] the outer wave replied, "Come see the might of your Master!" As if to say, "Do not suppose that I will be able to raise myself up one iota higher than my allotted measure, for even if it is *as much as a grain of sand the width of a thread*, I am not permitted to *pass* outside of my *sand*—outside of my domain."

As its double meanings ("sand/outer" [*hol*] / "tremble" [*tahilu*] / "strength" [*hayil*] or "might" [*gevurta'*]) bolster this theme of divine dominion by stressing that even the tiny sand can intimidate the great sea, this commentary draws out the central theme of divine ontology. When God *placed the sand for the bound of the sea*—a border between one cosmic "domain" and another—God drew, as we now say, "a line in the sand" between inside and outside, *sacrum* and *profanum*, *qodesh* and *hol*. Wet and dry are antithetical; one has no place transgressing the other.[357] God can of course suspend the antithesis, parting the sea or bringing the flood in apocalypses like Gen 6–9; just the sort of cosmic transgression that the waves seem to be expecting.[358] Such miraculous violations of divine order are a medium of re-revelation, no less than the restoration of order in law and covenant. But re-revelation can also work in the other direction: making the structure of the cosmic order perceptible as a trace of God's presence, transcending its inertia as mere nature. Such transcendence is what these tales achieve for one who can listen. By re-revealing a wave crashing against the shore as a sign of its submission to a primordial cosmic boundary—and, simultaneously, by amplifying the ocean's roar as a sign of its straining up to the stars—these tales again evoke God's ontology by means of its effects on creation. Like the watchman in the garden, like the sea at Moses's staff, the waves respond to something that their reader cannot see. Yet the spatial and temporal structure of the sea's response—its

---

357. Compare XVIII: "he held a skin-bottle of sand over [the sea-monster], and it went down." See n. 113.

358. As Rashbam (b. B. Bat. 73a ונחרביה) comments on the first wave's speech in II, "*And destroy it*—because of the sin of the generation." Rabbah seems to have read tale II in the same way, as he worries, later in our collection (XIIIb), that he will inadvertently annul God's oath never again to destroy the world with a flood (Gen 9:11; Isa 54:9). See n. 175.

immediate, total transformation from sublimity to humility, from the crest to the shoreline—brings a reader closer to experiencing that something. *The Sea resisted / the Sea saw and fled*: even in a two-line summary, our tale re-reveals God's presence while preserving its mystery.

Point/Counterpoint

In sum, whereas our collection's version of the Battle with the Sea (I–III) has been treated as the reprise of a dualistic theomachy, magic rite, or polemic against Israel's Others, by reconstructing its interpretive background for an early reader, I have shown how this reader also could have heard it as a dramatization of God's powerful and mysterious being. In light of midrashic re-revealation, this ancient Battle with the Sea is not only what it seems: not only proof of God's power, but the scattering of divine ontology across cosmic elements and planes: from a "man of war" at the Sea to a compassionate "old man" at Sinai. If concepts were characters, the plot of the understory—running throughout and connecting our introductory section of four tales—would be the interaction of those aspects of divine being across each cosmic domain: in the air, the heavens, and the deep; at the sea, on the shore; by fire or admixtures of elements (fire/water, wine/water, etc.). Rejecting hypostasis (this sea is not subdued by God's sidekick, the Word),[359] and dualism (this sea is not a fully rival god), our understory of the Battle with the Sea re-reveals divine being by staging a rigged contest between cosmological extremes: a contest that restores and shores up foundations of the cosmic order as revealed in Scripture. A listener informed by early Palestinian and Babylonian midrash would have grasped that message, affectively and in general. Even if they could not restate it in the form of one unambiguous message or interpretation, overlapping symbols and their oppositions carried across its structural logic and its rhetoric.

The telling achieved this, in part, by both identifying its reader with the characters in the tales and offering a new understory with which to make sense of what happens to them. From the sailors' viewpoint, they are about to pierce the firmament or sink beneath the sea. Hormiz, leaping, bounding, transgressing the domains of air and water, seems like a threat to the kingdom, just as the waves do at first seem poised to throw off their breakers and recapitulate the flood. In the cosmic order as re-revealed by midrash, by contrast, everything is in its place. Hormiz is not killed by

---

359. As in Tg. Neofiti, which elevates God's "Word" (*memra*) to the agent of the exodus. See Bruce Chilton, "The Exodus Theology of the Palestinian *Targumim*," in *The Book of Exodus: Composition, Reception, and Interpretation*, ed. Thomas B. Dozeman, Craig A. Evans, and Joel N. Lohr, VTSup 164 (Leiden: Brill, 2014), 386–403, at 399–400.

a mortal kingdom but "cut off" by a King (who "hears" and accepts the repentant "cry" of the sailors, i.e., Israel). God's Names at the Burning Bush fight fire with fire, subduing the waves' menacing "white shoot of flame" with what God is, was, and will be. (This strange fire itself, and the symbolic act of striking it on the "head," are stock signs of both rebellion against YHWH *and* YHWH's dominion.) By the same token, a "man of war"—to the enemies of Israel—is, for Israel (and the reader), re-revealed neither as man nor as warrior, but as a God of love. His weapons (*middot*) are his "measure" of compassion. The "cradle of a star" (proverbially vast as "forty fields of mustard [*hardla'*],")[360] shrinks to its opposite: a "grain of sand the width of a thread [*huta' dehala'*]," safeguarding creation from chaos. As one wave crashes against the shore and, receding, calls back to its fellow ("Come see the might of your master!"), it recapitulates this fugue's theme. God's power is no mere force. Like the angel's Might, like the pillar of cloud's Glory, it splits the sea, re-revealing the primal separation between elements of Wet and Dry. The waves fear God's "presence" and shrink from land, from the order of creation restored after the flood: a "perpetual decree" (Jer 5:22),[361] laid down in the beginning as God's landmark in the world.

By setting this drama in motion, the ancient myth of the Battle with the Sea was retold as vivid narrative, rich in epically scaled conflicts and crises of acute existential tension. By re-revealing it as divine ontology, midrash reconciled that myth's symbols and binaries with traditional patterns of explanation. This points to an ongoing cultural dialogue between myth and midrash in our entire composition—an iceberg, of which this unit is one crag. We can read this understory as poetic raw material that tellers used to retell and readers used to recollect both collections, crafting each unit as they harmonized texts with the theme, and fugue-like poetic form, of the Battle with the Sea. Returning to the understory, a deep myth running under the composition, allowed readers to link associations in a drama of divine ontology that was both old and new.

* * * * *

Myth or Exegesis? Wrong question. As I argued in chapter 1, rather than a dichotomy between genres of the text, both categories can help us to

---

360. A mustard seed is proverbially small (b. Meg. 28b) yet has a vast yield. Compare Rashbam's comment (b. B. Bat. 73a s.v. ביזרא "it is larger than other crops") to the parable of the mustard seed (Matt 13:1–32; Mark 4:30–32; Luke 13:18–19. Note that the Gospel parable ends like IV: the mustard seed becomes a great tree, in whose branches birds rest). In our collection, however, the poetry lies in the analogy—Stars ("mustard-seed") : Heavens :: Sand : Sea. Tiny stars cover a vast expanse of sky, just as a grain of sand resists the great sea.

361. In the midrash, the wave is tamed by God's "decree" (*hoq*); in the tale, by God's "engraven" (*haqiq*) Name. Again, story and understory complement one another in terms of the theme of divine dominion.

see a generative dialectic between genres for the reader. Rather than seek the meaning of this unit (I–III) in its origin, authorial/editorial intent, or social context (myth among "the folk" vs. midrash among "the rabbis," or a cryptic polemic against Zoroastrians or other Others), we put ourselves in the position of an audience who oscillated between the genre of the tale and the genre of its telling, in order to feel out its poetic texture. Our approach has disclosed how these tales could have had affected a specific early reader, whose intuitions and reactions to their content we managed to access by reconstructing their reading tradition. Our nascent poetics of reading has thus deciphered not a single meaning but a network of potential meanings, formed by association, conflict, and synthesis of images. Their early interpretive framework came from myth but was throughly transformed by midrash.

By comparing the tales (the text's form and content—what a reader can perceive) with parallel tales and tellings (how the tale is presented to direct a reader's attention to selected parts or aspects), we examined how many of these originally mythic images were refashioned through midrash to develop specific themes of divine ontology that early readers would have felt to be active. Yet this was not only a linear process. We also appreciated how the interplay between genres—their fugue of exegesis and understory, prooftexts and narrative events—reshaped meaning as a reader mediated both. As familiar symbols were drawn near, from the distant realm of myth into Scripture and its rabbinic reading tradition, they re-revealed divine being in a new dynamic form. That gradient of meaning from myth to midrashic retelling, is, I have argued, the basis of the interpretive process that generated the dense weave of this introductory section;[362] a collection that was recollected with Part 1 and, gradually, influenced an interpretive framework for the entire two-part composition. We will revisit this latter proposal when we study the composition (chapter 5). For now, with just a step forward in time and method, we turn to the medium-scale question of how Part 1 first became a collection in its own right.

---

362. In I. Heinemann's term, "bringing near of the distant." See Redfield, "Creative Historiography Today," 413. On how I think this section was edited into Part 1, see chapter 3 §*Chronological Layers* and n. 491.

3

Genealogy and Birth of the Literary Collection

In our story of how the meaning of these strange tales changed with their readers, we reconstruct the reader along two axes—synchronic (hermeneutic) and diachronic (historical)—in order both to develop our constellation of reading and to identify the lines of dis/continuity between readers' interpretive problems and frameworks over time. So far, this approach has yielded two historically specific implied readers whose different ways of interpreting the tales we studied in the Introduction and chapter 2, respectively. The first is a reader who knew the most stable feature of the tales: their attribution to the *teller* and related oral formulae as well as other stories that he told. This reader was familiar with a *raconteur* who played the role of traveler to the West but was, in fact, overwhelmingly a product of Babylonian tradition. By canvassing types of stories that he told, and the ways in which readers reacted to or built on such tales directly—in his tales themselves, or by adding tales built and retold along similar lines—we pointed to themes and tendencies that shaped his rabbinic reception in Babylonia. And we managed to do so without assuming that readers had access to any further material. For them, Rabbah was a popular narrator and visionary traveler to exotic realms, whose tales were not always taken seriously or understood, without reducing their speculative or entertainment value. Paradoxically, his tales' strangeness—lack of a strong received meaning—may have led to their retelling and survival; just as it makes them an apt case for my thesis that meaning is reading.

As we developed this profile for the first reader, we tested an idea in our constellation: the *reading tradition*, which refers to highly contingent ways that historically specific readers give meaning to parts or aspects of a text. Reading traditions may not leave explicit traces such as glosses of words. But we can detect them by seeing what readers do with a text (or do not). One reading tradition of Rabbah's narrative persona, for instance, was reflected in a new introductory formula for new tales by later tellers added at the end of his, suggesting that theirs, like his, were read with skepticism. Another reading tradition extracted legal norms—or raw data like big sizes—from his tales. This showed us a positivistic kind of reader, who admired the teller's proximity to the Land of Israel but had no interest—even avid disinterest—in his narratives as such. Discovering these faint and fragile reading traditions cautioned us against assuming that one true or original meaning of these tales was universally accepted but then degraded or lost. They are irreducibly strange; they mean only what each of their readers has made them mean.

In chapter 2, we reconstructed a reader with a robust set of tools for making sense of Rabbah's nonsense. This was a reader with some awareness, not only of the collection's first unit, but also of the dense biblical context and mythological background of its cited verses, as well as reception of those images and biblical sources by early Palestinian and Babylonian rabbis. Such a reader would have read the unit against the backdrop of these biblical verses and their reading tradition so as to create a fugue, a point/counterpoint hermeneutic structure. In this interpretive framework, the myth of YHWH's Battle with the Sea gained new meaning as it intersected with contemporary *realia* and thought patterns closer to the world of the study-house. This, in turn, led readers to reflect on the ontological structure of their deity. For such readers, I argued, this fugue's theme was divinity's ontological unity with itself and even with the rebellious Sea, despite apparent binary opposition to such mythic forces of nature. This is a more cogent approach to those tales' relation to their intertexts than dualistic, mechanistic, magical, or nationalistic readings of scholars who oppose Myth to Exegesis. By showing instead how this point/counterpoint between myth and midrash re-revealed YHWH's being and restored order to a chaotic, hostile cosmos, we developed part of our constellation: the tension between *tale* and *telling*. This section of the tales (I–III) began as myth. Yet its form and style, or telling, is that of midrash. By exploring how readers made sense of this genre gap and mediated it in their experience, we saw not so much *what* the text meant as *how* they made its meaning.

In this chapter, we encounter a reader who knew both more and less than these others: the entirety of our collection of tales—Part 1, what I call the Adventures of Rabbah & Friends. Here, we consider the meaning that readers could have created from this collection as such. In approaching them, my primary goal is to imagine how meaning was created from Part 1 by the first readers to access its contents in their current order. Its editors' choices imply a new reader. As the oral collection was performed "live," real readers responded to their creation. Over time, further gaps arose between audiences of this more-or-less-complete collection and its later editors, who made small textual changes. Those changes reflect editors' awareness of the original collection's literary conventions. They also show new questions and sensibilities. This analysis thus tracks the work of *collection* and *recollecting* by generations of editors; the *literary language* that they developed from past tellings to make their collection work as a whole; and how those changes affected its telling for their readers (listeners) in a live setting. Conversely, it shows how different readers responded to our collection differently over time: from its original Amoraic audience, to later anonymous answers to questions by later readers, to even later scribes, who "corrected" it in line with competing conventions of collection and canon.

While I thus allow for interaction between the collection's editors and "live" audience of their oral text, as well as changes within the editor-reader dynamic over time, I focus on our collection as a meaningful whole, structured into parts by its own literary language and structural conventions. Proceeding from general to local scales of analysis, we will examine this collection's placement in its tractate; boundaries (beginning/end); internal structure; and poetic combination of stress, sound, and sense. After a pause to summarize this analysis in terms of our constellation, I then offer a basis for a relative internal chronology of Part 1. These snapshots of how editors' poetic choices guided a reader's attention and interpretation of the collection as a literary unity, which was then lightly remarked upon and altered for new readers by new editors, will be useful when we turn to its late ancient cultural and later interpretive histories.

Placement

As we will see, our two-part composition is often called a digression or an interpolation. This is generally a negative description, stressing its disconnection from the literary context. Yet digression has many forms and uses, arguably more so in oral-performative literatures.[363]

"I shall show you the measures of the much-roaring sea," sings Hesiod, "I who have no expertise at all in either seafaring or boats" (*Op.* 646).[364] His disclaimer of expertise in sailing is a thinly veiled claim to expertise in poetry: the only time he took a (tiny) sea voyage, he adds, he retraced

---

363. David Morrison Kirk, "The Digression: Its Use in Prose Fiction from the Greek Romance through the Eighteenth Century" (PhD diss., Stanford University, 1960), 12–53; Julia Haig Gasser, "A Structural Analysis of the Digressions in the *Iliad* and the *Odyssey*," *HSCP* 73 (1969): 1–43; Shadi Bartsch, *Decoding the Ancient Novel: The Reader and the Role of Description in Heliodorus and Achilles Tatius* (Princeton, NJ: Princeton University Press, 1989), esp. 12–14, 144–55; and Shadi Bartsch and Jás Elsner, "Eight Ways of Looking at an Ekphrasis," *CP* 102.1 (2007): i–vi. I treat Part 1 as more *digressio* than *egressio*: a text stylized to be in creative conflict with its context. (See Quintilian, following Andreas Härter, *Digressionen: Studien zur Verhältnis von Ordnung und Abweichung in Rhetorik und Poetik* [Munich: Fink, 2000], 44-52.)

364. Hesiod, *Theogony, Works and Days, Testimonia*, ed. and trans. Glenn W. Most, Loeb Classical Library (Cambridge: Harvard University Press, 2006), 139.

the route of Homer's heroes and won a contest in song.³⁶⁵ Not despite but *because* this poet has no real "experience of many-bolted ships,"³⁶⁶ his poetic discourse on ships and naval commerce, before and after his pseudo-disclaimer, gains in poetic credibility; for "the Muses taught me to sing an inconceivable hymn." Further, by turning sailing into a metaphor for poetry, he steers nautical vocabulary back to his home turf.³⁶⁷ Thus—from a formal perspective, quite like our collection—a digression, in which a poet questions his own authority on the very subject that commands his audience, becomes a signature set-piece of didactic art.³⁶⁸

Over a millennium later and an *oikoumenē* away, another learned discourse on naval commerce swerves into lyric as its popular and loquacious teller, Rabbah bar bar Hanah,³⁶⁹ interrupts to recount the sea's measures (huge) and roaring (much). Not on his own authority, but on that of unnamed seafarers, he recounts their travels and then his own: at sea, in the desert, to the ends of the earth. Learned peers and successors interrupt—clarifying, debating, insulting him—but cannot resist adding similar tales of their own. Then, the Talmud seems to resume its discussion of the sale of a ship where it left off as if nothing strange had been said.

Yet the legal context is not unrelated to our collection, clearly distinct as the two are. One way that we can approach their relationship is by contrasting how other nonlegal and legal texts are related in the same chapter of this tractate. This contrast points to roads *not* taken by whoever placed our collection of strange tales in its legal setting. First, some nonlegal and legal materials are so tightly bound that the very distinction is arbitrary. Either readers drew no distinction between law (*halakhah*) and non-law (*aggadah*), or they did but concealed it.³⁷⁰ Second, in some cases, there is a more marked distinction of legal and nonlegal sources. The structure of

---

365. Following Deborah Steiner, "Nautical Matters: Hesiod's Nautilia and Ibycus Fragment 282 PMG," *CP* 100.4 (2005): 347–55, at 348–50.

366. On Hesiod's "measures" (unlike the measures in our text, which mainly function to convey scale), see Laura M. Slatkin, "Measuring Authority, Authoritative Measures: Hesiod's *Works and Days*," in *The Moral Authority of Nature*, ed. Lorraine Daston and Fernando Vidal (Chicago: University of Chicago Press, 2004), 25–49.

367. For this reading of the structure of Hesiod's nautical unit, his authorial *sphragis* or "seal," see Ralph M. Rosen, "Poetry and Sailing in Hesiod's *Works and Days*, " *ClAnt* 9.1 (1990): 99–113.

368. Richard Hunter, *Hesiodic Voices: Studies in the Ancient Reception of Hesiod's Works and Days*, Cambridge Classical Studies (Cambridge: Cambridge University Press, 2014), 52–57.

369. On the impossibility of being sure to whom the first two tales were originally attributed, see n. 74. By the time of the collection, listeners more likely attributed them to Rabbah, as the next set of tales is attributed to him.

370. For instance, the description of Shmuel's father's business practices (b. B. Bat. 90b) may have originally been a separate tradition but is cited there only for a specific legal point. Similarly, the unit that follows it, on migration to and from Palestine (90b–91b), connects legal with nonlegal texts in an equally inextricable way.

Genealogy and Birth of the Literary Collection 127

the Talmud's discussion makes the distinction hard to ignore, even as it bridges it.

In the latter cases, the distinction between legal and nonlegal materials is maintained and, in some cases, heightened. Through wordplay and thematic associations, however, it then becomes less pronounced. In these sections of the chapter (b. B. Bat. 78b–79a, 88b–89a), terse legal analyses of the Mishnah are subjoined by homiletical dilations on themes of divine judgment and punishment. In the first such pairing of sources (78b), a creative etymology of a word in the mishnah for "donkey foal" (*seyah*) that sounds like "conversation" (*sihah*) leads into an exegesis of verses and traditions related to speech. This series of exegeses uses further creative etymologies, recycling another etymological play on "donkey"/"conversation" twice to make a moral metaphor of a mishnah. (Compare "ass"/"jackass" in our collection, XIIb/XIIIb). By digressing on a word/theme, then, the Talmud spins normative discourse based on, yet also clearly distinct from, its basis in a word in a law in the Mishnah.[371] Similarly in the other section (88b), anonymous legal analysis of measurements in another mishnah leads to a series of traditions in the name of Rabbi Levi. This begins with a lesson on false "measures," supplemented by similar anonymous homiletical sources. Mishnah again becomes metaphor—as is common in the Talmud's transitions from legal to moral discourse.[372] This second pair of sources uses a formally similar bridge from legal to nonlegal material. Nonlegal material follows a mishnah directly, begins with a clear (and clearly strained) verbal or figural association, and ends a Gemara. After that, a new mishnah is quoted and a new topic starts.

No such patterns of recollecting legal and nonlegal texts—of Talmudizing a mishnah—hold for our Part 1. It is neither inextricably tied to legal material nor formally bridged with it in the same manner. It does not tie up a commentary on a mishnah. On the contrary, as I said, after Part 2, the Talmud resumes its prior legal discussion. This long independent sort of unit is usually at the head of a chapter or tractate, not in the middle.[373] So we should wonder about the meaning, for its editor and for

---

371. The repeated etymology of the Mishnah's word ("one who goes after pleasant talk [*sihah na'ah*]") stands both for the wicked—who create false etymologies to support heresy—and the Gemara itself, which pursues "true" etymologies to condemn them and to derive moral lessons from Scripture and tradition. The editors thus signal their own method of putting together the talmudic passage, and acknowledge that etymology can be dangerous.

372. Rubenstein, *Talmudic Stories*, 36; Wimpfheimer, *Narrating the Law*, 135–38; Wasserman, *Jews, Gentiles, and Other Animals*, 121–49.

373. See n. 147; Vidas, *Tradition and the Formation*, 48–81, esp. 57 n. 27; Uzziel Fuchs, "The Redaction and Objective of the Opening *Sugya* of Tractate *Baba Batra*" [Hebrew], *Sidra* 23 (2008): 83–105, at 94–96. Some disruptive texts are in the middle of tractates, e.g., a dreambook (Berakhot 55a–57b; see n. 792) or medical treatise (Gittin 68b–70a; see Amsler, *Talmud and Late Antique Book Culture*, 177–219). We lack a systematic study of how interpolations

their reader, of this choice to sandwich our composition between two thin blocks of mishnah commentary. Free association (the mishnah mentions a ship, so the Talmud adds sea yarns),[374] is too vague; it renders this choice almost meaningless.

I propose that the placement of the collection of tales arises from the internal structure of the preceding mishnah (m. B. Bat. 5:1), which has three parts: a list of items implicitly included in the sale of a ship; a list of items *not* so included; and a qualification that any item *may* be so included if the seller makes a declaration to that effect. The Gemara begins with a series of glosses on the first list, followed by a *baraita* listing more items implicitly included. Those items, too, are glossed, then their glosses debated. Rather than proceed to the second list, however, our composition now appears. Only after the entire long nonlegal composition, followed by a commentary loosely tied to the *third* part of the mishnah (about what it means to "acquire" a ship in the first place), do we rediscover a tiny fragment of a comment on the *second* list in the mishnah. It is a single Amoraic gloss (which reappears later in this chapter and may even be transferred from there).[375] The neglected part of the mishnah in the Gemara is, therefore, its second list: the items *not* included in the ship's sale, that is, sailors ("slaves," *'avadim*) and "pouches."[376] Having said what it can on the mishnah, the commentary trails off.

If we now see that Rabbah begins to recite tales of his "sailors" precisely where a *word* for sailors *should have* been glossed in the mishnah, our text's placement makes sense. Instead of glossing a term for sailors, the Gemara cites sailors' tales. Unlike the other bridges between legal and nonlegal material in this chapter, then, the Gemara's associative principle

---

relate to their contexts. See Shamma Friedman, "Aristotle in the Babylonian Talmud?: A Scholastic Interpolation by the Talmud's Anonymous Glossator," *Maarav* 21.1–2 (2014): 311–317; Shai Secunda, "The Talmud of Babylonia," *Oqimta* 10 (2024): 347–77, at 367–74, citing his forthcoming study of digressions.

374. Abramson, *Baba Batra*, 89 nn. 16–17: "Because this deals with a 'ship,' the Talmud attached tales of journeys through the seas and deserts"; Eli Yassif, *The Hebrew Folktale: History, Genre, Meaning*, trans. Jacqueline S. Teitelbaum (Bloomington: Indiana University Press, 1999), 217: "The problem deals with seafarers, so it is their stories that are presented here"; A. Weiss, *Literature of the Amoraim*, 273: the text follows the *halakhah* "in an unmediated fashion"; Stemberger, "Münchhausen und die Apokalyptik," 62: "The Gemara ... transitions immediately to *aggadaic* dicta in the name of seafarers.... The long *aggadic* text could be deleted from its context without the slightest detriment to a reader of the commentary." For another counterargument, see my discussion in chapter 1 at nn. 154–157.

375. 77b = 78b (Rav Pappa's gloss on *'antike*). The fact that it is so far out of order in relation to the *mishnah* suggests that it was transferred to supplement the commentary. At 78b, by contrast, it fits the discussion neatly.

376. Perhaps because the Gemara repeats and does discuss the same declaration regarding other transactions, which are covered in this chapter (78a) and elsewhere in the same tractate (65b, 67b), it was originally seen as redundant.

is neither creative etymology nor commentary, but a narrative link to a neglected word in the law, which makes up for its thin reading tradition of that particular law (or uses it as a creative opportunity).[377]

This lends the digression a more Hesiodic profile for readers of its literary collection. Like Hesiod's *sphragis*, in our tales the reader will encounter a set-piece, starring a poet who knows nothing of ships (but still has plenty to say about them). This boosts the performative-didactic ambience of what would be, otherwise, a mundane discussion of naval commerce. No wonder our tales became a parade example, for some medieval readers, of *aggadot* that "speak of some novelty contrary to custom or some paranormal phenomenon; which offer us no evident contribution of faith or moral succor, but merely recall a story, which contributes to the scholars' relaxation as they begin [their lesson] *with jesting words* [b. Shab. 30b]; a pause from the gravity of investigating the text and toil of recitation and memorization."[378] If we miss its subtle link to the mishnah, our tales' placement does suggest a mere pause for levity. Only if we grant that digression is itself a literary form, with many potential meanings, might an ironic comment on the telling (a dubious teller, as opposed to an authoritative law); a novel recollection (between legal content and nonlegal content about ships); and other such interpretive moves become audible again among the editors and their audience. It is uncertain how this digression form made sense to them. But we must assume that it did, and speculate.

Boundaries

Before we sharpen those speculations by analyzing Part 1's literary structure and chronology, a word on the division between Parts 1 and 2, which I view as originally distinct. Stemberger has made the best counterargument for treating both parts of our composition as a "planned literary unity." If we look at the text as we have it now, I agree that it is a unity, and I have found further support for his claim that both parts are linked by *Querverbindungen* ("lattices") so as to make them interpretable as one.[379]

---

377. At chapter 1, nn. 154-157 (see n. 374), I proposed a similar verbal link between the tales and their legal context: a word, *butsiyya'ta'*. The two explanations are not mutually exclusive and fit together in the compound logic of an oral text. The *mishnah* called for a comment on "sailors." The previous Gemara mentioned *butsiyya'ta'*. Why not add a sailors' yarn about a *tsutsita'*?

378. Yedayah Ha-penini (d. c. 1340), in Jacob Elbaum, *Medieval Perspectives on Talmud and Midrash* [Hebrew] (Jerusalm: Bialik, 2000), 198. On why he insisted that these "jesting words" receive an allegorical interpretation, see Isadore Isaac Twersky, "Yeda'ya Ha-Penini's Commentary on the 'Aggadah" [Hebrew], in *Studies in Jewish Religious and Intellectual History Presented to Alexander Altmann*, ed. Siegfried Stein and Raphael Loewe (Cambridge, MA: Harvard University Press, 1979), סג-פב, at סה.

379. These lattices between Parts 1 and 2 include: (i) The unit of measure *parasang*

I disagree with Stemberger, however, on how—and how suddenly—those lattices were created. Rather than by one editorial hand at one point in time, I see them as emerging gradually and intertextually over a few generations, in ways that will develop our constellation when we study the larger composition (chapter 5).

For now, some of the best evidence for my view requires no such detailed analysis: the two parts are in different languages. Part 1 is in Aramaic (with some Hebrew),[380] whereas Part 2 is in Hebrew (with some Aramaic).[381] Stemberger tries to subsume the entire two-part composi-

---

("Persian mile") is repeated in both parts (Stemberger, "Münchhausen und die Apokalyptik," 66 n. 3). Further, "three hundred *parasang*" appears at the very beginning of Part 1, while "three *parasang*" (followed by the number "three and thirty") appears at the conclusion of Part 2. We might see these base-three numbers as an *inclusio* device for the composition as a whole (base-three *parasang* measures run through Part 1: IV, VIIIb, XI, XVIIa). See further n. 250, n. 449. (ii) Not only is a major theme of Part 2, the Leviathan, also explicit in the final subsection of Part 1 (XVIIa, XX), but the Leviathan was easily read into Part 1 by the earliest commentators (VI, see n. 235). (iii) Not only is "gazelle of the sea" (*'urzila' deyama'*), which Part 2 compares to Leviathan, verbally and mythologically akin to the "day-old male aurochs gazelle," but some manuscripts in fact read "gazelle of the sea" *for* "day-old male aurochs"—a hybrid figure, defended by Rashi, who interprets it as a monster that is located "on the shoreline" (see n. 163; compare Rev 13:1). Even if that is a textual corruption (see Tosafot at n. 163), it supports an early association between the two figures, which spans the two parts. (iv) As Stemberger notes, both parts use the motif of the banquet for the righteous in the eschaton, when they will feast on primordial creatures like the fish (Leviathan), bird (Ziz), and beast (*Behemoth*; Ginzberg, *Legends*, 1:31–32 n. 127). Yet Part 2 pictures the Leviathan at this banquet (74b–75a), which in turn strengthens an eschatological interpretation of the banquet of a "giant fish" in Part 1 (VIa); and Part 1 (IXb) mentions the Ziz, which is also at the banquet in early sources (see n. 775); furthermore, an eschatological gloss in Part 1 (Xb) links the Ziz directly to the banquet motif. In sum, I added four lattices to support an *eventual* literary unity of both parts. However, the textual distribution of the lattices supports my counterargument that these links arose gradually over time. Only the eschatological gloss (Xb) and three-*parasang* measures are in Part 1. The rest are in Part 2 or early medieval commentators who already had both parts. Modifications of Part 1 in light of Part 2 are scant and minor, indicating that it is earlier. Part 2 was modified in light of Part 1 because it is later, and these retroactive changes to Part 1 were later added.

380. In the Aramaic Part 1, Hebrew is spoken only by characters whom a reader might expect to speak it: the Palestinian Rabbi Elʻazar (Xb); the Heavenly Voice (XIIIa); Qorah and his assembly (XIV); and Palestinian Tannaim (XX). This is not perfectly consistent: some Palestinian Amoraim speak Aramaic (XVI, XVIII)—which is also quite in character for them—and the Heavenly Voice speaks Aramaic, in some mss. (IXa) or all mss. (XVIII). On why its language alternates, see Vered Noam, "Why Did the Heavenly Voice Speak Aramaic? Ancient Layers in Rabbinic Literature," in *The Faces of Torah: Studies in the Texts and Contexts of Ancient Judaism in Honor of Steven Fraade*, ed. Michal Bar-Asher Siegal, Tzvi Novick, and Christine Hayes, JAJSup 22. (Göttingen: Vandenhoeck & Ruprecht, 2017), 157–68; Smelik, *Rabbis, Language, and Translation*, 131–34. In manuscripts, we find oral-formulaic interjections in Hebrew (ms. פ ln. ע"ר.קפ.יג"א; ms. וו, ה ln. א"קצ.ו"ט), but the fact remains that Part 1 is essentially in Aramaic.

381. In Part 2, even Babylonian exegesis (Rav Aha bar Yaʻaqov, 75a) and anonymous dialectic appear in Hebrew. Aramaic is reserved for introductory formulae typical of the

tion under his genre label, "Apocalyptic" (see chapter 1 §*Apocalyptic*). He therefore marshals the language gap to support his argument: this bilingual Aramaic/Hebrew genre, he says, mimics that of a famous Jewish apocalypse, the book of Daniel. Thus, Part 2 recasts Rabbah not just as a *raconteur* of bizarre sights but as a visionary, whose visions it parodies. By grafting an eschatological meaning onto his tales, Part 2 "controls," hermeneutically, Part 1.[382] If the tales in Part 1 are "a dream upon the ocean" (as some Geonim said),[383] Stemberger contends that Part 2 offers its interpretation—one that is openly hostile to dreams and visions.

Neat and tidy as this solution is, again it puts the generic cart before the textual horse. The talmudic parallels to Rabbah's tales do not allow us to date Part 1 as contemporary with or later than Part 2.[384] Scant evidence for intervention in the text of Part 1 indicates it was probably transmitted intact before the composition was put together in its two-part form.[385] Rather than an imitation of Daniel, the distinct linguistic profiles of the two parts, and lack of textual "lattices" running from Part 1 to Part 2 (almost all run in the reverse direction), point to transmission of distinct sources. Part 2 was clearly modified to link it with Part 1, but, as the reverse is less true, then it is legitimate to treat Part 1 as an originally independent earlier source, and to ask how it would have been edited and received on its own terms as we have it.

---

scholastic dialectic; a gloss on a word in Gen 1:21 that is marked as Babylonian *targum* (74b); a self-contained anonymous exegesis (74b); an exegetical remark by the Babylonian Mar Zutra (75a); a brief anonymous discussion of Rabbi Yohanan's comment on Zech 14:10 (75b), followed by an anonymous discussion in Hebrew, joined by Rav Pappa's comment in Aramaic (75b); and a story of Rabbah's, attributed to an "elder" (75b; note its formula, *I myself have seen*, which is a refrain in Part 1). From this linguistic profile, we can classify Part 2 more precisely as a Babylonian collection scaffolded onto a hefty body of Palestinian midrash (mostly attributed to Rav and Rabbi Yohanan), where Hebrew is used if it is not quoting an Aramaic speaker. In support, I would adduce (1) an etymological midrash which *only* makes sense in Aramaic (*kadkhod*, 75a) attributed to *Palestinian* Amoraim (or angels: see Joseph Yahalom, "Angels Do Not Understand Aramaic: On the Literary Use of Jewish Palestinian Aramaic in Late Antiquity," *JJS* 47.1 [1996]: 33–44, at 33); (2) a story that has a Palestinian parallel in Pesiq. Rab Kah., retold in a more fluid Hebrew/Aramaic (75a; note the Babylonian's archaic Hebrew, באשר, and the Palestinian's Aramaic insult, ריקא, see n. 699); (3) use of Babylonian Hebrew forms (! XX: see n. 496).

382. Stemberger, "Münchhausen und die Apokalyptik," 71: "The second Hebrew part bestows sense upon the Aramaic part, which appears at first glance to be rather colloquial and anecdotal as well as fantastical."

383. Cited by Rabbenu Hananel and, through him, Maimonides, Ritva, and others. See Yaakov Elbaum, "Rabbi David Darshan of Krakow and the Hermeneutic Rules That He Collected for *Aggadah* and *Midrash*" [Hebrew], *Asufot* 7 (1994): 281–302, at 293 n. 38.

384. See Introduction §*The Teller*.

385. These interventions, which I set in parentheses (IV.46/ד.מ"ב and V.54/ה.ג and XIIa.159/ד"נב.ק), are minor. They clarify the size of two places (IV, V) and cite an independent tradition to explain a narrative detail (XIIa).

Structure

Now that I have made a case for an original literary division of the composition's two parts, I offer an account of structural devices in Part 1, which signal its different types of textual subunit, its settings, other principles whereby its units are arranged, and the poetry of its performance. This analysis is mainly synchronic, although I also consider how variations in manuscripts reflect the reception of those structural conventions among oral editors and later scribes. I then assign §*Chronological Layers* to this account. First, I aim to show how an audience who had most of Part 1 was led to make meaning from the tales according to how its structure and poetry focus attention on the textual form and content. Those literary features reflect originally oral texts, of which some scribes transmit written-style tellings whereas others preserve or emulate an oral style.

Voice

The core subtypes of tales in Part 1 are the *adventure* and the *vision*. They correlate to distinct literary voices. Pace Yassif,[386] I would not call this entire collection a "story-cycle," as not every vision is a story, whereas an adventure is a story of a particular kind. (As shorthand, I do call them "stories" or "tales"; see Introduction §*The Tales*.) To define a story technically, with Jonah Fränkel, as a dramatic tension between two events,[387] it is hard to call a vision a story. Either it does not contain two events (IV, XVI, XVIIa) or there is no obvious tension between those events (V).[388] The vision impresses us with vivid imagery above all else: a vision is marked with words like "I myself have seen," "saw," "resembled." By contrast, an adventure is a narrative with vividness (especially visual or other sensory detail), an exotic setting, and a strong sense of movement. All adventures contain visions. Not every vision is an adventure.

This adventure/vision distinction is formally consistent but not always clear in the text as we now have it. As just noted, in three cases it was elided by adding a conclusion, turning a vision *into* an adventure.[389] Still,

---

386. See Rubenstein, "Story-Cycles," 227–30.
387. Fränkel, "Chiasmus in Talmudic-Aggadic Narrative," 183–97.
388. In this respect, the formal structure of V is complex but cogent. V.51–57 are an enigmatic vision, with two added explanations (V.58–61). Only with the explanations does a narrative tension between the elements of the vision become clear. IIIb has a similar structure. It begins as a vision (IIIb.32–38), continuing the previous vision (IIIa) in form and content. But in the conclusion, the vision is "narrativized" with the aid of a verse (IIIb.39–41), just as IIIa was at the end (see n. 230, n. 279).
389. To restate the analysis of n. 388: if we read the stories in III and V until their concluding lines (IIIa.31, IIIb.39–41, V.58–61), they are just visions of Hormiz doing impressive tricks and giant animals swallowing each other. Only remarks at the end introduce tension,

Genealogy and Birth of the Literary Collection 133

this distinction is useful to show how units were expanded and transmitted (§*Chronological Layers*) and how the very idea of vision became a problem over the cultural and canonical circulation of the whole two-part composition (chapters 4–6).

Unit divisions and subdivisions in our text of the collection (Appendix §*Translation, Part 1* and §*Edition of Part 1*) are based on their content. This forces us to analyze its form and chronology, rather than smuggle assumptions about them into the text's presentation. Each unit begins with "X said," "Y recounted," or a compound ("X said … Y recounted to me"; "He said to me"; "X recounts"). A subunit is added if a scene changes and/or speakers speak who were not originally present.[390] By those criteria, Part 1 has XXI units, each with no more than one subunit.[391] I call the subunit a *remark* to reflect that, as presently formulated,[392] it can only attach to a primary unit. (For instance, the remark at VIIIb.103–4 is not "The *gildna* fish of the sea has two fins" but "*That one*, he's the *gildna* fish of the sea, who has two fins.") The remark is both logically and chronologically a secondary unit; the Adventure/Vision, a primary unit.

There are two types of remark: *anonymous* (translated in parentheses) and *attributed* (always in a subunit, labeled with b/ב). They differ in both syntax and form. Anonymous remarks are always in the middle of an adventure/vision; attributed remarks are always at the end. Anonymous remarks are rhetorical question and answers ("And how big is X? – Y *parasang*," IV.46; V.54), or an independent tradition ("For it has been taught that …" XIIa.159).[393] Anonymous remarks are all directed at the reader of the polished text: they assume that the reader does not know something about the primary unit that one needs to know in order to

---

a hierarchy of the vision's elements, and an evaluative dimension. They tell readers that the message of the vision is the execution of Hormiz and great strength of the tree, making it a story.

390. One adventure/vision is not subdivided at Rav Pappa the son of Shmuel (V.60–61) as, unlike other remarks, his remark does not add a change of scene or new details about the content of the adventure/vision. It is directed to the same audience.

391. One adventure/vision (VI) is subdivided because of a break in time rather than a change of scene (VIb.73: "When we returned the next year, we saw …"). By that logic, technically, XXI should have three subunits. However, the short remark that marks a break in time (XXIa.260, "The next year, I came back …") simply completes the first scene, after which is the typical break between a *vision* (of herbs/coals) and a *remark* about the vision (XXIb.262: "the herbs were … and the coals were …").

392. Probably, some remarks did not originate with the current adventure/vision but in bodies of oral tradition like zoology (VIIIb.102–4); botany (XXIb.262–63); myth and exegesis (IXb; XVIIb.211–12). For example, note that in VIIIb and XVIIb, Rav Ashi remarks about a "fish of the sea" and "goat of the sea" (for the fish, see b. Ber. 44b, b. Hor. 12a; for the goat-fish, see n. 238) They seem to come from different discourses but extend their vocabulary into these tales.

393. See n. 91. These anonymous remarks were likely added as small notations by Stammaim or Geonim.

understand it. By contrast, attributed remarks are all directed at the teller or the telling of the primary unit. Some attributed remarks are glosses ("X said ... that is ..."; or, in mss. V, O,"When I came before X, he said ... that is ...").[394] One remark goes beyond the gloss, augmenting and supporting the primary unit's content.[395] One attributed remark (V.61) goes so far as to support its claim with a firsthand observation, defying an implicit contrary view ("If I hadn't been there,[396] I wouldn't have believed it"). Conversely, another pair of attributed remarks attack the truth of an adventure/vision, as well as the teller's stance toward it ("You should have" done X and Y ... !")[397] The latter are a limit-case of the attributed remark: they are introduced by the teller of the adventure, so they seem to be an anticlimax *within* his adventure and, in that sense, part of a primary unit, like Rav Pappa in V.60–61. But their style and function are like other attributed remarks: they support or attack the primary unit based on evidence (firsthand observation; secondhand observation; logic; or tradition). Thus the basic formal distinction holds. Anonymous remarks are outward-facing — they turn to the reader of the text. Attributed remarks are inward-facing — they focus on the primary unit that precedes them or primary adventure/vision to which they were added.

This distinction between kinds of remark is useful because it correlates closely to different ways that each type of remark responds to the text; to different readers of the text; and to different points in time. That is, the anonymous remarks have their own ideological tendencies. They are scholastic, measuring sizes in the adventure/vision.[398] They are pious, censoring its language. As Uzziel Fuchs has shown (see Appendix §*Thieves in Heaven (?!)*), one arose in debates in Geonic academies, and found its way into manuscripts. The others are formulae that are always anonymous in the Talmud,[399] and which intrusively notate a detail in an adventure with a scholastic turn of phrase ("For it has been taught that ...").[400] These anonymous remarks, then, are evidence of a substantially later reception of Part

---

394. VIIIb.102; Xb.134; XVIIb.211; XXIb.262. See further §*Attributions and Other Introductory Formulae.*

395. VIIIb.96–101: "When Rav Dimi arrived, he said ... and there is one who says ...."

396. V, O: *seen it,* harmonizing with other formulae in the unit: V.52, "I *myself have seen* ..."; V.58, "Come see...." See further §*Attributions and Other Introductory Formulae.*

397. XIIb.165; XIIIb.174.

398. See n. 88, n. 463.

399. The question כמה + verb ה.ו.י ["How big is/was it?"; IV.46, V.54, 59] is anonymous in all but two of approximately sixty-six instances in the Talmud, in both *aggadic* and *halakhic* contexts. The sole clear exception is b. Qidd. 12a. Redfield, "Stance in *Aggadic* Terminology."

400. "*For it has been taught* that one who takes something from them can't walk" (XIIa.159). As Bacher says (see n. 91) this participle of "complete; learn; teach" (גמירי) — in most complete mss. (H, V, M) and a Geniza fragment (N) — is "an introduction to material that differs from traditional dicta [*memrot*]." That material is often nonlegal — e.g., similar "traditions about biblical history" — and can be either anonymous or attributed. See David

1, and not for the reader whose perspective we emphasize in this chapter. They serve as a contrast to the attributed remarks, which do address our reader, take them into the action, and complicate or render more potentially meaningful all of the narrated content in the Visions and Adventures.

Setting

Now that we hear its voices (named tellers, and earlier/later named/unnamed commentators), we may further note four principles governing how the collection's twenty-one units were arranged. The first global principle is each unit's *setting*. As Stemberger notes, the settings alternate: Sea (I–II; VI–IX)–Desert (X–XIV)–Sea (XVI–XX)–Desert (XXI). In one unit (XV), the setting is not clear. This was already a point of debate between medieval authorities. What some manuscripts call the place "where the earth and firmament kiss" cannot be the ends of the earth.[401] For some, it is left unsaid; for others, the sacred center of the Land of Israel; for others, a scale model of the cosmos that Alexander the Great made and left behind.[402] Regardless,

---

Weiss Halivni, "Reflections on Classical Jewish Hermeneutics," *PAAJR* 62 (1996): 21–127, at 105–7.

401. This story shares much with the Greek myth of Geryon, whose realm is where sky and earth meet, in the western extremity of Ocean, also a land of theft (of cattle), to which Heracles sails in the "bowl of the sun," where the sun rests overnight as it revolves (M. Davies and P. J. Finglass, *Stesichorus: The Poems*, Cambridge Classical Texts and Commentaries 54 [Cambridge: Cambridge University Press, 2014], 230–43). XV is also set "where earth and firmament touch," with motifs of "thieves" and the "orb of the firmament revolving"—and Rabbah is a traveler to the West. In another, related image from a Syriac version of the Alexander Romance, the hero travels to "the place where the sun enters the window of heaven" (E. A. Wallace Budge, *The History of Alexander the Great, Being the Syriac Version, Edited from Five Manuscripts of the Pseudo-Callisthenes, with an English Translation* [Cambridge: Cambridge University Press, 1889], 148). See Appendix §*Thieves in Heaven* (!?), n. 3. A beautiful myth attributed polemically to Jewish tradition imagines a gap in the firmament that God left open at creation as a signature of authorship, for only God can close it (Petrus Alfonsi, *Dialogue against the Jews*, trans. Irven M. Resnick, Fathers of the Church: Mediaeval Continuation 8 [Washington, DC: Catholic University of America Press, 2006], 90–91. This gap is the realm of the north wind, whence all evil enters the world: Pirqe R. El. 3, ed. Börner-Klein, 25. See Ch. Merchavia, *The Church Versus Talmudic and Midrashic Literature* [500–1248] [Jerusalem: Mossad Bialik, 1970], 104 [Hebrew]).

402. "It cannot be that he is showing him the actual end of the world, for the world is 500 years' walking [distance from the firmament; b. Pesah. 94b]. Rather, he is showing him a place in a certain desert where they touch" (Rabbenu Gershom *ad loc.*). Rashbam (b. B. Bat. 74a s.v. היכא דנשקי ארעא ורקיעא) adds, "the Land of Israel is the *center* of the world (as it is written: *that dwell in the midst of the land*, Ezek 38:12), and this is the location of Rabbah bar bar Hanah." The Rif, citing a Geonic story also attested in versions of the Alexander Romance (see chapter 4), says, "A king of Alexandria built a place in the desert where he made a replica of the firmament and a revolving orb, to display his wisdom; and that is what Rabbah bar bar Hanah saw" (Alfasi, *Responsa* [Pittsburgh: Machon Ha-Rambam, 1954], §314). See n. 92. I thank Ezra Chwat for help with the latter source (personal communication, 12 June 2019).

136 *Adventures of Rabbah & Friends*

everyone agrees that this adventure is still part of Rabbah's travels through the Desert, so does not really violate the alternation between Desert and Sea, despite lacking their usual introduction ("Once we were/I was traveling in the Desert/in a ship ... and I/we saw ..."). This may be an exception for a reason: as the most extreme location to which Rabbah travels, it is beyond just another Desert story. It is an apt conclusion to a collection of extreme settings. It is also ambiguously set in the Desert or Air; and, in a more subtle sense, the latter element is also in play.

Indeed, a more glaring violation of this alternation between Sea and Desert appears in III–V: the vision of Hormiz in Mahoza, leaping from one bridge of a river to another (IIIa–b); followed by the vision of an aurochs "as big as" Mount Tabor (IV); followed by the vision of immense animals that swallow each other until the largest comes to rest in a great tree (V). All of those visions mention real places that are less cosmological than geographical: three in Babylonia, one in Palestine.[403] However, insofar as all three have a strong vertical orientation, we could call their shared setting the element of Air.[404] For Rabbah's travels, this would yield the pattern Sea–Air–Sea–Desert–Sea–Desert. (That pattern is stronger in ms. H: the aurochs in IV is "at"/"upon" Mount Tabor, not "as big as" Mount Tabor.)[405] In this analysis, the logic of the alternation between settings is more complex than antithetical cosmic extremes (the wet and the dry, the ends and the center of the earth). Rather, the vertical axis not only adds a contrast of high/low but also accents the opposing axis of center/periphery. The Sea and Air tales explore the upper and outer limits of the cosmos, whereas, in his quest into the interior (with his ear to the heart of darkness, XIV, and culminating at the very center of the cosmos, XV), Rabbah explores complementary terrain to the other tellers, expanding a reader's cosmological vision.

Whether one prefers Stemberger's analysis of the pattern of the collection's settings, or mine, both encounter a contradiction. Why is the final unit in the Desert (XXI) not at the end of Rabbah bar bar Hanah's travels in the Desert (between XIV and XV)? If it were, the collection would keep the alternation (Sea–Air–Sea–Desert–Sea), including in the final six tales after Rabbah disappears.[406]

---

403. The only other real place cited in the collection (and a mythical one too) is Mount Sinai (XIIIa.186). On the creative tension in I–III between its realistic Persian setting and mythology, see the introduction to chapter 2.

404. Stemberger does not explain the settings of IV–V; my model is less an alternative than a supplement to his.

405. Ms. ה, ln. א״מ.ד. The scribe of ms. ה distinguishes between "at"/"upon" and "as big as" in the same introductory line of the next vision (ה.מ״ט), writing כי אקרא (vs. mss. פ, כאקרא ב ;ב, ms. וו באקרא), so this is not just a mistake.

406. The explanation (Stemberger, "Münchhausen und die Apokalyptik," 65–66) has the same flaw as his lack of explanation for the settings of IV–V: it is too miscellaneous,

In literary terms, I suggest that this "inconsistency" is due to a second poetic principle, which shapes the contents of each unit as well as their arrangement. Much of this collection's lyricism arises from the interpenetration of alternating domains that its cosmological structure has established. I call this a *metamorphic poetics*, one in which "everything is mixed together. The sea strikes the stars, the sky."[407] This poetics operates in two ways. First, it creates and reverses binaries. The sailors *go down to the sea* but are *lifted ... up* to the stars by an immense wave restrained by *a grain of sand* (I); then *the wave that sinks a ship* is beaten back down and *subsides* (II). Hormiz begins by *bounding* in the air but goes *down to the depths* (III); a giant fish is *hurled ... ashore,* where each part of its carcass metamorphoses into food, oil, and towns (VI). Both Hormiz, in the Air, and a giant fish, in the Sea (VIIIb), race horsemen (on dry land, in both cases?) and their arrows (in the Air). Another giant fish is a true hybrid, covered in *sands* and sprouting *a thorn-plant* (VII); just as a bird spans two elements, *standing up to its ankles in the water / and its head reached the firmament* (IXa). The Desert is a portal to *water* (XI), hellish *smoke* (XIV), and a corner of *the firmament* (XV): a liminal space, allowing for passage between cosmic elements. The eyes of another giant fish are *moons*, its nostrils *fords* (XVI); Leviathan's are *eyelids of the dawn* (XX). Another fish is a *goat of the sea* (XVIIb). The action of one adventure, on the deck of a ship, pans dramatically from the depths of the Sea to the Air, as a *sea-serpent, bird,* and *salted birds* vie for underwater treasure (XIX).

The cumulative effect of these metamorphoses is more than the sum of its parts; by opposing and juxtaposing settings, which mirror planes of the cosmos, the text intensifies movement within and across scenes,[408] an impression of dynamism and surprise, much like the impact of rapid montage in a film.[409]

---

undermining his own analysis. To say "perhaps the redactor ... simply had in mind a different schema for the composition's structure than we would perceive today" is to admit defeat.

407. "Omnia miscentur. Pulsat mare sidera, caelum." See G. A. A. Kortekaas, ed., *The Story of Apollonius, King of Tyre: A Study of Its Greek Origin and an Edition of the Two Oldest Latin Recensions,* Mnemosyne 253 (Leiden: Brill, 2004), XI.16, 128.

408. There is great confusion in manuscripts of XIX (after XIX.233/ln. יט.רל״ה) about which character does which action: the second sea-serpent, the wondrous bird, or the rabbi and other sailors. This is probably because the pronouns that abbreviate each character were originally disambiguated by the oral performer's gestures, became unclear in transmission, and were disambiguated differently by scribes who put referents back into the text. The sheer amount of back-and-forth in the story itself and high number of characters (six or seven; other stories have three or four at most) also entail that this "confusion" is a result of the story's dynamic poetics. Compare VIIIb.101 and see n. 460.

409. Stein, *Textual Mirrors,* 69: "Experience is described through a mixture of the notions of time and space—such that the idea of time condenses the concept of space—in order to heighten certain aspects." On the concept of "rapid montage" in Eisenstein and phenomenology, see Redfield, "Towards a History of Presence."

The second, closely related aspect of this metamorphic poetics is its *wobbly binaries*. By this, I mean the technique of introducing inverted motifs in uneven progression such that, rather than "replace" or directly correspond to the one before it, each motif transfers selected pieces or aspects that fit its new context and help to propel a transition to the next context. In other words, it is not simply that binaries between cosmic domains/settings mix and are inverted as the text proceeds, but also that, despite their global clearly separated order, motifs inside each setting oppose and intermingle with their boundaries in a similar manner. Motifs themselves also have piecemeal, accumulative, less binary ("wobbly") interrelationships.

Consider the motif of Fire in the first adventure and vision (I–II). It is introduced only briefly, in the form of the "heat" of the star's corona, which nearly burns the sailors. Then, in II, a similar threat presents itself: the "flame" on the crest of the wave. Finally, a verse on the Burning Bush inverts the motif, with reverse effect. Rather than be fixed high on the vertical axis (the heavens/the crest or "head" of the wave), now the element of fire moves downward as the sailors strike the wave. Rather than threaten them, it protects them. Thus, the binaries between cosmic domains and vertical axis of the cosmos remain intact (Sea/Air; High/Low). Yet this foregrounded motif "slides" or "wobbles" along the lines established by its opposed settings. A reader who watches these transitions experiences surprise as the cosmic antithesis of Water and Air is pierced and gives way to Fire, which descends to the level of Water and rears its head again, only to be broken by the Fire of the divine presence. Is the order of this universe stable? The collection's metamorphic poetics gives this question concrete form and dramatizes it in a succession of overlapping motifs across sharply distinct cosmic domains.[410]

Attributions and Other Introductory Formulae

In addition to settings, another principle of the arrangement of tales in this collection is attribution.[411] I–XV are attributed to Rabbah bar bar

---

410. Compare the motifs of the thread of *tekhelet*/tuft of wool/basket in the "orb of the firmament" (XIIa/XVIII–XIV–XV). All three have a similar function for the dynamic between binary cosmic settings: they mark boundaries: of the Desert (XIIa), the depths of hell (XIV), or the earth/firmament (XV). For Rabbah, as for the reader, these motifs are inserted in the cosmic structure of the collection in order to probe its gaps. In testing a gap, the motif mutates to reflect interference with the structure: neither fully apart from nor fully absorbed into it. (The thread is cut but must return; the tuft is charred but it survives; the basket is absent but accounted for.) The motifs are an index of the cosmological structure of the collection which help readers to grasp its structure. See n. 589.

411. A. Weiss takes attribution as the sole organizing principle (*Literature of the Amoraim*, 273–74). He sees Rabbah bar bar Hanah, then Rabbi Yohanan (XVI), as the skeleton of this collection—ignoring anomalous and internally complex units.

Genealogy and Birth of the Literary Collection 139

Hanah;[412] and XVI–XXI to other rabbis. (XX is an exception: its narrator is anonymous, among other anomalies to be accounted for in §*Chronological Layers*.) Others contribute to Rabbah bar bar Hanah's section of tales as well (in the anonymous voice,[413] or by name),[414] but only in a secondary remark, never in a primary adventure/vision. An adventure/vision is attributed to one and only one teller,[415] whereas remarks by as many as four speakers (VIIIb) can be attached to one of those units. The same rule ("one tale, one teller") applies to the additions at the end of the collection (XVI–XXI).

A simple limit-case illustrates this "one tale, one teller" rule, as well as the rigor of the formal distinction between primary and secondary units. An adventure is attributed to Rav Ashi (XXIa) but so is a remark (XVIIb). His remark has the same form as his remarks in Rabbah bar bar Hanah's tales (VIIIb, IXb). He tells his adventure just as Rabbah bar bar Hanah told his. That is, Rav Ashi seems to both comment on Rabbah's tales and report another rabbi's similar tale. Uniquely, then, he appears in both primary and secondary units. Yet he does so without violating the distinction between them. He tells, and he remarks, but he does not mix the two.

This distinction between primary unit (adventure/vision) and secondary unit (remark) is reinforced by the collection's third principle of arrangement: introductory formula. Only a few verbs bear three crucial functions: introducing a unit, marking it as primary or secondary, and shaping its internal structure. These are verbs of speech ("tell/say"; "recount"), vision ("see"; "show"), or motion ("travel"; "come/arrive"; "return"). In theory, these verbs have thousands of logical combinations. Yet in practice, such combinations are tightly restricted: only five combinations appear in a primary unit, only one in a secondary unit. A primary unit is introduced by (1) say ... recount;[416] (2) say ... [I myself have] see[n];[417] (3) say ... once ... travel;[418] (4) say ... come ... show;[419] (5) recount ... once ... travel.[420] (Here again, XX is an anomaly, as it is a wholesale literary construction by the

---

412. On I–II, see n. 74.
413. IV.46; V.54; XIIa.159
414. V.60-61; VIIb; IXb.
415. In a primary unit, tellers cite sources (seafarers; other rabbis; the Arab), but its attribution is still singular.
416. I–II and XXI.
417. III–V. Unit III contains a subunit with an additional vision (introduced by the formula "once").
418. VI–XI. Unit VI has a subunit with an added adventure (introduced by "return ... see"). Unit VIII has a subunit with four additional remarks (introduced by "say"). Unit IX has a subunit with a remark (introduced by "say"). Unit X has a subunit with a remark, introduced by "When I came before Rabbi X, he said ..."
419. XII–XV. Units XII–XIII have subunits: attributed remarks (introduced by "when I arrived ... they said").
420. XVI–XIX, XXI.

editors, to be discussed below). As this list shows, units with the same introductory formula are grouped together.

There are slight variations, however, among manuscripts. When transitioning from one formula to another, a longer version of the new formula is sometimes used, repeating an element of the old formula ("see"). This transition device appears between sections III–V and VI–XI, and once more in most manuscripts.[421] The first formula is (2): "say ... I myself have *seen*." The second is an expansion of (3): "say ... once ... travel ... *saw*." The repetition in the expanded formula smooths out the transition to the ear.[422] Another exception that proves the rule is the final unit (XXI) belonging, as usual, with all preceding units of its group ("recount ... once ... travel"). However, unlike those units (XVI–XIX), it begins with an added verb ("say"). This repeats part of the formula all the way back at the beginning, in ("say ... recount ... once" or, in some manuscripts "say ... recount ... once ... travel") and adds a ring structure to the collection as a whole, as is common in oral composition.[423]

Verbs in these introductory formulae distinguish primary/secondary units consistently. As we have seen, a primary unit (adventure/vision) is often introduced by the verb "say/recount"—but this is always joined by one of the other verbs of speech, vision, or motion. By contrast, a secondary unit (a remark, whether attributed or anonymous) is introduced *only* by "say/tell." This is no artifact of natural discourse but a local oral-literary convention for our collection. Some manuscripts show awareness of this convention by adjusting limit-cases to maintain it. For example, consider how introductory verbs of speech and motion are "voiced" in ms. H:

> VIIIa. And Rabbah bar bar Hanah <u>said</u>:
> Once I was <u>traveling</u> in a ship
> and the ship passed between one fin of a fish and the other
> three days and three nights
> it went upstream as we went downstream.
>
> VIIIb. <u>And perhaps you'd say</u>:
> The ship <u>wasn't moving</u> much!

---

421. Between sections I–II ("say ... recount ... I/we *saw*") and III–V ("I myself have *seen*") in all manuscripts apart from H and P, where the order of I and II is reversed.

422. Note that a unit placed later in the second section (VIII) does not employ this transitional formula. It could have been placed at the transition, without violating the Sea–Air–Sea pattern, but it was not.

423. This ring structure is even stronger in mss. P, V, and O, where the first and last units begin "say ... recount ... once ... travel." However, we cannot have our formal analysis both ways: either a ring structure between I and XXI (mss. P, V, O) or this expanded transitional introductory formula from I–II to III–V ("I/we saw"). In addition to a scribal error (see n. 154), the unstable order of I–II could reflect a preference for one or the other oral-literary structure.

When Rav Dimi <u>arrived, he said</u>:
   Like heating a kettle
   the ship <u>moved</u> six *parasang*.
<u>And there is one who says</u>:
   A horseman shot an arrow
   but could not overcome it.
<u>Rav Ashi said</u>:
   That one, he's the *gildna* fish of the sea,
   who has two fins.

According to the rule, the primary unit, an adventure, is introduced by "say" + a verb of motion ("travel"), whereas the four remarks joined to it are introduced by "say" alone. Here, however, it would be very easy to "mishear" Rav Dimi's remark as a *primary* unit. It has a verb of motion ("come/arrive") + "say" + a verb of motion ("moved"), and it points back to a topic of the adventure. It sounds like an adventure or a vision of its own.[424] Indeed, it would be, if this remark lacked its preface ("And perhaps you'd say / the ship wasn't moving much! ..."). This preface (found in all manuscripts) preserves the local literary convention by framing the rest of VIIIb as a set of remarks on Rabbah's original adventure. It makes Rav Dimi's claim that the ship *did* "move six *parasang*" into a refutation of its counter-hypothetical—not a new adventure. Without it, he would be a teller alongside Rabbah, violating the "one tale, one teller" rule.

Such a violation does not occur in any manuscript or indirect witness. However, all manuscripts, apart from ms. H, do bend these rules to an extent—especially mss. V & O. First, all manuscripts except H lack the "attribution" of the following remark; a mere placeholder in any case (VIIIb.99: "And there is one who says ...").[425] Their version of the tale adds this to Rav Dimi's remark, making it more like an independent adventure. Indeed, it makes his remark longer and more vivid than the original adventure, recycling a vision from earlier in the collection (IIIa.30–31; see n. 9, n. 279) in Rav Dimi's voice. Mss. V and O "misbehave" with the local conventions even more: they turn Rav Ashi's later remark into the conclusion *of* Rav Dimi's long secondary adventure ("*When we came before* Rav Ashi *he said to us ...*"),[426] making *both* secondary units primary. In ms. H, by contrast, Rav Dimi "arrives" like an adventurer, but he ends as he "should," in the frame of a remark. By refuting an objection to the original adventure, he keeps it going, adding color and detail, but is set apart from the main

---

424. As in P: "When Rav Dimi arrived, he said ... *we traveled* ...."
425. This formula in ms. H, ln. ח"ב"צ is very common in the Talmud for reporting a variant unattributed tradition. See Yaakov Elman, "Orality and the Redaction of the Babylonian Talmud," *Oral Tradition* 14.1 (1999): 52–99, at 62–63.
426. VIIIb.102. Mss. V and O do the same thing at IXb.119, collapsing the remark into the adventure.

action. Thus, ms. H seems to notice and reassert the collection's convention for the nested structure of primary/secondary units. This is consonant with Friedman's view (see my study at n. 1) that ms. H is no *Urtext* but is carefully edited, and that the Ashkenazi manuscripts (here, mss. O, V) are not merely corrupt but make sense of textual issues differently.

Another limit-case shows a similar relaxation and reassertion of the same convention. Here again, all manuscripts except one blend a primary unit (vision) with a secondary unit (remark).

> V: Rabbah bar bar Hanah said:
> I myself have seen:
> A certain frog who was as big as the Fort of Hagrunya
> (And how big is the fort of Hagrunya? – Sixty houses).
> A serpent came, swallowed it;
> A wondrous bird came,[427] swallowed the serpent
> and flew up and settled in a tree.
> <u>Come see</u> the strength of the tree!
> How great it was!
> Rav Pappa son of Shmuel said:
> If I hadn't <u>been there</u> [mss. V, O: <u>seen it</u>], I wouldn't have believed it.

The primary unit by the teller begins as usual with "say" + a verb of vision. It is vivid, in the first person. Its elements unfold in a fixed sequence familiar from omen texts: "I saw X that swallowed Y that swallowed Z."[428] Except for the anonymous remark in parentheses, which interrupts to clarify a detail in the vision for a new reader (if they don't know the Fort of Hagrunya, they may not grasp the point about the size of these animals),[429] everything fits the pattern of a primary unit—all the way through the end, when the bird settles in the tree. However, this vision is incomplete. The

---

427. On the Iranian mythological background of this griffin-like creature, which I call "wondrous bird" following Buyaner but was glossed as a "female raven" by medieval Jewish commentators, see Kiperwasser and Shapira, "Irano-Talmudica II," 209; Kiperwasser and Ruzer, "Nautical Fiction," 302 nn. 20–22; Daniel E. Gershenson, "Understanding Puškaṇsa (bB.B. 73:2)," *AcOr* 55 (1994): 23–36; David Buyaner, "On the Etymology of Middle Persian baškučʹ (Winged Monster)," *SIr* 34 (2005): 19–30. It will reappear in XIX. See also n. 742.

428. This form appears in oral literature from *Had Gadya* to "There was an Old Lady who Swallowed a Fly," not always with an interpretation attached. See Gen 41:1–4 and the omen in Herodotus, *Hist.* 1.78 (*Landmark Herodotus*, 45): horses eat snakes = a foreign army will destroy autochthonous people. The pattern (vision of animals swallowing animals, followed by interpretation) is mantic or omen-like. On ornithomancy (bird divination), see Martin L. West, *The East Face of Helicon: West Asiatic Elements in Greek Poetry and Myth* (Oxford: Clarendon, 1997), 46–49. E.g., in b. B. Metz. 86a, Babylonian rabbis interpret the shade cast by birds in a tree as a sign of death from heaven. See also b. Git. 68a (hero in tree vs. demon).

429. The anonymous remark also adds "sixty," which links this vision to VIa and VIIIb, and has a mnemonic function. On *parasang* as mnemonic and structural device, see n. 9, n. 250, n. 379, n. 449.

Genealogy and Birth of the Literary Collection 143

signs are visible, but their meaning is not. It must involve the relation between the size of the animals and the tree. What sort of relation?

To fill this lacuna, an interpretation is now supplied under the stock talmudic formula "Come see …!" followed by Rav Pappa's remark ("If I hadn't <u>been there</u> …"; or, in mss. V and O, "If I hadn't <u>seen it</u> …"). Put together, these lines pose a problem with respect to the collection's local structural convention, because a verb of motion and vision ("come" + "see") would ordinarily introduce a primary unit, rather than a secondary unit (a remark, which must begin only with a verb of speech). All manuscripts except O solve this problem by *not* attributing the transitional phrase, "Come see …." Because "Come see …" is unattributed, most manuscripts leave room for ambiguity as to whether that is an anonymous remark—the Talmud's voice, explaining Rabbah's original vision—or part of his vision, in his own voice,[430] respecting the collection's convention. This leaves Rav Pappa firmly within the bounds of a remark.

If "Come see …" *is* in Rabbah's voice, however, it conflicts with another convention in the Talmud more broadly. An Amora hardly ever uses "Come see …" to explain his own tradition.[431] Rather, this formula is typically set apart from its explanandum, at the end of a running dialogue, where it summarizes the point of what was alluded to earlier (and often sings its praises at the expense of something else).[432] Despite the ambiguity about its speaker, that canonical usage of the formula is also in effect here. It is also how "Come see …" was already used earlier in the collection: "*Come see* the might of your master!"[433] This competing convention is adopted by ms. O, where "Come see …" opens a secondary unit—a remark,[434] which is further set apart by attribution, not to Rabbah bar bar Hanah, but to Rava,[435] who explains his namesake's vision.[436] Ms. O thus prefers the canon's convention over that of the collection.

---

430. As simply assumed by Frim, "'Those Who Descend,'" 2.

431. A possible exception is b. Meg. 28b, where "Come see" is at the end of an extended elegy by an Amora.

432. In b. Ber. 30b; b. Hul. 122a; b. Hul. 126b, "Come see" is used this way in dialogues between Amoraim. It is not clearly attributed in those cases. In some manuscripts, as here, it seems like an anonymous rejoinder blended in with the dialogue. In b. Eruv. 6b; b. Yoma 57a; b. Taʻan. 23b; and b. Nid. 20b, it does seem to be attributed in the dialogue.

433. I.13. Note how similar this is to the formula in V.58: "Come see the *strength* of the tree!" Rashbam, b. B. Bat. 73a s.v. שנאמר האותי, stresses that I.13 is a remark by the anonymous Talmud, not in the story: "The Gemara is saying it."

434. See ln. א"י.א and ln. ד'.ה.ד. In both cases, ms. ב prefers the Talmud's conventional usage.

435. Ms. O attributes the vision (V.51/ח"מ.ה.ה) to *Rabbah bar bar Hanah*. It is unlikely that the same scribe would quote the same person under two different names in the same unit. (Despite the genuine ambiguity of Rabbah/Rava generally; see n. 74).

436. Compare other similar cases, where the formula is clearly anonymous: b. Git. 57a; b. Sanh. 11a; b. Avod. Zar. 26a.

Rather than errant or arrogant scribes, my claim that this crux in the text tradition of mss. V and O reflects a competition of oral-literary conventions is supported in two ways. First, as we just saw in the previous limit-case (VIIIb), ms. O (as well as ms. V, with which it often aligns) was the least respectful of the collection's way of distinguishing primary and secondary units. It has the same tendency here. Rather than respect the local convention, such that Rabbah is the sole teller of an adventure/vision and other voices are remarks, in both cases, ms. O opts to split the primary unit into a new primary unit with a new teller: Rav Dimi in VIIIb, Rava in V. In both cases, mss. O and V uniquely harmonize the new story that they have thus (re)told with what remains, in other manuscripts, a remark *about* Rabbah's original story. Their harmonization creates a dialogue between voices in a new adventure/vision, rather than a comment about an old one. Instead of "Rav Ashi said ..." mss. O and V read, "*When we came before* Rav Ashi, he said ...." This puts his remark into their new story by Rav Dimi, which itself remains a remark in other manuscripts. Similarly, ms. O creates a new vision by Rava (*"Come see ..."*). Then, both manuscripts have Rav Pappa back him up by saying he *saw* it himself;[437] not just that he was "there," as in other manuscripts. Again, this repetition of the introductory formula within the remark creates a dialogue within their new primary unit, rather than a remark about the original one. This telling is meaningfully different. Rather than swept away by the adventure, the reader joins a critical debate about it (compare XIIb, XIIIb).

To craft and sharpen its dialogue, the telling in mss. O and V prefers the Talmud's conventions over the collection's in two ways. First, as we noted, it relies on a more canonical use of "Come see ...." Similarly, it uses two tropes where other manuscripts have just one: not only a sage who "arrives" from Palestine to Babylonia, but who also "comes before" a superior sage, who then assesses the Western tradition that he imported.[438] For mss. O and V, it seems more important to simplify, blend, and ventriloquize these limit-cases of awkward primary units into the Talmud's conventions of academic debate than it is to make their (re)tellings realis-

---

437. Supported by "Rabbenu Gershom," which supplements a text similar to mss. V and O with its own glosses.

438. In legal contexts, the formula "When X arrived, he said ..." nearly always supports a position raised earlier in the debate by adducing a Palestinian Amoraic tradition; much as Leib Moscovitz has shown for "X arrived [and] said ..." in the Palestinian Talmud. See Redfield, "Redacting Culture"; "'When X Arrived, He Said ...'"; see n. 710. In this nonlegal context, whether we attribute the tradition to Rav Dimi himself, or we see him as only its conduit when he "arrived" from Palestine, the formula also works that way: it lends Palestinian Amoraic weight to Rabbah bar bar Hanah's adventure. This seems to be another case of anonymous recollectors applying the same techniques to legal and nonlegal sources, which "arrive" here in similar ways. See Jeffrey L. Rubenstein, "Criteria of Stammaitic Intervention in *Aggada*," in Rubenstein, *Creation and Composition*, 417–40.

tic. Rav Dimi and Rav Ashi were generations apart, so this direct dialogue between them is impossible, but it fits this new version of the text better.

The competition over this local literary convention goes in the other direction as well. While it is so common in our collection that it is likely original to its basis in oral tradition, these limit-cases suggest that both units (V, VIII) were also edited to preserve or to reassert it: a harmonization of another order. Who did those edits? The oral composers of the collection's later layers (Stammaim or "anonymous" generations, often identified with the Talmud's Stam or unattributed voice)? Or the later medieval scribes of our manuscripts and their *Vorlagen*—individuals who were not uncreative either, and not shy about "correcting" awkward sources? In these two cases, the nature of these variants upholding the collection's conventions seems to point back to an oral stage of transmission that is linked with the anonymous voice. The line between editing and anonymous oral content is so fluid as to be practically invisible, suggesting that these editors are better located within the Stam than among the scribes.

Recall that the "problem" of these limit-cases is the same. They risk violating two of the collection's local conventions: the rule "one teller, one tale," and the rule that a verb of speech begins a remark and not a primary unit, which must start with a verb of speech as well as a verb of motion or vision. All manuscripts except O and V solve both problems in two lines:

V.58 /ה.נ"ד: <u>Come see</u> the strength of the tree!

VIIIb.94 /ח"ב.צ"ה: <u>And perhaps you'd say</u>: The ship wasn't moving much!

In both cases, the underlined anonymous formulae overcome challenges to those conventions by "blending" the content that follows with the content that comes before. They bend the audience's ear to the conventions in order to disguise the fact that the two parts do not quite fit. In V.58, the formula conveniently mimics the collection's rule for introducing a primary unit: it uses a verb of motion ("come") and verb of vision ("see").[439] Therefore, it sounds like it extends a primary unit (a vision). The fact that it is awkward for the storyteller (Rabbah) to be explaining his own vision—thus breaking the Talmud's typical usage of "Come see ...," and the collection's rule that a teller never remarks on his own tale—may escape the ear. It remains more prominent to the listener's attention as part of his ongoing tale.

Similarly, in VIIIb, this hypothetical question-and-answer framing

---

439. This would be another example where the Talmud fills in the language of an Amora—language that we have evidence, from elsewhere in the Talmud, was missing—due partly to "linguistic causes" in the local context (*ha-lashon gorem*). Friedman, *Talmud Arukh*, 20 n. 82). I call this *ventriloquism* (see n. 477).

("Perhaps you'd say") prevents the following tradition from Rav Dimi from becoming a new primary unit, keeping it within the frame of a secondary unit or attributed remark on Rabbah's original story. Whereas, as we saw, mss. O and V do eventually depart from that convention, the other manuscripts continue to clearly distinguish between the primary and secondary units. This stock phrase is tailored for that purpose: without it, Rav Dimi's tradition about the fish's speed, and the following tradition that is recycled from earlier in the collection (IIIa.31/ג"א.כ"ח; see n. 9, n. 79), would become a new primary unit. Ms. H, editing hyperactively in line with the same convention, goes even further, adding an "attribution" for the recycled remark (VIIIb.99/ח"ב.צ'"ח). These changes suggest that the collectors, listeners, and tellers were familiar with the collection's conventions and lightly or heavily adjusted each text to fit them.

In addition to establishing each unit and transitioning between sections, as well as marking primary versus secondary types of units, these verbal formulae with verbs of speech, motion, and vision also shape the *internal* literary structure of primary units. They create subunits inside units: spinning an adventure into chains of episodes, layering vision upon vision. This is not simply a matter of adding similar material. As material is added, the shape of the text changes. Isolated events or motifs become whole three- and four-dimensional worlds.

VIa-VIb illustrate the effects of this transformation on readers of the edited collection.

>VIa. And Rabbah bar bar Hanah said:
>> Once I was traveling in a ship
>>> and I saw a certain fish
>>>> whose nostril a mud-eater entered, and it died
>>>> and the water drew it and hurled it ashore.
>> Sixty towns were destroyed by it
>> Sixty towns ate from it
>> Sixty towns salted it
>> From one of its eyeballs, they made
>>> three hundred jugs of oil.
>
>VIb. When we returned the next year, we saw
>> they were hewing from its bones
>> beams to rebuild those towns.

The content of this unit as a whole is a grand cycle of destruction, metamorphosis, and renewal. The two formulae mirror one another as beginning and end: just as the narrator *saw* the death, the next year he *returned* and *saw* the renewal. In the middle, the metamorphosis is narrated very differently, in the third person, using another literary device (numbers; see §*The Uses of Repetition*). The poetic effect is like a time-

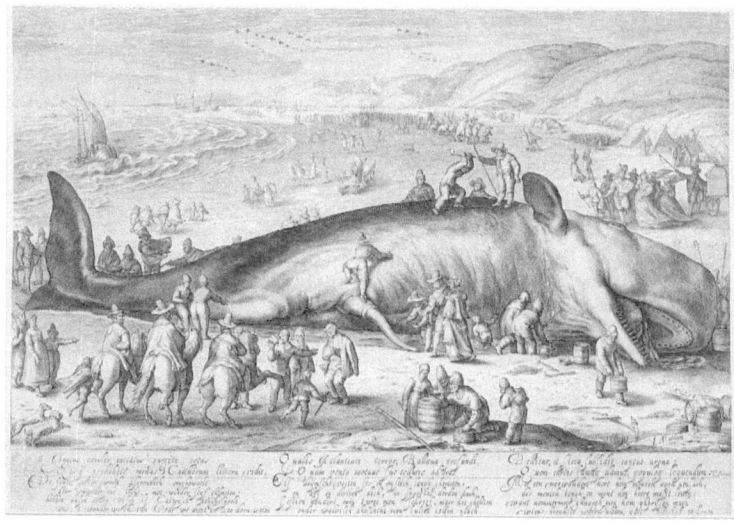

Figure 5. Jacob Matham, "Beached Whale," 1598. Metropolitan Museum of Art, https://www.metmuseum.org/art/collection/search/349137. CC licensed.

lapse photograph. The total arc of this radical change is shown, but it is "played back" at an accelerated rate to display the change itself. We see the fish crush the town; we see myriad figures scurrying about picking its bones clean, draining its eyes; we see the bleached outlines of a new town.

A break in time between oral formulae ("When we returned the next year") does not rupture the continuity of this time-lapse sequence but reinforces it, skipping straight to the weird and thrilling conclusion where it comes full circle.[440] Verbs of motion and vision (travel … saw; returned … saw) craft a narrative arc around the beginning and end of the central image. A structural role of verbal formulae is to create such timelines within primary units.[441]

---

440. See also XXIa.260–61. Here, too, a break in time emphasizes the continuity of the vision within the primary unit. In all manuscripts except H, the concluding formula is the same as VIb: *I/we saw*. . .

441. "Once" generally creates the timeline within which particular episodes/visions occur. But it can also do the opposite—adding an episode into a broader timeline (I.5) or concatenating one vision with another (IIIb.32). A tricky temporality is created by the formulae "When I came before Rabbi X, he said …" or "When I came to the house of study, they said…." As noted above (n. 426, n. 438), these formulae basically introduce remarks about the preceding adventures, secondary in form and content. However, some are still part of the adventure, and they even take it upon themselves to conclude or retell the narrative! Rabbi Elʻazar tells the narrator how it *will* turn out in the end-times (Xb.134); the sages in the

The Uses of Repetition

Repetitions of verbal formulae also shape a sense of pace and progress within primary units, even at the level of the individual line or phrase. This is clear in the travels through the desert with the Arab. Most of these begin "come ... show" followed immediately by "went ... saw" (XII–XV). The Arab names a destination; the teller immediately arrives and describes it. Their journey does not take time; again, the Desert is not so much a space as a network of portals. This intensifies the destination, concentrating attention on a single place or image.[442] In one adventure (XIV), the effect is more pronounced as it is repeated within a single adventure: first in a visual form and then in an auditory form.

> He said to us:
> "Come, I will <u>show</u> you the Maw of Qoraḥ."
> He <u>showed</u> us a certain crevice, from which a wisp of smoke was appearing.
> He brought out a tuft of wool,
> brushed it in water, and wrapped it around his spear, and inserted it.
> It was burnt and charred.
> He <u>said</u> to me: "Listen, now, to what you <u>hear</u> from here."
> And I <u>heard</u> that it was saying: "Moses and his Torah are truth, and they are liars!"
> He told me: "Every thirty days, Gehinnom stirs them *as flesh in the caldron.*"
> And it <u>said again</u>: "Moses and his Torah are truth, and they are liars!"

This adventure divides cleanly in half: "I will show you ... he showed us" and "Hear ... I heard." The first half builds suspense, revealing only a faint trace of the horror beneath the surface. The second half confirms this when the teller hears the agony below. At the climax, the Arab adds information which makes the agony more vivid and incessant. This, in turn, is amplified by a repetition of the rebels' infernal screams. The adventure ends on a high note. Its internal development is driven by the elegant doubling and repetition of formulae.

---

study-house tell him what he *should have* done (XIIb.165; XIIIb.174). All of their interventions are grounded, not in any detail of the narrative, but in a legal-didactic attitude: the world of the study-house that is constituted as outside of, and directly opposed to, that of the visions/adventures. (Stein, *Textual Mirrors*, 65–66: "For the Sages ... chaotic outburst is impossible.") They are in the story, but not of it.

442. Like the poetics of the Aqedah per Erich Auerbach, *Mimesis: The Representation of Reality in Western Literature* (trans. Willard R. Trask. Princeton, NJ: Princeton University Press, 1953 [1946]), 9–10: "... the impression that the journey took place through a vacuum; it is as if, while he traveled on, Abraham had looked neither to the right nor to the left, had suppressed any sign of life in his followers and himself save only their footfalls."

Again, groups of manuscripts vary in their handling of this literary convention. It is most consistent in ms. H, which preserves or—thanks to a conscientious scribe/editor—hyperactively reasserts it. Like this hand, the corrector of ms. O also seems to reassert the convention, by deleting a unique word that departs from it even though that word suits its context (XIV.185).[443] In Rabbah's last adventure (XV.189), the convention is preserved or reimposed in mss. H and P, whereas it is not in ms. O ("Come ... show" is followed only by "went"). In other manuscripts, it seems totally absent.[444]

Perhaps this split in uses of the convention is a split between oral and written poetics. Repetition can have the effects that I suggested in an oral medium. In a written medium, its function is less clear. It may seem monotonous and redundant. Thus, manuscripts that do not belabor the formula by repeating it move quickly to the action to form scene sequences. Rather than a uniform pattern, repeated at the start of each adventure, these manuscripts split actions into parts: one part continues another. For a written text's reader, this organization is more logical. For an oral text's audience, it may have been confusing or made memorization harder.

So far, we have examined the uses of repetition exclusively in terms of a small set of introductory formulae that demarcate, order, and hierarchize the units in our collection. But repetition and soundplay are, as Fränkel showed in scores of cases,[445] a bedrock of rabbinic poetics. They not only play the structural role that we have examined, but also link primary to secondary units, as well as linking sections of the collection comprised of multiple units. In these uses of repetition, too, manuscript traditions vary widely, but sometimes we can still suggest a poetic rationale for their variations. Beyond the introductory formula, then, we may consider two further devices where repetition and soundplay are variously used to shape the collection.

The first is the use of repeated numbers.[446] Rhetorically, as others have

---

443. יד.קפ"ב. Ms O: *He said to me: Listen and hearken to what it's saying. / And I heard ~~a voice~~ that they were saying ...*

444. At ln. טו.קפ"ח, only ms. P has the exact convention; the line is missing in mss. V, M, E. See יג.א"קס"ה: here, in the same group of mss. (V, O, M, E), the convention is again absent ("Come ... show," followed only by "saw"), but again appears in ms. P (and a Geniza fragment, ms. N: "Come ... show ... I came and saw"). Contrast mss. P, V, N, O/mss. H, M, E, B at ז"עק.יד. There, again, mss. PN align against mss. ME. The former keep the convention, the latter not.

445. Jonah Fränkel, "Paronomasia in Aggadic Narrative," in *Studies in Hebrew Narrative Art throughout the Ages*, ed. Joseph Heinemann and Shmuel Werses, ScrHier 27 (Jerusalem: Magnes, 1978), 27–50.

446. For a fresh discussion about earlier sources, see Beth A. Berkowitz, "The Rhetoric of the Mishnah," in *What Is the Mishnah?: The State of the Question; Proceedings of a Conference at Harvard University*, ed. Shaye J. D. Cohen, Jewish Law and Culture Series (Cambridge, MA: Harvard University Press, 2022), 187–203, at 188–90.

noted, large numbers can be figures of hyperbole.[447] We do not care that the fish destroyed *sixty* towns; we care that it was a lot.[448] Structurally, however, the exact number does matter. The repetition of numbers both organizes textual units and connects them. Sometimes a repeated number is the glue for a whole unit (IIIb):

> Once
> > two mules were saddled for him
> > on two bridges of the Ravnag,
> > and he bounded from one to the other and back again
> > and he held two goblets of water [or: *wine*] in his hands
> > and he poured from one to the other and back again [= *from one to the other and from one to the other*]
> > but did not spill a single drop [= *but did not drop a drop from them*] ...

The number *two* evokes the bounding arc of the vision: between two mules, on two bridges, holding two goblets, Hormiz leaps back and forth. The last line contrasts sharply with his outsized antics: not a drop falls. It causes a shift in focus, from *two* to a solitary drop at the center of the foreground, or a stream of liquid suspended in the air between the bridges. This small still point does not erase the massive, riotous background, but brings it forward. The vision remains in flux until its *denouement*, which arrests and inverts the ceaseless motion with an ironically apt verse:

> ... And upon that day,
> > *They mount up to the heaven, they go down again to the depths*:
> > the authorities heard of it and brought him to an end.

In another vision, numbers are used to structure and stretch a figure's proportions.[449] In other units, numbers represent structures of time: a long span and a regular cycle.[450] In the adventure which spans *three days*

---

447. Frim, "'Those Who Descend,'" 11; Ben-Amos, "Talmudic Tall Tales," 33.

448. See also V.54. On sixty as a figure for immensity in rabbinic literature, see b. Ta'an. 10a (*baraita*; compare y. Ber. 1:1, 2c); b. Ber. 57b; b. B. Metz. 84b. See Rashi, b. Shabb. 90b s.v. שיתין; Tosafot b. B. Qam. 92b s.v. שיתין רהוטי רהוט; Maharal, *Netsah Yisrael* VI.6; Israel Zeligman, *The Treasury of Numbers* [Hebrew] (Baltimore, MD: Schulsinger, 1942), 144–47. See further n. 751 on other meanings and uses of the number "sixty."

449. XVIIa: first, the fish says, it is merely a *minor creature of the sea*. But then, it continues, it is *three hundred* parasang / *and prepared for the mouth of Leviathan*. With each line, the vision's proportions elongate, as in a fun-house mirror, extending toward the immensity of the Leviathan. The number functions as an amplifier. Similarly, in XVI, a fish has *two* [mss. V, O] *eyes* and *two snouts* like *two moons* and *two fords*. The comparison amplifies its proportions dramatically, and the repetition of the number is what makes the comparison stick.

450. IXa.115 *seven years* and XIV.186 *thirty days*.

and three nights across a distance of *six parasang,* time converts into distance; the compound number of days/nights acts as an amplifier, intensifying the impression of the fish's size.[451] Numbers also form connections across units: a wave rises *three hundred parasang* to an area of *forty griv,* just as an aurochs spans *forty* and *three parasang;* much later, in the Desert, the traveler is *eight* or *three parasang* from water. (All of the *parasang* measures, including those later in Part 2.C, are a ratio of three or four). This repetition may also have a mnemonic function or appeal to a taste for symmetry. Regardless, it is not mechanical but varies at a fixed ratio, and is regularly applied to transform the scale of an image. This technique reveals the work of verbal artists with acute visual sensibilities.[452]

This literary feature does not vary widely across manuscripts, though it is worth noting that, in ms. H, the journey that spans *three days/three nights* and *six parasang* is actually *sixty parasang* in all other manuscripts.[453] That variant could be for the same poetic reason: 3 + 3 [time] = 6 [distance] works well within the unit to amplify the scale of this particular voyage, whereas *sixty* is repeated in the collection as a figure of hyperbole, and therefore works better to connect this unit with others; inviting, for example, comparisons to another giant fish (VI) and giant frog (V).[454] Yet again, ms. H seems to be edited in a way that is hyperactive in contrast to others, in order to reassert the collection's precise oral poetic conventions.

Another common use of repetition is the repetition of words/roots, often accompanied by soundplay. Again, this reinforces and embellishes the literary structure both within a unit and across units. For example, roots for *lift* (*d.l.y*/ד.ל.י), *cast* (ר.מ.י), and *raise* (ר.ו.ם) recur throughout the text. In the first unit (by the order in mss. H, P), the roots are intertwined:

I. ... Once, a wave <u>lifted</u> us up

---

451. *Pace* Ben-Amos, who sees *"realistic and empirical* descriptive measures" here, and says that "the chain or accumulative narration is another literary device which increases *realistically* the measurements" of the frog, serpent, bird, and tree in V ("Narrative Forms," 127–28). What is empirical or realistic about the day, night, year, kettle, or *parasang*? Either they are hyperbole or precise, but nonrealistic, amplifiers of time/proportion.

452. Compare Francesco Lubian, "Jeweled Sea Storm Descriptions in Zeno of Verona (and Juvencus)," in *A Late Antique Poetics? The Jeweled Style Revisited,* ed. Joshua Hartman and Helen Kaufmann, Sera tela (London: Bloomsbury Academic, 2023), 173–85; and, in the same volume, Michael Roberts, "Epilogue: The Jeweled Style in Context," 259–68.

453. VIIIb.98/ח.ב"צ.

454. In some manuscripts, textual units are also grouped by mnemonic formulae (at the beginnings of IV, XI, and XVI) and scribal section marks (ms. O, ב.ט"ז and ד.ל"ט). But it is hard to tell what the units under each mnemonic have in common, or why the scribe of ms. O inserted those section marks. As for mnemonics, though they overlap across manuscripts to an extent, they are inconsistent; mss. M and E even use words in them that are no longer in our text (see יא.קלי"ג). They possibly reflect later composition (Fishbane, "Great Dragon Battle," 49–53), but say little about the early oral collection.

and I saw the cradle of a star
and it was as great as the sowing of forty *griv* of mustard;
had it <u>lifted</u> us any higher, we'd have been burnt by its heat.
The waves <u>cast</u> their voices in chorus [= *one wave cast its voice to its fellow*]: . . .

Here, too, repetition functions as an amplifier of the adventure. The immense wave *lifted* the sailors into the heavens; the threat of being *lifted higher* intensifies the heat of the stars. Then, just when it seemed they could not go any higher, one wave *cast its voice* across to the next. Like the vision of Hormiz bounding in the air, repetition structures the staggering verticality of the image. Also like Hormiz, however, the waves' height is subdued by a verse invoking a superior power—the highest of all. One wave's dialogue with the other continues:

. . . "So, is there anything in the world you've left alone and not destroyed?"
"Let us go, you and I, and destroy it."
And replied:
"Come see the might of your master!
I cannot pass so much as a grain of sand the width of a thread,"
as it is said:
Fear ye not me? saith the LORD. Will ye not tremble at my presence?

Further repetitions of *lift* and *cast* similarly emphasize the vertical cosmic axis, foregrounding the structure of the text's settings in the act of traversing it. They bring a vision into focus or mark the climax of an adventure by transgressing the borders (Sea/Air/Desert) where the collection takes place. Some such uses verge on the seriocomic, even grotesque:[455]

IV. Rabbah bar bar Hanah said:
I myself have seen:
A day-old gazelle who was as big as Mount Tabor
(And how big is Mount Tabor? –Forty parasang).
The length of his neck: three *parasang*;
The cradle of his head: a *parasang* and a half;
and he *let loose* [= *cast, r.m.y*] a turd and stopped up the Jordan.

Or:

Xa. And Rabbah bar bar Hanah said:
Once I was traveling in the desert

---

455. Boyarin, *Fat Rabbis*; Zvi Septimus, "Revisiting the Fat Rabbis," in Fonrobert et al., *Talmudic Transgressions*, 421–56.

and I saw those geese
whose wings drooped
because of their fat
and a stream of oil
was flowing out of them.

We said to them:
Have we in you a portion of the world to come?
One *lifted* up its thigh at me, and one *lifted* up its wing.

Xb. When I came before Rabbi El'azar, he said to me:
In time to come, Israel shall be judged on their account.

In both of these units, as in two others,[456] the pivotal moment of the action is the verb *cast* or *lift*. Whatever these strange creatures represent, it is how they *move* on the vertical axis that establishes their immediate relation to the teller and reader, who watch them from ground level. As they rear up out of the Sea, as they hurl excrement or pour oil from the Air—with vaguely obscene or hostile gestures—such monsters transgress the order of the cosmos; that is, the narrative world. Just as prooftexts then appear to subdue the towering waves and leaping Hormiz, so, in these cases, do remarks attributed to rabbis ("in time to come"; "That one is the goat of the sea") comment on the monsters with the effect of domesticating them in the study-house's didactic idiom,[457] rhetorically enfeebling them and literally cutting the sea-goat down to size.[458] Juxtaposed with the collection's global structure, however, their transgression remains captivating. Like the repetition of numbers, this moment when the monsters *lift/cast* out of the element where they "should" remain, according to the rules of the narrative world, is highly consistent across manuscripts, suggesting an early oral-poetic origin.[459] Perhaps, here again, the group of variants

---

456. XVI.199 and XVIIa.206: *a certain fish lifted up its head*.

457. Stein ("Believing Is Seeing," 13): "In summing up this known paranormal experience, Rav Ashi endows it with an interpretation that is, by definition, drawn from the world of known concepts."

458. Reading XVIIb.212 ("it *is* lean") with mss. H, P, E. Jonah ibn Janah (d. ca. 1055) defines this word with m. Ter. 1:8 (in Shraga Abramson, *Mi-pi ba'alei leshonot* [Jerusalem: Mossad Harav Kook, 1988], 206), citing Saadia Gaon (in Abramson, *Mi-pi*, 281), who takes it as a synonym for "thin" (רזה), as in Ps 109:24 and b. B. Bat. 32b (פרה כחושה). Ms. M reflects not "lean" (כחישא) but the reading "roves about [בחישי] with its horns to seek its food" (Rashbam b. B. Bat. 74a s.v. דבחישא; see discussion in my study cited at n. 1; Rabbenu Gershom, *ad loc.*). That is an inferior reading: see b. Yevam. 120b; n. 87, n. 239.

459. Its only variations are a unique addition of "lift" (ד.ל.י.) at the end of one adventure (Ms. P XIX.240/ב"רמ.יט) perhaps to link with the next unit, and a resistance to that repetition (by adding "from the sea/the water"), in one group of manuscripts (mss. V, O, M, E, B to XVI.199/ח"צק.טז and XVIIa.206/ה"ר.א.יז).

that avoid repetition reflects a more written style, as formulaic repetition is replaced by smoother syntax, which links actions into sequences.[460]

Poetry

Now that we are beginning to appreciate this collection's literary language—a visual orality that uses introductory formulae and repeated numbers and words; set in a world of wobbly cosmic binaries, a montage of figures and motifs who metamorphose, transgress, blur, and clash around their edges—we can examine closely a few examples of how this literary language would have affected a reader when it was realized within a single vision or adventure. Our goal now is to uncover what would have happened in a single telling, as tellers addressed a reader who was attuned to these structural phenomena and performed them aloud in a live setting. What sort of poetic performance may the literary features that we identified have enabled? How could each of these tales—or, as we will call them now, poems—introduce creative variations upon the collection's overall structure that we have just studied?

What poetic potency, for instance, could the defecating land-monster possibly have?[461]

IV.
1 *ur-zeila ba̱r yomei*
2 *d-ha̱va̱ b-ha̱r ta̱vor*
3 *m-sha̱kha̱h d-tsa̱vrei*
4   *t-la̱ta̱ pa̱r-sei*
5 *u-vei ma̱r-ba̱'ta̱ d-reishei*

6 *pa̱r-sa̱ u-fa̱lga̱*

---

460. Notably, this is the same group of manuscripts that use what I suggest is a more written style (see n. 444). Another example is the phrase *but [he/we] could not overcome [him/it]*, repeated in ms. H (IIIa.31; VIIIb.101; XI.147). In the first two instances, this repetition is confusing, as there are two objects in motion, and it is hard to tell which is failing to "overcome" the other. To clarify it, other manuscripts use phrases such as *but that ship stayed in front of it* (see mss. P, V, O ln. ח"ב.ב.ץ"ט. See also ג"א.ב"ה, where ms. O has the reading of ms. P but is corrected in line with ms. H). In an oral-performative setting—perhaps supplemented by a gesture—the repetition in ms. H would not be confusing. But perhaps it works less well in writing and eventually had to be abandoned.

461. In this section, I modify SBL general-purpose transliteration (see §*Note on the Text*), as follows: *tsere/tsere-yod* = *ei*; *het* = *ch*; *shewa* = - and word-initial or word-final aleph unmarked. I do not cite my translation from the Appendix but retranslate each poem to make my analysis clear. My approach here is strongly influenced by the structural poetics of Roman Jakobson and Claude Lévi-Strauss, "'Les Chats' de Charles Baudelaire," *L'homme* 2.1 (1962): 5–21.

7 r-ma̱ k-futa̱
8 us-kha̱r lei l-ya̱r-d-na̱

    The poem's vowels are introduced in the first line, the only line where they all appear: /u/ as in "boot," /o/ as in "toe," /ei/ as in "neighbor," and /a/ as in "tall."[462] Its structure rests on one opposition, /ei/ versus /a/, together accounting for the vast majority of vowels (32 of 39). The distribution of this opposition is the key to the movement of the poem. Its obvious shift, audible on even a cursory hearing, is from lines 1–5, where the ending /ei/ predominates, to lines 6–8, ending in /a/. This shift creates a two-part structure for the poem: a listener can tell that its beginning and end are quite distinct without knowing the meaning of a single lexeme.
    The poetry of the poem is not this bare structure, however, but how it departs from it. The other seven vowels, which do not fit the /ei/ vs. /a/ opposition, are distributed so as to sharpen listeners' perception of that opposition. They keep it from being either predictable or jarring.
    The dominant vowel alternation is established in the first word of the poem (ur-zei-la) and repeated immediately thereafter (bar yomei). The first departure from this pattern falls at the ends of lines 1 and 2. Here a rhyme (bar/har) is paired with nonrhyming words (yomei/tavor). This yields two pairs (bar yomei/har tavor), which are audibly interrelated, yet just as audibly violate the opposition of /ei/ vs. /a/ by introducing the new vowel /o/. Yet in fact, that apparent first "exception" to the poem's rule reinforces the rule for a listener's ear, because the vowels in this new pair that are *not* /o/ are, again, /ei/ and /a/. Thus, the stressed rhyme (YO-mei/ta-VOR) carries along the /ei/ vs. /a/ contrast: a softer echo or undertone. Further, this extends the /ei/ vs. /a/ opposition from stressed syllables to unstressed syllables. This sets up a tension between stress and rhyme that will be intensified as the poem unfolds.
    The /ei/ vs. /a/ opposition intensifies through the rest of this first "stanza" (lines 3–5). All lines end in /ei/ with the opposing vowel /a/. Their alternation remains audibly marked: tsa̱vrei/pa̱r-sei/ma̱r-ba'ta d-reishei. Predictability continues to be avoided by the same means: a systematic tension between stress and rhyme. All lines end with rhyming /ei/ but never

---

    462. In any attempt to reconstruct poetry, especially from a tradition like the Babylonian Gemara, where poetry is not well studied, there are many questions such as stress, vowel length, and dipthongization, that would affect the realization of certain words. Of course, there are also poetic variations in the witnesses. However, none of the patterns that I identify, based on ms. H, rests on a single instance. In fact, textual variations are less common, in my poetic terms, than they are in terms of grammar or semantics (which makes good sense for an oral tradition). Historical linguists of this dialect can surely correct and adjust my analysis without, I think, invalidating it. My vocalization is informed by *JBA*; the Comprehensive Aramaic Lexicon; and the Yemenite tradition: *Talmud Bavli Me-nuqad 'al pi Masoret Yehude Teman*, ed. Yosef Amar Halevi, vol. 14 of 20 (Jerusalem, 1980).

on a stressed syllable. Attention is therefore divided between /ei/ and long /a/, which falls in every stressed syllable (*TSAV-rei* –> *t-LA-ta PAR-sei* –> *mar-BAʻ-ta*). This balance of alternating vowels is maintained by marking each vowel in a different way. Further tension between the two competing vowels is enhanced by the distribution of contrastive consonants around them. Rhyming /ei/ is concentrated in open final syllables (*YO-mei, TSAV-rei, PAR-sei, u-VEI, REI-shei*), mostly unstressed at the end of a line. As rhyme strongly bonds all /ei/ syllables, it would be monotonous to reinforce that bond by adding further assonance or patterned stress.

By contrast, /a/ is paired with consonants that echo each other or repeat themselves. From lines 2 to 3, the consonants around /a/ fuse alliteratively as the stress shifts (*ta-VOR* → *d-TSAV-rei*). From lines 4 to 5, unstressed -ta follows stressed syllables (*t-LA-ta* → *mar-BAʻ-ta*), a pattern extended in line 6 (*u-FAL-ga*). This keeps the sound /a/ alive to the ear. For the sake of further contrast with /a/, the /ei/ vowel is preceded by sibilants which lose stress and grow less emphatic as they fall back in the mouth (ts → s → sh; ***tsav-rei*** → *par-sei* → *rei-shei*). The power of line-final rhyme to drive the listener's anticipation as a poem unfolds and create a sense of closure, which threatens to throw attention too far toward the leading vowel /ei/, is thus offset by systematically focusing attention on /a/ vowels earlier in the line.

This balance between /ei/ and /a/ is reflected also in the global structure of the poem: /ei/ seems to trade places with /a/, which becomes the new rhyme at the end of the line. This transition from stanza 1 (ln. 1–5) to 2 (ln. 6–8), however, is more dynamic than a mere swap. It is aided by the poem's sole repeated word, which has *both* competing vowels as its endings. This word is introduced in stanza 1, ending in /ei/ (*PAR-sei*), where /ei/ is the leading vowel. Yet stanza 1 is an environment where, as we just saw, /a/ and /ei/ remain in constant tension through the opposition of rhyme to stress (*t-LA-ta PAR-sei u-VEI mar-BAʻ-ta d-REI-shei*). When the same word repeats in the next line, as stanza 2 begins, /a/ takes the lead, drowning out /ei/ almost entirely (*PAR-sa u-FAL-ga r-MA k-FU-ta us-khAR lei l-YAR-d-na*). But this victory of /a/ is short-lived. The final line restores balance, both by placing the competing /ei/ and /a/ together in equally weighted syllables (*us-khAR lei l-YAR-d-na*), and by mirroring the first line (compare line 8, *us-KHAR lei l-YAR-d-na*, with line 1, *ur-ZEI-la bar YO-mei*). This last line finally achieves closure by overcoming the poem's structural opposition. It enhances symmetry with the first line by starting the last line with /u/: the same rare ("leftover") vowel.

Our analysis so far has shown how this poem uses sound and stress to do what poems do: to create parts, with a sense of tension, balance, and movement between those parts, and to focus a listener's attention on subtle transition points between them. If we can correlate our analysis of its poetry with its semantics, especially at these transition points to which its sound and stress draw attention, it stands to reason that a listener heard such words as more meaningful. Here is a translation that aims to reflect this analysis of its meter and rhyme:

> kid gazelle, one day old,
> who was on Mount Tavor
> his neck-length stretched out straight
>   three miles far
> and the width of his head's cradle
> a mile and a half
> he flung out a crap
> and got the Jordan dammed

As we have established, the transition word between the two stanzas of the poem, which is also the only repeated word in the poem, is "mile/miles." This word, uniquely, shifts from one side of the opposition which structures the sound of the poem over to the other side. The plural, *par-sei*, has the /ei/ vowel, whereas the singular, *par-sa*, has only the /a/ vowel. In stanza 1, where /ei/ is the marked vowel because it rhymes at the end of the lines, it appears as *parsei*. In stanza 2, where /a/ becomes the marked vowel, this word reappears as *parsa*. The transition word thus tracks the poem's core sonic structure and brings it to a listener's ear.

In parallel, at the semantic level, "miles/mile" plays a structural role that we might call "scalar." This poem obviously has much to do with size and how big the animal was. But it is one thing to state that an animal was big, another to convey this in a poetic form that mirrors and intensifies its message. Nor are the lines with "miles/mile" the only way that one could have made this statement poetically. Consider a hypothetical version without them:[463]

ur-zeila bar yomei	kid gazelle, one day old,
d-hava b-har tavor	who was on Mount Tavor
r-ma k-futa	he flung out a crap
u-skhar lei l-yardna	and got the Jordan dammed

---

463. The version is not just hypothetical (we still have it!), and may be more original. If the formula "how big/much was X?" was added by anonymous editors, as seems highly likely (see n. 399), then at least the line about the size of Mount Tavor (IV. 46) is a late addition, and possibly the lines about the size of the beast's head and neck were added as well (IV. 47–48). Compare V, where the same anonymous question-and-answer ("How big/much ...?") is repeated. If we cut both repetitions there (ג.ה/V.54 and ה"ג.ה/V.59) we still have the poem; all we lack is an exact measure of a monster that we already know is big, or a heavy-handed gloss of a lesson that was clear enough from the poem itself (i.e., that a big tree is very strong). Those anonymous remarks interrupt and, I think, spoil the poem by addressing a reader who is somewhere else.

The short version has the same sound structure and same message about its size (even if we do not spell it out by adopting the reading of mss. P, V, M, E, "*as big as* Mount Tavor"). But its brevity squanders the effect. Even without the vulgarity added in English translation for rhyme ("crap" is really just "ball of dung"), the short version is more like a crude limerick. The first stanza conjures a strange, majestic newborn creature on a lofty mountain. The second stanza abruptly pivots to his nether regions; which, on the contrary, block the flow of an equally famous and sacred river. The limerick marks its violent transition from the sublime to the grotesque by hammering on stressed /a/ and /u/: *r-MA k-FU-ta us-KHAR lei l-YAR-d-na* mimics the first stanza's sound but, in so doing, mocks its possibilities for meaning.

By contrast, in the longer version that we have now, mile markers of the animal's size work together with the poetic meter to smooth the transition from high to low, lofty to less so. The poem preserves the element of surprise but uses it to evoke wonder rather than mockery. Instead of creating the huge newborn beast only to cut him back down, he grows and acquires fixed proportions as the lines grow in tandem: from six syllables to five, then from eight syllables to five. One sees him above the mountain, his broad head reaching up to the clouds:

his neck-length stretched out straight	*m-shakhah d-tsavrei*
three miles far	*t-lata par-sei*
and the width of his head's cradle	*u-vei mar-ba'ta d-reishei*
a mile and a half	*par-sa u-falga*

When the poem now concludes with its terse rhymes in /a/, their effect is different. The transition from the first stanza in /ei/ to the last stanza in /a/ is gradual and indirect. As we saw, the systematic opposition of rhyme to stress balances the poem's beginning and end. This, in turn, allows the acoustic parallel between the poem's first and last lines to be heard and interpreted as a true parallel rather than a harsh satire. Instead of focusing on the contrast between the impressive height of the beast and the unsightly consequences of his digestion, perhaps the heft of his dung, like the length of his neck, is another, equally impressive matter. The lines measuring the beast with the word "mile/s," are not poetic dead weight, no mere statistical digression. In expanding the visual scale, they balance the acoustic proportions.

Nevertheless, it is odd that a poem about a giant beast whose feces plugged a whole river would select such a dull word as its focus. "Mile," Persian *parasang* (Aramaic *parsa*), has neither an interesting sound nor an interesting denotation. If, however, we consider how this word could have functioned for a listener of the larger collection, its prominence makes much more sense. The word is not only a transitional device between stanzas of this poem. It can also be analyzed, in a similar way, as a connector of several poems within the collection. As a connector, it could have done some of the same things that it does within a single poem. This would be consistent with the highly formulaic nature of poetic collections, which often use the same patterns in order to both construct segments and put segments together, allowing the parts to be shortened, lengthened, or changed easily. Such patterns not only aid recall and transmission but also help listeners ("readers") to participate in creating a poem's meaning. By setting expectations for what is normal, they refocus a listener's attention on what is abnormal. Those abnormal elements—sounds, words, images—become salient to interpretation.

If, poetically, the word "mile/miles" (*parsa/parsei*) is one of those salient elements, could this word have connected several units poetically and thus recollected them? Whereas, as we saw from a narrative standpoint, units I–III can be read as a three-part drama, a poetic standpoint would amplify the connections between I, IV, VIIIb, XI, and XVIIa. In all five of these poems, not only does *parsa/parsei* appear, it also combines with repeated sound patterns and phrases. Those combinations help to make connections across the units audible.

First the word combines with the same dominant alternation in IV, between /ei/ and /a/. This pattern is already established in I,[464] where the first two lines, ending in *par-sei/par-sei*, contrast with the next lines, ending in /a/ (*ga-la/kokh-va/miv-zar*[465] ... *char-d-la*). As in IV, balance of vowels is maintained by throwing stress back in the line onto the opposing vowel, in this case /ei/ (*d-LEI-nan, cha-ZEI-tei*). Here, the effect of this pattern is very similar to its "scalar" effect in IV. In enumerating the vast dimensions of its subject, it elongates the sound; in concentrating on punctual events of transformation, it contracts to a staccato series in /a/. This panoramic soundscape makes the moment of action in each poem less abrupt. Compare:

IV	I
his neck-length stretched out straight	three hundred miles
three miles far	between the peak of each wave
the width of his head's cradle	three hundred miles
	the height of each wave

---

464. II, in all manuscripts except H and P. See n. 154. My analysis of poetic structures of attention and the experience of wonder is informed by Philip Fisher, *Wonder, the Rainbow, and the Aesthetics of Rare Experiences* (Cambridge, MA: Harvard University Press, 1998), 17–31. For studying Fisher's chapter and this Gemara in our 2023 *Wissenschaftskolleg zu Berlin* seminar, I thank Galit Hasan-Rokem, Freddie Rokem, Dina Stein, and our convener, Shai Secunda.

465. Sokoloff (*JBA*, 195) reads, with mss. M, E: *mivzaq*, "scattering." I read *mivzar*, "sowing," with mss. O, F⁰, and the corrector of ms. H. On this variant—which is, Friedman shows, due to a poetic association—see n. 252.

a mile and a half	time was, a wave lifted us up so far
he flung out a crap ...	we saw the cradle of the tiniest[466] star ...

Just as "mile" is used in IV to transition between stanzas, delay the moment of crisis, and balance it with description by setting parts of the poem in more harmonious proportion, it achieves similar effects in I. The vision of a single (tiny) star in the heights is prepared by the panoramic measure of the waves, just as the balance of vowels between /ei/ and /a/ (*wave/wave, was/saw, wave/cradle, far/star*) fits the last word of the last line into what precedes it.

In sum, a few devices shared by I and IV enhance visual scale and acoustic harmony. They help the listener to experience singular events in the poems—critical turning points—from a panoramic view and a greater sense of wonder or equanimity, instead of shock or mockery. This is highly relevant to the question of how a live audience would have created meaning from poetic qualities of our collection. It helps us to imagine how they felt about key moments in the telling. At the very least, it weakens interpretations that do not correspond to the poems' affective texture, but only to our own prejudices ("a huge ball of dung must be silly"). For a poetically attuned audience of I and IV, it may have been no less wondrous than a star.

This network of poetic connections allows us to go farther in such a listener's direction. Beyond the emotional level, it also indicates what their conscious interpretation of the poems could have been, if they were attuned to this unity of form and content. After all, this local poetic network also has a semantic dimension. It includes not only sound patterns, not only the transition word "mile," but also the rare word "cradle" (I, IV) and the formula "but could not overcome him." The latter is most prominent as the end of all three poems where it appears. In a rendition of one poem,[467] it revives a trope: Rabbah's ineptitude vis-à-vis his Arab guide.

h-vanan lei af-ra
amar m–rachakitun mi-maya t-man-ya par-sei
h-vanan lei

---

466. Adding, for meter, this adjective from mss. M, V, E, F, per gloss in Rashbam, b. B. Bat. 73a s.v. דכוכבא זוטא.

467. Ms. P has a shorter telling, the beginning of which is reflected in the longer telling in ms. E. At a fork in the road, the Arab picks up dust and sniffs it to tell Rabbah et al. where each path goes. They try to trick him by switching around the dust, but fail. The longer version, in other manuscripts, has this additional unit of dialogue, where he twice sniffs the dust and tells them how far they are from water as they walk along.

amar m-racheikitun[468] *mi-maya t-lat par-sei*
haf-kheinan lei af-ra
v-lo y-khaleinan lei

we handed him some dust–
"eight *parasang* far are you removed from water"
handed him [more]–
"three *parasang* far are you removed from water"
we scrambled the dust on him
but could not overcome him

The striking contrast is between the narration and the length and sound of the Arab's lines. He delivers fulsome pronouncements of twelve and thirteen syllables, double and triple the length of each narrative line in between. He uses an elaborate form, unique in the Talmud, "you are removed," which lends his voice a vatic tone and a hint of foreignness. By contrast, Rabbah et al. are reduced to silence, a mere "holding of the breath,"[469] any sign of their journey through the wilderness suppressed save their footfalls and movements of their hands.

The poem marks distance and passage of time by shrinking "eight miles" to "three miles" as the Arab leads them closer to water. This is yet another scalar use of "miles," as in I and IV. In fact, all of the information about the poem's world, its chronotope,[470] is delivered in the Arab's voice: space, time, orientation ("this road leads to such-and-such a place, that road leads to such-and-such a place" he declares—even in the short telling in ms. P). By the end, when Rabbah et al. test his expertise by trying to trick him, the language of the poem has made their failure a *fait accompli*. The narration simply restates in a tidy couplet (*haf-kheinan lei/v-lo y-khaleinan lei*) the superior ability that his poetic speeches have already established.

Indeed, why does Rabbah test the Arab at all? Sheer curiosity; a desire for objective verification; and fear of dying from thirst are all plausible motives. But, in poetic terms, Rabbah's failed ruse of "scrambling the dust on him" is an apt conclusion because it stresses the same contrast of panoramic to narrow perspective, processes and punctual events, which also defines the sonic and narrative structures of both I and IV. His pithy failure constrasts with the length of his journey. The inept narrator's failed interruption makes it clear that his movement through the chronotope is that of the Arab—the poet in the poem—and not his own.

A similar anticlimax, with a similar poetic use of the same words and phrases, arises from later efforts to interrogate The Tale of the Speedy Fish

---

468. The spellings (מרחקיתון/מרחיקיתון) are inconsistent in opposite ways in mss. H, E.
469. Auerbach (trans. Trask) on the poetics of the Aqedah; see n. 442.
470. This Bakhtinian idea was already fruitfully applied to our collection by D. Stein, *Textual Mirrors*, 67–72.

(VIIIa). After Rabbah recounts this tale, the Talmud (VIIIb) entertains a hypothetical objection, then cites two voices to lay it to rest.

> v-dil-ma am-rat:
> lo mas-g-ya s-fin-ta tuva!
> ki ata rav dimi amar:
> ki cham qum-quma
> s–gaya s-fin-ta shita par-sei
> v-ika d-am-rei:
> sh-daya gira parasha
> v-lo y-kheil lei

> And you, lest you say:
> "That ship wasn't going so fast!"–
> When Rav Dimi arrived, he said:
> "While a kettle boils
> That ship was going eight miles."
> And someone else says:
> "A rider shot an arrow
> but couldn't catch up."

Unlike the long, elegant lines of the desert Arab, the acoustic texture of this seafarers' yarn is homespun and quixotic. The question about the speed of the ship is posed in a stressed long /u/ (*TU-va*) and resolved by a repetition of the same ebullient vowel (*qum-qum-a*). A second proof is given by sounds that half-echo each other: "miles"/"rider" (*par-sei/parasha*). Whereas, in the desert journey, the length of the Arab's lines elevated him above the narrator, here, all three voices carry along in clipped rhyming syllables and nearly symmetrical meter. If the transition word "mile" conveyed scope, scale, and size in I and IV, whereas in XI, it marked the passage of time, in VIIIb, the same word has the opposite effect—rapidity—a leap from zero to eight miles that is compared to transfer of heat, like late-ancient warp speed.[471] As in IIIa and XI, the conclusion ("but couldn't catch up/overcome him"), underscores a gap between the movement of the poem itself, and a figure who lacks control of its movement.[472] Here, the anonymous Talmud, putting all three voices together, plays the Arab's role of guide.

---

471. The same effect is achieved in the third structural element, Air, by juxtaposing Hormiz's "bounding" to the speed of a rider below who "could not overcome him" (IIIa), the same recycled phrase: see n. 9, n. 230, n. 279.

472. VIIIb ("a horseman shot an arrow but could not overcome him") has a very similar formula to b. San. 95a. In Persian culture, "accuracy in archery indeed symbolized power itself": Herman, "Hunt of the Falconers," 12. Compare IIIa ("a horseman raced beneath him...but could not overcome him") to the proverb cited at b. B. Qam. 92b: "sixty runners run but cannot reach the man [who eats a proper breakfast]." On "sixty" as hyperbole see nn. 448, 562.

This poetic-structural analysis is especially useful because it traverses both reception and composition. If poetry connects not only units of the synchronic collection (I, IV, VIII, XI) but also its layers over the time it was being put together (VIIIb; which, as a whole, is later), then it appears that, as in other oral traditions, these local poetic techniques and conventions influenced how audiences both experienced and expanded fixed segments of a cycle of tales. Revealing their ways of doing so helps to address questions that are often treated separately, under the rubrics of literary and source criticism. Poetic analysis can integrate two questions.

First, how would a listener have connected this set of poems during a performance, if they did indeed hear the patterns that we documented? I have offered a few descriptive terms. At the emotional level, I showed that the balance of sounds and rhythm within this network of poems was coordinated with their visual imagery so as to maintain the singularity of key events without allowing those events to subvert the larger poetic structure. Instead of events that make the rest of the poem sound like the setup for a punch line, devolving into parody, the ear is constantly drawn back to poetic devices that set each event in its poetic world. For instance, the scalar use of transition words to balance both acoustic and visual structures—words that seized the listener's attention by virtue of their sound, position, and repetition—expanded the panorama and made it possible to receive metamorphoses with awe or curiosity. Similarly, I suggested that a listener was initiated into the peculiar rules of each poetic world by the orchestration of sound, stress, and sense. Each poem performs—in the sound, length, and content of speakers' lines—the parameters of its chronotope, its literary world: the breadth and height of waves, a path to a hidden oasis, a huge fish outracing an arrow through the sea. Rational skeptics interrupt this poetry and the coherent alternative reality that it has created: for instance, a hypothetical "you" who questions the speed of the huge fish (VIIIb.94–95). Yet poetry cuts them off at the knees: the speed of the telling of the fish's speed eclipses its critic, just as the Arab's long-drawn-out speech asserts his leadership despite efforts to mislead him. Like didactic texts that rhetorically construct their own authority, poetry conjures its reality.

On the collection level of our analysis, we can ask: How might the anonymous poets and editors, as they retold these traditions as poems and assembled them into our collection, have used their poetic features in order to develop and harmonize them? I have argued that a key function of repeated words and phrases, within and across units, is to enhance visual and narrative features like scale, distance, quantity, and time sequence. Collectors and tellers received certain words and phrases as a way to achieve those effects from a poetic tradition, then used those inherited devices and techniques to retell and recollect the text of the tales. For example, the phrase "but could not overcome him" works as a figure for the fish's speed because it is paired with a more traditional figure of speech for speed (outpacing an arrow, VIIIb.100–101); just as "of-much-craft" (πολύμητις) is a stock epithet for Odysseus, and so a listener is not surprised but amused when his own name becomes a pun on "Craft" (μή τίς, *Od.* 9.410). One poet/teller found the new figure of speech useful for something similar but original: the relentless forward march of the Arab as he finds his way through the wilderness. Another poet/teller used it more conventionally, in a new setting—for speed in the Air, as opposed to the Sea or the Desert (IIIa.31). Rather than mechanically repeat adjacent phrases, or harmonize them for mere mnemonic convenience, oral tellers shared an awareness of what figures of speech could do at specific narrative moments. The most acute hearers of their tradition, they were adept in the art of making new poems old.

Summary

This literary analysis has covered our collection's placement in the talmudic canon; independent cohesiveness; voices and nested hierarchy of unit types that they signal (primary adventure/vision vs. secondary remark, either attributed to a named Amora or unattributed); verbal formulae that introduce sets of tales and contribute to their order in the collection; the tales' cosmological settings, which also contribute substantially to how they are arranged; the poetic combination of sound, stress, and sense within individual tales (with illustrations of its effects on listeners), as well as related uses of repetition and soundplay to extend, join, and associate tales in the collection; and examples of how listeners, editors, and scribes interacted with those literary conventions of the collection over time, leaving traces in its text tradition.

In terms of our constellation, I have applied and developed a few interrelated ideas. Above all, collection is not only passively juxtaposing or free-associatively reading together adjacent sources. It guides readers' creation of meaning by redirecting their attention on three scales: to the whole text in its canonical context, to its parts and units, and to their contents. On the first scale, in relation to the canon (a legal discussion in a legal tractate), our strange tales are no mere hiatus or bald interpolation. They were recollected with law in the form of a digression, which prompts listeners to make creative leaps from law into tales (or vice versa). Second, on the scale of individual tales, the collection transforms prior ways of reading them when they circulated independently (see Introduction §*The Tales*–§*The Teller*), like focusing on Rabbah's dubious reputation or extracting raw data about legal norms, sizes, and numbers. Collection made possible a more coherent reading of these adventures and visions as a series. That series calls attention to the cosmos and its limits—as we see from its arrangement by the basic elements of creation—and, with its introductory formulae, to themes of movement and vision. Yet, as this cosmological pattern unfolds and its components rapidly move and mix, the collection also redirects a listener's attention to each tale's performative technique: its oral *telling*. Here, we examined the effects of repetition, metamorphosis, wobbly binaries, sound/stress/sense patterns, and other poetic devices on a listener of the series of tales in real time, which resonate with each other. In their use of these devices, the literary language of past tellers—Rabbah's stress on adventures and visions, for instance, or stock praises of rare sights and vast sizes—informed the collectors as they standardized and developed a poetic tradition.

If we put ourselves in the seat of the first reader of this literary collection as a whole—a live audience in a fifth- or sixth-century rabbinic study-house; see §*Chronological Layers*—we now have a better sense of what they would have perceived as meaningful and how they created its meaning. Nevertheless, at each crux in their experience of the text, individual readers could still make different choices. When, while studying a law on contracts, a word called for commentary, which digressed into stories about words with similar meanings and sounds, some may have felt sweet relief. Others may have tried to link the digression back to its legal topic, using it to illustrate nautical terms or drawing morals from it as motives for legal study. As this digression moved on to other realms—the Air and Desert—and became a set-piece of its own, listeners had to seek its meaning in its own terms, even before it was joined to Part 2, which would offer them a fresh interpretive framework (chapter 5). Yet room for debate remained. Within broad parameters of its literary content and structure—cosmic settings and binary elements in wobbly, metamorphic fusion; rapid motion and vivid narration, punctuated by ironic, pedantic, supportive or confused remarks; sonic echoes, wordplays, and repetitions, which heighten its size and scale, wonder and awe; and general thematics of liminality and transgression, chaos and order—audiences attended to it and made meaning from it selectively.

Some of those differences were preserved as attributed remarks in the collection itself. When Rabbah and the study-house debate which divine "oath" Rabbah should have revoked (XIIIb), is this merely a tongue-in-cheek satire of his tale and speculative academic exercise? Or is Rabbah's view—that the "oath" to which God alluded was to never again bring a flood—based on his reading of his first story, when waves were held back by a "perpetual decree," whereas the sages are not interpreting the collection as a whole but only its latest installment? (See n. 175.) Similarly, when Rav Pappa and Rav Dimi remark on Rabbah's strange tales to back them up with firsthand empirical evidence, are they arguing against the study-house, which is interested only in the tales' normative content? Or are they disputing a skeptical "live" audience of the tale as it was being told, reflected in anonymous remarks: listeners who, unlike the study-house, question the tale's veracity as such? The tenor and topics of such debates are more important than their content or resolution. They illuminate the kind of dispute that arose at each crux.

Nor did arguments stop when the collection, with its nested structure of adventures/visions and remarks, was edited in more or less its current form. On the contrary, we saw moments in its transmission when louder voices and heavier hands—later generations of oral editors and scribes—asked for clarification of *realia* or had to be reminded what was notable about its telling. We also saw how later edits to the text of ambiguous passages reasserted or exaggerated the collection's local literary conventions or, instead, harmonized them with the canon's usual conventions—either way, they showed awareness of predecessors' poetics. This analysis of the collection's reception from three convergent angles—performance of single units; remarks on units, and their recollection; small oral and scribal changes in their transmission—can now help us to divide Part 1 into layers, advancing a theory of its relative internal chronology.

Chronological Layers

We have studied five literary structures of our collection and how they vary in manuscripts:

1. Types of unit (primary/secondary; adventure-vision/remark; attributed/anonymous), as they are distinguished by narrative voice (only one teller vs. one to four remarkers)
2. Settings (Sea–Air–Sea–Desert–Sea–Desert, with metamorphoses/wobbly binaries)
3. Attributions and other introductory formulae
4. Repetition of motifs, including numbers, ratios, and verbal roots
5. Poetry: the interrelation of sound, stress, and sense to all of these literary structures

I propose that our analysis of features 1, 3, and 2 can be used, with descending order of confidence, to divide our collection into chronological layers. This division is based on the above analysis but also on the current theory and case studies of talmudic redaction engaged throughout this book, where literary features like these are often assigned to separate layers.

1. Primary and secondary units could be substantially earlier and later. Necessarily, in their current form, secondary units are later than primary units. The question is how much. Were these anonymous and attributed remarks added seconds or centuries after the material on which

they comment? If we assume that the handful of anonymous remarks are additions of the Stammaim (whom we, in turn, equate to the editors of the final text of those units),[473] then we can explain a glaring difference between the anonymous remarks and the primary units on which each comments. Simply put, the anonymous remarks are rather clumsy.

> IV.44–47 ... I myself have seen:
> A day-old gazelle who was as big as Mount Tabor
> (And how big is Mount Tabor? –Forty *parasang*).
> The length of his neck: three *parasang* ...
>
> V.52–55 ... I myself have seen:
> A certain frog who was as big as the Fort of Hagrunya
> (And how big is the fort of Hagrunya? – Sixty houses).
> A serpent came, swallowed it ...
>
> XIIa.156–160 ... I cut off and took a thread of *tekhelet* from them
> and our camel couldn't walk. He said:
> "Perhaps one of you took something from them? Have it returned to them."
> (For it has been taught that one who takes something from them can't walk).
> We returned it to him, and we walked on ...

These anonymous remarks interrupt the flow of the visions/adventures without adding much that we do not learn in the story. The gazelle

---

473. As does Rubenstein, "Story-Cycles," 241 n. 28, for one such remark (XIIIb.175). This case is less clear than what I classify as "anonymous remarks" and set in parentheses in my translation (IV.46; see already Rashbam b. B. Bat. 73b s.v. ואקרא דהגרוניא, V.54, XIIa.159). This remark in XIIIb.175 is in Rabbah's own voice in ms. H (יג'ב.קע'ב). More importantly, in all manuscripts, it sounds as if the scholars (*rabbanan*) are replying *to* Rabbah, not to each other, so it is not straightforwardly anonymous. The editorial dynamics here may be like what we saw in tale V above (§*Attributions and Other Introductory Formulae*): some editors and scribes "blended" anonymous remarks into a teller's voice by ventriloquism, whereas other editors and scribes separated them as distinct primary units based on the collection's conventions for dividing primary/secondary units (see nn. 432–439). As in tale V, here in XIIIb, an anonymous, typical scholastic debate *about* the story may be relocated *within* the story by "blending" anonymous with named voices. Note that an earlier telling of Rabbah's tales (XIIa, XIIIa) lacked these study-house scenes (XIIb, XIIIb) altogether. Most manuscripts begin XIIIa where XIIa leaves off, and XIV where XIIIa leaves off. Rabbah's travels with the Arab simply continue: "He said to me/us...." After the study-house scenes were added to each tale, mss. E, N (and the marginal addition of ms. B) harmonize those scenes with the tales by reintroducing Rabbah's dialogue with the Arab at the beginning of each: "And Rabbah bar bar Hanah said, 'He said to me ....'" On this kind of repetition as a sign of editing, see Bernard Septimus, "Iterated Quotation Formulae in Talmudic Narrative and Exegesis," in *The Idea of Biblical Interpretation: Essays in Honor of James L. Kugel*, ed. Hindy Najman and Judith H. Newman, JSJSup 83 (Leiden: Brill, 2004), 371–98, at 396.

was as a big as a mountain; the frog was as big as a fort. Furthermore, as we noted, *sixty* (like *forty* here) is a figure of hyperbole rather than an exact number. This amounts to saying, "the frog was as big as the fort of Hagrunya. (How big? Really big!)." (*OK, one hears a live audience reply, we get it: it's big*). Similarly, in the third case, it is clear from the prior line that, if you take something from the "dead of the desert," you are unable to go on—and no less obvious from the next line that, if you return it, then you are able to. Here, the anonymous remark amounts to saying, "(By the way: we know that what just happened, happens)." What is the rationale for these anonymous interruptions?

Two complementary explanations present themselves. The first is literary: as we have seen, numbers are a device that forms connections across units. Here, the additions of *forty* and *sixty* tie back to the first unit and forward to the following unit, respectively, perhaps as a mnemonic aid or even as a thematic link. Yet I see no thematic link between the wave/gazelle or frog/decaying giant fish, and I would be more comfortable treating those numerical devices as mnemonic only. The second explanation has less to do with the text itself than with its audience. Where the audience of the anonymous remark differs from that of the primary unit, it may indicate the passage of time: a chronological gap between literary layers, corresponding to what I called "outward"-facing anonymous remarks as opposed to "inward"-facing attributed remarks.

To glimpse an audience of these anonymous remarks, let us focus not on what they say but on how they say it: fixed formulae ("How big ...?"; "For it has been taught that ...") These formulae address a reader presumed *not* to know things that are plain from the tale's context. We could assume that their authors were pedants, and the scholasticism of the Stammaim surely extended to nonlegal matters as well. But it is more plausible that what is obvious *to us*, in the current form of the tale, was not obvious to these anonymous voices' own readers. They could figure out from the tale that one who takes something from "the dead of the desert" cannot walk; but the anonymous remark has to teach them that this is based on a further independent *tradition*, not only on the content of the tale. The technical terminology of this Talmud is redundant,[474] or perhaps a self-conscious performance of excess pedantry.[475] Regardless, it has a point: You (the audience) know what happened in this situation, *because* We (the scholars) know what *should* happen in all such situations. In order to preserve this tradition, the anonymous remark wedges it—however awkwardly—back into the narrative, putting it in the mouth of

---

474. See n. 91, n. 400.

475. I thank Barry Wimpfheimer (personal communication, 20 October 2023) for observing that this "clumsy" interruption reorients a tale to the study-house, and may therefore be a self-reflective parody.

a character (the Arab) who would never talk this way.[476] This could have had significant collateral effects on the reception of the narrative. In the next line, when the teller comes back to the study-house, and is called an "ass" and a "jackass," will we, the audience, side with him? Or with his critics? The latter is more likely: now we already know that he should have known better. Thus, the anonymous remark not only comments on a tale but also, in so doing, subordinates the meaning of the tale to an over-educated peanut gallery.

Even in another case, where clear scholastic terminology is lacking, we could also explain the need for anonymous remarks by a gap in time. As we saw above from instability in the text of tale V, it seems likely that Rabbah's vision of the frog, wondrous bird, and tree was originally transmitted with a lost or missing interpretation. That interpretation was added later under the formula "Come see ...." But this interpretation should not be attributed to the original teller according to its canonical usage: it should be someone else, who comments.[477] In fact, the comment may be an anonymous addition by oral editors, as it responds to what is clearly an anonymous question/remark ("And how big is ...?" "Come see the strength ...!"). Ms. H even has a third remark ("How great it was!"), which clarifies the second remark and ties that remark even more closely back to the first anonymous remark on the size of the fort. This mimics the text's oral style, as we have seen that the scribe of ms. H does in other cases. Thus, ms. H offers us *three* anonymous remarks, but two are "blended" back into the vision:

V. Rabbah bar bar Hanah said:
   I myself have seen:
      A certain frog who was as big as the Fort of Hagrunya
         <u>(And how big is the fort of Hagrunya? – Sixty houses)</u>.
      A serpent came, swallowed it;

---

476. By contrast, ms. E firmly separates the voice of this character from the anonymous remark and its intended audience: "For *we* have taught ..." (emphasis added).

477. As it actually is in ms. O; see n. 435. To illustrate how natural this "blending" of primary/secondary voices in a text can become, especially in an oral medium, consider an NPR broadcast: "The Water Crisis in Chennai, India: Who's to Blame and How Do You Fix It?" at https://www.npr.org/transcripts/742688141 (accessed 17 July 2024). It ends, "For advice on how to conserve water, this shortage is a wake-up call, he says: for millions of Indians, and others around the world." The whole sentence is a later paraphrase; the source ("he") was quoted with sound-bites up to this point. But we can still distinguish stylistically, within the paraphrase, between its first half ("this shortage is a wake-up call, *he says*") and its expansion in the voice of the reporter ("and others around the world"). In blending or ventriloquism, a reporter editorializes in the form of a quotation, addressing a different audience than the original speaker's. This effect was much clearer orally, on the radio, but can be recovered from the transcript. On ventriloquism in the Talmud, see Redfield, "Redacting Culture," 39–59.

> A wondrous bird came, swallowed the serpent
> and flew up and settled in a tree.
> <u>Come see the strength of the tree</u>!
> <u>How great it was</u>!
>> Rav Pappa son of Shmuel said:
>> If I hadn't been there, I wouldn't have believed it.

Again, apparent redundancy of these remarks with each other and with the primary unit is the sign of a new audience. What is impressive about the "strength of the tree," if *not* its magnitude? What are we being shown, if *not* the tree's greatness over the animals? But this repetition makes the third remark seem more organic to its local context. It makes the first remark ("How big?") into the question answered by the second remark—one that, in turn, repeats the anonymous remark in the prior unit ("How big?" IV.46). This repetition ventriloquizes a new telling of the tale with its commentary. (Similarly, other manuscripts employ repetition and redundancy here. Rather than strengthen connections *within* the tale, however, their telling uses a phrase that repeats later in the collection, creating mnemonic as well as thematic resonances *across* tales.[478]) Like ms. H, as I noted above, the formula in the first remark ("Come see ...") perfectly fits the rules for introducing a primary unit using verbs of motion and vision: it is *just like* what the teller *would* have said. Thus, all three anonymous remarks react to a vision that was without commentary, and are interwoven with it. Upon closer inspection, however, they speak to a different audience, an audience in dialogue with their anonymous oral editors.

3. As for the text's absolute chronology, <u>attributions</u> mark only a *terminus post quem*: it was not fully composed in its current form before the latest rabbis cited, the contemporaries Amemar and Rav Ashi (whose attributions are stable in all manuscripts).[479] But this could have been almost any time: between ca. 427 CE,[480] and ca. 990 CE,[481] when members of Qairouan's Jewish community were studying a copy of the Talmud and—understandably befuddled by our tales!—wrote to Babylonian Geonim

---

478. Compare ms. P to V.58 (" ... how *substantial* was the strength of the tree!") with ms. P to IXa.111 and IXa.117 ("we thought the water was not *substantial*"; "not because the water is *substantial*"). Note the shared motif of hidden strength: a tree's branches and water's current, praised by anonymous and heavenly voices.

479. See Albeck, *Introduction to the Talmud*, 426–30. The stability of these Amoraic attributions is not the only criterion for their relative chronology. I would also note that Rav Ashi often appears at the end of Talmud units, as he does here, and that his remarks interspersed throughout the text (VIIIb, IXb, XVIIb)—all secondary glosses—suggest a later stage. On Amemar, see B. Cohen, *Legal Methodology*, 37–98. Cohen dates him slightly before Rav Ashi (noting that he is said to die during Rav Ashi's lifetime: b. B. Metz. 68a).

480. The date for Rav Ashi's death in the Geonic chronologies: *Seder Tannaim veAmoraim* (ed. Kahan, 5), *Iggeret Rav Sherira Gaon* (ed. Lewin, 94).

481. See Appendix §*Thieves In Heaven (?!)*

Genealogy and Birth of the Literary Collection 171

for an explanation. Besides, we do not know what version they had. Their question is only on the last unit in the series attributed to Rabbah, XV. Strictly speaking, then, our collection is unattested before its earliest complete commentary misattributed to Rabbenu Gershom (eleventh century). The attributions, however, may be a clue to *internal* chronology, provided that they are analyzed as literary forms, rather than as historical data. We do not need to prove that these dicta are authentic words of their authors or whether they belong to their period (in any case, that would not help us to date the text). Rather, we need to assess whether its *uses* of attribution reveal its layers and dating, relative to other talmudic sources.

At one level, the answer is a clear yes. All attributed remarks have the tone, interests, and content of Amoraic dialogues in the Talmud. They are basically nonlegal versions of its typical give-and-take, plus a smattering of glosses and exegeses. They answer hypothetical objections with supporting evidence;[482] catalogue names for rare things;[483] restore a lacuna;[484] ground primary units in Scripture;[485] or mock, moralize, and derive legal implications.[486] They belong to a uniform texture within the composition, addressed directly to the Amoraic study-house. It is possible, as Stemberger argues, that the whole text was composed *en bloc* by one group of editors responsible for both primary and secondary units.[487] But it is more likely that this division between the visions/adventures and their internal commentary reflects the passage of time, as adventures and visions were assembled, discussed, and reworked over generations.

2. This chronology is supported by how the collection combines attributions and other introductory formulae with <u>settings</u>. First, IV–XV are attributed consistently to *Rabbah (bar bar Hanah)*. By contrast, his name varies in I–III, where he also mentions other tellers (I–II), and the final tales (XVI–XXI) are clearly attributed to other rabbis. All of the units in which Rabbah is not the only storyteller (I–II and XVI–XX, except the final unit, XXI) are set at Sea,[488] and use an introductory formula different from

---

482. V.60–61; VIIIb.96–101.
483. VIIIb.102–104; XVIIb.211–212; XXIb.262–263.
484. V.58 (if, as all manuscripts but ms. O want us to think, this explanation is attributed to the teller Rabbah).
485. IXb.119-122; XIIIb.175; XX.250-251.
486. Xb.134-135; XIIb.161-164; XIIIb.172-174.
487. This would be a chronological formulation of the phenomenological analysis in Stein, "Seeing Is Believing." It bears on the much-debated relation between *halakhah* (law) and non-law (*aggadah*): both attitudes are found *within* non-law, in this case. Similarly, Yassif, *Hebrew Folktale*, 217 considers a remark which "attempt[s] to define and establish the truth of the matter" integral to the literary form, although not all remarks (attributed or anonymous) can be reduced to this function.
488. Note that the first hand of ms. O (XXIa.255/כא.רג'ה) contains the absurd formula *on a ship in the desert*. A corrector (or the scribe himself) noticed and prevented this harmonization of the setting of XXI with the conventional setting of the other added tales. But the

that in his tales ("recount," not "say"; except for a total anomaly, XX). I–III have further signs of distinction in terms of these "non-Rabbah-only" tales. The order of I–II varies in manuscripts.[489] Ms. O has section headings at the start of Units I and IV.[490] All manuscripts that do have mnemonic lists, where key words serve as headers for sections of the text, begin with Unit IV. (Ms. V has mnemonics for all of the other sections, but none for I–III.) In other words, Rabbah's own tales (IV–XV) are one group; others' tales (XVI–XXI) a second group, whereas I–III are ambiguous, as they share features with both groups.

Taking together those irregularities of I–III vis-à-vis other tales attributed to Rabbah, I–III seem to have been transmitted separately from IV–XV. As I–III also share features with the concluding section XVI–XXI, we can speculate that, building outward from a nucleus of adventures and visions attributed to Rabbah (an early shorter version of III + IV–XV),[491] editors added an introductory/concluding frame of sea yarns, told by sailors and later rabbis. They did not just paste the frame onto the nucleus, however, but smoothed out the transition.

This chronology further explains the formal anomalies of tale XX (see chapter 1 §*Exegesis*). First, XX is not attributed. Rather, it is introduced anonymously under a formula that typically introduces a *baraita* (a Tannaitic tradition left out of the Mishnah). By convention, then, it is early. But it is unattested in early works.[492] It is also a vision at Sea, and repeats

---

fact that he made this mistake underscores the persistence of the old convention. As I argued (§*Settings*), this departure from the convention also fits with the collection's metamorphic poetics: its dynamic alternation and blurring of boundaries between fixed cosmological domains. If there is a horseman at sea (VIIIb.100–101), why not a ship in the desert? See n. 9.

489. II is added in the margin in ms. P. The order of I/II in mss. H, P may be a scribal error: see n. 154, n. 423.

490. I thank Yakov Z. Mayer (personal communication, April 2019) for answering my questions on this subject.

491. According to this reconstruction, Unit III has two stages. In the first stage, it was attributed to Rabbah bar bar Hanah, set in the Air, and introduced by "I myself have seen." All three features indicate that it belonged with the following two units in the original nucleus: IV–V. In stage 2, by adding a verse to the end (IIIb.39–41), the editors linked it back to Units I–II. (Compare Rashbam's idea that the verse is in the Talmud's voice, n. 433). Like the concluding verses of I–II, the verse that editors added to IIIb connects this tale's setting to the Sea (I–II) and extols a superior power (the Kingdom or "authorities"), who subdues the original and terrifying visions (like YHWH in I–II). Further evidence for these two stages of III is: (a) None of Rabbah's adventures/visions in the Talmud end with verses. He cites one as a gloss *on* a verse (b. Meg. 18a = b. Rosh Hash. 26a; see Ber. Rab. 79:7), never the reverse. (b) Already in an attributed Amoraic remark in our collection (IXb), one way of expanding Rabbah's tales was to attach a verse, using midrash to make sense of his visions/adventures. Thus, the editors of IIIb build on earlier ways of connecting Rabbah's tales to the collection among Amoraim in order to both link IIIa–b back to the previous units (I–II) and keep it with the next two units of its group (IV–V), recollecting it almost seamlessly.

492. Michael Higger, *'Otsar ha-baraitot*, 10 vols. (New York: Jewish Theological Seminary, 1938–1948), 10:337.

Genealogy and Birth of the Literary Collection 173

the image of the Leviathan earlier in its section (XVIIa.210), so it was a good fit.

Perhaps the fit is no coincidence. Rubenstein calls a similar tale a "pseudo-*baraita*." It has formal features like an early (pre-Amoraic) tradition but is a post-Amoraic composition: "a redactional construction fashioned from earlier Hebrew sources."[493] This is the story of a wave that almost sinks Rabban Gamliel when he is traveling on a ship, but is made to "rest" by invoking the Master (similar to tale II in our collection).[494] Rubenstein bases his "pseudo-*baraita*" classification on two criteria: the text uses a stock motif (a rabbi traveling by ship) and is intrusive with respect to the surrounding material; but it is worked in by light touches (one repeated word from the previous unit, and a phrase contextualizing it in its surrounding text;[495] the rest of it is cobbled together from earlier sources and stock motifs).

Tale XX functions in the same way as this pseudo-*baraita*. It is highly intrusive in the sense that it violates both of the text's literary conventions: it has no named attribution and is the only unit entirely in Hebrew. This includes its introductory formula. By translating an Aramaic introductory formula from the earlier tales *into* Hebrew, however ("Going by ship"),[496] and by ending it with a verse as some of those earlier tales do, its recollector irons over this wrinkle. Structurally, its vision of the Leviathan does a key double duty: it links XX back to another addition (XVIIa), and points forward to Part 2 of the larger composition, which begins with a long section on Leviathan (2.A). Although this unit looks like the earliest source, historically,[497] it was probably crafted and added at the tail end of the col-

---

493. See Rubenstein, *Talmudic Stories*, 55 and 261. Jacobs misclassifies and misinterprets XX as "an early Tannaitic tradition" based only on the formula and attributions (*Midrashic Process*, 161).

494. This pseudo-*baraita* and II share a similar formulation: "the sea subsided from its anger" (b. B. Metz. 59b); "it [ms. E: *the sea*] subsides" (II.25; both are similar to Tg. Jonah 1:15). See n. 319 and n. 730.

495. We might add its use of "immediately" (מיד): a formula that, as Rubenstein had already noted, is used in medieval and late-classical midrash "to connect independent traditions and place them in chronological sequence" and "create cause-effect relations" (Rubenstein, "Mythic Motifs," 153 and 157). See further n. 686.

496. Abramson (*Baba Batra*, 2–4) shows that the Hebrew of ms. H in XX ("Going [מהלכין] by ship," כ.ר.מ"ה) is only in Babylonian Hebrew versions of early Palestinian traditions, including a mishnah (in b. Ber. 28b). It does not appear in Babylonian *baraitot* paralleled in Palestinian works. As this is precisely the verb that ties XX into the collection by echoing an introductory formula from the nucleus, it is evidence for a pseudo-*baraita* (or, possibly, of even more editing by the hyperactive scribe of ms. H). All other manuscripts have a synonym, "Coming [באין, באים] by *ship*," a good Palestinian Hebrew form (so is the equivalent in 2.C, "depart [פ.ר.ש]": see n. 674).

497. Friedman, *Talmud Arukh*, 9: "Sometimes the form is one thing (entirely a *baraita*) and the historical composition is quite another." See also Friedman in Redfield, "Redacting Culture," 70 n. 65. See XVI, where, in all manuscripts, R. Yohanan compares a giant fish that

lection, along with other seafarers' tales (I–II; the expanded III; XVI–XIX and XXI), to form a bridge to Part 2.

* * * * *

We can sum up this excavation of the collection's chronological layers in five stages:

i. A selection of popular visions and adventures attributed to Rabbah was made and divided into sections by setting: Air–Sea–Desert (XV). This formed the nucleus (IIIa27–IIIb.38 and IV–XV).[498]
ii. A selection of remarks on this nucleus was attached. All of these are attributed to Amoraim or reflect its circulation among Amoraim whose attributions were not preserved.[499]
iii. Similar adventures and visions were added as a frame at the beginning and end.[500] This frame was adjusted to a key literary convention of the nucleus: introductory formula.[501] Many of its units were chosen because they suited other local, as well as canonical, literary conventions. They were tailored to fit: setting (Sea),[502] repeated numbers,[503] other repetitions which create mnemonic and thematic links within and across units.[504] In keeping with one of the collection's conventions (dynamic alternation between cosmological settings), as well as a canonical convention (Rav Ashi speaks at the end),[505] his

---

he saw *to Sura in Babylonia*, even though he is a Palestinian and earlier than Rabbah—and far earlier than the Babylonians who recount the added tales that follow him. This is likely pseudepigraphic, perhaps because R. Yohanan was Rabbah's teacher. See also n. 71.

498. Why were other tales *not* chosen, like Rabbah's adventure with a desert caravan, which sparks a legal debate (b. Ber. 53b; compare XIIb), or b. Ta'an. 25b (compare III; see Kiperwasser and Shapira, "Irano-Talmudica I")? A theory of this important question—the Talmud's cutting-room floor—lies beyond my study's scope.

499. V.60–61; VIIIb; IXb; Xb.

500. I–II; IIIb:39–41; XVI–XIX; XXI. Like the verse in IIIb, the verses at the end of I–II are supplements to these stories which reframe them as exegesis. See chapter 2 §*Midrash as Fugue* and Rashbam at n. 433, contra Fränkel, *Darkhe ha-aggadah*, 1:259.

501. All use the verb "recount," not "say/tell"; otherwise, they fit the standard verbal formulae. See §*Structure*.

502. See IIIb.39–41, which fits I–II into III–V by shifting the setting to Sea and ending with a verse like those of I–II. See also n. 488.

503. XVI; XVIIa.

504. For example: I.2, II.19 ("sea," *yama'*) → IIIb.39, IV.45 ("day," *yoma'*). Recall (§*Placement*, see n. 377) that such echoes also tie our collection back to the mishnah: II.20 ("shoot," *tsutsita'*) → "boats" (*butsiyyata'*). That is, the same poetic logic that links our collection to its literary context also links certain tales within it.

505. As noted by David Weiss Halivni, this is one reason that Rav Ashi is traditionally but wrongly believed to have edited the Talmud (*The Formation of the Babylonian Talmud*, ed. and trans. Jeffrey L. Rubenstein [Oxford: Oxford University Press, 2013], 83).

adventure in the Desert was chosen as the last unit, XXI. Later Amoraic remarks on this new frame were selected and attached.[506]

iv. A few remarks that may go back to Amoraim but were transmitted anonymously, and may also be later, were integrated in various ways: attribution to "the house of study,"[507] "blending" to attributed material via local conventions/verbal echoes,[508] and bald interpolation.[509]

v. A pseudo-*baraita* on Leviathan (XX) was worked into the end of the frame, using local conventions and repetitions, to set up the composition's Part 2.A, starring the Leviathan.

We can likely date stages i–iii to Amoraim (through the mid-fifth century) and iv–v to Stammaim (up to as late as the mid-eighth), recalling that relevant data fluctuate in manuscripts (some of these variants point to a shift from orality to writing; others to competing oral texts). There is a time to build up and time to tear down—one can argue against any internal layers.[510] The grouping of all material by a tiny set of introductory verbs shows that, even if the content accumulated gradually, its form was harmonized.[511] It seems to me that (apart from stages iv–v, which have little impact),[512] there is no compelling reason to date our collection later than the close of the Amoraic era. Despite a few signs of intervention by anonymous voices and by oral editors who may be Stammaim, theories of talmudic redaction that prioritize their role should not bias us in this case: it is just as wrong to date a text too late as to date it too early.[513] Yet some timeline, even relative and internal, was needed if we are to restore our

---

506. XVIIb and XXIb.

507. XIIb and XIIIb.

508. V.58–59; IV.46 (harmonized with V.54, V.59); XV.193 (a Geonic gloss; see Appendix §*Thieves in Heaven(?!)*)

509. XIIa.159. Even here, the remark is lightly "blended" into the voice of a character in the tale itself, the Arab.

510. Noting that the legal commentary surrounding the composition is "typical of the Savoraic layer" and usually found at the start of a Gemara, Stemberger holds that "the *aggadic* passage was integrated as an integral block, and not until a relatively late date" ("Münchhausen und die Apokalyptik," 62). This study, from 1989, reflects the field's then-ascendant tendency to stress editorial control at the expense of other factors in meaning.

511. See I.1–2, II.18–19, XXIa.253–254. These added units are rigorous in distinguishing the voice of an original Amora who "says" in the nucleus (Rabbah and Rav Ashi), from tales added to the nucleus that are "recounted." In one place, several manuscripts (XXIa.254/ כא"ר"ד) fail to make this distinction, harmonizing the later formula ("recounted") with the earlier one ("said"). Yet again, ms. H preserves or reasserts the original oral convention.

512. If you remove this material, you lose the scholastic interruptions and a little connective tissue, as well as a nice tale about two Tannaim at sea, but nothing indispensable to the lyricism and liveliness of this minor epic.

513. I owe this piquant formulation to David Brodsky (personal communication, circa 2012).

collection to its contemporary cultural history (chapter 4) and to the later history of its canon (chapters 5–6).

* * * * *

As we proceed in those directions, we should bear in mind three lines of debate about the meaning of this collection that we have uncovered during its editing and transmission. First, the issue of evidence. Why should anyone believe these strange sights and adventures? For whose claims might they serve as evidence? If belief is *not* at stake, why relate them at all? This issue was not new: it had been raised by earlier audiences of Rabbah's individual tales—figured here by his peers in the study-house, who tried to tame their strange content by reducing it to known legal/theological debates. It was also implicit in named and unnamed voices in the collection who attacked or defended his tales' veracity. By preserving and carving out a formal place for such critical remarks on the tales, collectors continued to make evidence an issue. The second and related issue is vision as a source of authority, as opposed to oral tradition. By formulae citing visions as evidence ("I myself have seen ..."; "Come see ..."); by amplifying those sublime sights poetically; and by interpreting visions in conflicting ways (defending a vision with a vision; supporting or attacking it with Bible verses or related lore), readers made clear that vision was a persistent point of contention. Lastly, the cosmic structure and scope of this literary collection gave newly epic proportions to its tellers' once episodic adventures. Its chronotope mingled mythic creation-accounts with everyday realities (see chapter 2). Its borders wobbled as characters crossed them, binary elements metamorphosing into hybrid motifs. Monsters—hybrids par excellence—and other strange beings, at limits of the seen and the known, proliferated; spurring doubt, curiosity, and new efforts to tame them via interpretation. Evidence, vision, the order and the limits of reality—these issues in the collection's early editing and reception, within rabbinic circles, will continue to characterize its circulation in Babylonian rabbinic culture at large as well as its evolution within the rabbinic canon.

4

A Wonderful World and the Romance of the East

One fine day around 533, the story goes, a Syrian by the name of Uranius arrived in the Persian capital Ktēsiphōn,[514] as a minor *attaché* to the court of the new Sasanian king, Khusro the first. Uranius was an unlikely diplomat, judging by his reputation in his hometown Constantinople. A Christian of some sort,[515] (unlike his hostile historian Agathias),[516] he loved to loaf around the bookstalls in the center of town and run his mouth:

> Like Homer's Thersitēs he was full of noisy abuse and endless chatter. Yet he held no firm opinion about God and had no idea how to construct a reasoned argument on this subject. One moment he would attack the first proposition on which a particular line of enquiry was based, another time he would insist on being given the reason for a question before he could answer it. In this way he would not allow the discussion to develop in an orderly fashion but confused the issue and prevented anything positive from emerging. He affected the manner of what is known as skeptical empiricism and modeled his pronouncements on the style of Pyrrho and Sextus, aiming to escape mental anxiety by denying the possibility of mental activity. But he had not mastered even these notions, having barely picked up the few isolated scraps of information necessary to enable him to deceive and mislead the ignorant.

On the basis of this sketch (for which Agathias is its sole, clearly biased source),[517] we can hardly classify Uranius as a philosopher, nor as

---

514. I.e., the setting of Rabbah's tale of Hormiz (III); see nn. 244–246.
515. Joseph D. Frendo, "Agathias' View of the Intellectual Attainments of Khusrau I: A Reconsideration of the Evidence," *Bulletin of the Asia Institute* 18 (2004): 97–110, at 100 nn. 20–21.
516. Anthony Kaldellis, "The Historical and Religious Views of Agathias: A Reinterpretation," *Byzantion* 69.1 (1999): 206–52.
517. Trans. Frendo, "Agathias' View," 98; see Joel Walker, "The Limits of Late Antiquity: Philosophy between Rome and Iran," *Ancient World* 33.1 (2002): 45–69, at 65–67; Begoña

a Sophist in all but the most polemical sense. Like Ktēsiās, another Greek traveler and attendant at Persian courts seven centuries before Uranius, he was a doctor by trade, notorious for outlandish tales. Yet Agathias had to admit that, in a certain setting, he was hilarious:

> But if his cultural standards left much to be desired his behaviour left still more. Frequenting the houses of the wealthy he would gorge himself on the choicest dainties and consort repeatedly with the wine-jug, drinking himself silly and uttering a stream of obscenities. He made such a laughing-stock of himself that at times he was even smacked on the jaw and it was not unknown for his face to drip with the lees of other people's glasses that had been poured over him. He was in fact the butt of the dinner-table no less so than if he had been a buffoon or hired entertainer. (Trans. Frendo, "Agathias' View," 98.)

Buffoon or not, when Uranius arrived at Ktēsiphōn, he won Khusro's heart—although the king had been visited a few years before by real philosophers of the Athenian Academy. The philosophers found Persia immoral and terrifying; its king, an inept student. Uranius, by contrast, was a huge hit at court. Not only did Khusro shower him with wealth and gifts; he seated him at his table, violating a rigid etiquette of separating the king from all but his chosen few.[518] After Uranius returned to Constantinople, no wonder he lived out his life as an insufferable name-dropper, claiming each piece of mail that Khusro sent him as proof of his philosophical credentials. Yet back home, too, Uranius had his fans, Agathias admits: "Those in fact who combined extreme gullibility with a weakness for the strange and marvelous [τὰ ξένα καὶ παραλογώτερα] were easily hoodwinked by his boastful & bombasic assertions...."[519]

Both the structure and the rhetoric of Agathias's account clearly have Khusro as their target, undermining his foray into Greek thought by juxtaposing the best philosophers with the very worst.[520] Yet the specific faults that Agathias finds in Uranius (a magnet for ridicule with a penchant for hyperbole) and his audience (readiness to believe the strange, incredible, and fantastical) grudgingly present him not merely as a bad philosopher, but as a good jester—the master of a vulgar species of elite entertainment.[521]

Ortega Villaro, "Some Characteristics of the Works of Agathias: Morality and Satire," *Acta Antiqua* 50.2–3 (2010): 257–87.

518. Touraj Daryaee, *Sasanian Persia: The Rise and Fall of an Empire* (London: I. B. Tauris, 2009), 11. For a similar display of knowledge of Persian royal table manners by rabbis to project their own cultural superiority, see Simcha Gross, "Rethinking Babylonian Rabbinic Acculturation in the Sasanian Empire," *JAJ* 9 (2018): 280–310, at 299.

519. Trans. Frendo, "Agathias' View," 100.

520. Frendo, "Agathias' View"; Walker, "Limits of Late Antiquity," 46.

521. The experts hold that he knew Uranius and selected him out of personal animus (Ortega Villaro, "Some Characteristics," 283 n. 84; Averil Cameron, *Agathias* (Oxford: Claren-

A Wonderful World and the Romance of the East 179

If both he and the philosophers took their shows on the road, but Uranius found greater success, does it prove merely the failure of Khusro's philosophy—or a broadening of Sasanian taste toward the marvelous and strange?[522]

In this chapter, we trace that question along two intersecting paths of cultural history. First, what are the conditions of possibility for the popularity of characters like Uranius—or his rabbinic counterpart Rabbah—and the kinds of material attributed to them: Uranius's hodgepodge of Aristotelian natural science, hyper-skeptical sophistry, the "strange and marvelous" stuff of grubby bookstalls and drunken symposia; Rabbah's transgressive mythology, exotica, marvels, and hyperbole, which were fodder for scholars' mock-rationalistic dialogues?[523] Second: what does

---

don: 1970), 104; Cameron, "Agathias on the Sassanians," *Dumbarton Oaks Papers* 23–24 (1969): 67–183, at 172; Frendo, "Agathias' View," 105: "The Uranius whom he appears to have come to know long years after the event was a habitual drunkard of advanced age further intoxicated with distant memories of his friendship with the Great King." Yet Uranius is no less a literary stereotype than Agathias's other characters: Khusro, the philosophers, and the wise old man. This is clear from Uranius's comparison to Thersitēs, who was not a mere fool but a court jester: a classical paradigm for grotesque comedy and blame of kings on behalf of the people, who shared his critique even as they vented their frustration on him (Gregory Nagy, *The Best of the Achaeans: Concepts of the Hero in Archaic Greek Poetry*, 2nd. ed. [Baltimore: Johns Hopkins University Press, 1999], 253–64. On Lucian as literary model for Agathias's satire of Uranius, see Ortega Villaro, "Some Characteristics," 283–87.). Consider the parallel: "he made such a laughing-stock of himself that at times he was even smacked on the jaw" (in Frendo, "Agathias' View," 98) and the slapstick rendition of Thersitēs by Pherecratēs (fifth century BCE): "Achilles gave him a good blow to the jaw / so that the fire shone forth from his mouth" (trans. Ralph M. Rosen, in his "The Death of Thersites and the Sympotic Performance of Iambic Mockery," *Pallas* 61 [2003]: 121–36, at 128). Could it be in his role as court jester, rather than court philosopher, that there is some truth to Uranius's supposed intimacy with Khusro? On jesters' shifting position in the elaborate Sasanian court hierarchy, see Arthur Christensen, *L'iran sous les Sassanides*, Annales du Musée Guimet: Bibliothèque d'études 48 (Copenhagen: Levin & Munskgaard, 1936), 397–99. On Khusro's practical and relatively low-brow expectations for what "philosophy" could teach him, see Richard Sorabji, "Introduction," in Priscian, *Answers to King Khosroes of Persia*, trans. Pamela Huby et al. (London: Bloomsbury Academic, 2016), 1–10, at 4.

522. As evidence for such taste at the time, Sindbad the Sailor of the Thousand and One Nights is a later tradition, but a teller by that name was also popular at Khusro's court, as a vehicle for Indian and other tales; see Hermann Gollancz, trans., "The History of Sindban and the Seven Wise Masters," *Folklore* 8.2 (1897): 100–130. See also François de Blois, *Burzoy's Voyage to India and the Origin of the Book of Kalīlah wa-Dimnah*, Prize Publication Fund 23 (London: Royal Asiatic Society, 1990). Both works share faint motifs with our collection but have a more refined, courtly style.

523. General conditions of possibility for this exchange are well established. Not only did Khusro have contact with the philosophers (Priscian, *Answers to King Khosroes*), but his court was a center for Greek translation: Muriel Debié, "Textual Exchanges in Late Antiquity East and South of Byzantium Seen through an Eastern Christian Lens," in *Proceedings of the 24th International Congress of Byzantine Studies Plenary Sessions 1* (Venice: Università Ca' Foscari, 2022), 59–80. For the sources see Mohsen Zakeri, "Translations from Greek into

this show about rabbinic academies' changing culture in the place and time our collection began circulating in its current form: late fifth- and sixth-century Sasanian Iran?

Beyond Jewish Hellenization

The approach that I will be taking to this question varies substantially from that of an earlier yet still formative series of studies along these lines, for example, Saul Lieberman's "How Much Greek in Jewish Palestine?," Louis Feldman's "How Much Hellenism in Jewish Palestine?," and Jacob Neusner's "How Much Iranian in Talmudic Babylonia?" Note that, for these mid-twentieth-century scholars—in the postwar United States, where "How Jewish are you (still)?" was a more burning question than "How are you Jewish?"—comparison had to be a quantitative enterprise. Hellenistic "culture" in the Roman East, like Iranian "culture" in the Sasanian Empire, was presumed to be a stable phenomenon. The basic question was how much of the culture Jews "had" or "knew." The shared assumption behind this question was that its answer lay in continuities with the meaning of items of foreign culture *before* Jews knew them. This was proven by showing that such items (ideologies, practices, myths, folklore, institutions) kept their earlier meanings—even as they moved from Greco-Roman (or, for that matter, Persian) "cultures" (i.e., texts and languages) into Jewish ones. Lieberman especially showed that Greek loanwords in rabbinic literature do reflect knowledge of their meaning in Greek, although this knowledge was forgotten by later transmitters of the texts, who introduced misreadings or errors into the words themselves. Philology thus became a precious tool of cultural paleology: a way to salvage the fossils of Hellenistic culture from ancient Jewish sources and, using nothing but their skeletons, to reconstruct how they had evolved among the Jews.

Important paleology remains to be done. But recent studies signal a salutary shift to a more context-specific, less linear, and more active way of conceptualizing how Jews dealt with Greek culture. Instead of "How much Greek?," the question is, "What kind of Greek?" (or, better, "What

---

Middle Persian as Repatriated Knowledge," in *Why Translate Science? Documents from Antiquity to the 16th Century in the Historical West (Bactria to the Atlantic)*, ed. Dimitri Gutas (Leiden: Brill, 2022), 52–169, at 68–74, 105–16. Regarding one genre that we will investigate, Alexander Romance, Kevin van Bladel has bolstered Theodor Nöldeke's case that a lost Middle Persian Romance linked a Greek version to a Syriac version, from which it passed into Arabic (van Bladel, "The Syriac Sources of the Early Arabic Narratives of Alexander," in *Memory as History: The Legacy of Alexander in Asia*, ed. Himanshu Prabha Ray and Daniel T. Potts [Delhi: Aryan, 2007], 54–75). On Hellenistic sources in the Talmud, see n. 525.

kinds?"). This question has two advantages. First, it avoids reducing Jewish uses of Greek culture to a symptom of Jewish power or powerlessness. Not even in Palestine, where Jews were deeply affected by Roman and, later, Christian occupations of their sacred sites and institutions, and where political domination did lead to the decline of Jewish social structures, was every item of Hellenistic culture uniformly politicized or "marked" in every Jewish context. Even early Palestinian rabbis drew a zone of *adiaphora*, items of normative neutrality, with respect to other cultures in their discourse on idolatry, *'avodah zarah*—a discourse that, while it does mark a binary between Israelite and Greco-Roman cults, also exempts some Greco-Roman practices as *not* "idolatry" (even some to which practitioners themselves gave cultic significance), and relocates other practices to other categories of transgression. Rabbis' discourse was a fence around the Torah. But it was also a bridge for cataloguing religious and cultural differences, for thinking about the logic of such differences, and for debating which differences should make a difference between the cultures.[524] *A fortiori*, outside the political pressures of Rome and Byzantium, we can expect more flexible rabbinic use of things Greek.

Asking our question in the plural ("What *kinds* of Greek?") also encourages us to distinguish contexts where Jews engaged Hellenistic culture, as they did not receive it in a passive or monolithic way but appropriated it selectively, lending it new meanings and functions. Such studies use philological methods, especially the comparison of parallels across corpora, to show how Jews in Iran were not only aware of Greek rhetorical forms but also resisted and adapted them.[525] At the level of explicit ideology, they

---

524. Redfield, "Sages and the World"; "Commentary as Ethnography: The Case of Early Rabbinic Law"; "Curiouser and Curiouser." This is the subject of my second monograph, based lightly on the above, and provisionally entitled *When the Rabbis Met the Jews*.

525. This work exposes Greek and Syriac roots of the Talmud's demonological discourse, which both overlap (Ishay Rosen-Zvi, *Demonic Desires: "Yetzer Hara" and the Problem of Evil in Late Antiquity*, Divinations [Philadelphia: University of Pennsylvania Press, 2011], 102–19) and diverge (Adam Becker, "The 'Evil Inclination' of the Jews: The Syriac Yatsra in Narsai's Metrical Homilies for Lent," *JQR* 106.2 [2016]: 179–207); uses mythic echoes with Plato to explore the Talmud's alternative political philosophy (Charlotte Elisheva Fonrobert, "Plato in Rabbi Shimeon bar Yohai's Cave [B. Shabbat 33b–34a]: The Talmudic Inversion of Plato's Politics of Philosophy," *AJSR* 31.2 [2007]: 277–96); positions the Talmud's ideal subject against that of the philosopher (Ron Naiweld, *Les antiphilosophes: Pratiques de soi et rapport à la loi dans la littérature rabbinique classique*, Le temps des idées [Paris: Colin, 2011]); analogizes the carnivalesque and ironic aspects of talmudic discourse with Platonic dialogue and Menippean satire (Boyarin, *Fat Rabbis*; Arkady Kovelman, *Between Alexandria and Jerusalem: The Dynamic of Jewish and Hellenistic Culture*, Brill Reference Library of Judaism 21 [Leiden: Brill, 2005], 52–66); reconsiders the Talmud's "holy man" in light of Greek and Syriac exemplars (Michal Bar-Asher Siegal, *Early Christian Monastic Literature and the Babylonian Talmud* [Cambridge: Cambridge University Press, 2013]); dissects "clusters of unusual motifs" in the Talmud and Greek sources that are not in rabbinic texts from Roman Palestine (Richard Kalmin, *Migrating Tales: The Talmud's Narratives and Their Historical Context* [Oak-

have shown how the very idea of "Greek" became something of a floating signifier in the formation of Babylonian Jewish and Syriac Christian identities. Just as a tradition in the Talmud offers the pungent analogy that "one who teaches his son Greek is like one who rears pigs" and the roughly contemporary Syriac *Life of Ephrem* attacks "the wisdom of the Greeks," both, in the same breath, license studying Greek language.[526] Greek in the East meant something more, and less, than being able to read Greek. Here, "how much Greek" you had or knew was not the only question.

Whereas the findings of these studies thus have far-reaching implications for rethinking the role of Greek culture among Jews in the Sasanian Empire, in terms of their models, many are still paleological (what Seth Schwartz has called a "cultural inventory approach").[527] They tend to present the Greek side of their textual comparison as more stable and more original than the Jewish side; list its distinguishing features; and reconstruct how it influenced the Talmud, even if influence is now defined in less direct and more dynamic ways. In particular, if we were to look closely at how these paleological studies use the concept of "culture" to describe Greco-Roman influence on the Talmud,[528] we would find that they all use texts as their model for culture. Texts are adduced as specimens of one or another culture; relations between texts are relations between cultures. But if cultures are, as Clifford Geertz showed, interpretable *like* texts,[529] this does not mean the reverse is also true, that a text is essentially equivalent to the culture that produced it. Rather, in my approach, culture is a shared

---

land: University of California Press, 2021]); traces the origins of the more evolved Babylonian dialogue form to Greco-Roman rhetoric (David Brodsky, "From Disagreement to Talmudic Discourse: Progymnasmata and the Evolution of a Rabbinic Genre," in *Rabbinic Traditions between Palestine and Babylonia*, ed. Ronit Nikolsky and Tal Ilan, AJEC 89 [Leiden: Brill, 2014], 173–231), factoring in the role of its oral, competitive literary settings (Hidary, *Rabbis and Classical Rhetoric*); compares rabbinic subversions of Mosaic authority to Lucian's restyling of the figure of Homer (Yair Furstenberg, "The Agon with Moses," in *Homer and the Bible in the Eyes of Ancient Interpreters*, ed. Maren R. Niehoff, Jerusalem Studies in Religion and Culture 16 [Leiden: Brill, 2012], 299–328); uncovers the Talmud's veiled contestation with the Syro-Roman lawbook (Yakir Paz, "The Torah of the Gospel: A Rabbinic Polemic against the Syro-Roman Lawbook," *HTR* 112.4 [2017]: 517–40); and more.

526. Moulie Vidas, "Greek Wisdom in Babylonia," in *Envisioning Judaism: Studies in Honor of Peter Schäfer on the Occasion of His Seventieth Birthday*, ed. Ra'anan S. Boustan et al., 2 vols. (Tübingen: Mohr Siebeck, 2013), 1:287–305.

527. Seth Schwartz, *Were the Jews a Mediterranean Society? Reciprocity and Solidarity in Ancient Judaism* (Princeton, NJ: Princeton University Press, 2010), 5–7.

528. In a lecture on which this chapter is based ("Dispatches from Whale Island: Babylonian Jewish Hellenization, Revisited," Princeton, 18 November 2019), I supported this by parsing the implicit concept of 111 uses of "culture/cultural" in Kalmin, *Migrating Tales*, inter alia, in light of modern anthropology's critique of "culture."

529. Clifford Geertz, *The Interpretation of Cultures* (New York: Basic Books, 1973), 10; Jeffrey L. Rubenstein, *The Culture of the Babylonian Talmud* (Baltimore: Johns Hopkins University Press, 2003), 12; Redfield, "Redacting Culture," 35–43.

medium through which *all* texts or artworks become interpretable along particular lines. When Jews in the East encountered Hellenistic culture, it shaped how they interpreted their own texts, not only how they engaged Greek texts; just as no text in Greek is a mere token of "Hellenistic culture," but only a partial reflection of some of its influence. In fact, we do not even need to be certain that Jews knew any specific Greek texts nor prove any influence. Yet we do need to show that their new ways of interpreting their *own* texts were becoming more Greek-like. This Greekness ("Hellenicity," in Jonathan Hall's term) is not a top-down ideology more like secularism, but a contested stance and process more like modernity; a term for how Jews absorbed a range of possible changes into their own tradition. Those changes left their mark, not only in the transfer of new texts, but also and even especially on old ones. To seek Greek in the Talmud, beyond asking whether or how Jews knew Greek or had items of Greek culture, we should read the Talmud through Greek eyes—asking not *How much Greek in the Talmud?* nor only *What kinds of Greek in the Talmud?* but more radically, *How Greek is the Talmud?*[530]

This brings us to the final rule of method that I would like to propose as we historicize our collection at the nexus of Hellenistic and rabbinic cultures in Sasanian Iran, one that I also feel is lacking in the paleological "text-as-culture"/"cultural inventory" model—namely, a chronology on *both* sides of the cultural comparison. Typically, as soon as some encounter between Greekness and the Talmud has been demonstrated, the way in which their encounter changed over time is absent or so vague—framed by "late antiquity," rather than by the internal chronology of our sources—that it results in static juxtaposition between specimens of two abstract cultures—a slide show, not a historical moving picture. In part, this is due

---

530. Naturally, this approach risks becoming too subjective. We should seek channels whereby, if not individual Hellenistic texts, then at least their genres, left an imprint on how the Talmud's readers would have taken up our collection (i.e., not "genres of the text" but "genres for the reader": see chapter 1 §*Genres for the Reader*). For a valuable critique of Boyarin, *Fat Rabbis*, on this point, see Adam H. Becker, "Positing a 'Cultural Relationship' between Plato and the Babylonian Talmud," *JQR* 101.2 (2011): 255–69. A figure like Uranius—if, as I suggested, his "jester" persona is not pure fiction but a distortion—represents such a channel to Sasanian elites. Further, precisely the sorts of Peripatetic writings that, as I will demonstrate here, comprise sources or inspiration for our collection (zoology and biology, where wonder-writing found its early natural home), were transferred to the Talmud in this period along the same channels. (See Simcha Gross, "Editorial Material in the Babylonian Talmud and Its Sasanian Context," *AJSR* 47.1 [2023]: 51–76, at 67–69.) We might add that the first known written accounts of the wonders of Alexander's travels in Persia, by his own peers Onēsikritos and Nearchos, were incorporated in the royal archives there, then reused by Theophrastus and others. See Truesdell S. Brown, *Onesicritus: A Study in Hellenistic Historiography*, University of California Publications in History 39 (Berkeley: University of California Press, 1949), 79–104. Multiple lines of literary genres intersect in our collection and its historical context.

to challenges of dating rabbinic texts, which are formidable, but, just as one can divide rabbinic traditions into layers and—through investigation of parallels, style, linguistics, realia, etc.—sketch some internal chronology that distinguishes rabbinic voices or *Tendenzen*, so can one trace shifts in Greek literature and seek similar broad trends. Parallel and divergent changes over time should be our focus if we are to read our collection in a doubly culturally comparative way.

In brief, such are the basic ingredients of a new method for mapping Hellenism in our talmudic collection from the standpoint of a reader whom we assume is aware of both. First, a qualitative rather than purely quantitative definition of what it means for a Jewish text to be "Greek." Second, consideration of the other side of the comparison as well, that is, ways in which Hellenistic texts were being shaped by the same cultural currents as Jewish texts were. Third, an internal chronology of actual sources indexing those cultural relationships—allowing for variation and change on both "Greek" and "Jewish" sides of the comparison, which may, in turn, show trends in shared underlying cultural factors that produced our texts and made them interpretable. I make this case by first showing that, once our collection was accessible as a whole, its audiences in Sasanian Iran would have interpreted some of their Jewish traditions in light of Hellenistic rhetorical and literary genres. Then I will undertake diachronic comparison between stories in those Hellenistic genres themselves and their parallels in the Talmud, comparing their trajectories over time in terms of how their respective readers received them.

How Greek Is the Talmud?

In other words, rather than set up this comparison as a slide show of "Hellenistic" and "talmudic" texts, I am asking us to begin with the opposite: a sort of methodological aphasia. Let us picture that we are stepping into an exhibition of texts entitled "How to Do Things with Wonders," containing our collection and the comparable genre of Greek wonder-writing (defined below), but all sources' labels and dates are covered up. What likeness do we see at a glance? Let us begin with a catalogue of the contents that we find in both literary traditions:[531]

1. Nature (strange properties of mountains and winds, extraordinarily fertile earth, and especially bodies of water;[532] the medicinal,

---

531. Versions of all of these phenomena are well indexed in *PGR* under their respective general categories and clearly attested in our collection (Appendix §*Translation* Part 1).
532. Like water that turns into blood or waves that roar high in the air, sending white snaking light along the crests.

apotropaic, and potentially deadly properties of plants and herbs;[533] animals of all kinds and their remarkable habits and abilities;[534] minerals, including rare, precious, and powerful stones;[535] but also, in a similar vein, humans, the unique physical properties and impressive or horrifying customs of groups from certain regions of the world)[536]

2. The limits of the known world, either above, below, or beyond the reach of civilization
3. The deep past, including the discovery of immense bones said to belong to ancient heroes
4. Miscellaneous phenomena, like a great voice from nowhere that calls out at a particular location, or an unquenchable fire

As we explore how this tradition took shape in the composition and reception of our collection, the striking point of departure for this comparison is that the content of this exhibition catalogue appears in both the Talmud and Hellenistic wonder-writing ("paradoxography").[537] The difference is that these motifs are diffused across the Hellenistic wonder-collectors, in Greek and Latin, from Kallimachos (third century BCE) to the late ancient compendia. By contrast, the Talmud's motifs fall into a single text compressed in a mere two folia: our collection. This overlap in content, but radical discrepancy in distribution, suggests that there was at least one paradoxographer in the Talmud: whoever cobbled together our collection from Rabbah's tales and other sources on these strange phenomena.[538] Furthermore, as XV of XXI tales in our talmudic collection are recounted by its infamous traveler to the West, Rabbah (whose colleague adds a remark

---

533. Like a plant that, if roasted with a pot of meat, knits its sinews back together.

534. Like fish swimming under ships that halt their passage through the sea; or a giant fish that makes the sea boil; or giant birds, or talking birds; or fish and reptiles from which precious oil is extracted; or huge horned beasts that fling excrement for great distances; or immense scorpions.

535. Like rocks that morph into glowing coals; or gems with healing properties; or underwater treasure seen from the deck of a ship; or precious minerals guarded by mythical monsters.

536. Like tribes who know the secrets of underground springs and wells. See n. 95.

537. For the literature, see Redfield, "Ethnography in Antiquity," §*Paradoxography*; more recently and richly, Kenneth W. Yu, "Textualizing Wonders: Ancient Greek Paradoxography in Comparative Perspective," in *After Wisdom: Sapiential Traditions and Ancient Scholarship in Comparative Perspective*, ed. Glenn W. Most and Michael Puett, Philological Encounters Monographs 4 (Leiden: Brill, 2023), 251–83, at 251 n. 2 and 252 n. 4. "Paradoxography" is a twelfth-century term, but, as Yu notes, the integrity of this literary-scientific tradition had long been named and defined in other ways.

538. Shared utopian motifs also appear in the Talmud's collection of the wonders of the Land of Israel, which also includes Rabbah. See n. 108.

on his items that is nominally also from the West),[539] we need not hunt far outside rabbinic circles for the *mechanism* whereby this material reached Jews in Iran. Just as clearly, however, neither its tellers, nor its collectors, nor its recollectors, "copied" their Greek or Latin sources. Indeed, it is hard to prove that they had any particular Greek or Latin source. Yet that is no obstacle to comparison in terms of *genres for the reader* (see chapter 1). Collections of wonders entered various literary forms; our collection is one of their many crossroads. Our task is to explore how it was read partly in a paradoxographical tradition (and partly in a talmudic one)—not that it is directly dependent on any given source.

The Genres of Wonder

How could the unified collection's reader have been a participant, then, not only in admiring the content of these wonders, but also in the Hellenism that mediated wonder through various literary forms; even though our collection is in Aramaic/Hebrew, and cites no sources apart from the Bible and the rabbis? I suggest three interrelated genres as interpretive frameworks through which our collection was mediated and became interpretable. Again, we are seeking not simply overlap in content, nor isolated parallels, but genres for the reader: conventions whereby, as I show, wonders were retold and recollected along cross-cultural lines.

First, *History and Ethnography*: critical inquiry or *historiē* into beliefs, customs, natural phenomena, and events, arranged by place or people.

Second, *Paradoxography* in a stricter sense: (pseudo-)scientific lists and realistic evocations of wonders.

Third, the *Romance* or cycle of adventure stories, especially those featuring Alexander the Great.

We begin with a synchronic hunt for each genre in our collection and proceed to show how the reception of wonder-accounts, in later Hellenistic genres of the romance and the novel, both tracks and diverges from how our own collection was received within the Talmud. This comparison reveals not only the Talmud's Greekness but also its gradual Talmudization.

History and Ethnography

Our collection's epistemology seems far from that of Hellenistic history or its subgenre, ethnography. Rather than make the strange familiar, it makes the strange even stranger. Tellers take no critical distance from

---

539. VIIIb.96, "When Rav Dimi arrived, he said . . ."; see n. 438, n. 648.

their sources to evaluate or compare them but report them all as true (or equally true and equally false, rather than empirically relative). It is a poetic digression within a discourse on Jewish law; not a realist treatise on war, geography, beliefs, customs, or *realia*.

Nevertheless, there are some subtle connections to the genre and knowledge of *historiē*. First and foremost, our main teller's persona is very peculiar.[540] For example, rather than use a standard formula for introducing a rabbinic story, whether a parable (*mashal; matla'*), a case (*ma'aseh; 'uvda*), or what the Palestinian Talmud calls a *delama'* (from Greek *drama*), and then present the body of his story indirectly through dialogue or omniscient narration (as is much more common in rabbinic storytelling),[541] our teller is unusually front-and-center. He announces his presence by beginning his stories with two sets of formulae: *opsis* or seeing ("I myself have seen") and *akouē* or hearing ("seafarers recounted to me"). Even when he does use a standard introductory formula ("once"), whether to link an episode to a larger story (I, IIIb), or to introduce a new tale (VI–XI), this stock introduction rarely stands alone, but is followed by a formula of seeing: "*once* I was/we were traveling in a ship *and I/we saw*" (VIa, VII, IXa) or "once I was traveling in the desert *and I saw*" (Xa). Rabbah is a teller who has traveled far and wide, reporting to his audience things that he has seen with his own eyes, or who qualifies his stories as hearsay, yet presents himself as their sole hearer.[542] Nor is he always alone: he sails with sailors and he is guided through the desert by the Arab—as if he also needed local informants to relay his knowledge of wonders to us.

The same rhetorical conventions were recycled by the hidden hands of two collectors. First, whoever recollected the added tales at the end (see chapter 3 §*Chronological Layers*) seems to take cues from Rabbah's genre markers. These appended tales are prefaced by the verb that Rabbah used for the seafarers (ש.ע.י, "to speak, recount"; "to tell a story").[543] It complicates matters, however, as in an earlier reading tradition of Rabbah, this verb "recounted" smacks of unreliability.[544] Those new tellers, therefore, keep trying to bolster their credibility with the same formula pioneered by Rabbah: "Once I/we was/were traveling in a ship/and I/we saw (XVIII and XIX).[545] Similar language appears in XX, which makes more sense if,

---

540. See Introduction §*The Teller*.
541. For a useful summary, see *Rabbinic Stories*, trans. Jeffrey L. Rubenstein, Classics of Western Spirituality (New York: Paulist, 2002), 15–16.
542. This is a common dynamic in sea yarns, which, due to their remote and fantastic setting, cannot be verified (see n. 6). Consider the epigraph to the end of *Moby Dick*: "And I only am escaped to tell thee" (Job 1:15–19).
543. XVI, XVIIa, XVIII, XIX, XXIa.
544. See nn. 133–134.
545. Most mss. (V, O, M, E, B) recycle the device in XVII as well, but it is not used for a third time in mss. H or P.

as I argued, it is an anonymous late Babylonian invention.[546] There, all manuscripts also refer to a vision ("I have *seen* a great light in the sea"), and one manuscript lays further stress on vision by first asking the teller "What did you see?"[547] Even a stock formula to introduce proof from *oral* tradition in the Talmud ("Come see!") recuperates the epistemic force of its literal sense in this context, witnessing God's "might" (I.13) and the somehow symbolic "strength" of a gargantuan tree (V.58).[548] Finally, we may recall that, when Rabbah's signature formula "I myself have seen" is used elsewhere in the Talmud, it indexes similar phenomena: rare expertise in nature held by Rabbah's desert guide the Arab, and the immensity of exotic data.[549] The formula generically tries to lend credibility to the incredible.

In short, all of our tellers seem obliged to express their claims to knowledge as firsthand visions. Between the lines, however, we can also detect critical distance, even skepticism, about that epistemic premise, insofar as they also retell others' stories and rely on local experts — not to mention their need to constantly reiterate that they really saw what their readers cannot possibly see. The same tension affects how a Sasanian Jewish reader would have perceived the settings of the tales. All of the settings within Iran (the walls of Mahoza; fort of Hagrunya; fords of Sura; and Ravnag river),[550] are well-known landmarks, whereas settings outside Iran are cosmic extremes (the sea, desert wilderness, the ends of the earth or the "place where the earth and the firmament kiss"), and the partly real, partly mythological Mount Sinai and Jordan River: the limits of the land of Israel and the limits of the settled world. The familiar landscape of Babylonia is estranged, whereas the exotic land of Israel is richly illustrated.

Although its content may not seem historical or ethnographic, we can therefore say — and see! — that our collection's genre foregrounds the cultural issue of evidence, which it explores by combining oral formulae with intricate reflections on the epistemic status of firsthand experience. On one hand, it stresses the special authority of having traveled to a distant place

---

546. See nn. 493–496.

547. Ms. P, כ.רמ"ח. All other manuscripts echo the narrator's phrase ("Why did you *give a start*?"), not the character's.

548. This formula is echoed indirectly later, when Rabbah's Arab guide says of equally wondrous sights, "Come, I will show you ..." (XIIa, XIIIa, XIV, and XV). Knowing and seeing are generically linked.

549. See n. 87, n. 249.

550. As vocalized in ms. V, גִ.בְ.לִ"א. As Alexander Kohut notes (*Arukh Completum* [Hebrew], vol. ס–פ at 131 n. 4 and vol. ב–ג s.v. גשו) this resembles Ῥώγονις in Arrian, *Indika*, XXIX (see n. 193). That source has parallels to our I and VI, is set in Persia, and is told, like much of the *Indika*, by Alexander's admiral "Nearchos" (see n. 530), the Greek equivalent to Rabbah's "seafarers" (*nahote yama'*, I–II). This supports our collection's affinity with Hellenistic history via collections of nautical wonders.

and seen it with your own eyes. On the other, it recognizes that its narrators are reporting things about which its audience is skeptical, as they are by nature extraordinary, even incredible, and ordinarily unavailable to the senses. The same dynamic defines the Hellenistic genres of history and ethnography, which, as they are specially concerned with evidence and authority, in striving to prove their credibility, reveals the teller's role in mediating knowledge to the audience—abandoning the *de facto* credibility of anonymous collective tradition for another kind of knowledge.[551] In Greek history and ethnography, as in the Talmud, this tension surrounding the presence of a human teller is closely associated with a teller's formulae for introducing evidence. Like Rabbah, Herodotus may insist that "I have seen it" (αὐτὸς ὥρων), or more emphatically, "I myself have seen it" (αὐτὸς ἐγὼ ὥρων), or even "I myself have seen it, and it is too great for words" (λόγου μέζω). Or he may support evidence from other sources with personal autopsy, in the formula "Furthermore, I myself have seen it" (εἶδον δὲ καὶ αὐτός). As John Marincola has noted, however, these autopsies, in Herodotus and in later historians, play a specific role: they dispute an earlier view, whether or not it is stated.[552] Most autopsies appear in Herodotus's book on Egypt, because there his inquiry confronted earlier geographers, like Hekataīos of Miletus, who—he complains—based their notions about reality on abstract speculation.[553] His first-person reports try to debunk their armchair research with his own travels and what he saw, as well as evidence gathered from his local informants.

Having broken down his default credibility as a narrator, Herodotus builds it back up as a historian who is uniquely positioned, not only to refute his predecessors, but also to critically evaluate and take a carefully measured distance from all of his newly available sources. In other words, rather than tradition or speculation, his authority rests on constructing a narrative persona who mediates knowledge to the audience in a balanced and multifaceted way. He holds fast to the evidence of what he has seen and heard, yet he acknowledges that this is only part of a larger story. Consider how he approaches the question of the sources of the Nile:

> I consulted Egyptians, Lydians, and Hellenes about the sources of the Nile, but no one I talked to professed to know anything about it, except for a scribe of the sacred treasury of Athena in the Egyptian city of Sais.

---

551. Eva Tyrell rightly challenges this distinction between Jewish traditionalism and the critical Greek spirit (*Strategies of Persuasion in Herodotus' Histories and Genesis-Kings: Evoking Reality in Ancient Narratives of a Past*, JSJSup 195 [Leiden: Brill, 2020]).

552. John Marincola, "Herodotean Narrative and the Narrator's Presence," *Arethusa* 20.1/2 (1987): 121–37.

553. Rosalind Thomas, *Herodotus in Context: Ethnography, Science, and the Art of Persuasion* (Cambridge: Cambridge University Press, 2000), 136–39, 163–67.

For my part, I thought this man was joking when he presented himself to me as one who knew exactly where the sources were....

He said that Psammetichos king of Egypt decided to conduct an experiment to test whether the sources really are bottomless. He had a rope many thousands of fathoms long woven and let it down there, but it did not reach the bottom. The scribe actually showed, insofar as I understood him (and if what he said was true at all), that the water dashing against the mountains there produced powerful eddies and back currents which would prevent a sounding line from reaching the bottom when it was let down.

But I could learn nothing from anyone else. However, I did learn as much as I could by traveling to the city of Elephantine and seeing it for myself [αὐτόπτης ἐλθών], but I investigated the region beyond that point through hearsay alone [ἀπὸ τούτου ἀκοῇ ἤδη ἱστορέων]. (*Hist.* 2.28–29)[554]

The basic paradox of Herodotus's authority here is the same as it is for all tellers in our collection. On one hand, he gives us reason to doubt his sources. He admits that he has only one—who was, perhaps, "joking," or perhaps it was not properly "understood." He also admits that his source relies on an old story about a king who conducted a scientific experiment—rather than, say, recent sources or his own eyewitness testimony. On the other hand, Herodotus reminds us that one source is better than none; that he is the only person who knows it; and that both he *and* his source were careful to distinguish their own reasoning and inquiry from those of their separate sources. Just as the scribe explained the legend of the bottomless Nile, not by its bottomless depth, but by strong intersecting currents, Herodotus is clear where his autopsy runs out—at Elephantine. After that, he relies on hearsay. We may not believe him, but he is transparent about the sources and limits of his knowledge. By inviting his readers/hearers to question his account, he makes them into critical inquirers like himself.

The same genre markers and oppositions—autopsy and hearsay as opposed to tradition; travel as opposed to idle theory; a teller's authority as opposed to a local informant's—are reflected by a parallel in one of our tales.[555] Yet this parallel also shows how rabbinic collectors exploited those features in order to reclaim their own traditional authority.

IXa. And Rabbah bar bar Hanah said:
Once I was traveling in a ship
and I saw a certain bird
who was standing up to its ankles in the water
and its head reached the firmament.

---

554. *Landmark Herodotus*, 128–29.

555. The parallels in Herodotus and Pausanias were noted quite independently and only *en passant* in E. E. Halevy, *Aggadot ha-Amoraim* [Hebrew] (Tel-Aviv: Dvir, 1979), 158–59.

We thought the water was not substantial;
we meant to go down to cool ourselves off.
A heavenly voice appeared and said to us:
Here, you mean to cool yourselves off?
For a carpenter's adze fell seven years
and has not reached the bottom;
and not because the water is deep
but because the water is forceful.

IXb.
Rav Ashi said:
That was *ziz saday*,
as it is written:
and ziz saday is mine [*'immadi*; Ps. 50:11, modified.]

Not only is the wonder the same as the Egyptian tradition reported by Herodotus (a body of water where an object cannot touch the bottom), so is its rational explanation. Nothing resurfaces in this lake, not due to its depth alone—as others suppose—but "because the water is forceful," due to "powerful eddies and back currents." In the Talmud, however, both this wonder and its explanation are presented very differently. In Herodotus, the explanation is attributed to his source, the Egyptian scribe. It is a human and fallible reason for an empirical fact; one that the teller doubts is correct but reports anyway. In the Talmud, both perspectives on the wonder are blended together or ventriloquized. The teller reports that he did not perceive it; the heavenly voice corrects his naïve view, signaling the wonder; and the explanation of the wonder sounds as if it is spoken by the heavenly voice as well. In fact, this explanation is not part of the wonder itself, but a later anonymous remark, added by the Talmud's editors, who integrated the explanation—as well as another later tradition on the danger of swimming in this lake—back into the tale itself through ventriloquism.[556] It is, if we stop to think about it, rather odd that a divine

---

556. Midr. Ps 93:6 has precisely Herodotus's story (featuring Hadrian instead of the Egyptian king), minus any explanation. This suggests that the latter was added by the anonymous Talmud, blended with the heavenly voice. This wonder is also listed in paradoxographical collections. More direct development to the rabbinic versions, however, is in *Pausanias's Description of Greece*, trans. J. G. Frazer, 6 vols. (London: Macmillan, 1898), 1:130. Not only does Pausanias substitute Nero for Psammetichos just as Midr. Ps. substitutes Hadrian, his version also preserves the *other* tradition blended into our talmudic telling: the same remark about the danger of swimming. "I was told [ἤκουσα], too, that smooth and still as the water of the lake looks to the eye, it yet has the property of sucking down anyone who is rash enough to swim in it: the water of the lake catches him, and sweeps him down into the depths." An oral source, from whom Pausanias "heard," becomes the Talmud's "heavenly voice."

voice from the ether would pause to explain its own vatic declaration in this manner.[557]

Yet, as a reader who is immersed in this literary language, we do not stop to think about it. And that is precisely the rhetorical effect of this blending of voices: one hears the Talmud's rational explanation as no less authoritative than the voice of heaven. The two are the same. Mss. H, V, O take this ventriloquism even further to blend the heavenly voice with the teller's inner monologue. The voice can hear directly inside Rabbah's head: "We meant to go down to cool ourselves off," he says, to which it retorts: "*Here*, you mean to cool yourselves off?!"[558] By aligning other voices in the story with its voice, the anonymous Talmud's retelling of this story makes the reader complicit in a more conservative interpretation of its message: "Don't plunge into the unknown. You're in over of your head." Herodotus does the opposite: he marks an X on the map where his seeing and traveling end and the hearsay of others begins, making it possible for the reader—or even inviting the reader—to challenge one voice without rejecting them all.

How might we account for the different motifs in the two stories? Instead of a rope, lowered by an Egyptian king who is famous in Herodotus for natural-science experiments,[559] now the water's strong currents are measured by a "carpenter's adze." Why would this have been used to measure the depth of the water? One would assume it was dropped by mistake. But for a Jewish reader, this is no mistake: it recalls Elisha's floating axe-head (2 Kgs 6:1–7), just as the bird, "up to its ankles in the water," recalls Ezekiel's vision, in which an angel leads him "up to the ankles" in water that, like Rabbah, he cannot cross (Ezek 47:1–6).[560] This biblical intertext,

---

557. In the story of the Oven of Akhnai (b. B. Metz. 59b), "A heavenly voice emerged and said: 'Why do you differ from Rabbi Eliezer, because the law is in accordance with him everywhere [that there is a dispute]?'" Here, too, the talmudic *deus ex machina* is not a pure apodictic authority but a dialectical one, participating on the same level. For a comprehensive study of this phenomenon's literary function, see Peter Kuhn, *Offenbarungsstimmen im antiken Judentum: Untersuchungen zur Bat Qol und verwandten Phänomenen*, TSAJ 20 (Tübingen: Mohr Siebeck, 1989).

558. See mss. H, V, O, ט״א.קר״י. Note harmonization in ms. V, which used a different verb ("chill" not "cool") in IXa.112. Mss. P, M, and E have a relatively boring imperative: "Do not go down here!"

559. Herodotus, *Hist.* 2:2–5 (trans. Purvis, *Landmark Herodotus*, 117–18).

560. See b. Sotah 13a: Elisha's ability to make the axe-head float is attributed to his study of Torah. A similar motif of giant brigands–so tall that the *sea* reaches only their *knees*–appears in the adventures of Keresaspa, who fells them by striking their ankles (a comic inversion is the Lilliputians' assault on Gulliver). *The Pahlavi Riwāyat Accompanying the Dādestān ī Dēnīg*, trans. A. V. Williams, 2 vols., Historisk-filosofiske meddelelser 60:1–60:2 (Copenhagen: Royal Danish Academy, 1990), 2:41. As Thrope notes (see n. 201), Rabbah bears a resemblance to Keresaspa.

followed by Rav Ashi's exegetical gloss of the bird's identity,[561] enhances the tale's traditional flavor and renders familiar a wonder that remains very strange indeed. The reader is puzzled by the wonders in the tale, but, unlike Herodotus, the Talmud offers no foothold in the story to dispute the teller's account or criticize its own explanations, which are ventriloquized ("blended") into the story.[562] Its rhetoric puts readers in a "take-it-or-leave it" position, what Meir Sternberg calls the "foolproof" poetics of biblical narrative, or what Erich Auerbach (in a veiled polemic against the Nazis) called its "tyranny."[563] A reader can radically disbelieve the Talmud's tale—possibly at a cost—but cannot pick and choose what to believe.

In sum, precisely the generic narrative features that Herodotus took such pains to distinguish, in order to display himself as a critical historian, were implicitly distinguished—hence, recognized—by our tale's recollectors, retellers, and even by the tellings of some manuscripts. Yet the Talmud's anonymous collectors then collapsed those distinctions in order to make its telling more familiar and rhetorically "foolproof." This is a case of the Talmudization of Hellenistic wonder-writing,[564] a narrative parallel to the art of *ventriloquism* in talmudic legal discourse.[565] In other words, this talmudic adventure does share genre conventions with Greek ethnographies of wonder, but pushes them in the opposite direction: back to seamless dialogue within its own tradition. This process of cultural interaction and distinction that we have just observed on the scale of an individual parallel will recur when we proceed to our larger-scale comparison over time.

Paradoxography

On the surface, the Hellenistic genre of paradoxography no more resembles our collection than history or ethnography. While the genres are historically related—for example, similar such lists appear in books of strange customs, arranged by peoples, including one attributed to Herod's Jewish

---

561. See n. 118, n. 187, n. 619.

562. IXb and, even more, VIb, structurally parallel a story about a counterpart to the ziz: a huge bird called *bar yokhni* (b. Bekh. 57b; compare Tg. Job 39:13 to Tg. Ps. 50:11). A Rabbah-like story, including his hyperbolic use of "sixty," tells of destruction wrought by this giant bird (compare also VIa). The parallels do not end there: Rav Ashi ends with a "scientific" gloss that "explains" this wondrous tradition. This shows that the process of Talmudization was not limited to our collection. In fact, it continued in a Zoharic commentary: see n. 756.

563. Sternberg, *Poetics of Biblical Narrative*, 233-35; James I. Porter, "Erich Auerbach and the Judaizing of Philology," *Critical Inquiry* 35.1 (2008): 115–47, at 137; Redfield, "Auerbach at Saints Peter and Paul."

564. On "Talmudization," see Introduction §*The Canon*. On ventriloquism, see n. 477.

565. See nn. 439 and 477.

friend, Nikolaos of Damascus—this genre took the form not of narratives but of lists of "wonders" (*thaumata, terata*) generated as extracts or epitomes.[566] It flourished in a rich Alexandrian book culture among scholars who reworked myths or took Peripatetic texts on nature and animals as their starting point but delved into their stranger, more speculative features and, by extracting such features, recollected lists of "strange but true" items with varied principles of organization. This genre occupies the realm, not so much of the supernatural (not clearly separated as such: the second-century CE Roman, Phlegōn of Tralles, prefaced a wonder-book with ghost stories), but of the paranormal. Rather than explain, the paradoxographer puts wonders on display, helping them to speak more loudly for themselves. His editorial choices evoke surprise and wonder in the reader while remaining authoritative. The reader is confronted with wonders as real phenomena in the world, in real places. The author occasionally verifies them with an autopsy or casts doubt on a source, but this genre is striking for its usual *lack* of explanation or evidence (let alone rationalistic deconstructions of its mythological basis like Palaiphatus' *Peri apistōn* ("On Incredible Things") or the so-called Euhemerist tradition).[567] Wonder is real: a paradoxography lists its *where, who,* and *what* but minimizes its *why*.

By contrast, our collection is concerned with evidence and explanations for its visions, and does employ a narrative form: the adventure. But it also has overlooked generic features with these wonder-lists.[568] As noted,[569] it is hard to ignore their dense shared types of content. We might also view the arrangement of Rabbah's tales—the original nucleus of our collection—as a partial reflex of paradoxography. After exploring the cosmos, divided by the biblical elements of creation (see chapter 3 §*Setting*), Rabbah ends at its outer limit: a mysterious place that most manuscripts call the place "where earth and firmament kiss."[570] Paradoxographers are also interested in mapping the known world and its limits: the structure

---

566. See Ben Zion Wacholder, *Nicolaus of Damascus*, University of California Publications in History 75 (Berkeley: University of California Press, 1962), 70–73. On wonder terminology, see Dimitria Eleftheriou, "Pseudo-Antigonos de Carystos: *Collection d'histoires curieuses*", 2 vols. (PhD diss., Paris–Nanterre, 2018), 1:67–80.

567. Palaephatus, *On Unbelievable Tales*, trans. Jacob Stern (Wauconda, IL: Bolchazy-Carducci, 1996). On how late ancient Christian authors invoked Euhemerus to debunk "pagan" religion, see Nicholas P. Roubekas, *An Ancient Theory of Religion: Euhemerism from Antiquity to the Present* (New York: Routledge, 2017), 57–66.

568. This section is inspired by a bold and original suggestion by Joshua Levinson, "There Is No Place Like Home: Rabbinic Responses to the Christianization of Palestine," in *Jews, Christians, and the Roman Empire: The Poetics of Power in Late Antiquity*, ed. Natalie B. Dohrmann and Annette Yoshiko Reed, Jewish Culture and Contexts (Philadelphia: University of Pennsylvania Press, 2013), 99–120, at 117. See now Amsler, *Babylonian Talmud*, 20–21.

569. See above, §*How Greek is the Talmud?*

570. Mss. P, E, V, O, M, B, נשק.פ"ז.

of some collections moves from one to the other.⁵⁷¹ When Rabbah reaches the edges of the earth at the very end, he assumes that it should be a utopia, like many Hellenistic authors who recounted wonders. That is why he is shocked when his basket is gone: "Really?! There are thieves here?!"⁵⁷² Even in its violation, a Hellenistic topos informs the expectations of the teller and his readers.

Since so many of these wonders appear from classical to late ancient paradoxographies, and are condensed in our text, collectors in the Talmud could have worked from a similar sort of list, or at least a similar genre. Early wonder-books are also arranged by elements, animals, plants, stones, and especially—as in our collection—water-wonders.⁵⁷³ This form of organizing wonders differs from rabbis' own occasional lists of won-

---

571. On geography as an organizing principle, see Guido Schepens and Kris Delcroix, "Ancient Paradoxography: Origin, Production, Evolution, and Reception," in *La letteratura di consumo nel mondo greco-latino: Atti del convegno internazionale*, ed. Oronzo Pecere and Antonio Stramaglia (Cassino: Università degli studi di Cassino, 1994), 373–460, at 394–98; for more recent literature, see Klaus Geus, "Paradoxography and Geography in Antiquity: Some Thoughts about the *Paradoxographus Vaticanus*," in *La letra y la carta: Descripción verbal y representación gráfica en los diseños terrestres; Estudios en honor de Pietro Janni*, ed. Francisco J. González Ponce et al. (Seville: University of Seville Press, 2016), 243–57, at 248 n. 16. For example, while the exact title and the structure of Callimachos's collection are not certain, it seems to have billed its wonders as arranged *"kata topous,"* from regions in the extreme west (utopian Erytheia) to the extreme east (Asia), and it may have moved from west to east. See Irene Pajón Leyra, «Paradoxografía Griega: Estudio de un género literario» (PhD diss., Universidad Complutense Madrid, 2009), 35–38. This structure, in contrast to its central focus on Greece, suggests a map of the known world, bookended by the obscure periphery. In a similar albeit nongeographical way, the structure of Antigonos's collection yields a "steady gradation in the levels of θαῦμα," ending in wonders "hardly accessible to observation" (Schepens and Delcroix, "Ancient Paradoxography," 398).

572. Ms. P שט.קצ"א. See Appendix §*Thieves in Heaven (?!)* See nn. 108 and 401. The claim that God is a "thief" is similarly represented by the Talmud as a topos of Jewish polemics with Romans (b. Sanh. 39a; parallels at Moses Gaster, *The Exempla of the Rabbis: Being a Collection of Exempla, Apologues and Tales Culled from Hebrew Manuscripts and Rare Hebrew Books*, 2nd ed. [New York: Ktav, 1968 (1924)], 196–97). A more direct parallel is in Rabbah's contemporary Solinus (ca. 300 CE), who starts in his homeland Rome and ends at the utopian periphery of the Islands of the Blessed. Solinus's utopia is also spoiled by a wonder that is also in Rabbah's collection (VI): "… the wavy sea spits out sea monsters on to the shores of this island. When the monsters are decomposing into putrefaction, everything there is imbued with a foul reek: for this reason, the nature of the islands does not wholly agree with their nomination" (translation by Arwen Apps, "Gaius Iulius Solinus and His *Polyhistor*" [PhD diss., Macquarie University, 2011], §56.14, at https://topostext.org/work/747 (accessed 7 September 2024). On the uses of utopia in Herodotean wonder, see Jessica Lightfoot, *Wonder and the Marvellous from Homer to the Hellenistic World*, Cambridge Classical Studies (Cambridge: Cambridge University Press, 2021), 59–65, literature at 59 n. 40. On the uses of wonder in utopian tales of the East after Alexander, see James S. Romm, *The Edges of the Earth in Ancient Thought: Geography, Exploration, and Fiction* (Princeton, NJ: Princeton University Press, 1992), 92–109.

573. See Giannini in *PGR*, 427–30, and n. 611.

ders,[574] as it is no static enumeration. Rather, it moves across the cosmos in a "hodological" format: wonder becomes a journey.[575] Unfolding in a wheeling motion across planes and elements of the cosmos, our collection, like paradoxographies, also creates dynamic links across sections by selecting aspects of their contents that criss-cross their thematic and geographical oppositions in a *metamorphic poetics*, propelled by *wobbly binaries* (see chapter 3 §*Setting*). It begins with Ocean; moves east, to the homeland of its own audience; then west, to the river Jordan, which is a boundary of the Land of Israel; then south, to the Sinai Peninsula and the site of national origins; then it comes full circle to Ocean (adding the Desert due to a competing genre-convention).[576]

This form is not the more realistic *periodos gēs* of geographers like Hekataios, tracing the Mediterranean coast from west to east and back in a circle. Nor is it the cartographic *periplous*, touching on ports, coastlines, or riverbanks—as in the account of the Carthaginian king, Hanno, who sailed the reverse direction, through the straits of Gibraltar down the west coast of Africa. Indeed, the Talmud is less interested in the limits of its own *oikoumenē* than in the limits of the cosmos itself: what the Greeks called *peīrati gaiēs*, the ends of the earth.[577] Its narrators are nearly burnt by a star; hear the screams of the damned in hell; and traverse the desert or what Greeks called the "wasteland" (*erēmos*): a terrain not merely unknown but barely knowable, empty as it is of any living soul but the Arab, with his expertise in paths, water, bones, and magical relics. These closer similarities with the content of wonders, their fascination with limits, their epistemological conventions of being located and verifiable, and their manner of arrangement, are strong enough to suggest that our collection has some Greek literary DNA. If rabbis had lists of wonder-material and wanted to turn them into stories, this integration of cosmologically ordered lists into an itinerary or "hodology" form, on one hand, featuring evidence of autopsies and hearsay, on the other, would have been a very

---

574. E.g., "Ten miracles performed for our ancestors in Egypt ... in the Temple ..." (m. Avot 5:4–5); "Ten things created at twilight on the eve of [the first] Sabbath" (m. Avot 5:6, b. Pesah. 54a). See further I. Heinemann, *Darkhe ha-aggadah*, 81; August Wünsche, "Die Zahlensprüche im Talmud und Midrasch," ZDMG 65.1 (1911): 57–100, 395–421; 66.3 (1912): 414–59.

575. Pietro Janni, *La mappa e il periplo: Cartografia antica e spazio odologico*, Pubblicazioni della Facoltà di lettere e filosofia 19 (Macerata: Bretschneider, 1984), 79–90. See Geus, "Paradoxography and Geography," 248, on *Paradoxographus Vaticanus* (second century CE); Klaus Geus and Colin Guthrie King, "Paradoxography," in *Oxford Handbook of Science and Medicine in the Classical World*, ed. Paul T. Keyser and John Scarborough (Oxford: Oxford University Press, 2018), 431–44, at 437–38, on Ps.-Aristotle, *Of Marvelous Things Heard*.

576. See n. 505. On analogy as a similar way to link parts of a paradoxography, see Christian Jacob, "De l'art de compiler à la fabrication du merveilleux: sur la paradoxographie grecque," *Lalies* 2 (1983): 121–40, at 128–29.

577. Romm, *Edges of the Earth*, 37–41.

A Wonderful World and the Romance of the East 197

Greek way to do it.[578] And, closer to their time, it was how some Hellenistic authors did — as we will see.

Parallel (Anti-)Heroes

Finally, as for the Alexander Romance, it is easy to briefly note what our text lacks and what it shares with this cosmopolitan but, like paradoxography, originally Alexandrian genre. It lacks the main character, Alexander, who was no stranger to Jews or rabbis, appearing as he does throughout their literature. Rabbah and the other travelers in our collection hardly seem like Alexander-type heroes. They do not stride boldly forward but startle and shrink back, as does Rabbah at the edge of the bottomless lake. Rather than preternaturally wise, they are easily mistaken and puzzled.[579] Still, if we look for generic affinities between our collection and Alexander traditions preserved in rabbinic literature,[580] we do find a few close ones that have not yet been noted. This genre is present in the Talmud — even if Alexander himself is absent.

First, unlike Greek historians, ethnographers, or geographers, Alexander is the best-known ancient figure who explored the ends of the earth and

---

578. Another related and comparable late ancient genre, the *itinerarium* used in pilgrimage narratives like Egeria's (ca. 381 CE), combines localized marvels with references to vision. See Georgia Frank, *The Memory of the Eyes: Pilgrims to Living Saints in Christian Late Antiquity*, Transformation of the Classical Heritage 30 (Berkeley: University of California Press, 2000); Mary B. Campbell, *The Witness and the Other World: Exotic European Travel Writing, 400–1600* (Ithaca, NY: Cornell University Press, 1988), 18–33. Rabbah and friends, however, are neither pilgrims nor anti-pilgrims, as Scripture is not their primary framework for seeing, recording, localizing, critiquing, and interpreting wonders. On reception of paradoxography in late ancient Christian narratives, see Scott Fitzgerald Johnson, *The Life and Miracles of Thekla: A Literary Study*, Hellenic Studies 13 (Washington, DC: Center for Hellenic Studies, 2006), 113–220; *Credible, Incredible: The Miraculous in the Ancient Mediterranean*, ed. Tobias Nicklas and Janet E. Spittler, WUNT 321 (Tübingen: Mohr Siebeck, 2013); *Recognizing Miracles in Antiquity and Beyond*, ed. Maria Gerolemou (Berlin: de Gruyter, 2018).
579. Nevertheless, Alexander is not always wise or brave in the romance tradition. See, e.g., the motif of his fear in Richard Stoneman, "The Alexander Romance and the Rise of Paradoxography," in *The Alexander Romance: History and Literature*, ed. Richard Stoneman et al., Ancient Narrative: Supplement 25 (Eelde: Barkhuis, 2018), 49–62, at 54.
580. Parallels between tales in our collection (VII, XVIII) and episodes in the Alexander Romance were first, to my knowledge, noted by James R. Russell, "Sasanian Yarns: The Problem of the Centaurs Reconsidered," in *La Persia e Bizanzio* (Rome: Lincei Academy, 2004), 411–38, at 427–28. On the direction of influence (west to east), see Richard Stoneman, "Oriental Motifs in the Alexander Romance," *Antichthon* 26 (1992): 95–113; and further evidence in *The Alexander Romance in Persia and the East*, ed. Richard Stoneman, Kyle Erickson, and Ian Netton, Ancient Narrative: Supplement 15 (Eelde: Barkhuis, 2012), esp. Stoneman, "Persian Aspects of the Romance Tradition," 3–18, on the Sasanian *Book of the Acts of Ardashir*. See Ory Amitay, "Alexander in Ancient Jewish Literature," in *A History of Alexander the Great in World Culture*, ed. Richard Stoneman (Cambridge: Cambridge University Press, 2022), 109–42.

the wasteland—that is, the settings of our text. Palestinian sources imagine him going to visit "King Qatsiyya"[581] (literally, "the extreme king"), who judges with Solomonic wisdom in a land that—again by the common convention—the Talmud pictures as a utopia.[582] Just as the earlier Palestinian Talmud knows of Alexander's ascent to the heavens in a diving bell, the Talmud (b. Tamid 32a) imagines Alexander as the sort of man who would ask questions about "what is above and what is below, what was before and what will be after" creation: a paradigm for the limits of forbidden knowledge.[583]

It is little surprise then that, when rabbis in both Talmuds retell Alexander's exploits, we rediscover motifs from our collection. Just as in XIV, where the Arab guide opens the "Maw of Qorah"—the place where the earth split open and swallowed up Qorah and company—to Rabbah's ears, who hears their cries in Gehinnom, so does Alexander insist on crossing Mountains of Darkness, which lead—according to an adjacent tradition—directly to Gehinnom.[584] Furthermore, in order to penetrate this darkness, Alexander, again like Rabbah, must rely on local expertise of mysterious desert sages: the Elders of the Negev. They guide him as follows (b. Tamid 32a):

> They told him: bring Libyan donkeys,[585] which can walk even in the darkness,[586] and take coils of rope and tie them on this side, so when you come [back], you can hold them, and come back to your location.

---

581. Y. B. Metz. 2:4, 8c; Ber. Rab. 33:1 (ed. Theodor-Albeck, 301); Vay. Rab. 27:1 (ed. Margulies, 618–19) = Pesiq. Rab Kah. 9:1 (ed. Mandelbaum, 148). Tanh. §'*Emor* 9 (ed. Buber, 2:44b–45a).

582. Or: "the king of the people of the end of the world" (*eschatoi andrōn*), who were "cast in idealized form" per Hellenistic convention (see n. 572; Saul Lieberman, in Pesiq. Rab Kah. ed. Mandelbaum, n. to 1:148 ln. 9). See Shai Secunda, "Gaze and Counter-Gaze: Textuality and Contextuality in the Anecdote of Rav Assi and the Roman (b. Baba Meṣi'a 28b)," in Herman and Rubenstein, *Aggada of the Bavli*, 149–71, at 162–66; Yael Wilfand, "Alexander the Great in the Jerusalem Talmud and Genesis Rabbah: A Critique of Roman Power, Greed, and Cruelty," in *Reconsidering Roman Power*, ed. Katell Berthelot (Rome: L'École française de Rome, 2020), 337-60, at 350 n. 50.

583. B. Hag. 11b and parallels. See Amitay, "Alexander in Ancient Jewish Literature," 118–19. Subtle Talmudizations of Alexander Romance traditions, in order to make rhetorical points for a Jewishly educated audience about Alexander's character, are deciphered expertly by Ory Amitay, "Alexander in Bavli Tamid: In Search for a Meaning," in Stoneman et al., *Alexander Romance in Persia and the East*, 349–65, at 355, 363-64.

584. B. Tamid 32b: "The school of Eliyahu taught: Gehinnom is above the firmament; and some say it is beyond the Mountains of Darkness."

585. Libyan donkeys are better (b. Shabb. 51b). If they are also white (יג׳קס.א״ה, ms. H: *Libyan*; all others: *white*), perhaps their color counteracts the darkness. Arabian horses can see in the dark: Agostini & Thrope trans., *Bundahišn*, 124.

586. הברא, "thick darkness": no etymology in the lexica. I suggest a metathesis of Ἔρεβος, god of darkness.

While this is surely a folk motif like Theseus's thread in his quest through the labyrinth, Rabbah contacts Gehinnom with his desert guide using a curiously similar device:

XIIIa.
He said to us:
"Come, I will show you Mount Sinai."
I went and saw that it was surrounded by scorpions as big as Libyan donkeys
. . .
XIV.
He said to us:
"Come, I will show you the Maw of Qorah."
He showed us a certain crevice, from which a wisp of smoke was appearing.
He brought out a tuft of wool,
brushed it in water, and wrapped it around his spear, and inserted it.
It was burnt and charred.
He said to me: "Listen now, to what you hear from here."
And I heard them saying: "Moses and his Torah are true, and they [sic][587] are liars!"
He told me: "Every thirty days, Gehinnom stirs them *as flesh in the caldron.* (Micah 3:3)"

"Scorpions as big as Libyan donkeys" block Mount Sinai from Rabbah's view, just as only "Libyan donkeys" can pass the "Mountains of Darkness" in the Alexander romance.[588] The motifs' order is the same: first, Libyan donkeys and mountain; then, the ropes or tuft of wool: a thin thread tying our world to the awful and wondrous ends, or depths, of the earth.[589]

As our collection has affinities with the Alexander Romance, and as the latter, like our collection, drew on a common stock of motifs from wonder-writing, by going on to compare how that common stock was adapted to narratives in the Romance and Talmud, we can trace the dynamic evolution of wonders within each literary tradition. It may turn out, not only that Rabbah was more aware of Greek culture than his reputation as "ass"

---

587. All manuscripts. This seems to be a euphemism for *we*, lest a reciter or reader identify even indirectly with these villains during their telling of the story.

588. The "Horn of Darkness," mentioned only by our Rabbah (b. Taʿan. 22b), recalls the "mountains of darkness." Compare *Gilgamesh* IX.38–45: "There were *scorpion-men* guarding its gate, whose terror was dread, whose glance was death, whose radiance was fearful, *overwhelming the mountains*" (trans. Andrew George [New York: Penguin, 1999], 70).

589. In Tan. Yel. §*Vayyishlah* 2, Moses puts "bundles of wool" in the earth to subdue the "fire" of God's wrath after another wilderness rebellion (Num 11:1). Whether probe or defense, it is a mediator of two cosmic domains. It plugs a demon's pit in b. Git. 68a.

and "jackass" implies, but also that his tales' retellers, recollectors, and readers knew how to do some Greek things with wonders.

From Wonder to Romance: Another Risky Swim

We already saw that the tale of Rabbah's narrowly averted death by swimming (IXa) is a talmudic retelling of the same traditions recorded by Herodotus and developed in Pausanias. It emphasizes the sole authority of its "heavenly voice" rather than a critical/empirical stance, and it incorporates motifs from Scripture to lend this Greek wonder a more traditional profile. Water-wonders—beneficial, dangerous, simply odd—were indeed a very popular feature of the original lists,[590] and influenced tales about Alexander in both romantic and historical genres. One case of a water-wonder's mutation into story sheds further light on our talmudic parallel.

An odd little tale is told about Alexander's military campaign in Kilikia near the Turkish-Syrian border. By the time of our collection, it existed in thirteen versions—to count just the ones we have—but most agree on the basic story: King Alexander was hot, so he went for a swim, but then he fell terribly ill. Why? Five tellings appear in the Alexander Romance tradition; one in Lucian; and seven among Alexander's historians. The romance and historical traditions share narrative contradictions and lacunae indicating a synthesis of distinct sources: a water-wonder, on the one hand; a historical event, on the other. Those problems are themselves our best evidence for authors' strategies—more or less successful—of narrativizing the wonder.

In the Alexander Romance (II.8.1–2), the earlier and shorter ("alpha") telling of Ps.-Callisthenes (third century CE) brings this narrative contradiction to the surface:

> 1. Passing through Kilikia, Alexander came to a certain river called Ōkeanos, whose water is [fast-]flowing and translucent. 2. Alexander was longing to bathe [himself] and [so], undressing, he leapt into the river and came back out. But the bath did him no good: immediately, he had a headache and he was in a bad way.[591]

---

590. See n. 573, n. 611, and Lightfoot, *Wonder and the Marvellous*, 49.

591. My trans. ed. Stoneman/Gargiulo, 1:26–28. The β recension adds, like Iulius Valerius (see below), that the water was "very cold" and that Alexander "ached all over inside," in addition to his headache. The latter looks like partial harmonization with the rational explanations in the historians (see below). All texts of the Romance from *Il Romanzo di Alessandro*, ed. Richard Stoneman and Tristano Gargiulo, 2 vols. (Milan: Mondadori, 2007–2012; vol. 3 forthcoming). In the Armenian version, Alexander is initially "restored to health" (ἐθεραπεύθη) by his swim but then he falls ill right afterward, suggesting a clumsy synthesis

A Wonderful World and the Romance of the East 201

Two problems are obvious. First, why is this river called "Ōkeanos," the name for the sea around the world, where Alexander travels elsewhere in his romance? Second, why would this mighty hero, who was already famous for crossing *into* Turkey by symbolic conquests of the Hellespont,[592] and who, in later versions of the Romance, had the power to leap into the river Scamander like Achilles (noting, as he did, that Achilles's shield was smaller than it sounded in Homer!)[593] be brutally beaten by a swim?

The next telling, by Iulius Valerius (fourth century CE), solves only one of those problems:

> While passing through Kilikia, after having traveled many roads on foot weighed down with armor under the summer sun, he happened to came to a bridge over the Kydnos, a river second to none in its volume and its clear frigid waters. Transfixed by its translucence and voluminousness, he dove from the bridge in his armor and swam across. But, while the deed added greatly to his reputation for valor, his health also suffered for it; upon immersing in those vigorous and frigid waters, his body again grew hot and sweaty, his nerves having received a grievous injury such that he was immediately afflicted with pains all over by an illness, the cause of which seemed difficult to explain.

Iulius Valerius has solved the geographical problem (Ōkeanus is an error for Kydnos—an actual river in the area). But if anything, he compounds the narrative problem by having Alexander swim in full armor. If he was strong enough to do that, why did he fall ill? If overexertion did cause nerve damage of some kind, why was its cause so "difficult to explain"?[594] What might his reader know about these waters that he does not; or at least, what he is not telling us?

---

of two versions, due to competing interpretations of the water as either curative or a local god who smites the invading king (see n. 601). See Richard Raabe, *Die armenische übersetzung der sagenhaften Alexander-biographie* (Leipzig: Hinrichs, 1896); Albert Mugrdich Wolohojian, *The Romance of Alexander the Great by Pseudo-Callisthenes*, Records of Civilization, Sources and Studies 82 (New York: Columbia University Press, 1969), 86.

592. See Diodorus Siculus, *Library of History* 17.17.2 and compare Arrian, *Anabasis* 1.11.6 (see n. 599: ed. Romm, 23) with Hdt. 7.54 (ed. Strassler, *Landmark Herodotus*, 480). A stock imperial motif: see Jean-Luc Desnier, «*Le passage du fleuve*» *de Cyrus le Grand à Julien l'Apostat: Essai sur la légitimité du souverain*, Annales littéraires de l'Université de Besançon 143 (Paris: Harmattan, 1995), 27–36. In this respect, Josephus (*Antiquities* 2.347–348) compares Moses to Alexander, supporting his exodus account by Greek histories (*Flavius Josephus: Translation and Commentary*, vol. 3: *Judean Antiquities 1–4*, translation and commentary by Louis H. Feldman [Leiden: Brill, 2000], 230 n. 897).

593. Recensions β/γ I.42.11 (see ed. Stoneman/Gargiulo, 1:216). Compare an idiom from today's American cult of celebrity: "I thought you'd be taller."

594. Iulius Valerius, *Res Gestae Alexandri Macedonis* (my translation after Gargiulo's Italian in Stoneman and Gargiulo, *Il Romanzo di Alessandro*, 2:329). As a nagging symptom of this narrative problem, forensic pathologists held a conference in 1996 to debate whether Alex-

Historical authors recognize this narrative problem but fail to solve it. Some suggest the cold of the water or the shock of going from hot to cold.[595] Their diagnosis is not unanimous. One speculates that Alexander imbibed too much;[596] another that he swam too long.[597] Crucially, our earliest source for these events, the historian Diodorus Siculus,[598] does not yet know this story about the swim, but he does note that Alexander fell ill around this time. This suggests that perhaps the story of the swim was introduced later, as an etiology for the great Alexander's inexplicable weakness. That is supported by the testimony of Aristoboulos, who, as a general on this very campaign, could have been there on the riverbank, yet who knows nothing of a swim; he cites only fatigue.[599] The font of this tale clearly does not lie in history.

A better clue to its origins is in the first Alexander historian who *does* know the swim:

> The river Kydnos ... flows through the middle of Tarsus; it was then summer, the heat of which burns no other shore more than that of Kilikia with the sun's fires, and the hottest time of the day had begun. The clear water of the river *tempted the king*, who was covered with dust and at the same time with sweat, to bathe his body when it was still heated; accordingly, laying off his clothing in the sight of the army—thinking that it would also be fitting if he were to show his men that he was content with attention to his own person which was simple and easily attained—he went down into the river. But *hardly had he entered it when his limbs began to stiffen with a sudden chill*, then he lost his colour, and the vital warmth left almost his entire body.[600]

In part, like all other accounts, Quintus does attribute Alexander's illness to natural causes: not cooling down, before swimming in the heat

---

ander had contracted malaria (hence his alternating chills and fever). They concluded that a proximal cause of his eventual death was more likely: fatigue, heavy drinking, stabbing, and the like. See David W. Oldach, M.D., et al., "A Mysterious Death," *New England Journal of Medicine* 338.24 (1996): 1764–69.

595. In chronological order: Plutarch, *Life of Alexander* 19; Justin, *Epitome of the* Philippic History *of Pompeius Trogus* 11.8.3–4; Arrian, *Anabasis* 2.4.7–8; Lucian, *De domo* 1.

596. Valerius Maximus, *Memorable Doings and Sayings* 3.8 ext. 6 (first century CE).

597. Undated fragment; *Die Fragmente der griechischen Historiker*, 151 F.1.6. See Cinzia Susanna Bearzot, "Fragmentum Sabbaiticum (151)," in *Brill's New Jacoby*, ed. Ian Worthington (Leiden: Brill, 2017), 1–11.

598. Diodorus Siculus (mid-first century BCE), *Library of History* 17.31.4.

599. In Arrian, *The Landmark Arrian: The Campaigns of Alexander = Anabasis Alexandrou*, ed. James Romm, trans. Pamela Mensch (New York: Pantheon, 2010), 2.4.7–11, p. 62.

600. Quintus Curtius Rufus, *History of Alexander*, trans. John C. Rolfe, 2 vols., Loeb Classical Library (Cambridge, MA: Harvard University Press, 1946), 1:93–95 (emphasis added). A mid-first-century CE dating is argued by J. R. Hamilton, "The Date of Quintus Curtius Rufus," *Historia* 37.4 (1988): 445–56.

of the day, in an unusually hot area. But its sudden onset and extremely rapid progression suggest something paranormal at work. Alexander is not even harmed by swimming but essentially by dipping a toe in the water. The water itself seems alive, seducing the king with its clear calm surface. The Kydnos is, after all, a local god—today, he is named "cold water" in Turkish, as he is depicted already in these tales and by Strabo. Alexander is not the last invader who would be harmed by entering his realm.[601]

The paradoxographical lists hold further possible sources for this episode of the risky swim, at least for some of its contents and details. There are wondrously destructive waters:

> 1. Theopompos says there is a spring in Thrace in which those who bathe give up their life.
>
> 2. Among the Kyklōpes in Thrace there is a small spring of water that is clear and transparent to look at and just like any other water. But when an animal drinks of it, [the animal] is instantly destroyed.[602]

There are waters with salutary effects that are highly selective about who enters them:

> [Ktēsiās] says that there is a spring in India […]. The most prominent of Indians, men, women, and children, bathe in the spring and jump in it feet first. When they jump into it, the water casts them back out. It not only repels men, but any other creature whether living or dead, is cast out onto dry land. This holds true for simply anything thrown into it except iron, silver, gold, and bronze; these items sink to the bottom. The water is very cold and sweet to drink. It makes a great noise like water boiling in a kettle […].[603]

The first two waters resemble the wonder in Quintus: instantly fatal but deceptively normal-looking, "clear and transparent." In this light, the point of the tale of Alexander's swim would be not his illness but his survival: what kills lesser creatures only makes him sick. Similarly, in the Indian water-wonder, only prominent individuals can jump into the river, and even they are cast back out. So are all nonprecious metals. Precious

---

601. Oğuz Tekin, "River-Gods in Cilicia in the Light of Numismatic Evidence," *Varia Anatolica* 13 (1999): 519–51, at 525–26. On this river's healing properties, see Strabo, *Geography* 14.5; Pliny, *Natural History* 13.8.

602. (1) Ps.-Aristotle, *Of Marvelous Things Heard* 121 (my trans.). (2) *Paradoxographus Vaticanus* 39 (in *PGR*; Anon., second century CE or later, my trans.).

603. In the epitome of Photius, *Bibliothēkē* 72; cited from *Ctesias: On India and Fragments of His Minor Works*, trans. Andrew Nichols (London: Bristol Classical, 2011), 58; on its health benefits, see 138. On "like the boiling of a kettle" as a figure of speech for the speed of a fish in our collection as well (VIIIb), see n. 7.

metals, by contrast, sink. Again, this would make Iulius Valerius's Alexander even more heroic. He swam across the wondrous river in full armor—perhaps including precious metals—and he survived!

Some such link between a water-wonder, Alexander the romantic hero, and this story's setting—Kilikia—also emerges from their juxtaposition within a contemporary paradoxographical list:

> They say that in India a spring filling with oil spontaneously appeared to Alexander.
> They say that there is a certain system of water around Kilikia. The birds and beasts that drown in it are cast back out returned to life.[604]

Influence could run in either direction between the wonder and the tale (or both). But a mere coincidence is unlikely. Alexander's illness during his campaign called for explanation: a tradition on a local wonder supplied one. Or, accounts of his Indian campaign supplied a report of one water-wonder (as they often did) and, by association with a new water-wonder, they influenced accounts of his Turkish campaign. Either way, wonders shaped his adventure.

In addition to the wondrous content of this risky swim story, paradoxographies were a source for specific details that tellers integrated into narrative versions in various ways. In this respect, too, retellings of wonders in the Alexander Romance will illuminate the Talmud. For instance, since Herodotus,[605] another combination of life-giving water and water that spouts oil was located in Ethiopia (often conflated with India).[606] This wonder is listed by Solinus, Rabbah's contemporary, who, as I noted, has a parallel to another of his tales.[607]

> Also in that place is a lake, in which people's bodies, if bathed, shine as if with olive oil. The water of this lake is extremely health-giving. It is so limpid that fallen fronds do not float on it; immediately the leaves fall, they sink to the bottom because of the thinness of the water.[608]

Like the wondrous waters of Kilikia where Alexander's risky swim is set,[609] unlike the fatal waters in Thrace or the dangerous waters of India,

---

604. *Paradoxographus Florentinus* 5-6 (Anon., first–second century CE or later. Entry 1680, ed. and trans. Robin J. Greene, *Die Fragmente der Griechischen Historiker, Part IV*, ed. Stefan Schorn [Leiden: Brill, 2018]).

605. Herodotus, *Hist.* 3.23, ed. Strassler, *Landmark Herodotus*, 218.

606. Pierre Schneider, *L'Éthiopie et l'Inde: Interférences et confusions aux extrémités du monde antique* (Rome: École française de Rome, 2004).

607. See n. 572.

608. Solinus, *Polyhistor* §30.11, trans. Apps, "Gaius Iulius Solinus" (emphasis added).

609. Ps.-Aristotle (*Of Marvelous Things Heard* 29) notes a "whirlpool" in Kilikia with restorative powers.

the effect of this water is beneficial: just the opposite of the river in Alexander's story. It is possible that this health-giving concept stands behind an awkward later version of the story, in which the river "cures him" (of what?) but he immediately falls ill after his swim for no apparent reason.[610] Or it may be a Hellenistic reflection of local lore surrounding the god Kydnos and its healing cold waters (see n. 601). However, this does not explain why the Kydnos would make an exception for Alexander and try to kill him—unless the exception is the point: just as he is exceptional with respect to other wondrous waters where he alone swims and survives, he alone is smitten when he swims in the local god.

While this risky swim's precise sources are impossible to recover, our examination of wondrous waters, which reappear in stories about Alexander, suggests three literary processes at work in the reception of paradoxography in the form of a romance; or, in the Talmud's case, an adventure. First, the hero plays a special role with respect to the wonder's properties. Whatever the wonder usually does, for good or for ill, it does the opposite to him, or he can push it to its limit. Other stories may share this technique of foregrounding the hero against the background of a wonder. Second, narrative contradictions can be a symptom of clumsily combined versions, of course, but not necessarily. They can also reflect opposed properties that cluster around a category or specimen of wonder: in our case, water's power to kill or to heal, to repel or to sink. Some tellers and readers likely expected a wonder to have one property, and some the reverse; both properties could be distributed across distinct tellings or combined within one telling.[611] Third, minor details of specific items in paradoxographical lists were also recycled in stories. Beyond the wonder's *what* and *where*, its description and location, or other ways that it is integrated into its collection, supplemental remarks on the properties of wonders stick out from the text. For example, in Herodotus and Pausanias, these are glosses to the effect that the water is wondrous *not* because of its depth *but* because of its current, and that one should not *swim* in it, *despite* its deceptive appearance. Both glosses were preserved in the Talmud's retelling but blended into its all-knowing "heavenly voice." Similarly, in Solinus (above), "because of the thinness of the water" is an intrusive remark, a gloss that explains—unusually for this genre—why the wonder does what it does. These features—the special hero; the incorporation of multiple, even opposed, properties of a wonder as possibilities

---

610. The Armenian version, dated to the fifth century. See n. 591.

611. I later found an apt formulation and term for my inchoate idea—"polarized description"—in Charles Delattre, "Paradoxographic Discourse on Sources and Fountains: Deconstructing Paradoxes," in *Recognizing Miracles in Antiquity and Beyond*, ed. Maria Gerolemou, Trends in Classics: Supplementary Volume 53 (Berlin: de Gruyter, 2018), 205–23, at 214: "… the hybrid nature of the spring, both cold and boiling, resolves itself into two possibilities for those who undertake an oath there."

for characters' action; and the intrusive remark—can help us to discover processes of retelling, recollecting, and reading wonders in the Talmud.

* * * * *

How were wonders integrated into Rabbah's own would-be risky swim story (IXa)? Do we see here any analogous techniques for retelling wonder-lists in the form of a narrative?

This tale synthesizes four wonders attested in the Hellenistic collections: giant birds, a lake where everything sinks, a disembodied warning voice at the water's edge, and a body of water that one cannot enter because it is shielded by an invisible deity.[612] Its telling has two parts (IXa–b). In IXa, the giant bird is shown but not explained. Rabbah assumes that it is safe to swim because it is only "up to its ankles" in the water, so it is "not substantial." As he is about to jump in, however, the heavenly voice interrupts to warn him of the strong current.

Yet here we see the first gap between the wonder's content and its retelling. The heavenly voice ventriloquizes glosses in Herodotus and Pausanias, similar to the gloss in Solinus. It tells Rabbah not to *swim* (as Pausanias would say) because he was wrong about the source of danger: not "because the water is substantial" but "because it is *forceful*" (as Herodotus would say; or "thin," as Solinus would). The sources of the story's voices are distributed as follows:

We thought the water was not substantial;	**Rabbah**
we meant to go down to cool ourselves off.	**Pausanias**
A heavenly voice appeared and said to us:	
Here, you mean to cool yourselves off?	**Pausanias**
For a carpenter's adze fell seven years	**Herodotus**
and has not reached the bottom	
and <u>not</u> because the water is deep[613]	
<u>but</u> because the water is forceful.	**Herodotus (compare Solinus)**

The blending of these Hellenistic glosses into Rabbah's voice and the heavenly voice—blended, in some tellings, together—wedges the stock water-wonder back into a tightly crafted dialogue. Rabbah says, in effect, "We thought [A], we meant to [B]" and the heavenly voice retorts, "Here, you mean to [B]? For ... and not because [A], but because ..."[614] In other

---

612. Indexed in *PGR*; see n. 531.

613. Or: "substantial." This repetition (ms. P: ק"ט/ק"א"ט) both stresses the chiasm and connects the heavenly voice with the teller's inner monologue, recovering an omniscience effect that is more pronounced in ms. H (see n. 558).

614. On intrusive remarks, see chapter 3 §*Chronological Layers*.

words, the chiastic structure of this dialogue ties together Rabbah's inner speech and the heavenly voice: all the more so in manuscripts that use exactly the same wording for "A" and "B."

Yet the gloss still stands out as a distinct element because it informs readers that this water-wonder is *not even* the wonder that Rabbah *would have* expected, once his wrong assumption about it had been corrected. The birds are extraordinary in their ability to stand, *not* due to their height ("not because the water is *deep/substantial*") *but* due to the current ("but because the water is *forceful*.")[615] Thus, the gloss still has a similar function with respect to Rabbah's reader as the glosses in classical paradoxographies: it marks and elevates the wonder's wondrousness by reminding a reader that it has *not* (merely) one property, *but* (also and even more unexpectedly) another. The wonder is thereby "polarized," in Charles Delattre's sense. Like Alexander, the Talmud's hero is foregrounded with respect to the wonder, but in the reverse way: he foolishly tries to swim, and has to be told to save his skin. Nevertheless, by weaving glosses together chiastically, the wonders retain their properties and narrative effects (exceptionally tall; deceptively shallow; strong hidden current). Wonders are further enhanced for Jewish readers by allusion to prophets (Elisha and Ezekiel) and attribution to the voice of heaven, even as those Talmudizing gestures hide their Greek origin.

We could thus interpret the first part of Rabbah's risky swim (IXa) as a self-contained unit: a retelling of a water-wonder by a teller rather like Iulius Valerius, who wove together paradoxographies to turn a history of Alexander's illness on the banks of a river into a romance of his risky but valiant swim. In the Talmud's case, however, we have more direct evidence for a reader who knew XIa as a unit: "Rav Ashi," i.e., whoever added Rav Ashi's remark on this story (IXb). What sense did *that* rabbinic reader make of the tale? And what might it suggest about further changes in the retelling of wonder in the Talmud's nascent Romance of Rabbah?

For this reader, the striking feature of Rav Ashi's gloss was surely its formal similarity to other scientific-sounding glosses on the wonders in our collection: two by Rav Ashi himself, one in reply to a story that he retells (VIIIb.102–4; XVIIb.211–12; XXIb.262–63). One effect of those glosses is to domesticate the wonder, making it familiar to a reader by giving it a scientific name (despite its apparently supernatural power) and placing it back in the realm of the para/normal, from which Hellenistic paradoxographies also emerged. Its rhetorical impact is not quite a rationalist etiology that tells a reader what the wonder "really" is (unlike Palaiphatus, who ends his myths "But that is not really so …"), yet it does serve to undercut its

---

615. This gloss is even more intrusive in ms. P ("*not because the water is substantial*," ט״א.קט״ר), as it refutes what Rabbah just said to himself in his own words, and therefore what he *would* have assumed the wonder *would* be: depth, not force.

wondrousness: both giant fish in the tales, Rav Ashi says, are very small![616] One could read his exegesis of the giant bird in the same light. Here, perhaps, Rav Ashi domesticates wonder not by science but by the Bible and its rabbinic reception: he names the bird after a familiar piece of lore, just as the study-house tames Rabbah's adventures by reducing their significance to the clarification of legal desiderata (XIIb, XIIIb).[617] Where Aristotle's followers turned science into wonder by subtracting explanations,[618] we might say that Rabbah's early reader converted wonder into rabbinic "science" by putting an explanation back. Perhaps this is merely, as we say, a "power move" on Rav Ashi's part: he subordinates wonder to a hermeneutic framework, that is, biblical exegesis and Talmudization, where God is in charge and the study-house is in control.

Yet Rav Ashi's reader could, and more likely did, interpret his gloss *within* the context of the wonder-adventure as a whole. It is neither as intrusive nor as domesticating as it seems. His gloss of "with me" in Ps 50:11 as "my pillar" (by a clever play on vowels) could *already* have been known to a reader as a possible meaning of this word.[619] In the story's context, it is all the more apt: as the heavenly voice said (contrary to Rabbah's assumption), the wondrous property of this bird is *not* that it is so tall *but* that it is so stable. Rav Ashi's gloss fits both features of the bird: its height (up to the heavens, where it is "with" God, as in the verse itself: reading *'immadi*) and its stability (it stands firm on "the bottom," literally "the earth," as God's "pillar," reading *'ammudi* with the exegetical tradition—even though "the water is forceful"). This midrash turns the giant bird into a cosmic *axis mundi*: rooted in the Sea, the lowest of the elements, it extends all the way up past the firmament.[620] A parallel—or perpendicular—appears in another midrash, where God created Leviathan on the fifth day in order to rest the world's horizontal axis on its fins (this is

---

616. Compare n. 87 ("it is lean"), n. 239, n. 458. Rav Ashi's "*gildna* fish of the sea" (VIIIb.102–4) is equally an "ironic hyperbole," says Löw, *Fauna und Mineralien*, 5, as the *gildna* is a tiny freshwater sprat. The fish in this story also resembles a wonder in the Hellenistic collections: ἐχενηΐς or *remora*, see n. 4.

617. That literary-historical analysis is consistent with the phenomenological one of Stein, "Believing Is Seeing."

618. This is a useful formula for how the effect of wonder was created: science – explanation = "strange but true." Compare Aristotle's *History of Animals* to its Pseudo-Aristotelian additions and Pseudo-Aristotle, *Of Marvelous Things Heard*. As Yu puts it: "Ancient paradoxographers take up the Aristotelian imperative to gather as many miraculous phenomena as possible, but they abandon the pursuit of their causes" ("Textualizing Wonders," 254). See examples in Schepens and Delcroix, "Ancient Paradoxography," 391–94; Lightfoot, *Wonder and the Marvellous*, 72–79.

619. Precisely that gloss of the same word-form appears in Ber. Rab. 74:3 on Gen 31:5, ed. Theodor-Albeck, 859.

620. See n. 188.

why the Leviathan is called "the slant serpent").[621] Leviathan is to the Sea as *ziz* is to the Air: mythological avatars of fish and fowl, each inserted into a cosmic element of our collection's literary structure (see chapter 3 §*Settings*). They uphold cosmic stability, both horizontality and verticality, until the messiah, when God will serve them to the righteous at a banquet. (It is more likely that a reader of Rav Ashi's gloss would have thought of all this in the context of the larger composition, given that the horizontal Leviathan or "slant serpent" will recur in Part 2A).

As he Talmudizes this wonder via exegesis, then, Rav Ashi does not merely undercut its wondrousness. He also helps his own readers to create a meaning that is more consistent with what they know from the Bible; re-revealing it to them, again, out of the old understory about the tension between order and chaos, divine being and the forces of the Sea (chapter 2). From there, one could go on to reread Rabbah's entire adventure in light of Rav Ashi's gloss, turning it into a didactic allegory that runs roughly as follows: This giant bird is God's "pillar" (so *it* can stand in the turbulent sea of life), but a heavenly voice warns that mere mortals like Rabbah (impelled by "hot" fires of sin?) will drown if *we* plunge in without divine "support." That is just the sort of reading to which our tales have been submitted since the high medieval period (chapter 6). At this stage of the tradition, however, any allegories are implicit, at the very most. Here, the plainer meaning that Rav Ashi's gloss restores to the adventure is more of a rhetorical shift in focus: back to God, away from curiosity about the hero's strange adventures and wonders in their own right (a curiosity that readers could be forgiven for drawing from IXa in isolation). Just as the retellers of wonder in the Alexander Romance may have used it to highlight the specialness of their hero, this reader of the same water-wonder, in his own Jewish literary language and reading tradition, did the same. He just had another hero in mind.

* * * * *

To summarize this cultural history so far: we began by observing that, in the place and time after the collection of Rabbah's and other tales was put together, there was a growing taste among Sasanian elites for the sort of performer that he had long represented among rabbis. This style—as Boyarin has argued of talmudic parallels to Greek "seriocomic" story-

---

621. Isaiah 27:1 (see Part 2A) and *Pirqe R. El.* 9: "On the fifth day, He set swarming from the waters Leviathan, the slant [בריח] serpent, from its dwelling-place in the lower waters. And between its two fins rests the central axis [בריח] of the earth." Note the motif of the world resting "between the fins" of Leviathan, like the ship between the fish's fins (VIIIa). On Leviathan as *axis mundi*, see Andrei Orlov, *Supernal Serpent: Mysteries of Leviathan in Judaism and Christianity* (Oxford: Oxford University Press, 2023), 47–124; Adelman, *Return of the Repressed*, 251–53.

telling—joined vulgar humor with (pseudoscientific) mock dialogues in a curious new way of seeing the world. I reconstructed and chronologized some of its stock motifs and its literary language—the description, classification, and narrativization of parallel water-wonders—from Hellenistic sources into the Talmud. Wonder was, I argue, transmitted not only from west to east, but also, contemporaneously, within the Alexander Romance tradition and the Talmud, in similar ways: as a catalogue of topoi on which tellers drew to craft characters and stories, and as a hybrid mode of inquiry, fusing natural science, ethnography, and geography, which mapped and made sense of paranormal phenomena at limits of the known world and the borders of literary genres.

By now, I hope I have persuaded you that three interrelated Hellenistic genres—history and ethnography, paradoxography, and the Alexander Romance—bear enough similarities with the content, structure, and style of our collection that it is possible that its tellers, collectors, and recollectors used these genres as a pattern to weave their traditions and folklore into a new literary whole. As I argued in chapter 1, we should not be looking for *genres of the text*—formal conventions that composers observed and educated audiences interpreted in fixed ways.[622] Rather, we should seek *genres for the reader*: a flexible set of performative options and ways to stylize, sometimes very subtly, a common stock of tales and images, in order to impact one's audience. If we want to trace the circulation of these ancient genres for the reader, rather than mere presence or absence of sources or raw data, we must try to imagine how audiences would have interacted with "cues" for their attention that they were provided as the story was told in real time. Were they cued to believe in wondrous plants, animals, rocks, and rivers, because each was "geotagged" with a real location and taxonomized in the dispassionate voice of Aristotelian science? Or did the same items acquire a quality of strange irreality as they moved closer and closer to the limits of the cosmos: the stars, heaven and hell, the wasteland, the ocean? Were audiences cued to be skeptical and critical, as in Herodotus's constant display of his sources—whether visual, oral, written, or material—yet ultimately to trust the teller's authority, precisely because he presented himself as a restrained and balanced mediator of competing positions? Or did the same cues provoke them to doubt—even to ridicule—tellers like Rabbah for strange visions and voices that he claimed to see and hear? Was he a conquering

---

622. On the terms "paradoxographer" (Tzetzes), "paradoxography" (Westermann), and genre beyond these labels, see Schepens and Delcroix, "Ancient Paradoxography," 380–82; Lorraine Daston and Otta Wenskus, "Paradoxographoi," in *Der neue Pauly: Enzyklopädie der Antike*, ed. Hubert Cancik and Helmuth Schneider, 16 vols. (Stuttgart: Metzler, 1996–2003), 9:309–14; see n. 575.

hero, like King Alexander? Or was he a rogue spinning yarns of parts unknown, like Ishmael in Moby Dick?

Our comparison between our collection and parallels in all three Hellenistic genres has helped us to imagine how the collectors and retellers of Rabbah's tales could have interacted with their readers by exploiting those characteristic tensions with the telling's rhetorical cues: reference to evidence or lack thereof, belief and disbelief, real or unreal places, marvel or science. And in the Talmud, as I argued in the examples of the heavenly voice and Rav Ashi, we find precisely the opposite tendency to what we saw in Herodotus's rhetorical construction of his authority. Rather than call forth a critical audience, who stands on the side of an equally critical narrator, over and against the world, the Talmud "Talmudizes" its sources such that its tellers stand on one side of the world, with the reader and commentators on the other. The reader's attention is called to the same tensions that define these Hellenistic genres: a spectrum of visual, auditory, and material evidence; the limits of the known world and the cosmos; an aura of wonder, mingled with scientific anatomy and taxonomy. Yet, because the Talmud peels apart its reader from its human tellers, re-endowing later sages and its own anonymous voice with the authority of tradition, its readers are left with only two choices. Either they can choose to disbelieve the tale in total—rebelling and reading it against the grain; in effect, a narratological heresy—or they can doubt tellers *in* the story, but not the story itself. What they *cannot* do, as Herodotus constantly invites his reader to do, is to enter a piecemeal critical reality, with a sliding spectrum of some items that are more or less real, and others that remain to be seen. The genre markers are the same; the performance of those genres can be radically different.

* * * * *

In the next stage of the argument, I expand this concept of Talmudization in order to trace one of the main ways in which the Talmud not only transformed itself in light of Hellenistic genres, but also transformed the Hellenistic genres that it received. On one hand, I illustrate how the fundamental narrative tensions that we have observed continued to develop in these Greek genres and in the Talmud along parallel lines in late antiquity—relatively earlier in the Greek novel-form moving east—such that we can say the Talmud does respond, not only to the novel's conventions, but also to their evolving reception by other Hellenistic readers. On the other hand, I offer more examples of how later layers of our collection implant rhetorical "cues" to its audience that subvert human tellers' authority and restore the authority of tradition. Talmudization is strongest in how our stories were retold and edited by anonymous collectors, although it had already begun as they were interpreted by earlier named rabbis, the Amoraim.

Believe It or Not: Fictionalizing Wonders in Late Antiquity

If three genre markers that the Talmud and Hellenistic literature share are, first, lists of wonders of nature; second, their setting at the ends or heart of the known world; and, third, a "hodological" or journey structure within this cosmic setting (mainly Sea, Air, and Desert), then how did those features evolve *within* Hellenistic literature? Originally, as I noted, their classical form was the list, although we also find early wonders in epic form (the *Argonautica* and the *Metamorphoses*); as symposium entertainment and fodder for poetry at royal courts; in explorers' chronicles cited by historians; and, perhaps, in Jewish and Christian miracles, though relations between miracles and wonders are disputed.[623] In narrative form, wonders are strongest in two genres that flourished in late antiquity: the Alexander Romance and the novel. From the beginning, both were questioned. Strabo calls Alexander's companion Onēsikritos the author of a "wonderbook" (*teratologia*), mocking him, not as Alexander's real sea captain, but his "sea captain of the paranormal" (*paradoxa*).[624] Similarly, as Plutarch tells it, Alexander's successor laughed when he heard this sea captain's chapter on the Amazons, asking him just one question: "But what about me? Where was I at the time?"[625] As wonders migrated from lists and Aristotelian science to popular narrative forms like the romance and novel, they grew open to their readers' doubts, but their popularity waxed as their credibility waned.

The doubts increased as time went on. From Antonius Diogenes's *Wonders beyond Thoulē* in the second century CE, to Philostratus's *Life of Apollonius of Tyana* in the third, wonder-narratives—featuring an intrepid but dubious traveler, much like our Rabbah—spread. And a funny thing happened on the way to late antiquity: Hellenistic audiences stopped taking wonders quite so seriously. If classical wonders featured in works of science or history, which represented them as paranormal phenomena—at the edge of the known world, intense and surprising, but still very real—in the romance and novel, wonders became resources for fiction. The success of those new forms meant that, by the time of our collection in fifth-century Iran, relatively few readers still encountered wonders in the form of the scholarly list. Lists continued (e.g,. the first- to third-century Vatican,

---

623. This is the subject of a 2022–26 EABS [European Association of Biblical Studies] research group, "Miracles and Paradoxography in Biblical Reception from Late Antiquity." See also *Storyworlds in Short Narratives: Approaches to Late Antique and Early Byzantine Tales*, ed. Stavroula Constantinou and Andria Andreou, Brill's Series on the Early Middle Ages 31 (Leiden: Brill, 2025).

624. Strabo, *Geography* 15.1.28; see T. S. Brown, *Onesicritus*, 6–7. See n. 530.

625. Plutarch, *Life of Alexander*, 46: καὶ ποῦ, τότε ἤμην ἐγώ (my trans.).

Florentine, and Palatine manuscripts). But, as Geus has noted (see n. 575), even the lists began to adopt a hodology or journey format, moving from wonder to wonder on a map. And older wonder-books—including that dubious sea captain's who served Alexander—were likely received more and more as Aulus Gellius tells us: "filled with marvellous tales, things unheard of, incredible"—and sold cheaply at bookstalls at a port: "filthy from long neglect, in bad condition and unsightly," but irresistible to read, extract, and plagiarize in his own miscellany.[626] In short, wonders became popular. As they became popular, their classical forms were cannibalized in the novel, which still located wonder at the ends of the earth yet parodied its credibility: a major shift in wonder's epistemological status.

The greatest cannibal of them all was the Syrian-born second-century novelist Lucian, who parodies paradoxographers and historians at every turn. Yet Lucian insists that he is the only one who is not a liar, because he never claims to tell the truth. He inverts the critical epistemology of historians like Herodotus, who, by projecting authority onto his sources, styles himself as their fair and balanced judge. Lucian is like the Cretan who said all Cretans were liars: he, and only he, must be telling the truth, or else everything is a lie from which it is impossible to escape. His fiction is "foolproof" in Sternberg's sense, "tyrannical" in Auerbach's: the reader must close the book or be on his side, as he offers no alternative whatsoever. This sets Lucian, and his reader, free to mock "real" historians' or paradoxographers' efforts to prop up their tales with real locations, autopsy, hearsay, and artifacts; free to laugh, postmodern *avant la lettre*, at their fake neutrality. It is in this parodic vein, rather than merely because he shares wonders with the Talmud, that Lucian can show us how retellers in the Talmud dealt with the same narrative possibilities.[627]

Two Seasons in Hell

In Lucian's *True History*, like Hanno or any truly adventurous explorer, he ignores the sane sailor's path of sticking to the coast and sleeping at night on shore. Instead, he sails dead west through the straits of Gibraltar ("pillars of Heracles"). Half-mad, it seems, he then forays into open ocean.[628] He ends up at the Islands of the Damned (not the Blessed, like

---

626. Aulus Gellius, *Attic Nights* 9.4.1–5. See Schepens and Delcroix, "Ancient Paradoxography," 411–25.
627. Contra Frim, who says simply that Lucian has no direct parallels to our tales ("'Those Who Descend,'" 8). Boyarin (*Fat Rabbis*, 193–214) argues for deep rhetorical connections between Lucian and the Talmud but suggests only one textual parallel (236–39).
628. Lucian's ship is borne aloft by a wave "three hundred and fifty miles," where it encounters "millet-throwers" in the heavens. (Later, his ship is attacked on the high seas by pirates wielding "pumpkin-seed missiles.") Rabbah's sailors' vision of the heavens, with

Solinus) where his guides—who ironically include one of Jason's Argonauts—offer him a tour of its sights:

> Our guides described for us the life of each of the victims and the reason for his punishment. The people who suffered the greatest torment were those who had told lies when they were alive and written mendacious histories; among them were Ctesias of Cnidos, Herodotus, and many others. You may guess that, seeing them, I had high hopes for the next world—I knew very well I had never told a lie.[629]

In the wilderness with his own local guide, Rabbah tells his audience a similar story:

> XIV. [The Arab] said to us:
> "Come, I will show you the Maw of Qorah."
> He showed us a certain crevice, from which a wisp of smoke was appearing.
> He brought out a tuft of wool,
> brushed it in water, and wrapped it around his spear, and inserted it.
> It was burnt and charred.
> He said to me: "Listen, now, to what you hear from here."
> And I heard that it was saying: "Moses and his Torah are true, and they are liars!"
> He told me: "Every thirty days, Gehinnom stirs them *as flesh in the caldron* [Mic. 3:3]."
> And it said again: "Moses and his Torah are true, and they are liars!"

Lucian has his Ktēsiās, as Rabbah has his Qorah: not simply a wild storyteller like him, but a real liar, who suffers accordingly. Why does he—why do we, his readers—need to see this? Perhaps because we know well that in this narrative world, the distinction is not self-evident. Lucian parodies serious historians, like Herodotus, by damning them in the same breath as notorious liars, like Ktēsiās. He himself stays safe in his fiction; and his reader, let in on the lie, can only laugh. The Talmud exploits the same tension between truth and fiction but in just the opposite way. The Torah of Moses, bedrock of rabbinic authority, remains true—and look what happens to anyone who denies it! Even the Arab guide knows Scripture, as he quotes the prophet Micah in order to paint the liars' torture in highly graphic terms: churning and boiling, they turn every thirty days *like flesh in the caldron.*[630] Lest the audience miss the point, the story

---

stars "as great as the [area yielded by] sowing of ... mustard-seed," when their ship is "lifted up" by a wave of "three hundred *parasang*" (I.3–4), uses similar motifs.

629. Lucian, *A True Story* 2.31, trans. B. P. Reardon, in *Collected Ancient Greek Novels*, ed. B. P. Reardon, 2nd ed. (Berkeley: University of California Press, 2008), 619–49, at 644.

630. Remarkably, this reference is often missed by traditional and modern commen-

repeats their agonized screams: "Moses and his Torah are true, and they are liars!," just as the verse quoted by the Arab continues: *Then shall they cry unto the Lord, but he will not hear them* (Micah 3:4). In the telling, this repetition can be made louder, so as to amplify the message, or softened, making the sound fade into the distance like a receding siren as the sinners churn below the earth.

This is not just parodic fiction, but a vivid horror story: a cautionary tale of what will happen to its readers if they blur the line between fiction and Torah. Its rhetoric is as "foolproof" as Lucian's: even if one does not believe the teller or his tale, one still gets the message, with no interpretive way out. It thus Talmudizes the parodic convention of Lucian's fiction, even as it suggests a reader's growing awareness of that convention. The transmission of the text itself also reflects this awareness: rather than "Moses and his Torah are true and *we* are liars!" all manuscripts make Qorah and company speak of themselves in the third person—"And *they* are liars"—lest the Talmud's (oral) reader inadvertently say that they, themselves, deny Moses. Where Lucian takes ironic pains to distance himself from Ktēsiās as a storyteller, the Talmud borrows a fictional narrative to condemn fictional theology. Its tales and tellers do not have to tell the truth to teach us—by way of what they say, see, and piously do *not* say— that the Torah is true.

Like Lucian, then, the Talmud exploits new epistemological problems of the novel. Like Lucian, it does so by exploiting a genre convention of serious literature: the wonder at the edge of the world. Here, we might also consider the convention of first-person autopsy: eye-witnessing what one claims to know, as opposed to what one has merely heard. Lucian parodies that convention often, as in his ethnographic excursus on "the novel and unusual things I noticed during my stay on the moon"; a textbook specimen of classical history on the customs and beliefs of people who, alas, do not exist.[631] Among historians, as we said, autopsy was used to strengthen the teller's authority: others had merely speculated about a place, wonder, or relic, or merely relied on past accounts, whereas the historian had gone and seen it for himself. History fostered the same criti-

---

tators alike (it does not even appear in the list of Scriptural references in the margins of the standard printed Talmud [ed. Vilna]), perhaps because they assume that an Arab speaker would not quote Scripture. See Tosafot b. Hul. 98a s.v. דנפל.

631. See Karen Ní Mheallaigh, *The Moon in the Greek and Roman Imagination: Myth, Literature, Science and Philosophy*, Greek Culture in the Roman World (Cambridge: Cambridge University Press, 2000), 205–60. For one Roman's reflections on how to use wonder in a serious history, see Rik Peters, "Beyond *ira* and *studium*: Tacitus and the Hellenistic Anxiety about Wonder," in *Tacitus' Wonders: Empire and Paradox in Ancient Rome*, ed. James McNamara and Victoria Emma Pagán (London: Bloomsbury Academic, 2022), 52–76, at 60–72. On rabbinic engagement with the novel, see David Stern, *Jewish Literary Cultures*, 2 vols. (vol. 3 forthcoming, University Park: Pennsylvania State University Press, 2015–), 1:23–53.

cal mentality on the part of its audience: the authority of tradition was no longer sufficient to define truth. The Talmud took this as a challenge.

Double Vision

While, as we noted, most of the truth-claims in our talmudic collection were also expressed in the language of vision, did its use of the Hellenistic convention of autopsy also encourage a critical reader? Yes and no; but, ultimately, no. Yes, it encouraged them to be critical of the human tellers *within* the stories. We have already noted a feature that casts doubt on Rabbah's autopsies: excessive or repetitive statements ("I myself have seen"), to which the collection of tales adds new voices who mock, contradict, or cast doubt on them;[632] and secondary tellers on whom their truth depends (some of whom, like the desert Arab and not at all like Herodotus's Egyptian scribe, are said to outsmart the teller himself).[633]

Over time, too, we can see that the reception of these tales within rabbinic circles tended to further undermine the authority of their tellers. Consider the first comment on the tales by Rav Pappa the son of Shmuel (V.61): "If I hadn't been there, I wouldn't have believed it." This comment itself shows that readers were doubting the teller's autopsies enough to have to bolster them with their own: if one hasn't "*seen it*" as some manuscripts say,[634] the vision is likely bunk. Yet at this early stage of their reception, it seems the convention of autopsy was still strong enough to be taken seriously. One autopsy might cause doubts, but adding another autopsy could lay those doubts to rest. VIIIb points to the same early stage of the talmudic reception of these tales. Again, it sows seeds of doubt, but nothing more. The Talmud mounts a standard hypothetical challenge to Rabbah's tale ("*And perhaps you'd say*: the ship wasn't moving much"), but defends him with two traditions. One of these two pieces of supporting evidence is brought by Rav Dimi, "when he arrived" (from Palestine, where, apparently, earlier rabbis had told a fuller version of the same tale, featuring a kettle). The other supporting remark is also in Rav Dimi's voice in some manuscripts; in ms. H, it is anonymous.[635] So, whether its reports come from autopsy or hearsay, first-person local experience or vague oral traditions, whether they have the warrant of a named rabbi or the Talmud's Stam, we see that readers were already skeptical about Rabbah's tales. Yet they dealt with their skepticism just as the Talmud often does with critical inquiry into law: comparing and testing versions and sources, striving to preserve the best-supported version of the tradition. Readers' critical faculties were engaged, but they used them to defend the tradition.

---

632. See further chapter 3 §*Voice* and §*Chronological Layers*; Introduction §*The Teller*.
633. XI.143-47, XIIa.157-160, and XV.193-95.
634. Mss. V, O, at מ.ג"ז.
635. ה.צ"ב"ה. See nn. 424–426.

They do not call Rabbah a liar; on the contrary, they travel far and wide for helpful evidence.

Even at this early stage of the reception of Rabbah's tales, however, we can already detect cracks in his authority. First and foremost, this is clear when Rabbah tells of himself recounting his travels to other Babylonian rabbis. In both cases, they respond not so much with wry laughter as with open scorn: "Every Abba is an ass, every bar Hanah is a jackass!" (XIIb.162; XIIIb.173). Yet we should not hastily conclude, as many scholars have, that they do not believe him. Rather, they subject his stories to meticulous traditional analysis. First, they criticize him for missing a precious opportunity to settle an old legal debate: when he stole a thread from the corner of the prayer shawl on their ancestors' giant bones, before he returned it, he should have checked to see if its joints had four threads (per the house of Shammai) or three (per the house of Hillel). To be sure, there *is* something absurd about insisting that, effectively, a man on the moon should stop to count magic threads of his mythic ancestors to settle a minor old scholarly debate.[636] There is something Lucianic about the rabbis' parody of his wonder; just as Lucian makes fun of Homeric scholars by asking Homer if he is truly the author of his poems. The reader could read the tale as making fun of its own narrow idea of truth in fiction. At the same time, however, rabbis who criticize Rabbah are making a more serious point. Their problem is not whether his tale is true. Their problem is that, even if it were true, he would not know what is meaningful about it. They grant, for the sake of argument, that it is true—but it makes no contribution to their own scholarly discourse. It is worse than false: irrelevant. Thus, their rational critique of his story further Talmudizes it for the audience: "truth" is redefined in terms that are familiar to them, and found wanting. Rabbah *could* have contributed to a famous legal debate. Instead, he told them no more than the saga of a missed opportunity. To paraphrase the 2011 film *Footnote* (possibly alluding to I. B. Singer):[637] "There are many new things and many true things in your story, dear friend; but the true aren't new and the new aren't true."

The next story, Unit XIIIb, is a more developed version of the same epistemological conflict. The rabbis in the study-house use the same attack. Even if Rabbah heard a heavenly voice, he did not stop and think to give the proper response. This time, however, he defends himself: he did not respond, not because he did not understand the gravity of the

---

636. See b. Menah. 41b. Compare b. Ber. 53b, where a story about Rabbah is drawn into another Shammai/Hillel dispute. The marginalia of Jacob Emden and his father Tsevi Ashkenazi (in ed. Vilna) defend Rabbah well against the study-house (XIIb): the caravan had been idling for a while and was anxious to proceed. He did not want to be left behind in the desert! See n. 91.

637. This is a line from Singer's Yiddish novel *Shadows on the Hudson*, but they may have a common source.

situation, but because he interpreted the heavenly voice differently. They counter that his reasoning was faulty: based on the language, as he himself reported it to them, his interpretation cannot be correct. Here, the stakes of this debate are far higher than a nicety of ritual procedure: if Rabbah *had* known the proper response to the heavenly voice—according to his colleagues—he could have released God from God's own vow to exile the Jews! Instead of saving humanity from destruction, according to *his* interpretation of the voice, he has condemned them to their exile. (See n. 175, n. 358, n. 667.)

The ironic wrinkle is that "exile" (a rabbinic academy in Babylonia) is where this entire debate takes place. As in the prior tale but, again, in a more developed way, there are two levels of irony here. First, the anonymous Babylonian rabbis who attack Rabbah for keeping them in "exile" are, as the tale makes plain, perfectly comfortable there. He is the one who traveled to the land of Israel and back. They could have gone—as many rabbis in the Talmud do—but stayed in the study-house. The "return from exile," important a messianic ideal as it may be for them—and, indeed, is in Part 2 of the composition—is not a missed opportunity at all but a parodic fantasy in the voice of a diaspora elite: "Ah, we wish we could go home, but this jackass ruined it for us. (Now, as we were saying ...)." The second irony is that the very idea that a storyteller who is such a fool could, simply by interpreting God's vow correctly and knowing how to say the proper formula, have released God from God's own vow, is absurd by *any* reading. Again, like pausing over giant bones of the ancestors to count the threads in their prayer shawls, this is not only a parody of the teller. It is a self-parody of the rabbis' own love of hair-splitting arguments. Who is this "ass," to release God from God's vow? But also: Who are *we* to say—based on our laws of vows, and our reading of nothing but the words of this "ass"—that we know any better?

In sum, as the seriousness of wonder-stories was undermined by their entry into the novel, Rabbah's readers reckoned with the same tension of truth and fiction in their own culture. Like Greek readers, they had come to doubt, even ridicule, their all-too-human tellers. A gap widened between story, on one hand, and truth, on the other, as fictional forms went east. Unlike Lucian, however, the Talmud did not therefore encourage its audiences to dismiss the *content* of its traditional tales, even in fictional form. On the contrary, it taught them how to save whatever they could: even apparently tiny legal details could have significant consequences. By criticizing its tellers, it did not discard their tales, but Talmudized them. Rather than curious tourists, mere sightseers, the collection spawned a generation of reinterpreting readers: those for whom a tale's truth did not depend on the reliability of its teller, because truth was ultimately interpretation and understanding: its meaning *for them*. The Talmud located its own critique of fiction, not purely in what one saw or heard, but in knowing how to ask. At the same time, it showed its readers how to reflect on and laugh at themselves by exposing the limitations of scholastic fixation on legal details; the hubris of efforts to discern God's intent in stories. It treated the authority of human reason no less critically than the authority of the visionary traveler. But it did not thereby license its reader to throw out the theological baby with the epistemological bathwater. Every story might hold a single thread of authentic tradition, one that can be recovered only by collective debate.

At this early stage of the reception of Rabbah's tales as a collection, then, their reader was faced, not with a hegemonic ideology ("culture") imported from "Hellenism," but with an unresolved tension. On one side, these strange tales came to represent a kind of authority that had always been a problem, and was growing more so: vision, a teller who claimed that he had "gone there" and "seen it" himself. On the other, the tales had become part of a living tradition, with its own authority assured, if nothing else, by the sheer fact of its inclusion in the Talmud. It was already impossible to simply apologize for or "interpret away" the tales—they are cautionary tales of rebels like Qorah who try to replace the Torah's authority with their own, after all, and thematize limits to the interpreter's confidence in his own abilities. What was one to do with that tension otherwise? How could one uphold and develop the narrative tradition, without believing in it?

Our collection holds two answers to this question. The first, too easy but partly right, is that, in some cases, the Talmud did not deal with this tension openly but simply preserved some of its sources in the genres from which it had inherited them: refraining from critique, commentary, or explicit Talmudization. This seems to hold, both for some Alexander Romance stories and for some wonder-lists. In XIX, for example, R. Judah (uniquely and suggestively called "the Indian") tells a story that is genetically related to the Water of Life episode in the Alexander Romance (e.g., in a late Syriac version: a sixth-century poem attributed to Jacob of Serugh, which is also found in the Qur'an).[638] The motifs and narrative structure are basically left intact: without going into the parallels here, we can see that the Talmud keeps its version of this tale-type for its entertainment value. Its new setting in a ship on the imaginary ocean, full of mythical monsters and magical gems, lends its audience more license to enjoy this story *as* a story, without having to assign it meaning or reconcile it with legal-theological issues.

A different case is offered by the glosses akin to fragments of scien-

---

638. See Budge, *History of Alexander the Great*, 170–74; Israel Friedlaender, *Die Chadhirlegende und der Alexanderroman: Eine Sagengeschichtliche und literarhistorische Untersuchung* (Leipzig: Teubner, 1913). On further sources and peregrinations of this tale-type, see Kiperwasser and Ruzer, "Nautical Fiction," 304–7.

tific wonder-lists (VIIIb.102–4, XVIIb.211–12, XXIb.262–63). In these cases, as we saw, rather than harmonize the genres of Hellenistic wonder, or confront the tension that arose around wonder-writing in relation to the Talmud's interpretive tradition, the genres are collected side by side, one awkwardly or critically commenting on the other. But of course, in the context of the passage as a whole, its reader could have interpreted these "scientific" glosses quite differently—for example, as an etiology of wonder that did not undermine its wondrousness at all. We have evidence for the reading that led to the gloss—not for the reading of it. Here the ambiguity arises around the same productive tension in the culture. Are these glosses clarifying or enhancing what the teller saw? (Compare IXb, Xb, XX.250–51, XVIII.222–24.) Or, like the sages in the study-house, are they criticizing the wonders by saying that they are nothing special: nothing new or nothing true? Once this tension between the fictional and the realistic interpretation of wonder-writing had become an established cultural pattern, there was no going back: even this apparently passive transmission of a scientific gloss might be interpreted as constructive or as an attempt to radically limit what the reader could derive, without discarding the tale entirely.

This leads to a second answer to the question of how the Talmud's readers dealt with the tension between the unbelievability of wonders and the popularity of their reading tradition. If we look beyond the collection of tales (Part 1), into Part 2 of the larger and later composition, where these wonder-tales were transmitted in an entirely new setting, we find subtle verbal links between the beginning and the end of both Parts. The way in which this later reader was spurred to interpret wonders in light of these intertextual cues scattered through the composition suggests that, ultimately, their collectors' impulse to Talmudize and thus restrict the strangeness of the wonders was strong; so strong that it made their very existence in the tradition a nagging problem. In this new recollection, wonder-tales received morals that altered, or even violated, their premises.

The cues for this Talmudization of Part 1's wonder-stories in the new interpretive framework of Part 2 are "catchphrases": repetitions that make both parts of the composition interpretable in light of one another, changing wonder's meaning in the process. Chapter 5 will focus on the history of this interpretive device within the talmudic canon. By way of transition and conclusion to our question of how talmudic wonder was fictionalized, and vice versa, here is one example.

One subtle catchphrase is repeated twice in Part 1 (VIb.73, XXIa.260). In both stories, the teller "sees" a wonder; then he returns "a year later" and "sees" how it has persisted over time. Again, without venturing into the details of these two stories, the function of their shared catchphrase ("When I/we returned the next year"; "Next year, I/we came back [and saw]") is a temporal form of a telling device that I called the "amplifier" (chapter 3 §*The Uses of Repetition*). It expands the wondrousness of the wonder-tale by showing how it really *continued* to radiate its special regenerative power, a year later. This may enhance its teller's credibility. It certainly makes his tale more effective: instead of static items on a map, a reader witnesses dynamic wonders across the world in a tale unfolding over time. A similar "amplifier" effect is created by a second catchphrase: "if I hadn't been there/if I hadn't seen it, I never would have believed it." Rav Pappa says this about Rabbah's tale—but he *was* there, and he *did* see it—and his belief in this wonder, in spite of himself, like the effects of this wonder a year later, only makes it all the more wonderful for his reader. Both catchphrases, then, appear to bolster the authority of first-person vision.

The second catchphrase, however, is repeated in a didactic story at the beginning of Part 2.C, where its function is precisely the opposite. In this story, the cultural tension between vision and the authority of oral "Torah"—rabbinic textual study and preaching, exegesis of the Bible and continuation of its interpretive tradition—has precisely reverse destructive consequences.

Appendix §*Translation* 2.C

> R. Yohanan was expounding: "In time to come, the Holy One, Blessed be He, will bring precious stones and pearls that are thirty by thirty [cubits], and carve out [a space from] them ten [cubits wide] by twenty [high], and set them up in the gates of Jerusalem." A certain disciple jeered at him: "Nowadays, we don't find them as big as a turtle-dove's egg; are we to find them that big?!"
>
> Some days later, his ship went off to sea. He saw the ministering angels who were chiseling precious stones and pearls thirty by thirty [cubits] and carving out [a space from them] ten [cubits wide] by twenty high. He said to them: "Who are these for?" They replied that in time to come, the Holy One, Blessed be He, would set them up in the gates of Jerusalem.
>
> He came before R. Yohanan and said to him: "Expound, Rabbi, it is fit for you to expound; yea, just as you have said, thus have I seen." He replied: "Good-for-nothing! If you *hadn't* seen, you *wouldn't* have believed! You jeer at the words of the sages." He cast his eyes at him and he was transformed into a pile of bones.

In this story (a close cousin of the doubting Thomas parable in the New Testament), the same catchphrase teaches a rabbinic reader that "Hellenistic" first-person vision is anything *but* impressive. On the contrary, it is heresy, punished by death. A reader is presented with an absolute dichotomy between rabbinic textual authority ("words of the sages") and visions, *even when* their content is exactly the same. The genre and source, not the story, are at stake. How should a rabbinic disciple get his information? By seeing and traveling, or by hearing and believing? By relying on his own prophetic experience, or by faithfully following his rabbi's preaching on a prophetic text? There can be no compromise between these two modes: seeing is not believing, and belief does not need seeing. Ironically, the story uses the very narrative conventions of wonder-stories to make this point: the voyage on the Ocean and the vision of the pearl in the depths of the sea (compare XIX), and the motif of "casting the Evil Eye"—a wonder that appears in story form as early as a classic sea-yarn, *Argonautica*.[639] The disciple's eyes should stay closed but of course the sage's eyes are as wonderful as ever.

This recollection of the tale, during the canonization of Part 1 in the new frame of Part 2, Talmudized the authority of Hellenistic wonder in two contradictory senses. On the surface, it restored a stark binary between the rabbinic oral tradition and a traveler's visionary experience. Later readers of the entire composition might take this story, retroactively, as passing a moral judgment on the tales of Rabbah and friends as a whole. Perhaps he was worse than an "ass" who bumbled around in the dark. Perhaps he, and the other seafarers whose tales he told, were dangerous heretics like this doubting disciple. On the other hand, his tales were still there, in the canon, next to their apparent refutations. No one had censored them or altered them enough to remove the tension. Another Talmudization remained possible: a reinterpretation that appropriated the power of vision back *into* the authority of rabbinic tradition. To know *anything*, after all—exegesis, or visions, or wonders—you had to know how and whom to ask. Vision need no longer be a threat if you knew where to look; in Torah, by listening to your rabbi the first time. These alternative ways of resolving the cultural problem of Hellenistic wonder would continue to inspire readers of our collection within the Talmudic canon (chapter 5) and even beyond (chapter 6).

* * * * *

In this chapter, we have been searching for a way to model the interaction between Hellenistic sources and the Babylonian Talmud that goes beyond paleology, the dissection of one-to-one correspondences or influences, in order to show how literary circles reacted differently to shared cultural changes. I have argued, first, that there are enough overlaps in content, structure, and rhetorical conventions between the Talmud, on one hand, and the interrelated Hellenistic genres of history, ethnography, paradoxography, and romance, on the other, to justify a cultural comparison in terms of how tellers used those literary resources to persuade, delight, intimi-

---

639. See Matthew W. Dickie, "Talos Bewitched: Magic, Atomic Theory and Paradoxography in Apollonius *Argonautica* 4.1638-88," *Papers of the Leeds International Seminar* 6 (1990): 267–96, esp. 268–69.

date, and otherwise influence their diverse readers. Second, I proposed that this interaction between readers and their shared literary conventions followed parallel tracks in late antiquity, as Greek wonder-writing turned from serious science or elite entertainment into fictional, easily parodied, and popular raw material for new compositions.

We saw, however, two different approaches to the problem of narrative authority that was caused by this shift from serious belief or curiosity about wonders to their literary afterlife. Whereas Greek audiences of fiction were free to side with the author or narrator, *without* believing the story—just as audiences of the romance could love its hero while hating the historical Alexander—in the Talmud, this clean split between the narrator and the narrative never really got off the ground. On the contrary, the Talmud's reception of these wonder-stories turned *against* the authority of a first-person narrator, turning its back on the very idea of storytelling for mere wonder or curiosity. The earliest readers of these stories, trying to make sense of Rabbah's nonsensical tales, were already beginning a process of Talmudization: moving the salience of these stories from what they wanted to say about the "real" world, on one hand, to what they said about the Torah according to rabbinic sources and methods, on the other. Rather than traveling, seeing, hearing, and knowing, the focus moved to interpreting their meaning. This allowed rabbis to continue transmitting and even adding to the stories, while keeping their own safe distance from the alien wisdom that we now see they contained.

Yet this strategy was not fully foolproof. Some wonders were transmitted more or less intact, perhaps for entertainment or scientific value; others generated mixed messages, a cultural tension that the reader had to confront. Some rabbinic authorities spoke in their own voices: seeing, repeating, and verifying that they had experienced these wonders. Not all were attacked; some were even supported or amplified. However, cues to the readers, embedded in the larger literary context of these wonders by means of repeated catchphrases, prompted them to draw a clearer brighter line between visions and the authority of Torah. These cues drew on visionary narrative conventions, and stock wonders like the Evil Eye, to undercut the possibility that vision could become its own independent source of authority. By Talmudizing vision as part *of* Torah, later collectors appropriated its authority, without having to systematically censor or condemn past claims to such experience by first-person narrators. Seeing was not believing, and the recollectors of wonder ensured that, in principle, it never would be. Yet wonders and visions now had a special place in the Talmud's tradition: a site to which future generations would return and continue to ask troubling questions. *Why not, exactly? And if not, what good are these stories?* At the tail end of late antiquity, those questions would grow more acute and hermeneutically productive within the Talmud as a canon.

5

The Iridescence of Scripture: Inner-Talmudic Interpretations

As we use our constellation to compare how readers create meaning from our collection over time, we have focused relatively little on the constellation's outer ring: the canon. Recall that I defined a canon from two angles with respect to the reader: inside-out and outside-in (Introduction §*The Canon*). Inside-out, as a product of the *inertia* of collecting and recollecting texts, a canon is a "collection of collections," simply a larger scale on which intertexts can be read together. As texts are re/collected in a unit, or made intertexts in other ways by calling a reader's attention to their relationships, they become a new flexible whole, from which readers can pluck and transpose parts or aspects to recreate meaning. Inertia has force: how some readers once did so influences how other readers can. For instance, some readers received Ps 107 with scribal marks on its verses about a storm at sea (chapter 2). By comparing the storm's phases with locations of the scribal marks, they read the storm as a theological debate on sin, repentance, and salvation. Under the inertia of their reading, collectors of our tales of storms at sea (I–III) had the same theological theme in mind when they used those verses as intertexts. Thus, a few canonical verses, and their reception in midrash, did exert inertia on contemporary or later readers. But this force was nonlinear, without direction. It had no predictable effect on new collectors—let alone on *their* "readers," who heard a fugue between the tales and verses in various ways, based on a much larger inventory of relevant intertexts and their own interpretive choices. The reading process is both structured and chaotic. The dead hand of tradition has no hold over it—*a fortiori*, reading processes generated by the canon that we will map on a larger scale below. The talmudic canon has a pervasive *plural canonicity*, such that—while Scripture is not only its verses' content/context but also their received meanings—other rabbinic traditions are always in the mix, and they can change, even subvert, the received meaning of Scripture. Talmudic readers follow past readings' inertia. But as they can always read more, and differently, rather than merely repeat received meaning they are incentivized to be creative. Inertia and plural canonicity thus cooperate in constant tension.

Conversely, from the outside-in perspective, the canon is the primary factor in the reading process. Its diversity of readers, plural subcanons, and fluid library of traditions are less meaningful than the interpretive frameworks and conventions whereby a canon exerts authority over all its readers. In this sense, the canon is not merely a structure for the chaos of reading but the basis of any possible reading. It sets limits and rules for any collection inside it. It exerts strong pressure on all lower circles of the reading process: collection, telling, tale, and teller. If they play strictly by a canon's interpretive rules, readers are less free to say what counts as a collection; which of a given collection's parts or aspects count as intertexts; what is meaningful about a tale's form and content; and how to evaluate its traditional storytellers. For instance, as we saw in chapter 4, some traditions and aspects of Part 1 were aggressively *Talmudized* as they entered the canon. That is, they were subjected to the interpretive frameworks and conventions typical of this canon—not of their origins in myth/midrash, nor their reception by earlier readers. For belated arrivals to the discussion like ourselves, one unfortunate effect of Talmudization is to hide past readers by harmonizing oral sources—for example, blending anonymous with Amoraic voices—which makes it hard to recover the readers prior to the canon.

Nevertheless, the canon's competing forces—inertia, plural canonicity, and Talmudization—do interact and open up spaces where we can uncover readers' diversity, creativity, and agency. (Indeed, without those constraints on readers, what would there be for us to uncover?) For instance, at the end of chapter 4, we saw how, as Part 1 was Talmudized, it became an intertext with Part 2 via what I called "catchphrases" inserted by the editors. These links make both parts into intertexts, newly interpretable in light of one another. At stake in those catchphrases was a cultural issue—the authority of vision versus oral tradition—that had long been thematized by the collectors of Part 1, and by earlier readers. Here, inertia and Talmudization converged: the latest composers chose to turn their readers' attention back to a venerable interpretive conflict. Yet readers remained free to rethink that conflict by navigating their intertexts in new ways.

In this chapter, I extend that line of argument, foregrounding readers' creativity not despite but because of how the tales were canonized within our larger two-part composition. This is an account of how the emerging canon of the Talmud altered their interpretive framework. I build on new work in the field which stresses that, rather than interpret the "final" version of each text as a direct expression of editors' intent, the centuries-long circulation and reading of texts *within* the canon is always part and parcel of their meaning.[640] A key insight of these studies is that oral tradi-

---

640. See nn. 33, 45, 47, 55–59, 70, 690, 736. Shamma Friedman seems to share this position when (contra Fränkel; see nn. 28, 33, 732), he rejects analysis of "the end product in splendid isolation" in favor of "the overall kinetic unfolding of *all* its stages" ("A Good Story

tions reflected in sources and textual variants did not disappear with our "final" text but kept circulating in new, more or less intertextually activated, forms. This growing interest, in what I call "inner-Talmudic interpretation,"[641] explores how editors and readers engaged their many coeval configurations of oral sources. It is characterized not so much by novel ideas or methods as by a different use of the "layers" model of source criticism (chapter 3) and by a shift in focus. Rather than privilege the agency of one recollector ("author/editor") and their intention for the meaning of the "final" text, it turns to readers' roles (as student, performer, listener, etc.), whereby they engaged the matrix of possible intertexts. By disentangling readers from the edited text, and by reconstructing how they engaged the text as it reached that form *and* thereafter, we can move past an editor-centric model of meaning.

In that effort, sources shared by the Talmud and contemporary Palestinian *midrash* are an invaluable basis for comparison. They reveal not only different editorial techniques and ideologies in West and East, but also different readers' interpretive problems and frameworks. To that end, I compare two units in Part 2 (2.B–2.C) with parallels in a Palestinian Midrash, Pesiqta of Rab Kahana (see Appendix §*Parallels to Part 2 in Pesiqta of Rab Kahana*). By contrasting how each work uses sources shared by both, I exemplify select processes of inner-talmudic interpretation that will help us to develop our broader ideas of recollection and Talmudization. As I have argued (chapter 3 §*Boundaries*), our composition did not spring intact from the head of one editor. Part 2 postdates Part 1, but editors tied it back by catchphrases and keywords. Less editing was done on Part 1 to link it in the reverse direction. My analysis of inner-talmudic interpretation develops that analysis. I show how both parts coevolved in the canon as, and after, the whole composition was knit together; not only by editors, but by their readers.

From Wonder to Eschatology

Part 2 is a complex passage interweaving anonymous and attributed material on topics that appear, at first glance, to wander ever farther from

---

Deserves Retelling: The Unfolding of the Akiva Legend," *Jewish Studies, an Internet Journal* 3 [2004]: 55-93, at 89. But he still assigns the end-product to "*a* skilled literary artist" who turned "*isolated* components into a polished and *seamless* creation" (emphases added), rather than stressing how readers made meaning from components and exploited textual "seams" even after it was finished. As I said (see n. 47), Friedman's work generated a vast trove of resources for this poetics of reading, but our emphases differ.

641. By analogy to "inner-biblical interpretation" with respect to *aggadic* creativity in the Tanakh (Michael Fishbane, *Biblical Interpretation in Ancient Israel* [Oxford: Clarendon, 1985]). Specifically, I also ask how the Talmud became a "synoptic" canon (Fishbane, *Biblical Interpretation*, 407), and how editors introduced dynamics of "correlation" or "polarity" between intertexts (Fishbane, *Biblical Interpretation*, 421–23).

the adventures and visions of Part 1. Yet editors establish thematic connections between both parts by shaping contents and their order. Its first unit (2.A), on Leviathan and other myths from the Battle with the Sea (see chapters 1–2), echoes the sea-creatures in Part 1, raising those strange sights to an eschatological power.[642] This Leviathan unit leads to discussion of how Leviathan's flesh and skin will be apportioned in the eschaton (2.B), which forms a bridge to the conclusion on the Heavenly Jerusalem (2.C). This shows a structural affinity with many homiletical midrashim, which also conclude with a messianic "peroration" [*hatimah*] intended to console the audience by looking forward to the eschaton.[643] One such peroration, what Edmund Stein calls the "theophoric," even has a similar refrain: "The Holy One, Blessed be He, said: 'In this world ... [but] in time to come....'"[644] Yet the consolation that Part 2 offers its audience is not solely eschatological. Rather, like some attributed remarks on the tales *in* Part 1 (V.60-61; XIIb; XIIIb), exegesis and commentary in Part 2 further thematize the scholastic status hierarchy, with its authority of the Torah and oral Torah, as a source of truth—against tellers' competing claims to the authority of autopsy and visionary experience as evidence.

I suggest that this tension between scholastic and visionary authority not only ties together the Heavenly Jerusalem section of Part 2 (2.C) in itself, but supplied the composition's editors with a recipe for reworking their sources so as to link Part 2 back to Part 1. As editors did so, they guided a reader of Part 2 to reinterpret Part 1 in light of the themes that editors had implanted. They did not control *how* readers would proceed— many options are open; ambiguity abounds—but they winnowed avail-

---

642. The only eschatological moments in Part 1 are an Amoraic gloss (Xb: "In time to come, Israel shall be judged on their account") and the conclusion to a story attributed to an Amora (XVIII.222-24: "A heavenly voice appeared and said: What did you do with the little basket that belongs to the wife of R. Hanina ben Dosa [...]"; compare b. Ta'an. 24b: "Rav Yehudah said in the name of Rav: Every single day a heavenly voice appears and says, 'The whole world is nourished by R. Hanina ben Dosa ...,'" followed by stories about his wife). Given that they appear in glosses and a device of the "heavenly voice," which functions as an anonymous remark on an earlier adventure or vision in our collection (see n. 478, n. 556), both eschatological elements point to an intermediate stage of Amoraic responses *to* Part 1 *before* its Stammaitic reception in Part 2. Thus, even these sources support my analysis over Stemberger's: the composition was a gradual process, not a "planned literary unity." Part 2's editors modeled their changes to Part 1 on how Part 1 was already read by later Amoraim, who planted those eschatological seeds for their recollection.

643. Edmund Stein, "Die homiletische Peroratio im Midrasch," *HUCA* 8–9 (1931–1932): 353–71.

644. Compare the series of homilies in 2.C: "In time to come, Holy One, Blessed be He, will ..." See E. Stein, "Die homiletische Peroratio," 359–61. This suggests that editors of the Talmud's conclusion aimed for a similar rhetorical effect: elevating and consoling their audience by bringing them back to visions of Jerusalem. For a similar reading of the Temple in the Pesiq. Rab Kah. parallel, see Marc Hirshman, "Pesiqta deRav Kahana and *Paideia*" [Hebrew], in Levinson et al., *Higayon L'Yonah*, 165–78.

able interpretive options. This interpretive process seems to be almost entirely retrospective. We cannot prove that it was foreseen by collectors of Part 1. Nor did it cause textual changes to Part 1 except for the addition of XX.[645] Yet inner-talmudic interpretation is not invisible. It left a trail of traces in Part 2—"catchphrases" and "keywords": terms for which I am indebted to others, as noted—which cement readers' retrospective connections to Part 1. This cement is bolstered by thematic associations between both parts, as well as other intertexts. With it, the audience of the loosely unified composition can read texts together and rebuild a more synoptic canon.

We see how editors restructured this interpretive process for the composition's reader by contrasting how they, and editors of Palestinian midrash, used a shared set of sources. By stripping Part 2 down to its prooftexts and retracing those verses through rabbinic tradition, we find that many sources of a section of Part 2 (2.B–2.C) are also preserved in the Palestinian Midrash Pesiq. Rab Kah., as well as a sermon of unknown provenance formally akin to the latter.[646] Rather than verbatim parallels,[647] or linear developments leading in or out of the Talmud,[648] these overlapping sources are edited into coherent literary units that accent distinct intertexts in order to stress markedly different themes. Pesiq. Rab Kah. parallels draw on voices that are marginal or anonymous in the Talmud, and distance themselves from its case for a status hierarchy based on oral Torah. The Talmud parallels trumpet this status hierarchy, as opposed to the authority of vision, and further wed the hierarchy to their Heavenly Jerusalem theme. This contrast supports my argument about how the Talmud's readers integrated both parts of their composition through interpretation—not by altering the text of Part 1 itself. It also shows the editors' work in reshaping sources along thematic lines, leaving it to readers to

---

645. See nn. 492–497.

646. From its placement in the manuscript, this unit (ed. Mandelbaum, §*Parashah Aheret*) seems to be a homily for the second day of Sukkot, which was not a festival day in Palestine (ed. Mandelbaum, 452 n. 1; see Appendix, §*Parallels to Part 2 in Pesiqta of Rab Kahana*). As I am comparing this unit's editorial choices with the Talmud's, whether the homily is from Palestine or from Babylonia does not affect my analysis. Its literary form and populism mirror the other Pesiq. Rab Kah. parallel that we study; it is cited as *Pesiqta* by Yalqut Shimeoni, and it is labeled Pesiq. Rab Kah in its (one) manuscript. It is either from a macroform of Pesiq. Rab Kah. (see n. 67), or reflects both its form and its ideology.

647. As opposed to the direct inner-talmudic parallel b. Sanh. 100a = 2.C, see Appendix §*Translation* Part 2.C. On this parallel, see n. 726.

648. We do find a small-scale linear relation between the anonymous list of seven seas surrounding the Land of Israel in a Palestinian tradition (y. Kil. 9:4, 32c) and the dictum attributed to R. Yohanan (2.A) with a similar longer list. In the Talmud, this dictum is introduced by the formula "When Rav Dimi arrived, he said": one example where the famed talmudic "travelers" between the regions (*nahotei*; see Redfield, "Redacting Culture"; "When X Arrived") do seem to carry a Palestinian text directly to Babylonia, where it developed.

debate those themes. As readers did so, they also applied their creativity less to the textual content than to the models for its interpretation. They made meaning by Talmudizing, not only by retelling or adding new tales.

Specifically, I show how editors developed the theme of vision versus scholastic-textual evidence and authority via two analyses of these parallels (2.B–2.C//Pesiq. Rab Kah.). In the first case, editing of shared sources reveals inverse positions on the scholastic status hierarchy in the two works. Further, the talmudic editors added a keyword (*Woe!*) on the theme of scholastic authority. This keyword ties Part 2 back to Part 1, and potentially to other intertexts, prompting readers to create new meanings on the same theme. It generates new, potentially ironic reinterpretations of the Talmud's apparently pro-scholastic, anti-visionary attitude, when new readers engaged the composition. My first case thus illustrates both of my chapter's claims: the talmudic editors' preference for scholastic authority but, on the other hand, a real dialogue on this issue as Part 2 evolved in the talmudic canon, given other intertexts and ways of rethinking it that were available to a reader of both parts.

How did that dialogue between editors and their readers actually unfold around the theme? Is the composition slanted toward scholastic elitism, or irony about itself in that regard? Vision or exegesis? To clarify those questions, our second case retraces more clear interpretive pathways between Parts 1 and 2, and their intertexts, in the wider talmudic canon. Here, too, options for inner-talmudic interpretation were signaled by keywords and catchphrases. Here, too, readers surely rethought the cultural issue of scholastic authority vs. vision in diverse ways. Yet in this case, verbally and thematically linked sources suggest more strongly what readers' interpretive options were—above and beyond any one foreclosed meaning determined by the editors' intent.

The Heavenly Banquet and Eschatological Tabernacle

In the Talmud (2.B), R. Yohanan (cited by Rabbah; in several witnesses "our" Rabbah—sealing the association between parts 1 and 2) interprets Job 41:6a (40:30a) in terms of the popular myth of the banquet of Leviathan for the righteous in the end-times. He interprets its "companions" (*habbarim*) as "disciples of the sages" (*haverim*).[649] They will be the only ones to feast on Leviathan, he claims, and stresses this point by going on to Job 41:6b (40:30b): leftovers from the banquet will be sold by lowly

---

649. On my approach to transliteration and citing biblical translations/versifications, see §*Note on the Text*.

The Iridescence of Scripture   231

"merchants" in Jerusalem. (An anonymous Aramaic gloss of "merchants" in light of Isa 23:8 chimes in with a different view than his).[650] Smaller portions of Leviathan will be worn as pendant amulets ("for thy maidens," a stereotype with some historical basis about women's fondness for these magical artifacts). But first—R. Yohanan argues as he goes on to the next verse, Job 41:7a (40:31a)—at the End of Days, God will make a cover (*sukkah*) for the righteous from Leviathan's skin. Again, he then reads the second half (Job 41:7b/40:31b) as a status hierarchy in the end-times. The righteous will get a cover; less deserving will get lesser trinkets from Leviathan's skin. But he ends his hierarchical reading with a universal panorama of Heavenly Jerusalem: Leviathan's skin will stretch along the city walls, shining across the world, summoning all the nations.[651]

One theme stands out in R. Yohanan's otherwise seamless exposition of both parts of both verses: status hierarchy in the eschaton (scholar/nonscholar; women/everyone else; more/less righteous; Israel/the nations). He leaves this theme suspended between hierarchy and egalitarianism. Does God reward all equally? Some more than others? Perhaps both: scholars deserve to be rewarded more but, ultimately, Jerusalem transcends this internal hierarchy. Even merchants (whom he seems to call "deceitful"), and even the nations, will partake of some Leviathan.

These exegeses attributed to R. Yohanan by Rabbah (2.B) are now interrupted by another unit of exegesis, featuring R. Yohanan's reflections on similar ideas at another scriptural location (Isa 54:12: see 2.C, text body through n. 63). This has parallels in b. Sanh. 100a and Pesiq. Rab Kah. 18:5, and is a thematically related distinct source that I will treat in our second case below. After it is over, Rabbah resumes reciting R. Yohanan's midrash on the "covers" from the Leviathan, and develops both key points from 2.B. Just as all righteous will have a cover, so will each righteous individual have a "canopy" (per Isa 4:5: *for upon all the glory shall be a canopy*).[652] In R. Yohanan's reading,[653] this verse means not only that God's

---

650. In all manuscripts, this anonymous gloss is introduced by a phrase typical of Babylonian give-and-take ("or, if you like, argue it from here ..."), which introduces an alternative source for an argument. This, as well as the language-shift, suggests a gloss by the anonymous Talmud, which preserves a secondary debate on whether merchants are lowly ("deceit") or of high status ("princes"), and tries to situate them in R. Yohanan's hierarchy.

651. Jacobs notes that this is a bookend motif to the primordial light from which Adam's garments were woven (*Midrashic Process*, 162 n. 35). Fishbane notes late midrashim in which Adam's garments *are* Leviathan's skin ("Great Dragon Battle," 197 n. 39). Similarly, just as in midrash, the primordial Adam was cosmically vast and had to be brought down to size (Ginzberg, *Legends*, 1:49 n. 4) at the end of our composition (2.C), Jerusalem regrows. On adaptation of this motif in *piyyut*, see Schirmann, *Battle between Behemoth and Leviathan*, 3.

652. KJV, trans. modified.

653. Here, the addition is in Hebrew, and seems part of a coherent exegesis. Contrast n. 650. See n. 381.

Glory will be a cover (*sukkah*) for Zion in the eschaton,[654] but also that, just as the "cover" of the Leviathan's skin will be apportioned based on merit, as he said before, so will God bestow a "canopy" upon each of the righteous according to personal glory/honor/*dignitas* (*kavod*).[655]

Here, again, R. Yohanan pairs the Heavenly Jerusalem with a status hierarchy in the eschaton. But now, the balance tips: hierarchy outweighs egalitarianism. The verse itself extends God's Glory to all Heavenly Jerusalem,[656] but R. Yohanan restricts it to the "righteous." In fact, he continues (in two more exegeses recited by Rabbah), *only* the righteous will be invited ("called") up to the Heavenly Jerusalem, just as *only* the righteous will be "called" by the Glory of God at the end. This, again, contrasts with the verse (Isa 43:7, which is addressed to all Israel), and with the earthly Jerusalem, where "anyone" at all can go.[657] Commenting on this internally coherent set of R. Yohanan's exegeses (recited by Rabbah, on verses of Job and Isaiah, on the theme of status hierarchy in Jerusalem in the end-times), in additions to the same edited unit, talmudic editors restrict the scope of what he means by "the righteous" still further: to "disciples of the sages" only, insofar as they thematize the "envy" of non-rabbis or their "envy"

---

654. He seems to build on the midrash of Rabbi Akiva (*Mekhilta* §*Pisha* 14, ed. Jacob Z. Lauterbach [Philadelphia: Jewish Publication Society, 2004], 74 = *Mekhilta* §*Beshallah* 1, ed. Lauterbach, 124), who reads *sukkah* in the continuation of this verse as equivalent to the "cover" (*And there shall be a sukkah for shadow by day* [Isa 4:6, KJV modified]). On these motifs of the Glory and the cover for Israel, see nn. 219–221, n. 356.

655. Women also have *kavod* (look no further then the fifth commandment; and see Shamma Friedman, "Dama ben Netinah," 435–39). The original dictum may not have referred only to men, let alone to rabbis. This is added by the anonymous Talmud and the editors.

656. Underscored by the repetition (Isa 4:5): *And the Lord will create upon every dwelling place of Mount Zion, and upon her assemblies, a cloud and smoke by day, and the shining of a flaming fire by night / for upon all the glory shall be a canopy*. Of course, in the post-apocalyptic context of the verse, the language of universality applies only to the righteous "remnant in Jerusalem" (Isa 4:3). So the Talmud's elitist reading also has an exegetical basis.

657. Already in Rabbi Yohanan's context, when Jewish residence in Jerusalem was banned, this contrasts temporary pilgrimage with eternal salvation. In the post-Constantinian context of the composition's redaction, Jewish pilgrimage had been affected by an imperial Christianization of space (Oded Irshai, "The Christian Appropriation of Jerusalem in the Fourth Century: The Case of the Bordeaux Pilgrim," *JQR* 99 [2009]: 465–84). As noted by Catherine Hezser, in "the only explicit Yerushalmi reference to Jewish pilgrimage to Jerusalem … Jerusalem is described as a disgusting place, full of violence and blood, where one will almost certainly become unclean—the exact opposite of a holy place where pilgrims might want to visit" ("The [In]significance of Jerusalem in the Talmud Yerushalmi," in *The Talmud Yerushalmi and Graeco-Roman Culture*, vol. 2, ed. Catherine Hezser and Peter Schäfer, TSAJ 79 [Tübingen: Mohr Siebeck, 2000], 11–49, at 27). That shift may account for a renewed praise of the Heavenly Jerusalem. Ephraim E. Urbach argues that R. Yohanan and his followers saw Heavenly Jerusalem as a messianic restoration of the one on earth ("Yerushalayim shel matah ve-yerushalayim shel ma'alah," in Urbach, *The World of the Sages: Collected Studies* [Hebrew] [Jerusalem: Magnes, 1988], 376–91, at 390–91).

for one another upon receiving the reward of the righteous. In sum, this editing of 2.B–2.C not only reiterates the central theme of status hierarchy but also consistently privileges the sages' position within that hierarchy. In turn, the specific phrases with which its editors make this argument generate a network of verbal connections back to Part 1. Such connections will goad readers to rethink that theme, as we will see.

Another homily, closely related to Pesiq. Rab Kah.,[658] turns the Talmud's innovations on their head. It uses the same verses and interpretations to reverse effect. R. Levi similarly interprets Isa 4:6 (*and there shall be a cover [sukkah] for shadow*, trans. modified) in light of Job 41:7a ([40:30a], *canst thou fill his skin with barbed irons [sukkot]?*): anyone who sits in a *sukkah* in this world will be seated by God in a *sukkah* of the Leviathan's skin at the end.[659] A long excursus on Leviathan's skin, sundry qualities, and war with Behemoth ensues. It ends by repeating Job 41:7a: God will make a *sukkah* for the righteous with Leviathan's skin. Its themes and prooftexts are identical to the Talmud's. But this is repetition with a real difference: R. Yohanan had defined "righteous" as disciples of the sages, R. Levi as *anyone* who sits in a *sukkah*.[660]

Like the Talmud, this Pesiq. Rab Kah. homily then attaches a reading of Job 41:7b (40:31b).[661] All rabbis cited agree that the most righteous, who will receive the choicest part of the Leviathan, are *anyone* who fulfills the commandment of pilgrimage to Jerusalem.[662] They gloss "companions" (Job 41:6a [40:30a]) in the same way—*anyone* who fulfills commandments. Again, quite unlike R. Yohanan in the Talmud, they do not limit the term's meaning to disciples of the sages. "Companions" are not only "adepts in Torah ... Mishnah ... Talmud ... *Aggadah*," but also "adepts in commandments" and "good deeds." There are many "companies"

---

658. Appendix §*Parallels to Part 2 in Pesiqta of Rab Kahana*. On its provenance, see n. 646.

659. Note the change in the Masoretic consonantal text, as well as the ending of the word (בְּסֻכּוֹת/בְּסֻכֹּה). For other midrashim featuring these alternations, see Yosef Sheq ed., *Siah ha-talmud: 'Otsar ha-miqra', ha-derashah, veha-lashon be-Talmud Bavli* (Bene Beraq: Morashah Qehillat Yaʻaqov, 1999–2000), 344–46.

660. On *sukkah* as a "minimal commandment," see n. 220. This further supports my argument that, by using *sukkah* to define who is "righteous," R. Levi is appealing to a markedly popular Judaism—between the elite scholars and the nations writ large.

661. The following exposition of Job 41:7b is not part of the homily but joined by the formula "another matter." On this formula, which he unconvincingly claims always conveys the editor's true opinion, see Eli Ungar, "When 'Another Matter' Is the Same Matter: The Case of Davar-Aher in Pesiqta DeRab Kahana," in *Approaches to Ancient Judaism*, ed. Jacob Neusner, BJS 9 (Missoula, MN: Scholars Press, 1978), 2:1–43.

662. As Marc Hirshman points out, Pesiq. Rab Kah. strongly emphasizes the earthly Jerusalem and its Temple as the way to contact God's Presence ("Yearning for Intimacy: Pesikta d'Rav Kahana and the Temple," in *Scriptual Exegesis: The Shapes of Culture and the Religious Imagination; Essays in Honour of Michael Fishbane*, ed. Deborah A. Green and Laura S. Lieber [Oxford: Oxford University Press, 2009], 135–45). See further n. 644.

of "companions": at the end of days, "*every* single company comes and serves itself a portion" (emphasis added). This argument that there will be no competition among "companions" continues by glossing the term as "merchants" and, again like the Talmud, its gloss uses Isa 23:8: *whose merchants are princes, whose traffickers are the honorable of the earth*. In the Talmud, however, that gloss was cited anonymously. It seemed to apologize for R. Yohanan's gloss of *merchants*, which gave this term a negative connotation and painted them as anything but "honorable,"[663] reaffirming the Talmud's hierarchy of the rabbis over the merchants, and picturing envy even among scholars, also due to status hierarchy. In this homily by contrast, the Talmud's anonymous aside becomes the dominant position. Every companion is a "merchant" (scholars included!) and in the End, they all appear in an irenically egalitarian light.[664]

In sum, this homily draws from the same set of prooftexts and interpretations as the Talmud to present an inverse vision of the status hierarchy in the Heavenly Jerusalem. Anyone who is righteous, in any way, will take their share of the goods—not only scholars. We could read this as a bald rejection of the Talmud's implicit snobbery. Or, we could see it as indirectly building on R. Yohanan's idea that, in the Heavenly Jerusalem, anyone will be able to buy Leviathan's flesh (even if it is miniaturized as an amulet), or see its skin shine across the world. Whereas he simply defused the tension between hierarchy and egalitarianism by painting the Heavenly Jerusalem as an egalitarian island in a sea of hierarchy, this homily rejects the hierarchy altogether. Good deeds are no less righteous than study; pilgrimage to the earthly Jerusalem is no less meritorious; merchants are no less deserving than scholars. The murky provenance of this homily makes it hard to assess whether it is reacting directly to the Talmud or drawing from the same well of Amoraic exegeses but taking them in the opposite direction. Regardless, it pointedly rejects the anonymous Talmud's and its editors' scholastic view of the hierarchy of merits.

In terms of how readers engaged our composition's version, the Talmud's contrast with this homily further calls our attention to one keyword in the Talmud that does *not* reflect its preference for a scholastic status hierarchy. This is also, not coincidentally, one of few elements that is clearly an anonymous voice: the chorus (*Woe for such shame! Woe for such disgrace!*), appended by the editors to two earlier traditions.[665] In con-

---

663. Citing Hos 12:7: *He is a merchant, the balances of deceit are in his hand; he loveth to oppress* (KJV).

664. Contrast R. Hanina's interpretation of Isa 4:5 (*the shining of a flaming fire by night*): "This teaches that, if anyone [of the scholars] envies the canopy of his *companion*, Woe for such shame!," etc. (2.C, emphasis added).

665. The chorus is not marked as an earlier source, whereas the statements that it glosses are. The first is attributed to a Palestinian Amora, in Hebrew (compare t. Pisha 3:20, ed. Lieberman, 4:157). The second appears under the formula "And thus have we learned

text, this chorus puts a wrinkle on the Talmud's implication that scholars dominate the status hierarchy. They seem to envy each other even in the messianic age, and the decline of the generations has afflicted them since the days of their exemplar Moses, whose successor Joshua was less fair than he (as a past generation, ironically, reminds them).

This chorus would strike another ironic note for a reader who recalls that it also echoes a story in Part 1 (XIIIa–b). At the foot of Mount Sinai, Rabbah heard a heavenly voice proclaiming, "*Woe is me* for having sworn," and—back in Babylonia—the study-house derided him as an "ass" and "jackass" for failing to utter a formula that would have released God from an oath, which they interpret as the exile of God's "children," Israel, from their Land (b. Ber. 3a).[666] While their debate about the substance of the oath—which, as they point out themselves (XIIIb.176), turns on the very same keyword, "Woe"—may have seemed speculative or even playful in its original context, now that it has been coded negatively as "shame" and scholarly envy (even *after* redemption from exile) the reader might gain some sympathy for Rabbah as the butt of his colleagues' derision. Such a reader might reinterpret both passages as a sign of the decline of the generations: reading "the face of Joshua," which pales in comparison to Moses's face (2.C), as Mount Sinai, thronged by scorpions like "asses": not Rabbah, but his cruel colleagues (XIIIa; for sages as scorpions, see Avot 2:10). On the other hand, they might read the sages' derision of Rabbah as refuting a legitimate counter-argument: if God regrets exiling Israel, why has God not ended the exile? It must be someone's fault. Who better than that "ass," Rabbah, who thought he knew better and did not end the exile when he could?[667]

None of these conclusions is foregone, but the point, for our purposes, is that readers' attention to these intertexts is cued by the editorial keyword. Just as editors' work on Part 2 links a universal Heavenly Jerusalem

---

[נמצינו למידין]" in Sifre Numbers. *Sifre on Numbers: An Annotated Edition* [Hebrew], ed. Menahem I. Kahana (Jerusalem: Magnes, 2011), vol. 1, ס.

666. At least according to one interpretation of that "oath"; the earliest that I know explicitly is a late twelfth-century *piyyut* by R. Ephraim b. R. Yaʿaqov of Bonn, where this line is paralleled with "woe is the father who exiled his son" (b. Ber. 3a). For translation and commentary, see Hans-Georg von Mutius, *Hymnen und Gebete* (Hildesheim: Olms, 1989), 80. See nn. 173–175. See also b. Eruv. 30a, another of Rabbah's outsized stories, in which he reports that Rabbi Yohanan was able to eat a tremendous quantity of a certain fruit (see n. 110). This story of Rabbah's is structurally similar to XIIIa–b: it also ends with an "oath" about an abnormal phenomenon in the Land of Israel that is then "corrected" or debated in the Talmud's anonymous voice.

667. In blaming Rabbah, this reading allows the study-house to anticipate a polemic against a parallel (b. Ber. 3a) actually recorded among later Christians: "If, however, [God] will have [the power to free you from captivity] at a certain time, it remains for you to say what prevents him from having it now …" (Alfonsi, *Dialogue against the Jews*, 69). See Peter the Venerable in Saul Lieberman, *Shkiin* [Hebrew] (Jerusalem: Wahrmann, 1970), 28–29.

theme with a preference for scholarly status, here, their keyword (*Woe ...*) redirects a reader back to Part 1 in light of the same theme. This enriches stories in light of exegesis (and vice versa) and complicates the Talmud's own apparent pro-scholastic ideology. By contrasting this editor-reader interaction with the populist homily, we glimpsed how the process of canonization guided readers to recollect Part 2 and Part 1 in new and creative ways.

In other units of Pesiq. Rab Kah., we find further parallels to the Talmud's Heavenly Jerusalem section (2.C). In Pesiq. Rab Kah., these show the same populist and anti-scholastic rhetoric.[668] In the Talmud, they shed further light on editorial keywords and catchphrases which reshape our composition by generating a stronger reading of Part 1 in light of Part 2.

Doubting Thomas in the Study-House

The Talmud's Heavenly Jerusalem section (2.C) begins on an odd note: a dispute about the meaning of *kadkhod* in Isa 54:12 (*And I will make thy battlements of* kadkhod *and thy gates of carbuncles*) in the name of the Palestinian Amora R. Shmuel b. Nahmani. Parties to this dispute are also odd: two unnamed Palestinian Amoraim (as it says, "in the West" — from the perspective of this Talmud), or two angels, Gabriel and Michael.[669] Regardless, God intervenes to settle their dispute with a brilliant stroke of equivocation: *The Holy One, Blessed be He, said to them: Let it be both as this*

---

668. Two more examples along these lines. (1) A homily in Pesiq. Rab Kah. 4:4 (ed. Mandelbaum, 66 ln. 11–67 ln. 2) on Eccl 8:1 (*A man's wisdom maketh his face to shine*: see this book's epigraph) cites Moses as the scholastic paradigm to whom this verse applies, due to his expertise in purity law (see n. 752). However, Pesiq. Rab Kah. 4:4 also glosses the same verse as *all* Israel, who have the same expertise. Again, this populist treatment of the motif contrasts sharply with the Talmud's status hierarchy. (2) The same unit of Pesiq. Rab Kah. has another extensive parallel to the Talmud's Part 2.C (Amoraic midrashim on Ezek 28:13). In this parallel, Pesiq. Rab Kah. 4:4 draws out the logic behind Amoraic expositions that the Talmud, for its part, attributes to late Babylonians (e.g., Mar Zutra). That could indicate later development on the side of the Pesiq. Rab Kah. parallel. Yet the Talmud also adds an exposition of the next words of Ezek 28:13 that is *not* in Pesiq. Rab Kah. 4:4. In its place, Pesiq. Rab Kah. develops an interpretation of the same words that the Talmud cites anonymously *en passant* (under the formula ואיכא דאמרי הכי קאמר). Here again, the relation between the two works is not a linear evolution, but different elaborations of shared sources. See the parallel in Pesiq. Rab. 14:33–36; Rivka Ulmer, ed., *A Bilingual Edition of Pesiqta Rabbati*, vol. 1: *Chapters 1–22* , SJ 86 (Berlin: de Gruyter, 2017), 396–401.

669. Urbach identifies this as an allusion to the *angelus interpres* in apocalyptic sources, e.g., Rev 21:19, noting that this angel specifically reveals the precious stones in the Heavenly Jerusalem (including jasper, ἴασπις, equivalent to *kadkhod* in LXX Isa 54:12) ("Yerushalayim shel matah," 389). For the rivalry of Gabriel and Michael, see Pesiq. Rab Kah. 1:3, Pesiq. Rab 21, ed. Meir Ish-Shalom (Vienna: self-published, 1880), 100a.

and as that (keden u-kheden). Now that the meaning of this word is based on the dispute *about* its meaning, not vice versa, it can have both.[670]

In Pesiq. Rab Kah., God's position is attributed to Abba b. Kahana;[671] aside from that, the parallels are identical. Then, after an independent story, departing from a fourth etymology of *kadkhod*, Pesiq. Rab Kah. returns to the next part of the verse: *and thy gates of carbuncles*. Here, as in the parallels discussed above, Pesiq. Rab Kah. shares the Talmud's interpretation of a word in Scripture (*carbuncles* → *I shall bore/sprout*), but attributes it to someone other than R. Yohanan. Only after citing an independent yet identical gloss on this word by this alternative authority (R. Shmuel b. Yitshaq) does Pesiq. Rab Kah. trace it back to a source that it shares with the Talmud: R. Yohanan's gloss of the subject of this new action (bore/sprout) as God, and its object as the Heavenly Jerusalem. By that action, R. Yohanan held, God will "make" a single pearl so large that it forms the Temple's east gate and both its wickets (in the Talmud, he says something similar).[672]

A story follows to illustrate the truth of R. Yohanan's dictum, as we have already seen (chapter 4 §*Double Vision*).[673] A certain "seafaring heretic" (מינוי פרוש) in Pesiq. Rab Kah.,[674] who is called a "disciple" (תלמיד) in the Talmud, questions R. Yohanan's dictum or openly "jeers

---

670. Rashbam, b. B. Bat. 75a s.v. כדין וכדין: "And even though this [interpretation of] the verse was [already] before the sons of R. Hiyya [the disputing Amoraim "in the West"—J.R.], it is preferable to say that this is what Isaiah was prophesying about: that it shall be built according to *all* the words of the commentators." The same kind of etymology is used for *ziz* (IXb), "of this and that" (*mizzeh u-mizzeh*; Lev. Rab. 22:10).

671. Pesiq. Rab Kah. 18:5, see Appendix §*Parallels to Part 2* (3.B).

672. 2.C: "In time to come, the Holy One, Blessed be He, will bring precious stones and pearls that are *thirty by thirty* [cubits], and carve out [a space from] them *ten* [cubits wide] by *twenty* [high], and set them up in the gates of Jerusalem" (emphasis added; compare Rev 21:21: "And the twelve gates were twelve pearls"). In the Talmud, these numbers are a structural device: most of the following units use repeated numbers to shape and connect units ("seven canopies"; "ten canopies"; "three *parasang*"; and the final unit of 2.C, which revives the topic of the length/breadth of the Heavenly Jerusalem). See chapter 3 §*The Uses of Repetition*. The Talmud's version of R. Yohanan's dictum is tailored to this schema.

673. As Hirshman notes ("Pesiqta deRav Kahana and Paideia," 174), the theme of belief in text over vision (D. Stein, "Believing Is Seeing" and *Textual Mirrors*) is thematized not only by the Talmud but also in this unit of Pesiq. Rab Kah. (18:5, ed. Mandelbaum, 296–99), by inserting similar stories before and after this one. Hirshman (also in "Yearning for Intimacy") reads Pesiq. Rab Kah. as a text that recreates the Temple, arguing that these stories are a key to that program, as they teach, by example, the imperative of belief in its restoration.

674. Per Lieberman (*Tosefta Ki-feshutah: Zeraim*, 1:54 n. 84), פרוש here means one who "departs" (פ.ר.ש) for the sea. This association of visions and seafarers ties the story all the way back to I–II, adding to a ring-structure. More commonly, of course, the term connotes "sectarian/separatist" (as in "Pharisees," פרושים; see Shaye J. D. Cohen, "The Significance of Yavneh: Pharisees, Rabbis, and the End of Jewish Sectarianism," HUCA 55 [1984]: 27–53, at 39 n. 32). On this possible double-meaning of "heretical seafarer," see D. Stein, "Believing Is Seeing," 24 n. 46.

at" it in the Talmud: nobody finds pearls that big![675] When he goes off to sea,[676] however, and when what R. Yohanan foretold to him is revealed to his very eyes in a miraculous encounter with the angels (who, in Pesiq. Rab Kah., seem to save him from a shipwreck),[677] he returns and begs the rabbi to repeat his exposition. Alas, this heretic/disciple now believes for the same wrong reason that he did not at first: because he has seen it with his own eyes. R. Yohanan is quick to point out his error, and, unforgiving—as we have seen in our brief discussion of this story at the end of chapter 4—he turns the doubter into a pile of bones with his magical gaze.

Given that the two versions relate a more or less identical story, it is easier to identify differences between their plots,[678] all of which imply opposed attitudes to status hierarchy. In the Talmud, the rabbi's foil is a "disciple," an insider; in Pesiq. Rab Kah., he is a "heretic" and a seafarer, a paradigmatic outsider to the world of the study-house. In fact, Pesiq. Rab Kah. sets the whole story, not in R. Yohanan's study-house in Tiberias, but at "the great synagogue in Sepphoris," leaving scholars still unsure

---

675. "Nowadays, we don't find them as big as a turtle-dove's egg ...." For a Talmudic reader, the disciple's keyword could trigger a wordplay reinforcing other clever word choices by the disciple that we will hear. "Egg" (ביעתא) generally means "oval" (hence also "testicle" or "skull"; compare the Syriac rendering of "skull" [*qadqod*] in Peshitta Pss 7:17 and 68:22 (William Emery Barnes, *The Peshitta Psalter according to the West-Syrian Text* [Cambridge: Cambridge University Press, 1904])). This Syriac "skull," *qadqod* (JBA קרקפא: JBA, 1046), is spelled and pronounced differently than the gem (*kadkhod*) in the passage above. But by association with "egg," it can evoke soundplay (like *śukkôt/sukkôt*, *ṣilṣal/ṣilṣāl*, 2.B. To disambiguate homophones from here on, I adopt the academic transliteration of the *SBL Handbook of Style*, 26, cited in §*Notes on the Text*). The Aramaic-speaking reader may hear about a jewel the size of an "oval" and think of a "skull" (*qadqod*)—reminding them of the jewel that was just discussed (*kadkhod*). Alternatively, the word "skull" (*qadqod*, a direct soundplay on *kadkhod*) could stand behind "egg" in an earlier, now lost telling of his insult. The unit of measure (pearl/tiny egg) is not rhetorically neutral. See n. 756

676. This motif is itself a midrash, on the verse just prior to the one on which R. Yohanan comments (Isa 54:11, trans. KJV: *O thou afflicted, tossed with tempest, and not comforted; behold* [הִנֵּה], *I will lay thy stones*). This story was not just appended to an exposition of Isa 54:12; it is a unified narrative exegesis of the prophecy. An innocuous word in the verse (הִנֵּה) is interpreted in opposite ways by the sinner and the sage. One takes it visually ("Look"), as a token of evidence for believing the prophecy. The other takes it as a given truth: "Here."

677. This motif of an underwater pearl, connected to eschatological symbolism (see n. 642), is also prominent in Part 1 (XVIII–XIX). Readers could have recollected the composition based directly on this content. For instance, the diver's miraculous salvation and loss of the pearl in XIX could foreshadow the wicked disciple, as could the fact that the diver in XVIII failed to recover the right object—according to rabbinic norms (compare Rabbah in XIIb). I avoid such connections where there is no verbal link prompting a reader's attention to them, whereas Septimus might call them "simultexts." See n. 736.

678. Defining "story" as the bare succession of events and "plot" as the causal nexus that connects them; see E. M. Forster, *Aspects of the Novel*, Clark Lectures 1927 (London: Harcourt, Brace, 1927), 130–31. This mirrors the *syuzhet/fabula* distinction in Russian Formalism and the Tel Aviv School of Poetics; see Redfield, "Behind Auerbach's 'Background.'"

whether to call his exegesis of the Bible "study" or "preaching."[679] In the Talmud, the disciple calls him "Rabbi" and begs him to "expound" (*d.r.sh*) in highfalutin or archaic Hebrew: the characters seem to share a sense of what midrash is.[680] In Pesiq. Rab Kah., the heretic refers to him with a vague term ("Elder"),[681] his teaching with a vague verb ("to praise," שבח) and another vague Aramaic verb ("to tell, proclaim," ג.ל.ג.)—with no mention of midrash as such. Finally, in the Talmud, the disciple's transgression is called "jeering at the words *of the sages*" by both the narrator and R. Yohanan. By contrast, in Pesiq. Rab Kah., the heretic transgresses not "words of the sages" but "words that I said *about* the Torah" (מילייא דמרתי באורייתא). This term is ambiguous (oral Torah or written?) but clearly not respect for "the sages" per se. The Talmud narrator's reference to "words of the sages" sets up R. Yohanan for his punch line, when he can punish the disciple with his withering gaze for neglecting the authority of tradition. Pesiq. Rab Kah. pulls the very same punches, softening a sense that scholastic status is at stake here. All of these differences reassert the talmudic editors' interest in promoting scholars to the top of the status hierarchy. Rather than assert that "the message is basically the same" in both versions because both uphold the rabbi's authority, or assume that the Talmud "lost something in the process of transfer" because it sets this conflict in a study-house rather than a synagogue,[682] I think that this *is* the subtle message of the Talmud's editors, just as they chose to call attention to the scholarly status hierarchy in several other ways above.

---

679. Lee I. Levine, *The Ancient Synagogue: The First Thousand Years*, 2nd ed. (New Haven: Yale University Press, 2005), 486 and 488.

680. The disciple's כאשר אמרת refers to R. Yohanan's midrash by a formula rarely found in rabbinic sources (outside biblical quotations) but a standard formula for citing Scripture in the Dead Sea Scrolls (כאשר אמר הכתוב). See Moshe Bernstein, "Scriptures: Quotation and Use," in *Encyclopedia of the Dead Sea Scrolls*, ed. Lawrence H. Schiffman and James C. VanderKam, 2 vols. (Oxford: Oxford University Press, 2000), 2:839–42, at 840. On the disciple's כאשר... כן as a typological formula in the Bible, see Fishbane, *Biblical Interpretation*, 352, 362, 366.

681. Elder (*Saba'*) is not itself derogatory. It disambiguates rabbis' names, like our "Senior" (R. Dostai Saba' as opposed to R. Dostai; y. Hag. 1:8, 76d; Nahman Saba' as opposed to Nahman bar Adda, y. Meg. 2:1, 73a = y. Ber. 2:3, 4d). It is even a scholastic title (b. Sanh. 17b). Yet wherever a character *repeats* the term (סבא סבא, only in Palestinian works), it is clearly disrespectful: a son disrespects his father (y. Qidd. 1:7, 61b = y. Peah 1:1, 15c); a *matrona* disrespects a rabbi (y. Shabb. 8:1, 11a = y. Pesah. 10:1, 37c) or, in a similar turn of phrase, Turnus Rufus disrespects R. Akiva (y. Sotah 5:5, 20c; see y. Ber. 9:5, 14b, with Amram Tropper, *Like Clay in the Hands of the Potter: Sage Stories in Rabbinic Literature* [Hebrew] (Jerusalem: Shazar Center, 2011), 134 n. 71); Hadrian disrespects an old man (Lev. Rab. 25:5; see Balberg and Weiss, *When Near Becomes Far*, 177); R. El'azar bar. R. Shimeon disrespects Elijah (! Pesiq. Rab Kah. 11:22, ed. Mandelbaum, 197; on Elijah-as-Elder, see n. 707, nn. 722–23). Ours seems to be a lone exception, where a character does not intend to be disrespectful—but it turns out that he was. For anyone familiar with the reading tradition of "Elder, Elder," then, it lends a grating tone to the heretic.

682. Richard Kalmin, *Jewish Babylonia between Persia and Roman Palestine* (Oxford: Oxford University Press, 2006), 88–90.

Both versions of the story share other peculiar features that shed light on how, precisely, they directed their readers' attention to editors' preferred themes. In Pesiq. Rab Kah., Aramaic/Hebrew alternation is noteworthy. A pattern is not obvious.[683] The narrator begins in Aramaic to introduce the setting and continues in Aramaic after R. Yohanan's dictum, which is in Hebrew, as in the Talmud. The heretic speaks Aramaic to R. Yohanan, and their dialogue at the end of the story is in Aramaic. So far, language use is consistent: a tale set in Palestine with an old quotation in Hebrew, but most narration/dialogue in the Aramaic vernacular. However, in Pesiq. Rab Kah., the part about the sea-voyage and vision of the angels is all in Hebrew; in the Talmud, all in Aramaic. This further supports our proposal that Pesiq. Rab Kah. shares the Talmud's source of that story, but not its telling;[684] otherwise, why not keep it in Aramaic?[685]

This selective use of Hebrew tips the hand of the editors of the Pesiq. Rab Kah. story, showing how they integrated a shared source into their retelling. At the end of the shipwreck, Pesiq. Rab Kah. says something that is not in the Talmud: *Immediately* [מיד] *a miracle was performed* [נעשה] *for him and he departed unharmed*. As the heretic is under water, this line is crucial to the plot. (In the Talmud, his ship is not in peril, so it would make no sense.) This addition has a simple exegetical basis (see n. 676). But it also points forward to the end of this telling of the story: *Immediately* [מיד] *he was transformed* [נעשה] *into a pile of bones*.[686] Unlike the preceding dialogue and narration, *transformed into a pile of bones* is in Hebrew in Pesiq. Rab Kah., as it is in the Talmud, where it appears a few times, in similar contexts.[687]

---

683. Burton L. Visotzky, "The Misnomers 'Petihah' and 'Homiletic Midrash' as Descriptions for Leviticus Rabbah and Pesikta De-Rav Kahana," *JSQ* 18.1 (2011): 19–31, at 29: "For the most part, Pesiq. Rab Kah. uses Aramaic loanwords either to spice the dialogue or for a particular lexical nuance." Gerhard Svedlund catalogues Aramaic features but lacks a thesis on language use (*The Aramaic Portions of the Pesiqta de Rab Kahana according to MS Marshall Or.24, the Oldest Known Manuscript of the Pesiqta de Rab Kahana, with English Translation, Commentary and Introduction*, Acta Universitatis Upsaliensis: Studia Semitica Upsaliensia 2 [Stockholm: Almqvist & Wiksell, 1974]).

684. Already noted by Stemberger, "Münchhausen und die Apokalyptik," 81.

685. On "code-switching" as one answer to this question, see Smelik, *Rabbis, Language, and Translation*, 116–21; Smelik, "Code-Switching: The Public Reading of the Bible in Hebrew, Aramaic, and Greek," in *Was ist ein Text? Alttestamentliche, ägyptologische und altorientalistische Perspektiven*, ed. Ludwig Morenz and Stefan Schorch, BZAW 362 (Berlin: de Gruyter, 2007), 123–54; Kalmin, *Migrating Tales*, 37–38. See now Steven D. Fraade, *Multilingualism and Translation in Ancient Judaism: Before and after Babel* (Cambridge: Cambridge University Press, 2023), 11–14, 142 n. 43 (citing Smelik's forthcoming book on the subject).

686. Similarly, "medieval *midrashim* routinely use this term [מיד] to connect independent traditions and place them in chronological sequence" (Rubenstein, "From Mythic Motifs," 153). As in our story, מיד can create cause–effect relations in a passage (Rubenstein, "From Mythic Motifs," 157). Compare the analysis of the Talmud's use of "once" (פעם אחת) in Friedman, "Dama ben Netinah," 439–40; Tropper, *Like Clay in the Hands*, 117 n. 19.

687. On this motif, see Sinai (Tamas) Turan, "'Wherever the Sages Set Their Eyes, There

This language shift in the Pesiq. Rab Kah. telling suggests that its editors worked from a source like the Talmud's (R. Yohanan's exegesis of a verse; disbelief, vision, and destruction), but repeated this within the narrative for the sake of symmetry with the source's conclusion. Now, in their telling, the heretic's salvation at sea foreshadows his destruction in the end. This adds another layer to what is already an ironic narrative structure, as this rabbinic Doubting Thomas is struck down by precisely that in which he placed his trust—the eyes.[688] By leaving their source's Hebrew intact at the end, these editors cost themselves some realism (that sentence of narration begins in Aramaic and ends in Hebrew—a bit of a hiccup). Yet their Hebrew ending may also lend their conclusion an elevated tone for members of their audience who would recognize allusions to similar rabbinic stories.[689] At a safe distance from the Talmud's status hierarchy, these editors still exploit it for a special effect: the explosive eyes of a wrathful sage.

Keywords, Catchphrases, and the Rebirth of a Theme

Our reconstruction of this story's source has shed light on how editors of its retelling in Pesiq. Rab Kah. tailored its beginning and end to fit a measure-for-measure punishment. The Talmud's editors did so as well. How-

---

Is Either Death or Poverty': On the History, Terminology, and Imagery of the Talmudic Traditions about the Devastating Gaze of the Sages" [Hebrew], *Sidra* 23 (2008): 137–205; and, on our story, 157–59. For prior discussion, see Shamma Friedman, "The Further Adventures of Rav Kahana: Between Babylonia and Palestine," in *The Talmud Yerushalmi and Graeco-Roman Culture*, ed. Peter Schäfer et al., 3 vols., TSAJ 71, 79, 93 (Tübingen: Mohr Siebeck, 1998–2002), 3:247–71, at 263–64; Daniel Sperber, "On the Unfortunate Adventures of Rav Kahana: A Passage of Saboraic Polemic from Sasanian Persia," in *Irano-Judaica: Studies Relating to Jewish Contacts with Persian Culture throughout the Ages*, ed. Shaul Shaked (Jerusalem: Yad Ben-Zvi, 1982), 83–100, at 90 (with sources at 90 n. 40); Rubenstein, *Talmudic Stories*, 340 n. 62. Compare Vision of Theophilus; see *1. Vision of Theophilus, 2. Apocalypse of Peter*, trans. Alphonse Mingana, Woodbrooke Studies 3 (Cambridge: Hefer & Sons, 1931), 22, where Jesus turns camels to stone with his gaze, or Thekla, who "knocked the wind out" of men with her gaze and "would have taken their lives ... if she had not spared them" (trans. Linda Ann Honey, in her "Thekla: Text and Context" [PhD diss., University of Calgary, 2011], 414).

688. To paraphrase R. Yohanan, "Because thou hast seen me, thou hast believed: blessed are they that have not seen, and yet have believed" (John 20:29). Note the parallel context (master/disciple) and cultural issue (vision/belief). (The same parallel and theme were noted independently by Hirshman, "Pesiqta deRav Kahana and Paideia," 175; Levinson, "No Place Like Home," 115–16; and already long before, by Hermann L. Strack and Paul Billerbeck, *Kommentar zum Neuen Testament aus Talmud und Midrasch*, 3 vols. [Munich: Beck, 1922–1928] 2:586).

689. Friedman acknowledges the possibility of transference of this particular motif between other Talmud sources ("Historical *aggadah*," 413). Turan shows that it was developed in the Talmud generally in tandem with the sages' greater prestige and danger ('"Wherever the Sages Set their Eyes,'" 190–91), as I argue it is here.

ever, the interpretive frame that they had in mind for this story was much larger—our entire two-part composition—and their tailoring of the story not only invited new meanings for each part but also goaded readers to rethink relations across the whole composition in structured and creatively nonlinear ways. Devices whereby editors reworked their source spurred and guided readers to recollect the composition.[690] These devices include catchphrases, or what I called "flourishes" in chapter 1: repeated, discrete, always anonymous remarks separable from sources. Catchphrases were tagged and often prefaced by "keywords," which, unlike catchphrases, appear in any voice including those of Amoraim, not just the Stam.

Two keywords stand out: a pair of verbs with inverse root-letters and opposite connotations, "tell/proclaim" (ג.ל.ג) and "jeer" (ל.ג.ל.ג), as well as a noun (סבא, "Elder"), doubled in Pesiq. Rab Kah., which is not in the Talmud's telling at all but does resurface later in its Heavenly Jerusalem section (2.C). There, like the first keyword, the Talmud links "Elder" to a catchphrase, which *also* appears much earlier in Part 1. Together, these catchphrases turn a reader's attention to the Talmud's theme of Part 2 (scholarly status hierarchy), in light of a long-standing cultural problem that surrounds the tales: belief in *vision* or *words of the sages*? A reader of this Heavenly Jerusalem section was thus provoked to revisit instances of the catchphrase back in Part 1, and to reassess the tales where they appear, in light of Part 2, thereby realizing latent interpretive potentialities of the composition as a whole. As they did so, isolated textual units, unrelated by content alone, entered new inner-canonical dialogue.

One-half of the first keyword, "tell/proclaim" (ג.ל.ג), appears uniquely in the Pesiq. Rab Kah. telling. There, it has the positive connotation. The heretic goes to R. Yohanan and admits that his interpretation of the verse was true, saying:

> Elder!, Elder!, proclaim all you can proclaim [כל מה דאת יכיל למגלגלא גליג], praise all there is to praise [למשבחה שבח]. For had my eyes not seen, I would not have believed–

This positive sense "proclaim" is from Palestinian Aramaic ג.ל.ג,[691] like the inverse Syriac root ("speak in plain terms," ל.ג.ל.ג).[692] In the Talmud,

---

690. My approach in the following section is inspired by a distinctive reading method developed by Zvi Septimus ("Trigger Words"; "Poetic Superstructure") and inspired by several of his talks and our conversations. For how my approach differs, see n. 736.

691. For our story, see Sokoloff, *JPA*, 128. Ber. Rab. 64:10 (ed. Theodor-Albeck, 712): "Go and proclaim [תהוי מגלג] that you put your head in the lion's mouth unharmed and took it out unharmed." In an oral text, association between opposed meanings is easily exploited (ג.ל.ג is *also* "to disdain" in Palestinian Aramaic: Sokoloff, *JPA*, 129). In two manuscripts of Pesiq. Rab Kah., the heretic's keyword is in fact inverted: למלגלג, למילגלגל (see ed. Mandelbaum, 298, ln. 9).

692. *CAL* s.v. לגלג notes that the Syriac *Life of Rabban Hormizd* combines the opposite keyword "speak in simple terms, stammer" (ל.ג.ל.ג: "jeer" in Jewish Aramaics) *and* "praise"

including earlier in our story, the very same ל.ג.ל.ג has the opposite sense: "to jeer," and, specifically, to jeer at the sages.[693] In the Talmud's telling, R. Yohanan reuses the keyword in that opposite negtive sense:

> "Expound (*d.r.sh*), Rabbi, it is fit for you to expound; yea, just as you have said, thus have I seen." He replied:
> "Good-for-nothing![694] If you *hadn't* seen, you *wouldn't* have believed! You jeer [מלגלג] at the words of the sages.'"

In Pesiq. Rab Kah., this keyword is synonymous with R. Yohanan's exegesis, his oral Torah. In the Talmud, the reverse letters have the reverse meaning: to mock "the words of the sages." Further, in the Talmud's telling only, it also frames the beginning of the story: "a certain disciple *jeered at him*"—a sin for which his later vision and confession will not atone. Thus, the Talmud's editors use the keyword to call audiences' attention to a conflict between the basic sources of truth in the two-part composition as a whole: *vision* versus "*words* of the sages." For a reader of the composition, that conflict is further highlighted by a *catchphrase* linked to this keyword ("If you *hadn't* seen, you *wouldn't* have believed"). In Part 1, after all, the composition's reader has already encountered the only other instance of this catchphrase in the Talmud. A colleague remarks on one of Rabbah's visions (which began "I myself *have seen*"):

> V.61. Rav Pappa son of Shmuel said: "If I hadn't *been there* [mss. V, O: *seen it*], I wouldn't have believed it."

This nearly or fully verbatim echo across the two parts of the Talmud's composition is hardly a coincidence. Rather than an open schism between apocalyptic authority (vision) and rabbinic authority ("words of the sages"), staged by an editor of both parts as a literary unity, however,[695] I prefer to interpret this echo as a moment in a multi-generational dialogue between editors and their readers. After all, if editors simply

---

(ש.ב.ח), in a formula just like Pesiq. Rab Kah: "in my stammering manner I stammered out his glories in a praising way." Further examples at Sokoloff, *Syriac Lexicon*, 673. This supports the notion that the pair of verbs was readily inverted by retellers and editors of the rabbinic works' shared sources.

693. "I am not angry at the one who says the blessing, I am angry at the one who jeers [ל.ג.ל.ג] at him! If your companion is equivalent to one who has never once tasted an iota of meat, at what did you have to jeer?" (b. Ber. 39a; "to jeer" and "to taste meat" are also conjoined at b. Eruv. 21b; this is an idiom of some sort).

694. ריקא (*reqa'*). See Michal Bar-Asher Siegal who notes that, in general, unlike here, "the insult does not seem to be used specifically in reference to Scriptural arguments" ("Matthew 5:22: The Insult 'Fool' and the Interpretation of the Law in Christian and Rabbinic Sources," *RHR* 234 [2017]: 5–23, 20).

695. Stemberger, "Münchhausen und die Apokalyptik," 78–82.

wanted to strengthen the lesson of the Doubting Thomas story, why would they pair it with one that seems to contradict its message? It raises more questions than it answers. Clearly, this disciple was wrong to privilege the evidence of vision over belief in the words of the sages. But how is a reader to square him with his counterpart in Part 1, Rav Pappa? When Rav Pappa said the same catchphrase, did he mean that he "would not have believed" Rabbah's vision either—*but* that others (like the study-house, who deride Rabbah as an "ass" and "jackass" in XIIb and XIIIb) *should* believe it, because he saw it, too? If so, then is vision legitimate evidence for (some) words of (some) sages after all? Or was Rav Pappa making the same mistake as the heretic/disciple: only believing Rabbah's words after he saw them with his own eyes? Yet if vision is *not* evidence for words of the sages, why would Rabbah have repeated that "I myself have seen" these things so often in Part 1? Is Rabbah just like the bad disciple, who thinks that vision is evidence? But if it is not evidence at all, then why were we, the audience, told in the same story (V.58) to "come see" for ourselves the lesson of Rabbah's vision—a formula that is typically used to introduce proofs in rabbinic *oral* Torah, but which blurs the line between oral Torah and actual autopsies? (Especially as the Talmud's editors' and its tellers' voices blend there—see nn. 430–39, n. 548).

The editors do not answer those questions. However, by repeating the keyword in Part 2, using it to restructure their telling, and "tagging" it with a catchphrase from Part 1, they do intensify the questions and guide their reader to recollect the composition via interpretation. Their technique does not remove inherited ambiguities—it creates new ones.[696] Nor does it foreclose alternative resolutions.[697] Regardless, for a reader of Part 2, Part 1 will never be the same: the keyword and catchphrase bind the composition by restructuring its reading process.

The same argument holds for the second keyword in the shared

---

696. For example, if Rabbah *said* that he saw something, and Rav Pappa *said* that he believed it, then why don't their dicta qualify as "words of the sages" in the rabbinic oral tradition, even if they refer to seeing?

697. For example, one may read the sages as mocking Rabbah, not because he claims to have *seen* things, but because he looked for the wrong ones (XIIb: "Now then, those threads of the joints [in the fringes of the prayershawl]: Is it according to the House of Shammai or according to the House of Hillel? If only you'd counted them! And come and told us!") For them, it seems, vision is a legitimate source of evidence so long as it serves the truth of oral Torah (a legal dispute at b. Menah. 41b on the question, "How many threads does one put in [the fringes of the prayershawl]?" See Rashbam, b. B. Bat. 74a s.v. למאי הלכתא). In the same serious spirit, Tosafot (b. B. Bat. 74a s.v. פסקי חדא קרנא דתכלתא) ask another legal question ("*Does this story prove that a man should be buried in a prayershawl?*") and return to b. Menah. 41a to debate this. Ramban (Nahmanides) (*Kitve Rabbenu Moshe ben Nahman*, ed. Charles Ber Chavel, 2 vols. [Jerusalem: Mossad ha-Rav Kook, 1963], 2:79) similarly reads the tale as proof that burial face-up (XIIa.152, *supine*) is proper (*Kitve Rabbenu Moshe* 2:115). Vision is not always bad per se. See chapter 4 §*Double Vision*.

The Iridescence of Scripture   245

source of both works ("Elder," סבא), although, in this case, the keyword survives only in Pesiq. Rab Kah.'s telling. In the Talmud, this keyword was displaced from the story to later in the same section (2.C).[698] In terms of talmudic editors' dialogue with their reader, this keyword has the same function. Again, they link it with a catchphrase and a theme that guide a reader to create retroactive links from the end of Part 2 all the way back to Part 1. Again, their composition is Talmudized — tied into a canonical interpretive framework and theme — without acquiring one fixed meaning.

In the Pesiq. Rab Kah. story, the keyword "Elder" has a clear rhetorical effect. Not in itself derogatory, it creates distance between the heretic and the rabbi by naming the rabbi in a generic register, just as the rest of their dialogue quotes the heretic's words for rabbinic tradition in a register that is elevated,[699] yet generic.[700] Further, as we saw (n. 681), the heretic's repetition of the keyword ("Elder! Elder!") has ironically derogatory connotations. In these subtle ways, Pesiq. Rab Kah.'s telling uses the honorific keyword "Elder" to convey less respect for scholastic status. Again, we see how it differs from the Talmud in this respect.

This keyword's function in the Talmud is more nuanced. In the Talmud's telling of the same story, it is missing or suppressed: "Rabbi" stands in its place. This change to the source is rhetorically consistent with the Talmud's telling: it becomes a dialogue between master and "disciple," who "comes before" him to hear his words in a study-house, not a synagogue.[701] It would be bizarre to call him "Elder"; in the Talmud, "Elder" is never used for direct address in this setting. It is a title connected to

---

698. Rubenstein shows great fluidity around another talmudic instance of this term (b. Shabb. 34a): in the Palestinian Talmud parallel, it is a "Samaritan" or "scribe"; in Ber. Rab., an 'am ha-'arets (*Talmudic Stories*, 340 n. 61). This supports my claim that the Talmud's editors replaced "heretic" with "disciple" and recycled the flexible keyword in their telling.

699. Note that the heretic repeats every verbal element — unnecessarily, in strictly semantic terms: סבא, the intensive forms ג.ל.ג.ל and ש.ב.ח. Even the verb ח.מ.י and noun עיני are semantically redundant (the Talmud parallel has simply ר.א.ה). These repetitions heighten the heretic's register and, correspondingly, the force of R. Yohanan's interruption. A similar effect is created in the Talmud's Hebrew telling but by a different literary language: the disciple's florid archaism כאשר אמרת and poised parallel clauses conflating Scripture with Oral Torah (כן...כאשר...לדרוש...דרוש) make the rabbi's guttural vernacular retort (ריקא!) all the more blunt.

700. In the Talmud, "words of Torah" are laws based on the Bible rather than on rabbinic tradition (b. Pesah. 115a). Similarly, in both Tannaitic and Amoraic works (e.g., Pesiq. Rab Kah. 4:3, ed. Mandelbaum, 63–64 = Ber. Rab. 7:1, ed. Theodor-Albeck, 51–52), a "word of Torah" (מילה דאוריתא) is a rabbinic law based on *the* Torah, rather than on the Prophets or Writings ("tradition," קבלה; Bacher, *Die Exegetische Terminologie* 1:166 n. 1). Pesiq. Rab Kah. has a more popular outlook here and either does not know or does not emphasize those distinctions within plural canonicity — all is "Torah."

701. The ubiquitous formula "X came before R. Y" (אתא לקמיה ר' פלוני) in the Talmud implies a scholastic setting where R. Y has special authority (see Avinoam Cohen, "Towards

"Rabbi,"[702] or a respectful way to distinguish a senior from a junior rabbi by referring to him in the third person,[703] not a form of address. Its absence is not surprising.

Its presence later in the same section of Part 2, however, is. After an independent unit on the Garden of Eden—tied into the Heavenly Jerusalem unit by its image of a divine *canopy* bestowed on the righteous, like their *cover* of Leviathan's skin—the editors circle back to a final link in their chain of R. Yohanan's exegesis of Isa 4:5, reiterating their theme of status hierarchy in the Heavenly Jerusalem. This exposition, based on R. Yohanan's gloss of *her assemblies* (מִקְרָאֶהָ) as the elect, who are "called" or invited to the Heavenly Jerusalem,[704] is hooked onto a chain of other exegeses of this root (ק.ר.א), also praising the special intimacy of God and the righteous in the eschaton and in the Heavenly Jerusalem. This unit ends with yet another exposition of Isaiah (4:3) by Rabbi El'azar, which, yet again, exalts the status of the righteous "elect" in the Heavenly Jerusalem.

The next unit seems to divert from this theme to the measures of Heavenly Jerusalem:

> And Rabbah said: R. Yohanan said: "In time to come, the Holy One, Blessed be He, will raise up Jerusalem three *parasang*, as it is said: *and it shall raise* [וְרָאֲמָה] *and it shall settle* [וְיָשְׁבָה] *in its place* [תַּחְתֶּיהָ]."[705]

---

the Historical Meaning Hidden in the Phrase 'Rabbi So-and-so Happened to Come to . . .'" [Hebrew], *Sidra* 15 [1999]: 51–64, at 63). See n. 710.

702. Examples at *JBA*, 783.

703. See b. Hul. 18a: "But oughtn't a master be worried about [overruling] an Elder?" (senior rabbi); b. Eruv. 63a: "But oughtn't one be worried about [overruling] an Elder?" (vs. a subordinate class of scholar, צורבא מרבנן). See also b. Git. 79a and b. Nid. 61b: "From where does the Elder [i.e. Rav Hisda] get this [idea]?"

704. Clarified by Joel ben Samuel Sirkis (BaH; ed. Vilna *ad loc.*), whose emendation cites the verse in full.

705. Zech 14:10 [my trans.; KJV: *and it shall be lifted up, and inhabited in her place*]. The verse is difficult. The first verb was taken in the Old Greek LXX Zechariah as the name of the place near Jerusalem: "But Ramah shall remain in her place" (Ραμα δὲ ἐπὶ τόπου μενεῖ)—as opposed to other dramatic transformations in the Land of Israel that the prophet depicts in this verse. That is a weak solution, as the second *vav* (וְרָאֲמָה וְיָשְׁבָה) suggests that both are verbs, and י.ש.ב is repeated at the start of the following verse: *And they shall settle there* (וְיָשְׁבוּ בָהּ), where the LXX renders י.ש.ב by a synonym (κατοικώ), flaunting the parallel construction. However, this translator's weak solution highlights the same textual problem that gave R. Yohanan an opening for his exegesis. Does it mean that God will lift Jerusalem up in the air and set it back down on the spot? Why? Wouldn't this "hurt"? Perhaps, R. Yohanan suggests instead, it means that the city's vertical and horizontal will correspond: it will rise *in* (= as much as) its "place" (= area). For expositions of the same verse that respond to similar problems, see t. Sotah 11:16 (ed. Lieberman, 223); Pesiq. Rab Kah. 20:7 (ed. Mandelbaum, 317–18).

What is [meant by] *in its place* [תַּחְתֶּיהָ]? [That *it shall rise*] as [high] as its base [is wide]. And how [do we know] that this [= three *parasang*] is its base?

Rabbah said: A certain Elder told me: I myself have seen the previous Jerusalem, and it is three *parasang* [wide].

But perhaps you'll say: It hurts to go up? [It doesn't. That is what] the statement teaches: *Who are these that fly as a cloud, and as the doves to their windows?*[706]

In this context, Rabbah's invocation of "a certain Elder" is no different than any other source. It solves a problem that was just raised by the prior anonymous voices; that is, it proves their claim that the base of the Heavenly Jerusalem will be three *parasang*. If one reads Part 2 in isolation, it is natural to interpret the Elder just as Rabbah cites him. He is the source for an equation between the future city's height and the ancient city's base: hence, Jerusalem will "raise *and* settle" in the same measure.[707] This vision of the city's sublime symmetry, what our Elder claims to have "seen," is old indeed, well known in other prophecies and apocalypses.[708]

Yet three unusual features of this Elder's tradition, in light of parallels and relevant sources, reveal his further thematic role within the Talmud's composition. This Elder is not just an ordinary Amoraic source, but another editorial device whereby a keyword/catchphrase leads the reader to link Parts 1 and 2. The running theme of scholastic status hierarchy— and, relatedly, the authority of vision versus oral Torah as a source of evidence—is not far behind.

The first unusual feature is that an Elder is hardly ever a rabbinic source like this one. The term "Elder" can designate a reciter of the oral

---

706. Isa 60:8 (KJV).
707. As Fränkel says (*'Iyyunim*, 18), "a certain Elder" is often "a figure of special spiritual authority." Tosafot (b. Hul. 6a s.v. אשכחי ההוא סבא) read an unnamed Elder as "Elijah" (in Pesiq. Rab Kah. 11:22, he is). The two figures appear together in b. Shabb. 33b. See also the story featuring Elijah in the parallel at Pesiq. Rab. Kah. 18:5, summarized parenthetically at Appendix 3.B §*Parallels to Part 2*: a possible source for the "Elder" cited here in the Talmud). On Elijah in rabbinic literature, see Adelman, *Return of the Repressed*, 185–208; Kristen Lindbeck, *Elijah and the Rabbis: Story and Theology* (New York: Columbia University Press, 2010), focusing mainly on the Talmud.
708. Similarly, Ezek 42:15–18; Rev 21:16; 4Q554 col. III, 20–21 (ed. Florentino García Martínez and Eibert J. C. Tigchelaar, *The Dead Sea Scrolls Study Edition*, 2 vols. [Leiden: Brill, 1997–1998], 2:1108) and 4Q554a frag. 2 II, 16 (ed. García Martínez and Tigchelaar, 2:1110) imagine the eschatological Jerusalem as displaying horizontal symmetry of city, Temple, or areas inside them. Whereas here the Talmud extends this symmetry to a vertical dimension by picturing the city in the form of a cube, Ezekiel envisions the heavenly city as "altitude markers on a relief map": gradations of holiness tapering to a peak, on the mythic model of the cosmic mountain. See Jonathan Z. Smith, "Earth and Gods," reprinted in his *Map Is Not Territory: Studies in the History of Religions*, SJLA 23 (Leiden: Brill, 1978), 104–28.

law,⁷⁰⁹ but even in that sense, no Amora ever cites an Elder's personal tradition as he would cite a tradition from a rabbinic peer.⁷¹⁰ When an Elder does have something to say on a topic of interest to the rabbis, he comes from outside their conversation—disrupting, supplementing, querying, or correcting their sources.⁷¹¹ No other Elder is associated directly with one Amora, as if he were his teacher or colleague.

One of the best parallels to our Elder shows just how unusual his appearance here is:

> R. Haninah and R. Yohanan and R. Yehoshua ben Levi went up to Jerusalem. Produce had been set aside for them and they wanted to redeem it within the [city] walls. An Elder said to them: "That is not what your forefathers used to do. Rather, they would renounce [ownership of] it outside the wall and redeem it there."⁷¹²

Here, as in our case, the Elder claims knowledge of ancient Jerusalem superior to that of the Amoraim. However, even he does not claim to have "seen" ancient Jerusalem with his own eyes. He is simply more familiar with the practice of previous generations. Nor is his the last word on this subject: the Palestinian Talmud goes on to analyze the logic of the practice reflected in his tradition, compare it with the logic of later Amoraim, and reconcile it with the positions of earlier rabbis.⁷¹³ That Elder's role as a rabbinic source, superficially similar as it is, therefore stays within a realistic chronology and a conventional mode of rabbinic rhetoric.

Our Elder defies both chronology and the Talmud's general rhetorical conventions. He claims firsthand knowledge of ancient Jerusalem, which he saw with his own eyes (somehow, in fact, he surveyed the city's entire

---

709. See examples in Epstein, *Introduction to the Mishnaic Text*, 679 n. 2.

710. Y. Qidd. 4:4, 65d (ר' חמא אתא סבא אמ' ליה) may be an isolated exception, especially if, as Leib Moscovitz argues ("'Ata' R' Peloni," in Sussmann and Rosenthal, *Talmudic Studies* III, 2:505–18, at 516–17), אתא ("he arrived") is not a physical arrival but a formula for introducing support for an Amoraic dictum (see n. 438).

711. E.g., b. Ber. 43a: "By and by, a certain Elder came and posed [a contradiction between] a *mishnah* and a *baraita* and taught it [as follows] ..."; b. Shabb. 45b: "A certain Elder of Qairouan asked R. Yohanan: May a hen's nest be carried on Shabbat?"; b. Shabb. 141b: "A certain Elder said [to R. Abbahu]: Delete your [tradition] due to what R. Ḥiyya taught ..."; b. Pesah. 50a (= b. Qidd. 71a): "Rava intended to expound it in a public lecture. A certain Elder said to him ..."; b. Mak. 11a: "A certain Elder said to him: I heard at the public lecture of Rava ..."; b. Hag. 25b: "A certain Elder said to Rabbah bar Rav Huna: Do not dispute Ulla's [tradition]. For, like him, we have taught ..." (same formulation, different tradition, at b. B. Qam. 114a); b. B. Metz. 110a: "A certain Elder said to him: So said R. Yohanan ..."; b. Hul. 28b: "R. Yirmiyah asked ... a certain Elder replied: So said R. Yohanan ..."; b. Nid. 27b: "R. Ammi said: R. Yohanan said ... a certain Elder replied to R. Ammi: I will explain to you R. Yohanan's reasoning ...." See also b. Zev. 12b.

712. Y. Maʿas. Sh. 3:6, 54b.

713. See Hezser, "(In)significance of Jerusalem," 29–30.

perimeter). If he means Jerusalem before the Temple was destroyed, this is extraordinary, as Rabbah reports being told of his vision over a century and a half later.[714] But it is not extraordinary enough to make Rabbah a bald-faced liar.[715] Our Elder's claim is no more or less ordinary than the one by R. Yohanan that he supports. What Zechariah foresaw in eschatological Jerusalem (according to one rabbi), this Elder already saw in the Jerusalem of old (according to another). Per the mythic pattern, *Endzeit wird Urzeit*: its end corresponds to its origin. Neither rabbi claims to have seen pre-Destruction Jerusalem himself (and Rabbi Yohanan had little desire to see Jerusalem in his day).[716] They claim to know a mysterious figure who did. The Elder is to Rabbah as the prophet is to R. Yohanan and the angels are to the heretic/disciple: a herald of the unseen.

Thus, without radically straining their reader's credulity, the editors deftly insert the Elder seemingly only to support a tradition about Heavenly Jerusalem. Yet in the same breath, by analogizing their mysterious eyewitness to R. Yohanan who just vaporized his disciple for what he had to see himself to believe, the editors also resurrect the composition's basic theme. It is unsettled. Given the violent conflict of vision *against* exegesis as a source of evidence—marked by the disciple's catchphrase, "Had my eyes *not* seen I would *not* have believed"—how can this Elder's catchphrase ("I myself *have seen*") cite a vision *for* exegesis? Why is a much later Babylonian named Rabbah unusually, indeed uniquely,[717] intimate with the Elder? What might their association teach the reader?

Indeed, this is the third unusual feature of our Elder's cameo. Everything else in it—a catchphrase, a source, and his tradition's content—is directly associated with our Rabbah in Part 1. These repetitions—again signaled by a catchphrase, "I myself have seen"—open portals for a reader from Part 2 to Part 1. They focus a reader's attention on correlations or polarities between the composition's two parts in terms of its theme of vision versus rabbinic exegesis. Just as the first keyword in Part 2 ("jeer/proclaim") was linked to a catchphrase on this theme, which led back to Part 1 ("If I *hadn't* seen, I *wouldn't* have believed"), editors again set this reading process in motion with the same devices, turning their reader's gaze back to Part 1. Like a new actor cast in an old role (with the star of

---

714. Hanokh Albeck, *Introduction to the Talmud*, 305; Bacher, *Die agada*, 87–93.

715. Because, in his local context, the Elder otherwise seems to be an ordinary Amoraic source, cited by Rabbah to support R. Yohanan's reading of Zech 14:10, a reader who is not attuned to chronology can take him as such without challenging his claim to first-person autopsy. This is not to say that the gap in time could not have raised an eyebrow.

716. See n. 657.

717. Stemberger, "Münchhausen und die Apokalyptik," 68. On the ambiguity of the name's spelling here ("Rava" in mss. M, E, B; "Rabbah" in mss. H, P, O, V; and a combination, ראבה, in the Geniza fragment ms. C), see n. 74.

Part 1, Rabbah, as scene partner), the Elder's cameo entices the reader to compare the two performances across the composition.[718]

After all, this Elder's catchphrase ("I myself have seen") is Rabbah's signature, attributed to him in over half its roughly nineteen instances in the Talmud,[719] including three in Part 1. By the same token, a catchphrase thematizing vision ("Come, I will show you ...") was attributed to Rabbah's Arab guide (in fact, ms. H has "Arab" *for* "Elder" in Part 2; for this scribe, who participates in the reading process that I am arguing was structured by the Talmud's editors, this Elder is certainly read in light of Part 1!).[720] In other talmudic sources,[721] Rabbah also says "I myself have seen" about a three-*parasang*-sized location in Scripture, just as our Elder says, "I myself have seen" the three-*parasang*-wide ancient Jerusalem. Another Elder's tradition has a variant attribution to Rabbah;[722] here, Rabbah cites the Elder.

In sum, whether a reader focuses only on links between Parts 1 and 2 or also incorporates allusions to other sources in the talmudic canon, the Elder bears an unusual bond to Rabbah. Their bond is highlighted by a shared catchphrase in Parts 1 and 2 that thematizes the relationship of vision to exegesis. Thus, the editors' keyword and catchphrase guide a reader of their composition to review what Rabbah claimed to have "seen" in Part 1, and to reconsider the theme of vision versus oral Torah, as Part 2 swells to its conclusion.[723]

---

718. Bacher (*Die agada*, 100–101 n. 12), goes so far as to say, "Perhaps this Elder [in Appendix 2.C] is none other than Rabbah b. bar Hanah." (He views the Rabbah who cites the Elder as, arbitrarily, Rabbah bar Nahmani). Here, a modern scholar performs the interpretive assimilation of the two parts that, I argue, any reader is strongly goaded to do by the editors' combination of the keyword "Elder" with a catchphrase belonging to our Rabbah.

719. See n. 83. Exceptions include b. Shabb. 22a; b. Ketub. 111b; b. Sotah 58a; b. Git. 57a; b. B. Qam. 21a; b. B. Metz. 85b; b. B. Sanh. 67b. Some of these (e.g., b. Git. 57a) are attributed to Rabbah b. bar Hanah in some manuscripts (Ma'agarim) although this may be due to harmonization.

720. Rabbis also use the catchphrase "I myself have seen" to report visions *of* an Arab (b. Shabb. 82a; b. Yevam. 120b).

721. B. Yom. 75b = b. Erub. 55b (in the manuscripts, unlike the prints, the parallel is more or less exact). See also b. Yoma 39b = b. Yoma 20a; b. Ketub. 111b = b. Meg. 6a (on the attribution, see Bacher, *Die agada* 88 n. 9).

722. B. Pesah. 53b: "Rav Yehuda said: 'Shmuel said: We only say a blessing on the light at the end of the Sabbath, for that [i.e. evening] is when its creation began.' A certain Elder said to him (or, if you like, it was Rabbah b. bar Hanah): 'Just so! And R. Yohanan said the same.'" (Three latter attributions are consistent in all manuscripts.) This "Elder" tradition, like other traditions where he appears in close proximity to Rabbah b. bar Hanah, supports exegesis by R. Yohanan, who himself is called "an elder man" (*gavra' saba'*, b. B. Qam. 117a).

723. Mira Balberg and Haim Weiss show that, in the Talmud, the elder/old man "catalyzes" the plot and exposes the limits of the social order ("'That Old Man Shames Us': Aging, Liminality, and Antinomy in Rabbinic Literature," *JSQ* 25.1 [2018]: 17–41). It is a "narrative function," not simply a character. This accounts for the elder's malleability: he can appear in

These editorial goads do not direct the reader to one linear argument about the theme. Nor, however, were they fixed at random. Rather, they provoke the reader to hypothesize a teleology—an ordered progression—between verbally correlated moments in the composition. For instance, a reader might look back from Part 2's vision of Jerusalem to what Rabbah "saw":

IV. Rabbah bar bar Hanah said:
    I myself have seen:
        A day-old gazelle who was as big as Mount Tabor
            (And how big is Mount Tabor? —Forty *parasang*).
        The length of his neck: three *parasang*;
        The cradle of his head: a *parasang* and a half;
            and he let loose [ורמא] a turd and stopped up the Jordan.

Further aural correlations (the catchphrase "I myself have seen"; the number in both visions, "three *parasang*" and verbs "to cast; let loose/to raise" [ר.ו.ם/ר.מ.י]) invite the reader to draw an unexpected arc between this defecating gazelle in Part 1 and Part 2's Heavenly Jerusalem. What relation could this beast, its excrement blocking the sacred river in the Land of Israel, bear to the Heavenly Jerusalem that will be "lifted" (ר.ו.ם) three *parasang* in the air? Is one to read this grotesque image in Part 1 by filtering it through the eschatological prism of Part 2? By contrasting it to a sacred stream, running through the eschatological Temple?[724] By comparing it to the river of sacred effluent that fertilized the land and sustained the first Temple?[725] In our version of Part 2, there are no direct links to either of those traditions—today, both are dead ends. Yet even looking at these dead ends illustrates the process whereby readers could have integrated the composition by inner-talmudic interpretation of keywords/catch-

---

one parallel telling (Pesiq. Rab Kah. 18:5, Appendix §*Parallels to Part 2*, 3.B), precede another (b. Sanh. 100a), and follow a third (b. B. Bat. 75b, Part 2.C). He can be "doubled" with other characters (Rabbah, in b. B. Bat. 75a–b; Elijah, in Pesiq. Rab Kah. 11:22 and 18:5 and b. Shabb. 33b: see n. 707). See also Balberg and Weiss, *When Near Becomes Far*, 118, 174. This "doubling" of characters is a stock editorial device in talmudic *aggadah* (Rubenstein, *Talmudic Stories*, 258; Levinson, *Twice Told Tale*, 259; Friedman, "Dama ben Netinah," 445–46). Some of the Elder's narrative effects noted by Balberg and Weiss within a story may also have been created by inner-talmudic interpretation of multiple stories. Because his role is so marked, it was easy to read together "Elder" scenes as intertexts. For Elijah's similar role ("one of [few ...] biblical characters that break through the rabbis' narrative and chronological boundaries—both in the Palestinian and in the Babylonian tradition"), see Holger Zellentin, "Typology and the Transfiguration of Rabbi Aqiva (*Pesiqta de Rav Kahana* 4:7 and BT Menahot 29b)," *JSQ* 25.3 (2018): 239–68, 262.

724. Ezekiel 47.
725. M. Yoma 5:6; also m. Mid. 3:2.

phrases. For instance, a reader attuned to these links between Part 2 and Part 1 (IV) could have been inspired to reincorporate a talmudic parallel to Part 2 (where the sacred stream *is* cited),[726] into a still more comprehensive reading of our composition, performing a more synoptic Talmudization.

A stronger—that is, still intact—series of correlations between Parts 1 and 2 repeats both the keyword "three [hundred] *parasang*" and the verb "lift, raise" (ר.ו.מ). Further, in both verbally correlated texts, the theme of vision and exegesis is also central. This correlation of keyword, catchphrase, and theme more emphatically invites a reader to interpret the end of the series of midrashim by R. Yohanan in Part 2 as the restatement, elevation, and resolution—the crescendo, as it were—of the beginning of Part 1. By retracing those correlations, a reader may create a peroration-like conclusion to the composition as a whole, which plays on its theme of vision versus exegesis; one that calls on its audience like the conclusion of a homiletic midrash not so different from the form of Pesiq. Rab Kah. If editors did not necessarily intend this meaning, and their reader did not necessarily create it, the composition makes it possible and transmits that possibility down to us.

(Appendix §*Translation Part 2.C*)

And Rabbah said in the name of R. Yohanan: In time to come, the Holy One, Blessed be He, will raise up Jerusalem three *parasang*, as it is said: *and it shall raise and it shall settle in its place.*"[727]

What is [meant by] *in its place*? [That *it shall raise*] as [high] as its base [is wide].

And how [do we know] that this [= three *parasang*] is its base?
Rabbah said: A certain Elder told me: I myself have seen the previous Jerusalem, and it is three *parasang* [wide].

---

726. B. Sanh. 100a. In this source, like R. Yohanan in ours, one rabbi gives a messianic interpretation of a verse about the sacred stream. Then, an "Elder" validates him, adding that Rabbi Yohanan had said the same thing. One rabbi then asks another whether, despite validating the first rabbi's exegesis, the Elder's way of doing so "smacks of irreverence" (*'afqaruta*; see b. Eruv. 63a). Our story of the disciple who validates but initially disrespects R. Yohanan is then cited as a case that does, and the Talmud appends the same debate between R. Meir and Rav Yehudah about a detail in R. Yohanan's tradition. Then, the b. Sanh. 100a parallel returns to discussing the first rabbi's messianic interpretation of the first verse about the sacred stream. This structure of this parallel strongly suggests that its editors used the same ingredients of the Pesiq. Rab Kah. and b. B. Bat. parallels (the figure of the "Elder"; the topic of disrespecting-while-validating messianic exegesis based on rabbinic authority). They chose to focus on developing an interpretation of the sacred stream, rather than the Heavenly Jerusalem, but this shared keyword/theme could have led readers who knew all three parallels to read them back together and recollect them.

727. Zech 14:10 (my trans.; see n. 705).

But perhaps you'll say: It hurts to go up?

[It doesn't. That is what] the statement teaches: *Who are these that fly as a cloud, and as the doves to their windows?*[728]

(Appendix §*Translation Part 1.I*):

Rava (mss. V, O: *Rabbah*) said:
> *They that go down to the sea in ships* recounted to me:
>> Between one wave and the next are three hundred *parasang*,
>>> the height of each wave is three hundred *parasang*.
>> Once, a wave lifted us up [דלינן]
>>> and I saw the cradle of a star
>>> and it was as great as the sowing of forty *griv* of mustard;
>> had it lifted us [דלי לן] any higher, we'd have been burnt by its heat.
>> The waves cast their voices in chorus [רמא לי גלא קלא לחבריה]
>>> "So, is there anything in the world that you've left alone and not destroyed?"
>>> "Let us go, you and I, and destroy it."
>> And replied:
>>> "Come see the might of your master!
>>> I cannot pass so much as a grain of sand the width of a thread,"
>>>> as it is said:
>>> *Fear ye not me? saith the LORD. Will ye not tremble at my presence? . . .*[729]

At first, Rabbah reports terrifying visions of nature, barely held at bay by God's will. Vision and exegesis are not aligned but opposed: the words of Scripture are the only thing standing between humanity and this image of a violent, alien cosmos.[730] Yet precisely in this, a reader can find conso-

---

728. Isa 60:8.

729. *. . . which have placed the sand for the bound of the sea by a perpetual decree, that it cannot pass it: and though the waves thereof toss themselves, yet can they not prevail; though they roar, yet can they not pass over it?* (Jer 5:22).

730. Another way in which the Talmud's composition helps the reader to make sense of its traveling antihero caught between a hostile cosmos and a divine power are its structural allusions to the book of Jonah. This biblical intertext is not cited as such ("and it subsides," 1.II, echoes Tg. Jon. to Jonah 1:15 faintly; more loudly, the reading in Rashbam, b. B. Bat. 73a s.v. וניח). But the composition's three-part structure suggests a Jonah model. Parts 1.I and 1.V–VII reflect the tempest and (nearly) being swallowed by a whale; 2.B describes a salvific divine covering (see Jonah 4:5 and the Mosaic of Aquileia, ca. 314 CE, which depicts this covering as a *sukkah*); 2.C concludes with hope for the salvation of a city, mapped out in typologically large numbers (on ancient readings of Nineveh-as-Jerusalem, see Elias Bickerman, *Studies in Jewish and Christian History*, 2 vols. [Leiden: Brill, 2007], 1:66–67). This Jonah model

lation. Just as Scripture halts the waves from crashing over the shoreline, midrash guarantees that Heavenly Jerusalem will be raised three *parasang* and set back down without a scratch.[731] Like the sailors, it is not in danger. As it ascends, so will it "settle in its place"; not violently transforming but returning to its ancient size, projected back onto the heavens. And if a skeptical reader—again recalling Part 1—objects ("Perhaps you will say") that no such change is painless ("… it hurts to go up"), again, Scripture is their consolation (it will be *as a cloud, and as the doves to their windows*).[732] What began as a war between the cosmos and Scripture, in Rabbah's retelling of the Battle with the Sea myth, is yet again won by Scripture: the same cosmic forces that threaten our life are our salvation.[733] In this

---

grows much stronger in the reception of some of the composition's core motifs in chapter X of *Pirqei deRabbi Eliezer*. See Rachel Adelman, "The Poetics of Time and Space in the Midrashic Narrative: The Case of *Pirqei deRabbi Eliezer*" (PhD diss., Hebrew University of Jerusalem, 2008), 352 (underwater pearl), 367 (swallowed sons of Qorah) and, especially, 355–59; see also Adelman, *Return of the Repressed*, 211–64. A similar Jonah model for another composition was used by printers in Prague (1595) who juxtaposed Midrash Jonah with another fantastic rabbinic travelogue. See Ossnat Sharon, "Elephant, Leviathan, and Nineveh the Great City: *Sibbuv Rabbi Petahiah* and *Midrash Yonah*, Printed Side by Side," in *Jerusalem Studies in Jewish Folklore: In honorem Tamar Alexander* [Hebrew], ed. Galit Hasan-Rokem et al. 30 (2016): 37–73. On Jonah-esque stories, see Reuven Kiperwasser and Serge Ruzer, "Sea Voyage Tales in Conversation with the Jonah Story: Intertextuality and the Art of Narrative Bricolage," *Journeys* 20.2 (2019): 39–57; Noegel, "Jonah and Leviathan," 256–57.

 731. For a similar example of the use of a number as a literary device to confer a "measure-for-measure" structure on an extended Talmud composition, see Sperber, "On the Unfortunate Adventures," 95–96.

 732. As Fränkel says (*Darkhe ha-aggadah*, 1:259), tale I encapsulates, in its two-part structure, the same movement of destruction and consolation that I am arguing a reader may have derived from the composition's beginning and ending. "In the first stage [*a wave lifted us up*], mankind still thinks that it might only be by chance that they were not burnt [*by its heat*], whereas in the second part [*Come see the might of your master!*], the conversation reveals the *perpetual decree*," affirming divine order and comforting the reader. As Z. Septimus says ("Trigger Words," 164), the problem is not Fränkel's idea of "closure," but applying it to isolated stories rather than other sources. (For a potent demonstration, see Marienberg-Milikowsky, "'Beyond the Matter,'" 28–58.) Fränkel's "closed" reading of the first story also applies on the scale of our entire composition.

 733. An earlier midrash on the "pillar of fire and cloud" (Mekhilta §*Beshallah* 6, ed. Lauterbach, 158–59) makes the same point using the same verse of Isaiah. "Come and see: the healing of the Holy One, Blessed be He, is not the same as the healing of a mortal. A mortal does not heal by that with which he wounds; he wounds with a scalpel and heals with a plaster. But the Holy One, Blessed be He, is not that way. Rather, that with which he wounds, He also [uses to] heal [… expounds on the example of the destructive storm from which God "answered" Job …] And when He exiled Israel, He exiled them by means of nothing but a cloud, as it is said: *How hath the Lord covered the daughter of Zion with a cloud in his anger* [Lam 2:1] and when He brings about their ingathering, He does so by means of nothing but a cloud, as it is said, *Who are these that fly as a cloud* [Isa 60:8]. And when He scatters them, He scatters them like nothing but doves, as it is said, *But they that escape of them shall escape, and shall be on the mountains like doves of the valleys, all of them mourning, every one for his iniquity* [Ezek 7:16]. And when He brings them back, He brings them back as nothing but doves, as

light, readers might try to resolve the theme of visionary versus exegetical authority. The point is not what Rabbah saw or did not see; the point is where you look in the canon to make sense of it.

Beyond the *Sugya* and Back to the Sources

In this chapter I argued that, as our collection of strange stories (Part 1) was joined to eschatological midrashim (Part 2), they accrued shared meanings as a coherent composition. Rather than the result of a single editorial intention with a clear message behind its changes to all of this inherited material, however—a model that is sometimes more effective when applied to shorter or more focused literary units (*sugyot*) in the Talmud, resulting in "closed" readings—I argued for a structured but also chaotic and gradual reading process of inner-talmudic interpretation. Through a dialogue with the composition's anonymous editors, who guided their attention to specific words and phrases in both parts of the composition, readers were led back to a core cultural issue and literary theme of tension between vision and exegesis,[734] and the Talmud's related but more parochial concern with scholastic hierarchy (even in the eschaton). The Talmud's editors did not structure this theme for their readers in an even-handed manner. They did incline readers to filter the evidence and authority of vision through the lens of rabbinic exegesis—to tame, so to speak, visions in Part 1 with the midrashic hermeneutic of Part 2. However, readers could have read both parts against that grain, and in other ways altogether.

Editors stressed both related themes—scholastic status-hierarchy; vision versus exegesis—not only by subtly retelling one of their narrative sources (a rabbinic Doubting Thomas tale), but also by restructuring the reading process. They called readers' attention to two *keywords* and *catchphrases*, appearing in *both* parts of the composition, and connected with its themes. These devices prompted readers to make sense of strange visions in Part 1 in terms of Scripture—even, in the end, to take refuge from the visions of Part 1 in an exegetical form that recalls familiar homilies of consolation. By reconstructing how editors used their sources (shared with the roughly contemporary Palestinian work of midrash, Pesiq. Rab Kah.), I showed how their keywords/catchphrases led readers to integrate—to Talmudize, thus canonize—the composition.

---

it is said, *and as the doves to their windows* [...]." In light of this source, "waves" and "clouds" in the Talmud's comment on R. Yohanan's midrash are another Amoraic variation on a Tannaitic midrash (compare n. 654).

734. For nuances of this rhetoric in the Talmud's telling of the Doubting Thomas tale, see Turan, " 'Wherever the Sages Set their Eyes,'" 158, nn. 67-68.

How did this reading of the composition's two parts via shared keywords/catchphrases work, concretely? What were its implications for our composition's evolving relationship with the emergent canon of the Talmud? My approach to these questions resists a linear or singular model of meaning in terms of editorial intention, a closed textual unit, or one interpretation that seems the most likely or natural for an "average" implied reader. Inner-talmudic reading is unpredictable, emergent, and dependent on the viewer's angle on its data, much as a multistable figure like Wittgenstein's duck-rabbit can be either a duck or a rabbit and is intrinsically both or neither. To show this—building on terms and methods of Friedman and Z. Septimus, *inter alios*—I argued that, conjoined with other features (the theme of vision versus exegesis, attributions, echoes with other sources still preserved in whole or in part by our Talmud), two keyword/catchphrase pairs generated correlations and polarities between Part 2 and Part 1 for the Talmud's reader. These interpretive pathways accented the composition's cultural themes along lines tilted by the editors. But they did not strictly determine the reading process, or its results. At most, we can venture different guesses about how different readers might have Talmudized the composition by reading its parts together and integrating it with the canon, drawing in elements of related sources, and rediscovering its themes in those sources as well. This synoptic process of Talmudization, which goes beyond the mere inertia of recollecting, is how the dialogue of editors and readers changed our composition's interpretive framework. Rather than a closed *sugya* or a stand-alone story-cycle, visions and exegeses became Talmud.

Our turn to the study of the whole composition, rather than only the collection of tales, has thus illustrated both concepts of canonicity—"inside-out" and "outside-in," more fluid and more rigid, inertia and Talmudization—with which this chapter began. We have seen how the Talmud's editors could make one of their compositions more coherent without fabricating, deleting, or even radically reorganizing its sources. We have also recovered a culturally specific concern for scholastic status hierarchy buried in their edits (unlike Pesiq. Rab Kah.). Finally, we have shown how new readers of our composition *as Talmud* were led to rethink its theme by linking our composition with other canonical sources. Many of these are now "dead ends" but they retain the heuristic value of suggesting past routes of inner-canonical travel. In short, this constellation has helped us to read in three different directions: within, between, and beyond the conceptual borders of a *sugya* or self-contained, rhetorically coherent unit of talmudic text.

Let me restate that our way of focusing on how keywords/catchphrases helped readers to canonize an extended composition is not *sui generis*. Rather, it extends recent advances in literary study of the Talmud without abandoning close analysis of literary sources as well. I fundamentally affirm literary scholars' calls for a more holistic way of reading Talmud, beyond the single legal or nonlegal *sugya* (whether this means studying wider literary contexts; forms of discourse ["genres"] across a tractate,[735] the Talmudic canon,[736] or the Babylonian and Palestinian rabbinic canons).[737] By arguing for the reader's experience, not the edited *sugya*, as the vehicle for mediating talmudic intertexts and making sense of their relationships, I share rising resistance to Fränkel's "closed" readings. Like these literary scholars, I temper the *halakhah/aggadah* dichotomy by showing that Talmud editors reworked sources with the same toolkit: stressing words, or drawing out themes, to make sources speak to one another. On the other hand, I tried to show how literary interpretation benefits from source criticism and should not relapse into a new "closure" even if it turns to larger or different textual units. I argued that by focusing on how sources were used, we can access the dynamic between editor and reader where literary creativity in this canon happens—as opposed to "the Talmud" in the abstract or on the scale of a distant reading. Specifically, by comparing the reception of two exegetical complexes in Babylo-

---

735. Wasserman, *Jews, Gentiles, and Other Animals*; Charlotte Elisheva Fonrobert, *Menstrual Purity: Rabbinic and Christian Reconstructions of Biblical Gender*, Contraversions (Stanford, CA: Stanford University Press, 2000), 15–39.

736. Z. Septimus, "Trigger Words"; and "Poetic Superstructure." Rather than adopt this model (as Zellentin, "Typology," at 263 n. 67, summarizes it: "Given the likely process of ongoing editorial revisions of the Bavli, we should read (almost) all its stories in light of (almost) all its stories"), I develop and change it in two ways. First, I apply Septimus's theory, not to an "implied reader" of the Talmud as a whole, but to this specific composition's reader as implied by its editors. These editors are also a construct, but one with a thicker profile in scholarship that can be tested against local signs of their activity. My goal is to understand, not how "the" Talmud's editors created "the" reader, but how *these* editors created *their* implied reader using verbal devices akin to those that Septimus has deftly named and analyzed in his work. (We are both deeply reliant on Friedman; see n. 47). Second, as for those editorial devices, my revision of Septimus's method is to show that what he calls "simultexts" in the Talmud can emerge not only by reading "triggers" of rare words, but also by pairing what I (like him and others) call "keywords" with "catchphrases" and ideas, related to a larger theme of one simultext. This generates an interpretive key that makes an earlier (adjacent) simultext newly legible in its light, and vice versa. I am more tentative about extending this approach to passages that are not—that is, no longer—edited as part of the same source, although I concede Septimus's argument that, in the Amoraic period, and perhaps even later, sources were not always studied in the order or configuration that was imposed by the editors of our versions. (To illustrate this distinction between our approaches, see nn. 724–726 for speculative links among Part 2, Bible, Mishnah, and b. Sanh. 100a that I call "dead ends." Septimus's method is more open to such intertexts).

737. Levinson, *Twice Told Tale*, 278–93, and, for primarily legal sources, see Alyssa M. Gray, *A Talmud in Exile: The Influence of Yerushalmi Avodah Zarah on the Formation of Bavli Avodah Zarah*, BJS 342 (Providence, RI: Brown Judaic Studies, 2005); Christine Hayes, *Between the Babylonian and Palestinian Talmuds*. For a compelling approach to reading across *aggadah* and *halakhah*, see Yonatan Feintuch, *Face to Face: The Interweaving of Aggada and Halakha in the Babylonian Talmud* [Hebrew] (Jerusalem: Magid, 2018).

nian and Palestinian works during the obscure period between Amoraim and the Talmud's more or less final redaction, I hope I have shown that the Talmud's editors (or, as some now say, "author/redactors"), could *both* retain the integrity and linear flow of their sources according to their canon's conventions *and* repeat keywords, paired with catchphrases, in order to guide the reading process—whether it was retrospective (from Part 2 back to Part 1) or canonical (across other verbally linked sources in the Talmud).

These linear, retrospective, and lateral interpretive pathways in the emerging canon need not produce split meanings or a "hermeneutics of suspicion," aimed at ferreting out suppressed counter-readings. If subordinated to a culturally relevant and widely shared theme (here, the authority of vision vs. exegesis), multiple reading processes could also cooperate: verbal correlations piqued readers' interests, jogged their memories, nudged their arguments. Nor were editors wholly original in how they structured this chaotic and emergent meaning. Rather, my reconstruction of their activity based on their sources hints that keywords and catchphrases once built bridges across traditions of the Talmud that they did not use (and that therefore turned into dead ends), while other pathways were alive and well in the academies, but can be restored only tentatively (e.g., as relics of oral performances, reflected in manuscripts).[738] One can continue to test this profile of the Talmud's editors as creative traditionalists, guiding students through structured rereadings of inherited material. For us, their intentions are somewhat beside the point. At least along the narrow line of inner-talmudic interpretation that we have retraced, it is less the Talmud's editors who subsumed Scripture under their new literary forms than the reverse: in talmudic midrash, Scripture's iridescence spreads to all texts that it contacts. Saturated by a spectrum of possibilities as broad as (written and oral) Torah, any text is at once supercharged and blurred, straining its frame of reference to enfold an excess of potential interpretation. Its reading process issues in new senses and—no less significantly—new incomprehensibilities or blocked pathways whose entrances remain visible. Such is interpretation. Now you see it; now you don't.[739]

---

738. Already Zecharias Frankel called attention to passages (b. Shabb. 147a, 148a; b. Hul. 106b) where the Talmud's redactors presume familiarity with oral explanations that were lost or only retained elsewhere ("Traditionelle Erklärung der Mischna und des Talmuds," *MGWJ* 11 [1862]: 274–75). On this phenomenon, see Rosenthal, "'Al ha-qitsur ve-hashlamato."

739. "'When your eyes light upon it, it is gone'" (Prov 23:5, after trans. and exposition in Visotzky, "Misnomers," 21). See Stein, "Seeing is Believing"; Stein, *Textual Mirrors*, 58-83; Shamma Friedman, "Now You See It, Now You Don't: Can Source-Criticism Perform Magic on Talmudic Passages about Sorcery?," in Nikolsky and Ilan, *Rabbinic Traditions*, 32-83, at 58, where "seeing is *not* believing" in a *halakhic* context.

6

The Allegorical Canon

> Nature: a temple where animate pillars
> Let slip the occasional tremulous word;
> Its path runs through forests of symbols, a wood
> Which gazes at man as if he were familiar.
> – Baudelaire, "Correspondences"

A sea change in how our collection was received had taken hold by *Shevet Yehudah*,[740] a work on the memory of Jewish persecution penned in response to the expulsion from Spain.[741] Here, Rabbah's strange tales earned dubious pride of place in a disputation between King Alfonso of Portgual and an unnamed Jewish interlocutor:

> And I say that, because it is your practice to speak lying and vain words, you are already under the presumption of being liars in all things, and I have heard it said in a disputation that you say, in this "Talmud" of yours, that there was once a frog as big as sixty houses, and that a serpent

---

740. Maharsha has been miscredited for it (Ben-Amos, "Talmudic Tall Tales," 27), but allegorical commentary on our tales began far earlier. The first extended example that I know is *Mehoqeq Tsafun* [as the author notes, a wordplay on *tsafun*, "hidden"/*safun*, Deut 33:21]. Part of this commentary, copied already in 1360, is interpolated in ms. Munich 94 of Gersonides, *Milhamot ha-shem*, 209a–212b. It has been assigned to the Provençal scholar Moshe ben Ya'aqov ben Yosef ha-Kohen and correctly identified with the full work by this title in ms. Günzburg 367 (at folio 67b): see Charles Touati, *La pensée philosophique et théologique de Gersonide* (Paris: Gallimard, 1992), 62–63. Both manuscripts are now available at the Bavarian State and National Israel library websites, respectively. Touati calls it a "very flat commentary," but study of the first three (of thirty-one) folia shows that this is not a fair account. For instance, it interprets "that wave that sinks the ship" (II.20) as the Evil Impulse and the "sea" as Torah, like later allegorists. I thank Noam Sienna for transcribing these folia and hope to undertake a full study of this commentary in the future. My epigraph is from Charles Baudelaire, "Correspondences," in *Œuvres complètes* (1857; repr., Paris: Laffont, 1980), 8–9 (my trans.; see my website for a complete retranslation of the poem).

741. On our tales in anti-Jewish polemic, see Jeremy Cohen, *A Historian in Exile: Solomon ibn Verga, Shevet Yehudah, and the Jewish-Christian Encounter*, Jewish Culture and Contexts (Philadelphia: University of Pennsylvania Press, 2017), 70–72.

swallowed it, and a female raven came,[742] and swallowed the serpent, and rose to the top of a tree [V]. But all these words are a well-known lie, as has been verified.

And furthermore, you say that in the sea, Ocean [sic], a piece of iron fell and rolled around for seven years but did not touch the bottom [IXa]. Who looked into the depths of the sea [to see] whether it went down or not? And furthermore, you say that a wise man saw in the sea,[743] that the waves were roaring, and that between one wave and the next were three hundred *parasang* [I]. But this is a lie, for that entire sea is not three hundred *parasang*![744]

As we saw in the previous chapter, layers of commentary and transmission in the study-house had read our strange tales skeptically yet made sense of them via midrash, or even sustained a (partly ironic) hope that they could be scavenged for legal and other norms. By now, however, they had become a scapegoat for the canon as a whole. In attacking their truth, the Christian king impugns the truth of the Talmud as such. Some of these tales, he argues, are "well-known" lies—and had been a target of anti-Jewish polemic at least since the Talmud was tried at Paris in 1240.[745] Others must be lies: their claims are unverifiable or flout common sense. Any canon so credulous as to admit these stories deserves no credibility at all.

In his reply, however, the Jew defends our strange tales so as to suggest a new idea of how to read them and thus a new idea of their distinctive role in the talmudic canon. He does so by drawing a provocative analogy to the role of music in Greco-Roman culture:

> Some sagacious minds have written that it was the practice of their ancestors, when they desired to draw the people near so that they might hear

---

742. An early gloss of the bird in this tale ("female raven," Rabbenu Gershom ed. Vilna *ad loc*.; Arukh s.v. פשנא; Rashbam, b. B. Bat. 73b s.v. פשקנצא) became its meaning for European readers, who made much of its symbolism but forgot its Persian origins. (Gershenson, "Understanding Puškansa," 33–36, shows why.) The gloss stuck so firmly that a lexicographer traced it back *into* Persian (Kohut, *Arukh Completum*, 6:459–60).

743. This attributes the tale to Rabbah rather than the sailors, due to his signature formula, "I myself have seen."

744. Solomon ibn Verga, *Liber Schevet Yehudah* [Hebrew], ed. M. Wiener (Hannover: Lafaire, 1924), 62–63. On the size of a *parasang*, see n. 8.

745. At the trial, the heavenly voice which speaks to Rabbah (XIIIa) was brought forward in support of the charge that "God curses Himself because He vowed and asked to be released from His vow" (Judah M. Rosenthal, "The Talmud on Trial: The Disputation at Paris in the Year 1240," *JQR* 47.2 [1956]: 145–69, at 156. See "The Christian Evidence," trans. Jean Connell Hoff, in *The Trial of the Talmud: Paris, 1240* [Toronto: Pontifical Institute of Medieval Studies, 2012], 102–21, at 112–13). Tosafot b. B. Bat. 74a s.v. ועכשיו raises and parries a similar objection to the story.

their words, to take a lyre and play. And once the people drew near to the delight of the melody, then they would proclaim what they held, as to setting aright the affairs of state, and as to the rectitude of the soul.

And so, our ancestors, when they knew not how to play, grasped a different way to put forward their words: by way of parable and figure of speech. And one who knows came to know their true contents.

And we have learned both of these things from the language of the poet, who said,

"I will incline mine ear to a parable; I will open my dark saying upon the harp." (Ps 49:4 [49:5])

And the parable of the frog is an allegory [*remez*] for natural reason, which sings of the works of God as does the frog. And it said that it was *as big as sixty houses*, which is an allegory for the sixty divisions or parts that are contained within it....[746]

Like strings of a poet's lyre, the Jew argues, which drew together your ancestors to debate religion and civic affairs, our lore (*aggadah*) was the instrument of our own ancestors.[747] The parallel in the psalm is a parallel between cultures: as you bend your ear to the harp, so are we drawn by the parables and riddles of our sages.[748] This parallel further justifies not only the inclusion of our strange tales in the canon but also their local legal context in the Talmud.[749] Rather than pause *halakhah* and distract the scholars ("sustaining them with raisin-cakes," as the saying goes),[750] *aggadah*, like the lyre, enlivens and refocuses their attention on the task of holding forth

---

746. *Shevet Yehudah* ed. Wiener, 63.
747. Alluding to b. Yoma 75a: "[*Manna* is called] *gad* [linseed] because it is like *haggadah*, which draws [n.g.d] a person's heart to it like water" (recall the desert context of the *manna*). See Menahem Hirshman, "Aggadic Midrash," in *The Literature of the Sages*, ed. Shmuel Safrai et al., 2 vols., CRINT 2.3 (Assen: Van Gorcum; Minneapolis: Fortress, 2006), 1:107–32, at 113.
748. Conversely, see b. Ketub. 5b: if one's ears are drawn to "an improper matter" (דבר שאינו הגון), one has thumbs and earlobes so that one can plug the ears and not let it penetrate. For a Jewish apologist, the polemic of the "king" is weak because the Talmud anticipated his argument against listening to *aggadah* in multiple ways.
749. For a contemporary allegorical explanation, i.e., that their legal context concealed and protected the tales' mysteries in the vulnerable period of exile, but they can now be safely revealed, see the introduction to a handy anthology of commentaries on our tales: *Sefer 'Aggadata' de-ve Rav: ma'amre R.b.B.H. Bava batra 73–74: 'im be'ure gedole ha-dorot* (Ashdod: Makhon Limmud Aggadah, 2008–2009), 14–15. Compare the editor's preface in Yaakov ibn Chaviv, *Ein Yaakov*, trans. Avraham Yaakov Finkel (Jerusalem: Aronson, 1999), 569.
750. Rachel A. Anisfeld, *Sustain Me with Raisin-Cakes: Pesikta deRav Kahana and the Popularization of Rabbinic Judaism*, JSJSup 133 (Leiden: Brill, 2009), 38–39. Hence this verse is the title of Elyaqum Getz's commentary on our tales; see below. (The author also chose it because the sum of the letters in "sustain me," רפדוני, equals his name, אליקום געץ.)

on national affairs. Hence the frog's immensity ("sixty houses") is an allegory for the Mishnah's sixty tractates; the very opposite of "lying and vain words."⁷⁵¹ It draws the ear of "natural reason" to higher things. If one can hear its music, its very croaking is a Psalm. For the Jew, these arguments are ready to hand, as the Talmud already uses a giant frog to represent the study of *aggadah* as such.⁷⁵² His allegory takes the next step of using it to represent the whole canon, turning *aggadah* from an embarrassing footnote into an apologia. Further, the Jew argues, just as it is absurd to hold music and poetry to the same standard of reason as classical rhetoric, nor should one hold *aggadah* to those standards. If one attunes to them, our strange tales will yield a meaning that will fully explain and justify their place in the canon. One must only learn how to listen.

That new way of listening, or reading, can be called allegory.⁷⁵³ Following Marc Saperstein's use of this term in his classic study of how one allegorist in this tradition "decoded" the *aggadah* as a set of symbols, in this chapter, I ask how allegories of our tales developed in medieval and early modern Ashkenaz.⁷⁵⁴ I pose the same questions that I posed earlier readers. How does this new interpretive framework mediate our tales' archive of potential meanings with meanings that readers create? To what extent is allegory continuous with past interpretive frameworks? In what ways, if any, is it fundamentally different? Our answers to these questions will lead us to center the outer ring of our constellation—the canon—in

---

751. The Talmud itself is often called *ShaS*, an acronym for *Shishah Sidre Mishnah* ("sixty orders of Mishnah"). On six/sixty as an ordering principle for the canon, see Menahem Kahana, "The Arrangement of the Orders of the Mishnah" [Hebrew], *Tarbiz* 76.1–2 (2006): 29–40, at 34 nn. 28–30.

752. As opposed to the study of recondite purity laws (b. Sanh. 67b). See Moulie Vidas and Mira Balberg, "Impure Scholasticism: The Study of Purity Laws and Rabbinic Self-criticism in the Babylonian Talmud," *Prooftexts* 32.3 (2012): 312–56, at 321–22. This identification of the frog—who is swallowed in V—and "wisdom" may also be based on this tale's intertext, Ps 107:27 ("all their wisdom was swallowed up"), or based on an old etymology of "frog" (Hebr. צפרדע) as "a bird with wisdom" (צפור שיש בו דיעה, Yal. 182 ed. Shiloni et al., III:88). See Maharsha *ad loc.*: "*A frog* is an allusion [*remez*] to the Greek kingdom … and Greek wisdom"; and Gra, *Be'ure 'Aggadot: Kamah 'Aggadot*, ed. Yosef Eliyahu Movshovitz (Jerusalem: Mossad ha-Rav Kook, 2020), 18.

753. On medieval Jewish terminology for allegory, see Elbaum, *Medieval Perspectives*, 36 n. 38, 78–79 n. 5; Isaak Heinemann, "Die wissenschaftliche Allegoristik des jüdischen Mittelalters," *HUCA* 23.1 (1951), 611–43, at 615–17; Marc Saperstein, *Decoding the Rabbis: A Thirteenth-Century Commentary on the Aggadah*, Harvard Judaic Monographs 3 (Cambridge, MA: Harvard University Press, 1980), 14–15. On Greek/Latin terms, see Jon Whitman, *Allegory: The Dynamics of an Ancient and Medieval Technique* (Cambridge, MA: Harvard University Press, 1987), 263–68.

754. Saperstein defines allegory as "the representation of an abstract concept by a concrete image somehow related to it" (*Decoding the Rabbis*, 15). On our collection, see 53 and 232 n. 33: "The interpretations of the stories of Rabba bar bar Hana can be taken as a fine case study of varying approaches to the aggadah."

the creation of meaning. How do readers use allegory to collect and recollect our tales with the rest of the Talmud and a wider body of intertexts? What do their uses of allegory show about their ideas of what truly defines a canon?

In a curated sample of commentaries,[755] I retrace a line of thought that is increasingly canon-centered, a meaningful whole that becomes more and more than the sum of its parts. As we have seen, this impulse to solve the tales' strangeness by widening their interpretive frame began in the Talmud itself. Not only the teller Rabbah but his teacher Rabbi Yohanan were criticized and mocked, the sheer scale of their visions leading some readers to "jeer at the words of the sages." In the bigger picture of the composition and its eschatological themes, however, their big claims made sense.[756] Now that Christians were using the tales to attack the canon from the outside, it became all the more vital to make them fit back in. If the Talmud could not accommodate its strange tales, how was one to prove that *aggadah* was not the weakest link in its chain of tradition? On the positive side, this was an opportunity for interpretive creativity: allegorical commentators agreed that if you can make sense here, you can make it anywhere.

Thus, the high-medieval turn to allegory responded, in part, to the limits of piecemeal apologetics. Yet in larger part, its canon-centricity deepened the tales' established interpretive tradition within the Talmud. It added symbolic coherence, without subtracting either the close attention to context or the intertextually derived moral lessons that had long

---

755. Rav Tuvia Lifschitz cites sixty nine books and nine articles in his helpful collection of medieval and modern interpretations of the tales: https://www.daat.ac.il/daat/toshba/rababach/bib.htm (accessed 24 April 2024). In English, see Yitzchok Adlerstein, *Maharal of Prague: Be'er Hagolah. The Classic Defense of Rabbinic Judaism through the Profundity of the Aggadah* (Brooklyn, NY: Artscroll, 2000), 69–80; Naor, *Rabbi Abraham Isaac Hakohen Kook: Commentary*; Rabbi Nahman of Bratslav, *Liqqute Moharan*, trans. Moshe Mykoff and Symcha Bergman, 8 vols. (Jerusalem: Breslov Research Institute, 1990–2012), Part I:1:5–18:8 (vol. 1:41–vol. 3:117); Aharon Feldman, *The Juggler and the King: The Jew and the Conquest of Evil; An Elaboration of the Vilna Gaon's Insights into the Hidden Wisdom of the Sages* (Spring Valley, NY: Feldheim, 1991). Once I had studied and translated Rashbam and all or most of only five allegorical commentators on the tales (Ritva [thirteenth century, Spain] and the Ashkenazi scholars Maharal, Maharsha, Elyaqum Getz, and the Gra), I narrowed my focus to a hermeneutic dialectic that I hope will be relevant for a proper study of this tradition.

756. For instance, a Zoharic commentary refutes the bad disciple in order to develop its own hermeneutic of an esoteric canon. Recall that the disciple mocks Rabbi Yohanan's speech about a giant pearl because "we don't find them as big as a turtle-dove's egg" (see n. 675). This must be why the mystical commentary cites the *giant* egg of the bird *bar yokhni*, which crushed sixty houses (b. Bekh. 57b; compare VI), as its example of a misapprehended allegory—adding that, if mystical masters "speak a *pearl* to their students, but they are insensate of its allegory [ולא אשתמודעון ברמיזא], the matter is repeated to them as a jest." Ra'aya Mehemna, *Pinhas* 216a, in Isaiah Horowitz, *Shenei Luhot Ha-berit*, 2 vols. (Jerusalem: n.p., 1962–1963), 2:17b.

been used, not only to read our tales in light of Scripture (chapter 2), but also to integrate them with each other (chapter 3) and with the rest of the Talmud (chapter 5).[757] Many of these techniques (keywords, repetitions, attention to stylistic flourishes) and interpretive themes (evidence, vision, the cosmic order's limits and transgression), as we will see, remained generative among the allegorists. Keywords in the two-part canonical composition became symbols linking intertexts across the canon. Understories resurfaced in allegories which retold the tales in light of their mythic past.

The distinctive, if not radically new, innovation of this framework is that an allegorist uses select correspondences between the tales and the symbols that they contain to create a meaning that spans our entire interpretive constellation: the tale; the collection of tales; the Talmud as a whole; the exegesis of Scripture; and other traditional Jewish texts. By wielding the symbol as a code that mediates these intertexts, he achieves two things.[758] On one hand, he makes sense of each and every strange detail in our tales and their telling. On the other, he makes their allegorical meaning cohere with other meanings of other canonical texts. He recollects not only intertexts, but their past interpretations as well, evoking a sense of seamlessness across the canon. Our allegorists differ, however, in terms of how seamless their results truly are: in whether they succeed (or even evidently try very hard) to balance the old with the new, their symbolic meaning with its basis in a recollection of intertexts and interpretations. One allegorist mirrors techniques of classical midrash, both exegetically and didactically. Another enjoys the freedom to create independent meanings from the symbols that inspired his allegory. And a singular mind joins both contradictory tendencies while erasing the contradiction.

To show this, I trace the allegorical canon's development in four stages. First, a strong reading of the non-allegorical framework against which this new method emerged: contextual interpretation (*peshat*), as practiced by Rashbam. Second, Maharsha's critique of the limits of *peshat* and, in response, his development of allegory as midrash. Third, the emancipation of allegory in its own right in another, slightly later Polish authority, Elyaqum Getz. Finally, I explore how the Gra reflects and transcends this dialectic between *peshat*, midrash, and allegory by recollecting our tales in a canon so well harmonized with techniques of midrash that allegory feels like *peshat*. In his hands, our tales' strangeness finally yields to familiarity, as if the Jewish canon had been waiting all along to receive Rabbah & friends back into its embrace.

---

757. On the relation between midrash and allegory among Tannaim and Amoraim, see n. 24; Ishay Rosen-Zvi, "Midrash and/as Allegory: The Case of 'Ella,' " *Oqimta* 10 (2024): 187–209, at 205–8 nn. 40–48.

758. All allegorists in this chapter are male. I weigh this fact's implications in §*Allegory Emancipated* below.

Twice upon a Time: The Art of *Peshat*

Given the fantastic content of our tales and their perhaps willfully exaggerated telling, a method that accounts for them rationally in their own terms and context (*peshat*) risks tumbling headlong into the Inquisitor's trap. Who but a liar would say that a giant frog is real, or that its size ("sixty houses") is accurate? And yet, were conventionally accepted meanings of all of these rhetorical figures established in the Talmuds and Midrashim? Were the tales' terms, style, or syntax a natural fit for *peshat*? No, and Rashi, the foremost *peshat* exegete, supposedly died before he reached this part of the tractate, leaving the task of explaining the tales as he would have to his grandson Rashbam.[759] Rashbam rises to the occasion. Rather than defend the tales as literally true, he reads them in two ways that were both broadly influential among allegorists: first, as praising God's greatness; second, as a morality tale for the Jewish people.

Rashbam begins by recollecting Parts 1 and 2 of our composition; a strategy that was already crucial to their interpretation by editors and readers within the Talmud (see chapter 5).

> All of these matters may be accounted for in terms of "How great are thy works, O Lord!" (Ps 104:24),[760] which includes making known what will be given as a reward for the righteous in the world to come, or interpreting verses that are pronounced in the book of Job, which speak of giant birds, beasts, and fish, for *every discussion of the disciples of the sages requires study* (b. Sukkah 21b = b. Avod. Zar. 19b).[761]

In the Talmud itself, this saying refers to the sages' mundane speech. It teaches that even if they were not teaching Torah, their apparently trivial words contain pearls of wisdom. By reapplying the saying to our tales, Rashbam invokes the canon in order to avoid the charge that Rabbah & friends are not credible or exaggerating. Leave aside your suspicions of the tellers, he warns—they were all "disciples of the sages." We know (and he knows) that, before canonization, they were suspect. But they are in the Talmud now, so we must take them seriously. He presses his point:

---

759. Avraham Grossman holds that Rashi did finish his Baba Batra commentary but it was lost (*Rashi* [Oxford: Littman Library, 2012], 135–36). In any case, it breaks off at folio 29a, long before our composition. Ms. O contains an unstudied, unidentified commentary on the parts of the tractate where both Rashi and Rashbam are missing; see my supplement to this book cited at n. 1. On Rashbam's *peshat*, see Sara Japhet, *Commentary of Rabbi Samuel ben Meir (Rashbam) on the Song of Songs* [Hebrew] (Jerusalem: ha-'iggud ha-'olami le-mada'ei ha-yahadut, 2008), 82–104; Jonathan Jacobs, "Rashbam's Major Principles of Interpretation as Deduced from a Manuscript Fragment Discovered in 1984," *REJ* 170.3–4 (2011): 443–63.

760. My trans.; see below.

761. Rashbam, b. B. Bat. 73a s.v. אמר רבא אשתעו.

the canon not only tells us to study them, it also tells us how. By weaving together sea yarns with psalms that praise God's triumph over the sea, and especially by setting the beasts in Part 1 beside the mysteries of Behemoth and Leviathan and other eschatological visions in Part 2, the Talmud's editors left us a context for coherent *peshat* reading. All of these strange beasts were intended to praise God's works and depict the rewards awaiting the righteous—for example, watching Leviathan fight like a gladiator and feasting on its flesh, or resting beneath the radiant canopy of its skin. If all that is strange, it is no stranger than those ancient myths preserved in Scripture, expanded in midrash, and performed in *piyyut*. Indeed, Rashbam suggests, the strangeness of the telling suits the tales' main function: to exalt their creator by visualizing things that cannot be seen, things beyond this world. Those are not matters that narrow literal language can portray. Their content fits the local context: if we treat the composition as a whole, he suggests, perhaps Part 1 *should* be strange.

Rashbam supports this argument when he focuses on the telling in its own right and shows how its strangeness was calculated to bring about a sense of awe in the reader. Rather than try to systematically or logically account for every detail in light of every other detail, let alone in light of the canon as a whole, he discerns patterns in the telling's poetic effect. In this mode, he operates as a skilled close reader, treating the text's literary language as an internal key to its meaning.[762] To explain why the tales were told just as they were, and in no other way, he refutes implicit questions by a non-*peshat* reader. Let us consider an imaginary sample of his dialogue with such a reader. In bold quotes, I set the lemma with which Rashbam's comment begins; in plain type, imaginary questions by a non-*peshat* reader; in bold, his actual response, with my imaginary expansion/dilation in plain type. Each dialogue is numbered by the tale on which it comments.

I. Why does it say **"between one wave and the next are three hundred parasang"**? Is this number a literal measurement, a figure of speech for emphasis, or a coded symbol?[763]

---

762. It is no coincidence that Jonah Fränkel was not only a pioneer of the close reading of rabbinic texts but also a scholar of Rashi's methodology. See Jonah Fränkel, *Darko shel Rashi be-ferusho la-Talmud ha-bavli*, 2nd ed. (Jerusalem: Magnes, 1980), 95–162.

763. Rashbam (b. B. Bat. 73a s.v. דלינן גלא) weakens a literal interpretation by acknowledging the vast discrepancy between the height of the wave (300 *parasang* = 30 days' walk, b. Pesah. 94a) and the distance to the firmament (500 years' walk, b. Pesah. 94b). Rashi (b. Hul. 90b s.v. גוזמא, s.v. שלש מאות כהנים), following Rava *ad loc.*, interprets the number 300 as figurative. On the figurative interpretation of numbers in *aggadah* generally, see Elbaum, *Medieval Perspectives*, 82 n. 12, 99–100.

—None of the above, but **because it says in the context,** *a wave cast its voice to its fellow*,[764] **this is necessary to make us understand** [לאשמועינן, "make us hear"] **that they heard their fellows' voices from** *three hundred parasang* **away.**

V. Why does it say that the giant bird landed **"in a tree"**? Surely this is no ordinary tree …

– Obviously not, but only in the sense that the Talmud tells us to focus on, not because it is a coded symbol. We may assume this giant female raven landed **on a branch, in the manner of birds,**[765] not the trunk. Now, if just a *branch* could hold a bird that swallowed a serpent that swallowed a frog as big as sixty houses, imagine how strong the tree was! That is precisely what "in a tree" teaches us.

VIa. Why does it say **"sixty towns were destroyed by it"**? As I asked about the first story: is this number literal, figurative, symbolic? …

–As I told you, none of the above. **The sea hurled it upon** *sixty towns* **and it** *destroyed* **them because that is just how big it was. And** *sixty towns ate from it* **while it was still moist.**
Whereas the *sixty towns salted it* **are others that were far from there, so they salted some of it and transported it to their areas.**

In all three cases, Rashbam's *peshat* intensifies the effect of the telling by retelling the story's basic lesson and linking its literary language directly to the reader's experience of awe, helping the reader to make contact with the content. He does not change the lesson but sharpens it. Now it is directly linked to how the tale is told. His comments do this by activating sensory elements of the tales—hearing, seeing, touch—and expanding them in space and time.

In the first story, he explains the distance between the waves as an amplifier of their roaring voices, a means to help his reader understand (literally, "hear") how loud they are.[766] It is not just that they must "cast their voices" to hear one another but that the reader, too, needs a large number to "hear" their dialogue at the right volume. The space of the story is no blank canvas where events unfold—it is intrinsically meaning-

---

764. A more literal translation of ורמא ליה גלא קלא לחבריה than in my Appendix §*Translation* I.9. No textual variants in the early prints of Rashbam (Pesaro 1510, Venice 1521) affect my analysis.

765. On "normal behavior" (דרך ארץ) in Rashbam's method, see Jacobs, "Rashbam's Major Principles," 53 n. 30; Japhet, *Commentary*, 100–104. On the classical concept, see Redfield, "Pragmatic Points of View: Kant and the Rabbis, Together Again."

766. On numbers as amplifiers see chapter 3 §*Poetry*.

ful, dense with messages to the reader.[767] The louder the waves are, the more the end of the story's prooftext (*though they roar, yet can they not pass over*) and its demonstration of God's dominion over the sea ring true.

Similarly, in the fifth story, Rashbam retells its lesson and adds a subtle sense of scale. The Talmud had interpreted this strange story as proof for its own obscure conclusion: *Come see the strength of the tree! How great it was!* Rather than gloss the *tree* as a symbol (e.g., Torah, the "tree of life"),[768] Rashbam deftly bolsters the Talmud's own lesson in its own terms. Since birds typically rest, not "*in* a tree" as the tale literally says, but *on* its branches, then the tree is even greater! Without engaging the tale's inner content, Rashbam strengthens its effect.

Finally, in the sixth story, Rashbam achieves a similar effect with a larger number than he did in the first. Rather than either literally or figuratively, he interprets the sixty towns that the fish destroyed as an index of its size. "Because that is just how *big* it was" does not literally claim an exact number. It reminds the reader of the proper emphasis and of what to visualize. Yet here, Rashbam's retelling of a tale goes even further. In the original, the dead fish is flung ashore and dismantled by people who will use its skeleton to rebuild the very towns that it destroyed. This is an example of the vivid, rapid, surprising crossing between cosmic domains and states of being that I called the "metamorphic poetics" of Part 1 in general.[769] Rashbam picks up on this feature of the telling and incorporates it into his commentary's retelling. His giant fish is cut up and eaten in a limited time frame: "while it was still moist." It is not only eaten fresh, preserved in salt, and then eaten by the same "sixty towns" where it landed;[770] it is exported to sixty more towns, beyond the extreme limits that it has already crossed. The textures of his new fish—wet and dry—and its narrative setting—from shoreline to hinterland—are more dynamic.[771] Against the backdrop of the telling, he conjures a new chronotope in just a few words.

To a reader who seeks the tales' hidden meaning, Rashbam's *peshat* is disappointing. He does not answer obvious and urgent follow-up questions such as "So, the tree is stronger than I thought—what does it represent?" Instead, he maintains that the tales themselves contain enough

---

767. This is similar to the technique of a *peshat* attributed to Rabbenu Gershom, who sets this dialogue between "inner" and "outer" waves in a dynamic space as they crash on the shoreline. See chapter 2 §*Parting the Sea(s)*.

768. See *Perush Qadum Le-midrash Vayyiqra' Rabbah*, ed. M. B. Lerner (Jerusalem: Meqitse nirdamim, 1995), 89.

769. See chapter 3 §*Setting*.

770. Like Leviathan in the eschaton in Part 2; see Appendix §2.A.

771. The dichotomy of wet/dry (לח/מלח), in Rashbam's retelling of VI, is also imported from the surrounding collection: the dichotomy between the cosmic elements Water/Dry Land, which animates I, VII, IX, XI, and XVIII.20.

context and content to be read on their own terms. Leaving their explicit lessons and structure intact, he helps a reader to experience their telling: the sound of the waves, vision of the tree, and texture of the fish elevate a reader's awe at God's vast and manifold creation. In addition to expanding details, he creates this sublime effect by recollecting his retelling in local context, where language points his reader's attention to this kind of meaning. In essence, each aspect of the telling that Rashbam foregrounds, at least in these examples,[772] answers the rhetorical question with which he began: "*How* great are your works, O Lord!?" For a close reader, he ensures that Rabbah's tales will be much greater on a second reading.

The Breakdown of *Peshat*

The other aspect of Rashbam's approach, reading the tales as moral lessons for Israel, was also influential in general, but not all of his applications of this approach were successful. Recall that, based on Part 2 of the composition, he aimed to interpret the giant beasts and sundry exotica of Part 1 as foretelling "what will be given as a reward for the righteous in the world to come"; in effect, as a prophecy for the Jewish people. On its face, this is quite sensible. As we know, some, like Leviathan, *are* a reward for the righteous in the world to come in ancient traditions that are cited in Part 2 itself. It is hardly a stretch to extend that idea to the rest of Part 1 and derive from this a moral lesson about the world to come.[773] In one case where he does so, however, Rashbam bumps into a tension between the literary context and the moral that he derives from it. Context does not always support the moral that he finds, leaving his method vulnerable. Those vulnerabilities would be exploited by Maharsha, who moves below the tales' surface and between their gaps to argue for a more consistent but hidden moral. Where *peshat* breaks down, Maharsha finds a warrant for midrash and allegory to reenter the tales.

This argument with *peshat* across five centuries comes to a head in the tale of the fat geese.

---

772. I would interpret another original feature of Rashbam's *peshat*, his insertion of a demonology into II and III (b. B. Bat. 73a s.v. חיורתא דנורא צוציתא, s.v. הורמין), in the same light. By making occult forces in the telling more visible to his reader, he highlights the same message of awe and praise for God's dominion. See Rashbam b. B. Bat. 73a s.v. אקופי דשורא: "This matter is to inform the righteous of the Holy One Blessed Be He, that He is compassionate to His creations and does not give [demons] leave to harm them." Maharsha (b. B. Bat. 73a s.v. הורמיז) critiques Rashbam's demonology as he critiques his *peshat* in general, and Getz's allegory transforms it totally; see below.

773. Recall that Part 1 also has an explicit eschatology, albeit not very much: see nn. 642, 677, 708.

Xa.
And Rabbah b. bar Hanah said:
Once I was traveling in the desert
and I saw those geese
whose wings drooped
because of their fat
and a stream of oil
was flowing out of them.
We said to them:
Have we in you a portion of the world to come?[774]
One lifted up its thigh at me, and one lifted up its wing.

Xb.
When I came before R. Elʿazar, he said to me:
In time to come, Israel shall be judged on their account.

On Rabbi Elʿazar's comment, Rashbam comments:

[In time to come, Israel shall] be judged on their account:
For due to their sins, the Messiah is delayed; and they bear
    [responsibility for] animal cruelty to those geese, due to their fat.

Israel's righteous will have a portion of the geese in the eschaton (like Leviathan;[775] the geese lift up their *wing* and *thigh* to point out the menu), but this end is not nigh. Worse, its delay is due to Israel's sins in this world. The oil (משחא), flowing out of the geese like sand in an hourglass, marks time that Israel's sins are delaying the Messiah (משיח). With this reading, Rashbam uses his clever equation between "oil" and "Messiah" to explain away the glaring problem that Rabbi Elʿazar's comment poses for his *peshat* approach: the fact that, far from a reward for the righteous in the world to come, the geese seem to signify Israel's punishment.[776]

---

774. This might also be a statement ("We have in you a portion" etc.), which would not affect my argument.

775. The cosmic bird (*ziz*) was added to the banquet of Leviathan already in the classical *midrashim* and *piyyutim*. See Ginzberg, *Legends*, 1:32–33 n. 139; Schirmann, *Battle between Behemoth and Leviathan*, 8 n. 20.

776. In that respect his *peshat* is similar to, but an advance over, his contemporary Joseph ibn Migash (*Hiddushe Ha-R. Y. Migash ʿAl Massekhet Baba Batra*, Jerusalem: Or Yisrael, n.d.), 36: "When they [= Israel] are redeemed in the World to Come, *One* [i.e., God] *will deduct it* [i.e., their punishment] *from their merits* [b. Shabb. 32a = b. Taʿan. 20b]." Unlike Rashbam, ibn Migash does not find a reason for the punishment. He merely specifies its mechanism: as if paying off a debt, Israel will lose spiritual credit at the very moment of its final redemption. In other words, he reads R. Elʿazar's comment on the story as a *reversal* of Rabbah's expectation that these giant geese will be the reward for Israel's temporal righteousness. "To be judged" (ליתן את הדין) does often mean to pay the deferred price for a sin. See Shimon Sharvit, *Language and Style of Tractate Avoth through the Ages* [Hebrew] (Beer-Sheva: Ben-Gurion

The Allegorical Canon 271

Yet even if we accept this solution, he must still account for the rest of Rabbi El'azar's comment: "on their account," that is, on account of the geese. Why will Israel be judged on *their* account? Don't the geese stand for the sins of Israel, who are punished on their own account? Rashbam fends off this further objection with the out-of-context notion of "animal cruelty."[777] The longer the "oil" runs out of the geese (i.e., the longer the Messiah is delayed by Israel's sins), the more the geese will suffer in *this* world "because of their fat,"[778] which painfully makes their wings droop or even molt.[779] Therefore, Rashbam argues, there is no contradiction between both meanings of the geese: Israel's reward and punishment. In the world to come, Israel's righteous will be rewarded. In this world, the scape-geese suffer for Israel's sins: sins that Israel will have to repay.[780]

Rashbam's acrobatics in resolving this dilemma show how hard he is straining to stay within the bounds of *peshat* interpretation. He tries to use R. El'azar's commentary, within the story's context, to find its moral. In the process, however, he stumbles over a contradiction; a contradiction

---

University of the Negev Press, 2006), 133. For instance, t. Avod. Zar. 7:7: "[God] leaves the world to proceed in its usual way and, in time to come, those fools, who acted corruptly, will be judged."

777. For Rashbam, it is less out of context than it is in our collection. The main discussion of "animal cruelty" in the Talmud also explores a hypothetical relationship between a suffering animal, on one hand, and (an individual) "Israel," on the other. Just as there, according to Rashi (b. B. Metz. 32b s.v. משום צערא דישראל), one "Israel" suffers by "having to wait there" while an animal is loaded, so here, according to Rashbam, the *animal* suffers because *all* Israel "delay" the Messiah. That is, Rashbam is explaining R. El'azar's comment on the tale by recycling a rhetorical pattern ("X suffers because Y delays") in connection to an idea ("animal suffering.") That is one reading tradition for Xb. (Hence, it is stated as a gloss of the plain sense in Kiperwasser, "Travels of Rabbah," 237.)

778. Kenneth Moss notes (personal communication, 24 January 2022) that Rashbam might gloss the "fat" of the geese itself as "animal cruelty," if they were fattened by force-feeding. This yields a smoother reading of the phrase: "And they [i.e., the *geese*] bear animal cruelty, because of their fat[tening]." Alternatively, the contemporary Mainz Anonymous—a Jewish account of the First Crusade—cites a famous legend that this Crusade was led by a goose (Robert Chazan, *In the Year 1096: The First Crusade and the Jews* [Philadelphia: Jewish Publication Society, 1996], 60). If that is the allegory, then *Israel* suffer "animal cruelty," slaughtered "on account of *their* [i.e., the Crusaders'] Messiah [משחא = משיח]." On popular legends of gushing oil—including one that may be from the Jewish community of Rome, see Sylvia Elizabeth Mullins, "Myroblytes: Miraculous Oil in Medieval Europe" (PhD diss., Georgetown University, 2017), 310, 448. We should avoid reducing the allegory to any one historical meaning because it can bear so many so easily.

779. In ms. H (וי"א.קכ"ה), their wings seem to "droop" due to their weight; in all other manuscripts, they are "plucked," that is, they molt. Ms. H suggests a slightly less exaggerated telling, which could be a motive for its variant.

780. Rashbam may gloss the subject of "*their* fat" as Israel, with "fat" signifying Israel's sins, as in Deut 32:15: "But Jeshurun [= Israel] waxed fat, and kicked." Even if so, his point is the same: their sins delay the Messiah.

that his notion of "animal cruelty" resolves at the cost of further contradiction. Why would Israel be punished for the effect of its sin on the geese, rather than the sin itself?[781]

Noting these acrobatics, what he calls a "forced" reading, Maharsha follows Rashbam, but only up to a point.[782] From that point forward, his midrashic mode of allegory takes over:

> There is no denying the *peshat* of these matters, for Ezekiel has already prophesied that in the eschaton, Israel will similarly walk in the wilderness, and [God] will destroy those among them who are sinners, as it is said [Ezek 20:35–38 NRSV]:[783]
>
>> "[35]And I will bring you into the wilderness of the peoples, and there I will enter into judgment with you . . . [36] As I entered into judgment with your ancestors in the wilderness . . . [38] I will purge out the rebels among you, and those who transgress," etc.

Maharsha follows Rashbam that this story is about Israel's reward and punishment in the end-times. That is *peshat*, and no interpretive stretch: the geese and Rabbi El'azar say so! He supports this by noting the tale's setting: the desert, where the tale unfolds, is where Israel will get their just des(s)erts (as Ezekiel predicted). Yet now Maharsha does critique Rashbam:

> One might, however, inquire logically [לעיין] into the specifics of these matters: that he specified the *geese* among all birds. Further, what is the meaningful content [ומה ענין] of *Lifted up its wing*, etc.? And what Rashbam commented [about R. El'azar's comment; see above] is forced.

Maharsha charges Rashbam on two counts. First, for the reasons that we noted, his moral seems "forced."[784] Second, Rashbam did not assign a

---

781. This second contradiction is avoided by the allegory in Ritva, b. B. Bat. 73b s.v. אוזא דשמטי גדפייהו משומנייהו (ed. Ilan, 593). Rabbah wandering in the wilderness = Israel in exile. The geese = the righteous "remnant" of foreign (Persian and Arab) empires, who will be saved at the Messiah. Yet because Israel's exile, due to its sins, delays their salvation, Israel will be "judged on their account." In contrast to this elegant solution, Rashbam's *peshat* is forced because he needs the geese to remain, in some real sense, geese.

782. See further Yaakov Elbaum, *Openness and Insularity: Late Sixteenth Century Jewish Literature in Poland and Ashkenaz* [Hebrew] (Jerusalem: Magnes, 1990), 140-42; on our story see 142 nn. 188–89. Elbaum shows that Maharsha tries not to go too far from *peshat*. He turns to allegory where previous *peshat* is illogical or arbitrary, aiming to restore sense to details of each telling and harmony to the talmudic canon. See further n. 791.

783. Here, the NRSV translation is closer to Maharsha's interpretation. See the text of Maharsha in *Sefer hiddushe 'aggadot Maharsha ha-shalem: 'al massekhet Baba kamma, Baba Metzi'a, Baba batra* (Jerusalem, 2008), 153–54.

784. For medieval commentators on forced explanations (דחוקים) in the Talmud, see

meaning to every other part of the story. He did not say why it features *geese* rather than another animal. He did not explain *wing* and *thigh*, let alone distinguish between the two meanings. He explained both images as Israel's reward in the world to come, but again, that is hardly an explanation at all: it is what Rabbah asks, the geese answer, and R. El'azar confirms. Why name *two* "portions"? Why distinguish *wing* from *thigh*? Maharsha calls for a more full, exacting interpretation than *peshat* had offered.

And the [more] apt [explanation] is in light of what we said:

1. [b. Ber. 57a]: *One who sees a goose in a dream should expect wisdom, as it is said, "Wisdom crieth without; she uttereth her voice in the streets"* [Prov 1:20]. From this we learned that there is a matter of wisdom in the voice and honking of a goose.

1.a. And we also say in [b.] Sotah [48a], *Rav Huna banned singing: a hundred geese went for a single zuz but there were no takers. Rav Hisda brought it down [i.e., the prohibition]: if one sought a goose for a zuz, it could not be found.*[785]

1.a.i. The [price of a] goose was pegged to the unit of the *zuz*, as they said in [b.] Hullin [49a]: *A goose for a zuz, its lung for four*. This means that [after Rav Hisda brought down the prohibition on singing], one could not buy a goose for more than its value,

1.a.ii. just as *zuz* [זוזא] and *goose* [אווזא] have the same numerical value [21]; whereas the *lung*, which is the name of the place from which the voice goes out, is worth four *zuz*, for that is the place and the source of the *voice* of *Wisdom* [Prov 1:20, above], as well as the *chit-chat* [of Torah scholars], as we have written.[786] And therefore it said that Rav

---

Halivni, *Formation of the Babylonian Talmud*, 221–22 n. 90. The concept here is the same: the explanation does not fit the context of the statement, making it about something it is not. For another usage, that is, an interpretation that does not correlate a speaker's words with their inner speech (intention), see Daniel Boyarin, " 'Pilpul': The Logic of Commentary," in his *The Talmud: A Personal Take; Selected Essays*, ed. Tal Hever-Chybowski, TSAJ 170 (Tübingen: Mohr Siebeck, 2017), 47–65, at 56.

785. In his first two paragraphs, Maharsha draws on his own comment at b. Sotah 48a s.v. ביטל.

786. Maharsha alludes to his own comment on IXa ("And we saw a certain bird"), where he extols the virtue of authentic logical analysis (*pilpul*) as "chit-chat" (*pitput*) between study partners for the sake of truth. *Pitput*, like *pilpul*, is a reduplicated form, which can connote onomatopoeia, repetition, or derogation: here, a birdlike chirping. As a bird chirps constantly, Maharsha insists, so should the oral Torah be constantly on your lips; *not depart out of thy mouth ... day and night* (Josh 1:8; see y. Ber. 9:5, 14d: "All chatter [פיטטיא] is bad, except chatter about Scripture which is good.... All storytelling [כדבייא, see n. 185], is good, except storytelling about Scripture, which is bad"). Following the Zohar, the Gra's comment on the

Huna *banned singing*, which is the voice of the forbidden, because a voice should serve a person in order to study wisdom. And therefore such merit accrued to the *voice of Wisdom* that the price of a hundred geese stood at a *zuz*. Vice versa as well: Rav Hisda brought [the prohibition on singing] down, and reestablished the voice of the forbidden, and therefore a goose was valued above what it was worth, such that even *for a whole zuz it could not be had*.

2. And this refers to the eschaton, when knowledge and wisdom will increase such that all *shall know* the wisdom of the Lord, *from the least of them unto the greatest* [Jer 31:34 (31:33)], and they shall walk in the wilderness like our ancestors [see Ezek 20, above], in order to gain enlightenment.

2.a. And it said that [God] will give them *geese* in order to consume something spiritual and intellectual from them, for the sake of the wisdom of one who is deserving,

2.a.i. just as He gave the quail in the wilderness to the righteous among our ancestors, about whose *fat* they argued in the chapter *Yom ha-kippurim* [b. Yoma 75b]: "It was as small as a little bird, but they put it in an oven to roast and it swelled and filled [the oven, and they placed it on thirteen loaves, yet even the bottom loaf could only be eaten in the form of a mixture"],[787]

2.a.ii. which corresponds to the *river of oil* that [Rabbah bar bar Hanah] saw [*was flowing*] *out of them*. That is an allegory [*remez*] for the pleasure of the spirit and the soul,

2.a.iii. according to what we said in [b.] Taʿanit [25a], that [God] showed Rabbi Elʿazar ben Pedat "thirteen rivers of oil [in the World to Come as a reward for his righteous conduct] etc." So too, here, the *river of oil* of the *goose* is an allegory [*remez*] for enlightenment and pleasure of the soul.

3. And *Rabbah bar bar Hanah, who was one of the wise, said [to the geese]: Am I, too, deserving to have [a portion] of you*, that is, to benefit and derive merit from this spirituality? And he said that *one of them lifted up*, that is,

---

"frog" in V uses the same allegory: "Why were Egyptians punished by frogs? Because they prevented Israel from learning Torah, like a frog that is *not* quiet by day or by night … And so, Rabbah bar bar Hanah said in a figure of speech that he saw a disciple of the sages" (Gra, *Beʾure Aggadot*, 18). Both animal allegories support Rashbam's view (see n. 761) that "*every discussion of the disciples of the sages requires study*," even their "chit-chat."

787. b. Yoma 75b. Square brackets [ ] extend the quotation. Rashi comments (s.v. ותחתונה אינה נאכלת) that the bottom loaf had to be diluted "because of how much fat it had absorbed — let alone the loaves on top!" This is a stock Talmud motif; we might call it The Princess and the Pita. See b. B. Metz. 84b; Boyarin, *Fat Rabbis*, 185.

they showed him, that the matter does not depend upon wisdom alone, but also upon practice, as they said [Avot 1:17]: *"Not study is the foundation, but practice."*

> 3.a. And the foundational means of practice are the hands and feet, and thus *one lifted up its wing*, so that I should lift up my hands in good deeds, *and another lifted up its thigh* to me, so that I should lift up my feet to walk on the path of those who are good.

4. *When he came before R. El'azar, he said: Israel shall be judged on their account,* just as Ezekiel [Ezek 20:35, above] prophesied, *and there will I enter into judgment with you.* For there are many among Israel who are not deserving due to good deeds, and they are *those who transgress* and *the rebels* to whom he [Ezek 20:38, above] referred.

> 4.a. And [God] *will enter into judgment with* them for their consumption of the *geese* for the sake of their appetites, just as He *entered into judgment* of our *ancestors* regarding the *quail* [Num 11:31–34], that is, of they who consumed it for the sake of excessive appetite.

And that is what we are to understand from it.

Allegory as Midrash

But what are we to understand from it about Maharsha's method? He combines midrash and allegory, integrating both to derive a single moral lesson that explains the story precisely and comprehensively. Maharsha's allegory is more midrashic than later commentators, however, in the sense that he does not create a hidden meaning fully independent of the story. He explains and thus retells the tale by integrating it with intertexts. The canon that the tale and his intertexts share is the background for those connections, one that his interpretation reinforces. But the format of his commentary stays tied to each gap in *peshat* with which he began. Each closure of each gap points back to the tale directly, filling in a dialogue between Rabbah and the geese to restore its moral subtext without changing its surface meaning. He does clearly mark separate layers of interpretation, surface and depth.[788] Yet the deeper layer—Geese as symbol for Wisdom—is not peeled off and reapplied to interpret his intertexts in their own right, in their own contexts. His allegory sticks to the exegetical and didactic aims of midrash. Once it has served that purpose, a reader can leave it behind. His intertexts are more background for

---

788. In his opening comment, Maharsha, Baba Batra 73a s.v. אישתעו לי נחותי ימא האי גלא contrasts *peshat* to allegory or "inward matters" (i.e., "hidden things to which it is necessary to set one's mind" [Rashi, b. Ketub. 111a s.v. דברים בגו]).

his allegory than foreground. If a reader attends to what he selects from the intertexts, they partly correspond to the tale. Those correspondences help to explain the tale in terms of Wisdom.[789] Maharsha's canon thus grows more densely meaningful, collecting texts and intertexts. But he does not place the whole canon under the sign of Wisdom as one interpretive key. His allegory can reapply to its intertexts but does not have to. He aims to develop the story, not to demonstrate the canon's perfect harmony and integrity.

To unpack this analysis of Maharsha's allegorical midrash, we should examine how symbols function in his argument. How do symbols and their hidden meanings explain gaps in the tale left by *peshat*? In the process, what happens to the structure of the relationship between this tale and its canonical intertexts? Finally, how does the tale's moral lesson both emerge from and authorize his interpretive framework? We can schematize our evidence for those questions as follows. (Numbering corresponds to his commentary's sections, presented above.)

Gap in *Peshat*	Maharsha's Solution	Intertext(s)
Why "I **saw** those geese"?	The entire tale is a dream	Geonic tradition in Ritva; Dreambook, b. Ber. 55a–57b
Why "I saw those **geese**"?	1. Goose + Dream = Wisdom	b. Ber. 57a
Why "I saw those geese"?	The teller is a wise man	He is in the Talmud[790]
Why "traveling in the **desert**"?	2. Prophecy of Israel's reward/ punishment in the eschaton	Ezek 20:35-38 (Jer 31:34 [31:33])
Why "wing" **and** "thigh"?	3. Pursuit of Wisdom = Torah-study **and** practice	Avot 1:17
Why shall "Israel be judged on [the geeses'] account"?	4. Punished for base appetite for literal geese, **not** Wisdom	Num 11:31–34 (b. Yoma 75b)

---

789. His allegory also recollects certain tales with one another. The previous tale (IXa), which is also about giant birds, is a similar allegory for levels of Wisdom: the revealed oral Torah below ("water," for which one needs the sharp "adze" of *pilpul*, a key subtext here as well) versus the heights of mysticism ("Work of the Chariot"). But this allegory does not cover the whole collection; Maharsha follows his intertexts as much as he leads them.

790. Whereas Rashbam had to argue for this, due to the tales' strangeness and Rabbah's dubious reputation in the Talmud, now it is a given, as stated in 3. Maharsha does support the claim indirectly (see i.a.ii above and n. 786).

This allegory's fundamental but silent premise is that the tale is a dream.[791] Relying on a reading tradition that Rabbah's formula for introducing his tales ("I myself have seen") refers to "matters that are allegorical [נרמזים], that do not appear with the vision of the eye but with the vision of the dream,"[792] Maharsha goes further. He essentially looks up the tale's content, using the Talmud as his decoder ring.[793] "Geese" in a dream are a symbol and omen of wisdom; therefore, this is a tale about wisdom.[794] But this allegory is no mere gloss: it is a whole framework. It must close gaps in the telling left by *peshat* with the tale's new meaning. Like midrash, it does so by solving each interpretive crux to retell a tale of Wisdom with a moral lesson.

---

791. For the tradition of interpreting a certain category of *aggadah*, and Rabbah's especially, as a dream, see nn. 383, 792. On dreams and/as allegory, see Patricia Cox Miller, *Dreams in Late Antiquity: Studies in the Imagination of a Culture* (Princeton, NJ: Princeton University Press, 1999), 91–105. Maharsha also uses the dreambook to decode the meaning of another story in the Talmud (Elbaum, *Openness and Insularity*, 139). This illustrates Maharsha's method of allegory whereby he, as Elbaum says, creates a precise one-to-one translation from the symbol into its meaningful content by comparing and harmonizing *aggadot* across the canon.

792. *Hiddushe ha-Ritva 'al Massekhet Baba Batra* to b. B. Bat 73a s.v. אמר רבה אשתעו לי נחותי ימא (ed. Ilan, 591). Ritva cites a source that suggests that this is an old reading tradition: "The Geonim wrote that everything of which we say, 'I myself have seen,' was in the vision of the dream, when [Rabbah] was traveling on the sea Okeanus." See *Otzar ha-Geonim he-Hadash: Massekhet Baba Batra*, ed. Robert (Yerahmiel) Brody et al. (Jerusalem: Yad Ha-Rav Nissim, 2017), 290. This tradition is surely prompted by the formula "I saw," which also introduces dreams in the talmudic dreambook (b. Ber. 55a–57b). The dreambook also has a dream at sea (b. Ber. 56a) and other shared content (the same animals; a vision of an "Arab"). Near its end, Rav Ashi says, like Rabbah in IX, "I have seen [a goose]." Maharsha's allegory takes flight from there. On the dreambook, see Haim Weiss, *All Dreams Follow the Mouth: A Reading in the Talmudic Dreams Tractate* [Hebrew] (Kinneret, Zmora-Bitan: Dvir, 2011); *Traum und Traumdeutung im Talmud*, ed. and trans. Alexander Kristianpoller (Weisbaden: Matrix, 2006), 9–34; Holger Zellentin, "Jewish Dreams between Roman Palestine and Sasanian Babylonia: Cultural and Geographic Borders in Rabbinic Discourse," in *Borders: Terminologies, Identities, Performances*, ed. Annette Weissenrieder, WUNT 366 (Tübingen: Mohr Siebeck, 2016), 419–57, at 422–23 n. 4.

793. Ritva had already used a Wisdom allegory in his comment on the "basket" and "precious stone" (XVIII–XIX, Baba Batra 74a–b s.v. עובדא דקרטליתא, s.v. אבן טבא, ed. Ilan, 594–95). But he kept allegory "closer to the *peshat*," due to concern that it would be used to further denigrate *aggadah* (a wise move, considering his political context: see n. 745). His allegories stay close to biblical apocalyptic convention, for example, animals = foreign nations (the gazelle in IV = Muslims; see also n. 781). On his teacher Rashba's related worry about allegorical excess, see Gregg Stern, "Philosophic Allegory in Medieval Jewish Culture: The Crisis in Languedoc," in *Interpretation and Allegory: Antiquity to the Modern Period*, ed. Jon Whitman, Brill's Studies in Intellectual History 101 (Leiden: Brill, 2000), 189–209, at 194–98.

794. The symbol as omen ("One who sees a goose in his dream may *expect* wisdom") further supports the eschatological aspect of Maharsha's reading. After all, not only what a prophet sees in his vision, but also the word for it, convey its meaning (e.g., "summer-fruit"/"the End," קַיִץ/קֵץ, Amos 8:2). Similarly for Maharsha, the actual word for "geese," its numerical value, *and* its received meaning are Wisdom. It is a symbol in triplicate.

278 *Adventures of Rabbah & Friends*

Maharsha's midrashic allegory is a tale of two textures with different implied readers.[795] If a reader grasps only the top-line summary of its basic points (1, 2, 3, 4 in our chart above), it reads smoothly as a retelling that inserts his allegory of Wisdom into the gaps of *peshat*. The only intertexts with which such a reader would need a passing familiarity are in the Bible and an almost proverbial adage in tractate Avot, familiar from liturgy. If one grants the premise that the tale is a dream, and geese in a dream are an allegory for Wisdom—why wouldn't its teller have read the first tractate of the Talmud, which says so, and encoded it accordingly?— one needs minimal knowledge or attention to arrive at its moral, which he underscores by repeating it at the end. To illustrate this surface reading, consider a version of the tale that adds Maharsha's commentary directly to the tale, as if it were set in the margins of a Talmud page like Rashi/Rashbam (instead of a separate volume or appendix) and we could read tale with commentary straight across the line.[796] Note that, except "stream of oil," each keyword to which he attaches a comment was set up as a gap in *peshat* by his critique of Rashbam. That original recollection of interpretive gaps—marked by the keywords "I/saw/geese/fat/oil/thigh/wing"—emplots Maharsha's allegorical retelling, signaling each new turn of Rabbah's old adventure.

> Once I was traveling in the desert **like our ancestors,**[797] **in order to gain enlightenment**
> and I, **who was one of the wise,** saw **in a dream** those geese, **to consume something spiritual and intellectual from them, for the sake of the wisdom of one who is deserving,**
> [whose wings drooped]
> because of their fat, **just as He gave the quail in the wilderness to the righteous among our ancestors**
> and a stream of oil, **an allegory [*remez*] for the pleasure of the spirit and the soul in the World to Come**
> [was flowing out of them].[798]
> I[799] said to them:

---

795. These readers are not necessarily two groups of people. They could be the same people with different levels of attention to the text or reflect renditions of the text performed in different settings (e.g., preaching vs. study).

796. That is actually how many readers would have encountered Maharsha's commentary from 1684, when it began to be printed in the margins of the anthology *'En Ya'aqov* alongside the editor's commentary. See Marjorie Lehman, *The En Yaaqov: Jacob ibn Ḥabib's Search for Faith in the Talmudic Corpus* (Detroit: Wayne State University Press, 2012), 183–84.

797. This is not an allegory—it is Rashbam's *peshat*, based on Ezek 20:35–38. As Maharsha said, "there is not denying the *peshat*." He develops it by adding the symbol of the quail and building a Wisdom allegory around it.

798. The two bracketed lines remain gaps in the allegory, not only in the *peshat*. None of the commentators in my relatively small sample was very interested in them, perhaps because they do not contain any new symbols but are subjoined to *wings* and *oil*.

799. As noted (Appendix §*Translation*), this form can mean "I" or "we." Maharsha

The Allegorical Canon 279

Have I in you a portion of the world to come? **Am I, too, deserving to have [a portion] of you, i.e., to benefit and derive merit from this spirituality?**
One lifted up, **i.e., showed**, its thigh at me, **that I should lift up my feet to walk on the path of those who are good**, and one lifted up its wing, **that I should lift up my hands in good deeds, for the matter does not depend upon wisdom alone but also upon practice** [Avot 1:17].
When he came before R. El'azar, he said:
In time to come, Israel shall be judged on their account,
For there are many among Israel who are not deserving due to good deeds, and they are *those who transgress* **and** *the rebels* [Ezek 20:38]. **And [God]** *will enter into judgment with* **them** [Ezek 20:35] **for their consumption of the geese for the sake of their appetites, just as He entered into judgment of our ancestors regarding the quail** [Num 11:31–34]**, i.e., of those who consumed it for the sake of excessive appetite.**

All gaps in *peshat* that Maharsha opened are closed by becoming symbols. As soon as the formula "I saw" makes this story interpretable as a dream, any keyword can be unlocked as one unlocks an image in a dream: symbolism, that is, a hidden meaning based on some form of resemblance. In this case, it is easy, as the Talmud holds the master key in its dreambook: *geese* means to *expect wisdom*, and Rabbah, who was a wise man, *expected* that Wisdom would be the reward for his righteousness in the world to come. However, the geese lifted up their *wing and thigh* to remind Rabbah that, as the adage goes, "not study is the foundation, but practice."[800] Wisdom alone is not enough to be righteous or to expect reward. Deeds also matter. Therefore, the geese showed him a *wing*–a symbol of action like a hand–and a *thigh*, like legs, a symbol of the foundation for action. Their message, alas, is lost on the sinners of Israel, who fail to pursue not only wisdom, but even good deeds. On the contrary, they follow base appetites. Just as Ezekiel foretold that the desert, where the tale is set, will be where Israel is judged in the eschaton, so too will sinners—like some Israelites in the wilderness, whom God punished with death for craving the quail's meat—*be judged on account* of the geese (Wisdom) that they did *not* consume in *this* world. Thus, the allegorical retelling yields a less forced reading of R. El'azar's comment on the geese: he was referring not to all Israel, nor to the suffering of the geese, but to sinners of Israel who crave only carnal things. The righteous, who at least do good deeds and at most seek Wisdom, may continue to expect Wisdom as their reward.

---

takes it as "I," even though Rabbah says "we" in his following question (in all manuscripts, except ms. V). This is just a paraphrase, but its effect is to make Rabbah speak from inside the allegory, as if, by "world to come," he is already referring to Wisdom.

800. Avot 1:17: playing on a literal sense of "foundation" (עיקר) and the goose's "thigh/leg," the basis of wisdom.

Any reader can grasp this lesson without following Maharsha's digressions or the fine points of his intertextual connections. For such a casual or less-informed reader, allegory operates as a sermon that teaches a clear moral lesson. It recollects the tale and intertexts from the biblical canon, based on evident correspondences between the two. This is also how classical midrash works. It allows for a surface reading of the biblical story that need not contradict its deeper meaning but does draw out its moral implication, calling select words to a reader's attention by creating interpretive gaps and then retelling the story with its moral lesson in the foreground. Maharsha's allegory of our tale in the Talmud is pure midrash in this sense. It closes interpretive gaps that *peshat* could not and adds a moral to the story that makes more sense than Rashbam's. It does so by building on his *peshat* that our tale is about God's ultimate judgment of Israel—hence, it was set in the "desert." Then, it recalls a biblical tale where Israel's appetite for birds provoked God's punishment there. Such simple connections integrate our strange talmudic tale with a familiar biblical canon, making it seem as if this allegory for Wisdom is a natural outgrowth of the Bible's own morality tale.[801] The new interpretive framework authorizes itself as uncannily familiar. Wisdom is not mentioned in Ezek 20 or Num 11. But their symbolic correspondences with the tale are so elegant that a reader accepts the allegory intuitively. *I think I heard a story about this somewhere before ...*

For a reader who knows its talmudic intertexts, the allegory works on another level. As we see in the full translation above, two integral subsections (1.a–1.a.ii and 2.a.i–2.a.iii) cite only the Talmud, even though they point back to biblical texts in the main body sections. Those are digressions commenting, not on the tale directly, but on further biblical intertexts: Prov 1:20 (the dreambook's own prooftext for its allegory, *goose* = Wisdom), and Num 11, the story of the quails (a juicy occasion for midrashim; Maharsha cites just one of many). Initially, these digressions do not seem to add much to our questions about how the Wisdom allegory restructures the canon and how it authorizes itself. The first digression teaches that "a voice should serve a person in order to study wisdom." The second shows that quails in the Bible were as plentiful—"fat"—for the righteous as geese will be for them in the world to come. In terms of content, both are minor refinements to the allegory. One clarifies its moral lesson; the other notes that "fat" symbolizes not only a punishment for vice but also a reward for virtue. Both raise the bar of the simpler moral

---

801. The biblical story itself is easy to read as a moral allegory. After sinners of Israel spurn *manna* and demand meat, God punishes them with an excess of quails and, tantalizingly, smites them as they are about to eat. They are buried in the "Graves of Craving [קִבְרוֹת הַתַּאֲוָה], because there they buried the people who craved" (Num 11:34; my trans.). Maharsha builds on this lesson in his condemnation of "excessive appetite" [תאוה יתירה].

lesson for a more scholastic reader. Not only should you do good deeds and study Torah—you should *not* use your voice for base ends like singing. You should not pursue carnal appetites (for which you will be judged in the world to come). But, if you do not, you *will* be rewarded with wisdom more sensual than your wildest dreams.

On closer inspection, it seems to me that these digressions do play an important role in self-authorizing the allegorical framework, and do affect the canon's role as background for an advanced reader's interpretation of the tales, and indeed, that those two functions are connected. They are meta-allegorical: symbols in them refer simultaneously to their talmudic intertexts and to the commentary itself. This turns the allegory around; instead of simplifying the tales by anchoring them in Scripture, these symbols make the tales denser by anchoring them in the Talmud (and Talmudized Scripture, i.e., midrashim that have accrued to the prooftexts). In this situation of plural canonicity, where both the Talmud and the Bible hold meanings for each symbol, and a reader must uphold both, only the commentary can teach them how to do so. As they learn how, both the symbols and the code that the commentary gives its reader point back to itself. The commentary thus authorizes itself as sole go-between for the reader to decipher its allegorical canon. It is both lock and key for the interpretive difficulties that it has created.

The new symbol in the first digression—the "voice" of the goose/Wisdom—is not Torah in general. It is Maharsha's own technique of logical analysis in this commentary (*pilpul*).[802] Citing his recent defense of *pilpul* via an allegory to the "chatter" (*pitput*) of giant birds, he goes further to allegorize *pilpul* as the "lung" of a goose or "source of the voice of Wisdom"—as opposed, that is, to carnal use of the voice ("singing").[803] By reading his method back into the allegory, he defends *pilpul* from the stock insult that it is more like singing: "some call this craft *pilpul*, others call it

---

802. Specifically, "comparative *pilpul*." Rather than analyze one *sugya* logically in its context—"local *pilpul*," his methodology for law in the Talmud—in this method, Maharsha critiqued and harmonized *aggadic* material along a theme. See nn. 791, 808; H. Z. Dimitrovsky, "On the Method of Pilpul" [Hebrew], in *Salo Wittmayer Baron Jubilee Volume on the Occasion of His Eightieth Birthday*, ed. Saul Lieberman and Arthur Hyman (Jerusalem: American Academy for Jewish Research, 1975), 111–81, at 118 n. 30; 123 n. 61; 126–27; 180–81 n. 65. On institutional changes as a cause of polemic against *pilpul*, see Elhanan Reiner, "Temurot bi-yeshivot Polin ve-Ashkenaz be-me'ot ha-טז–ha-יז veha-viquah 'al ha-pilpul," in *Minhag Ashkenaz u-folin*, ed. Yisrael Bartal et al. (Jerusalem: Shazar Center, 1993), 9–80.

803. "The lesson is completed, let it be a song" is an idiom for reciting a text without understanding it (Rashi to b. Avod. Zar. 32b s.v. א"ל גמרא גמור זמורתא תהא). Maharsha does not actually say that this is an allegory against *pilpul* but, once he has cross-referenced the parallel and virtually identical allegory (*pitput* = *pilpul*, IX; see n. 786), he does not need to. That parallel allegory, with its opposition between good *pilpul* and bad *pitput*, was not original to him: *Orhot Tsadiqim* (Cleveland: Spero Foundation), 1946, 165; Reiner, "Temurot," 10–11 n. 2.

confusion [*bilbul*]."[804] That is how he turns around the allegory: the symbol in the tale points back to a prooftext (Prov 1:20), by way of the symbolism of the word "goose" in the Talmud,[805] and finally back to his own commentary. Such a reversal makes his own voice newly audible as the "voice of Wisdom." If at first his commentary had seemed to impose his allegory on the canon, now that it is grounded there, the canon can act as an allegory for his commentary. In other words, if a goose means wisdom, then wisdom is a goose; and if that is so, his reader should not be surprised that the voice of wisdom is loquacious, hypercritical, even abrasive–precisely those qualities for which *pilpul* was increasingly criticized in his own time.

Now that the first meta-allegory has cleared a space for his commentary within the tale, the second extends it to the tale's eschatological fulfillment. Maharsha achieves this by alluding to his own method, this time more subtly, as he develops a symbol in the tale: "rivers of oil." For a reader who does not catch this allusion to his commentary on the previous tractate, his interpretation of this symbol simply enhances the moral lesson. It renders the reward for Wisdom more vivid, nuancing his thesis that wisdom is better than carnality ("singing," "appetite.")[806] The reward for Wisdom in the world to come is like the quails: not only a curse on sinners' carnal appetites (as in the Bible) but also a blessing for the righteous (as in midrash). Here again, at this simpler level, allegory grows organically from a midrash in its intertext, which says that righteous and sinners alike ate the quail [*selav*], but it had opposite effects on them. "The righteous eat it at ease [*be-shalvah*]; the wicked eat it and it seems to them like thorns [*ke-silevin*]" (b. Yoma 75b). Similarly, "the ease [*shalvah*] of the wicked in this world ends in their destruction" (b. Yoma 86b).[807] What, then, may the

---

804. '*Alilot devarim*, in Eric Lawee, *Rashi's* Commentary on the Torah: *Canonization and Resistance in the Reception of a Jewish Classic* (Oxford: Oxford University Press, 2019), 687–88 (on this work, see Reiner, "Temurot," 26–27 n. 27). On that older polemic against *pilpul* as hairsplitting analysis of the talmudic dialectic, see Aviram Ravitsky, *Aristotelian Logic and Talmudic Methodology: The Application of Aristotelian Logic to the Interpretation of the Thirteen Hermeneutic Principles* [Hebrew] (Jerusalem: Magnes, 2009), 224–26. (Much later, the Gra will read IV as a polemic against *pilpul* in that older sense, not distinguishing *pilpul* from *hilluq*.)

805. The word, its numerical value, and its contextual meaning symbolize Wisdom because together they establish an opposition to what is *not* Wisdom: singing. This is another symbol in triplicate (see n. 794). Here, however, any resemblance between the symbol and its meaning comes from what it is *not*, not from what it is. If singing is forbidden, then Wisdom is abundant (hence geese are cheap); if it is permitted, then Wisdom is scarce (hence geese are expensive).

806. In this intertext (b. Ta'an. 25a), R. El'azar has a vision of reward in the world to come because he accepts his lot, despite being weak with hunger (see n. 290). This reinforces the commentary's moral lesson of wisdom versus "appetite." Maharsha laminates this intertext's correspondence to our tale with yet another layer of symbolism: *thirteen* rivers of oil/ *thirteen* loaves of quail fat (b. Yoma 75b). On the latter source, see Picus, "Ink Sea," 223–27.

807. These ideas about the quail are already developed in Tannaitic midrash about *manna*. Like the quails, which taste different to the wicked and the righteous, "every time

righteous hope to "eat" in the end? The allegory elegantly answers a logical follow-up question in the same midrashic vein: they will have as rich a portion in the world to come as their ancestors had in the wilderness.

For a more advanced reader, however, Maharsha's allegory points back directly to his own commentary. In the previous tractate, he defended *pilpul* from its critics by distinguishing it from an imposter. That imposter, "division" (*hilluq*),[808] gives *pilpul* a bad name. Its aggressive yet vapid style of logically analyzing texts "wears one out from [seeking] truth, and does not lead to its desired end." True *pilpul* is in the tradition of the Talmud's sages, who "scrutinized and tested every matter to get to the bottom of it, and the law came to light by means of their *pilpul*."[809] True *pilpul* is argument for the sake of truth; *hilluq* is argument for its own sake. In the Talmud source that he cites for this distinction, *hilluq* is Babylonia, where scholars were "bitter to one another ... like olives." *Pilpul* is the Land of Israel, where they were "pleasant to one another ... like olive oil." That is why Zechariah saw them as a vision of olive branches.[810] This strong correspondence between visions of olive oil, in all three of Maharsha's more advanced intertexts, prompts advanced readers to connect their interpretations of these intertexts as well. For such readers, his allegory builds on allegory, not just on midrash. If wisdom is a goose, then the voice of wisdom–*pilpul*–may be abrasive, but its reward is a river of olive oil. Any contention in this world is for the sake of wisdom in the world to come, unlike the bitterness of *hilluq*. By reading both the means and the ends of his commentary back into the tale, meta-allegory authorizes itself. Now, Rabbah's tale anticipates critics of *pilpul*, who fall into traps that meta-allegory has laid. If they cannot go beyond *peshat*, they are guilty of base carnal lust, craving quails not wisdom. If they reject *pilpul*, they are guilty of bad *pilpul*, a.k.a. *hilluq*, motivated not by wisdom but by vanity. The hermeneutic circle draws tighter, pulling intertexts together with a symbolic language that makes them speak to each other in the same way as it speaks of itself. For one who has followed it this far, allegory leaves no gap through which to escape.

---

that Israel eat [the *manna*], they find in it different flavors." Unlike the quails, *manna* is said to be barely corporeal: digested without leaving waste, food of angels and the righteous in the world to come (Mekhilta §*Vayassa* 4. See Ginzberg, *Legends*, 571 n. 197, 577 n. 134).

808. On the origins of *hilluq*, see Daniel Boyarin, "Studies in the Talmudic Commentaries of the Spanish Exiles" [Hebrew], *Sefunot* n.s. 2/17 (1983):166–83. On its new controversial sense in Poland, of which this comment is early evidence, as logical analysis of the Talmud changed from part of a study session under the *yeshivah* head to a wider practice, see Dimitrovsky, "On the Method of Pilpul," 113–14, 118; Reiner, "Temurot," 38–42.

809. Maharsha, b. B. Metz. 85a s.v. דלשתכח תלמוד בבלאה מיניה (*Hiddushe 'Aggadot Maharsha Ha-shalem*, 66). See Dov Rappel, *The Debate over the* Pilpul [Hebrew] (Tel-Aviv: Dvir, 1979), 111–12.

810. B. Sanh. 24a (on Zech 4).

Not every reader has to venture so far, however. If one only reads the commentary on the tale of the geese, its allegory is classic midrash: it gives a satisfying account of details left out by *peshat*, without contradicting *peshat*. It retells the story as a nation's journey into the wilderness, not only in the biblical past but also in the messianic future. Each symbol, each opposition between symbols, and even R. Elʻazar's original commentary on the story, are now fully explained by a Wisdom allegory. Now the teller has a motive—seeking Wisdom—and his dialogue with the geese makes sense. He already knew that they symbolize Wisdom—he read the Talmud, which says so!—but asked if he was deserving. Their reply: Wisdom is not enough, you must also do good deeds. In conclusion, Rabbi Elʻazar tells him what will happen if he doesn't do even that much. This ensures that the lesson sticks, even if the allegory does not.

Throughout the commentary, on this level, the canon stays in the background and does not have to enter the interpretive foreground. It generates the premise for the allegory: "I saw" means a dream. It enriches the allegory: quail fat in midrash, and rivers of oil in Rabbi Elʻazar's own dream, symbolize rewards of Wisdom, as opposed to carnality. This makes the allegory more concrete and intense. Yet the canon remains a source of the allegory rather than a target. Readers do not have to reinterpret the biblical quails as Wisdom, only to see them as an example of non-Wisdom. Similarly, when Rabbi Elʻazar says to resist carnal appetites, he has more clout if one reads his allegory back into his life story (for saying "I do not want" while starving, he, too, was once rewarded by a messianic dream of "rivers of oil").[811] But that is not required. Only if a reader centers Maharsha's commentary itself and reads it freely, stretching the allegory to cover relations *between* canon and commentary, rather than only relations among intertexts *within* the canon, does Wisdom become a meta-allegory that obliges one to reapply it to the canon as a whole—lest one be smitten for anti-allegorical carnal sins of literalism or hollow logic. Most of us, most of the time, can read and enjoy Maharsha's reading of the tale while ignorant of its polemical scholarly background. He uses allegory like midrash to close gaps in *peshat*, expanding the telling and moral lesson without forcing every reader into an allegorical canon.

Allegory Emancipated

By contrasting two levels on which Maharsha's commentary can be read, we saw that the more self-referential a canon is, the more allegorized it

---

811. Extending the Wisdom allegory to the entire canon thus motivates R. Elʻazar's otherwise cryptic remark in Xb in terms of his own dream (b. Taʻan. 25a; see chapter 2 §*A White Shoot of Flame*).

The Allegorical Canon 285

becomes. If an allegory emerges from its sources, it can work in classically midrashic ways: recollecting intertexts, drawing out new meaning from their relationships, retelling tales to solve traditional interpretive cruxes, and summarizing it all with a clear moral. Yet as soon as an allegory refers back to itself, showing that the commentary has a stake in its own story and its own interpretive framework, its reader has a new task. Rather than interpret a tale via intertexts and contexts with an allegorical twist, one begins to foreground the allegory's own internal symbolic vocabulary and oppositions. One learns to seek them wherever they may be found, repressing anti-allegorical readings or subsuming non-allegorical ones. One trawls the canon for fragments of the allegory and recollects them in retellings that go far beyond closing familiar interpretive gaps. This way of reading, in turn, reifies an impression of the canon as a harmonious whole. If one sees how intertexts fit together in terms of their symbols, then they can be read together; no other connection is required, though more will surely emerge. Like Talmudization—applying a Talmudic lens to all sources, including Scripture—allegorization puts pressure on the canon from outside its borders, straining each source through its logic. Rather than read symbols out of each intertext to explain their meanings in context, allegory reads its coded symbols back into the canon as a whole.

A striking example of this eisegetical and self-referential mode of allegory is the commentary on our tales by Rabbi Elyaqum Getz (1643/44–1705), whose father studied at Maharsha's *yeshivah* in Poznan (Posen) and who finished the work in 1679 while serving as a rabbi in the nearby city of Swarzędz (Schwersenz).[812] Despite his proximity to Maharsha,[813] Getz does something quite different with allegory. In the framing of this work, he posits that sages of the Talmud already spoke allegorically (with "riddle and wisdom") in order to teach a lesson to non-rabbis.[814] When he repeats

---

812. After my manuscript was accepted for publication, with over 10,000 words on Getz's commentary, its first critical study appeared: Steinmetz, "To Strengthen the Words of the Sages" (see n. 3). Her superb thesis superseded much of my work and seems to agree with my view of how Getz's allegory differs from Maharsha's (her view is summarized on 20, 60–61, 71, 93–95, 151). Steinmetz characterizes Getz's allegory as less exegetical ("looser") than Maharsha's and more "tendentious" (Elbaum's technical term). In my revised argument in this chapter, I try to offer a more positive description of Getz in terms of how he emancipates allegory from exegesis and reads it into the canon.

813. For two proofs that Getz knew Maharsha's commentary on our tales, see Steinmetz, "To Strengthen the Words of the Sages," 45–46.

814. His introduction of Rabbah's tales as "words of parable and figure on the *aggadah* that Our Sages of Blessed Memory spoke in the manner of riddle and wisdom, in order to discipline the multitude" is an apt summary of his own interpretive framework. As Steinmetz says "[Maharsha] is the solution for someone trying to make sense of Aggadah; [Getz] teaches the intrinsic moral value of Aggadah and proves that the Talmud supports the pressing matters of ethical rebuke found within [his commentary's] pages" ("To Strengthen the Words of the Sages," 71). I cite the text of Getz, *Rappeduni ba-tapuhim*, in *Sefer 'Aggadata' de-ve*

the same method with their stories, bringing their morals to light, he will follow in their footsteps. Rather than limit his interpretive obstacles to gaps in *peshat* that he will close by correlating specific intertexts and contexts, Getz gives allegory free rein. He turns to a canon that he presumes to be always already allegorical, connecting intertexts and deriving meanings from them which fit a unified symbolic and ethical code. He does not draw his allegory out of the tales but rediscovers it, and its lessons, throughout the canon. He thus emancipates allegory as an interpretive framework, one that neither contradicts nor depends on those of *peshat* and midrash, but subsumes and transforms both.

Consider Getz's reading of the vision of Hormiz/Hormin in Mahoza (III).[815] Superficially, his argument is structured exactly like Maharsha's.[816] He begins by accepting the *peshat* of Rashbam that this figure is a demon. Then he marks gaps: symbols that *peshat* did not explain. Yet he makes it clear from the outset that he is not committed to those gaps alone: "there are further difficulties that I have refrained from writing, but anyone who has a brain in his skull can sense and express them." Whereas Maharsha's commentary stays close to his gaps—especially on a less advanced level, such that any reader can follow how he closes gaps with his allegorical retelling to arrive at a simple moral—Getz's gaps are simply his gambit for a more expansive allegory. Hence, at the end, where he retells the story with his allegory inserted into the gaps, he freely opens and closes new gaps that he did not mark before, adding new phrases into his base text. For instance, there he glosses *bounded upon the turret of the wall* (IIIa.29) as "he did it in public, because no one had the strength to slay him, for that is how evil the demon's power was." As Getz's allegorical subtext has become the text, there is no longer any need to frame it as exegesis.

This extra gloss also shows the self-referential structure of Getz's alle-

---

Rav, 1–5, 15–176. The newer edition, Elyaqum Getz, *Sefer 'Even ha-shoham u-Me'irat 'enayim: She'elot u-teshuvot ve-hidushim u-ve'urim* (Jerusalem: Zikhron Aharon, 2014), 8–12, 13–65, has no relevant variants (see especially n. 828).

815. Originally, there were two figures, the good Ahura Mazda (Hormiz) and the evil Ahriman (Hormin). Both are known in the Talmud (b. Sanh. 39a and Tosafot b. Sanh. 39a s.v. דהורמיז; Tosafot b. B. Bat. 8a s.v. איפרא), but their Jewish names differ only by similar letters. Confusion led to compound identities. Rashbam (b. B. Bat. 73a s.v. הורמין or הורמיז; see my study cited at n. 1) identifies a demon, adopting his father's oral tradition (see also Rashi, b. Sanh. 39a s.v. דהורמיז). Ritva (b. B. Bat. 73a s.v. הורמין) cites competing traditions: a demon *or* a person close to the demons. Compare Kiperwasser ("Travels of Rabbah," 230 n. 59); Shai Secunda's debate with Reuven Kiperwasser and Dan D. Y. Shapira, "Encounters between Iranian Myth and Rabbinic Mythmakers in the Babylonian Talmud," in *Encounters by the Rivers of Babylon: Scholarly Conversations between Jews, Iranians, and Babylonians in Antiquity*, ed. Uri Gabbay and Shai Secunda, TSAJ 160 (Tübingen: Mohr Siebeck, 2014), 285–304, at 298–301.

816. I summarize the long and densely intertextual source; see Appendix §*Commentary on Tale III by Elyaqum Getz* for full annotated translation.

gory in a related way. It is a stylistic flourish that adds no new content to his allegorical interpretation of the tale. Rather, it highlights an element of the telling—the power of the demon—in order to make his allegory more vivid. As we saw, this is what Rashbam's *peshat* did so well with the tale itself. However, at the beginning of his allegory, Getz had argued against precisely that way of interpreting the following line in the tale. "If this were introduced in order to show us his great strength," he argued (i.e., if he were to read the tale like Rashbam),[817] then there would be "no point [in saying] whether or not the *mules* had a *saddle*." Initially, each element of the telling must have a fixed place in Getz's allegory. Nothing can be interpreted as if it were merely for poetic effect; that risks repeating *peshat*. By the end, on the other hand, Getz is glad to do so. At first, he had to argue against *peshat* in order to set up his allegory as a needed alternative. Now that it is established, he can use *peshat*-style reading to enhance his allegorical retelling. Once he has read his allegory into the story, he reads his allegory as if it were the story.

So far we have examined two ways in which Getz's allegory is self-referential. First, it uses the convention of interpreting the tales as a point of departure rather than a destination. The allegory has a meaning that exceeds that of the tales, and they fill it in, not vice versa. That is why Getz cites them with an open structure that does not distinguish rigorously between when he closes an interpretive gap in a tale and when he cites a tale as part of his allegory. Unlike an exegesis of the tales, his allegory determines what counts as a gap in the first place and therefore it can open or close gaps freely at any time as it unfolds. The same holds for Getz's orientation to traditional interpretive frameworks, in this case *peshat*. Here too, superficially, he follows Maharsha in cleaving *peshat*—an interpretation of the text's surface—from allegory, an interpretation of symbols and their hidden meanings. In practice, however, Getz also creatively uses *peshat*-style interpretations to heighten the impact of his allegory.

The reverse is also true. Getz's allegory never contradicts Rashbam's *peshat* approach to III, i.e., that this tale is the biography of a demon. Getz "reads downward" from *peshat*. In other words, he keeps the *peshat* intact and deepens it by adding allegory. The result is that not only the telling but also the *peshat* are stronger, not weaker; more vivid, better sourced. Overlooked or invisible aspects of the tale enter the interpretive foreground, and Rashbam's reading of the story in terms of a half-hidden world of the demons comes to seem all the more precise. This is possible because Getz's allegorical symbols are overdetermined: so dense with meaning that they can supplement *peshat* without being used up or contradicting other meanings that they also accumulate. These symbols, condensations

---

817. Getz says Rashbam *would* read the line this way, though he does not. This supports my reading of Rashbam.

of meaning, form the canon's connective tissue, enfolding potential interpretations that Getz redistributes across the surface of the tale. In so doing, he recollects the tale's parts with each other as well as a vast, complex canon of intertexts—not only the Bible and the Talmud but especially the Zohar and Ari. Yet, despite its overdetermination, his commentary generates a transparent retelling and clear moral—that is, it subsumes the functions of *peshat* and midrash—because his allegory is constantly running in the background. Like a deep syntax that regulates grammatical combinations of intertexts, every meaning that Getz's symbols create, by activating intertexts and bringing them to bear on the tale, is structured by his allegory and its lesson. This is yet another sense in which Getz's allegory is self-referential. It interprets a canon with infinite potential meaning so as to trap that potential within the symbols of its allegory and thereby allegorizes the canon itself.

To illustrate how Getz does this, we must keep his allegory in view as we summarize his reading. In short, to the old *peshat* that Hormiz is a demon, Getz adds his backstory: what kind of demon he is and how he was born. Hormiz is an *incubus*, son of a *succubus*: a female demon of the night,[818] who conceives by stealing men's semen that they have not controlled, making them fathers of half-demonic offspring.[819] This ancient myth was known to the rabbis,[820] but revived by the Zohar, which is stricter about accidental seminal emission than the Talmud and depicts a conjugal rite for warding off the *succubus* that may reflect

---

818. This association arose from the similarity of לילית (Lilith) and לילה (night). Israel Ta-Shma, "Day and Night," *Encyclopedia Judaica*, ed. Michael Berenbaum et al. (Detroit: Macmillan, 2007), 5:486–88; Raphael Patai, "Lilith," *Journal of American Folklore* 77.306 (1964): 295–314. The name may actually come from Akkadian, but that is a Jewish etymology, not a "falsche Annahme" (Kathrin Trattner, "Von Lamastu zu Lilith: Personifikationen des weiblichen Bösen in der mesopotamischen und jüdischen Mythologie," *Disputatio Philosophica* 15.1 [2013]: 109–18, at 109 n. 1).

819. See Trattner, "Von Lamastu zu Lilith"; Marcel Poorthuis, "Eve's Demonic Offspring: A Jewish Motif in German Literature," in *Eve's Children: The Biblical Stories Retold and Interpreted in Jewish and Christian Traditions*, ed. Gerard P. Luttikhuizen, TBN 5 (Leiden: Brill, 2003), 57–74; Shalom Sabar, "Childbirth and Magic: Jewish Folklore and Material Culture," in *Cultures of the Jews: A New History*, ed. David Biale (New York: Schocken, 2002), 671–722, at 672–75.

820. Lilith seduces men in sleep (b. Shabb. 151b) and she is the mother of a *halakhically* human fetus (b. Nid. 24b). Adam fathered children with female demons by his seminal emissions (Ber. Rab. 20:11 = Ber. Rab. 24:5 = Tan. §*Bereshit* 26), even involuntary (b. Eruv. 18b). Ber. Rab. 26:4 blames seminal emissions indirectly for human/divine couplings that led to the Flood (and directly, b. Sanh. 108b; Kallah Rab. 2:7, ed. Higger, 199–201). Ruth Rab. 6:1 answers its own question—why does the verse say "a woman lay at his feet"?—as excluding that she might be a demoness. In nocturnal sexual context, this midrash clearly reflects the *succubus* myth: "[Boaz] began touching her hair and said, 'Spirits don't have hair.... What are you, spirit or woman?,' he asked her."

popular anxieties.⁸²¹ The fear was certainly widely shared; as sober an authority as Thomas Aquinas gave it credence.⁸²² In Getz's world of early modern Poland, Lurianic Kabbalah had become so influential that this myth remained very much alive. The problem of controlling or atoning for seminal emissions "attracted almost obsessive attention" and was "addressed in nearly every work of moral or ethical guidance," inspiring entire books on the subject.⁸²³ Getz cites the myth in the Zohar and Ari's teachings only in passing because it is, as he says, "well known." He does not need to convince his reader of the problem. Rather, his task is to read this myth back into the Talmud and lead readers to discover his practical remedy in our strangely familiar tale.

Our tale is ripe for this retelling for a few obvious reasons. First and foremost, Hormiz is named *bar Lilith*, "son of Lilith," the demoness who is a *succubus*, and so he is an *incubus*. He acts the part: Lilith has wings, as does her *incubus*,⁸²⁴ and he seems to fly. Beyond its content, the tale lends itself to the myth because Getz can "read downward" from *peshat* interpretations that suit or already contain the myth. For instance, in the talmudic source that Rashbam cites for his *peshat* that Hormiz is a demon, he is said to dwell in the lower half of the body.⁸²⁵ In the Talmud's cultural context, this had nothing to do with the *incubus*; it refers to a Zoroastrian evil deity. For Getz's reader, however, this demon's link to the nether region makes even more sense: he was born from sexual sin. The kabbalistic realm of evil (*sitra' 'ahra'*, Other Side) maps neatly onto an inherited dualism. Similarly, at the end of the tale, where Hormiz is killed by "the authorities" or "kingdom," Rashbam cites a *peshat* that the (unstated) reason for his execution is that people "feared, lest he take the kingdom from them, for he was the demon who comes from a man who has intercourse with a

---

821. Isaiah Tishby, *The Wisdom of the Zohar: An Anthology of Texts*, trans. David Goldstein, 3 vols., Littman Library of Jewish Civilization (Oxford: Oxford University Press, 1989), 3:1363–67; Joshua Trachtenberg, *Jewish Magic and Superstition: A Study in Folk Religion* (New York: Behrman's, 1939), 51–54; Gershom Scholem, *Kabbalah and Its Symbolism*, 154–57. Patai cites an antidote: a rite to conjure a succubus safely for just a night ("Lilith," 303).

822. Trachtenberg, *Jewish Magic and Superstition*, 282–83 n. 17.

823. Gershon David Hundert, *Jews in Poland-Lithuania in the Eighteenth Century: A Genealogy of Modernity* (Berkeley: University of California Press, 2004), 131–32; and see 131–37 for a decisive treatment. This problem also animates Getz's commentary on XII, as noted by Steinmetz, "To Strengthen the Words of the Sages," 92 n. 117.

824. Rashi, b. Nid. 24b s.v. דמות לילית: the *incubus*/child of Lilith is "a demon who has a human face and wings."

825. B. Sanh. 39a: "A certain *magus* said … 'From your waist up is [the domain] of Hurmiz, from your waist down of Ahurmiz.'" See literature in Yishai Kiel, "Redesigning Tzitzit in the Babylonian Talmud in Light of Literary Depictions of the Zoroastrian Kustīg*," in Secunda and Fine eds., *Shoshannat Yaakov: Jewish and Iranian Studies in Honor of Yaakov Elman*, ed. Shai Secunda and Steven Fine, Brill Reference Library of Judaism 35 (Leiden: Brill, 2012), 185–202, at 187 nn. 5–9.

demoness, and he dwelled among men."⁸²⁶ This reflects a common belief that, due to his human father, an *incubus* is king of the demons.⁸²⁷ And it shows that this myth had already entered the *peshat* of this story, paving the way for Getz's expansive allegory.

Peering downward from that reading tradition, Getz's allegory uses the tale's leftover symbols to write out a prescription for men to avoid siring demons. First, he marks gaps in *peshat* that Rashbam had left unexplained: the setting *Mahoza*; a redundant word, *beast*;⁸²⁸ and the *saddles* or *bridles*. "It seems," he argues, "one can resolve these difficulties if [Rabbah] is showing us matters of moral discipline."⁸²⁹ The moral is to prevent the "great sin" of spilling seed that "is still leaping among us." His allegory explains each symbol accordingly. The setting is Mahoza because Mahozan men go to hell (Gehinnom),⁸³⁰ due to laziness and concupiscence.⁸³¹ "Mahozan" is a word for the sort of man who spills his seed, like the horseman pursuing the demon. He rides a *beast* because he did not ride a *saddle* but bareback, stimulating himself.⁸³² Therefore he *could not overcome* the demon. Con-

---

826. Rashbam, b. B. Bat. 73a s.v. הורמיז בר מלכא וקטלוהו ה"ג שמעין בי מלכא וקטלוהו. Ritva, b. B. Bat. 73a s.v. לילתא (ed. Ilan, 592) also cites two *peshatim* here but neither reflects the myth of the *succubus/incubus*. In fact, one of those traditions debunks the tale by making the demon into a mere human "conjurer." This highlights Rashbam's new approach. See n. 772.

827. Trachtenberg cites a fourteenth-century source (*Jewish Magic and Superstition*, 283 n. 19). See earlier sources in Patai, "Lilith," 314 n. 62. Getz will refer directly to this belief in this context: "I have found [a source] that the demon who is their king must be one who is born from [the seminal emissions] of humans."

828. חיותא, as in mss. M, E, *'En Ya'aqov*, and *Haggadot ha-Talmud* (See *DS ad loc.*). In mss. H, P, V the reading is *steed* (סוסיא), noted in *Masoret ha-Shas*). Getz's text of the tale is close to Vilna but not always. His approach is fluid: he seems to select readings like "beast" that suit his allegory; to combine readings from different text traditions; and to stretch the meaning of minor features of all texts available to him, even if they are unknown to those with whom he argues. In this line, for instance, he will later read כי רכיב חיותא ("*while* riding a beast") in the stronger sense "because" (מחמת), as reading that idea into the particle כי forestalls a hypothetical objection to his allegory, even though כי appears only in the prints (and ms. V).

829. On moral discipline [*mussar*] as the basis for Getz's allegory and its relationship to the interpretive tendencies of the period, see Steinmetz, "To Strengthen the Words of the Sages," 61–76, 96–118. Over two centuries later, the Hasidic authority Rabbi Zadok ha-Kohen of Lublin took the same approach to the battle between Moses and Og King of Bashan, reading in the same Lurianic concepts of "seed"/"covenant" and sexual restraint to explain gaps in the *aggadah*. Admiel Kosman, "The Story of a Giant Story: The Winding Way of Og King of Bashan in the Jewish Haggadic Tradition," *HUCA* 73 (2002): 157–90, at 184–85. I thank my student Avidan Halivni for calling my attention to this wonderful essay.

830. B. Betzah 32b (wealthy Babylonian Jews in general. Getz infers Mahozans, who "do not work"; see next note).

831. Rashi, b. Shabb. 12a s.v. בני מחוזא; Rashi to b. Shabb. 109a s.v. מפנקי; Rashi to b. Rosh Hash. 17a s.v. בני מחוזא. Compare Rashi to b. Ketub. 62a s.v. מפנקי דמערבא: the "pampered men of the West" (Palestine) are "decadent in food and drink, and therefore healthy and full of virility for the bedchamber," ergo, pampered = concupiscent.

832. According to Rashi (b. Nid. 14a s.v. דמכף), that is why a righteous donkey-driver

versely, the *saddles* of two mules on two bridges, with bridles,[833] must have been put on by two other men, whose existence Getz infers. They are the antithesis of a bareback rider: they tame their impulses ("bridle the inner beast," we might say). They stand on *two bridges*, which symbolize danger.[834] But the demon cannot harm them. Because they did not *spill a single drop* of their seminal emissions, even during sex,[835] they withstand Hormiz as he *bounded from one to the other* trying to kill them. Finally, because they used the best defense against Lilith stealing their seed at night, which is to recite Shema at bedtime,[836] God's *kingdom heard [shemaʿu]* their prayer and *killed* the demon on their behalf.

Note again how freely Getz opens and closes gaps in the story. He explains not only the gaps with which he began, but also the *single drop* and the ending. Those gaps open up in his retelling and are closed within his allegory itself–not in response to his or others' exegetical problems. This self-referential structure of his allegory even allows him to patch a glaring contradiction between his allegory and the tale. In the tale, it is Hormiz who *did not spill a single drop*. In the allegory, it is the new characters—the two virtuous men standing on the two bridges. Getz patches this gap by implying that the teller was himself an allegorist who spoke in symbols. "He made it plain for the eye to see" that Hormiz's feat of juggling liquid between two vessels, across two bridges, in the middle of a storm, without spilling a single drop, symbolizes the practical lesson of Getz's allegory. It does not matter which character does so in the story. It matters that one sees the symbol and grasps the moral. The tale is always already allegorical, encoded through and through. Any petty exegete who attacks the allegory as self-contradictory is trying to redraw a line between text and commentary that no longer exists.

If one step toward allegory's total emancipation is to recast the teller as Ur-allegorist, who "[spoke] words of parable and figure ... in the manner of riddle and wisdom, in order to discipline the multitude," the next is to subsume other interpretive frameworks into allegory. We just saw how

---

(see, e.g., b. Ber. 56b) is "saddled" and a wicked donkey-driver is not (b. Nid. 14a; b. Qidd. 82a; it also applies to elephants [b. Ber. 57a]).

833. Rashbam to b. B. Bat. 73a s.v. סריגן: "for there was a saddle *with bridle* placed upon the mules."

834. B. Shabb. 32a: "And men? Where are they tested? At the moment that they are crossing a bridge." (Satan kills men in a "ferry" [b. Shabb. 32a]). Getz may derive a sexual sense of that scenario from b. Qidd. 81a. Maharsha (b. B. Bat. 73a s.v. לדידי) calls Hormiz a "minion [בר גונדא] of Satan"–a term for the Angel of Death [b. B. Metz. 86a]).

835. Reading the *goblet* where they did not "spill a single drop" as the vagina (for which "cup" is a standard idiom; see Michael Satlow, *Tasting the Dish: Rabbinic Rhetorics of Sexuality*, 2nd ed., BJS 303 [Providence, RI: Brown Judaic Studies, 2020 (1995)], 127). Getz also refers to the vagina as "a limed cistern which does not *lose a single drop*" (Avot 2:8).

836. B. Ber. 5a. Getz relies more directly on the Ari here; see Appendix §*Commentary on Tale III by Elyaqum Getz*.

Getz subverts the threat of *peshat*; above, we saw how he subsumes *peshat*. He "reads downward" from a shared myth; selects symbols that suit his allegory because of their literary context or their previous *peshatim*;[837] and even reads his own allegorical retelling through a *peshat* lens for poetic effect. Here we also see a case of how he subsumes midrash. After all, his allegory's heroes are nowhere to be found in the tale. Rather, Getz reads them in by drawing an inference from a narrative gap: the story says *two mules were saddled* on *two bridges*—so presumably, two people saddled them. That is a textbook technique of midrash.[838]

Getz's creation of new characters from gaps in the story functions differently, however. His midrash replicates his allegory more neatly than Maharsha's—for whom allegory still works as an exegesis of the tale—and far more than classical midrashim, which maintain tension between the biblical story and its retelling by reading in characters who represent not one but many possible interpretations of the story.[839] Rather than a plurality of new perspectives, Getz reads in the only truly crucial character: his reader, who is focalized by the men on the bridge.[840] Through these men's eyes, the reader sees attacks by a demon and his supernatural power as he flies and juggles liquid in the throes of a storm. Through their eyes, he perceives what Hormiz's actions signify: a symbol of what he must do to protect himself. Through their eyes, he witnesses divine salvation. Rather than read in characters who might focalize other readers of the story and different interpretations, Getz uses midrash to validate his allegory's self-referential structure of meaning. He typecasts his reader as a silent character and leaves him no one else in the retelling with whom to identify. As a result, the reader is as restrained as the characters who play him. By subsuming the dialogic potential of midrash into allegory, Getz also bridles his reader's interpretive role.

No surprise that Getz's allegory is as repressive hermeneutically as it is practically. He wants a reader's creativity and procreation to fit a strict norm, not to foster hybrids or critique. As a result, however, gender comes

---

837. Similarly, consider his use of Rashi's *peshat* that the wicked donkey-driver does not use a saddle because he stimulates himself (n. 832). How apt this odd comment now seems, in a story about virtuous riders who bridle their sin! Even where Getz's allegory is sourced directly from *peshat*, putting it back into narrative form subsumes *peshat*.

838. For example, Abraham's anonymous servants ("lads"), who accompany him after he "saddled his ass" (Gen 22:3) and wait with it at the foot of Moriah, turn into Ishmael and Eliezer in midrash (Ginzberg, *Legends*, 1:228).

839. Heinemann, *Darkhe ha-aggadah*, 21–22, 50–51, 94–95. See further Levinson, *Twice Told Tale*, 150–91.

840. On focalization, see Mieke Bal, *Narratology: Introduction to the Theory of Narrative*, trans. Christine Van Boheemen, 4th ed. (Toronto: University of Toronto Press, 2017), 132–54, at 135: "The reader watches with the character's eyes and will, in principle, be inclined to accept the vision presented by that character."

into focus as a problem within his own framework. While one critique may be that, by developing the *succubus* myth, Getz demonizes women and fuels a misogynistic castration anxiety fantasy—an allegorical *vagina dentata*—I find it more curious that he says nothing about real women. They should play a role in his story; he acknowledges *en passant* that a wife is involved in this act, which can cause spilled semen and sire demons. Yet he rests all prophylactic responsibility on the husband, contrary to his talmudic source.[841] Why does he delete women from his allegory for the mechanics of conjugal sex? Patriarchy and a normatively male readership are necessary but not sufficient conditions for this choice.

Getz is trying to resolve a bizarre asymmetry between men and women in the Talmud. Women are said to die in childbirth as a punishment for being lax in menstrual impurity. With cruel logic, one dictum interprets this as measure-for-measure punishment: by the womb, for the sin of the womb.[842] The Talmud then adds that a corresponding site of punishment for men is "when they are crossing a bridge." One thing is not like the other. Even if—as the Talmud says, and Rashi emphasizes—"bridge" is only an example of a dangerous place, like childbirth inasmuch as it is a precarious transition ("liminal," as anthropologists say),[843] the asymmetry remains. Why would a "bridge" cause a man's measure-for-measure punishment? For what?! Getz solves this problem by drawing an analogy between genders. If the womb is the site of women's procreative transgression and causes their death in childbirth from the demon Lilith, then seminal emissions are the same for men and cause them to sire demons by Lilith. Therefore, *bridge* is a symbol for the male analogy to childbirth: the interval during sex after a man withdraws but before he has reentered to ejaculate, as the Talmud dictates.[844] It is a time when he is vulnerable to

---

841. A dictum in b. Nid. 71a says that man and wife are rewarded (by a son) if he withdraws and waits for her to ejaculate before he does. On the "two-seed" theory of conception here, see Gwynn Kessler, *Conceiving Israel: The Fetus in Rabbinic Narratives*, Divinations (Philadelphia: University of Pennsylvania Press, 2009), 107–16. This norm requires communication between the partners and benefits both. Getz turns the norm into a stricture for the man alone, who is solely liable. If he ejaculates prematurely, even a "single drop," he will sire not a son but a demon. I thank Moulie Vidas for discussing this with me (personal communication, 29 June 2022).

842. M. Shabb. 2:6; b. Shabb. 31b–32a. See Fonrobert, *Menstrual Purity*, 29–36.

843. Arnold van Gennep, *The Rites of Passage*, trans. Monika B. Vizedom and Gabrielle L. Caffee (Chicago: University of Chicago Press, 1960). Rashi, b. Shabb. 32a s.v. כעין גשר adds the example "one who goes out on the road." Rashbam, b. B. Bat. 73a s.v. אקופי דשורא explains the *horseman* who *could not overcome him* and is even—he adds—*unaware* of the demon, by a similar liminal logic. This shows why one "should not go out on the road alone" (see Avot 3:4).

844. As Getz says, "A man who *projects* from one vessel to another must control himself so that he does not *spill a single drop* on the ground [= the wife's belly; Gen. 38:9 and sources in Kessler, *Conceiving Israel*, 117]; so, too, must a man [control himself] who *projects* from his

Lilith, who, like the troll in European folklore, lurks between *two bridges* (an image suggestive of two bodies),[845] waiting to pounce. At that moment a man must stand firm and bridle himself so as not to *spill a single drop*. If not, his own spawn will kill him.[846] Getz thus uses allegory to fill a gap in the canon. In his eyes, he is not deleting women from a story of how demons prey on sexual impurity—women are there in the Talmud!—but adding men.

Getz's stringent sexual ethics and radical emancipation of allegory go hand in hand. Because the symbols of this allegorical framework hold a stable meaning across all contexts, he can use them to read intertexts together, translating them into a fixed symbolic vocabulary. *Bridge* is a symbol for the hidden meaning: "men's danger due to sexual impurity." Because the symbol contains that meaning, it can be read back into both intertexts in their own contexts: the tale and the Talmud's other discussion of ferries, demons, rivers, and bridges. This deep syntax of symbols makes possible new conjunctions of symbols and new meanings that neither contradict, nor are reducible to, the meanings derived from *peshat* and midrash. Rather, allegory subsumes *peshat* and midrash by reading itself back onto the surface of the tale or between its lines. Allegory retells the tale as if its symbols were characters, or discovers new characters who focalize its lesson for the reader. Allegory mimics past frameworks even as it hollows out their exegetical core because, for the allegorist, a true story can never be fully told.

I have argued that Getz's emancipated allegory is not merely loose or tendentious by contrast to Maharsha's exegetical allegory but methodical in its own way. Like his kabbalistic models, he creates a self-referential and expansive retelling of a canonical tale that uses the gaps of older interpretive frameworks but also freely opens and closes its own. Into those gaps, Getz reads an ancient myth with fresh currency in his culture. His eisegesis condenses a deep syntax of symbolic meanings into a demonological reading of III, which achieves several things at once: teaching male

---

'vessel of the covenant of skin' into a vessel which does not 'lose a single drop' [= the vagina; Avot 2:8]." By "vessel of the covenant," Getz refers to the kabbalistic concept *pegam ha-berit*, "blemishing the covenant/circumcision"; see literature in Hundert, *Jews in Poland-Lithuania*, 133 n. 12.

845. If the bridges are bodies, then "bounded from one to the other and back again" places the demon at the scene. In Lurianic rite, Lilith is quite literally in bed with the couple, who address her: "You, who are wrapped in the sheet ... and are present [to seize the child], let go [of your hold on the sheet]." Hayyim Vital in Tishby, *Wisdom of the Zohar*, 3:1376 n. 88.

846. "And the statement of the Zohar is well known, *for according to a man's deed, He will repay him* [Job 34:11]: the same demon whom a man creates himself is the demon who will *repay him* his comeuppance." See Appendix §*Commentary on Tale III by Elyaqum Getz*, section [3]. Just as his source (b. Shabb. 32a) goes on to extol repentance and "angels" as a lifesaving remedy, Getz develops the same idea in his conclusion, section [9].

sexual ethics; subsuming and borrowing older ways to interpret the tale; and correlating gaps in the tale with other gaps in the canon. As a reader, Getz has a panoramic vision of a canon unified by symbolic correspondences and hidden meanings. This allegorical canon offers a vast canvas for his creative retelling and interpretation of the tale. On the other hand, Getz blinkers his own implied male reader. Like the original teller,[847] he narrows the reader's vision to focus on a tiny detail in the foreground — *a single drop* — and learn from it a strict rule of conduct. His radical emancipation of allegory makes his implied reader more rigid.

The Plain Sense of Allegory

The line of allegorical reading that we have traced throughout this chapter vibrates with a tension between the two poles of interpretation as such: surface and depth. For *peshat*, this became a tension only where a tale's meaning could not be found on its surface. Once the reader of a tale, in its own literary context, contradicted its teller by interpreting the tale as a punishment and not a reward, this opened a gap in its surface that led to a breakdown of *peshat*: Rashbam's contextual close reading and sublime retelling of *peshat* cried for deeper coherence. In order to restore a unified meaning to the tale and retell it to teach a single moral, Maharsha reinterpreted it symbolically. He assigned hidden meanings to its images and setting, based on their correspondences to those meanings elsewhere in biblical and rabbinic sources. This method presumed a more allegorical canon: a universe of intertexts speaking a language of symbols that can communicate across contexts. In his turn to allegory, surface and depth had already begun to separate. To read the tale as a dream, then decipher its symbols with the talmudic dreambook, had the potential to split the surface of the narrative from its meaning, collection from canon.

Yet Maharsha held these two layers together in a seamless retelling that stayed close to gaps in *peshat*, rather than using gaps as an occasion for radically new ideas or to find one hidden meaning everywhere. His allegory worked as midrash in both classical senses of the term: exegesis and preaching. For general readers, he created an elegant retelling with a moral based on biblical stories where the tale's symbols bear similar surface meanings. Only for initiates, more likely to focus on talmudic intertexts and to read his allegory as a commentary *on* his commentary in its timely polemical context, did he more fully allegorize the Jewish canon. For such readers, there was a stake in his allegory beyond the tale — to defend the Wisdom of its own method from other methods — that advanced readers were obliged to uphold by reading his meta-allegory

---

847. See analysis of IIIb in chapter 3 §*The Uses of Repetition*.

into each intertext and reapplying his commentary's categories and binaries across the canon. This appeal to a meta-reading of the allegory was our first glimpse of an allegory beyond midrash, where deep meaning builds on deep meaning without returning to the surface of the tale itself.

Getz went further in this direction to emancipate allegory from exegesis by developing its self-referentiality in three ways. First, he subverted *peshat* or subsumed *peshat* and midrash into allegory, using their sensibilities and conventions rhetorically to make his allegory more vivid and dogmatic, even as he foreclosed or ignored the alternative implications of both methods for his uses of them (e.g., he shifted attention away from Hormiz and "read in" new characters who focalize his tale's lesson monologically, rather than dialogically as in classical midrash). Second, he "read downward" from the surface to the depths, using gaps in *peshat* as an occasion for fresh ideas rather than to restore coherence to the tale (e.g., a new rendition of an old myth). Third, he read the Talmud as if it were always already allegorical, arguing that its teller spoke in code and that his symbols' hidden meanings ("bridge") did not change across intertexts, even if they did not suit the context (decoding "bridge" as a symbol of one moment in coitus, whereas the Talmud has only a vague analogy, men on a bridge : women in childbirth). Getz could read his allegory so freely into our tales because it emanates not from them or their intertexts but from elsewhere: a mystical framework more expansive than the canon he interprets. As, in that framework, symbolic meaning is immanent and unbound by the law of contradiction,[848] one deep interpretation called out to another until the tale no longer had a surface.

We have compared these stages in the emergence of an allegorical canon in terms of how they direct a reader's attention from narrative foreground to canonical background, from a tale's surface to its symbolic depths. *Peshat* reads from surface to surface: the story expands and grows more sublime on the same narrative plane. Allegory, in the mode of midrash, closes gaps in the story's surface by deriving deeper meanings and a moral lesson. Mystical allegory, by contrast, posits that its deep meaning is always there–its stable symbols patch or subsume any surface resistance.

The Gra's style of allegory holistically reads together texts from the entire Jewish canon to transcend and sublimate this tension between surface and depth. He evokes, we might say, the plain sense of allegory, by finding symbols and their deep meanings on the very surface of rabbinic and biblical intertexts alike. The precision of a *peshat* close reading, which creates a vivid and moving but not distorted retelling of a tale in context, also applies to his allegories. He reads each intertext as saturated with symbolic meaning and performs a close reading to make each symbol fit

---

848. Idel, *Absorbing Perfections*, 78, 110, 285, 453–55.

its context naturally. His allegory seems to come from its sources, rather than to have been imposed on them; read out, not read in. As a result, his canon is so fully allegorical—so dense with symbolic correspondences—that sources and interpretations seem to speak together as if before Babel. By reading our tales as if they belong in an allegorical canon, the Gra's overcoming of interpretation by interpretation tames their strangeness momentarily.

He models this method in his commentary on tale II, which comes first in his text.[849]

> Rabbah said:
> They that go down to the sea in ships recounted to me:
> That wave that sinks the ship appears like a white shoot of flame upon its crest, but we strike it with poles on which is engraven: "*I am that I am, YAH, YHWH of Hosts, Amen, Amen, Selah,*" and it subsides.

The core logic of the Gra's commentary on this vision is the same as that of the earliest implied reader of tales I–III, who engaged their telling in terms of a mythic "understory." As we saw in chapter 2, a reader attuned to cited verses and their reading tradition in early midrash would have heard the telling in stereo: each event and image in the tale correlates with images and events in the understory. The verses and their associated midrashim supplied readers with a score to create a fugue of meaning, conducting readers to interpret the tale by correlating it with the understory. Crucially, we saw that, while readers surely shaped the understory in different ways by correlating it to different moments in the telling differently, it retained thematic and narrative coherence. The verses had a tale to tell that readers could not ignore. This understory is a mythological battle between chaos and God's saving power, personified by signs (a "white shoot of flame" on the wave's "head" vs. God's Name). It stages the antithesis between cosmic elements (Water and Dry Land) on both vertical ("going up/down" in peril) and horizontal axes (the sea subdued by God's Name and sand of the shore). Ultimately, a reader aware of sources that identify God with the other "side" of the cosmic conflict was led to contemplate and praise the deeper unity of divine being.

---

849. I translate from the text of the tale in Gra in *Be'ure Aggadot*, 1. It is identical to Vilna. Only prints and the corrector of ms. E (minus *Selah* at the end) have these four divine Names, followed by "Amen Amen." Other manuscripts have different divine names, and/or no *Amen* or three *Amenim*. Those variants would not support the Gra's argument in his commentary §7 below. In this case, the Gra seems to have preferred a close reading of his *textus receptus*. But, on his Talmud text criticism, see Eliyahu Stern, "The Mitnagdim and the Rabbinic Era as the Age of Reason," in *Time and Eternity in Jewish Mysticism: That Which Is Before and That Which Is After*, ed. Brian Ogren, Studies in Jewish History and Culture 48 (Leiden: Brill, 2015), 136–47, at 139.

The Gra's allegory inverts the same structure. Now, the understory *is* the story, and the story is a myth, grounded more directly in *kabbalah* than in Scripture or midrash; although, as we will see, he blends those layers. He begins:

> It is befitting to interpret that all of these events are according to their order [דכל המעשים כסדרן] on the verse of *Those who go down to the sea* [Ps 107:23],[850] as I wrote in my commentary on Jonah that this world is called "Sea" and the body is called "Ship,"[851] by means of which the soul enters this world.

The Gra frames the tale's symbols with a core myth of Lurianic *kabbalah*: "contraction" of the divine presence (צמצום). As sailors "go down" to the Sea, the soul "goes down" to this world: a world of sorrow ("smallness," *tsa'ar*) and sexualized evil (the "Impulse" or *yetser*).[852] The Gra's commentary proceeds to retell our talmudic tale as a rendition of that Lurianic myth, "ordered" by verses (Ps. 107:23–26) and their understory—the memory of their myth in midrash. By allegorizing the entire canon, he reshapes all four of those textual layers into a single story.

> *It is they who have seen the deeds of YHWH, and His wonders in the deep* (Ps 107:24): for they always see how he judges each according to his deeds, measure for measure. And he is ordering all wicked measures [of charac-

---

850. Gra, *Be'ure Aggadot*, 1. I translate from the manuscript as it is cited in this edition, not from the print. There are many issues with the textual transmission of the Gra's oral Torah that I cannot deal with here (see Movshovitz's introduction to Gra, *Be'ure Aggadot*, 11–14). Certainly, the print contains clear expansions and deviations from the manuscript.

851. Gra, *Aderet Eliyahu*, Hebrew text in *Yonah: "Journey of the Soul"; An Allegorical Commentary Adapted from the Vilna Gaon's* Aderes Eliyahu, ed. Moshe Schapiro (Rahway: Mesorah, 1997), 86–95, at 86 s.v. וימצא אניה. I do not venture into the Gra's reading of Jonah in the Zohar beyond broad outlines of the myth that he also reads out of our tales. See n. 730 and Aryeh Wineman, "The Zohar on Jonah: Radical Retelling or Tradition?," *Hebrew Studies* 31 (1990): 57–69.

852. Gra (*Be'ure Aggadot*, 1) comments on Ps 107:23 here, *Who do tasks in the mighty waters* [מים רבים]: "As they [tasks of the Sea = this world] are those of sorrow [צער; for ימים = צער, see Vay. Rab. 19:5 (ed. Margulies, 429); Exod. Rab. I.34.1 (ed. Shinan, 98–99)], so are they called "mighty" [רב ים = "great Sea"], as is written on my commentary to the *Megillot*." In the latter commentary (Gra, *Be'ure Aggadot*, 317), he comments on the same letters (ימים רבים, *many days*, Esther 1:4) that those days when Jews observe menstrual impurity or fasting, that is, denial of the body, "are days of sorrow to the Evil Impulse [ימי צער ליצר הרע]": ימים and מים reverse a symbolic identity. For צר = צער, see Gra, *Be'ure Aggadot*, 5: "All the waves are sufferings [צרות, literally "compressions"] ... *all thy breakers and thy waves passed over me* [Jonah 2:4 = Ps 42:7 [42:8]; my trans.]. And they are the emissaries of Satan, and their heads are 12 "princes" [= archangels: Rashbam, b. B. Bat. 73a s.v. צוציתא דנורא חיורתא, s.v. גלא ליה ורמא; compare Tosafot, b. Avod. Zar. 17a s.v. עד]" (for Satan = the Evil Impulse, who "goes down" to tempt Job to sin, see b. B. Bat. 16a). In sum, the Gra reads the Sea as a symbol of this world's sorrow/suffering/evil, to which the soul/*Shekhinah* descends/contracts.

ter] and the comeuppance of each one: *He speaks and raises [the storm wind and it makes the waves loom high]"* (Ps 107:25). And thus orders Rabbah bar bar Hanah here.

The Gra begins to read his allegory out of the tale while preserving its understory. First, he divides the tellers. Each is responsible for one side of the story: the tale on the one hand, the understory on the other. After all, Rabbah himself retells this particular tale and "orders" its message by prooftexts: it was told to him by sailors. The Gra turns those sailors into the main characters in his own allegory. Like the soul, sailors "go down to the sea" — suffering of this world — where they experience the allegory's symbols, binary oppositions, and moral lesson, in a stance of mystical devotion. "It is they who contemplate the upheavals of this world":[853] that is, the sailors focalize the allegory.[854] Rabbah, for his part, becomes the allegory's editor ("orderer"): the guiding hand behind its understory.

This role of Rabbah as "orderer" is also a meta-allegory for the Gra's own interpretive framework. As he says, not only the verse at the beginning, but the next verse as well—in fact, this entire unit of mythic and midrashic tradition around Ps 107:23–26[855] — "orders" the allegory according to its understory, just as we saw in chapter 2 that it did long ago for early readers of I–III.[856] As early readers created meaning from our tales using this "storm at sea" as a narrative frame, interpreting them in counterpoint with received meanings of its imagery and ending, so the Gra

---

853. הם המתבוננים בתהפוכות עולם הזה. Gra, *Be'ure Aggadot*, 2–3. On "contemplation," see Jonathan Garb, "From Fear to Awe in Luzzatto's *Mesillat Yesharim*," *European Journal of Jewish Studies* 14.2 (2020): 285–99, at 295.

854. Compare the role of the "bridled" mule-drivers on the "bridges" in Getz's allegory; see n. 840. Each allegorist's choice to focalize his reading through these two characters responds to a dichotomy in the Talmud: "Most donkey-drivers are wicked ... most sailors are pious" (b. Qidd. 82a; Rashi *ad loc.* s.v. הספנין רובן חסידים).

855. On this subunit, see chapter 2, §*The Storm as Framing Device*, n. 74, and chapter 3 §*Chronological Layers* 2, especially n. 491.

856. See the end of his comment on I (the second tale in his version): Gra, *Be'ure Aggadot*, 8: "And Rabbah bar bar Hanah ordered this according to the measure of pride ... he ordered it according to the order of the verses. And the first story (II) is on the verse *He speaks and raises the storm wind* (Ps 107:25a) ... and the second story (I) is on the following verse, *And it makes the waves loom high* [Ps 107:25b]." The Gra pauses the understory in III. For IV, his attack on *pilpul*, he applies the same moral about pride, based on the same verse (Gra, *Be'ure Aggadot*, 17). He continues the allegory in V (Gra, *Be'ure Aggadot*, 23): "The entire subject of this dictum [i.e., story] is those who lack faith, for they cannot learn due to their 'vexation' [= Evil Impulse; Gra, *Aderet Eliyahu*, 86, s.v. וימצא אניה].... And so is its order in Psalms [107:26]: *They reel and sway like a drunkard / and all their wisdom is swallowed up.*" After his comments on tales I–V, we only have one, on Rabbah's final tale in the collection (XV). It seems that the focus of his attention on our tales was to pursue an allegorical reading of I–V in light of Ps 107:23–26.

reads his allegory out of our tales by "ordering" its own symbols according to its understory.

As the understory is still so generative, his allegory fits it better than one might expect. Elements of Lurianic myth that the Gra chooses to emphasize correspond closely to the mythic understory. He re-reveals the same battle between God and evil/chaos (the *yetser*, the Other Side). He uses the same signs for each: a "white shoot of flame" and divine Names held by the sailors. He stresses the same cosmic antithesis of Sea and Dry Land and hence, the same literary language: dangerous "ascent" and "descent" versus the safety of the horizontal plane. This continuity is not merely a result of referring to shared sources or loosely recollecting stock motifs. His allegory has the effect of a plain-sense reading because it retells a story its reader knows.[857] That is not the story in Ps 107:23–26 or in its midrash. It is not in the tales or in the Zohar. It is an interpretive history of all of those stories, itself a story, retold on the most familiar lines.

Knowing the tales' history as we now do, we can experience this plain-sense effect of the Gra's allegory by reading through the rest of his commentary on this tale as a whole, *without* initially thinking about its meaning in terms of sources. His lemmata from the tale are in italics. I preserve the flowing and holistic quality of his tissue of quotations by replacing only his formulae for quoting any source with ellipses, and moving those sources to my own footnotes in the relevant section of the Appendix, where each is cited in full, greatly aided by the editor of his published text. [Square brackets expand the context of his sources and add my clarifications.] After an initial reading and reflection on his allegory in its own terms, I will discuss a few sources of its eight sections [also added].

>§1. *The wave that sinks a ship*: ... The body is called a 'ship' and all the sufferings which overwhelm it are called 'waves'.... All thy breakers and thy waves passed over me. And that is the Angel of Death who puts a person to death, *that sinks* ... and it is the Evil Inclination, who leads a person astray ... that is the Evil Inclination [that is the Angel of Death, who "goes down" and leads astray, "goes up" and prosecutes, "goes down" and takes the soul], who *appears like a white shoot of flame* ... as in the case of Rav Amram the Pious [who took an oath against the Evil Inclination to make it go out from him, and] it went out from him like a pillar of fire.

>§2. [*White*] *on its head*: At the beginning [literally *head*], when it leads him astray, it shows him fifty signs of purity that it is permitted.... For the lips [of a strange woman] drop as an honeycomb.... But her end is bitter

---

857. On the continued centrality of contextual canonical reading within theosophical, as opposed to ecstatic, *kabbalah*, see Moshe Idel, *Kabbalah: New Perspectives* (New Haven: Yale University Press, 1988), 208.

as wormwood / [sharp as a two-edged sword], which is the sword of the Angel of Death, and a bitter drop hangs between her feet, and her feet go down to death.

§3. And all this causes subjugation to empires and sufferings for us.... [Lord of the Universe], it is revealed and known before you that our will is to do your will, and what holds us back? [The leaven in the dough and the subjugation of the empires. May it be your will to save us from their hands, and may we repent and perform the statutes of your will with a perfect heart].... For without subjugation to empires, we would not let the leaven rise: And they baked unleavened cakes ... because they had been cast out of Egypt, and there was no subjugation to empires upon them.

§4. But in this [tale] we have two guarantees: First, that even in exile, we will be delivered from all evil.... And yet for all that, when they be in the land of their enemies, I will not cast them away [neither will I abhor them, to destroy them utterly, and to break My covenant with them], and similarly, [He shall call upon Me, and I will answer him]; I will be with him in suffering [בצרה]; [I will rescue him.] And second, that we are guaranteed to be redeemed from exile. The first was guaranteed to us in Egypt ... I am that I am, I am what I will be with you in this subjugation [and I will be with you in subjugation to empires in the future.] And for the second [to redeem us from exile], we have a pledge: ... The Hand upon the Throne of the LORD: the LORD will have war with Amalek. And ... His Throne is not perfected until He has redeemed us.

§5. And the matter of His Name is known ... from the day that the Temple was destroyed, it is enough for the world [to use two letters of the Name.... Let the completion of the soul praise YAH.] And the matter of His Throne [is also known], for his greatness and kingship is through the nation of Israel, and when Israel are in subjection, his kingdom is not perfected, and therefore at the sea they said: YHWH will reign [forever and ever]. For there is no king without a host [i.e., army]. And YHWH will not be called Hosts until He redeems and rules His host.... Our Redeemer, YHWH of Hosts [is His Name, the Holy One of Israel], then [the moon] shall be confounded [and the sun ashamed, for the Lord of Hosts will rule.]

§6. And that is ... *But we strike [the sorrow/suffering of this world, i.e., the Evil Impulse and subjugation to the empires] with oaths ("poles") on which is engraven: I am that I am, YAH, YHWH of Hosts.*

§7. And for what merit can we expect all this, given that all arousal must be from below? ... [Since the day the Temple was destroyed], each day is more [cursed] than the last.... But on what does the world stand? On the "sanctification of the order," *Qedusha desidra,* and on saying, "May His great Name be blessed" after *aggadah...* A land of darkness, as darkness itself; and of the shadow of death, without any order. See: if there are orders (of prayer and the study of *aggadah*, then the land) shall appear from out of the darkness.]

§8. And similarly, [*Qedusha desidra*] saves us for the world to come.... Anyone who answers 'Amen' in this world merits [and answers 'Amen' in the world to come.... Blessed be the Lord God of Israel, Lord of Israel, from [this] world to eternity]: Amen and Amen. And ... One who answers Amen with all his strength, they open to him the gates [of the Garden of Eden.... Open ye the gates, that the righteous nation which keeps the faith may enter in. Do not read: "Which keeps the faith [*shomer 'emunim*]," but "Who say Amen, *she-'omerim amen*]." Those who say Amens (*she-'omerim Amenim*): that is, two Amens. And that is what he is saying [at the end of the tale]: *Amen Amen Selah and [the Wave of exile and sufferings and subjugation to foreign empires] subsides.*

Even on the surface of this allegory we can appreciate how much of the understory it preserves and develops. The understory is, as it were, its plain sense. In broadest outline, they tell the same story: the nation of Israel's exile and redemption. Their casting of characters is different but not radically so. The ancient Sea was once a foreign god, subdued by God at the mythic battle of Creation and, in turn, by midrash in its retelling of the Parting of the Sea. The Sea is still a symbol for Israel's suffering under foreign dominion. It only receives a new accent: the exilic condition causes lust, which causes death. The waves' ascent and descent in the tales and in Ps 107 still symbolize a dangerous oscillation between heaven and earth. Now it is an evil intermediary, Satan, who "goes up/comes down" to exact God's judgment on Israel's sinners, rather than Hormiz, who figured primordial chaos and transgression as opposed to divine order. For the same reason, the "white shoot of flame" still echoes the exodus, but it is no longer a symbol of God's dominion.[858] It is no Burning Bush but a Lurianic "pillar of fire": lust, the Evil Impulse.[859]

Given this new theme of lust, "evil" in the Gra's allegory becomes a more specific concept than it was in the original understory. Here, the Gra is at his most Lurianic: he fuses the "strange woman" of Proverbs (whose seduction is both cause and effect of Israel's exile) with the Angel of Death, echoing the *succubus* myth that Getz already read into the tales.[860]

---

858. *Shekhinah* can be black fire, the space between the letters: see n. 337; Idel, *Absorbing Perfections*, 45–79.

859. Conversely, "a shoot of flame went out" from a sage as a sign of his ascetic virtue (b. Ta'an. 25a, see n. 811).

860. The "bitter drop" on tip of the "sword" in §2 = semen. (For "fetid drop" = semen, see Avot 3:1). The sexual allegory is reinforced when the Gra infers—from the fact that Lilith i.e., the "sword" of the Angel of Death, is said in the Talmud to "stand" above a man's head—his own commentary's new phrase, "between her feet." This may allude to the popu-

The sexual aspect of "arousal from below"/"arousal from above"—the erotic union of God and Israel, whose prayer and repentance seduce the Shekhinah to descend, just as the soul "goes down to the Sea"—is pure *kabbalah*, albeit with older roots.[861] Indeed, it might be possible to read the Gra's allegory in this way: as a dialogue, not between the tale's symbols and its understory, but between its symbols and other symbols (i.e., Sefirot such as Throne that he correlates with the tale).

I would argue, however, that the ancient understory's mythic battle of God and chaos remains no less generative for the Gra's allegory. He is not only rewriting a Lurianic myth, and the keyword of his commentary is not only in a Lurianic vocabulary. Rather, he thematizes the old antithesis of chaos: "order."[862] Just as it was for the old fugue, restoring "order" is a key to his allegory's theosophy, its re-revelation of the ontological structure of the cosmos. As in the understory, God's role in this structure is to restore order and dominion over the Sea as an agent of chaos. That, for the Gra, is the tale's hidden-not-so-hidden narrative of exile and redemption.

As in the understory, each weapon in God's arsenal refines a nuance of that story within the allegory. One Name on the sailors' poles is no magic wand, but a declaration of ontology across the vicissitudes of time: "I am that I am" in exile and redemption, in this world and the world to come.[863] Other Names (YAH, YHWH, Hosts) symbolize complementary aspects of God's dominion. The shorter YAH symbolizes descent ("contraction") of the soul/Shekhinah to this world of suffering. Ultimately, the longer YHWH, Israel's king and ruler, will "encamp" with his Host in messianic splendor, putting sun and moon to shame.[864] By the same token, the sailors' "poles" symbolize two "oaths": to be with Israel in this world

---

lar belief preserved in rabbinic sources that Lilith demands to have intercourse in an upright position on top (see Sabar, "Childbirth and Magic," 674), as "feet" is a common symbol for genitals: see Elliot R. Wolfson, "Images of God's Feet: Some Reflections on the Divine Body in Judaism," in *People of the Body: Jews and Judaism from an Embodied Perspective*, ed. Howard Eilberg-Schwartz, SUNY Series, The Body in Culture, History, and Religion (Albany: State University of New York Press, 1992), 143–82, at 164.

861. On this "general principle," see commentary and sources in Zohar 1:244a (*Zohar: Pritzker Edition*, 3:493 n. 863; Melila Hellner-Eshed, *A River Flows from Eden: The Language of Mystical Experience in the Zohar*, trans. Nathan Wolski (Stanford, CA: Stanford University Press, 2009), 222–25. I thank Daniel Matt for these references. On the allegory of Song of Songs as the seduction of God and Israel in classical midrash and its influence on *kabbalah*, see literature at Kaplan, *My Perfect One*, 37–38 n. 31.

862. See chapter 2 §*Order Over Chaos*.

863. Note, in his gloss of this name, the Gra's recourse to the same body of early midrash that we studied in chapter 2 (especially n. 326).

864. See notes to §5 in Appendix §*Commentary on Tale II by the Gra*. Compare the talmudic tradition in our Part 2 (Appendix §*Translation* 2.C): "The face of Moses is like the face of the sun, the face of Joshua is like the face of the moon." This tradition from 2.C is often cited in the Zohar, which identifies the moon with the *Shekhinah* or divine Presence. See Elliot Wolfson, "The Face of Jacob in the Moon: Mystical Transformations of an Aggadic Myth," in

and the world to come, to redeem Israel from suffering and subjugation. This allegorical retelling of the understory draws it back to the surface, rather than veiling it in a newly emancipated set of mystical symbols like Getz's.

By the same token, we have already seen a vital structural function for the Gra's keyword: "order." It links our tales to the order of verses in the storm (Ps 107:23–26).[865] It thus confers a global structure on the tales whereby, as the Gra says, the teller Rabbah meant to teach a lesson consistent with that of the Psalmist in the understory. The Gra's allegory replays this fugue of story and understory by assuming that, in effect, Rabbah preached his tales on those verses. In the very same way, "order" is the Gra's allegory's implicit argument for itself; indeed, for reading these strange tales at all. This meta-allegorical or self-reflexive function of "order" creates an allegorical canon.

This becomes clear if we revisit the Gra's section §7 in light of its talmudic source. The only words that he actually quotes from this source seem only to support his argument that prayer is how Israel survives in this world, as well as how Israel will be redeemed in the next. "Arousal from below" of the prayer *Qedusha desidra*, sanctifying and praising God's Name, excites "arousal from above" by the *Shekhinah*, who, as if in a call-and-response, "goes down" to this world, strikes its evil, "and it subsides." Yet in its original context, as the Gra well knew, *Qedusha desidra* ("sanctification of the order") lends this keyword "order" a meta-allegorical role. In that prayer (as Rashi explains), "order" refers to both prayer *and* the study of lore and tradition (*aggadah*). This version of the prayer, he says, was instituted so all Israel could qualify as having "engaged in" *aggadah* by reciting the prayer after a public sermon on Shabbat—itself a form of *aggadah*. Today, this prayer contains a verse that the Gra cites here (from the Song at the Sea, no less!) as his proof for how prayer "perfects the Name": *YHWH will reign forever and ever*.[866] The prayer used to include the line "May His great Name be blessed" (still the *Amen*, or congregational response, in *kaddish*).

Based on either textual version of this talmudic prayer/"order," then, the Gra implies that to bless or "perfect the Name" *is* to study *aggadah* and vice versa. Not only did Rabbah preach on ("order") these tales in order to exposit Ps 107–the Gra implies that his commentary, too, by unlocking the tales' hidden meaning, is helping his reader to grasp the "order" behind Rabbah's *aggadah* and thus to perfect the Name. Mystical allegory thus re-reveals the same resolution to a mythic battle that midrash did long

---

The Seductiveness of Jewish Myth: Challenge or Response?, ed. Daniel S. Breslauer (Albany: State University of New York Press, 1997), 235–70.
    865. See chapter 2 §*The Storm as Framing Device*, especially n. 263.
    866. Exod 15:18; see §5 of the Gra's commentary above.

ago. If one praises God's Name–not only by prayer, but also by study of *aggadah*–the Name is perfected and descends. "Arousal from above" answers "arousal from below": the Sea parts, subsides from its anger, and as the Talmud says, "land shall appear from out of the darkness." Evil yet again yields to order. By mirroring his own mystical allegory in the structure of older midrash on verses embedded in the tale, and in turn, mirroring this plural canon in a mythic understory that animates all three layers of the canon as a unified whole, the Gra uses symbolic correspondences to allegorize and harmonize ("order") the canon itself.

Not for nothing did the Gra say of our tales: "They seem ... negligible matters, but in them is preserved all the light and teaching of the Torah of Moses and all the secrets of Scripture."[867] If a symbol is "a depth that both shows and hides itself,"[868] he shows its hidden face, which smiles: a plain-sense effect of renewed familiarity, not despite but because of the tales' unfathomable meaning. More than any reader we met on our adventure, the Gra reads Rabbah into an allegorical canon where nothing is truly new and therefore, anything can still be true. He does not ask whether or not to believe him. He does not debate what he ought to have said or seen, making his tales object-lessons for practical norms (prayershawls, vows, conjugal sex). He does not strain the context or interpretive frame in which to dignify his "negligible matters." All that is done. Now that Rabbah's tales are Torah plain and simple, he can read their teller back into one of the Torah's oldest stories and make him recognizable again. No longer a stranger, never a prodigal son: he was always with us, and every word he said was ours.

---

867. In Movshovitz, introduction to Gra, *Be'ure Aggadot*, 7.
868. Paul Ricoeur, *Freud and Philosophy: An Essay on Interpretation*, trans. Denis Savage (New Haven: Yale University Press, 1997), 7.

The Other Story (*Déjà Vu*)

I began by making you two promises: first, that these stories would tell a story of their own—a history of the continuities and discontinuities in their meanings. Second, I promised to demonstrate a method for telling this story that is broad enough to be more generally useful (see §*Introduction* fig. 3)—a constellation of ideas that centers readers within their inherited interpretive frameworks in order to compare how readers create meaning from the tales as frameworks grow and change. Only you know whether I delivered. Here is how I tried. On one hand, each chapter unfolded a larger circle of our constellation as we moved forward in time. On the other, every element of the constellation was meaningful at every stage of the tales' evolution. We used it to take snapshots of each stage's interpretive dynamics and then to watch them develop.

We began from the earliest reader who associated colorful travel stories with a certain teller: Rabbah bar bar Hanah, who circulated between his and his audience's native Babylonia to the Land of Israel and back in the third century CE. Even this link between a teller and a general sort of tale, regardless of our lack of certainty about the tales' content or literary form, led us to three more early aspects of his telling that his peers consciously mocked or imitated: movement in space, the praise of vision, and related issues of evidence and narrative reliability. All three links between tales, teller, and telling resonated throughout this history. Most of all, Rabbah and his tales were paradigmatically strange: in content, and in the sense that no given genre, body of texts, or set of conventions could control how their readers made sense of them. Rather, readers used genres, intertexts, and interpretive conventions to recreate their meaning. Chapter 1 argued this by opposing the study of textual genres to that of "genres for the reader."

As time marched on, we began to use our constellation to trace the dis/continuities across interpretive frameworks whereby each new type of reader recreated the tales' meaning. I aimed to show that our constellation's common denominators of the reading process reveal both gaps and links across interpretive frameworks' characteristic assumptions and procedures. Moving outward in the constellation, chapter 2 analyzed links between telling and collection. By integrating stories' familiar Babylonian language and world with their scriptural intertexts and mythological origins, we saw how readers may have used an early midrashic framework to recreate one unit's meaning in terms of themes of divine ontology, order, chaos, sin, and repentance. Chapter 3 studied links between the collection and the work of editing or recollecting. Old interpretive tensions—familiar and strange, home and away, exegesis and mythology—were still alive in the polished literary creation of XXI stories that emerged in the fifth century. But they were given new form and new meaning among collectors and readers who digressed from their legal studies to traverse the cosmos through Rabbah's eyes: performing and engaging polished poetic structures that linked the tales, sharpened their messages and effects, and opened a coherent view of Rabbah & Friends' adventures and visions as a new literary whole.

In chapter 4, we considered how that literary whole could have emerged from a cultural context where Hellenistic genres of wonder-writing, romance, and the novel influenced how Sasanian Jews read their own traditional texts and, vice versa, how Jews traditionalized ("Talmudized") those inherited genres, koshering the new wine by bottling it in Scripture and older rabbinic exegesis. Greek genres' inertia was strong enough to affect how wonders were retold and collected in the Talmud. It meaningfully revitalized questions of travel, vision/hearing, and knowledge. But, as the Talmud's own way of answering those questions in some of our stories showed, pressure in the opposite direction was even stronger: Greek epistemology was no path to truth, and those who ventured otherwise were refuted, subtly undermined, or turned to bones.

Chapter 5 showed that this cultural dialogue grew more ambivalent as it developed over a longer period within the talmudic canon behind the doors of its study-houses. In contrast to contemporary Palestinian sources, the Talmud showed far more interest in scholastic hierarchy and rabbinic authority in its own right–above and beyond its basis in Scripture. Yet rather than mere chauvinism, its editors' way of retelling and recollecting our tales to form one composition with the next unit of midrash (Part 2) also goaded their readers to rethink those issues. By following repeated verbal links from midrash to story, from story to midrash, interpreters canonized Rabbah's strange tales by reading them and reflecting on their canon's own strangeness. The tension between belief in texts or visions, the rabbi or the traveler, was stronger than ever. Now, the Talmud encompassed both kinds of meaning with its messianic content and structure, its hyperbolic glosses and expansions—even as it recalled readers' attention to themes of forbidden knowledge and wonder at realms where angels fear to tread. Tension between collections (Parts 1 and 2) thereby generated a more synoptic way to read the talmudic canon in light of shared themes and was, in turn, generated by this canon's emergence as an interpretive horizon. Yet the cultural problems—vision, evidence, and narrative authority—were long-standing, from the earliest oral tradition of the teller and his tales to their encounter with Hellenistic genres.

Our constellation thus reflects both the continuity of the tales' meaning at the level of culture and its discontinuity at the level of history. Basic problems were more or less constant; frameworks for solving them changed, and never fully succeeded. Between the two, I argued, common denominators of the reading process itself can help us to assess what was relatively new about a given interpretive framework; how it built on past frameworks; and what sort of difference it made for stories' meaning among specific readers, whether known or only implied. The most radical discontinuity of all—yet also the most continuous with how our tales are still interpreted today, in traditionalist circles—is the high-medieval turn to allegory and mysticism. In chapter 6, we explored how this framework—by using the Talmud's dreambook to decipher the tales as dreams; by converting them to a set and syntax of symbols; and by correlating symbols with virtues, vices, or practical lessons—broke from the contextual (*peshat*) framework and generated a more internally consistent meaning for the tales as their readers wrote them back into a traditional Jewish canon. As this allegorical framework developed under the sign of Lurianic *kabbalah*, not only the tales' content but also their full interpretive history–including myth and midrash that we saw in chapter 2—were read back into a holistic Jewish canon: as if their received meaning was itself their plain sense, and needed only to return to its place.

By ending our history on this note of familiarity, one might suppose that taming the tales' strangeness was their inevitable final stage; that their nonsense was merely waiting for a certified genius (the "Gaon" of Vilna, the Gra) to finally make sense. Returning to our starting point that one's own experience of a text, partial as it is, is the only way we can begin to understand others', I would say that, for me, the familiarity conferred on our tales by the Gra's allegory was itself strange: less a familiar bedtime story, more a momentary eruption of *déjà vu*. Because we have traveled inside the history of these tales together for so long (if you're still here), I hope that you, too, experienced some of that strange familiarity as we felt the Gra recover myth and midrash from the very beginning of our history in a mystical framework at the very end. But what is it to have an experience of reading like *déjà vu*? What might it mean for reading? Our book has focused on which meanings were made by reading our tales, and how, without ever asking a prior question. Why read at all—let alone spend a book reading readers reading?

Regardless of how *déjà vu* is triggered (scientists do not agree), the phenomenon itself—again, at least for me—is an interruption of the flow of my experience by another story. Ordinary life is an unbroken succession of events that happen to me from my limited first-person point of view. *Déjà vu* breaks this flow with something else. It is like having the ghost of an experience or dreaming while awake. Suddenly I interpret what is happening, not as a new series of events, but as a repetition of a past series: a misplaced memory. I follow this other story as it proceeds.

I try to extend the other story further, expecting something to happen because it already has. For instance, someone I am talking to seems poised to deliver a certain line, but I cannot quite remember the words. Soon—often at the precise moment when I become conscious of my desire for a new future in my imagined past—the two stories split apart. Reality reasserts itself. I return to the present; life, as we say, goes on. Like a dream, the other story is easily forgotten. Unless I tell it to someone else and we interpret it together, its meaning will always be closed to me.

On the other hand, this shared experience may help to explain why we tell or interpret a story of any kind. Regardless of what we do or do not believe, we are reminded every night, and even during these everyday hallucinations, that we live in a story of our own making; and, further, that we will always have another story to tell. Repressing this self-awareness to force life into a master narrative takes its toll. Instead we ask questions. How can we induce, extend, harness our experience of other stories? What if our canonical texts were collections of these other stories—revelations—through which we can learn to interpret and retell our reality? Those questions make reading a ritual and commentators our shamans: experts in ecstasy who help us to grasp our story *as* a story by stepping out of it for a time. We become our own readers.

Reading our story from within the other story, it loses reality's deadened immediacy. We may have strong feelings about the characters but, because we no longer identify too strongly with just one, we can interpret them more generously and rethink their relationships. Rather than live in fear of our story ending, we can hold together the pain that all stories end with the certainty that ours is not the only story. A better story can always be told: after the end, before the beginning, or from someone else's point of view. If meaning is reading and life is no more or less than a story, every reading changes the meaning of life.

Acknowledgments

First thanks are due for the existence of the actual book. Brown Judaic Studies and its editor Michael Satlow offered flexibility with deadlines, word count, and specialized original-language content, including an edition of the tales, which made this series the perfect fit. I further thank Paul Kobelski and Maurya Horgan of The HK Scriptorium, Inc., who copyedited and typeset the text; Tim DeBold of Atramenti Editing, who edited each chapter with his customary acuity and prepared the index of names and subjects; and my graduate assistant, Jasmine Jiménez, who drafted the source index. Production costs were supported by the Jordan Schnitzer First Book Publication Award, administered by the Association for Jewish Studies.

I have many institutions and hosts to thank for supporting the book's gradual production by inviting me to present draft material from chapters 3–5, looking after me, and giving feedback: Wissenschaftskolleg zu Berlin (Shai Secunda); École Pratique des Hautes Études (Daniel Barbu, Geoffrey Herman); Universität Potsdam Institut für jüdische Theologie / Alexander von Humboldt Foundation (Admiel Kosman, Markus Krah / Sina Rauschenbach); Cornell University Program in Jewish Studies / Society for the Humanities (Jonathan Boyarin / Paul Fleming, Emily Parsons); Elizabeth A. Clark Center for Late Ancient Studies (James Rives, Laura Lieber); Princeton University Department of Religion (Moulie Vidas); New York University Department of Hebrew and Judaic Studies (Jeffrey Rubenstein). Jonathan Boyarin made an odyssey to Ithaca like home.

I thank the University of Chicago Divinity School and its former Dean David Nirenberg for a six-quarter visiting appointment, during which I held graduate seminars, finished the book in my favorite library, and workshopped a draft of chapter 6. Warm thanks to Clifford Ando, Samuel Catlin, Christopher Faraone, Sarah Hammerschlag, Jessica Kirzane, Nitzan Lebovic, Carolina López-Ruiz, Kenneth Moss, Sarah Nooter, James Robinson, Naʻama Rokem, Erin Galgay Walsh.

Most of all, I thank my home institution, Saint Louis University, and its Research Institute for allowing these external leaves as well as direct material support and extra time to finish writing when global and personal crises collided. I am truly grateful to my college dean, Donna Lavoie; department chairs, Peter Martens and Daniel Smith; and colleagues, especially Grant Kaplan, Atria Larson, Eleonore Stump, and Jeffrey Wickes.

Never before had I been part of an academic community with sincere moral purpose. It makes higher education's structural rot less unbearable.

For seven years, this book's main implied reader has naturally been a projection of myself. Introverted, idealistic, and strange, he also proved to have an ugly streak of cruel pedantry which slowed and nearly thwarted my progress. I needed people in my life to exorcise him by modeling a better reader: a generous critic who asks fundamental questions. They are Mira Balberg, Emanuel Fiano, Simcha Gross, Ishay Rosen-Zvi, Moulie Vidas, Mira Beth Wasserman, Steven Weitzman, and Barry Wimpfheimer. As readers of my own work, Barry, and especially my mentors Charlotte Fonrobert and Daniel Boyarin, have invested much time and thought, for which I will always be grateful. I am lucky to consider these better readers my friends. Yet two fine scholars would remain friends even if they were as illiterate as they oft surmise that I am: Todd Berzon and Heidi Wendt.

I have dedicated this book to my father, James M. Redfield, in his ninetieth year, as a way to recognize the influence of his thinking on mine and to continue our more difficult work of saying goodbye. Every book I do not write is for Isaac; for Beni, Javy, and Rose—and more adventures.

Appendix 1

Translation. Part 1.

1 I.[1] <u>Rava</u>[2] said:
2   <u>They that go down to the sea in ships</u>[3] recounted to me:
3   Between one wave and the next are <u>three</u>[4] hundred *parasang*,
4   <u>the height of each wave is three hundred *parasang*</u>.[5]
5   <u>Once</u>,[6] a wave lifted us <u>up</u>[7]
6   <u>and</u>[8] <u>I</u>[9] saw the cradle of <u>a</u>[10] star
7   <u>and it</u>[11] was as great as <u>the sowing</u>[12] of forty *<u>griv</u>*[13] of mustard;
8   had it lifted us any higher, we'd have been burnt by <u>its heat</u>.[14]
9   The waves cast their voices in chorus:
10   "<u>So</u>,[15] is there anything in the world you've <u>left alone</u>[16] and not
                     <u>destroyed</u>?"[17]

---

   1. Vilna: b. B. Bat. 73a, ln. 17-74b ln. 22. For sigla and order of witnesses, see §*Note on the Text*. Text based on ms. H. For the principles of this presentation of the text of the tales, see chapter 3. – indicates an omission in the witness in this line, not due to a lacuna. [x] indicates a seeming error in the witness, but a reading clearly like others listed in the line. (For a more complete indication of errors, see Appendix §*Edition*). In P, II is a marginal addition after I. In V, O, M, F, E, the order of I and II is reversed.

   2. V, O: *And Rabbah said*. M: *And Rava said*

   3. Tg. Ps 107:23.

   4. F: —

   5. M, O: —. P, V, E: *and* the height (etc.)

   6. P, V, O: *Once, we were traveling in a ship and*

   7. P: *up three hundred* parasang *in the air*. V, O: *up in the air*

   8. V, O, M, E, F [x]: *until*

   9. V, M, O, E, F: I/*we*. Wherever the participle form is ambiguous ("I was/we were") in context, from now on, it will be translated 1s ("I was"). Readings that are unambiguously 1c pl. due to form or context will be cited as such.

   10. V, M, F [x]: *the smallest star* (literally, "small star"; trans. follows the gloss of Rashbam *ad loc.*), O: *stars*.

   11. V, O, M, E [x], F: *which*

   12. M, E: *scattering*. V: –

   13. O: –

   14. H: *the damage*. Following all other mss. See however Appendix §*Edition*, n. 27.

   15. V, M, F: —. E: *My friend*,

   16. M, E, F: *left behind*

   17. P: *drowned*. E, F, M: *flooded*

11	"Let us go, you and I, and destroy it."[18]
12	And replied:
13	"Come[19] see the might of your master!
14	I[20] cannot pass so much as[21] a grain of sand[22] the width of a thread,"
15	as it is said:[23]
16	*Fear ye not me? saith the LORD. Will ye not tremble at my presence?*[24]
17	
18	**II.** And Rava[25] said:
19	*They that go down to the sea in ships* recounted to me:[26]
20	That wave that sinks[27] the ship has[28] a[29] white shoot of flame upon its crest,[30]
21	but we have[31] poles upon which is engraven:
22	*I am that I am*,[32] God, the LORD of Hosts,
23	Amen, Amen, Amen, Selah, Selah, Selah,[33]
24	and we strike it,[34]
25	and it[35] subsides.
26	

---

18. Following M, but reading *destroy* for *flood* per V, O, and Rashbam *ad loc.* V, O: *But let me come and we will destroy it.* H, P, E, F: —

19. M, E, F: *Go*

20. P, M, E, F: *One*

21. P, E, F: —

22. H: *mustard* [x]. Following all other mss.

23. O, V: *written*

24. Jer 5:22 (KJV). The verse aptly concludes: ... *which have placed the sand for the bound of the sea by a perpetual decree, that it cannot pass it: and though the waves thereof toss themselves, yet can they not prevail; though they roar, yet can they not pass over it?* Part or all of this conclusion is filled in by other mss., with minor idiosyncrasies. Closure of the quotation marks in I.14 follows Rashbam (who stresses that the verse is added in the Gemara, not in the dialogue; see chapter 3, n. 433). Fränkel disagrees (*Darkhe ha-aggadah*, 1:259); he would place the quotation marks after the end of the verse.

25. V: Rabbah. E: Rabbah bar bar Hanah. O: Rava ~~bar bar Hanah~~

26. O: –.

27. H, O [x]: *about to overwhelm* (on this construction, see Elitzur Bar-Asher Siegal, *Introduction to the Grammar of Jewish Babylonian Aramaic*, 2nd rev. ed. (Münster: Ugarit, 2016), 288). Following all other mss.

28. P, M, E, F: *projects*. On this reading (b. Ta'an. 25a), see chapter 2 n. 291.

29. Following V, O [x]. H, P, M [x], E [x], F [x]: *like a*.

30. P: —

31. Following P, V, O. H: *they have.* M, E, F: *we strike it with*

32. Exod 3:14 (KJV).

33. Following the longest version in the marginal addition to V. All mss. vary in the number of divine names, *Amen*, and *Selah*. Shortest version in H: *I am that I am, the LORD of Hosts.*

34. M, E, F: — [but see ln. II.21 above. Only F is truly missing ln. II.24.]

35. E: *the sea.* See chapter 3 n. 494.

27 **IIIa.** And[36] Rava[37] said:
28 I myself have seen:
29 Hormiz,[38] son of Lilith, who was bounding upon[39] the dome[40] of Mahoza,
30 and a horseman raced[41] beneath him,[42] riding a steed,[43]
31 but could not overcome him.[44]
32 **IIIb.** Once
33 two mules[45] were saddled for him[46]
34 on[47] two bridges of the Ravnag,[48]
35 and he bounded from one[49] to the other and back again
36 and he held[50] two goblets[51] of water[52] in his hands[53]
37 and he poured[54] from one to the other and back again[55]
38 but did not spill[56] a single drop.[57]
39 And upon that day,[58]
40 *They mount up to the heaven, they go down again to the depths:*[59]
41 the authorities[60] ["kingdom"] heard of it[61] and brought him to an end.[62]
42

---

36. P: –
37. V, F: *Rabbah*
38. V, O, M: *Hormin.* See chapter 6 n. 815.
39. P, O, M, E: *racing along.* V: *upon*
40. P, O [x], M, E [x]: *turrets of the wall.* V: *turrets.*
41. O: *was.* M: *rode*
42. P: *on the ground*
43. M, E: *beast*
44. E: *but did not overtake him.* P: *without outstripping him.* O: *but could not* ~~outstrip~~ *overcome him.*
45. M: *beasts.* E [x]: *beasts: white mules.* For the gloss in E, see XIIIa.169 and chapter 4 n. 585.
46. V: —
47. P, V, M, E, O: *and set upon*
48. Following the vocalization in V.
49. V: *one side*
50. V: —
51. P, V, O: *cups*
52. Uniquely in H. P, V, O, M, E: *wine*. On the logic of ms. H's reading, see Kiperwasser and Ruzer, "Irano-Talmudica I," 104–13.
53. V, O: *were poured for him*
54. P, O, M, E: *spat/projected.* V: *threw.*
55. V: —
56. P: *sprinkle.*
57. M, E: *drop on the ground*
58. V, O: *And, they say, upon that day,*
59. Ps 107:26. E: *and they* (not in the Masoretic Text). The verse pointedly concludes: *... their soul is melted because of trouble.* See n. 3 above.
60. P, V, O, M [x], E [x]: *house of the kingdom*
61. P: *heard about him.* V, O, M, E: *heard.*
62. P, E, O [x]: *killed him*

43	**IV.**[63] <u>Rabbah bar bar Hanah</u>[64] said:
44	I myself have seen:
45	A day-old <u>gazelle</u>[65] who was <u>as big as</u>[66] Mount Tabor
46	(And how big is Mount Tabor? –Forty *parasang*).
47	The length of his neck: three *parasang*;
48	The cradle of his head: a *parasang* and a half;
49	and he let loose a turd and stopped up the Jordan.
50	
51	**V.** Rabbah bar bar Hanah said:
52	I myself have seen:
53	A certain frog who was <u>as big as</u>[67] the Fort of Hagrunya
54	(And how big <u>is</u>[68] <u>the fort of Hagrunya</u>?[69] – Sixty houses).
55	A serpent came, swallowed it;
56	A wondrous bird came, <u>swallowed</u>[70] the serpent
57	and flew up and settled in a tree.
58	<u>Come see</u>[71] <u>the strength</u>[72] of the tree!
59	<u>How great it was!</u>[73]
60	Rav Pappa son of Shmuel said:
61	If I hadn't <u>been there</u>,[74] I wouldn't have believed it.
62	
63	**VIa.** And Rabbah bar bar Hanah said:
64	Once <u>I was</u>[75] traveling in a ship
65	and <u>I</u>[76] saw a certain fish
66	whose nostril a <u>mud-eater</u>[77] <u>entered</u>,[78] <u>and it died</u>[79]
67	and the water <u>drew it and hurled it</u>[80] ashore.[81]

---

63. In V, M, a mnemonic with supralinear markings and keywords of Parts IV–X is inserted at the beginning of Part IV. V: *Mnemonic [day-old] Gazelle Frog Gnawing Sands Between Fins* Ziz Saday *and Geese*. M: *[day-old male] Aurochs Frog who Gnawed Sands Between Fins Saday and Geese Mnemonic*.

64. E: *Rava*

65. P: *aurochs gazelle*. V: *female gazelle*. O, M, E: *gazelle of the sea*

66. Following all other mss. H, O [x]: *upon* [literally, *in*]

67. V: *at* [literally, *in*]

68. M, E: *was*

69. O: *it*

70. P, E: *took up*

71. O: *Rava said, "Come see how substantial was*

72. P, V, M, E: *how substantial was the strength*

73. Only in H. Literally, *how big it was*, as in IV.46, V.54. See chapter 3 §*Chronological Layers* 1.

74. V, O: *seen it*

75. P, E: *we were*.

76. P, M, E: *we*

77. See *JBA*, 131. O: *tiny fish*. See chapter 1 n. 235.

78. P, M, E: *occupied*. V, O: *went up*

79. O: –

80. P: *and the water hurled it*. V, O: *and the sea hurled it*. M [x], E [x]: *and the water drew it and hurled it*. The first verb in M, E may or may not be a corruption of the same first verb as in H.

81. V, O: *upon the shore*. P: *out [of the sea]*

68	Sixty towns were destroyed by it[82]
69	Sixty towns ate[83] from it
70	Sixty towns salted[84] it
71	From one of its eyeballs, they made[85]
72	three hundred jugs of oil.
73	**VIb.** When we[86] returned the next year,[87] we[88] saw
74	they were hewing from its bones
75	beams[89] to rebuild[90] those towns.[91]
76	
77	**VII.** And Rabbah bar bar Hanah said:
78	Once I was[92] traveling in a ship
79	and I saw[93] a certain fish
80	with sands settled upon its back
81	and a thorn-plant[94] had sprouted[95] on it.
82	We thought it was dry land
83	and we went up, we kneaded, and we baked;[96]
84	The[97] back of the fish[98] got hot
85	and[99] it flipped[100] over
86	and if the ship hadn't been close to[101] us
87	it would have drowned us.[102]
88	
89	**VIIIa.** And Rabbah bar bar Hanah said:
90	Once I was[103] traveling in a ship

---

82. P: *And it destroyed sixty towns.* O, E: –. For E, see VIa.70.
83. V: *salted from,* see following note.
84. V: *ate from.* E: *salted and sixty towns were destroyed by.* Trans. follows Rashbam *ad loc.*: it is not that salt was drawn from the fish, but that remote towns—who could not *eat from* it on site—salted its flesh and took it home. See chapter 6 n. 770.
85. P: *they drew.* E: *they built.* M: *they filled*
86. P: *I.*
87. Following V, O. H: *When we came back after a year.* P, M, E: *came back after a full year* [lit.: *after a year of twelve months*]
88. P: *I.*
89. V, O: *logs.* M, E: *huts*
90. P: –. M, E: *and resettling.* V, O: *to rebuild*
91. M, E: —. P: *for those sixty towns, and building.* V, O: *those towns*
92. P, E: *we were*
93. P, E: *we saw*
94. P, M, E: *a marsh.* V, O: *herbage*
95. O: *was standing*
96. P, V, M, E: *and we baked and we cooked.* O: *and we cooked and we baked*
97. P, O: *When its.* M, E: *And when its.* V: *when the*
98. V: *of the oven.* P, O, M, E: –
99. P, V, O, M, E: –
100. V, O: *turned*
101. V: *by us.* O: *with us*
102. V, O, M, E: *we would have drowned*
103. P, E: *we were*

91	and the ship[104] passed[105] between one[106] fin of a fish and the other[107]
92	three days and three nights
93	it went upstream[108] as we went downstream.
94	**VIIIb.** And perhaps you'd say:
95	The[109] ship wasn't moving[110] much![111]
96	When Rav Dimi arrived, he said:
97	Like heating a kettle[112]
98	the ship moved[113] six[114] parasang.
99	And there is one who says:[115]
100	A horseman shot[116] an arrow[117]
101	but could not overcome it.[118]
102	Rav Ashi said:[119]
103	That one, he's[120] the *gildna* fish of the sea,
104	who has two fins.
105	
106	**IXa.** And Rabbah bar bar Hanah said:
107	Once I was[121] traveling in a ship
108	and I saw[122] a certain bird[123]
109	who was[124] standing[125] up to its[126] ankles in the water[127]
110	and its head[128] reached[129] the firmament.[130]

---

104. O: —
105. O: —. V: *went along*. P, M, E: *moved*
106. V: *each*
107. V: —
108. V, O: *into the swell*. For this "swell/stream" distinction, see Rashbam *ad. loc.* s.v. בזקיפא. The issue is whether the two bodies in motion are kept apart by wind or current.
109. V, O: *that the*
110. V, O: *didn't move*
111. P: —
112. P, V, O [x], M, E: *a kettle of water*
113. P: *we traveled*. V, O: *it moved*. M, E: *it was moving*
114. Uniquely in H. All other mss.: *sixty*
115. Uniquely in H. All other mss.: *And*
116. P: *aimed*
117. O: —
118. [I.e., the fish]. P: *but that ship stayed in front of it* [i.e., the arrow]. V [x]: *but the ship stayed in front of it* [f.s.]. M, E: *but it* [i.e., the ship] *stayed in front of it* [i.e., the arrow]. O: *but it* [i.e., the fish] *stayed in front of it* [i.e., the ship].
119. M, E: *And Rav Ashi said*: V, O: *When we came before Rav Ashi, he said to us*:
120. E: *he was*
121. E: *we were*
122. P, E: *we saw*
123. P: *those birds*
124. P: *were*
125. V: *in the water*. O: *standing in the water*
126. P: *their*
127. V, O: —
128. P: *their heads*
129. M, E: —
130. P, M, E: *in the firmament*. V: *the joint of heaven*. See Tg. Onqelos Gen 28:12 (*and its head*

111	We thought[131] the water was not substantial;[132]
112	we meant to go down to cool ourselves off.[133]
113	A heavenly voice appeared[134] and said to us:[135]
114	Here,[136] you mean to cool yourselves off?[137]
115	For[138] a carpenters'[139] adze fell seven years[140]
116	and has not reached the bottom;
117	and not[141] because the water is deep[142]
118	but because the water is forceful.
119	**IXb**. Rav Ashi said:[143]
120	That was[144] ziz saday,
121	as it is written:
122	and ziz saday is mine.[145]
123	
124	**Xa**. And Rabbah bar bar Hanah said:
125	Once I was[146] traveling in the desert
126	and I[147] saw those geese[148]
127	whose wings[149] drooped[150]
128	because of their fat[151]
129	and a stream[152] of oil
130	was flowing[153] out of[154] them.

---

reached the joint of heaven). O: ~~the firmament~~ *the joint of heaven*.

131. M, E: *And we said*. Line IXa.111 is absent in V.
132. M: *there wasn't any water*; E [x]: *there wasn't any*
133. P: *And we meant to chill ourselves off*. V: *And we meant to go down and chill ourselves off.* O: *And we meant to go down and cool ourselves*. M: "*Shall we go down to chill ourselves off?*" E: "*Let us go down to chill ourselves off.*" Note that only mss. H and O use the same verb as "make [the female Leviathan] frigid" in Part 2; the others use a synonym.
134. E: —
135. V, O: —
136. V: *How can.* P, M, E: –
137. P, M, E: *Do not go down here!*
138. P: *For lo, it is seven years since.* V: *For if.* O: *Once*
139. P, V, M, E: *carpenter's*
140. P: —. V: *seven years ago*. O: *for seven years*. M, E: *lo these seven years*
141. P: *you shouldn't say*
142. P, M, E: *substantial*
143. V, O: *When we came before Rav Ashi, he said to us:*
144. P. *That is.* V: *That is called*
145. Ps. 50:11 (KJV, modified).
146. P, V, M, E: *we were*
147. P, V, M, E: *we*
148. E: *a certain goose*
149. P, V, O, M, E: *feathers*. [Same word as H but meaning *feathers*, based on the verb in these mss. See the next note. For the meaning *wing* in H, see b. Yoma 84a: משחא דגדפא דאווזא, *oil from the wing of a goose*.]
150. P, V, O, M, E: *were plucked out*. See b. Hul. 22b: שמיט גדפא מיניה (*he plucked out a feather*).
151. M: *fattiness*. E [x]: *their fat* [pl.; vs. sg. *a certain goose* in ms. E above]
152. P, M: *rivers*. O, V: *streams*
153. M, E: *was pouring* [different verb, same meaning, almost identical spelling].
154. M, E: *beneath*

131	We[155] said to them:
132	Have we[156] in[157] you[158] a portion of[159] the world to come?[160]
133	One lifted up its thigh[161] at me, and one lifted up its wing.[162]
134	**Xb.** When[163] I[164] came before[165] Rabbi[166] El'azar, he[167] said to me:[168]
135	In time to come, Israel[169] shall be judged[170] on their account.
136	
137	**XI.**[171] Rabbah bar bar Ḥanah said:
138	Once I was[172] traveling in the desert
139	and with us[173] was a certain Arab,[174] who was sniffing the earth.[175]
140	He said:
141	"This[176] goes[177] to such-and-such a place,
142	and this[178] goes to such-and-such a place."[179]
143	We gave him some dirt.[180]

---

155. P, V: *I*
156. V: *I*
157. P: *part of*
158. V: *your bodies*. The underlined addition is due to a scribal insertion above the line, a misreading of the term *in you.*
159. V, O: *anything of*. See *anything*, ln. I.10. P, M, E: —
160. Spelling error in H. Corrected on the basis of all other mss.
161. P, V, M, E: *wing*. O: *wing* [related synonym]
162. Uniquely in H. P, V, M, E, O: *thigh*
163. O: —
164. E: *he*. O: —
165. O: —
166. O: *And Rabbi*
167. O: —
168. E: *to him*
169. V: *it is Israel who*
170. In Hebrew, H treats "judgment" as an indefinite rather than definite noun.
171. At the beginning of XI, some mss. have another mnemonic for Parts XI–XV. V: *Mnemonic Dirt of* Tekhelet *Scorpion Qorah and his Basket*. E: *Mnemonic in* Tekhelet *Him Stung a Scorpion Qorah and his Basket*. M: *In Dirt of* Tekhelet *Whistled a Scorpion to Qorah and his Basket Mnemonic*. "Stung" and "Whistled" may be scribal errors for "Smoke," indexing tale XIV. See J. Brüll, *Die Mnemotechnik des Talmuds* (Vienna, 1864), 41.
172. P, E: *we were*
173. P: —. V, O: *going along with us*. M, E: *accompanying us*
174. P: *a certain Arab was with me*
175. P: *and he was holding dirt from two paths and sniffing it*. E: *who was taking dirt from two paths and sniffing it*. V, O, M: *who was taking dirt and sniffing it*.
176. Uniquely in H. P: *this road*. O, V, M, E: *this path*
177. O, V, E, M: —
178. P: *this road*
179. Following H, P. Instead of this ln. XI.142, all other mss. have a response to the statement by the Arab. M, E, V, O, N: *We said to him, "What distance are we from water?"*
180. Following H. In P, this line is absent. All other mss. continue the dialogue. V: *He said to us, "Give me some dirt."* O: *He said to us, "Give some dirt." We gave him some dirt.* M: *He said*

144	He said: "You are at a distance of eight *parasang* from water."[181]
145	We gave him some [more]. He said: "You are at a distance of three *parasang*."[182]
146	We shuffled the dirt around on him,[183]
147	but we[184] could not overcome him.
148	
149	**XIIa.** He said to us:[185]
150	"Come, I will show you[186] the dead of the desert."
151	I went and I saw that[187] they were reposing, like[188] one who is[189] intoxicated,[190]
152	and they were lying down.[191] And one of them was lying down supine, knees bent.[192]
153	And the Arab[193] went through[194] while riding a camel, and held[195] a[196] spear in his hand,
154	but did not touch him.
155	

---

to me, "Give me some dirt." We gave him some dirt. E, N: He said to us, "Give me some dirt." We gave him some dirt.

181. Following H. In P, ln. XI.144 is absent. All other mss. continue the dialogue. V, O: *He said to us, "Eight* parasang." M: *And he said to us, "Eight* parasang." E: *He said to us, "We are at a distance of eight* parasang." N: *"You are at a distance of eight* parasang."

182. Following H. In P, ln. XI.145 is absent. Other mss. extend the exchange. V: *Again we gave him some dirt. He said to us, "Three* parasang." M: *Again we gave him some dirt and he said to us, "Three* parasang." E: *Again we gave him some dirt. And he said to him [sic]: "We are at a distance of three* parasang." N: *Again we gave him [some]. He said, "You are at a distance of three* parasang." O has a lacuna and some abbreviations, but otherwise it matches V.

183. P: *The dirt was turned around on him.* V, O: *We shuffled it around on him.* M, E, N: *And it was shuffled around on him*

184. P: *one.* M, E, N: *I*

185. P: *He said to me.* E: *And Rabbah bar bar Hanah said: Once I was traveling in the desert and he said to me.* N: *And Rabbah bar bar Hanah said: That Arab said to me.*

186. Uniquely in H: [plural]. All others: [singular]

187. Uniquely in H. All others: *them*

188. V: —. N, O, E [x]: *that they were like.* M: *and they were* one who *like.* P: *that they were wrapped up in their linens, and they were like*

189. O: —

190. Common spelling errors in H and P. Following all other mss.

191. V, N: —

192. P: *and they were lying down supine, and one of them had his knees straight.* V: *and they were sleeping supine; one of them was straightening his knees.* O: *and they were lying down supine; one of them had his knees straight.* M, E: *and they were lying down supine, and one of them had his knees straight.* N [x]: *and one of them was lying down supine, and he had his knees straight.*

193. P: *a man.* V, O: *that Arab*

194. P: *passed by.* O: *went under his knees.* V, M, E, N: *went beneath his knees*

195. Uniquely in H. All other mss.: *straightened*

196. M, E, N: *his.* O is ambiguous (*a* or *his*).

156   I cut off and took a thread[197] of *tekhelet*[198] from them[199]
157   and[200] our camel[201] couldn't walk. He said:[202]
158   "Perhaps[203] one of you[204] took something[205] from them? Have it
                returned to them."[206]
159   (For it has been taught[207] that one[208] who takes[209] something[210] from
                them[211] can't walk).
160   We returned it to him,[212] and we walked on.[213]
161 **XIIb**. When I arrived at the house of study,[214] I was told:[215]
162   "Every Abba[216] is an ass; every bar[217] Hanah is a jackass.
163   Now then, those threads of the joints:[218]
164   Is it according to the House of Shammai or according to the House of
                Hillel?[219]
165   If only you'd[220] counted them![221] And come and told us!"[222]
166
167 **XIIIa**. He said to us:[223]
168   "Come,[224] I will show you[225] Mount Sinai."

---

197. P: *And I took a thread*. V: *I took one corner*. M: *I cut off and took one corner*. E: *I cut off and brought away one corner*. O: *I cut off one* ~~thread~~. N: *I cut off and brought away one corner*
198. P: —
199. P, E: *one of them*
200. E, N: –
201. V, P, M, E, N: *we*. V: *the camel*. O: *our camel*
202. M, N: *he said to me*. O, E: *he said to him*
203. Uniquely in H, P. All others: *If*
204. Uniquely in H, but E has this word later in the line; see following note. O: *anyone*. All other mss.: *you* (m.s.)
205. V. E lacks this word, but "one" appears here; see previous note.
206. P: —. All others: *Return it to them*
207. P, O: —. E: *we have taught*
208. V, O: *anyone*
209. V [x]: *borrows*
210. V: —. E: *one [thing]*
211. V: *them, his camel*. O: *them, his* ~~donkey~~ *camel*
212. P: *and I returned it to him*. V: *I returned them*. O: *I returned it*. M, E, N: *I went [back and] returned it*
213. P: *and we could walk*. V, M, E, O, N: — (From the fact that Rabbah is telling the story, this is obvious, hence omitted).
214. M, E, N: *before our teachers*
215. P, V, O, M, E, N: *they told me*
216. V: *Rabbah*. E: ~~bar bar Hana~~ *Abba*. O has a similar confusion between Abba and Rabbah.
217. P, V, O, M, N: *bar bar*. Unique reading in H.
218. P: *What were you thinking? To find out:* V, O: *For what rule did you take it?* M, N: *For what rule?* E: *For what rule? Was it necessary [to take it] to count its threads?*
219. O: –
220. P, V, O, M, N: *You should have*. E: *One should have*
221. P, O, M, N: *the threads and counted the joints!* V: *the threads and the joints!* E: *the threads!*
222. P, M, N: —
223. P, V: *he said to me*. M: *he said*. E, N: *And Rabbah bar bar Hanah said, He said to me:*
224. H: *Come, [pl.]*. P, V, E, N: *Come, [sg.]*.
225. V [x]: *me*. P, O, M, E, N: *you [sg.]*. H: *you [pl.]*

169	I <u>went and</u>²²⁶ saw that it was surrounded by scorpions <u>as big as</u>²²⁷ <u>Libyan</u>²²⁸ donkeys.
170	<u>A heavenly voice appeared</u>²²⁹ and said:²³⁰
171	"Woe <u>is me</u>²³¹ for having sworn; <u>and now that</u>²³² I have sworn, who will annul it for me?"²³³
172	**XIIIb.** When I arrived <u>at the house of study,</u>²³⁴ <u>they said</u>:²³⁵
173	"Every <u>Abba</u>²³⁶ is an ass, every <u>bar</u>²³⁷ Hanah is a jackass.
174	You should have said, 'It's <u>annulled</u>²³⁸ for you, it's <u>annulled</u>²³⁹ for you!'"²⁴⁰
175	But I <u>figured,</u>²⁴¹ "Perhaps it was <u>the oath</u>²⁴² of <u>the generation of</u>²⁴³ the Flood?"
176	Yet our teachers [retorted]: "'<u>One doesn't say 'woe'</u> [about that!]"²⁴⁴
177	
178	**XIV.** <u>He said</u>²⁴⁵ to us:²⁴⁶
179	"<u>Come,</u>²⁴⁷ <u>I will show</u>²⁴⁸ <u>you</u>²⁴⁹ the <u>Maw</u>²⁵⁰ of Qorah."

---

226. V, O, M, E: —
227. P, V, E, N: *and they were standing as big as.* O: *I saw that they were standing as big as*
228. Uniquely in H. O: *a white.* All other mss.: *white.* M is ambiguous (*white, a white*).
229. P, M, E, N: *I heard a heavenly voice.* V, O: *I went and heard a heavenly voice*
230. Uniquely in H. All others: *that was saying:*
231. P: —
232. V: *but because*
233. P: *who will release me? Who will annul it for me?*
234. M, E, N: *before our teachers*
235. Uniquely in H. All others: *they said to me*
236. V: *Rabbah*
237. P, V, N: *bar bar.* O: *Rab bar bar*
238. P: *released*
239. P: *released*
240. O: —
241. P, V, M: *But he figured.* E, B: *He figured.* O: *But he was one who said*
242. P: *about the oath.* All others: *the oath.* [Aramaic]
243. Uniquely in H and O. P, V, M, E, B: —
244. P, N, B: *"If so, why do I have 'woe'?"* V: *"If it is the oath of the flood, then why would one say 'woe is me'?!"* M: *"Why do I have 'woe'?!"* E: *"Why do I have 'woe is me'?!"* O: *"If it is the oath of the generation of the flood, why should one say 'woe' is him?!"*
245. E: *And Rabbah bar bar Hanah said: He said.* N: *And Rabbah bar bar Hanah said: Once we were traveling in the desert and he said.* B: *And Rabbah bar bar Hanah said: Once while we were traveling in the desert that Arab said*
246. Uniquely in H. P, V, E, M, N, B: *me.*
247. H: [plural]. All other mss. (P, V, O, M, E, N, B): [singular]
248. B: *see for yourself*
249. H: [plural]. All other mss.: [singular]
250. P, E, N: *Swallowed Ones.* Rabbinovicz (*DS*, B. Bat. p. 115) rules this a textual error because they do not appear. But "Rashi" preserves the reading and glosses it like the other reading, as *"the place where* the Assembly of Qorah were swallowed up" (b. Sanh. 110a, s.v. בלוע; emphasis added).

180	He showed us[251] a certain[252] crevice,[253] from which a wisp of[254] smoke[255] was appearing.[256]
181	He brought out[257] a tuft[258] of wool,
182	brushed it[259] in water, and wrapped it[260] around his spear,[261] and inserted it.[262]
183	It was burnt and[263] charred.[264]
184	He said to me: "Listen, now,[265] to what[266] you hear[267] from here."[268]
185	And I heard that it was[269] saying: "Moses and his Torah are true, and they are liars!"
186	He told me: "Every thirty days, Gehinnom stirs them[270] as flesh in[271] the caldron."[272]
187	And it said again:[273] "Moses and his Torah are true, and they are liars!"
188 **XV.**	He said to us:[274]
189	"Come,[275] I will show you[276] where the firmament is overturned upon the earth."[277]
190	He showed us; I saw a certain slit.[278]

---

251. P, V, O, N: *I went and saw*. M, E, B: *I saw*
252. P, E, M, B: *two*
253. P, E, B, N: *crevices*. V: *slit*
254. P, M, E, N, B, V, O: — Unique reading in ms. H. Note that *wisp* (literally, *thread*) harmonizes with I.14, XIIa.156, XVIII.224.
255. V, O: *smoke* [synonym]
256. V, O: *rising*
257. P, M, E, B: *he took*. N: *and he took*
258. V: *two tufts*. O: *tufts*
259. E, N, B: *brushed it*. V: *and brushed them*. O: *raised them and brushed them*. P: *dipped it*
260. V: *wrapped them*. P: *attached it*. M: *placed it*. E, O [x]: *and stuck it*. B: *grasped it*
261. Uniquely in H, P. All other mss.: *on the tip of his spear*
262. O: *and roasted them*. V, M, N, B: *and entered it*. E: *and entered it there*
263. Uniquely in H. P: *and it was*. V, O: *when he took them out [they were]*. M, E, N, B: *when he took it out, it came out*
264. Uniquely in H, P. All others: *all burnt up*
265. Only in H, B. M, E: *show me*. O: *and hearken*. P, V: —
266. B: *whom*
267. V, O: *it's saying*
268. P, V, O: —
269. O: *a voice that they were*
270. V, O: *turns*. P: *overturns*
271. P, E: *as flesh within*. P and E bring the verse in line with the Masoretic Text.
272. Micah 3:3 (KJV). See §Introduction n. 93, chapter 4 n. 630.
273. Literally, *thus*. P: —
274. E, B: *And Rabbah bar bar Hanah said, "That Arab said to me*. All others: *That Arab said to me*. Unique reading in ms. H.
275. Uniquely in H: *Come* [plural]. P, V, O, M, E: *Come* [singular]. B has a lacuna here, but see following note.
276. Uniquely in H: *you* [plural]. All other mss., including B: *you* [singular]
277. V, O: *the earth and the firmament touch* [lit. *kiss*]. P, M [x], E: *the earth and the firmament touch* [lit. *kiss*] *one another*
278. V, M, E: —. O: *I went to that slit of the firmament*. P [x]: *I went and saw that it was made a wall opening* (see b. B. Bat. 6a).

191	I took my basket and rested it inside until I had prayed.²⁷⁹
192	The orb revolved and²⁸⁰ I did not find it.
193	I said:²⁸¹ "Perhaps–God forbid–²⁸² there are thieves here?"²⁸³
194	He told me:²⁸⁴ "Keep watch until tomorrow around now;²⁸⁵
195	the orb will revolve to its position,²⁸⁶ and you'll take it back."²⁸⁷
196	
197	**XVI.**²⁸⁸ Rabbi Yohanan recounts:²⁸⁹
198	Once I was traveling²⁹⁰ in a ship
199	and a certain²⁹¹ fish lifted²⁹² up its head²⁹³
200	and its eyes²⁹⁴ resembled²⁹⁵ two moons
201	and water fell²⁹⁶ from its²⁹⁷ two snouts²⁹⁸
202	like the two fords of Sura.
203	
204	**XVIIa.** Rav Safra recounts:²⁹⁹
205	Once I was traveling³⁰⁰ in a ship³⁰¹
206	and³⁰² a certain fish lifted up its head³⁰³

---

279. P: *I rested my basket in the slit of the firmament until I had prayed.* V: *I put my basket inside until we had prayed.* O: *I put my basket inside until we had prayed.* M, E: *I took [and] rested my basket in the slit of the firmament until I had prayed.* B: *I rested ... slit of the firmament until I had prayed.* Despite lacuna (...) B seems most similar to M, E.
280. P, V: *I sought it but.* O, M, E, B: —
281. P: *I said to him,* V, M, E, B: *I said to him,*
282. P, O: *Can it be that.* M, E, B: —
283. V, E: *in the firmament.* O: ~~in the firmament~~ *here.* M, B: *here*
284. V, O: *A heavenly voice appeared and said:*
285. P: "*That is the orb of the firmament revolving. Keep watch until tomorrow around this time,*" M, E: "*That was the orb of the firmament revolving. Watch here until tomorrow around now.*" B: "*That is the orb of the firmament revolving. Watch until tomorrow around now,*" V, O: "*That is the orb of the firmament revolving. Tarry here until tomorrow around now*"
286. P, M, E, B: —. O: "*until the orb revolves,*" V: "*until the orb has revolved,*"
287. Uniquely in H. All others (P, M, E, V, O, B): "*and you'll find it.*"
288. Here, V has a mnemonic for Parts XV–XIX: *Mnemonic Safra Yohanan Yonatan Indian*
289. P: *recounted*
290. P, V, M, E, B: *we were traveling.* O: —
291. V, O, M, E, B: *we saw a certain*
292. V, O, M, E, B: *which brought out*
293. V, M, E, B: *its head from the water.* O: *its head from the sea.* P: *its head from below the water*
294. V, O: *two eyes*
295. V: *were like.* O: *detached.* I understand neither the sense nor the transmission of the unique reading in ms. O.
296. P: *spurted.* V: *washed.* O, M, E, B: *spilled*
297. E: —
298. Following O, M, B. P: *nostrils.* V: *ears.* H [x]: *columns* (unique scribal error). E: —
299. P: *recounted*
300. P, V, O, E, B: *we were traveling*
301. E: ~~on a road~~ *in a ship*
302. V: *we saw.* M, E, B: *and we saw.* O has a lacuna here.
303. V, M, E, B: *which brought out its head from the water.* O: *which brought out its head*

207   and it had two horns³⁰⁴
208   and³⁰⁵ upon them³⁰⁶ was engraven³⁰⁷: *I am a minor creature of the sea,*
209   *and I am³⁰⁸ three hundred³⁰⁹ parasang,*
210   *and prepared for³¹⁰ the mouth of Leviathan.*
211 **XVIIb. Rav Ashi said:³¹¹**
212   That one³¹² is the goat of the sea, and it is lean.³¹³
213
214 **XVIII.** Rabbi Yonatan³¹⁴ recounts:
215   Once we were traveling in a ship
216   and we³¹⁵ saw a certain little basket
217   which was studded³¹⁶ with precious stones and pearls
218   and encircled by a kind of³¹⁷ fish³¹⁸ named³¹⁹ *kharsha.*
219   A diver went down to bring up [the basket]. It was about to³²⁰ kill him.³²¹
220   He surfaced, held³²² a skin-bottle of³²³ sand³²⁴ over³²⁵ it, and he/it went
              down.
221
222   A heavenly³²⁶ voice appeared and said:³²⁷
223   What did you do³²⁸ with the³²⁹ little basket³³⁰ *that belongs to the wife of R*
              Hanina ben Dosa,

---

304. E, B: *a horn*
305. V, O: —
306. P, E, B: *it.* V, M: *which*
307. V: –
308. V [x]: *we are*
309. V: *as much as three hundred*
310. P, M, E, O, B: *and I am going into.* V: *and we are going in.* The variant in V is likely an error by harmonization, but may be intended to include Rav Safra (see chapter 1 n. 236).
311. V, O: *When we came before Rav Ashi, he said to us:*
312. O: —
313. Uniquely in H. P: *which has two horns and is lean.* E: *which is lean and has horns.* M: *which roves about and has horns.* B: *which creeps and has horns.* V, O: *which has the horn of a serpent.* M, V, O, and B are corrupt; see chapter 3 n. 458.
314. O, M, E, B: *Yohanan*
315. B: *one*
316. Uniquely in H. P, V, O, B: *affixed.* M, E: *inlaid*
317. V, O: *a certain.* M, E, N: *kinds of*
318. B: *fishes*
319. M, E, B, N: *that is called*
320. E: *they were coming [to].* N: *it was coming [to].* B: *they were fixing to*
321. P, M: *wrench his thigh.* E, N, B: *wrench him [apart].* See Gen. 32:26, 32:33; XXIa.257.
322. V: *threw.* P: *plunged*
323. V: —
324. On competing translations of this word and their apotropaic principles, see chapter 2 n. 278.
325. V: *at*
326. O: —
327. P, M, E, B, N: *and said to us:* V: *And it said to him:* O: *and the voice said to us:*
328. V: *did you want.* M, E, B, N: *have you [to do]*
329. V: *this*
330. V [x]: *little triangular couch*

224	in which <u>is tekhelet *that she spins into threads*</u>[331] *for the righteous in the world to come?*
225	
226	**XIX.** <u>R.</u>[332] Yehudah the Indian recounts:
227	Once <u>I was</u>[333] traveling in a ship
228	and <u>I</u>[334] saw a certain precious stone that was encircled by <u>a</u>[335] sea-serpent.
229	A diver went down <u>and brought it up.</u>[336]
230	and the <u>sea-serpent</u>[337] <u>was swallowing the ship.</u>[338]
231	A <u>wondrous bird</u>[339] came and <u>killed it:</u>[340]
232	the water <u>was transformed into</u>[341] blood.
233	Another <u>sea-serpent</u>[342] came,
234	<u>took</u>[343] [the sea-serpent],[344] <u>placed</u>[345] it upon[346] [the precious stone[347]],[348] and <u>revived it</u>.[349]
235	Again it <u>was swallowing</u>[350] the ship;
236	that <u>wondrous bird</u>[351] came <u>back</u>[352] and <u>killed it;</u>[353]

---

331. P, M, E [x], O [x]: *in future, she will spin* tekhelet. V [x], B, N: *in future, she will spin a thread of* tekhelet

332. Uniquely in H: *R[abbi]*. P, V, O, M, E, B, N: *Rav*

333. P, V, E, B: *we were*. N: *one was*

334. P, V, E, B: *we*. N: *one*

335. V: *that*

336. P, V, O, M, E, N: *to bring it up*

337. V: *that [one]*

338. P: *was about to swallow it*. B: *was about to swallow the ship*. V: *was about to sink the ship*

339. O, E: *bird*. N: ~~bird~~ [correction illegible; probably "wondrous bird," as in ms. N to IX.236]. On the earlier Persian reading "wondrous bird," see chapter 3 n. 427 and chapter 6 n. 742.

340. E: *killed the sea-serpent*. P: *cut off its head*. V: *and swallowed the head of the sea-serpent*. O: *snipped off*. M, B, N: *snipped off its head*

341. V, O, M, E, B, N: *was transformed and became*. Ln. XIX.232 is absent in P. See Exod. 7:17; 7:20; Rev. 16:4.

342. P, O, M, E, B: —

343. P: *brought*

344. M: *the head of the sea-serpent*. E: *it [i.e., the head of the sea-serpent]*. P: *it [i.e., the precious stone]*. V: *a certain precious stone*. O: *it [i.e., the precious stone]*

345. P: –. V [x], O, M, E, B, N: *hung*

346. P: *to*

347. P: –. V again mistakes its gender for masculine (as do all mss. except O at ln. XIX.228 above and H at ln. IX.237 below).

348. M: *hung it upon [the head]*. V, N, E [x]: *hung a certain precious stone upon it*. P: *[the sea-serpent]*. O, B: *and hung it upon [the head]*.

349. P, V, O, M, E, B, N: *it revived*. Unique reading in ms. H.

350. P, V: *It came back and was about to swallow the ship*
O: *came back to terminate the ship*. H: *was swallowing the ship*. M, E, N, B: *came back [and] was swallowing the ship*

351. O, M, E, B: *bird*. N: ~~bird~~ *wondrous bird*. Only H, P, V, and the corrector of N retain the Persian reading.

352. P, V: —

353. P, N: *cut off its head*. M, E, B: *cut it off*. O: *cut it off and threw it onto the ship*.

237	[the wondrous bird] took [the precious stone]³⁵⁴ and flew off³⁵⁵ with it,³⁵⁶ and as it flew,³⁵⁷
238	[the precious stone] landed in³⁵⁸ the ship,
239	on top of some salted birds, and they revived.³⁵⁹
240	They took it³⁶⁰ and they flew off.
241	
242	**XX.** Our rabbis taught:
243	A story about Rabbi Eliezer and Rabbi Yehoshua,
244	who were traveling in a³⁶¹ ship,
245	and Rabbi Eliezer was sleeping,
246	and Rabbi Yehoshua was awake.
247	Rabbi Yehoshua gave a start and Rabbi Eliezer woke up.³⁶²
248	He asked him: "What is it, Yehoshua?"³⁶³
249	He replied: "Rabbi,³⁶⁴ I have seen a great light in the sea."
250	"Perhaps³⁶⁵ it was the eyes of Leviathan you saw," he said. "As it is written of him:³⁶⁶
251	and³⁶⁷ his eyes are like the eyelids of the morning."³⁶⁸
252	
253	**XXIa.** Rav Ashi said:
254	Huna bar Natan recounted³⁶⁹ to me:
255	Once I was³⁷⁰ traveling in the desert³⁷¹

---

354. Ln. IX.237 is absent in O. N [x]: *and took that precious stone and threw it into the ship*
355. N, M, B: –
356. N, E: –
357. M, E, B: –
358. Ln. XIX.238 is absent in O (and N, where it falls in ln. XIX.237). M, E, B: *[the bird] threw [the precious stone] into*.
359. Uniquely in H. P: *And there were some salted birds with us*. V, O, M, E, B: *And so it was that there were some salted birds with us*. N: *We had several salted birds with us*. The underlined word in N is in the margin, as part of an obscure addition.
360. P: *We brought it to them. They lifted it up* V: *We took it and hung it* O: *We took it and hung it on them. They took it* M: *We hung it on them. They took it* E: *We took it, hung it on them; they took it* B: *I took it and hung it on them. They took it* N: *We hung it on them. They took it*
361. Unique error in H. P, V, O, M, N, B: *Going by*
362. M [x]: *woke up Rabbi Eliezer*
363. P: *"Yehoshua, what did you see, my brother?"* O, M, B, N: *"Why did you give a start?"*
364. Uniquely in H.
365. O: *Understand*: This is a correction away from *Perhaps*, the reading in the other mss. Ms. M is ambiguous due to abbreviation: it reads either *Perhaps* or *Understand*: (which differ only by one letter). See chapter 1 n. 233.
366. P: —
367. P: —
368. Job 41:18 (41:10).
369. P, M, E, B, C: *said*
370. P, E, B, C: *we were*
371. O: ~~in a ship~~ in the desert.

256	and <u>with us was</u>³⁷² a <u>thigh</u>.³⁷³
257	I <u>opened</u>³⁷⁴ it and <u>removed the veins</u>,³⁷⁵
258	<u>put it on</u>³⁷⁶ <u>herbs</u>,³⁷⁷ <u>and it closed up</u>;³⁷⁸
259	<u>we brought kindling and roasted it</u>.³⁷⁹
260	<u>The next year, I came back</u>;³⁸⁰
261	<u>the coals were still glowing</u>.³⁸¹
262	**XXIb.** <u>When</u>³⁸² I³⁸³ came before Amemar, he said <u>to me</u>:³⁸⁴
263	The³⁸⁵ <u>herbs were</u>³⁸⁶ <u>dragon's blood</u>,³⁸⁷ and³⁸⁸ the³⁸⁹ coals <u>were</u>³⁹⁰ of³⁹¹ broom.

---

372. V: *there was*. P, O, M, E, B, N: *there was with us*
373. P, O, M, E, B, N: *of meat*. This is simply implied in H, uniquely so.
374. V: *sliced*
375. P, N: —
376. P: *We placed it on*. V, M, E: *I put it on some*. O [x]: *and we put it on some*
377. M: –. E, B, N [x]: *greenery*
378. Uniquely in H [but see the continuation of other mss. in ln. XXIa.259. Only in V is *and it closed up* truly absent (—)].
379. P: *while we were getting kindling, it closed up, and we roasted it*. V: *and we brought kindling and roasted*. O: *before we could get kindling and roast, when we returned, it had become thick*. M: *while we were getting kindling, it closed up and became thick. We roasted it*. E, C: *while were were getting kindling, it closed up. We roasted it*. B: *while we were getting kindling, the thigh became thick. We roasted it*.
380. P: *When I came back after a full year* [lit.: *twelve months of a year*]. M, E [x], B, C: *When we came back after twelve months of a year*. O: *We arrived after a full year* [lit. *a year of months*]. V: *The next year, when we came back,*
381. P, B [x]: *I saw that those coals were still glowing*. V [x]: *We saw those coals that were just as alive*. O [x], M, E, N: *We saw that the coals were just as alive*. O: *we saw that those coals were still preserved* [lit. *salted*]
382. P: —
383. Following all other mss. except C (which has a lacuna here) and E. H [x]: *one/he*
384. V, O: —
385. P, V: *Those*. O, M, E, B, N, C: *That*
386. O, M, E, B, N, C: *herb was*
387. O [x]: *of dragon's blood*
388. P, O, M, E, B, N, C: —
389. P, O, M, E, B, N, C: *those*
390. P, M: –
391. M: –

Translation. Part 2.
b. B. Bat. 74b.22–75b.40

(per folio-side.line in Vilna, on which text is based;
for mss. in notes, see §*Note on the Text*)

2.A. The Leviathan

And God created the great sea-serpents ...[1]

Here, they rendered [this as]:[2] *gazelles of the sea.*[3] R. Yohanan said: Those are *Leviathan the straight serpent*[4] and *Leviathan the bent serpent*,[5] as it is written: *In that day the Lord with His sore [and great and strong] sword shall take care of [Leviathan the straight serpent and Leviathan the bent serpent]*.[6]

(Mnemonic: **All things, Moment, The Jordan**).

Rav Yehudah said in the name of Rav: **All things** that the Holy One, Blessed be He, created in his universe, *male and female created He them* (Gen. 5:2). So, too, Leviathan the straight serpent and Leviathan the bent serpent–*male and female created He them*. And were they to copulate, they would destroy the entire universe. What did the Holy One, Blessed be He, do? He castrated the male, killed the female, and salted her for the righteous in the world to come, as it is written: *And He slayed the sea-serpent that was in the sea.*[7]

And so, too, *Behemoth upon a thousand hills*,[8] *male and female created He them*, and were they to copulate, they would destroy the entire universe. What

---

1. Gen 1:21 (KJV, trans. modified).
2. For all instances of this formula, see Smelik, *Rabbis, Language, and Translation*, 193 n. 38. It more commonly contrasts a Babylonian translation/interpretation ("here") with one attributed to a Palestinian authority. In this case, the contrast to the Palestinian authority (R. Yohanan) is implicit. See further Kalmin, *Migrating Tales*, 43–44 n. 34.
3. This is not in any extant Targum that I could find, but it is a variant of *aurochs/aurochs gazelle*, 1.IV (Rashi, b. Zevah. 113b, s.v. אורזילא). It may be influenced by, or in fact reference, 1.IV (Stemberger, "Münchhausen und die Apokalyptik," 69).
4. Isa 27:1 (KJV, modified; trans. after Rashi *ad loc.*).
5. Isa 27:1 (KJV, modified; trans. after Rashi *ad loc.*).
6. Isa 27:1 (KJV, trans. modified). For *p.q.d* + '*al* ("to take care of" in a negative sense; "to visit [punishment] upon"), see, e.g., Isa 10:12.
7. Isa 27:1 (KJV, trans. modified). In its biblical context, the verse is in the future aspect, and refers to a *third* kind of aquatic creature.
8. Ps 50:10 (KJV, trans. modified).

did the Holy One, Blessed be He, do? He castrated the male and made the female frigid,[9] and looked after her for the righteous in the world to come, as it is said: *Lo now, his strength is in his loins*—that is the male—*and his force is in the navel of his belly*—that is the female.[10]

[But] there, too, [in the case of the Leviathan], He should castrate the male and make the female frigid [rather than killing her]!—Fish are dissolute [so making them frigid is not an option].[11] —Then He should do it the other way around [kill the male and preserve the female]! —[Indeed,] if you like, argue: a salted female is superb. If you like [to differ], argue: *there is that* [male] *Leviathan, whom thou hast made to play with.*[12] —[Further, because] it is not proper conduct [to *"play"*] with a female, here, too [in the case of Behemoth], shouldn't he salt the female [rather than *make her frigid* and *look after her*]? —[Not necessarily, because] salted fish is superb, whereas salted meat is not.

And Rav Yehudah said in the name of Rav: At the **moment** that the Holy One, Blessed be He, decided to create the universe, He said to the Prince of the Sea: "Open your mouth and swallow all the waters in the universe." But he said to Him: "Lord of the Universe, it's quite enough for me to swallow my own waters."[13] Immediately, He kicked[14] him and killed him,[15] as it is written: *He divideth*[16] *the sea with his power, and by his understanding he smiteth through Rahav.*[17]

R. Yitshaq said: Learn from this that the Prince of the Sea's name is Rahav. And if waters were not covering him, no creature could remain due to his stench, as it is written: *They shall not hurt nor destroy in all my holy mountain* [*for the earth shall be full of the knowledge of the Lord*] *as the waters cover the sea.*[18] Do not read *as the waters cover the sea* but rather *cover the Prince of the sea.*

And Rav Yehudah said in the name of Rav: **The Jordan** issues from

---

9. The same root as *cool ourselves off* (1.IXa.112, mss. H and O); in the telling of these mss., a link back to part 1.
10. Job 40:16. To read this language as castration and sterility seems counter to the context (extolling the virility and fecundity of these creatures). Rashbam *ad loc.* explains that his strength is *in* his loins because it has never been ejaculated, just as her force is *in* her belly because she has never given birth.
11. Bracketed explanations after Rashbam.
12. Ps 104:26 (KJV, trans. modified). I.e., the playmate "Leviathan" is clearly marked as male, so God cannot kill him.
13. Underlined text after Rashbam *ad loc.* (Vilna: *that I shall remain with what is mine*).
14. Ms. P: *yelled at*; Ms. O: *grew angry at*. See Fishbane, "Great Dragon Drama," 279 n. 11.
15. Compare the defiance of the company of Qorah and their punishment, linked to the same verb: "swallow" (ב.ל.ע), Num. 16:30–34, and noun: "maw" (1.XIV.179).
16. The translation *divideth* accords with Rashbam *ad loc.*, whereas Rashi to Job 26:12 renders "wrinkles," as in Job 7:5: *My skin is wrinkled* (KJV, modified).
17. Job 26:12 (KJV, modified).
18. Isa 11:9.

the cave of Panyás.¹⁹ It is also taught thus:²⁰ The Jordan issues from the cave of Panyás and goes through the sea of Samməko and the sea of Tiberias, and circulates and runs down into the Great Sea, and circulates and runs down until it reaches the mouth of the Leviathan,²¹ as it is written, *he trusteth that he can draw up Jordan into his mouth*.²²

> Rava bar Ulla challenged him:²³ That [verse] is written about *Behemoth on a thousand hills*! Rather, what Rava bar Ulla said [that the verse meant] was: When *"trusteth"* Behemoth on a thousand hills? At the moment that the Jordan penetrates the mouth of Leviathan.²⁴

(Mnemonic: **Seas, Gabriel, Hunger**).

When Rav Dimi arrived,²⁵ he said in the name of R. Yohanan: What [are we to make of] what is written, *For he hath founded it upon the seas, and established it upon the rivers*?²⁶ Those are the seven **seas** and four rivers surrounding the Land of Israel. And these are the seven seas: The sea of Tiberias²⁷ and the sea of Sodom²⁸ and the sea of Shilyat²⁹ and the sea of Ḥulta'³⁰ and the sea of Samməko and the sea of Apamea and the Great Sea.³¹ And these are the four rivers: the Jordan and the Yarmuk and the Qeramyon and the Pegá.

---

19. Spelling of rare Palestinian and Babylonian place-names, respectively, follows Reeg, *Die Ortsnamen*; Oppenheimer, *Babylonia Judaica*. Common place-names are spelled with house style (see §*Note on the Text*).

20. This *baraita* is paralleled at b. Bekh. 55a, minus the conclusion ("until it reaches the mouth of the Leviathan, etc."), which seems to be added to harmonize it with the larger context.

21. See 1.XVIIa.210: *and [I am] prepared for the mouth of the Leviathan*, another retrospective link between the two parts.

22. Job 40:23.

23. I.e., whoever added the conclusion about the Leviathan to the *baraita*.

24. I.e., although, in the context of Job 40:23, the verse is clearly about Behemoth, not about Leviathan, according to this reinterpretation of Rava bar Ulla's challenge, he *accepts* the interpretation that it is about Leviathan, but he asserts that it is *Behemoth* who "trusteth" when *Leviathan* "drinks." (Why, he does not say; perhaps because Leviathan cannot devour Behemoth while it is busy drinking the waters.) These confusions are elegantly harmonized by an allegory (Behemoth : Leviathan :: Body : Soul) in Rashba, *Commentary on the Legends in the Talmud* [Hebrew], ed. Leon A. Feldman (Jerusalem: Mossad Ha-Rav Kook, 1991), 101.

25. In the Babylonian Talmud, this formula is traditionally understood as implying [from Palestine], and often associated with Rav Dimi, who transmits teachings of the Palestinian sage, R. Yohanan. See chapter 3, n. 438, and Redfield, "'When X Arrived,'" 5 n. 9.

26. Ps 24:2 (KJV, modified). For an Iranian parallel to this talmudic hydrology, see Kiperwasser and Shapira, "Irano-Talmudica II," 211.

27. A.k.a., the Sea of Galilee.

28. A.k.a., the Dead Sea.

29. Reeg (*Die Ortsnamen*, 303) identifies this with the Gulf of Eilat.

30. Location uncertain. Reeg (*Die Ortsnamen*, 302) locates it north of the sea of Samməko.

31. A.k.a., the Mediterranean.

When Rav Dimi arrived, he said in the name of R. Yohanan: In time to come, **Gabriel** shall arrange a hunt[32] of the Leviathan, as it is written: *Canst thou draw out Leviathan with an hook? or his tongue with a cord which thou lettest down?*[33] But if the Holy One, Blessed be He, does not help him, he will not be able [to overcome] him, as it is written: *He that made him can make his sword to approach unto him.*[34]

When Rav Dimi arrived, he said in the name of R. Yohanan: At the moment that Leviathan is **hungry**, he puts forth vapor from his mouth and makes all the seas that are in the deep boil, as it is written: *He maketh the deep to boil like a pot.*[35] And if he did not put his head into the Garden of Eden, no creature would be able to withstand his odor, as it is written: *he maketh the sea like a pot of ointment.*[36] And at the moment that he is thirsty, he makes furrows upon furrows in the sea, as it is written: *He maketh a path to shine after him.*[37]

Rav Aha bar Ya'aqov said: [Due to the Leviathan], the abyss only returns to its strength after seventy years, as it is said: *one would think the deep to be hoary;*[38] and *hoary* is not less than seventy.[39]

2.B. The Leviathan and The Covering

Rabbah said in the name of R. Yohanan: In time to come, the Holy One, Blessed be He, will arrange a banquet for the righteous from the flesh of Leviathan, as it is said: *Shall the companions make a feast of him?*[40] For *feast* is none other than a banquet, as it is said: *And he had them feasted with a*

---

32. *Qenigiya*, from Gk. κυνήγιον; see Samuel Krauss and Immanuel Löw, *Griechische und lateinische Lehnwörter im Talmud, Midrasch und Targum*, 2 vols. (Berlin: S. Calvary 1898–1899), 2:553–54. Rav Dimi's Babylonian contemporary prized the agentive form as a rare loanword (b. Hul. 60b): "But was Moses our teacher a hunter (*qenigi* = κυνηγός) or an archer (*balistari*)?! [...] Rav Hisda said to Rav bar Tahlifa bar Avina: 'Go, write *qenigi* and *balistari* in your [book of] *aggada* and define it." On possible Iranian background to this motif, see Kiperwasser and Shapira, "Irano-Talmudica II," 223–27.

33. Job 41:1 (40:25). In the Vilna print and other witnesses, the word for *Canst* has a prefixed *heh*, indicating a rhetorical question. Other mss. (the Genizah fragment Cambridge T-S F1(1).30; the early Spanish ms. Hamburg; and the late Provençal ms. Escorial) lack this feature. The same variant appears among mss. of the Hebrew Bible itself. (The following verses all begin with the same rhetorical prefix; perhaps it was added due to harmonization).

34. Job 40:19, reading restrictively to imply "... [*only*] He that made him [= Leviathan] can make his [= Gabriel's] sword" etc.

35. Job 41:31a (41:23a).
36. Job 41:31b (41:23b).
37. Job 41:32a (41:24a).
38. Job 41:32b (41:24b).

39. In other words, a person is not called *hoary* until they reach seventy. See m. Avot 5:21: *At the age of seventy, one is hoary* (ed. Albeck, *Shisha Sidrei Mishnah*, 4:381).

40. Job 41:6a (40:30a; KJV, trans. modified).

great feast: and they ate and they drank;[41] and *the companions* are none other than disciples of the sages, as it is said: *Thou that dwellest in the gardens, the companions hearken to thy voice: cause me to hear it.*[42] And they divide the rest and arrange it as merchandise in the markets of Jerusalem, as it is said: *shall they part him among the merchants?*[43] For *merchants* are none other than wheeler-dealers,[44] as it is said: *He is a merchant, the balances of deceit are in his hand: he loveth to oppress.*[45] Or, if you like, argue it from here: *whose merchants are princes, whose traffickers are the honourable of the earth.*[46]

And Rabbah said in the name of R. Yohanan: In time to come, the Holy One, Blessed be He, will arrange a cover for the righteous from the skin of Leviathan, as it is said: *Canst thou fill his skin with barbed irons* [śukkôt]?[47] If he is deserving, a cover is arranged for him; if not, a shading is arranged for him, as it is said: *or his head with a fish spear* [ṣilṣal dagim].[48] If he is deserving, a shading is arranged for him; if not, chains are arranged for him, as it is said: *and chains about thy neck.*[49] If he is deserving, chains are arranged for him; if not, an amulet is arranged for him, as it is said: *or thou wilt bind it for thy maidens.*[50] And the rest will the Holy One, Blessed be He, spread across the walls of Jerusalem, and its radiance will shine from one end of the universe to the other, as it is said: *And the nations shall come to thy light, and kings to the brightness of thy rising.*[51]

---

41. 2 Kgs 6:23 (KJV, trans. modified).

42. Song 8:13. These verbs (*hearken; hear*) often refer to Torah-study. This strengthens the merely etymological correspondence between "disciples of the sages" (*haverim*) and "companions" (*habbarim*). For another example, see Gershom Scholem, "The Idea of the Golem," in *On the Kabbalah and Its Symbolism*, 158–216, at 166 (on b. San. 65b).

43. Job 41:6b (40:30).

44. The same gloss appears in the Masorah Parva to Job 41:6b (40:30; "a term for a wheeler-dealer," *lashon tagrayya*). It is not always pejorative (closer to "middleman"); see Friedman, "Dama ben Netinah," 465.

45. Hos 12:7 (12:8).

46. Isa 23:8.

47. Job 41:7a (40:31). "Barbed irons" [śukkôt] is a homophone of "covers" [sukkôt]; here, the midrash changes the consonantal text of the Masoretic tradition. To disambiguate homophones, I adopt the academic transliteration system of *The SBL Handbook of Style*, 26 (cited in §*Note on the Text*).

48. Job 41:7b (40:30, trans. modified). Biblical "spear" is a homophone of rabbinic "shading" (*ṣilṣāl*), from *ṣēl* ("shade; shadow"; see also t. Eruv. 2:3; y. Sukkah 5:5, 55c; b. Eruv. 10b). Rather than *ṣilṣāl*, Rashbam to b. B. Bat. 75a s.v. *sukkāh* seems to read *ṣēl*, just as in Isa 4:6 (see 3.A below), i.e., "a kind of covering [*sikkūah*] without a [vertical] partition."

49. Prov 1:9.

50. Job 41:5 (40:29, KJV, trans. modified in line with Rashbam's interpretation: the verse is referring not to the binding of the Leviathan but to "a small thing that one ties to wear around one's throat, like an amulet").

51. Isa 60:3 (KJV, trans. modified).

2.C. The Heavenly Jerusalem

And I will make thy battlements of kadkhod:[52]

R. Shmuel bar Nahmani said: Two angels are debating in the firmament, Gabriel and Michael. And some say it was[53] two Amoraim in the West. (And who are they? Judah and Hizqeyyah, the sons of R. Hiyya). One said [*kadkhod* is] beryl.[54] One said [*kadkhod* is] onyx.[55] The Holy One, Blessed be He, said to them: Let it be both as this and as that [*keden u-kheden*].

And thy gates of carbuncles.[56] Just as in this [tradition]:[57]

//R. Yohanan was expounding: "In time to come, the Holy One, Blessed be He, will bring precious stones and pearls that are thirty by thirty [cubits], and carve out [a space from] them ten [cubits wide] by twenty [high],[58] and set them up in the gates of Jerusalem." A certain disciple jeered at him: "Nowadays, we don't find them as big as a turtle-dove's egg; are we to find them that big?!" Some days later, his ship went off to sea. He saw the ministering angels who were chiseling precious stones and pearls thirty by thirty [cubits] and carving out [a space from them] ten [cubits wide] by twenty high. He said to them: "Who are these for?" They replied that in time to come, the Holy One, Blessed be He, would set them up in the gates of Jerusalem. He came before R. Yohanan and said to him: "Expound, Rabbi, it is fit for you to expound; yea, just as you have said, thus have I seen." He replied: "Good-for-nothing! If you *hadn't* seen, you *wouldn't* have believed! You jeer at the words of the sages." He cast his eyes at him and he was transformed into a pile of bones.

It is objected:[59] *And I will make you go upright*:[60] R. Meir says: "[The word *upright* means that the height of the gates of the Heavenly Jerusalem

---

52. Isa 54:12 (KJV, modified).
53. On this introductory formula for variant attributions/traditions, see literature at Redfield, "Redacting Culture," 74 n. 92.
54. *Shoham*, an unknown gem in the priestly breastplate (see Exod 25:7; 28:9, 20; 35:9, 27; 39:6, 13). I translate *beryl* after LXX βηρύλλιον (Exod 28:20; cf. Exod 28:9: σμάραγδος, *emerald*).
55. *Yashfeh*, an unknown gem in the priestly breastplate (see Exod 28:20; 39:12). I translate *onyx* after LXX ὀνύχιον (Exod 28:20).
56. Isa 54:12 (KJV, modified).
57. The section enclosed within // // is paralleled at b. Sanh. 100a. On its significance, see chapter 5, n. 726 and n. 736.
58. Trans. after Rashbam *ad loc.* and the clarifying wording of the repetition below ("twenty *high*").
59. I.e., someone disputes R. Yohanan's previous claim about the height of the Temple in the Heavenly Jerusalem on the basis of R. Meir's interpretation of a different verse.
60. Lev 26:13 (KJV, modified from the past tense to the future tense, in line with R. Meir's interpretation).

will be] two hundred cubits, equalling twice the height of Adam."[61] Rav Yehudah says: "[The gates of the Heavenly Jerusalem will be] a hundred cubits, matching [the height of] the Temple and its walls, as it is said: *That our sons may be as plants grown up in their youth; that our daughters may be as corner stones, polished after the similitude of a palace.*"[62] But R. Yohanan is only speaking about the slits of the [much smaller] area for a draft.[63]//

And Rabbah said in the name of R. Yohanan: In time to come, the Holy One, Blessed be He, will arrange seven canopies [*huppot*] for every righteous one, as it is said: *And the Lord will create upon every dwelling place of mount Zion, and upon her assemblies, a cloud and smoke by day, and the shining of a flaming fire by night: for upon all the glory shall be a canopy.*[64] This teaches that for every one of them, the Holy One Blessed be He will arrange him a canopy, according to his honor. [But] why is there *smoke* in a canopy?[65] R. Hanina said that if anyone squints[66] at disciples of the sages in this world, his eyes will be filled with smoke in the world to come. [And] why there is there *fire* in a canopy? R. Hanina said: this teaches that if anyone envies the canopy of his companion, Woe for such shame! Woe for such disgrace!

Along the same lines, you [may] say: *And thou shalt put some of thine honour upon him.*[67] But not all of your honor? Elders who were in that generation said: "The face of Moses is like the face of the sun, the face of Joshua is like the face of the moon."[68] Woe for such shame! Woe for such disgrace![69]

R. Hama[70] the son of R. Hanina said: The Holy One, Blessed be He,

---

61. As Rashbam notes *ad loc.*, R. Meir derives this doubled height from the doubled letter *mem* in "upright" (*qomemiyyut*). For Adam's height after the fall as 100 cubits, see sources in Ginzberg, *Legends*, 1:98 n. 137.

62. Ps 144:12. I.e., the height of the gates for God's *sons* and *daughters* in the Heavenly Jerusalem will equal the height of God's previous *palace* [= Temple] *in their youth*.

63. This unique term has a longer reading/gloss in ms. P: *Slits that a draft goes through*, i.e., the ventilation ducts of the Temple. The rare words "slit" and "draft" (or a homonym of the latter: "skin-bottle") already appeared in 1.XV.190 and 1.XVIII.220, respectively—yet another example of verbal synergy between the two parts of the composition.

64. Isa 4:5 (KJV, trans. modified).

65. I.e., if it is a reward, why does it contain this noxious element?

66. I.e., is stingy and does not share his assets with them. Rashbam *ad loc*.

67. Num 27:20. The verse addresses Moses and refers to Joshua.

68. I.e., the word "some" shows that the generations had already begun to decline with Joshua. Note the inversion of the redemptive eschatological prophecy in Isa 30:26 (KJV: *the light of the moon shall be as the light of the sun, and the light of the sun shall be sevenfold*).

69. I.e., the decline of the generations due to lack of honor for the sages, and envy among them, is shameful. Note another inversion of Isaiah (24:23, KJV: *Then the moon shall be confounded, and the sun ashamed*). Obviously, Moses's shining face is already biblical (Exod 34:29; see also Deut 34:7), whereas the description of Joshua's face as "like the moon" is attested elsewhere in rabbinic sources (see chapter 6, n. 864).

70. The tradition of this sage (Hama) may be joined to the prior tradition by association with "sun" (*hammah*). For somewhat similar examples, see §*Introduction* n. 120; Friedman,

arranged ten canopies [*huppot*] for Adam in the Garden of Eden, as it is said: *Thou hast been in Eden the garden of God; every precious stone [was thy cover: carnelian ...].*[71] Mar Zutra said: [He arranged] eleven [canopies], as it is said: <u>*Every*</u> *precious stone.*[72] R. Yohanan said: "And the least of them all was gold"—because it was not accounted for until the end [of the list in that verse].

What [is meant by] *the workmanship of thy tabrets and of thy pipes [was prepared] in thee?*[73] Rav Yehudah said in the name of Rav: "The Holy One, Blessed be He, said to Hiram King of Tyre, '*In thee* did I look, and [upon that very day] did I create orifices upon orifices[74] within humanity.'"[75] And there is one who says, this is what [the verse] is saying: '*In thee* did I look, and I imposed death upon Adam.'"

What [is meant by] *and upon her assemblies?*[76] Rabbah said in the name of R. Yohanan: "Not like Jerusalem of this world is Jerusalem of the world to come. Jerusalem of this world: anyone who wants to go up, can go up. Jerusalem of the world to come: only those who are invited[77] to it can go up."

And Rabbah said in the name of R. Yohanan: "In time to come, the righteous will be called[78] by the name of the Holy One, Blessed be He, as it is said: *Even every one that is called by my name: for I have created him for my glory, I have formed him; yea, I have made him.*[79] And R. Shmuel bar Nahmani said in the name of R. Yohanan: "Three were called by the name of the Holy One, Blessed be He, and they are: The righteous, and the Messiah, and Jerusalem." The righteous—as it was [just] said. The Messiah—as it is written, *and this is his name whereby he shall be called, The Lord Our Righteous-*

"Nomen est Omen," 74; J. D. Wynkoop, "A Peculiar Kind of Paronomasia in the Talmud and Midrash," *JQR* 2.1 (1911): 1–23, at 14.

71. Ezek 28:13. The verse itself refers to Adam, ironically contrasting him to Hiram (Rashbam *ad loc.*; see also the beginning of this prophecy, "Son of man" [*ben-'Adam*]). But the [bracketed continuation of the verse], not quoted in Vilna, is the key to this midrash. "Carnelian" (*'odem*; LXX: σάρδιον) is close to "Adam," while the root of "cover" [*mĕsūkātekā*] was already used for "canopy" in the midrash on Job 41:7a (40:31) above. Midrash thus yields: "*every precious stone [was thy canopy for Adam]*." For gems as divine protection in 2.C above, see Isa. 54:11 and chapter 5 n. 676.

72. Reading "every" as an addition to the contents of the list; a standard *midrashic* technique (e.g., m. Ber. 1:5; ed. Albeck, *Shisha Sidrei Mishnah* 1:15).

73. Ezek 28:13.

74. Combining the language of a rabbinic blessing uttered upon excretion (b. Ber. 24b = b. Ber. 60a = b. Ber. 75a) with the unique instance of this biblical noun for a jeweller's cavity.

75. I.e., foreseeing Hiram's rebellion and bad character, God saw the need to install a means to excrete noxious waste from the rest of humanity (following Rashbam *ad loc.*).

76. Isa 4:5 (KJV, trans. modified).

77. I.e., "called"; playing on the root of *assemblies* (ק.ר.א).

78. Continuing the wordplay on ק.ר.א, which links the two exegeses.

79. Isa 43:7 (KJV).

ness.⁸⁰ And Jerusalem—as it is written, *It was round about eighteen thousand measures: and the name of the city from that day shall be, The Lord is there.*⁸¹ Do not read *there* [*šāmmāh*] but rather *its name* [*šemāh*].⁸² R. El'azar said: "In time to come, one will say 'Holy' before the righteous in the same way that one says it before the Holy One, Blessed be He, as it is said: *he that is left in Zion, and he that remaineth in Jerusalem, shall be called holy.*⁸³

And Rabbah said in the name of R. Yohanan: In time to come, the Holy One, Blessed be He, will raise up Jerusalem three *parasang*, as it is said: *and it shall raise and it shall settle in its place.*"⁸⁴ What is [meant by] *in its place*? [That *it shall raise*] as [high] as its base [is wide]. And how [do we know] that this [= three *parasang*] is its base? Rabbah said: A certain Elder told me: I myself have seen the previous Jerusalem, and it is three *parasang* [wide]. But perhaps you'll say: It hurts to go up? [It doesn't. That is what] the statement teaches: *Who are these that fly as a cloud, and as the doves to their windows?*⁸⁵ Rav Pappa said: "Learn from it that a cloud lifts⁸⁶ three *parasang* atop [the earth].⁸⁷

R. Haninah bar Pappa said: "The Holy One, Blessed be He, wanted to give Jerusalem a proper measure, as it is said: *Then said I, Whither goest thou? And he said unto me, To measure Jerusalem, to see what is the breadth thereof, and what is the length thereof.*⁸⁸ The ministering angels said before the Holy One, Blessed be He: 'Master of the Universe, in your world, you made many towns⁸⁹ of the Nations of the world, and you gave them neither a measure of their length or a measure of their width. To Jerusalem—within which is Your Name, Your Holiness, and Your righteous—are you immediately giving a measure? As it is said: *And said unto him, Run, speak to this young man, saying, Jerusalem shall be inhabited as towns without walls*

---

80. Jer 23:6. The verse refers to David, often identified with the Messiah. Compare Jer. 23:5/Isa. 11:1 and see further Sigmund Mowinckel, *He That Cometh: The Messiah Concept in the Old Testament and Later Judaism*, trans. G. W. Anderson (Grand Rapids: Eerdmans, 2005 [1956]), 155–86.
81. Ezek 48:35.
82. I.e., "the name of the city from that day shall be, *The Lord is its name.*" The proof retains the consonantal text.
83. Isa 4:3.
84. Zech 14:10 (my trans.; see chapter 5 n. 705).
85. Isa 60:8 (KJV).
86. From the root נ.ש.א, "to lift," yet another verbal link to part one (I.1.5, I.1.8, Xa.133, XVI.199, XVIIa.206).
87. I.e., if we know from the tradition of the Elder that its base is three *parasang*, and we know from the tradition of R. Yohanan that its height was the same as its base, and we know from Isa 60:8 that it is lifted up by a cloud, then we also know that a cloud rises three *parasang* in the air.
88. Zech 2:2 (2:6).
89. *Kerakhim*, which by definition (b. Meg. 2a–2b) do have walls/fortifications, contrary to the verse below. The term can also mean "city; settlement," and it seems to be used in that more general sense.

for the multitude of men and cattle within.'"⁹⁰ Resh Laqish said: "In time to come, the Holy One, Blessed be He, will expand Jerusalem by:⁹¹ a thousand [times] טפ"ף gardens [= 169], a thousand [times] קפ"ל towers [= 210] a thousand [times] ליצו"י citadels,⁹² [= 146] a thousand and two [times] שיל"ה four-cornered mansions [= 345].⁹³ And every single one of them will be like Sepphoris at its most irenic. It is taught:⁹⁴ R. Yose said: "I saw Sepphoris at its most irenic, and in it, there were a hundred and eighty thousand markets of vendors of mincemeat puddings. *And the side chambers were three, one over another, and thirty in order.*⁹⁵ What [is meant by] *three, one over another, and thirty in order*? R. Levi said in the name of Rav Pappi following R. Yehoshua of Siknin: [In time to come] if there are three Jerusalems, every single one of them has in it thirty stories above [one another]; if there are thirty Jerusalems, every single one of them has three stories above [one another].

---

90. Zech 2:4 (2:8; KJV, modified). I.e., the ministering angels are challenging God's imposition of a three-*parasang*-square or any size upon Jerusalem. They argue that the nations' towns do not have a fixed size, and the verse proves that Jerusalem is supposed to be like those. The conclusion of the argument refutes this by expanding Jerusalem's size hyperbolically.
    91. Rashbam *ad loc.* explains the following acronyms as a particular conventional way to express numbers in words. This understanding is also reflected in ms. H, which marks all except one (ליצו"י) as numbers.
    92. *Biraniyyot*; Alexander Kohut plausibly glosses "Burg, Castell" (*Aruch Completum* [Vienna 1880], 2:195), based on lexical equivalents in Targumim, but he neglects this source (or biblical sources, e.g. 1 Chr 29:1). Trans. after Stephen A. Kaufman, *The Akkadian Influences on Aramaic*, Assyriological Studies 19 (Chicago: Oriental Institute of the University of Chicago, 1974), 44.
    93. טוטפראות, a corruption of טיטרפלין = τετράπυλα (see Krauss and Löw, *Lehnwörter* 2:262).
    94. Conventionally, this formula introduces a *baraita*, but in this case, the *baraita* is unattested elsewhere: see Higger, *Otsar ha-baraitot*, 8:92; Rabbinovicz, *Diquduqe Soferim Baba Batra*, 240 n. ס.
    95. Ezek 41:6 (KJV). R. Yose alludes to the renaming of Sepphoris as Eirēnopolis ("city of peace") in the Roman period.

Appendix 2

Edition

(Part 1 only: text body = ms. H/ה
with starred *corrections from others as cited)

א **א**[1]

ב אמ' רבא[2] אשתעו[3] לי נחותי *ימא[4]

ג בין גלא לגלא[5] תלת[6] מאה [7]פרסי

ד רומיה[8] דגלא[9] תלת מאה[10] [11]פרסי

ה זמנא חדא[12] דלינן[13] [14]גלא

ו וחזיתיה[15] בי[16] מרבעתיה[17] [18]דכוכבא

---

1. Unit א follows Unit ב in all indirect witnesses cited in *DS* and all mss. *except* פ , ה. In פ, Unit ב is added in the margin.

2. וו, ב: ואמ' רבה. מ: וא' רבא

3. פ: אישתעו. ב, מ, א: אישתעי. ⁰פ: אישעו

4. וו: ימה.

5. מ: לגל'

6. — :⁰פ. The omission is between lines, probably due to eye-skip.

7. מ: פרסאי

8. ורומיה :וו .ורומיה :א ,פ. Ln. ד is absent in mss. ב ,מ, perhaps due to eye-skip over a phrase between identical words (פרסי). But note that is also absent in some indirect witnesses. See §*Select Variants in Other Sources* in my study, "Textual Witnesses, Editions, and Translations of the Tales of Rabbah bar bar Hanah & Friends," cited in n. 1 to the Introduction.

9. א: דגלהא

10. וו: מאת

11. וו: פרסין

12. פ, וו, מ: זימנא חדא. ב: זימנ' חדא. א: וזימנא חד'. ⁰פ: זימנא

13. פ: הוה אזלינן בספינתא ודלינן. ב: הוה קאזלי' בספינת' ודלינ' קגלא דלינ'. וו: הוה קאזלינן בספינתא ודליין. Correction in ms. ב above the line. This entire introductory formula (up to דלינן) is missing in ⁰פ, א, מ.

14. פ: גלא לעילא תלת מאה פרסי. וו: גלא לעילא. ב: גלא לעילאי. Underlined text in ms. פ is not necessarily a dittography. Rashbam comments (b. B. Bat. 73a s.v. גלא דלינן): "[the wave] lifted us *more than* the measure of its own height, up to the firmament." Ms. פ preserves the opposite view: the wave, which was 300 *parasang*, lifted the ship *only* to its height.

15. פ: וחזינא. וו: עד דחזינא. ב, מ: עד דחזינ'. א: עד דיחזיניה. ⁰פ: עד דחזינן. Unique reading in ms. ה.

16. וו: —. מ, ⁰פ: לבי. א: לבית

17. פ, וו: מרבעתא. ב: מרבעת'. א, ⁰פ: מעברתיה

18. ב: דכוכבי. וו, מ: דכוכבא זוטא. א: רכוכבא זוטא. ⁰פ: דכוכמא זוטא. Unique errors in mss. ⁰פ, א.

ז וְהוָה^{19} כִּי מִיבְזַר^{20} אַרְבְּעַי^{21} גְּרִיוֵי^{22} חַרְדְּלָא^{23}

ח וַאֲיֵי^{24} דְּלִי לָן^{25} טְפֵי הֲוָה קְלֵי לָן^{26} מֵחַבְלָא^{27}

ט רְמָא לִי גַּלָּא קָלָא לְחַבְרֵיהּ^{28}

י מִי^{29} שָׁבְקַתְּ^{30} מִידֵי בְּעָלְמָא^{31} דְּלָא חֲרִיבְתֵּיהּ^{32}

י״א אֲמַ' לֵיהּ^{33} תָּא^{34} חֲזִי בִּגְבוּרְתֵיהּ^{35} דְּמָרִיךְ^{36}

י״ב דְּאַפִּלּוּ^{37} כַּמְלָא חוּטָא *דַּחֲלָא*^{38} ^{39}לָא עָבְרִי

י״ג שְׁנֵ'^{40} הָאוֹתִי לֹא^{41} תִּירָאוּ נְאֻם יי^{42}

---

19. וו, ב: דהוה. מ: דהוי'. א, פֿ: דהויא.

20. כמבזר. פֿ: כי מבזק. מ, א: כמבזר בזרא. וו: — . ב: כבי ביזרא. פ. The last letter in ms. ה is a correction over the original (מיבזר).

21. ארבעהן וו: ארבעין. פֿ, ב, מ, פ.

22. גריוז בחדא. פֿ: גריוו בורא. א: גריוי ביזר'. — : .מ. וו: גריוז ביזלי.

23. דחרדל דהדד לא :ב. דחרדלא. :פֿ, א, מ, וו. In ms. ב, the correction is added in the margin.

24. וו, ב: אילמלא.

25. דלינן. All others: דליי'. Unique reading in ms. ה.

26. מקלינן. וו, ב: פֿ, מ, פ: קלינן.

27. מהבליה. :ב, וו, מ, א, פֿ. פ: מחבליה. ב: Gloss by Rashbam (מחום הכוכב) and comment by Ritva (והרגישו בחומו) ad loc. support the majority of mss. However, the reading of ms. H is also supported by b. San. 93b (חבלא דנורא—a gloss of Dan. 3:27).

28. פ: ורמי ליה קלא גלא לגלא חבריה. וו: רמא ליה קלא גלא לחבריה. מ: ורמ' לי' גל' קל' לחבריה. א: ורמי ליה קלא גלא לחברי' חבירתי. ב: רמא ליה קלא גלא לחבריתין חברתין. פֿ: ודמא ליה קלא לגלא לגלא חברתא. In ms. וו the underlined letter is a correction (a modified ל). Ms. פ contains unique errors (underlined).

29. וו, מ, פֿ: — . א: חבירתי.

30. מ, א, פֿ: שיירת.

31. וו. בעלמ'. In ב, that reading precedes rather than follows מידי.

32. אטבעתיה. א, פ: שטפתיה. מ: שטפתיה וניתי אנא ואת ונשטפי'. וו: חרבתיה וניתי אנא וניחרביה וניחרביה אנא' ביתי' אחרביתי :ב For the reading in mss. מ, ב, וו, see the Venice print (with corruption of version in ms. וו) and the BaH (Joel ben Samuel Sirkis), ed. Vilna ad loc.

33. וו, ב, מ: א"ל. א, פֿ: אמ' ל'.

34. מ, א, פֿ: פוק.

35. ב: גבורתא. א: גבורת'. מ: גבורתי'. וו, פֿ: גבורתיה.

36. פ, א, פֿ: דמרך. מ: דמריך.

37. פ, א, פֿ: — . מ: ואפי'. ב: דאפי'. וו: דאפילו.

38. פ: דמלא חוטא דחלא. וו: מלא חוטי דחלא. ב: מלא חוט דחלא. מ, פֿ: כמלא חוטא דחלא. א: מליא חוטא דחלא. *Unique error (דחרדלא) in ms. ה (see ln. ז.א), corrected on the basis of all other mss.*

39. פ, מ, פֿ: לית דעבר. א: ולית דעבר.

40. וו, ב: דכת'. שנ: .מ.

41. וו: אל. Unique error in ms. וו by metathesis of two words with identical meanings.

42. (Jer. 5:22). Ms. פ has the same reading as ms. ה, followed by "etc." (וגו'). Ms. פֿ fills out the verse: ואם מפני לא תחילו אשר שמת חול גבול לים חוק עולם. Ms. וו fills out the verse: בל. ואם מפני מה לא תחילו. Ms. מ fills out the verse: מפני אם יעברנהו. Ms. א fills out the verse: אם מפני. ואם מפני לא תח' אש' שמ' חו' גבו' לים וגו'. Ms. ב fills out the verse: אשר שמתי לא תחילו אשר שמתי חול גבול לים חוק עולם לא יעברנהו. חול גבול לים. In ms. ב, the underlined words are added in the margin. In mss. ה and פ, the abbreviation יי is written with a third yod above the line. A marginal note to ms. וו also indicates to add a third yod, as does a note above the line in ms. ב (and for יי in ms. ב, ln. כ.ב.). Note: underlined words in ms. פ

י"ד
ט"ו ב
ט"ז   וְאָמַ'[43] רָבָא[44] אשתעו[45] לִי[46] נחותי[47] יַמָּא[48]
י"ז   הַאי[49] גַּלָּא[50] דְּאָתֵי לְטַבּוּעֵי[51] סְפִינְתָא[52]
י"ח   אית ליה ברישיה[53] כִּיצִיצָתָא[54] דנורא חִיוָּרָא[55]
י"ט   וְאִית לְהוּ[56] אִילּוֹאתָא[57] דַּחֲקִיק[58] [59]עֲלַיְהוּ
כ   אֶהְיֶה אֲשֶׁר אֶהְיֶה[60] יי צבאות
כ"א   וּמָחֵינַן[61] לֵיהּ[62] בְּגַוֵּיהּ[63] וְנַיַּח[64]
כ"ב
כ"ג ג'א

---

and ms. וו are not in the Masoretic text. Rabbinovicz (DS) presumes "scribal error," but fluidity in prooftexts has various causes. For the significance of the variant מה in ms. פ, see Mekhilta *Beshallah* §5 (§4) at ch. 2 n. 347.

43. וו, פ. א, פ⁰: אמ'. ב: אמר. In ms. ב, this word has a sinuous scribal ornament, also found in this word at ln. מ.ד and elsewhere in the ms. It is a section marker or "secondary title"; see ch. 3 n. 490.

44. ב: רבא בר־בר־חנא. וו: רבה. א: רבה בר חנה.

45. ב, א: אישתעי

46. — :ב

47. מ, א: נחתי

48. וו: ימה.

49. וו: הא.

50. מ: גל'.

51. פ, מ, א, פ⁰: דמטבע. ב: ואתא לטב' לטבועי.

52. מ: ספינ'.

53. פ: נפיק מינה. וו: אית לֵיהּ ברישא. מ: נפק' לי'. א, פ⁰: נפקא ליה. The underlined correction in ms. וו is written over a letter.

54. פ: כי צוצייתא. וו: צוצייתא. מ: ביצוצית'. ב: צוניתא. א, פ⁰: בצוציתא.

55. פ: חיורת'. וו: חיורתי. ב: חוורתי. מ: חיורתי ברישי'. א: חיורתי ברישיה. פ⁰: חיורתי ברישא.

56. פ, וו: ואית לן. ב: אית לן. מ, א: ומחינן ליה. פ⁰: ומחינן לה

57. פ: אלותא. וו: אלוותא. ב: אלוות'. מ: אלוות'. א: באלוות. פ⁰: באלוותא

58. ב: דחקוק

59. פ: עלוהי. ב: עלייהו. מ, פ⁰: עלוהי. א: עליה

60. פ: יה יה יי צבאו'. וו: יק' יי צבאות אמן אמן אמן סלה ס"ס. ב: יה' יה' יי' צבאות אמן אמן אמן סלה. מ: אהיה אשר אהיה יה יי צבאות. א: אהיה אשר אהיה יֵה יי אמן צבאות אמן אמן. פ⁰: יהיה' צבאות וניח אמן אמן סלה. In ms. וו, the underlined words are added in the margin. The underlined word in ms. א is added above the line. In ms. H, the abbreviated Tetragrammaton (יי) is written with a third *yod* in the middle, above the line.

61. — :פ⁰. מ, א, פ⁰: מחינא. פ: ומחינא. Also absent in the text body of ms. וו, but added in the margin (see below).

62. — :פ⁰. מ, א: לה. פ. Also absent in the text body of ms. וו, but added in the margin (see below).

63. — :פ⁰. מ, א: בגה. ב. Also absent in the text body of ms. וו, but added in the margin (see below).

64. פ: וניח. וו: וְנַח. ב: וניחי. מ: וניחי. א: ונח ימא. In ms. וו, only the underlined word is in the text body. However, below the addition of the verse to ms. וו, all of this line is added in the margin: ומחינן ליה בגביה וְנַח. In the margin, the underlined word is marked above and below (to indicate deletion, as it is now redundant with text body). — :פ⁰.

כ"ד	ואמ'⁶⁵ רבא⁶⁶ לדידי חזי לי
כ"ה	הורמיז⁶⁷ בר ⁶⁸לילוואתא
כ"ו	⁶⁹דהוה קא משואר אקובנאה דמחוזא
כ"ז	ורהיט⁷⁰ פרשא⁷¹ בי⁷² רכבי⁷³ סוסיא⁷⁴ ⁷⁵מתתאי
כ"ח	ולא יכיל ליה⁷⁶
כ"ט	ג"ב
ל	זמנא חדא⁷⁷ סרגי⁷⁸ ליה⁷⁹ תרתי⁸⁰ ⁸¹כודניאתא
ל"א	אתרי⁸² גשרי⁸³ ⁸⁴דאגנג
ל"ב	ושוור⁸⁵ ⁸⁶מהאי להאי ומהאי להאי
ל"ג	ונקיט⁸⁷ תרי מזגי מיא⁸⁸ ⁸⁹בידיה

---

65. פ: אמ'. וו, ב, א: ואמ'. מ: וא'.
66. וו, פ°: רבה. After the following word (לדידי), ms. °פ is missing.
67. וו, ב, מ: הורמין.
68. פ: ליליתא. וו: לילותא. ב: לילת'. מ: ליליאת'. א: לילאתא. Unique spelling in ms. ה; note also the *plene*-aleph spelling in ms. מ and ms. א.
69. פ: כי קא רהיט אקוקפי דשורא דמחוזא. וו: דהוה אקופי דמחוזא. ב: דהוה רבהיט פרׁשא יאקפי' דשורא דמחוזא. מ: כי הוה רהיט אקוף דשור' דמחוז'. א: כי קא רהיט אקופקי דשורא דמחוזא. In ms. ב, the first correction דמחוזא מדחזא modifies the letter.
70. ב: והוה. מ: ורכיב.
71. מ: פרישא.
72. ב: —.פ, מ, א, כי.
73. פ: רכיב. וו: —. ב, מ: רכיבו. מ: ורכיב.
74. מ: חוות'. א: חיותא.
75. פ: על ארעא. וו, ב: מתותיה. מ, א: מתתאי.
76. פ: ולא קא מדריך ליה. מ: ולא יכיל לי'. א: ולא מדוור ליה. ב: ולא יכיל ליה למידרכי.
77. מ: זימנ' חד'.
78. פ: סריגן. וו: סריגין. מ: הוה מסרג'. א: הוה מסרגא. ב: שריגו
79. וו: —. פ: לי'.
80. מ: תרתין.
81. פ: כונדיאתא. וו: כודיאתא. מ: חיות'. ב: כונדייתא. א: חיותא כודכתא חוורתי. Note the affinity of Venice, Pesaro to mss. א, מ here (see my study cited at §*Introduction* n. 1).
82. פ: וקומן אתרי. וו: וקיימין אתרי. מ, א: וקיימי אתרי. ב: וקיימי אתרי
83. ב, מ: גישרי
84. פ, מ: דרונג. וו: דרונָג. ב: דריר'. א: דרוג גוש (Note vocalization in ms. וו). In ms. א, underlined word is at the end of a line.
85. מ, א, ב: ושואר
86. וו: מהאי גיסא להאי גיסא ומהאי להאי. This may be an error due to displacement of the added phrase ומהאי להאי from ln. ל"ב.ג', or it may be a stylistic device which emphasizes the back-and-forth bounding motion by repeating it. מ: מהא לה ומה להא. א: מיהא לא ומיהא להא
87. ב: מזג' לי'. וו: ומזגי ליה
88. פ, וו: כסי דחמרא. ב: כסי דחמרא. מ: תרתי מזגי חמר'. א: תרי מזגי חמרא. Underlined words in ms. ב added in the margin.
89. וו, ב: —.

ל"ד וּשְׁפִיךָ[90] מהאי להאי [91]וּמֵהַאי להאי
ל"ה ולא נָטַף[92] [93]נטופתא מיניהו
ל"ו [94]וההוא יומא יעלו שמים[95] [96]ירדו [97]תהומות
ל"ז שמע מלכותא עילוה[98] [99]וקטעתיה
ל"ח
ל"ט דּ[100]

מ אמ'[101] רבה בר בר חנה[102] [103]לדידי חזי לי
מ"א אוזילא בר יומיה[104] דהוה[105] [106]בהר תבור
מ"ב והר תבור כמה[107] הוי[108] ארבעין[109] [110]פרסי

---

90. פ, מ, א: ומוריק. ב: ומריק׳. וו: ומזרק.
91. וו: — . מ: וּמוּרִיק-מ ומהאי להאי
92. פ: מבדר. וו: נטיף. ב: נטיף ליה. מ: נטפ'. א: נטפא
93. פ: ניטופתא מיני'. א: ניטופתא לארעא. מ: מניטופת׳ לארע'. וו: טיפתא מיניהו. ב: טיפה מינייהו. In ms. ה, one letter (נטופחא) is added above the line. In ms. מ, the correction is by erasure.
94. פ: אותו היום. מ: ואותו היו'. א: ואותו. וו: ואמרי אותו היום. ב: אמרי אותו היום
95. מ: שמי'.
96. א: וירדו
97. מ: תהומו'.
98. פ: שמעי' ביה בי מלכותא. וו: שמעו בי מלכא. ב: שמע' בי מלכא. מ: ושמע' ביה מלכות'. א: ושמעת ביה מלכותא. In ms. ב, underlined word is added in the margin. Unique reading in ms. ה.
99. מ: וקטעתי'. פ: וקטלוה'. א: וקטליה. ולקטיה Here, ב has a unique error by metathesis. Here, the Venice print corresponds only to ms. א, although Venice probably reflects the same tradition as mss. ב, פ.
100. At the beginning of this section, ms. וו reads סימן ("mnemonic") with a dot over it, followed by the mnemonic: אוזילא בר אקריקתא אכל חלתה ביני שיצי זיז שדי ואוזי. Ms. מ writes out a slightly different mnemonic in abbreviated form: אוזי"ל ב"ר אקרוק'ת' דא"כ' חל"ת ביני"י שיצ"י שד"י ואוז"י, followed by the abbreviation of "mnemonic" (סי"מ').
101. ב has an ornament here. Compare ln. ז.ט.ב.
102. א: רבא
103. מ, וו: לדידי חזי. In ms. וו, the underlined word is added above the line.
104. פ: אורזילא דרימא בר יומיה. וו: אוזילא בת יומא. ב: אורזילה דימ' בר יומ'. מ: אוריל' דימ' בר יום א: אורזילא דימא בר יומיה. Ms. ה had a unique error (אֲחַיִלא), corrected faintly in the text body by erasure, as noted already by Rabbinovicz (DS XI:225 n. ת).
105. פ, א: דהוי. מ: דהואי. וו: דהוה. In ms. וו, the underlined letter is a correction.
106. פ, וו, א: כהר תבור. מ: כי הר תבור. ב: בהר יום. In ms. ב, the underlined correction is added above the line. The word in italics looks like an uncorrected dittography.
107. מ: כמ'.
108. ב: הוה
109. ב, מ: ארבעי'. From this point onward, my edition ceases to distinguish every abbreviated spelling from every non-abbreviated spelling. I may not distinguish that a given form is abbreviated *if and only if* the full spelling appears in another ms. in the footnote *and* both words are unambiguously the same. Otherwise, I do continue to list the abbreviated forms separately.
110. וו: פרסין.

מ"ג   משכא[111] דצואריה[112] תלתא[113] פרסי[114]

מ"ד   בי מרבעיה[115] *דראימא*[116] דרישיה פרסא[117] ופלגא

מ"ה   ורמא[118] כפותא[119] וסכריה[120] לירדנא

מ"ו

מ"ז   ה

מ"ח   ואמ'[121] רבה בר בר חנה[122] לדידי חזי לי[123]

מ"ט   האי[124] אקרוקתא[125] דהוה[126] כי אקרא[127] דהגרוניא[128]

נ   ואקרא דהגרוניא[129] כמה הוי[130] שתין[131] בתי

נ"א   אתא תנינא[132] בלעה

נ"ב   אתא[133] פשקצא[134] בלעת[135] לתנינא

נ"ג   וסליק ויתיב באילנא

נ"ד   תא חזי[136] חיליה[137] דאילנא

נ"ה   כמה הוי[138]

---

111. פ: ומשחתא. וו: ומשכא. מ: וכי משכ'. ב: ומשכי

112. וו: דתצ̇ורא. ב: דצוארי. In ms. וו, the underlined correction is added above the line.

113. פ: תלתה. ב: תלת

114. וו: פרסאי

115. פ, א: ובי מרבעתא. מ: וכי מרבעת'. ב: בי מרבעת'. וו: בי מרבעתא

116. In ms. ה, this word, likely an error for the next one, has flourishes on the first and last letters—possibly for deletion.

117. מ: פרס'. פ, ב: פרסה

118. וו, ב, מ, א: רמא

119. ב: כופת'. וו: כופתא. מ: בפות'. א: כפתא

120. מ, א: וסכר ליה

121. פ: אמ', ב: א'

122. מ: חנ'. ב: חנא

123. א: —. וו: ליה

124. פ, וו, ב: ההוא. א, מ: ההיא. Unique reading in ms. ה.

125. פ: אקרתיא. ב: אוקרוקת'. וו: אקרקתיא. In the margin here, ms. וו has a Hebrew gloss (צפרדע הגדולה) and variant spelling.

126. פ: דהוי. ב, מ, א: דהואי

127. פ, ב: כאקרא. וו: באקרא

128. Ms. וו has another marginal variant spelling (או: הגרוניא).

129. ב: —

130. מ, א: הוי

131. Unique reading in ms. H. All others: שיתין.

132. פ: ובלעה. ב, מ: ובלע'. וו: ובלעא. א: בלעא

133. מ, א: ואתא. The underlined letter in ms. א is a correction and in ms. מ an abbreviation.

134. פ: פושקנצא. וו: פרושקנצא. ב: פי שקנצ'. מ: פושקיב'. א: פישכנתא

135. פ: ודריה. א: ודרייה. ב: ובלע'. וו, מ: ובלעיה

136. פ, וו, א, מ: תא חזי כמה נפיש. ב: אמ' רבא תא חזי כמ' נפיש

137. מ: חלי'. ב: חילא

138. Unique reading in ms. ה. This line is absent in all other mss.

נ"ו אמ' רב פפא בר שמואל[139]

נ"ז אי לאו[140] דהואי התם[141] לא הימני[142]

נ"ח

נ"ט ו''א

ס ואמ'[143] רבה בר בר חנה

ס"א זמנא[144] חדא הוה קא אזילנא[145] בספינתא

ס"ב וחזינא[146] ליה לההוא כוורא[147]

ס"ג דעילא ליה[148] אכלה טינא[149] באוסיה[150] ומית[151]

ס"ד ואגדיה מיא ושדייה[152] לגודא[153]

ס"ה חריבו[154] מיניה[155] שתין[156] מחוזי

ס"ו אכלו[157] מיניה שיתין[158] מחוזא

ס"ז מלחו[159] מיניה שתין[160] מחוזי

ס"ח מגולגלא[161] דעיניה[162] עבדי[163]

---

139. מ, וו: שמו'.

140. מ, א: לא.

141. מ, א: הואי התם. וו: דחזיתיה. ב: דחזיתי.

142. א: הימניה. ב: מהימנתי'. וו: הימניתיה.

143. פ. ב: א'. אמ'.

144. זמנא. א: זימנ'. מ, ב: In ms. א, the underlined letter is a correction.

145. פ. אזילנן. וו: קאזילנא. מ, ב: קא אזילנ'. א: קא אזלינן.

146. פ. וחזי'. ב: וחזי'. מ: חזינן. א: וחזינן.

147. פ: ההיא כורא. וו: לההוא כוורא. מ: ההו' כוור'. ב, א: ההוא כוורא

148. פ: דיתיבא ליה. וו: דסליק עליה באוסיא. ב: דסליק עליה. מ: דיתב" לי'. א: דיתיבא ליה

149. פ. אכלה טינא. מ: אכל' טינ'. ב: כולכיטנא. Ms. ב could be corruption of (אכלה טינא) by metathesis, but, after the correction, it reflects a gloss of אכלה טינא as כילבית—likely an interpolation of commentary such as Rashbam's. See ch. 1 n. 235.

150. ב: כעסיה. וו: —

151. ב: —

152. פ: ושדיוה מיא. וו, ב: ושדייה יוא. מ: וארחיה מיא ושדיוה. א: ואד ואדחוה מיא ושדיוה.

153. פ: לברא. מ: לגיד'. א: לגודא. וו: אגידא. ב: אגדא

154. פ: וחרב. וו, מ: חרבו.

This line is missing in ms. ב. Rabbinovicz (DS XI:226) posits scribal error, as ms. ב does have ln. ר"ב.ע"ג. In ms. א, this line is also missing but it reappears at ln. ח"ס.א"ו.

155. פ, וו, ב, א: —

156. פ, מ: שיתין. Compare ln. ה"ע. However, the reading in ms. ה is שיתן in the very next line; the spelling is clearly inconsistent.

157. פ, מ: ואכלו. וו: מלחו. א: ואכל.

158. ב: מחוז'. פ, וו: מחוזי. א: מחוזאי

159. פ. מ א: אכלו. ב: ומלחו. וו: מחלו. Unique error by metathesis in ms. ב.

160. פ, ב, מ: שיתן. Underlined letter in ms. ב is a correction. The italicized letter in ms. ב is an abbreviation symbol (').

161. פ: ונגדו מגלגלא. א: וחרוב מיניה שיתין ונגרו מיניה מחד גלגלא. מ: ומלו מחד גולגל. וו: עבדי מחד גלגלא. ב: עבדן מחד גלגל

162. וו: דעינוהי

163. פ, וו, ב, מ, א: —

ס"ט   תלת מאה גרבי מ<u>שחא</u>[164]

ע   ו"<u>ב</u>

ע"א   <u>לישנא כי הדרינן ואתינן</u>[165]

ע"ב   <u>הוה קא מנסרין</u>[166] [167]<u>מגרמיה קורי</u>

ע"ג   <u>למבניה</u>[168] [169]<u>להנך מחוזי</u>

ע"ד

ע"ה   ז

ע"ו   ואמ' רבה בר בר [170]<u>חנה</u>

ע"ז   זימנא חדא <u>הוה</u>[171] <u>קא אזילנא</u>[172] בספינתא

ע"ח   <u>וחזינא</u>[173] [174]<u>להההוא כוורא</u>

ע"ט   <u>דיתיב</u>[175] חלתא [176]<u>על גביה</u>

פ   <u>וקדח</u>[177] [178]<u>עליה חיזרתא</u>

פ"א   <u>סברינן</u>[179] <u>דיבישתא</u>[180] [181]<u>הוא</u>

פ"ב   <u>וסלקינן</u>[182] [183]<u>לישינן ואפינן</u>

פ"ג   [184]<u>חם גבה דכוורא</u>

---

164. פ, ב: מישחא. מ: דמישח'.

165. פ: כי הדרי ואתאי לבתר תריסר ירחי שתא חזאי. מ: וכי הדרן אתן לבת' תריס' ירחי חזינן א. Rabbinovicz (DS XI:226) points out that the succinct language of Rashbam (Pesaro print: לשנה אחרת הוו מנסרי) best supports the reading of ms. H.

166. פ: דהוו קא מנסרי. וו, ב: דהוו מנסרי. מ: דהוו קמנסרי. א: דהוה קא מנסרא.

167. פ: מגרמיה. וו: כשורי לגרמי. ב: כשורי מיגרמי. מ: מגרמ' מטללי. א: מגרמיה מטללטלי.

168. פ: —. וו: למיבנא להו. ב: למיבני בהי. מ: ויתבי. א: ויתבו.

169. פ: להנך שיתין מחוזי ובנו. מ, א: —. ב: להך מחוזי. וו: ולהנך מחוזי.

170. מ, ב: חנ'. פ, וו, א: חנא

171. In ms. ב, this is added above the line. — וו.

172. פ, א: קאזלינ'. ב: קאזיל'. מ: קאזיל'. וו: קאזילנא

173. מ, ב: וחזיב'. פ, א: וחזינן. וו: חזינן.

174. פ: ההוא כוארא. Note that both gender and spelling differ from the same word, in the same witness, at ln. ו"א.ס"ב.

175. פ: דיתיבה ליה. וו: דייתבה ליה. ב, מ: דיתב' ליה. א: דיתיבא ליה

176. Unique reading in ms. ה. All others: אגביה.

177. ב: וקאי. וו: וקדוח

178. פ, מ, א: אגמא עילויה. וו: עלייהו עישבי. ב: עליה עשבי

179. פ: וסברנן. מ: סברנן.

180. וו: יבשה. ב: יבשת'. פ, מ: יבישתא.

181. פ: הוה. ב, מ, א: היא

182. וו: סלקינן

183. Unique reading in ms. ה. ב: ובשלי' ואפי'. פ, וו, מ, א: ואפינן ובשלינן

184. פ: כד חם גביה. מ: וכדחם גבי'. א: וכד חם גביה. וו: כי חם גביה תנורא. ב: כי חם גבי דכוורא

פ"ד ואיתהפיך{185}

פ"ה ואי לאו{186} *דהוה*{187} {188}ספינתא מקרבא לן

פ"ו {189}הוה {190}מטבעא לן

פ"ז

פ"ח ח"א

פ"ט ואמ' רבה בר בר {191}חנא

צ זמנא חדא הוה{192} קא אזילנא{193} בספינתא

צ"א ואזלא{194} ספינתא{195} בין שיצא{196} לשיצא{197} {198}דכורא

צ"ב תלת{199} יומי {200}ותלת {201}לילוואתא

צ"ג איהו בדלא{202} ואנן {203}בשפלא

צ"ד ח"ב

צ"ה ודילמ'{204} אמרת {205}לא מסגיא{206} ספינתא {207}טובא

צ"ו כי אתא רב דימי אמר

צ"ז כי חם{208} קומקומא{209} סגיא{210} ספינתא{211} שיתא{212} פרסי

---

185. וו, ב: הפך. מ, א: איתהפיך. פ: איתהפיך.
186. וו, ב: אי לאו. מ: ואי לא.
187. פ, ב, מ, א: דהוה. Error (דהות) in ms. ה shared by ms. וו, corrected on the basis of the others.
188. וו: ספינתא גבן. ב: ספינ' בהדן. פ: מקרבא ספינתא. מ: מקרב' ספינת. א: מיקרבא ספינתא.
189. מ, א: —.
190. פ: מטבע לן. וו: טבעינן. ב: טבעני. מ: טבעי'. א: טבעינן.
191. ב, מ: חנ'. פ, וו, א: חנה. Note that the spelling in ms. ה is inconsistent with all previous units.
192. In ms. ב, added above the line.
193. פ: קאזלינן. וו: קאזילנא. ב: שאזלינ'. מ: קאזלי'. א: קא אזלינן.
194. פ: והוה סגיא. מ: וסגאי. א: וסגא. ב: —. וו: ועלה לה.
195. —: ב.
196. ב: שיצא דכוורא.
197. —: וו.
198. פ: דכוא'. וו, ב, מ, א: דכוורא.
199. פ: תלתה. מ, ב: תלת'. וו, א: תלתא.
200. פ: ותלתה. מ, ב: ותלת'. וו, א: ותלתא.
201. מ: לילוות. ב: לילוות.
202. וו: בזקיפא. ב: בזקיפא. In ms. ב, the underlined correction is added almost imperceptibly between two letters.
203. וו: בשפיל'. ב: בשיפולי. מ: בשפל'. א: בשיפלא.
204. וו: דילמ'. א: ודילמ'.
205. וו, ב: דלא.
206. וו, ב: סגיא.
207. —: פ.
208. פ, מ, א, וו: כמיחם. ב: כי מיחם.
209. פ, א, וו: קומקמא דמיא. ב: קומין דמיא. מ: קוקמא דמיא. Unique reading in ms. ה.
210. פ: אזלינן. וו, ב: סגיא לה. מ, א: מסגיא.
211. Uniquely in ה. All others: —
212. Uniquely in ה. All others: שיתין.

צ״ח	ואיכא דאמרי²¹³ שדיא²¹⁴ גירא פרשא
צ״ט	ולא יכיל ליה²¹⁵
ק	אמ' רב אשי²¹⁶
ק״א	ההוא²¹⁷ גולדנא²¹⁸ דימא²¹⁹ הוא
ק״ב	דאית ליה תרי²²⁰ שיצי
ק״ג	
ק״ד	ט״א
ק״ה	ואמ'²²¹ רבה בר בר²²² חנה
ק״ו	זמנא חדא הוה קא אזילנא²²³ בספינתא²²⁴
ק״ז	וחזינא²²⁵ ²²⁶ להוא צפורתא
ק״ח	דהוה קימא²²⁷ עד קרסולה²²⁸ ²²⁹ במיא
ק״ט	ורישיה²³⁰ ²³¹ מטי לרקיעא
ק״י	סברנא דליכא מיא דנפישן²³²
קי״א	בעינא²³³ ²³⁴ למיחת לצנוני נפשין

213. Uniquely in ה. All others: —
214. פ: ופתק פרש' גירא. וו, מ: ושדיא פרשא גירא. א: ושדי פרשא גירא. ב: ושדא פרשא.
215. פ: וקדמא ליה ההיא ספינתא. וו: ומקדמה לה ספינתא. ב: וקדמ' לה איהו. מ: וקדמ' ליה. א: וקדמא ליה. Rabinovicz (*DS* XI:227) corrects ms. ב to איהי (as does *FJMS*) but, upon close inspection of the ms., that seems to be incorrect. (Compare איהו in ms. ב at ln. ח״צ.א״ג.) For other transcription errors in *DS* and later editions, see my essay cited at n. 1 to the Introduction.
216. מ, א: וא' רב אשי. וו: כי אתאו לקמיה דרב אשי אמ' לן. ב: כי אתינ' לקמי' דרב אשי אמ' לן. Again, ms. וו and ms. ב uniquely agree.
217. ב: איהו
218. ב: גלדנ'. וו, מ, א: גילדנא
219. א: הוה
220. א: שיצין
221. פ: אמ'.
222. ב: חנ'. א: חנא
223. מ: קאזלי'. מ: קאזילנ'. ב: אזילנ'. א: קאזלינן
224. מ: בספינ'. Note that in the previous unit (ln. ח.א״צ, see also ln. ה״צ.א״ח), the abbreviation in ms. מ is unambiguously Aramaic (בספינתא) whereas here it can be Hebrew (בספינה). Compare ln. קצ״ז.ט', ln. רי״ח.י״ז.
225. פ, א: וחזינן. מ, ב: וחזינ'. וו: וחזינא
226. פ: הנהו ציפרי. ב: להוא ציפרי. וו: להוא ציפורא. מ: ההוא ציפר'ב. א: ההוא צפרא. The ב in ms. מ may be a scribal indication and not a letter.
227. פ: דהוו קיימי. וו: דהוה במיא. ב: דקא' במ'. מ: דקא'. א: דקאים
228. פ: קרסוליהו. וו: קרסוליה. מ: קרצולי'. ב: קרסולי'. א: קרסוליה.
229. וו, ב: —.
230. מ: ורישי'. פ: ורישיהו
231. וו adds the Ms. פ: מטי ברקיעא. ב: מטי עד רקיע ציץ שמי'. וו: מטי עד ציץ שמיא. מ: ברקיע'. א: ברקיעא underlined word above the line. Underlined correction in ms. ב is also above the line.
232. וו: —. פ: וסברינן דלא נפישי מיא. ב: סברינ' לא נפישי מיא. מ: ואמרי' ליכ' מיא. א: ואמרינן ליכא.
233. מ, א: —. פ: ובעי'.
234. פ: לקרורי נפשין. וו: למיחת לאיקורי נפשין. ב: למיחת לצנוני נפשי'. מ: ליחות לאיקרויי נפשי'. א: ניחות לאקרורי נפשין.

קי"ב נַפְק235 בַּת236 קָלָא וְאָמְרָה לַן237
קי"ג הָכָא238 בְּעִיתוּ לְצַנּוּנֵי נַפְשַׁיְכוּ
קט"ד דְּנְפַל239 לֵיהּ240 חֲצִינָא241 דְּבֵי נַגָּרֵי242 שְׁבַע שְׁנִין243
קט"ו וְלָא244 מָטָא245 246אַרְעָא
קט"ז וְלָאו247 מִשּׁוּם דְּעַמִּיקֵי248 מִיָּא
קי"ז אֶלָּא מִשּׁוּם דְּרַדְפֵי249 מִיָּא
קי"ח ט"ב
קי"ט אֲמַ' רַב אַשִׁי250 הַהוּא זִיז שַׂדַי הֹוֶה251
ק"כ דִּכְתִ' וְזִיז שַׂדַי252 עִמָּדִי
קכ"א
קכ"ב י"א
קכ"ג וַאֲמַ'253 רַבָּה בַּר בַּר חָנָה254
קכ"ד זִמְנָא חֲדָא הֲוָה קָא אָזֵילְנָא255 בְּמִדְבְּרָא
קכ"ה וַחֲזֵינָא256 לְהָנֵךְ257 אַוָּוזֵי דִּינְתוּר258 גַּדְפַיְהוּ259 מְשׁוּמְנַיְהוּ260

---

235. מ: וְנָפַק. א: —. פ, וו: נָפְקָא.
236. וו: קוֹל.
237. וו, ב: —.
238. פ: לָא תִּנְחֲתוּ. וו: הֵיאַךְ בְּעִיתוּ לְצַנּוּנֵי נַפְשַׁיְכוּ. ב: הָכָ' בְּעִיתָן לְצַנּוּנֵי נַפְשַׁיְכוּ. מ: לָא תִּיחֲתוּ הָכָ'. א: לָא תַּחְתּוּן הָכָא.
239. פ: דְּהָא שִׁבְעִין שְׁנִין דְּנָפַל. וו: דְּאִי נְפַל. ב: זִימְנָ' חַד' נְפַל.
240. פ, וו, ב: —.
241. מ: חֲצָצ'. ב: אֲזִינָא.
242. פ: דְּבַר נַגָּרָא. וו, מ, א, ב: לְבַר נַגָּרָא.
243. פ: —. וו: כְּבַר שְׁבַע שְׁנִין. מ, א: הָא שְׁבַע שְׁנֵי'. ב: עַד שְׁבַע שְׁנִין.
244. ב: לֹא.
245. וו: מָטָא עַד. ב: מְטֵי. מ: קַמְטִי'. א: קָא מָטְיָא.
246. וו: עַד אַרְעָ'. ב, מ, א: לְאַרְעָ'. פ: לְאַרְעָא.
247. פ: וְלָא תֵּימָא. א, וו: וְלָא. ב: לֹא.
248. פ, מ, א: דְּנָפִישֵׁי.
249. וו, ב, מ: דְּרַדְפֵי.
250. וו: כִּי אַתְיָנַן לְקַמֵּיהּ דְּרַב אַשִׁי אֲמַ' לָן. ב: כִּי אֲתֵינַ' לְקַמֵּי' דְּרַב אֲשֵׁי אֲמַ' לָן. In ms. ב, the word רב is written over something; it could have said אשי רב, confusing אמ'/אשי. The underlined correction is added in the margin of ms. ב.
251. וו: מִיקְרֵי. פ: —. Ms. ב has a lacuna here and for the first word of the next line.
252. וו: עִימָדִי. Note that the plene spelling undercuts the midrash on this word found elsewhere and, I argue, implied here (chapter 4 n. 619).
253. ב: אֲ'.
254. פ: חֲנָא.
255. פ, א: קָאזְלִין. מ: קָאזֵלִי'. ב: קָאזִילְנָ'. וו: קָאזִילְנָא.
256. פ, מ, א: וַחֲזֵינָן. ב: וְחָזֵינָ'. וו: חָזֵינָן.
257. א: הַהוּא.
258. פ: דְּשָׁמִיטֵי לְהוּ. ב: דְּאִשְׁמַטִי'. וו, מ, א: דְּשָׁמִיטִי. Unique reading in ms. ה.
259. וו, ב, א: גַּדְפַיְיהוּ.
260. פ: מְשׁוּמְנַיְהִי. וו: מְשֻׁמְנַיְהוּ. ב: מִשְׁמַנַיְיהוּ. מ: מְשַׁמְנוּנַיְיהוּ. א: מְשׁוּמְנוּנַיְהוּ.

קכ"ו   וַנְגִיד[261] וְאֵתִי חוּטָא דְמִשְׁחָא[262] [263]מִינַיְיהוּ

קכ"ז   אָמְרִי לְהוּ[264] אִית לִי[265] בְּגַוַויְכוּ[266] חוּלְקָא[267] לְעָלְמָא[268] *דְּאָתֵי[269]

קכ"ח   חֲדָא דְּלֵיא לִי אַטְמָא[270] וַחֲדָא דְּלֵיא לִי גַּדְפָא[271]

קכ"ט   י"ב

ק"ל   כִּי[272] אֲתַאי[273] לְקַמֵּיהּ[274] דְּר'[275] אֶלְעָזָר אֲמ' לִי[276]

קל"א   עֲתִידִין[277] יִשְׂרָאֵל לִיתֵּן[278] עֲלֵיהוֹן דִּין[279]

קל"ב

קל"ג   יא[280]

קל"ד   אֲמ'[281] רַבָּה בַּר בַּר חָנָה[282]

קל"ה   זִמְנָא חֲדָא[283] הֲוָה קָא אָזִילְנָא[284] [285]בְּמַדְבְּרָא

---

261. פ: וקא נגדי. מ: וקנגרי. א: וקא נגרי. Ms. ב has a lacuna here.
262. Ms. ב: נחלי מישחא. ב: ... חוטי דמשח'. מ: נחלי דמשח'. א: נחלי חוטי דמשחא. וו: ואתי חוטי דמישמחא has a lacuna here (...)
263. פ: מיניהי. וו: מיניהו. ב: מיניהו. מ: מתותיהו. א: מתותיהו
264. אמרי להו .פ. All others: אמינא להו.
265. וו: לי
266. פ: מיניכי. ב: בגוייכי. וו: בגוייכו. Ms. וו has a scribal notation above the underlined letters resembling a *peh* (פ). Rabbinovicz (*DS* XI:227) interprets this as an insertion (בגופייכו).
267. פ, מ, א. — וו, ב: מידי.
268. Ms. ב has a lacuna here.
269. Unique error (דאית) by metathesis in ms. ה. Corrected on the basis of all other mss.
270. וו, מ, א: גדפא. ב: גפא. Unique reading in ms. ה that is also in indirect witnesses (*'Aggadot ha-Talmud*; *'En Ya'aqov*). See my study cited at §*Introduction* n. 1.
271. Unique reading in ms. ה, see previous note. All others: אטמ', אטמא.
272. ב: —
273. וו: אתיתי. ב: אתא .— א: אתא. Ms. א harmonizes with the stock formula. See chapter 3 n. 438.
274. ב: —
275. ב: ורבי'.
276. א: ליה. Ms. ב has a lacuna here.
277. Ms. ב has a lacuna here.
278. וו: שיתנו
279. מ, א, ב: את הדין. וו: את את הדין .פ. Ms. וו has a unique error by dittography.
280. At the beginning of Part יא, ms. וו has another mnemonic: סימן עפרא דתכלתא עקרבא קרח וסילתיה. Versions in other mss. differ slightly. 'סימ 'מ: בעפר' דתכלת' שרקתי' עוקרב' לקרח וסלתי'. א: סימן עפרא בתכלא טרקתיה עקרבא לקרח וסלתיה. Note that one keyword in mss. M, E (טרקתיה/שרקתיה) does not appear in our text. J. Brüll (*Die Mnemotechnik des Talmuds* [Vienna, 1864], 41) suggests that it is an error for קוטרא in ln. קע"ז, indexing Unit י"ד (which presumably lacked its other mnemonic index, קרח, in Brüll's proposed text).
281. מ: וא'. וו, א: ואמ'. The underlined letter in ms. א, וו is followed by an abbreviation symbol (').
282. מ, ב: חנ'. וו: חנא
283. Ms. ב has a lacuna here.
284. פ: הוה קאזלין. וו: הוה קאזילנא. ב: אזלינא... מ: הוה קאזלי'. א: אזלינ'. Ms. ב has a lacuna here. The unusual 1ms. form in ms. וו is explained at Bar-Asher Siegal, *Grammar*, 123, by "paradigm leveling" (harmonization) with the 1c pl. form.
285. ב: במדבר.

Edition

קל"ו והוה בהדן²⁸⁶ ההוא טייעא²⁸⁷ ²⁸⁸דהוה מורח בעפרא

קל"ז אמ' האי²⁸⁹ אזיל²⁹⁰ לדוכתא²⁹¹ ²⁹²פלן

קל"ח והאי אזיל לדוכתא פלן²⁹³

קל"ט הבנן²⁹⁴ ליה עפרא

ק"מ אמ' מרחקיתון ממיא תמניא פרסי²⁹⁵

קמ"א הבנן ליה אמ' מרחקיתון תלת פרסי²⁹⁶

קמ"ב הפכינן²⁹⁷ ליה²⁹⁸ ²⁹⁹עפרא

קמ"ג ולא יכלינן³⁰⁰ ליה

קמ"ד

קמ"ה יב"א

קמ"ו אמ' לן³⁰¹ תא אחוי³⁰² לכו³⁰³ מתי³⁰⁴ מדבר

קמ"ז אזלאי³⁰⁵ וחזאי³⁰⁶ דדמוכי³⁰⁷ כמאן³⁰⁸ ³⁰⁹*דמיבסמי

---

286. פ: והוה. וו: לוה לן בהדן. ב: ולווה בהדן. מ: ואתלווי בהדן. א: ואתלווי בהדן.
287. פ: ההוא טייעא בהדאי.
288. פ: וקא נקיט עפרא מתרתי אורחתא ומורח לה. א: דהוה שקיל עפרא מתרתי ארחתא ומורח ליה.
מ: דהוה שקיל עפר' ומורח לה. וו: דהוה שקיל עפרא ומורח לה. ב: דהוה שקיל עפר' ומרח ליה.
289. פ: האי דירכא. מ: האי אורח'. וו, א: הא אורחא
290. וו, מ, א, ב: —. פ: אזלא.
291. Ms. נ⁰ begins with this word (לדוכתא) and continues through the end of our collection (with lacunae as noted).
292. פ: פלנתא. ב: פלנבת'. מ: פלנית. וו, א: פלונית. נ⁰: פלנתא.
293. פ: והאי דירכא אזלא לדוכתא פלני. מ, א: אמרינן ליה כמה מרחקינן ממיא. אמינא ליה כמה מרחקנן ממיא
וו: אמרי' ליה כמ' מרחיקנ' ממיא. נ⁰: אמר' ליה כמה מרחקי' ממיא. ב. In ms. מ, underlined letter might be a correction (possibly of ל).
294. פ: —. וו, א: אמ' לן הבו לי עפרא. מ: אמ' לי הבו לי עפרא יהבינן ליה עפרא
ב: אמ' לן הבו עפר' יהבינ' ליה עפרא. נ⁰: א' לן הבולי עפרא הבנא ליה עפרא
295. וו, ב: אמ' לן תמניא פרסי. וא' לן תמני' פרסי'. א: אמ' לן מרחקינכן תמניא פרפסי. נ⁰: מרחקיתון תמניא פרס'. This line is absent in ms. פ.
296. וו: תנינא ויהבנא עפרא אמ' לן תלתא פרסי. ב: תנינא ויהבינ' ליה עפר' אמ' לן תלת פרסי
מ: תניב' יהיבנ' ליה עפר' ואמ' לן תלת' פרסי. א: תנינן ויהבינן ליה עפרא ואמ' ליה מרחקינן תלת' פרסי
פ: תנינין יהבינא ליה א' מרחקיתון תלת פרסי. נ⁰: This line is absent in ms. פ.
297. פ: וחליפי. וו: הפכינן. ב: הפכינ'. מ, נ⁰: ואפכי'. א: והפכי
298. פ: לי'
299. וו, מ, א, ב, נ⁰: —.
300. פ: יכיל. וו: יכילנא. מ: יכולי. ב: יכולי'. נ⁰: יכלינן. א, נ⁰: יכלית.
301. פ: אמ' לי. וו, מ: א"ל. נ⁰: ואמ' רבה בר בר חנה זימנא חדא הוה קאזילנא במדברא ואמ' לי ואי רבה בר בר חנה א' לי ההוא טייעא. Ms. ב has a lacuna here and for the following word.
302. וו: ואיחוי. ב: ואחוי
303. Unique reading in ms. ה. All other mss.: לך.
304. פ: מיתי
305. פ: ואזלי. וו, א, נ⁰: אזלי. ב: אזלי'. מ: אזל
306. פ, וו, ב: וחזיתינהו. מ, א: חזיתינהו. נ⁰: חזנתיהו
307. פ: דקא מיכרכי להו בסדיניהו ודמ'. וו: —. מ: ודמכב ודמיין. א: דדמיין. ב: דדמין. נ⁰: דדמו
308. —. ב.
309. פ: דמיבשמי. וו, א: דמיבסמי. ב: דמיבסמי. מ, נ⁰: כמבסמי׳. The underlined letter in ms. נ⁰ is damaged

קמ"ח וגנו והוה חד מיניהו גני אפרקיד וכיפן בירכיה‎310

קמ"ט ועאל טייעא‎311 כי רכיב גמלא ‎312ונקיט רומחא בידיה

ק"נ ולא נגע‎313 בי

קנ"א פיסקי ושקלי חוטא דתכלתא‎314 ‎315מיניהו

קנ"ב ולא‎316 ‎317איסתגיא גמלן

קנ"א אמ'‎318 דיל'‎319 חד מיניכו‎320 שקל‎321 מידי‎322 מיניהו‎323 ‎324ניהדר להו

קנ"ד דגמירי‎325 דמאן‎326 דשקיל‎327 מידי‎328 מיניהו‎329 ‎330לא מסתגי‎331 ‎332ליה

קנ"ה הדרינן ליה‎333 ‎334וסגינן

קנ"ו יב"ב

and hard to decipher. Lacuna at underlined letter in ms. ב. Unique spelling error (דמיכסמי) in ms. ה by confusion of similar letters, corrected on the basis of mss. ו, א.

310. ברכיה זקיפא הוה מיניהו חד אפרקיד וגנו :פ. מיני' דחד בירכא זקיף והוה וזקיף אפרקיד וגנו :וו. מיניהו. דחד בירכיה זקיף והוה אפרקיד וגנו :א. מיניהו. דחד בורכא זקיפא הוה מיניהו חד אפרקיד וגני :ב: Ms. ב has a lacuna at the underlined word; it is added by conjecture based on all other mss.

311. ברכי תותי' טייע' ועייל :וו. בירכיה. תרותיה טייעא ההוא ועל :ב. גברא וחליף :פ. ברכיה תותי טייעא ועייל :נ'. בורכי. תותי טייעא ועייל :א. Underlined letter in ms. וו is corrected by erasure. Ms. ב has a lacuna at the underlined location.

312. וו is ms. in letter Underlined .ב: וזקיף רומח' בידיה'. וו: וזקית רומחא. מ: וזקיפ' רומחי'. א, נ0: וזקיפא רומחיה. an error for פא or ף, not noted by Rabbinovicz (DS XI:228).

313. מ: בי'. וו, ב: ביה.

314. ושקלי חוטא. וו: שקלי חדא קרנא דתכלתא. מ: פסקי' חד' קרנ' דתכלת'. א: פיסקא אתאי חדא קרנא דתכלתא ב: פסקית חדא הוטא דתכילת'. נ': פיסקי איתאי חדא קרנא דתכלתא has been erased but it is still legible.

315. פ: דחד מיני'. א: דחד מינייהו.

316. א, נ0: לא.

317. פ. ולא מסתגי לן. מ: ולא הוה קמסתגי לן. א: לא הוה קא מסתגי לן. וו: ולא הוה מסתגי ליה גמלא. נ': ולא הוה קא מסתגי לן ה אזלי. ב: ולא הוה קמסתגי לן גמלא.

318. אמ'. ב: א"ל. וו, מ: אמ' לי. א: אמ' ליה. נ': א' לי.

319. פ: דלמא. וו, מ, א, ב, נ': אי.

320. —. פ, וו, מ, א, ב, נ': Unique reading in ms. ה.

321. מ: שקל'. פ, וו, א, נ': שקלת. ב: שקליתי.

322. א: חד

323. וו, ב, א: מינייהו

324. פ: —. וו: הדדיה. מ: אהדרי'. א, נ0: אהדריה. ב: אהדררייה.

325. פ, ב: —. א: דגמרינן

326. ב: דכל מאן. וו: כל מאן

327. וו: דשאיל

328. וו: —. א: חד

329. וו, ב, א: מינייהו

330. לא אהדריה :ב. Error in ms. ב by eye-skip (see previous line).

331. מסתני :ב. The underlined letter in ms. ב has been corrected (possibly to ג).

332. ליה המד גמלא :ב. ליה גמלא :וו. The error in ms. ב may be due to transposing the word חמרא from ln. קנ"ח.יב"ב

333. פ: ואהדרתי ניהליהו. וו: הדרתינהו. ב: אהדריתי. מ: אזלי אהדרתיה. נ0: אזלי אהדרתיה ליה.

334. וו, ב, מ, א, נ': —. פ: ומסתגי לן.

קנ"ז   כי אתאי לבי מדרשא[335] אמרי[336] לי

קנ"ח   כל אבא[337] חמור[338] כל בר[339] חנה[340] סיכסא[341]

קנ"ט   מכדי הנך חוטין לחלייתא[342]

ק"ס   אי כבית שמאי אי כבית הלל[343]

קס"א   הוה מיבעי לך[344] [345]למימנינהו ומיתי ומימר

קס"ב

קס"ג   יג"א

קס"ד   אמ' לן[346] תנ[347] אחוי לכו[348] הר[349] סיני[350]

קס"ה   אזלא וחזאי[351] דהדרי[352] עקרבי כחמרי[353] לובייתא[354]

קס"ו   נפק[355] בת[356] קלא[357] [358]ואמרה

---

335. מ, נ⁰: לקמיה דרבנן. א: לקמאי ורבנן.
336. פ, וו, מ, א, ב: אמרו.
337. א: בר בר חנה אבא. וו: רבה. Ms. ב reads, at the end of the line in the manuscript, אבא, and, at the beginning of the next line, רבה בר בר חנה.
338. All others: חמרא. Unique reading in ms. ה.
339. פ, וו, מ, נ⁰: בר בר. ב: רבה בר בר.
340. מ: חנ'. ב: חנא
341. וו: טיכסא. פ: סיכסה. Unique error of ms. וו (repeated in ln. יג"ב.ק"ע). Inconsistent spelling in ms. פ (vs. ln. יג"ב.ק"ע).
342. פ: מאי דעתיך למידע. וו: למאי הילכת' שקלתיה. ב: למאי הילכת' שקלתה. מ, נ⁰: למאי הלכתא. In ms. נ⁰, the underlined letters are damaged and hard to decipher. אי'בעי לי' למימני חוטי
343. וו: אי כבית הילל אי כבית שמאי. Ms. וו has a marginal correction, reversing the order of the words שמאי/הילל. — ב.
344. פ, וו, מ, נ⁰: איבעי לך. א: איבעי ליה.
345. ב: למימני חוטין ולמימני חליות. מ: למימני חוטין איבעי לך למימני חוליות. וו: למימ' חוטי וחליות ותיתי ותימא. נ⁰: למימני חוטין איבעי לך למימני חליות ותיתי ותימא. ב: למימ' חוליות ואיבעי לך למימני חוטי ותיתי ותימ' לן. א: למימנא חליות ותיתי ותימא. In ms. ה, the word ומימר is written with a triangle of dots above it, possibly for deletion.
346. פ, וו: לי. מ: ל'. ב: א"ל. א, נ⁰: ואמ' רבה בר חנה אמ' לי
347. פ, וו, מ, א, נ⁰: תא
348. פ, מ, א, נ⁰: אחוי לך. ב: ואחוי לך. וו: וחוי לי
349. פ, וו, מ, ב, נ⁰: טורא
350. פ, וו, מ, נ⁰: דסיני. א: סינאי
351. פ: אזלי וחזאי. נ⁰: אזלי חזאי. וו, ב, מ, א: חזאי
352. פ: דהוו הדרין לי'. וו: דהדרי עלי. ב: דהדרא ליה. מ: דהדיר' לי. א :דהדירא לי'. נ⁰: דהדירא ביה. In ms. נ⁰, the underlined word is added in the margin.
353. פ: וקימן כחמרי. וו: וקיימי כחמרי. ב: חזאי דקיימ' כחמרא. מ: וקיימן כחמ'. א: וקיימן כי חמרי. נ⁰: וקיימן בי חמרי
354. פ: חיורתא. מ: חיורת'. א: חיוראתא. וו: חוורתי. ב: חיוורת'. נ⁰: חורתא. Unique reading in ms. ה.
355. וו: אזלי שמעי. ב: אזילנ' שמעי. פ, נ⁰: שמעית. מ, א: שמעתי
356. Beginning with this word, ms. נ⁰ is lacunary through the word דילמא in ln. פ"ק.ד"י, with exceptions as noted.
357. וו, מ, א: קול.
358. פ: דקאמרה. וו: דהוה אמרה. ב: דהוה קאמר'. מ: שאומר'. א: שאומרת

קס"ז אוי לי³⁵⁹ שנשבעתי³⁶⁰ ועכשיו³⁶¹ שנשבעתי³⁶² מי מפר³⁶³ לי³⁶⁴

קס"ח יג'ב

קס"ט כי אתאי לבי מדרשא³⁶⁵ אמרו³⁶⁶

ק"ע כל³⁶⁷ אבא³⁶⁸ חמור³⁶⁹ כל בר³⁷⁰ חנה³⁷¹ סיכסא³⁷²

קע"א הוה³⁷³ לך למימר³⁷⁴ מופר לך מופר לך³⁷⁵

קע"ב ואנא סברי³⁷⁶ דילי³⁷⁷ שבועה³⁷⁸ דדור המבול³⁷⁹ הוה³⁸⁰

קע"ג ורבנן אוי לא לימא³⁸¹

קע"ד

קע"ה יד

---

359. — :פ. In the margin ms. ⁰נ reads ליה, maybe a correction of אוי לי, but this is unclear due to a lacuna in the text body.

360. וו: כי נשבעתי.

361. מ: ועכש'. פ, א: ועכשו. וו: כי.

362. וו: נשבעתי.

363. פ: מי מתיר לי מי מפר. וו: ומי מיפר. ב: מי מיפר.

364. א: בי.

365. מ: לקמי' דרבנן. א: לקמייהו דרבנן. נ⁰: לקמי דרבנן.

366. Uniquely in ms. ה. All others: אמ' לי, אמ' לי ,אמרו. Ms. ⁰נ is lacunary here (א...ל), but seems to share the majority reading.

367. כי ב. In ms. ב, the underlined letter is hard to read and may be damaged.

368. אנא :⁰נ .רבה :וו .אבא אמר :ב. In ms. ב, the correction is an erasure, but the word is still visible. In ms. ⁰נ, the underlined letter is hard to read and may be damaged.

369. מ: חמר'. פ, וו, א: חמרא.

370. רב בר בר :נ⁰ ,פ. רב בר בר :ב. In ms. ב, the correction is an erasure, but the word is still visible.

371. מ: חנ'. ב: חנא.

372. וו: טיכסא. Note unique error in ms. וו here, as in in ln. יב.ב.קנ"ח, and inconsistent spelling of ms. פ with ln. יב.ב.קנ"ח.

373. מ: היה.

374. מ: לומ'.

375. פ. שרי לך שרי לך. ב: מופר לך מופר. מ: סיכס' היה לך לומ' מופר לך מופר לך. Underlined error in ms. מ by dittography. Ms. ⁰נ has a lacuna here, but appears to read מופר לך (underlined letters are damaged). In ms. ה, there is a triangle of dots, above the line, between the two words in the second instance of מופר לך: possibly a sign for deletion.

376. פ: ואיהו סבר. מ: והו' סבר. א, ב⁰: הוא סבר. ב: והוא דאמ'. וו: והוא סבר. Ms. ⁰ב begins to be more legible here through the end of the passage, with lacunae as noted.

377. Ms. ⁰נ begins to be legible again here (דילמא :⁰נ), with lacunae as noted.

378. שבועתא אנ. פ: אשבעתא. וו: שבועת'. מ, א, נ⁰, ב⁰: In ms. ⁰נ, the underlined letters are damaged; in ms. מ they are abbreviated.

379. פ, מ, נ, ב⁰: דמבול. וו: המבול. Ms. ⁰נ has a lacuna here. The underlined letters in ms. ⁰ב are damaged. Here, only ms. ב certainly agrees with ms. ה.

380. פ, וו, ב: היא. מ: הו' דקא'. ב⁰: קא'. א: הוא. Ms. ⁰נ has a lacuna here.

381. פ, נ⁰, ב⁰: ורבנן אם כן אוי למה לי. וו: ורבנן אי שבוע' המבול היא אם לא נימא. In ms. ⁰נ, the underlined letters are damaged.

ב: ורבנ' אי שבוע' דור המבול אוי לו למה לי למימ'. מ: ורבנן אוי למ' לי. א: ורבנן אוי לי למה לי

קע"ו אמ'[382] לן[383] תו[384] אחוי[385] לכו[386] בי בלועי[387] [388]דקרח
קע"ז אחוי לן[389] ההוא[390] בזעא[391] דהוה נפיק[392] [393]מיניה חוטא דקוטרא
קע"ח איתי[394] גבבא[395] [396]דעמרא
קע"ט אמשייה[397] במיא[398] [399]וכרכיה[400] ארומחיה[401] ודחציה
ק"פ [402]איקלי ואיחרך
קפ"א אמ' לי[403] אצית[404] איזי[405] מאי דשמעת[406] [407]מהכא

---

382. ב: א"ל. א: ואמ' רבה בר בר חנה אמ'. נ⁰: וא' רבה בר בר חנה זימנא חדא הוה אזלי' במדברא ואמר. ב⁰: ואמ' רבה בר בר חנה זמנא חדא דהוה קאזלינן במדבר ואמ' לי ההוא טייעא. In ms. ב⁰, this entire reading is added in the margin. The underlined words are hard to decipher; they seem to be crossed out, because they are redundant with the text body.
383. ב, ב⁰: א' לי. פ, וו, א, מ, נ⁰: לי.
384. Uniquely in ms. ה. All other mss.: תא.
385. וו: וחוי. ב: ואחוי. ב⁰: חזי.
386. Uniquely in ms. ה. All other mss.: לך.
387. פ: בלעי. מ: בי בלעי. ב: בבלעי. א, נ⁰: בלועי. ב⁰: כי בלועי.
388. Ms. נ⁰ is damaged here.
389. פ, וו: אזלי וחזי. ב: אזלי וחזי. מ, א, ב⁰: חזאי. נ⁰: אזלי וחזי. The underlined letters in ms. נ⁰ are damaged.
390. פ, א, ב⁰: תרי. מ: תרתי. ב, וו: להההיא. Ms. נ⁰ has a lacuna here. In ms. ב⁰, the underlined word is damaged but discernible.
391. וו: כוותא. ב: ביזעת'. פ, ב⁰: בזע. מ, נ⁰: בזעי. א: ביועי. In ms. נ⁰ and ms. ב⁰, the underlined letters are damaged. In ms. ב, the underlined letter seems to be a correction of the letter ק.
392. פ: דקא נפיק. וו, ב: דסליק. מ: והוו קמפקי. א: והוה קא מפקי. ב⁰: והוה קא מפקי. נ⁰: והוה קא נפיק. The underlined letter in ms. א is added above the line.
393. פ: קוטרא מיניה. וו, מ: קוטר'. א: קוטרא. נ⁰: קוטרא מיניהו. מ: תבנא מיניה. ב⁰: קוטרא. In ms. ב⁰, the underlined word is added above the line. Unique reading in ms. H.
394. פ, מ, א: שקל. ב⁰: שקלא. נ⁰: ושקל. ב: אייתי. וו: אתאי.
395. וו: תרי גבבי. ב: גבבי.
396. וו: דעמרא.
397. פ: ואמשייח. וו: ומשינהו. ב: סליקנו אמשינהו. מ: אמשי'. א, נ⁰: אמשה. ב⁰: אמשייה.
398. א. נ⁰: מיא. ב⁰: במי איס. Underlined word in ms. ב⁰ is an error, with a letter above the line (מ): apparently a correction.
399. פ: ונקטי'. מ: ואנהי'. א: ודאציה. ב⁰: אחזנייה. וו: וכרכינהו. ב: ואצינהו. The word in ms. ב is written over a word ending in הן-. Ms. נ⁰ has a lacuna here.
400. פ: ארומח'. וו, נ⁰, ב⁰: ברייש דרומחא. ב, מ: בריש' דרומח'. א: ברישיה דרומחיה. The underlined letter in ms. ב⁰ is damaged.
401. פ: ועיליה. מ: ועיילי'. א: ועיליה להתם. וו: ועייל. ב: וצולונהו. ב⁰: ועיליה. נ⁰: ועייל ליה.
402. פ: ואיחרך. מ: כי אפיק אתי איחרוך. א: כי אפיק אתייה איחרך איחרוכי. וו: כי אפקנהו איחרוכי איחרוך. ב: כי אפקינהו איחרוך איחרוכי. נ⁰: כי אפיק ואתיא איחרך איחרוכי. ב⁰: כי אפיק איתי איחרך חרוכי.
403. ב: לי. In ms. ב, the correction is replaced by an abbreviation symbol (').
404. After this word (אצית), ms. נ⁰ is lacunary until אמת והן בדאין in ln. קפ"ב, and again lacunary after those three words, until it resumes with ומרגליות in ln. רכ"ח below.
405. פ, וו, ב: —. מ: איחזי. א: אחזי.
406. פ: מאי שמעת. מ: מאי שמע'. א: מאי שמעת. ב⁰: מאן שמעת. וו, ב: ושמע מאי קאמרי.
407. —: פ, וו, ב.

קפ״ב	ושמעית דקאמרי⁴⁰⁸ משה ותורתו אמת והן בדאין
קפ״ג	אמ' לי כל תלתין יומין מהדר⁴⁰⁹ להו גיהנם⁴¹⁰ ⁴¹¹כבשר בקלחת
קפ״ד	ואמרי הכי⁴¹² משה ותורתו אמת והן⁴¹³ בדאין
קפ״ה	
קפ״ו	טו
קפ״ז	אמ'⁴¹⁴ לן⁴¹⁵ תו⁴¹⁶ אחוי⁴¹⁷ לכו⁴¹⁸ היכא דסחיפא⁴¹⁹ ⁴²⁰רקיעא עילוי ארעא
קפ״ח	אחוי לן חזאי להחיא כותא⁴²¹
קפ״ט	שקלתיה לסלתאי ואנחתה בגווה עד דצליי⁴²²
ק״צ	הדר גילגלא ולא אשכחתיה⁴²³
קצ״א	אמרי⁴²⁴ דיל' חס ושלום⁴²⁵ ⁴²⁶גנבי איכא הכא
קצ״ב	אמ' לי⁴²⁷ ⁴²⁸אינטר עד למחר כי השתא

---

408. ב: שמעי קלא דהוו אמרי. From the next word, ms. °ב is lacunary, as noted, through ln. קצ״ז below.

409. פ: מיתפכא. וו: הפכינהו. ב: הפכינהן. Ms. °ב has a lacuna here.

410. In this line, ms. °ב has a lacuna up to and including this word.

411. פ: כבשר בתוך קלחת. א: כבשר תוך קלחת.

412. Ms. °ב has a lacuna here. — פ.

413. וַהֵן. א. In ms. א, the underlined letter is added above the line.

414. ב: °ל. א: ואמ' רבה בר בר חנה אמ'. ב: °ב. The reading in ms. °ב is added in the margin.

415. פ, וו, מ: לי. א, ב': לי ההוא טייעא. The reading in ms. °ב is added in the margin. Unique reading in ms. ה.

416. א, מ, ב, וו, פ. Ms. °ב has a lacuna here.

417. וו: ואחוי.

418. וו, ב, מ, א, ב': לך. Ms. ה uniquely has the Arab address the traveling party in plural, rather than singular. (Compare ln. יב.ב.קמ״ו, יג״א.קס״ד, י״ד.קע״ו).

419. א: דנשקא. וו, ב, מ: דנשקי. ב°: ונשק.

420. פ: ארעא ורקיעא אהדדי. מ: ארק' ורקיע' אהדדי. א: ארעא אדרקיעא אהדדי. וו, ב: ארעא ורקיעא. The underlined word in ms. מ is an error (probably by haplography). °ב reads ארעא, followed by a lacuna.

421. וו, מ. Ln. קפ״ח.טו is absent in א, פ: אזלי וחזאי דעביד כי כוי. ב: אזלי להההוא כוותא דרקיע. For this line and the next, ms. °ב is lacunary (שקלתיה א...כוותא דרקיעה אדמ..לנא לא ..תיה), but most closely resembles ms. א.

422. פ: אנחתה לסלתאי בכוותא דרקיעא אדמאלינא. וו: אחיתיה לסילתאי בגוה עד דמצלינן מ: שקלתא אתנחת' לסלתאי בכוות' אדמצלי' א: שקלתה אתנחאתה לסלתאי בכוותא דרקיעא אדמצלינא שקלתיה א...ח ... כוותא דרקיעה. Ms. °ב is lacunary but appears to read: אחזי לסילתאי בגוה עד דמצלינא אדמצלינא (as in the prior and following readings, here ms. °ב most closely resembles ms. א).

423. פ: בעיתה ולא אשכחתה. וו: בעיתיה ולא אשכחתה. מ: לא אשכחתיה. א: ולא אשכחתי. ב: לא אשכחתה. ב': לא אשכחתיה. In ms. °ב, the underlined letters are a lacuna, restored by conjecture.

424. פ: אמרי ליה. ב: אמינ'. וו, מ, א, ב°: אמינא ליה.

425. מ, א, ב°: —. פ: וכי.

426. א: איכא גנבי ברקיע. וו: איכא גנבי ברקיע. ב: איכ' גנבי ברקיע הכא. מ: איכ' גנבי הכא. ב°: איכא גנבי הכא. Ms. פ corresponds to ms. ה, but the word הכא is written over an erasure, presumably of the word ברקיעא as in mss. ב, וו.

427. ב: נפק' בת קלא ואמר'. וו: נפקא בת קלא ואמרה.

428. פ: האי גלגלא דרקיעא הוא דהדר אינטר עד למחר כי האי עידנא

א: הא גלגלא דרקיעא הוה דהדר נטר עד למחר כי השתא הכא. מ: האי גולגלא דרקיע' הו' דהדר נטר עד למחר כי השת' הכ'

Edition 359

קצ"ג ⁴²⁹<u>הדר גלגילא לדוכתיה ושקלת ליה</u>

קצ"ד

קצ"ה <u>טז</u> ⁴³⁰

קצ"ו רבי יוחנן ⁴³¹<u>משתעי</u>

קצ"ז זימנא חדא <u>הוה קא אזילנא</u>⁴³² ⁴³³<u>בספינה</u>

קצ"ח <u>ודלי ההוא</u>⁴³⁴ <u>כוורא</u>⁴³⁵ ⁴³⁶<u>רישיה</u>

קצ"ט <u>ודמיין</u>⁴³⁷ <u>עיניה</u>⁴³⁸ ⁴³⁹<u>לתרי</u> ⁴⁴⁰<u>סיהרי</u>

ר <u>ונפלו</u>⁴⁴¹ <u>מיא</u>⁴⁴² ⁴⁴³<u>מתרי</u> *זימיה

ר"א <u>כתרי</u>⁴⁴⁴ ⁴⁴⁵<u>מברי</u> ⁴⁴⁶<u>דסורא</u>

ר"ב

ר"ג יז''א

ר"ד רב ספרא ⁴⁴⁷<u>משתעי</u>

ר"ה זימנא חדא הוה <u>אזילנא</u>⁴⁴⁸ ⁴⁴⁹<u>בספינתא</u>

ב: האי גלגלא דרקיע הוא דהדר איעכבי למחר כי השת' וו: האי גלגלא דרקיעא הדר איעכב עד למחר כי השתא
ב⁰: האי גלגלא דרקיע הוא דהדר נטר עד למחר כי השתא

429. 'פ: ומשכחת לה. א, ב⁰: ומשכחת ליה. מ: ומשכחת לה. ב: עד דמהדר גלגלא ואשכחתי
וו:. . Unique reading in ms. ה. עד דנדהר גלגלא משכחתי

430. Before this unit, ms. וו has another mnemonic with keywords from Units XVI-XIX: סימן יוחנן ספרא יונתן הינדוואה

431. פ: אשתעי. ב⁰: מש<u>ת</u>עי. The underlined letter in ms. ב⁰ is added above the line.

432. ב: —. פ: הוה קא אזילנא. וו: הוה קאזלינ'. מ, ב⁰: הוה קאזלינ'. א: הוה קאזילנן

433. Uniquely in ms. ה. Ms. מ is abbreviated, hence ambiguous (בספינה/בספינתא). All others: בספינתא

434. וו, ב, מ: וחזינן ההוא. א, ב⁰: וחזינן לההוא.

435. פ: כוארא

436. פ: רישיה מתותי מיא. ב: דאפיק רישיה מימ'. מ: דאפיק רישיה ממיא. וו: דאפקי' לראשי' ממיא
א, ב⁰: דאפקיה לרישיה ממיא

437. פ: והוה דמיין. וו, ב: והוו תרי.

438. ב: עיני. א, ב⁰: עייניה

439. פ, וו, מ, ב⁰: כתרי. א: בתרי. ב: נתוק. I am baffled by ms. ב.

440. וו, ב, מ, ב⁰: סהרי

441. פ: ונפיץ. וו: ומשו. ב, א, ב⁰: ושפך. מ: ושפיך. Unique reading in ms. ה.

442. מ, א: —

443. פ: מתרין אוסיה. וו: מאודניה. ב: מתרי זיהומ'. מ: מתרתי זימ' מיא. א: מתרתי מיא. ב⁰: מתרתי זימי. Unique error (קימה) in ms. ה by confusion of similar letters, corrected on the basis of mss. ⁰ב, מ, ב.

444. פ: כתר. ב⁰: כ<u>רתי</u>. In ms. ⁰ב, the underlined letters include a scribal correction above the line (ב א), reversing them.

445. פ: מכדי. מ: מיכרי. ב⁰: מיברי. Ms. פ and ms. מ contain unique errors by confusion of similar letters.

446. In ms. ב, there is a lacuna here.

447. פ: אשתעי. ב⁰: מיש<u>ת</u>עי

448. פ: קא אזילנן. וו: קאזילנא. ב⁰: קאזלינ'. ב, מ: אזלינ'. א: קא אזלן

449. א. <u>באורחא</u> בספינתא. The underlined word is marked with two dots above the line (presumably for deletion, as it is absurd; see chapter 3 n. 488).

ר"ו וְדלי ההוא⁴⁵⁰ כּוורא⁴⁵¹ ⁴⁵²רישיה
ר"ז *והוה אית* ליה⁴⁵³ ⁴⁵⁴תרי קרני
ר"ח וְחקוק⁴⁵⁵ עליהו⁴⁵⁶ אני בריה קלה⁴⁵⁷ שבים
ר"ט והוינא תלת⁴⁵⁸ מאה ⁴⁵⁹פרסי
ר"י ומזמן⁴⁶⁰ לפומיה⁴⁶¹ ⁴⁶²דלויתן
רי"א יז"ב
רי"ב אמ' רב אשי⁴⁶³
רי"ג ההוא עיזא דימא הוא⁴⁶⁴ ⁴⁶⁵וכחישא
רי"ד
רט"ו יח
רט"ז ר' יונתן⁴⁶⁶ ⁴⁶⁷משתעי
רי"ז זימנא חדא הוה אזלינן⁴⁶⁸ ⁴⁶⁹בספינה
רי"ח וחזינא⁴⁷⁰ להיא⁴⁷¹ קרטליתא

---

450. וו: חזינן ההוא. מ: וחזינ' ההוא. א, ב⁰: וחזינן ההוא. ב: להההוא. Ms. ב has a lacuna before the underlined word.
451. פ: כוארא.
452. וו: דאפיק רישיה ממיא. ב: דאפקי רישי'. מ: דאפקי' לראשי' ממיא. א, ב⁰: דאפקיה לרישיה ממיא.
453. פ, וו, ב: והוו ליה. מ, א, ב⁰: ואית ליה. Unique error in ms. ה. Here, ms. ה retains competing readings which support both variants in other mss. (קרנא/תרי קרני) and are disambiguated there.
454. ב⁰: קרנ'. א: קרנא.
455. פ, מ, א, ב⁰: וחקוק. וו: דחקיק. ב: דהוו. The underlined letters in ms. ב⁰ are mostly lacunary.
456. פ, מ: עלוהי. וו: עלייהו. ב: עילוותא. א, ב⁰: עליה.
457. וו: אני ברייה קלה. מ: אנא ברי' קל'. א: אנא בריאה קלה. ב: אנא בוריא קלה. ב⁰: אנא בוריא קלא.
458. וו: זהוינן כתלתא. מ: וחיינא תלת. ב⁰: והונא. Unique common spelling error in ms. וו.
459. Added above the line in ms. מ. The text on the line (שני, presumably an error for פרסי) is not deleted.
460. פ, א: ואזילנא. וו: ואזילנן. ב: ואזילנ'. ב⁰: ואזילנה. מ: ואזיל' תלת מאה פרסי ואזילנא. Dittography, ms. מ. Unique reading, ms. ה.
461. וו: בפומיה.
462. Here, ms. וו has דלויתן in the text body but also לויתן in the margin, with horizontal lines above and below the word.
463. א. רב אשי אמ'. וו: כי אתינא לקמי' דרב אשי אמ' לן. ב: כי אתינ' קמי' דרב אמ' לן. Contrast ms. ב in ln. רכ"ב to ms. ב in ln. ח"ב.ק.קי"ט and ln ט"ב.קי"ט.
464. א: היא. —. ב: . Unique error in ms. א.
465. פ: דאית ליה תרי קרני וכחישא. וו, ב: דאית ליה קרנא דנחשא. מ: דבחיש' ואית ליה קרנין ב⁰: דרחשא ואית לה קרני. א: דכחישא ואית ליה קרני
466. ב: יוחנ'. מ, א, ב⁰: יוחנ'. Ms. וו includes a notation in the margin: יונתן ר' (also the reading in the text body). Perhaps this is used to disambiguate between copies that were available to the scribe, some of which read יוחנן as in mss. ב⁰, א, מ.
467. ב, ב⁰: מישתעי.
468. וו: קאזלין. מ: קאזילנא. ב: אזלינ'. ב⁰: קאזלי'. א: קא אזלינן
469. All others: בספינתא. Unique reading in ms. ה, which prefers the Hebrew form. Compare ln. קצ"ז and further ln. ט"ע, ln. קנ"ד, ln. קס"ד, ln. ק"ע.
470. פ, וו: וחזינן. ב, מ: וחזי'. ב⁰: וחזיה.
471. פ, מ, ב, ב⁰: ההיא. וו, ב: להההוא. א: ההוא.

רי"ט דְּהוּהּ[472] מִדְבָּק בָּהּ[473] אֲבָנִים טוֹבוֹת[474] וּמַרְגָּלִיּוֹת

ר"כ וְהַדַּר[475] לֵהּ[476] מִינָא דְּכַוָּורָא[477] דְּשָׁמֵיהּ[478] כְּרָשִׁי[479]

רכ"א נָחִית[480] בַּר אַמּוּדַאי[481] לְאֵיתוּיֵי[482] בְּעָא[483] [484]לְמִקְטְלֵיהּ

רכ"ב סָלִיק דָּרָא זִיקָא דְּחָלָא וּנְחִית[485]

רכ"ג נָפְקָא בַּת[486] קָלָא[487] וַאֲמָרָה

רכ"ד מַאי[488] עֲבַדְתִּיכוּ בַּהֲדֵי קַרְטָלִיתָא[489] דִּדְבֵיתְהוּ[490] דְּר' חֲנִינָא בֶּן דּוֹסָא

רכ"ה דְּאִית בַּהּ תְּכֶלְתָּא *דְּשַׁדְיָא* חוּטֵי[491] [492]לְצַדִּיקֵי לְעָלְמָא דְּאָתֵי

רכ"ו

רכ"ז יט

רכ"ח רַ'[493] יְהוּדָה הִינְדּוּאָה[494] [495]מִשְׁתָּעֵי

---

472. בּ°: דְּהוּ. פ: דהוו.

473. פ: מקבע בה. וו: מיקבען ביה. ב: מקבעין ביה. בּ°: קא מקבען בה. מ, א: מטבעו בה.

474. Ms. נ° resumes here (וּמַרְגָּלִיּוֹת) and continues through the remainder of the passage, with lacunae as noted.

475. פ: והוה הדר. מ: והדיר.

476. בּ: —. פ: לה. מ: לי'. וו, א, ב°, נ°: ליה.

477. וו, ב: דהוא כוורא. מ: מיני דכוור'. א: מיני דכוורי. נ°: מיני דכווורי. בּ°: מינא דכוורי.

478. מ, א: דמקרי. בּ°: דמתקרֵי. נ°: דמיקרי. Ms. ב° has a scribal correction above the line (ב א) reversing the underlined letters.

479. פ: כירשא. וו: כרשאי. ב: כרשא. מ: כריש.

480. פ: והוה נחית. ב, בּ°: ונחית.

481. וו: בר אמי אמוראה. ב: בר אמי אמורא. א: בת אֲמִירָאי, The underlined letters in ms. א have been modified and are hard to read. בּ°: בר אמידאי. מ, נ°: בר אמוראי. Common spelling errors in mss. וו, ב, מ, נ; dittography in ms. וו.

482. פ: לאיתוייה. ב: לאתויי. מ: לאתויי. נ°: לאיתרי.

483. א: אתו. נ°: אתי. בּ°: אתו קבעו.

484. מ: דנישממטה לאטמיה. מ: למישמטי אטמי. א, ב, בּ°: קא שמטי ליה. פ: Ms. ב has a lacuna.

485. פ: סליק ושקא זיקא דחלא בהדיא. וו: זרק ליה חלה ונחית. The underlined word in ms. פ probably belongs in ln. רכ"ד below. The bold word in ms. פ is probably due to dittography and assimilation of letters, but suits the context. In this line, mss. ב°, א, מ correspond to ms. ה. So does ms. נ°, except the last word (ונפיק, not ונחית; possible dittography). Ms. ב has a lacuna in this line, except for the penultimate word (קזלא; a possible error for דחלא, as in majority of mss.).

486. —: ב. Here, ms. וו has the marginal reading בת קלא, also in the text body. Compare ms. וו, ln. י"ח.רט"ז.

487. פ: ואמר' לן. בּ°: ואמרה לן. מ: אמר' לן. א, נ°: אמרה לן. וו: ואמרה ליה. בּ°: ואמר' קלא לן.

488. נ°: מאן.

489. וו, ב: בעיתון בהאי טרקליתא. מ, א, בּ°, נ°: אית לכו בהדי קרטליתא. Ms. ב has a lacuna at the underlined word, followed by the deleted word הוה, so it is impossible to construe its reading here.

490. פ, וו, ב: דביתהו. נ°: כדביתהו.

491. וו: דעתידא למישרא ביה חוטא דתכלית'. ב: עתיד' למישר' בי חוט'. מ: דעתיד' למישד' בה תכלת '. A. Underlined word in ms. נ° is damaged, added by conjecture. פ: דעתידה למשדא ביה תכלתא. בּ°: דעתירא דשדיא בה תכלתא. בּ°: דשריא. Likely error by confusion of similar letters in ms. ה:(דשריא) shared with mss. ב, וו (למישרא) but corrected on the basis of mss. פ, מ, א, בּ°, נ°.

492. Ms. ב, although the first word is lacunary, seems to share this reading with all other mss.

493. פ, וו, ב, מ, א, בּ°, נ°: רב. Unique reading in ms. ה.

494. פ, בּ°: הנדואה. וו, נ°: הינדוואה. א: הנדוואה.

495. פ, וו, ב, בּ°: מישתעי.

רכ״ט זִימְנָא[496] חדא הוה קא אזילנא[497] בספינתא

ר״ל וַחֲזֵינָא[498] לְהַהוּא[499] אבן טָבָא[500] דַּהֲדַר[501] לַהּ[502] תנינא

רל״א נחית בר אמודאי[503] וְאַיְתִי לֵהּ[504]

רל״ב וְאָתָא[505] תְּנִינָא[506][507] וקא בלעה לספינתא

רל״ג אתא פְּשַׁקְצָא[508] וְקַטְלֵיהּ[509]

רל״ד אִיתְהַפִיכוּ מיא לדמא[510]

רל״ה אתא תנינא חבריה[511]

רל״ו שַׁקְלֵיהּ אתנחתה עילויה ואחייה[512]

רל״ז הדר וקא בלע לספינתא[513]

---

496. זִימְנָא וו. The underlined letter is added above the line.

497. קא אזלי. In ms. ב, there is a notation above the underlined letters, perhaps indicating that they should be reversed (as they are in ms. וו). For this variant, see note to ln. יא.קל״ה.

498. וחזי׳ וו, א, ב[0]: וחזינן. ב, מ: וחזאי. נ[0]: וחזי.

499. להההוא כוורא ב: The word כוורא seems to be an uncorrected error by line-skip.

500. טבה ב[0]: טובה. נ[0]: טובא. מ, א.

501. דהיה הדיר ב[0]: דהוה הדיר. מ: דהדר נ[0]: דַּהֲדַר פ, א. וו, ב: Ms. נ has lacuna at underlined letters restored by conjecture.

502. ליה נ[0]: א, ב.

503. נחית בה אמודאי ב[0]: נחית בר אמוראי. ב, א: נחית ההוא בר אמוראי. וו: ונחית בר אמוראי. פ: Following this reading, ms. ב contains an uncorrected dittography: נחית בר אמוראי תניב׳ ליה הדר הנה.

504. לאתייה נ[0]: לאיש ת. ב[0]: לאיתוי. מ, א: לאיתווייה. פ, וו, ב: The underlined letter in ms. ב[0], a correction, is at the start of a line. Unique reading in ms. ה, possibly as others are troubled by similarity with the following line (ואתא/ואיתי) and emend away from it.

505. Unique reading in ms. ה. All others: אתא

506. ההוא :וו.

507. קא בעי למיבלע לה. וו: וקא בעי לספינתא לטבועה. ב[0]: קא בעי למיבלע לה לספינת פ. ב: וקבלע לַהּ לספינת׳. מ: קבלע לה לספינת׳. א: קא בלע לה לספינת׳. נ[0]: קא בלע ליה לספינתא ב: The underlined letters in ms. ב are added above the line.

508. צפרא א: צִיפְרָא. נ[0]: ציפרא. ב: חנב׳. פוני :מ. פושקנצא :וו. פשקנצא. פ: Ms. נ is corrected above the line to a word ending in א (Presumably פַּשְׁקַצָּא, like the above-line-correction of ms. נ[0] in ln. רל״ח).

509. לרישיה פסקיה :נ[0] ,ב[0]. פסקיה. מ, ב: פסקיה לרישיה תנינא. וו: ובלעיה לרישיה דתנינא. פ: קטעיה לרישיה. א: וקטליה לתנינא. The underlined word in נ[0] is added above the line.

510. ואהפכי מיא והוי דמא ב: אהפיכו מיא והוי דמא. נ[0]: ואיתהפיכו מייא והוו דמא. א: איתהפיכו מיא והוו דמא. פ, מ, ב[0]: וו. דמא וַהֲווּ ב: In ms. ב, the underlined word is added above the line. Ln. רל״ד.ט״ר is absent in ms. פ.

511. אתא תנינא חבריה נ[0]: אתא חבריה. ב[0]: א, ב. ב, פ: In ms. ב[0], the underlined word is added above the line.

512. שקלה ותלי ליה וחיה. ב: אוחתה ניהליה וחייא. פ. א: שקליה תליא לה ההוא אבן טבא וחיה. נ[0]: שקלה לאבן טובא ושקלי להה אבן טבא ותלת ליה וחיה וחייה תליא ליה ותלל In ms. נ[0], underlined words added above the line.

513. והדר איתא קא בעי לְמַבְלע לה לספינתא. וו: הדר אתא בעי למיבלע ליה לספינתא. פ. מ: הדר את׳ קבלע לספינת׳. א, נ[0]: הדר אתא קא בלע לַהּ לספינתא. ב: הדר את׳ לקטע לה לספינתא ב[0]: והדר אתא קא בלע לה לספיני Underlined letter in נ[0] is lacunary. Underlined letters in פ are added above the line.

Edition   363

רל"ח   הדר אתא ההוא פשקצא וקטליה[514]
רל"ט   שקליה ופרח בהדי דקא פרח[515]
ר"מ   נפלה בספינתא[516]
רמ"א   עילוי הנך צפורי דהוו מליחי חיין[517]
רמ"ב   שקלוה ופרוח[518]
רמ"ג
רמ"ד   ס
רמ"ה   תנו רבנן מעשה בר' אליעזר[519] ור' יהושע שהיו *הם* מהלכין[520] בספינ'[521]
רמ"ו   והיה ר' אליעזר ישן[522] ור' יהושע נעור[523]
רמ"ז   נזדעזע[524] ר' יהושע ונינער[525][526] ר' אליעזר
רמ"ח   אמ' לו[527] [528]מה זה יהושע

---

514. פ: אתא ההוא פשקנצא קטעי לרישיה. וו: אתא ההוא פושקנצא וקטליה.
ב⁰: הדר אתא ציפרא פשקנצא לרישיה. מ: הדר את' צפר' פסקיה. ב: הדר את' ציפר' פסקי' ושדייה לספינתא.
א: הדר אתא ציפורא פסקיה. ב⁰: הדר אתא ציפרא פסקיה. The underlined words in ms. ב⁰ are added above the line.

515. פ: שקלה להההיא אבן טבא ופרח בהדי דפרח. וו: ושקיל ההוא אבן טבא ופרח בהדי דקא פרח. ב⁰: ושקליה שדייה לההוא אבן טובא לספינתא ופרח בהדי דקא פרח מ: ושקלה לאבן. א: ושקלה ופרח. ב⁰: שקלה לאבן ms. ב⁰, beginning with ההוא, reading is added above the line. The underlined letters are damaged and added by conjecture. The final word appears to be added in the margin. This line is absent in ms. ב.

516. פ: נפל בספינתא. וו: נפלה ההיא אבן טבא בספינ'. מ: שדיי לספינת'. א: שדייא לספינתא. ב⁰: ושדייה לספינ'. This line is absent in ms. ב. It also absent in ms. ב⁰, as a similar text falls in the previous line.

517. פ: והוו הנך ציפורי מליחי בהדן. וו: והוה איכא בהדן ציפורי דמליחי. ב: הוה איכ' ציפור' מליח' בהדן. ב⁰: הוה איכא ציפורי מליחי בהדן. א: הוה איכא טובא ציפורי מליחי בהדן. In ms. ב⁰, the underlined word is added in the margin here. It is difficult to construe this marginal addition in ב⁰, which may contain an additional (but now completely illegible) word.

518. פ: אותיבנה עלי' דליוה ופרח. וו: שקלינהו ותלינו ליה ופרחו. ב: שקלינ' תלי' תלל ניהליהו שקלו ופרחו. א: שקליניה תליניה ניהליהו שקלוה ופרוח. ב⁰: שקלנא תלינא ניהלייהו שקלוה ופרחו. מ: תלינן ניהליהו שקלו ופרחו. ב⁰: שקלן פליגא תלינן נהליהו שקלוה ופרחו In ms. ב⁰, the underlined correction is added above the line.

519. Ms. ב⁰ has a lacuna at this word.

520. פ, וו, ב, מ, ב⁰: באין. א, ב⁰: באים. Unique error in ms. ה; this word is extraneous and syntactically awkward.

521. Ms. ב has this word in Aramaic, whereas all others have it in Hebrew; except ms. ק⁰, which has a lacuna, and mss. ה and מ, which have an ambiguous abbreviation. It is possible that the scribe of ms. ב copied from an abbreviated form, and accidentally harmonized this word to its Aramaic equivalent throughout the text. See ms. ה, In. יי״ח.רי״ז.

522. מ: ש ישן.

523. ב⁰: נינער.

524. וו: ביזדעזע.

525. מ: ומנער.

526. Ms. ב⁰ has a lacuna here.

527. פ: אמ' לו יהושע. ב: א"ל.

528. פ: אחי מה ראית. מ: מפני מה נזדעזעת. ב⁰: מפני מה נזדעזעתה. ב: מפני מה נזדעזע'. In ms. ב, the underlined word is added in the margin.

רמ"ט א' לו⁵²⁹ ר⁵³⁰י⁵³¹ מאור גדול ראיתי בים
ר"נ אמ' לו⁵³² שמא⁵³³ עיניו של לויתן ⁵³⁴ראית
רנ"א דכת⁵³⁵י ביה⁵³⁶ ועיניו⁵³⁷ כעפעפי שחר
רנ"ב
רנ"ג **כא"א**
רנ"ד אמ' רב אשי אשתעי⁵³⁸ לי הונא בר נתן
רנ"ה זמנא⁵³⁹ חדא הוה קא אזילנא⁵⁴⁰ ⁵⁴¹במדברא
רנ"ו והוה בהדן אטמא⁵⁴²
רנ"ז פתחנא ונקירנא איתנחה עילוי עשבי והלמה⁵⁴³
רנ"ח איתינן ציבי וטוינא⁵⁴⁴
רנ"ט לישנא הדרנא אתאי⁵⁴⁵

---

529. מ, ב: א"ל.

530. Unique reading in ms. ה (ms. נ᠎ has a lacuna). Rabbinovicz (*DS* XI:232) posits a scribal error. However, in light of אחי at ln. רמ"ח.כ in ms. פ (to which Rabbinovicz did not have access), it could in fact be an abbreviated form of address: "my master," similar to "my brother." Whether each form of address is suitable for their relative status is another matter.

531. Ms. נ᠎ is highly lacunary here, but seems to share this reading.

532. מ, ב: א"ל.

533. שמאע .ב: שמ' .מ: Ms. נ᠎ has a lacuna here. Ms. ב seems to be corrected away from the other mss. See Chp. 1 n. 233.

534. ראיתה .וו. פ: ראיתאה .ב⁰: , In ms. ב⁰, the correction is added on top of the letter.

535. א: דכת'.

536. — :פ. Ms. נ᠎ has a lacuna here.

537. עיניו :פ. Ms. נ᠎ has a lacuna at the underlined letters.

538. פ, ב⁰, א, ו"ו. מ: אמ'. ק⁰: ב, אישתעי. This corrects Rabbinovicz (*DS* XI:232), for whom "all mss." read like ms. ה. Ms. נ᠎ has a lacuna.

539. פ, וו, ב, מ, א, ב⁰, ק⁰: זימנא.

540. וו, ב, מ: קאזלינ'. פ: קאוליב'. א, ב⁰, ק⁰: קא אזלינא. Ms. נ᠎ has a lacuna here.

541. במדברא: במדבר. ב: בספי' במדבר. The underlined correction in ms. ב is added above the line. Ms. נ᠎ has a lacuna here.

542. וו: והוה איכא אטמא. פ: והוה אטמא דבשרא בהדן. ב: והואי אטמ' דפת דבישר' בהדן.
מ: והואי אטמ' דבשר' בהדן. ב⁰: והואי אטמא דבישרא בהד'. א, נ⁰: והואי אטמא דבישרא בהדן.

543. פ: ופתחנא ושדינא אעישבי. וו: חתכנא ונקירנא ואיתנחנא על הנך עישבי.
מ: ונקירנא ואנחנא. א: פתחנא נקירנא ואנחנא אירקנא. ב: פתחנ' ואנקטנא נקירנ' ומתחנן על הנך הנך עישבי. ב⁰: פתחנא ונקירנא ואנח' איקרא. נ⁰:פתחנא ואנח' אירקא Underlined letters in ms. נ⁰ are damaged, restored by conjecture. Ms. ב has a dittography, ms. ב⁰ an error by metathesis. The similarity of נקירנא in one branch of mss. to אירק in the other points to either a corruption in the branch with the latter reading, i.e. mss. נ⁰, ב⁰, א. Or, by *lectio difficilior*, we should posit a correction to עשבי/עישבי in the branch represented by mss. ב, פ, וו, ה. (The minus at this word in ms. M may be an attempt to avoid the problem altogether.)

544. פ: אדמיתינו ציבי חלם וטוינא. וו: ואיתינן ציבי וטוינא. ב: אדמייתנן ציבי וטוינ' כי הדרן איאלם.
א: אדמייתינא ציבי איחלם טוינא. ב⁰: אדמיי' ציבי איאלם אטמא טוינא. מ: אדמייתי' ציבי חלם ואיאלם טוינא.
נ⁰: אדמייתי' ציבי חלם טוינא. ק⁰: אדמייתנן ציבי חלם טוינה The underlined letter in ms. ב is added above the line. Underlined letters in ms. נ⁰ are damaged, restored by conjecture.

545. פ: כי הדרנא ואתינא לבתר תריסר ירחי שתא. ב: אתאן לבתר ירחי שת'. מ: כי הדרן אתן לבת' תריסר ירחי שת'.

ר"ס   הוה קא מלחשן גומרי[546]
רס"א   **כא"ב**
רס"ב   כי[547] *אתאי*[548] לקמיה[549] דאמימר אמ' לי[550]
רס"ג   עשבי[551] סמתרי[552] הוה[553] וגומרי[554] דריתמא[555] הוה[556]

א: כי הדרן אתאן לב' אתאן לבתר תריסר ירחי שתא. ב°: כי הדרן אתאן לבתר תריסר ירחי שתא. וו: לשנא כי הדרינן שתא °ק: כי הדרן אתן לבתר תריסר ירחי שתא. The underlined word in °ק is damaged, restored by conjecture. Ms. °נ is highly lacunary but seems to share the reading of °ב. The underlined letters in ms. א are an uncorrected dittography at the beginning of a line, followed by a blank space.

546.   פ: חזינא להנהי גומרי דההוא קא מלחשי. ב°: חזינחו לחנחו גומרי דהוו קא מלחשי
וו: חזינן להנך גומרי דההוא כחיי. מ: חזינבהי להנהו גומרי דהוו קא לחי. א: חזינן להנבה גומרי דההוא קא חיאן
נ°: חזינהו לַההוא גומרי דהוּהַ קא מחיה. ב: חזינן להנחו גומרי דהוו קאמלחיא. Underlined letters in ms. °נ are restored by conjecture. Ms. °ק has a lacuna at this line. In ms. ה, the word מלחשן is a correction in the margin (the text body reads מלחינן).

547.   — :פ. Ms. °ק has a lacuna here.

548.   אתאי :א. אתאי ,°ב ,°נ ,מ ,ב ,וו ,פ. Ms. °ק has a lacuna here. Unique error (אתא) in ms. ה by harmonization with common formula (see Redfield, "'When X Arrived,'" 10) corrected on the basis of mss. °ב ,°נ ,ב ,מ ,וו ,פ.

549.   Ms. °ק shares the reading of ms. ה for this word and for the remainder of the line.

550.   אלי :°ב .— :ב ,וו.

551.   ההוא עישבא :°ק ,°נ. ההוא עשבא :°ב. ההוא עישבי :ב. הנך עישבי :וו ,פ. In ms. °נ, the underlined letter is a lacuna, restored by conjecture.

552.   דסמנתרי :ב.

553.   הנהו הנד :א. הווי והנהו :ב. הוו. :וו. הנך :פ. Ms. °נ has a lacuna here.

554.   גומרי :°ק ,°נ ,°ב ,א ,מ ,ב ,פ. Unique reading in ms. ה.

555.   דריתמא :°ק. ריתמ' :מ. It is unclear whether or not ms. °ק is also abbreviated here, due to a lacuna.

556.   הוו :°ב ,ב ,וו. — :מ ,פ. Mss. °ק and °נ have a lacuna here.

Appendix 3

Parallels to Part 2 in Pesiqta of Rab Kahana

(Text and variants in ed. Bernard Mandelbaum. 2nd ed., 2 vols. Philadelphia: JPS, 1987)

3.A. [ed. Mandelbaum, §*Parashah Aheret*, p. 455 ln. 8–ln. 9 [... long excursus ...] p. 456 ln. 22 → p. 457 ln. 8] // Appendix §*Translation* Part 2.B]

Another matter: *and there shall be a cover [sukkāh] for shadow in the day time from the heat.*[1] R. Levi said: Anyone who fulfills the commandment of *sukkāh* in this world, the Holy One, Blessed be He, will seat him in the *sukkāh* of the Leviathan in the time to come, as it is said: *canst thou fill his skin with barbed irons [śukkôt]?*[2]
[... long excursus, concluding with the verse just cited.]
Or his head with a fish spear [tsiltsal dagim]?[3] R. Nahman and R. Huna the Priest and R. Yehudah the Levite the son of R. Shalum [comment]:

One of them [says]: They pound on their cymbals [*tsiltsalim*] and say, "Anyone who has performed the commandment of pilgrimage [to Jerusalem] shall come and serve [him/herself] and eat from [Leviathan's] head, and its taste is like the taste of the head of a fish from the Sea of Tiberias." And another says: They pound on their cymbals and say, "Anyone who has performed the commandment of pilgrimage [to Jerusalem] shall come and eat from his head, and its taste is like the taste of the head of a fish from the Great Sea." Immediately, they come and form a company and make a feast of him,[4] as it is said, *Shall the companions make a feast of him?*[5] [Namely,] one who has made himself a *companion* of the commandments.

---

1. Isa 4:6 (KJV, trans. modified).
2. Job 41:7a (40:31).
3. Job 41:7b (40:31).
4. Possibly by analogy to the "company" formed to sacrifice the Passover offering.
5. Job 41:6a (40:30; KJV modified).

Another matter: *Shall the companions make a feast of him?* Companies upon companies:[6] There are adepts in Scripture, there are adepts in Mishnah, there are adepts in Talmud, there are adepts in *Aggadah*, there are adepts in commandments, there are adepts in good deeds. Every single company comes and serves itself a portion. And perhaps you would say that there is dissension among them? One would reply: *shall they part him among the merchants?*[7] — those are the businessmen,[8] the ones who, when they are partners in a precious stone and they sell it and they come to divide the assets, have no dissension. Rather, each of them comes and takes out his portion according to the assets that he put in. And similarly, in time to come, there will be no dissension among [the adepts]. Rather, each of the righteous will come and take out his reward according to his deeds. Hence, *shall they part him among the merchants?* [which means] not [merely] *merchants* but businessmen, as it is written: *whose merchants are princes, whose traffickers are the honorable of the earth.*[9]

3.B. 18:5 [ed. Mandelbaum p. 296 ln. 4 [... elided story ...] p. 297 ln. 8 → p. 298 ln. 11] // Appendix §*Translation* Part 2 2.C

And I will make [thy battlements of] kadkhod:[10] R. Abba bar Kahana said: as this and as that [*keden u-kheden*]. R. Levi said: *kadkhediyyanon*.[11] R. Yehoshua ben Levi said: Stones of *kadkhodiyyah*.[12]

[... A story about R. Yehoshua ben Levi; Elijah; a shipwreck and a Jewish boy; magical luminous stones; a cave, and other motifs with similarities to Part 1 and Part 2 and especially 2.C is elided, as we focus on the Talmud, not on Pesiq. Rab Kah.'s reception of those motifs ...][13]

---

6. The term "companion" also refers to a member of Palestinian rabbinic study circles, which appears to be the basis of this midrash. See n. 42 to Appendix §*Translation* Part 2.B.

7. Job 41:6b (40:30).

8. *Pragmatotin*, from πραγματευτής. See Aaron Michael Butts, "Language Change in the Wake of Empire: Syriac in Its Greco-Roman Context" (PhD diss., University of Chicago, 2013), 156. Compare n. 44 to Appendix §*Translation* Part 2.B.

9. Isa 23:8 (KJV).

10. Isa 54:12 (KJV, modified).

11. From *καρχηδινόν ("carbuncle"); see Löw in Krauss and Löw, *Griechische und lateinische Lehnwörter*, 2:299; Sokoloff, *JPA*, 251.

12. From χαλκιδική, χαλκηδών ("chalcedony"). See Jacob Levy and Heinrich Fleischer, *Neuhebräisches und Chaldäisches Wörterbuch über die Talmudim und Midraschim*, 4 vols. (Leipzig: Brockhaus, 1876–1889), 2:449.

13. See Kiperwasser and Ruzer, "Sea Voyage Tales," 43–47; Kiperwasser and Ruzer, "Nautical Fiction," 297–300.

And thy gates of carbuncles [*'eqdah*, Isa 54:12].[14] R. Yirmiyah [said] in the name of R. Shmuel bar Yitshaq: "In time to come, the Holy One, Blessed be He, will make[15] the Eastern Gate of the Temple and its two wickets from a single stone of pearl."

R. Yohanan was expounding inside the Great Synagogue of Sepphoris: "In time to come, the Holy One, Blessed be He, will make the Eastern Gate of the Temple and its two wickets from a single stone of pearl." And a certain seafaring heretic was there. He said: "We do not even find [pearls] as big as a single egg of a turtle-dove. And someone's been talking[16] such [nonsense]?"[17]

When he set sail upon the Great Sea, his ship sank in the sea. He went to the depths, and he saw the ministering angels chiseling, etching, and hatching it, and he said to them: "What is this?" They replied: "This is the Eastern Gate of the Temple and its two wickets being made from a single stone of pearl." Immediately a miracle was performed for him and he departed unharmed.

A year later, he arrived and found R. Yohanan, who was expounding on the same matter: "In time to come the Holy One, Blessed be He, will make the Eastern Gate of the Temple and its two wickets from a single stone of pearl."

He said to him: "Elder!, Elder!, proclaim all you can proclaim, praise all there is to praise. For had my eyes not seen, I would not have believed—"

"And had your eyes not seen, you would not have believed the words that I said about the Torah!" he replied.

He raised his eyes and looked at him, and immediately he was transformed into a pile of bones.

---

14. The remainder of 3.B is paralleled at Pesiq. Rab. 32:8-10, in Rivka Ulmer, ed., *A Synoptic Edition of Pesiqta Rabbati Based upon All Extant Manuscripts and the Editio Princeps* (Atlanta: Scholars Press, 1999), 2:764–66; Midr. Ps. 87:2 (ed. Buber, 376–77). The former is close to Pesiq. Rab Kah.; the latter identical to the Talmud parallel at 2.C.

15. Glossing *'eqdah* not as a noun, *carbuncles*, but as an Aramaized verb: *I shall bore* (hence, "chiseling, etching, and hatching" below. See "Rashi" b. San. 100a s.v. שמשותיך).

16. Often translated literally (William G. Braude and Israel J. Kapstein add extravagantly "in a teacher's chair no less"! [*Pesikta de-Rab Kahana* (Philadelphia: Jewish Publication Society, 2002), 427]), here י.ת.ב may not mean "to sit," but function as a marker of progressive aspect, as in Jewish Babylonian Aramaic ("*was expounding*/*has been talking*"). See Bar-Asher Siegal, *Grammar*, 249.

17. The soundplay "somebody" (*hadein*)/"such" (*hakhdein*) echoes "I shall bore" (*'eqdah*) and *kadkhod*/*keden*, which are prominent keywords in this passage, adjacent material in Pesiq. Rab Kah., and the Talmud parallel at 2.C. See chapter 5, n. 675.

Appendix 4

Thieves in Heaven (?!) Heaven Forbid: A Geonic Apologetic

One of our only witnesses to the tales' interpretation by medieval Jewish authorities of Babylonia—in a collection of responsa identified with tenth- to eleventh-century Geonim of the academy of Pumbedita, Sherira and his son, Hayya (a.k.a. Hai)—is a creative apologetic for a theologically problematic line in Rabbah's final story (XV.193). Lest one suppose that the many variants in the text of our tales were due only to errors in transmission, or should be analyzed mainly as "better" or "worse" versions of an original text, this apologetic illustrates instead how textual problems have always informed interpretation and vice versa—already here, among our earliest evidence for the reception of Rabbah's tales outside of the Talmud itself.

As Uzziel Fuchs has shown,[1] responding to the utter perplexity of the Jewish community in Qairouan in Tunisia, who received this story and wrote to ask "how it is possible," these Geonic responsa (or, more precisely, two versions of one responsum, from 991–992),[2] chose not to address that question directly. Instead, they retold a new version of Rabbah's final story that is influenced by Eastern versions of the Alexander Romance (see chapter 4).[3] They went on to focus on solving one problem about the story that had arisen in the academy.

---

1. Uzziel Fuchs, "What?! Is there Thievery in the Firmament?!: On the Textual Correction of an Impiety" [Hebrew], in *Ve-Hinneh Rivka Yotzet: Essays in Jewish Studies in Honor of Rivka Dagan*, ed. Leib Moscovitz (Jerusalem: Tsur-Ot 2017), 103–5.

2. See Brody et al., *Otzar ha-Geonim he-Hadash*, 290–91 n. 4. There is a shorter version in Rif, *Gates of Repentance*, §128 (Leipzig, 1858), 13 (cited by ibn Migash cited by Betsalel Ashkenazi, see §*Introduction* n. 92).

3. See also chapter 3 n. 402. Brody et al., *Otzar ha-Geonim he-Hadash*, 290: "Thus have we heard in the name of our teachers, long may they live, that one of the kings of Greece made a great orb of copper, three hundred sixty cubits in diameter, in the form of the firmament.... And he made orbits for it which caused it to orbit all by itself by means of air and water, and it made a complete revolution every twenty-four hours. And that is what the Ishmaelite

Here, as we recall, is the original story:

XV. [The Arab guide] said to us:
"Come, I will show you where the firmament is overturned upon the earth."
He showed us; I saw a certain slit.
I took my basket[4] and rested it inside until I had prayed.
The orb revolved and I did not find it.
I said: **"Perhaps–God forbid–there are thieves here?"**
He told me: "Keep watch until tomorrow around now;
the orb will revolve to its position, and you'll take it back."

The line in bold was viewed as problematic, as Fuchs notes, because it insinuates that, in such a place, whose holiness Rabbah instantly acknowledges by praying—in some tellings, piously removing the skullcap under his turban, or his sandals,[5] *à la* Moses (Exod 3:5)—he could still be worried about theft.[6] The question could even be rendered as a shocking statement: "There are thieves" (!) The author of the responsum, Sherira or Hayya, hints that three similar texts were already in circulation in his academy, reflecting two basic versions:

#1a: "Are there thieves in the firmament?" / #1b: "Is there thievery in the firmament?"[7]

א"א גנאבי איכא ברקיעא / א"ב איכא גונבא ברקיע

#2: "What?! Is there thievery in the firmament?!"

מי איכא גונבא ברקיעא

As Fuchs notes, after noting one of these two basic readings, each version of the responsum continued to solve the problem in its own way. The easy solution was to simply delete the problematic line. This was adopted by both versions. (A comment on #2, likely the earlier version, states

---

showed Rabbah bar bar Hanah. And it contained holes [ms. P: כי כוי, see b. B. Bat. 6a] like windows [see Maharal, *Hiddushe Aggadot*, 4 vols. (Jerusalem, 1972–77), 3:101 ; Gra, *Be'ure 'Aggadot*, 25 nn. 279–82], and its orbits were so slow that it turned three hundred cubits within twenty-four hours. And Rabbah bar bar Hanah did not know where he was, so he put his *tefillin* bag into one of those holes and he turned aside to pray for a while, but by the time he had finished, that place had risen more than the height of a man, and Rabbah bar bar Hanah could not find the bag."

4. See chapter 1, n. 92.
5. Brody et al., *Otzar ha-Geonim he-Hadash*, 291; *Teshuvot ha-Geonim* §12 (in *Zikaron la-rishonim ve-gam la-aharonim*, ed. Avraham Harkavy [Berlin: Itzkowski, 1886], 5).
6. Kiperwasser ("Travels of Rabbah," 239) elegantly draws out the full irony; one that did not appeal to the sober Geonim.
7. Fuchs asserts that #1a is not a variant, but a paraphrase by the Gaon. Yet it is basically identical to mss. E and V, and mss. P and O before their corrections: see Appendix §*Edition* טו.קצ"א. It may have already existed as a variant.

explicitly: "But we ourselves, *and most sages,* do not adopt this reading.") Yet both versions of the responsum *also* show that the line *was* recited by other members of the academy. This generated an almost predictable alternative solution: keep the text, yet reinterpret it so as to neutralize the problem. Hence, version #2 continues: "One who *does* adopt this reading must interpret it as something said in astonishment: *Can something that is like the firmament have thievery in it?!*" As Fuchs observes, as a result of this instruction to pronounce the line with astonishment, a word ("What?!") was added to the actual text of the line in #2, writing the apologetic back into the text. Yet this was meant not so much as a textual variant, but more as a cue for intonation—in effect: *Say it like me [?!]; don't say it like them.*[8]

Some manuscripts preserve the apologetic more directly; others, less so; and ms. E, not at all.

Ms. E
Are there thieves in the firmament?
איכא גנבי ברקיעא

Ms. P
Really?! Are there thieves here?!
וכי גנבי איכא הכא

Ms. H
"Perhaps—God forbid—there are thieves here?"
דיל' חס ושלום גנבי איכא הכא

Ms. V
"Perhaps—God forbid—there are thieves in the firmament?"
דילמ' חס ושלום איכא גנבי ברקיעא

"A heavenly voice appeared and said: 'That is the orb of the firmament revolving.'"
נפקא בת קלא ואמרה האי גלגלא דרקיעא הדר

Ms. O
I said to him: "Perhaps—God forbid—there are thieves ~~in the firmament~~ here?"
A heavenly voice appeared and said: "That is the orb of the firmament revolving."
אמינ' דילמ' חס ושלו' איכ' גנבי **ברקיע** הכא
נפק' בת קלא ואמר' האי גלגלא דרקיע הוא דהדר

---

8. For another case of this intonational cue in Geonic responsa, see Daphna Ephrat and Yaakov Elman, "Orality and the Institutionalization of Tradition: The Growth of the Geonic Yeshiva and the Islamic Madrasa," in *Transmitting Jewish Traditions: Orality, Textuality, and Cultural Diffusion*, ed. Yaakov Elman and Israel Gershoni, Studies in Jewish Culture and Society (New Haven: Yale University Press, 2000), 10737, at 114–15.

Only ms. E preserves the problem without a solution—not even the "heavenly voice," which provides at least some divine reassurance that this problem will *eventually* be solved.⁹ Ms. P preserves almost exactly the original solution of version #2 of the responsum. It adds a standard marker of a rhetorical question, to be followed by a negation or restriction.¹⁰ Like "What?!" (*Mi*; see §*Edition* I.10, mss. H, P, O), this rhetorical marker reflects the tradition of intoning the text to show astonishment: "What?!" (*ve-khi*). In other words, ms. P marshals the narrative into a standard interpretive framework, foreclosing any impious ideas on the part of a character by anticipating their solution within the story—just as the anonymous voice in a *sugya* of legal give-and-take anticipates solutions to the legal problem. This apologetic retelling Talmudizes any transgressive narrative content.

Ms. H interjects more forcefully and obviously ("Perhaps—God forbid—"). This is a solution similar to that of ms. P, but it sanitizes its hero's voice in a way that is more out of character: he already saw Mount Sinai surrounded by scorpions the size of asses (XIIIa), and a clod of dung damming the Jordan (IV). Why wasn't he shy to describe those desecrated sites? Ms. V also forcefully interjects like ms. H, but takes a further step. Rather than the voice of the Arab guide, a "heavenly voice" now appears to reassure our hero that there are not, in fact, "thieves in the firmament." This solution, like the solution of ms. P, applies a standard device in the editing of talmudic texts, both legal and non-legal: harmonization with surrounding material, in this case, the "heavenly voice." This element has already appeared in the adventures of the giant bird (IXa) and Mount Sinai (XIIIa) and, as we saw, already functioned as a device for the Talmud's anonymous retellers and editors who managed to ventriloquize or "blend" their voices into the story and conceal the foreign origins of its content.¹¹ Ms. O, a highly synthetic Ashkenazi textual tradition, naturally combines both solutions of mss. H and V: the interjection *and* the heavenly voice.

In sum, as Fuchs argues, these European manuscripts of the late twelfth to fourteenth centuries reflect direct developments of a problem and solution that began in an academy in tenth-century Iraq. Further, the ways in which they solve the problem are consistent with what we know about the reworking of talmudic legal texts.¹² To resolve an impiety in the narrative, manuscripts use three devices that are amply documented for solving legal problems in the talmudic text tradition: adding phrases to clarify the prob-

---

9. Contra Fuchs ("What?!," 105), there is no heavenly voice in ms. E.

10. Standard patterns of the use of וכי in rabbinic literature include "Really?! ... But rather ..." or "Really?! ... [Rather, this verse] teaches that ..." See Bacher, *Die Exegetische Terminologie*, 2:61.

11. See chapter 4 §*From Wonder to Romance: Another Risky Swim*; see nn. 556–558, 613.

12. For further such comparisons, see Levinson, *Twice Told Tale*, 278–93.

lem;¹³ linking it to its solution by a stock rhetorical term;¹⁴ and adjusting the text to its context.¹⁵ In short, like both versions of the responsum, these manuscripts reflect an academic debate about the story that treated it like any other source, thereby Talmudizing it. Rather than delete a difficulty, they edited it using techniques much like those used for law.

In fact, this line was even more persistently difficult than Fuchs showed. It posed not one but two problems. The second problem, in a sense, presupposes the first: how can this place be "the firmament" at all? Both versions of this responsum, as well as a slightly later version attributed to the Rif, and the eleventh- to twelfth-century commentators Rashbam and the school of Rabbenu Gershom, reflect objections to the very idea that "the place where the earth and the firmament touch [lit. *kiss*]" should be identified with the firmament. In its place, all three versions of the responsum imagine an immense scale replica of the cosmos, using similar material found in later Eastern versions of the Alexander Romance.¹⁶ Therefore, the other problem motivating the responsum and these commentators alike, to which each offers a slightly different solution, is how this place could look *like* the firmament, yet not be it. That solution is, in turn, related to the first: if this location is, so to speak, "not in heaven"—then was there anything really problematic about our hero's fear of theft there to begin with?

This second problem/solution of the commentaries is *also* subtly reflected in the manuscripts.

Ms. O
I said to him: "Perhaps—God forbid—there are thieves ~~in the firmament~~ here?"
A heavenly voice appeared and said: "That is the orb of the firmament revolving."

אמינ' דילמ' חס ושלו' איכ' גנבי בּרקיע הכא
נפק' בת קלא ואמר' האי גלגלא דרקיע הוא דהדר

Ms. P
Really?! Are there thieves (here)?!¹⁷

וכי גנבי איכא (הכא)

---

13. Friedman: "introductory and organizational phrases" (*Talmud Arukh*, 1:32; see also "re-enforcement of the Talmud's stereotypical language," 1:28–30).

14. Friedman: "explanation of the question" (*Talmud Arukh*, 1:33).

15. Friedman: "harmonization of style within the *sugya*" (*Talmud Arukh*, 1:30).

16. See chapter 3, nn. 401–402. I thank Faustina Doufikar-Aerts (personal communication, 29 July 2019) for extraordinary generosity in sending me a bibliography and original collection of manuscript sources from the Arabic Alexander Romance tradition containing very similar motifs.

17. The word "here" is written over an erasure, presumably of "in the firmament," as in mss. V and O, ברקיע(א).

Mss. M, B
Are there thieves here?
איכא גנבי הכא

    Note that mss. M and B do not have our hero refer to "the firmament" at all; he says only "here," avoiding besmirching the heavens and thus the original need for the apologetic. Similarly, ms. O deletes "firmament" in favor of "here," and adds the first solution of ms. V: the heavenly voice. Only ms. E persistently shows no trace of interest in either apologetic agenda. It has the Arab speak directly to Rabbah, who voices his concern unapologetically. Then the Arab solves his problem with talmudic astronomy,[18] without correcting his impiety.

Ms. E
Are there thieves in the firmament?
איכא גנבי ברקיעא

He said to me: That was the orb of the firmament revolving. Watch here until tomorrow around now and you'll find it.
אמ' לי הא גלגלא דרקיעא הוה דהדר נטר עד למחר כי השתא הכא ומשכחת ליה

    From tenth-century Babylonia to high medieval Ashkenaz, by way of North Africa and Spain, we have seen how both the direct and the indirect witnesses to this line raise and solve two shared problems by several different means: deletion, reinterpretation, reworking of the passage, and rewriting by means of commentary. Only one Sephardi manuscript with a mixed textual tradition, which may well be the latest in this chain of transmission,[19] remains silent in this lively conversation. Is it because it does not know the solutions? Or because it has forgotten the problem—coming full circle to the original reading and question that prompted the Geonic response? The clear lesson, yet again, seems to be that we cannot recover the text of the Talmud beyond the prism of its interpretations. All witnesses—direct and indirect, earliest to latest—are constantly subject to interpretation, preserving textual changes that both cause and result from interpretation. We can only recover one reading's meaning by retracing it through the whole constellation of reading.

---

    18. See §*Introduction*, n. 93.
    19. Fifteenth- or sixteenth-century Provence or Catalonia? See Sussmann, "Ve-shuv li-yerushalmi neziqin," 116; and the provisional stemma in my study cited at §*Introduction* n. 1.

Appendix 5

Commentary on Tale III by Elyaqum Getz[1]

[1.] And one may raise difficulties with the words of Rashbam, who explains [the name] "Hormiz" as a demon. If so, why did he *see him* precisely *on the wall of Mahoza*, and not in some other location? And why does he waste words? He could have simply said that he *saw him*. What is the point of the location where he saw him? And it is also difficult that he said *a horseman was riding a beast beneath him*. If he was riding, obviously he was *riding a beast,* for if not, how was he riding? And if there was no *beast beneath him,* then this was not riding, but simply walking on foot! And another difficulty: what is the point of [saying] whether *he bounded* upon *mules* which had a bridle or did not have a bridle, as it says that they *were saddled*.[2] For if this were introduced in order to show us his great strength (that *he bounded from one bridge to the other*), then there is no point [in saying] whether or not the *mules* had a *saddle*.[3] And there are further difficulties that I have refrained from writing, but anyone who has a brain in his skull can sense and express them.

[2.] But it seems one can resolve these difficulties if he is showing us matters of moral discipline [*mussar*]. In his generation, as in ours, the great sin against which our predecessors set boundaries is still leaping among us *as if it is permitted*.[4] As we have said in the Gemara, tractate Qiddushin:

---

1. In *Sefer 'Aggadata' de-ve Rav*, 42–49. See chapter 6 n. 814.
2. Following Rashbam, who glosses the word *saddled*: "there was a saddle with bridle placed upon the mules."
3. I.e., the Talmud's own gloss of the imagery in V (*Come see the strength of the tree! How great it was!*) does not apply here. Or, Getz may be arguing against Maharsha b. B. Bat. 73a s.v. לדידי חזי לי הורמין בר לילותא, who allegorizes Hormiz's "bounding" as skirmishes in a war between the kings of North and South (Dan 11:40), and the "saddled" mules to their weapons of war.
4. Alluding to b. Yoma 86b, "Rav Huna said: 'After a person sins and repeats it, it is permitted to him.' Does it enter your mind that it is [actually] permitted?! Rather, say it becomes to him as if it is permitted." This allusion is especially apt because (a) the literal meaning of "permitted" is "unbound," which fits the allegory of the bridle; (b) the sin at issue, masturbation, is repetitive but private, and seems to go unpunished, making it hard to break.

*Most donkey-drivers are wicked.*⁵ But isn't it taught that they are *righteous*?⁶ That is not difficult: The latter is saddled, the former is not saddled.⁷

[3.] And the reason [for saying *saddled*] is that this concerns a man who *stimulates himself and spills seed in vain.*⁸ And the Zohar's statement, in multiple places, is well known, and in the sacred writings of the Ari OBM, who comments [... in his commentary on the recitation of *Shema* at the bedside] that from spilling the seed a demon is created, for Lilith consorts with a man and she makes him spill seed and she incubates with it, and a demon is created. And after the man dies, they come and exact judgment from him, and that is [the sense of] *for according to a man's deed, He will repay him* [Job 34:11]. But by reciting Shema at his bedside, a man slays those demons,⁹ and that is [the sense of] *Let the high praises of God be in their mouth ... to execute vengeance upon the heathen* [Ps 149:6-7], see [the Ari] *ad loc.*

[4.] That said, not all destructive demons¹⁰ are the same. Those created by wicked men who *stimulate themselves and spill seed in vain* (even if it is forced in the end, in the beginning it was willing),¹¹ they are the thoroughly evil demon, who requires great strength to be slain. And there are those who are created by conjugal union, even of pious and righteous men, if they but linger momentarily upon their wives' bellies and spill a drop. A demon is created from that as well. However, it is not quite so thoroughly evil, but comprises both evil and good. Therefore, a man must control himself so that he *does not lose even a single drop*,¹² for it has been

---

5. B. Qidd. 82a.
6. B. Nid. 14a: "Some donkey-drivers are wicked, some are righteous." See b. Ber. 56b: "One who sees a donkey in his dream should expect salvation, as it is said: *Lo your king comes to you ... riding upon a donkey* [Zech 9:9]."
7. B. Nid. 14a, continued: "There is one who says: This one [the righteous driver] bridles [his donkey]; that one [the wicked driver] does not bridle." Rashi explains (b. Nid. 14a s.v. דמכף): If the animal is saddled/bridled, then the rider does not stimulate himself against it. Compare b. Ber. 56b–57a: "One who sees an elephant in a dream, miracles will be performed for him [...] But wasn't it taught, 'All animal species are good [signs] in a dream, *except for an elephant*? [...] It is not difficult. This [good elephant] is saddled, that [bad] one is not saddled."
8. Kallah Rab. 2:7 (ed. Higger, 199–201), commenting on the sin of Onan in Gen 38:9.
9. B. Ber. 5a. There, the demon is the Evil Inclination, strongly associated in the Talmud with the male sex drive. Getz alludes to the end of our story, "The house of the kingdom *heard of* it and brought him to an end," connecting the Aramaic verb ש.מ.ע [in all mss.] to the Jewish creed *Shema*: a means to slay the demon.
10. Compare Rashbam's gloss, not only on Hormiz, but also on the "white shoot of flame" (II.20): "a destructive demon." This may relate to the similarity of the unique reading of ms. H ln. א.ת ("burnt *by its damage*," מחבלא) to a word for "demon," מחבלנא.
11. In other words, ejaculation may be involuntary when it occurs, but never when it is initiated, so that is no excuse. Compare b. B. Metz. 36b; 42a: "In the beginning it was by negligence and in the end it was by force."
12. Alluding to both our story (IIIb.38) and Avot 2:8, where "a limed cistern which does not lose a single drop" is usually understood as referring to skill in Torah memorization.

explained that a man must control himself even at the moment of conjugal union.[13] And in the Gemara, tractate Shabbat [12a], it says *"One may not delouse by lamplight ... even in order to distinguish between his own garment and those of his wife ... we stated this only with regard to the citizens of Mahoza,* because, Rashi explains, they were *pampered and did not do any work.*[14] And similarly, it says in the Gemara to the first chapter of Rosh Hashanah, *The finest men of Mahoza, they are "those who go down to Gehinnom";*[15] see further *ad loc.* And it is known that a person who is too pampered and does not work *proceeds according to the dictate of his heart,*[16] and Lilith joins herself to him, and at night, in a dream, she consorts with him, and it is as if he is having intercourse with a woman and spilling seed in vain; and then the demon is created from it. And great repentance is needed in order to slay it, by reciting Shema with intense concentration and self-mortification, and repentance will not succeed unless he *turns from his ways and lives,*[17] that is, [unless] he controls himself so that he does not again lapse into such a sin, may the Merciful One save us. But if not, then it is not in his power to kill it — and, heavens forfend, the external forces gather reinforcements — as is clarified for those who know the hidden wisdom [= *kabbalah*].

[5.] And thus [all the difficulty in [1] above] is laid to rest: *Rabbah bar bar Hanah said: I myself have seen Hormiz son of Lilith.* He meant, "I saw that demon who is created by Lilith from the spilling[18] of seed in vain." *Who was bounding upon the dome of Mahoza.*[19] He meant that "'the men of Mahoza are pampered,' i.e., by the 'decadences' of this world, and 'they do not do any work,' as is clarified in the Gemara to Rosh Hasha-

---

13. It is a commonplace in the Talmud that how the couple thinks or acts during intercourse will affect their child. See, e.g., b. Ned. 20b.

14. Rashi, b. Shabb. 12a, s.v. בני מחוזא. Similarly, Rashi depicts the Mahozans as "decadent" and "fat," qualifying them for another exception (b. Shabb. 109a, s.v. מפנקי; see also Rashi to b. Rosh Hash. 17a, s.v. בני מחוזא).

15. In b. Rosh Hash. 17a, these "finest Mahozans" are dubbed "sons of Gehinnom." Getz conflates this with the expression "those who go down to Gehinnom" (b. Betzah 32b), which similarly refers to "the wealthiest men of Babylonia." Compare Rashi to b. Ketub. 62a, s.v. מפנקי דמערבא: the "pampered men of the West" (i.e., Palestine) are "decadent in food and drink, and therefore healthy and full of virility for the bedchamber." Given the context of Getz's exposition, Rashi's sexual connotation for the word "pampered" is probably active here as well.

16. See Deut 29:18. A similar verse (Num 15:39) is used in the same context of conjugal excess (b. Ned. 20b.) The specific sin here seems to be thinking of other women. See Tishby, *Wisdom of the Zohar,* 3:1400–1402.

17. See Ezek 33:11. On the twofold importance of the phrase "and live" for Getz's mode of commentary on our tales, see §*Introduction* n. 3.

18. Getz reverts to the biblical language, ש.ח.ת (Onan in Gen 38:9) rather than י.צ.א, but the sense is the same.

19. Like "bridge" (see chapter 6 n. 844), the sexual imagery of Lilith "bounding upon the dome" likely did not escape Getz, as he chooses to use this word only after establishing the scenario. Above, he mentioned only "the wall [*shura'*] of Mahoza."

nah cited above,[20] and at length in the Gemara to Shabbat.[21] "'Perhaps an ejaculation due to exertion on the journey was observed by the master?' ..." 'The Omnipresent shall judge you for a spotless palm.'"[22] But the difficulty [with that counterargument] is—what spotlessness? Aren't [the Mahozans] 'they who go down to Gehinnom'; 'a man who spills seed in vain?' Nevertheless, it was necessary [for the Gemara] to state [both apparently contradictory sources] because any man who spills seed from the force of exertion and toil bears no punishment for the deed, and so it is not an excuse for the Mahozans that their ejaculation came from the force of great exertion and toil. And so the demon was created from it. And that is why he was *bounding upon the wall of Mahoza. And he bounded upon the turret of the wall* means that he did it in public, because no one had the strength to slay him, for that is how evil the demon's power was. *And a horseman raced ... but could not overcome him* means that one man rode and supposed that he would slay him, but it was not within his capacity, which is *could not overcome him*. And so he said that *he was riding*, meaning that he took all of the measures, such as reciting Shema and the other means of repentance,[23] yet the might and dominion were not in his power to slay him. And should you raise the difficulty, 'Well, are those really means of killing the demon?'—this is why he said that the *riding of the horseman* was ineffective, *because*,[24] he was *riding a beast*, meaning that he rode on the animal directly, without anything separating him from the animal,[25] and given how thoroughly evil the demon was, he was unable to overcome him.

[6.] And it says in the Gemara to Shabbat, "And men? Where are they

---

20. B. Rosh Hash. 17a.
21. B. Shabb. 12a; 109a.
22. A hypothetical counterargument based on a story in b. Shabb. 127b. See below. This hyperliteral translation of "favorably" (*le-khaf zekhut*) preserves the underlying metaphor that is so apt for the halakhic issue at hand. In ed. *Zikhron Aharon*, 19 (chapter 6 n. 814), Getz cites a source for his counterargument and refutation: one of his own sermons on Deut. 25:17.
23. See Maharsha (*Sefer hiddushe Aggadot*, 149): "And he says that *a horseman raced*: this is an allegory [*remez*] for the righteous of Israel, who run to perform the commandments of the Lord like horses, as we have said in [b.] Sanhedrin [96a] "as Scripture says, If thou hast run with the footmen, and they have wearied thee, then how canst thou contend with horses [Jer 12:5]." See also b. Eruv. 54b, "'Ye that ride on white asses' [Judg 5:10]: Those are disciples of the sages, who go from town to town and from province to province in order to teach Torah."
24. Getz glosses the apparently redundant כי as "because" (מחמת), interpreting it as Rabbah's way to forestall this objection. This illustrates how he supports the allegory with every element of his specific text of the story, which corresponds only to mss. P and V but is found in the early prints [Venice, Pesaro] and later in Vilna.
25. This is the explanation of Rashi (b. Nid. 14a, s.v. דמכף) for why the righteous donkey-driver is saddled and the wicked donkey-driver is unsaddled (see chapter 6 n. 832 and n. 7 in this Appendix).

tested? At the moment that they are crossing a bridge."[26] And the statement of the Zohar is well known, *for according to a man's deed, He will repay him* [Job 34:11]: the same demon whom a man creates himself is the demon who will *repay him* his comeuppance. That is why he said *and he saddled [two mules]*, meaning there were also some who were riding on the animal with no more than a saddle, although they were *crossing the bridge*. And so, when he said: and he was standing on the bridge *and he bounded from one to the other*, he meant that the demon wanted to jump and to slay those who ride on the animal with a bridle, but, although they were standing on the bridge—for they test a man "at the moment that they are crossing a bridge" [b. Shab. 32a]—it was not in the capacity of the demon to harm them.

[7.] And so, *that horseman was riding* means that he took all of those measures and attempted to perform a semblance of repentance in order to slay the demon, but could not. Whereas, the men who were riding with the *bridle*—even though they were standing in a dangerous place, on a *bridge*—the demon could not overcome them, nor did they have to take any measure against it. And he made it plain for the eye to see: a man who *projects* from one vessel to another must control himself so that he does *not spill a single drop* on the ground; so, too, must a man who *projects* from his "vessel of the covenant of skin" into a vessel which "does not lose a single drop." Or, one vessel is actually equated with another,[27] because [the "vessel" of skin] requires control at the moment of conjugal union,[28] so that he does not *spill a single drop*, and such are those whom the demon wanted to molest, but he was unable to overcome them, *because* they were too pious and controlled themselves so as not to *spill a single drop* and therefore, it was not within his capacity to do them evil.

[8.] And he said, *And upon that day, "They mount up to the heaven, they go down again to the depths"* (Ps 107:26, KJV). He means that this one did repent and his repentance *mounted up to the heaven* and from the power of his repentance, the spiritual husks [qelippot] *went down again to the depths*. And this is [the implied subjects of the verse] *"They mount up to the heaven, they go down again to the depths."* And *the authorities* [lit. "kingdom"] *heard* means that the Holy One, Blessed Be He, received his prayer and his repentance, *and killed him*, meaning that he *killed* the demon referred to above, and look into it further.

Alternatively, it seems to me more apt as follows. *And the kingdom heard*: Rashi comments,[29] *The demons heard* etc. And it seems to me that

---

26. B. Shabb. 32a.
27. I.e., rather than each "cup" in the story representing male and female organs, both "cups" are the male organ.
28. I.e., the dangerous "bridge" where a man can be tried and punished for his sins.
29. Getz means Rashbam, who appears as "Rashi" in the margin of the printed tractate.

he means that *demons* heard that he had revealed the matter to humans, how one needs to guard against the impurity of seminal emissions, and it would be bad for the demons if people were not to enter into such impurity, because then how would the demons give birth from humans? For that is how they survive, from their impurity. And therefore they *killed* the demon. And thus it refers to his *kingdom* because I have found that the demon who is their king must be one who is born from [the seminal emissions] of humans,[30] and look into it further.

[9.] Whereas it seems to me that disciples of the sages are called "angels," as we say in tractate Nedarim [20b]: "Who are the ministering angels? Our teachers."[31] And it says a few times in the Zohar,[32] that the disciples of the sages *mount up* in their Torah *to the heaven* and *go down* to the external forces, who are the Other Side: to the "hollow of the great abyss."[33] Thus it is said, *And upon that day, they mount up to the heaven*. He means the disciples of the sages, who were "reapers of the fields,"[34] mounted up to the heavens and went down to the external forces—to the great depths. *And the kingdom heard*: he means that the Holy One, Blessed Be He, heard the Torah of a disciple of the sages *and killed him*, the demon.

Alternatively, one might say that *and the kingdom heard* means the disciple of the sages heard him, that there was a destructive demon like this who wanted to destroy people, and they prayed and they performed acts of unification,[35] and through the recitation of *the high praises of God in their throat*, as it says in the writings of the Ari OBM, in his rite of the recitation of Shema at the bedside, that there is power in the hand of a righteous man to slay several thousands, and that is [what is meant by] *"A thousand shall fall at thy side, and ten thousand at thy right hand"* (Ps 91:7), and he killed him with the recitation of the Shema as referred to above, and look into it further.

---

30. Trachtenberg cites a fourteenth-century source (*Jewish Magic and Superstition*, 283 n. 19). See earlier sources in Patai, "Lilith," 314 n. 62.

31. B. Ned. 20a–b. The context is highly relevant: misbegotten offspring are a punishment for their father's sin. See n. 13 to this Appendix.

32. See following note.

33. Zohar §*Pequdei* (2:242b), ed. and trans. Matt (*Zohar: Pritzker Edition*), 6:403. See Nathaniel Berman, *Divine and the Demonic in the Poetic Mythology of the Zohar: The "Other Side" of Kabbalah* (Leiden: Brill, 2018), 256.

34. I.e., mystics, "the Companions who harvest the secrets of Torah sprouting in the field of *Shekhinah*." Zohar §*Va-yehi* (1:216b), ed. and trans. Matt (*Zohar: Pritzker Edition*), 3:303 n. 4 (with copious references).

35. An aspect of Lurianic rite for drawing down the *Shekhinah*; see Idel, *Absorbing Perfections*, 150.

Appendix 6

Commentary on Tale II by the Gra (Vilna Gaon)[1]

§1. *The wave that sinks a ship*: ... The body is called a 'ship' and all the sufferings which overwhelm it are called 'waves.'[2] ... "All thy breakers and thy waves passed over me."[3] And that is the Angel of Death who puts a person to death,[4] *that sinks* ... and it is the Evil Inclination, who at the beginning leads a person astray[5] ... that is the Evil Inclination [that is the Angel of Death, who "goes down and leads astray, goes up and prosecutes, goes down and takes the soul],"[6] who *appears like a white shoot of flame* ... as in the case of Rav Amram the Pious, [who took an oath against the Evil Inclination to make it go out from him, and] it went out from him "like a pillar of fire."[7]

§2. [*White*] *on its head*: At the beginning [literally *head*], when it leads him astray, it shows him fifty signs of purity that it is permitted.... "For the lips [of a strange woman] drop as an honeycomb.... But her end is bitter as wormwood / [sharp as a two-edged sword],"[8] which is the sword of the Angel of Death, and a bitter drop hangs between her feet,[9] and "her feet go down to death."[10]

---

1. Gra, *Be'ure Aggadot*, 1–3.
2. See b. Yevam. 121a; Maharsha, b. B. Bat. 73a, s.v. אשתעו לי; Gra, *Be'ure Aggadot*, 87.
3. Jonah 2:4 = Ps 42:7 (42:8; KJV trans. modified).
4. See chapter 6, nn. 834, 860.
5. Gra, *Aderet Eliyahu*, 86, s.v. וימצא אניה.
6. B. B. Bat. 16a. In context, this refers to Satan, but a dictum just after this tradition equates Satan = Evil Inclination = Angel of Death. See Gra, *Aderet Eliyahu*, 87, s.v. הטיל רוח גדולה and chapter 6, n. 834.
7. B. Qidd. 81a.
8. Prov 5:3–4.
9. Gra, *Aderet Eliyahu*, 87, s.v. הטיל רוח גדולה: "*Sent out a great wind* [*to the sea*; Jonah 1:4].... And the sword of the Angel of Death is Lilith, who seduces a man and then takes his soul, and she is the bitter drop which hangs from the sword from which he dies, as they said [b. Avod. Zar. 20b]: 'At the moment a sick man expires, the Angel of Death stands above his head, with a drawn sword in hand and a drop of poison [literally: *bitterness*] dangling from the sword.' And of this [the Gra continues], Solomon says, [*her end is bitter as wormwood /*] *sharp as a two edged sword* [Prov 5:3–4]. Two swords: in this world and in the world to come."
10. Prov 5:5.

§3. And all this causes subjugation to empires and sufferings for us.... "[Lord of the Universe], it is revealed and known before you that our will is to do your will, and what holds us back? [The leaven in the dough and the subjugation of the empires. May it be your will to save us from their hands, and may we repent and perform the statutes of your will with a perfect heart]"[11] ... For without subjugation to empires, we would not let the leaven rise: "And they baked unleavened cakes ... *because* they had been cast out of Egypt,"[12] and there was no subjugation to empires upon them.[13]

§4. But in this [tale] we have two guarantees: First, that even in exile, we will be delivered from all evil.... "And yet for all that, when they be in the land of their enemies, I will not cast them away [neither will I abhor them, to destroy them utterly, and to break My covenant with them],"[14] and similarly, "[He shall call upon Me, and I will answer him]; I will be with him in suffering [בצרה]; [I will rescue him]."[15] And second, that we are guaranteed to be redeemed from exile. The first was guaranteed to us in Egypt ... "I am that I am,[16] I am what I will be with you in this subjugation [and I will be with you in subjugation to empires in the future.]"[17] And for the second [to redeem us from exile], we have a pledge: ... "The Hand upon the Throne of the LORD: the LORD will have war with Amalek."[18] And ... His Throne is not perfected until He has redeemed us.[19]

---

11. B. Ber. 17a (y. Ber. 4:2, 7d).

12. Exod 12:39 (KJV trans. modified, emphasis added).

13. The Gra or, more likely, one of his transmitters, adds here an apt proof that leaven = lust/the Evil Inclination: "But in exile, both of these have returned: the leaven in the dough, as it is said, *They are all adulterers* [mena'afim] *like an oven heated by the baker* [me-'ofeh], *who ceaseth to stir from the kneading of the dough until it be leavened* (Hos 7:4)—and also subjugation to empires." I did not find this double meaning and the idea of "subjugation to empires" combined in classical midrashim but similarly, Pesiq. Rab Kah. 16:11 (see parallels at ed. Mandelbaum, 279 n. 1) and Pesiq. Rab Kah. 3:11 (ed. Mandelbaum, 49) connect *'af* ("passion/heat/nose/penis") with the Israelites' sins in exile, and attribute those sins to Amalek and Esau, who are paradigms for the Jewish Other.

14. Lev 26:44.

15. Ps 91:15 (KJV trans. modified).

16. Exod 3:14.

17. B. B. Ber. 9b; Mekhilta *Shirata* 4, ed. Lauterbach, 188–89. See chapter 2 §*A Man of War*.

18. Exod 17:16.

19. See Gra, *Be'ure Aggadot*, 3 n. 29. "*For the hand upon the throne of the Lord* [my translation]: The Hand of the Holy One, Blessed Be He, is raised to swear upon His throne that He shall have war and enmity with Amalek eternally. And why is ["throne" written] כס not כסא? And the divine Name is also divided in two [written here as YAH, not YHWH] ? The Holy One, Blessed Be He, has sworn that His Name is not perfected and His throne is not perfected until He blots out the name of Amalek completely. But when He blots out his name, His Name will be perfected and His throne will be perfected." Rashi, Exod 17:16 (= Pesiq.

§5. And the matter of His Name is known ... "from the day that the Temple was destroyed, it is enough for the world [to use two letters of the Name ... 'Let the completion of the soul praise YAH]."[20] And the matter of His Throne [is also known], for His greatness and kingship is through the nation of Israel, and when Israel are in abjection, His kingdom is not perfected, and therefore at the sea they said: "YHWH will reign [forever and ever]."[21] For there is no king without a host [i.e., army].[22] And YHWH will not be called Hosts until He redeems and rules His host ... "Our Redeemer, YHWH of Hosts [is His Name, the Holy One of Israel],"[23] then [the moon] shall be confounded [and the sun ashamed, for the Lord of Hosts will rule].[24]

§6. And that is ... *But we strike [the sorrow/suffering of this world, i.e., the Evil Inclination and subjugation to the empires] with oaths*[25] *on which is engraven: I am that I am, YAH, YHWH of Hosts.*

§7. And for what merit can we expect all this, given that all arousal must be from below? ...[26] [Since the day the Temple was destroyed, each day is more (cursed) than the last....[27] But on what does the world stand? On the "sanctification of the order"[28] and (saying) "May His great Name be

---

Rab Kah. 3:16, ed. Mandelbaum, 52–53 = Tan. §*Ki Tetse'* 18, ed. Buber 2:כב = Midr. Ps. 9:10. See already Mekhilta §*Amalek* 2, ed. Lauterbach, 270).

20. Ps 150:6 (my translation), cited in b. Eruv. 18b.

21. Exod 15:18.

22. Pirqe R. El. 3 (ms. JTS Enelow 866, Ma'agarim): "If there is no host or camp for a ruler, what does he rule?"

23. Isa 47:4 (KJV, trans. modified). See Vay. Rab. 32:8 (ed. Margulies, 755): "Two Amoraim—one says 'exile' and one says 'redemption.' One who says 'exile' [says] Israel were exiled to Babylon and the Shekhinah was exiled with them.... One who says 'redemption' [says] the savior [is] *Our redeemer, the Lord of hosts is his name* (Isa 47:4, KJV)."

24. Isa 24:23 (KJV, trans. modified). b. Pesah. 68a (= b. Sanh. 91b): "Shmuel said that there is no difference between this world and the days of the Messiah except subjugation to empires ... [but, the Talmud continues, at the Messiah "the moon shall be confounded and the sun ashamed" in the encampment of Shekhinah]. After all, sun/moon are merely the "host of heaven" (Isa 34:4, in b. Avod. Zar. 17a.)

25. Movshovitz (Gra, *Be'ure Aggadot*, 3 n. 40) notes that the Gra reads Aramaic plural *poles* (אלוותא) in the tale as Hebrew plural אלה, "oaths." The "poles" with which the sailors strike the wave symbolize God's two "guarantees" to deliver Israel from evil/suffering and from exile, corresponding to God's Name and Throne. By that logic, the act of striking with the Names may symbolize the "Hand on the Throne"; see chapter 2, §*Parting the Sea(s)* and n. 342.

26. The rest of §7 is a tradition at b. Sotah 49a. I add Rashi's commentary in parentheses to clarify the Gra's meaning.

27. See commentary to Zohar 1:181b in *Zohar: Pritzker Edition*, 3:100 n. 103.

28. *Qedusha desidra*. See Ismar Elbogen, *Jewish Liturgy: A Comprehensive History*, trans. Raymond P. Scheindlin (Philadelphia: Jewish Publication Society, 1993 [1913]), 70–71 and 404 n. 23 for sources as well as more recent literature.

blessed" after *aggadah*.²⁹ As it is said: "A land of darkness, as darkness itself; and of the shadow of death, without any order."³⁰ See: if there are orders (of prayer and the study of *aggadah*,³¹ then the land) shall appear from out of the darkness].

§8. And similarly, [*Qedusha desidra*] saves us for the world to come.... "Anyone who answers 'Amen' in this world merits [and answers 'Amen' in the world to come.... 'Blessed be the Lord God of Israel, Lord of Israel, from [this] world to eternity]: Amen and Amen.'"³² And ... "One who answers Amen with all his strength, they open to him the gates [of the Garden of Eden.... 'Open ye the gates, that the righteous nation which keeps the faith may enter in.' Do not read: 'Which keeps the faith [*shomer 'emunim*],' but 'Who say Amen, *she-'omerim amen*].'"³³ Those who say Amens (*she-'omerim Amenim*): that is, two Amens. And that is what he is saying [at the end of the tale]: *Amen Amen Selah and [the Wave of exile and sufferings and subjugation to foreign empires] subsides.*

---

29. Rashi, b. Sotah 49a, s.v. אקדושא דסדרא, presents this practice in a way that is both relevant to the Gra's argument and consonant with a modern historical interpretation (previous note). "*Qedusha desidra*: An order [i.e., version] of [the prayer for] the sanctification [of God's Name] that they instituted only in order for all Israel to engage in Torah [study] a little each day. For [the preacher] would recite [a sermon, after which the congregation recited a few verses—including Exod 15:18, "YHWH will reign for ever and ever"], as well as their [vernacular Aramaic] translation. And they are considered engaging in Torah [study]. And, because this was the rite for all Israel, both learned and unlearned, and it contains both sanctification of the Name and study of Torah, it is prized. And thus it was their rite [to say] 'May His great Name be blessed,' which one replied [by way of 'Amen'], after the sermon that the preacher preached in public every Sabbath. And as it was not a workday, all the nation would gather there to hear. And [this rite] has both Torah [study] and sanctification of the Name."

30. Job 10:22.

31. Rashi, b. Sotah 49a, s.v. סדרים, adds: "orders of the sections of the Torah," i.e., passages recited and preached on during these public Sabbath gatherings that the people "studied" through their recitation of *Qedusha desidra*.

32. Ps 41:13 (41:14) (my translation), in Tan. §*Tsav* 7 (Ma'agarim).

33. Isa 26:2 (my translation), in b. Shabb. 119b.

Bibliography

If a Hebrew work has a title page in English or another language in Roman characters, it is cited. If not, the title is transliterated using SBL general-purpose guidelines (see §*Note on the Text*).

Abramson, Shraga. *Mi-pi ba'ale leshonot*. Jerusalem: Mossad Harav Kook, 1988.

———, ed. and trans. *Talmud Bavli Massekhet Baba Batra*. Tel-Aviv: Dvir, 1958.

Adelman, Rachel. "The Poetics of Time and Space in the Midrashic Narrative: The Case of *Pirqei deRabbi Eliezer*." PhD diss., Hebrew University of Jerusalem, 2008.

———. *The Return of the Repressed: Pirqe de-Rabbi Eliezer and the Pseudepigrapha*. JSJSup 140. Leiden: Brill, 2009.

Adlerstein, Yitzchok. *Maharal of Prague: Be'er Hagolah. The Classic Defense of Rabbinic Judaism through the Profundity of the Aggadah*. Brooklyn, NY: Artscroll, 2000.

Aegineta, Paulus. *The Medical Works*, vol. 1. Translated and commentary by Francis Adams. London, 1834.

Agostini, Domenico, and Samuel Thrope, eds. and trans. *The Bundahišn: The Zoroastrian Book of Creation*. Oxford: Oxford University Press, 2020.

Ahuvia, Mika. "Reimagining the Gender and Class Dynamics of Premodern Composition." *JAJ* 14 (2023): 321–54.

Albeck, Chanokh. *Introduction to the Mishnah* [Hebrew]. Jerusalem: Mossad Bialik, 1959.

———. *Introduction to the Talmud, Bavli and Yerushalmi* [Hebrew]. Tel-Aviv: Dvir, 1969.

Alexander, Elizabeth Shanks. *Transmitting Mishnah: The Shaping Influence of Oral Tradition*. Cambridge: Cambridge University Press, 2006.

Alfonsi, Petrus. *Dialogue against the Jews*. Translated by Irven M. Resnick. Fathers of the Church: Mediaeval Continuation 8. Washington, DC: Catholic University of America Press, 2006.

Alter, Robert. *The Hebrew Bible. Volume 3: The Writings. A Translation with Commentary*. New York: Norton. 2018.

Amitay, Ory. "Alexander in Ancient Jewish Literature." In *A History of*

Alexander the Great in World Culture, edited by Richard Stoneman, 109–42. Cambridge: Cambridge University Press, 2022.

———. "Alexander in Bavli Tamid: In Search for a Meaning." In *The Alexander Romance in Persia and the East*, edited by Richard Stoneman, Kyle Erickson, and Ian Netton, 349–65. Ancient Narrative: Supplement 15. Eelde: Barkhuis, 2012.

Amsler, Monika. *The Babylonian Talmud and Late Antique Book Culture*. Cambridge: Cambridge University Press, 2023.

Anisfeld, Rachel. *Sustain Me with Raisin-Cakes: Pesikta deRav Kahana and the Popularization of Rabbinic Judaism*. JSJSup 133. Leiden: Brill, 2009.

Apps, Arwen. "Gaius Iulius Solinus and His *Polyhistor*." PhD diss., Macquarie University, 2011. https://topostext.org/work/747 (accessed July 9, 2024).

Aristotle. *How to Tell a Story: An Ancient Guide to the Art of Storytelling for Writers and Readers*. Translated by Philip Freeman. Princeton, NJ: Princeton University Press, 2022.

Arrian. *The Campaigns of Alexander = Anabasis Alexandrou*. Edited by James Romm. Translated by Pamela Mensch. New York: Pantheon, 2010.

Ashkenazi, Betsalel. *Shitta Mequbbetset*. 2nd ed. 8 vols. Tel-Aviv: Tsiyoni, 1955.

Auerbach, Erich. *Mimesis: The Representation of Reality in Western Literature*. Translated by Willard R. Trask. Princeton, NJ: Princeton University Press, 1953.

Azriel, Abraham ben. *Arugat ha-Bosem*. Edited by E. E. Urbach. 4 vols. Jerusalem: Mekize Nirdamim, 1939–1963.

Bacher, Wilhelm. *Die agada der babylonischen Amoräer*. Budapest: Royal University Press, 1878.

———. *Die exegetische Terminologie der jüdischen Traditionsliteratur*. 2 vols. Leipzig: Hinrichs, 1905.

Bal, Mieke. *Narratology: Introduction to the Theory of Narrative*. Translated by Christine Van Boheemen. 4th ed. Toronto: University of Toronto Press, 2017.

Balberg, Mira. *Fractured Tablets: Forgetfulness and Fallibility in Late Ancient Rabbinic Culture*. Oakland: University of California Press, 2023.

Balberg, Mira, and Haim Weiss. "'That Old Man Shames Us': Aging, Liminality, and Antinomy in Rabbinic Literature." *JSQ* 25.1 (2018): 17–41.

———. *When Near Becomes Far: Old Age and Rabbinic Literature*. Oxford: Oxford University Press, 2021.

Bar-Asher Siegal, Elitzur. *Introduction to the Grammar of Jewish Babylonian Aramaic*. 2nd rev. ed. Münster: Ugarit, 2016.

Bar-Asher Siegal, Michal. *Early Christian Monastic Literature and the Babylonian Talmud*. Cambridge: Cambridge University Press, 2013.

———. "Matthew 5:22: The Insult 'Fool' and the Interpretation of the Law in Christian and Rabbinic Sources," *RHR* 234 (2017): 5–23.

Bar-Ilan, Meir. "Between Magic and Religion: Sympathetic Magic in the World of the Sages of the Mishnah and Talmud." *Review of Rabbinic Judaism* 5.3 (2002): 383–99.
Barnes, William Emery. *The Peshitta Psalter according to the West-Syrian Text*. Cambridge: Cambridge University Press, 1904.
Bartsch, Shadi. *Decoding the Ancient Novel: The Reader and the Role of Description in Heliodorus and Achilles Tatius*. Princeton, NJ: Princeton University Press, 1989.
Bartsch, Shadi, and Jás Elsner. "Eight Ways of Looking at an Ekphrasis." *CP* 102.1 (2007): i–vi.
Baudelaire, Charles. "Correspondences." In *Œuvres complètes*, 8–9. Paris: Laffont, 1980 [1857].
Bearzot, Cinzia Susanna. "Fragmentum Sabbaiticum (151)." In *Brill's New Jacoby*, edited by Ian Worthington, 1–11. Leiden: Brill, 2017.
Becker, Adam H. "The 'Evil Inclination' of the Jews: The Syriac Yatsra in Narsai's Metrical Homilies for Lent." *JQR* 106.2 (2016): 179–207.
———. "Positing a 'Cultural Relationship' between Plato and the Babylonian Talmud." *JQR* 101.2 (2011): 255–69.
Ben-Amos, Dan. "Narrative Forms in the Aggadah: Structural Analysis." PhD diss., Indiana University, 1966.
———. "Talmudic Tall Tales." In *Folklore Today: A Festschrift for Richard M. Dorson*, edited by Linda Dégh, Henry Glassie, and Felix J. Oinas, 25-43. Bloomington: Indiana University Press, 1976.
Bergson, Henri. *Le rire: Essai sur la signification du comique*. 1900. Repr., Paris: Presses Universitaires de France, 1954.
Berkovitz, A. J. *A Life of Psalms in Jewish Late Antiquity*. Jewish Culture and Contexts. Philadelphia: University of Pennsylvania Press, 2023.
Berkowitz, Beth A. "The Rhetoric of the Mishnah." In *What Is the Mishnah? The State of the Question*, edited by Shaye J. D. Cohen, 187–203. Jewish Law and Culture Series. Cambridge, MA: Harvard University Press, 2022.
Berman, Nathaniel. *Divine and the Demonic in the Poetic Mythology of the Zohar: The "Other Side" of Kabbalah*. Leiden: Brill, 2018.
Bernstein, Moshe. "Scriptures: Quotation and Use," in *Encyclopedia of the Dead Sea Scrolls*, ed. Lawrence H. Schiffman and James C. VanderKam, 2:839–42. 2 vols. Oxford: Oxford University Press, 2000.
Bickart, Noah Benjamin. *The Scholastic Culture of the Babylonian Talmud*. Judaism in Context 31. Piscataway, NJ: Gorgias, 2022.
Bickerman, Elias. *Studies in Jewish and Christian History*. 2 vols. Leiden: Brill, 2007.
Bladel, Kevin van. "The Syriac Sources of the Early Arabic Narratives of Alexander." In *Memory as History: The Legacy of Alexander in Asia*, edited by Himanshu Prabha Ray and Daniel T. Potts, 54–75. Delhi: Aryan, 2007.

Blau, Ludwig. *Masoretische Untersuchungen*. Strasbourg: Trübner, 1891.

Blenkinsopp, Joseph. *Isaiah 40–55: A New Translation with Introduction and Commentary*. AB 19A. New York: Doubleday, 2000.

Blois, François de. *Burzoy's Voyage to India and the Origin of the Book of Kalīlah wa-Dimnah*. Prize Publication Fund 23. London: Royal Asiatic Society, 1990.

Bloom, Harold. *A Map of Misreading*. Oxford: Oxford University Press, 1975.

Bohak, Gideon. *Ancient Jewish Magic: A History*. Cambridge: Cambridge University Press, 2008.

Börner-Klein, Dagmar, ed. and trans. *Pirke de-Rabbi Elieser*. SJ 26. Berlin: de Gruyter, 2004.

Boyarin, Daniel. *Intertextuality and the Reading of Midrash*. ISBL. Bloomington: Indiana University Press, 1990.

———. "'Pilpul': The Logic of Commentary." In *The Talmud: A Personal Take; Selected Essays*, edited by Tal Hever-Chybowski, 47–65. TSAJ 170. Tübingen: Mohr Siebeck, 2017.

———. *Socrates and the Fat Rabbis*. Chicago: University of Chicago Press, 2009.

———. "Studies in the Talmudic Commentaries of the Spanish Exiles" [Hebrew]. *Sefunot* n.s. 2/17 (1983): 166–83.

———. "Towards the Talmudic Lexicon" [Hebrew]. *Tarbiz* 50 (1980): 164–91.

———. "Towards the Talmudic Lexicon II" [Hebrew]. In *Teudah*, edited by Mordecai Akiva Friedman et al., 3:113–19. Ramat-Gan: Bar-Ilan University Press, 1983.

Braude, William G., and Israel J. Kapstein, trans. *Pesikta de-Rab Kahana*. Philadelphia: Jewish Publication Society, 2002.

Bregman, Marc. "Pseudepigraphy in Rabbinic Literature." In *Pseudepigraphic Perspectives: The Apocrypha & Pseudepigrapha in Light of the Dead Sea Scrolls; Proceedings of the International Symposium of the Orion Center for the Study of the Dead Sea Scrolls and Associated Literature, 12–14 January, 1997*, edited by Esther G. Chazon and Michael E. Stone, 27–41. STDJ 31. Leiden: Brill, 1999.

Brodsky, David. "From Disagreement to Talmudic Discourse: Progymnasmata and the Evolution of a Rabbinic Genre." In *Rabbinic Traditions between Palestine and Babylonia*, edited by Ronit Nikolsky and Tal Ilan, 173–231. AJEC 89. Leiden: Brill, 2014.

Brody, Yerahmiel (Robert). "The Contribution of the Yerushalmi to Dating 'The Anonymous Talmud'" [Hebrew]. In *Melekhet Mahshevet: Studies in the Redaction and Development of Talmudic Literature*, edited by Aaron Amit and Aharon Shemesh, 27–37. Ramat-Gan: Bar Ilan University Press, 2011.

———. "Sifrut ha-geonim veha-teqst ha-talmudi." In *Talmudic Studies*, edited by Yaakov Sussmann and David Rosenthal, 1:237–303. 4 vols. in 6. Jerusalem: Magnes, 1990–2024.

Brody, Yerahmiel (Robert), Carmiel Cohen, and Yehudah Zvi Stampfer, eds. *Otzar ha-Geonim he-Hadash: Massekhet Baba Batra*. Jerusalem: Yad Ha-Rav Nissim, 2017.

Brown, Peter. "Saint Augustine." In *Trends in Medieval Political Thought*, edited by Beryl Smalley, 1–21. Oxford: Clarendon, 1965.

Brown, Truesdell S. *Onesicritus: A Study in Hellenistic Historiography*. University of California Publications in History 39. Berkeley: University of California Press, 1949.

Brüll, Jacob. *Die Mnemotechnik des Talmuds: Eine historisch-kritische Untersuchung*. Vienna: n.p., 1864.

Budge, E. A. Wallace. *The History of Alexander the Great, Being the Syriac Version, Edited from five Manuscripts of the Pseudo-Callisthenes, with an English Translation*. Cambridge: Cambridge University Press, 1889.

Burke, Peter. "Context in Context." *Common Knowledge* 8.1 (2002): 152–77.

Butts, Aaron Michael. "Language Change in the Wake of Empire: Syriac in Its Greco-Roman Context." PhD diss., University of Chicago, 2013.

Buyaner, David. "On the Etymology of Middle Persian baškuč (Winged Monster)," *SIr* 34 (2005): 19–30.

Cameron, Averil. *Agathias*. Oxford: Clarendon, 1970.

———. "Agathias on the Sassanians." *Dumbarton Oaks Papers* 23–24 (1969): 67–183.

Campbell, Joseph. *The Hero with a Thousand Faces*. Bollingen Series 17. 1949. Repr., Princeton, NJ: Princeton University Press, 2004.

Campbell, Mary B. *The Witness and the Other World: Exotic European Travel Writing, 400–1600*. Ithaca, NY: Cornell University Press, 1988.

Cassuto, Umberto. *Biblical and Oriental Studies: Bible and Ancient Oriental Texts*. 2 vols. Translated by Israel Abrahams. Jerusalem: Magnes, 1975.

Catlin, Samuel P. "The Rest Is Literature: *Midrash* and the Institution of 'Theory' in America." PhD diss., University of Chicago, 2022.

Chazan, Robert. *In the Year 1096: The First Crusade and the Jews*. Philadelphia: Jewish Publication Society, 1996.

Chernus, Ira. "'A Wall of Fire Round About': The Development of a Theme in Rabbinic Midrash." *JJS* 30.1 (1979): 68–84.

Chilton, Bruce. "The Exodus Theology of the Palestinian Targumim." In *The Book of Exodus: Composition, Reception, and Interpretation*, edited by Thomas B. Dozeman, Craig A. Evans, and Joel N. Lohr, 386–403. VTSup 164. Leiden: Brill, 2014.

Chin, C. M., and Moulie Vidas. "Introduction." In *Late Ancient Knowing: Explorations in Intellectual History*, edited by C. M. Chin and Moulie Vidas, 1–13. Berkeley: University of California Press, 2015.

Christensen, Arthur. *L'iran sous les Sassanides*. Annales du Musée Guimet: Bibliothèque d'études 48. Copenhagen: Levin & Munskgaard, 1936.

Cohen, Arthur. "Arabisms in Rabbinic Literature." *JQR* 3.2 (1912): 221–33.
Cohen, Aryeh. *Rereading Talmud: Gender, Law and the Poetics of Sugyot*. BJS 318. Atlanta: Scholars Press, 1998.
Cohen, Avinoam. "Towards the Historical Meaning Hidden in the Phrase 'Rabbi So-and-so Happened to Come to....'" [Hebrew]. *Sidra* 15 (1999): 51–64.
Cohen, Barak S. "Citation Formulae in the Babylonian Talmud: From Transmission to Authoritative Traditions." *JJS* 70.1 (2019): 24–44.
———. *The Legal Methodology of Late Nehardean Sages in Sasanian Babylonia*. Brill Reference Library of Judaism 30. Leiden: Brill, 2011.
Cohen, Jeremy. *A Historian in Exile: Solomon ibn Verga, Shevet Yehudah, and the Jewish-Christian Encounter*. Jewish Culture and Contexts. Philadelphia: University of Pennsylvania Press, 2017.
Cohen, Shaye J. D. "The Significance of Yavneh: Pharisees, Rabbis, and the End of Jewish Sectarianism." *HUCA* 55 (1984): 27–53.
Constantinou, Stavroula, and Andria Andreou, eds. *Storyworlds in Short Narratives: Approaches to Late Antique and Early Byzantine Tales*. Brill's Series on the Early Middle Ages 31. Leiden: Brill, 2025.
Dahood, Mitchell J. *Psalms: Introduction, Translation, and Notes*. 3 vols. AB 16, 17, 17A. Garden City, NY: Doubleday, 1966–1970.
Daryaee, Touraj. *Sasanian Persia: The Rise and Fall of an Empire*. London: I. B. Tauris, 2009.
Daston, Lorraine, and Otta Wenskus. "Paradoxographoi." In *Der neue Pauly: Enzyklopädie der Antike*, edited by Hubert Cancik and Helmuth Schneider, 9:309–14. 16 vols. Stuttgart: Metzler, 1996–2003.
Davies, M., and P. J. Finglass. *Stesichorus: The Poems*. Cambridge Classical Texts and Commentaries 54. Cambridge: Cambridge University Press, 2014.
Debié, Muriel. "Textual Exchanges in Late Antiquity East and South of Byzantium Seen through an Eastern Christian Lens." In *Proceedings of the 24th International Congress of Byzantine Studies Plenary Sessions 1*, 59–80. Venice: Università Ca' Foscari, 2022.
DeBold, Robert Timothy. "The Hermeneutics of Textual Hierarchies in the Babylonian Talmud." PhD diss., Stanford University, 2015.
Delattre, Charles. "Paradoxographic Discourse on Sources and Fountains: Deconstructing Paradoxes." In *Recognizing Miracles in Antiquity and Beyond*, edited by Maria Gerolemou, 205–23. Trends in Classics: Supplementary Volume 53. Berlin: de Gruyter, 2018.
Desnier, Jean-Luc. *"Le passage du fleuve" de Cyrus le Grand à Julien l'Apostat: Essai sur la légitimité du souverain*. Annales littéraires de l'Université de Besançon 143. Paris: Harmattan, 1995.
Dickie, Matthew W. "Talos Bewitched: Magic, Atomic Theory and Paradoxography in Apollonius *Argonautica* 4.1638–88." *Papers of the Leeds International Seminar* 6 (1990): 267–96.

Dimitrovsky, H. Z. "On the Method of Pilpul" [Hebrew]. In *Salo Wittmayer Baron Jubilee Volume on the Occasion of His Eightieth Birthday*, edited by Saul Lieberman and Arthur Hyman, 111–81. Jerusalem: American Academy for Jewish Research, 1975.

Dolgopolski, Sergey. *The Open Past: Subjectivity and Remembering in the Talmud*. New York: Fordham University Press, 2013.

Dor, Tzvi Moshe. *Torat 'erets-yisrael be-bavel*. Tel Aviv: Dvir, 1970.

Duval, Rubens, ed. *Lexicon Syriacum Auctore Hassano Bar Bahlule*. Vol. 1. Paris: Leroux, 1901.

Dweck, Yaacob. *The Scandal of Kabbalah: Leon Modena, Jewish Mysticism, Early Modern Venice*. Princeton, NJ: Princeton University Press, 2011.

Elbaum, Yaakov. *Medieval Perspectives on Talmud and Midrash* [Hebrew]. Jerusalem: Mossad Bialik, 2000.

———. *Openness and Insularity: Late Sixteenth Century Jewish Literature in Poland and Ashkenaz* [Hebrew]. Jerusalem: Magnes, 1990.

———. "Rabbi David Darshan of Krakow and the Hermeneutic Rules That He Collected for *Aggadah* and *Midrash*" [Hebrew]. *Asufot* 7 (1994): 281–302.

Elbogen, Ismar. *Jewish Liturgy: A Comprehensive History*. Translated by Raymond P. Scheindlin. Philadelphia: Jewish Publication Society, 1993 [1913].

Eleftheriou, Dimitria. "Pseudo-Antigonos de Carystos: *Collection d'histoires curieuses*." 2 vols. PhD diss., Paris–Nanterre, 2018.

Elman, Yaakov. "Orality and the Redaction of the Babylonian Talmud." *Oral Tradition* 14.1 (1999): 52–99.

———. "Striving for Meaning: A Short History of Rabbinic Omnisignificance." In *World Philology*, edited by Sheldon Pollock et al., 62–91. Cambridge, MA: Harvard University Press, 2015.

———. "The World of the 'Sabboraim': Cultural Aspects of Post-Redactional Additions to the Talmud." In *Creation and Composition: The Contribution of the Talmud Redactors (Stammaim) to the Aggadah*, edited by Jeffrey L. Rubenstein, 383–415. Tübingen: Mohr Siebeck, 2011.

Elman, Yaakov, and Shai Secunda, "Judaism." In *The Wiley Blackwell Companion to Zoroastrianism*, ed. Michael Stausberg and Yuhan Vevaina, 423–35. London: Wiley, 2015.

Ephraim b. R. Yaaqov of Bonn. *Hymnen und Gebete (Hymns and Prayers)*. Translated and commentary by Hans-Georg von Mutius. Hildesheim: Olms, 1989.

Ephrat, Daphna, and Yaakov Elman. "Orality and the Institutionalization of Tradition: The Growth of the Geonic Yeshiva and the Islamic Madrasa." In *Transmitting Jewish Traditions: Orality, Textuality, and Cultural Diffusion*, edited by Yaakov Elman and Israel Gershoni, 107–37. New Haven: Yale University Press, 2000.

Epstein, Y. N. *Introduction to the Mishnaic Text* [Hebrew]. Jerusalem: Magnes, 1948.
Faraone, Christopher Athanasious. *Hexametrical Genres from Homer to Theocritus*. Oxford: Oxford University Press, 2021.
Farrokh, Kaveh, et al. "Depictions of Archery in Sassanian Silver Plates and Their Relationship to Warfare." *Revista de Artes Marciales Asiáticas* 13.2 (2018): 82–113.
Feintuch, Yonatan. *Face to Face: The Interweaving of Aggada and Halakha in the Babylonian Talmud* [Hebrew]. Jerusalem: Magid, 2018.
———. "The Story of the Encounter Between Resh Lakish and Rabbah bar bar Hannah (bYoma 9b) in its Broader Talmudic Context" [Hebrew]. *Jewish Studies an Internet Journal* 12 (2013): 1–23.
Feldblum, Meyer S. "Prof. Abraham Weiss: His Approach and Contributions to Talmudic Scholarship." In *The Abraham Weiss Jubilee Volume*, edited by Samuel Belkin et al., 7–80. New York: Jubilee, 1964.
Feldman, Aharon. *The Juggler and the King: The Jew and the Conquest of Evil; An Elaboration of the Vilna Gaon's Insights into the Hidden Wisdom of the Sages*. Spring Valley, NY: Feldheim, 1991.
Feldman, Louis. "How Much Hellenism in Jewish Palestine?" *Hebrew Union College Annual* 57 (1986): 83-111.
Fiano, Emanuel. *Three Powers in Heaven: The Emergence of Theology and the Parting of the Ways*. Synkrisis. New Haven: Yale University Press, 2023.
Fine, Elisha, and Steven Fine. "Rabbinic Paleontology: Jewish Encounters with Fossil Giants in Roman Antiquity." In *Land and Spirituality in Rabbinic Literature: A Memorial Volume for Yaakov Elman*, edited by Shana Strauch Schick, 3–37. Brill Reference Library of Judaism 71. Leiden: Brill, 2022.
Fish, Stanley. *Is There a Text in This Class? The Authority of Interpretive Communities*. Cambridge, MA: Harvard University Press, 1980.
Fishbane, Michael. "The Arm of the Lord: Mythic Creativity and Exegetical Form in the *Midrash*." In *Language, Theology, and the Bible: Essays in Honour of James Barr*, edited by Samuel E. Balentine and John Barton, 271–92. Oxford: Clarendon, 1994.
———. *Biblical Interpretation in Ancient Israel*. Oxford: Clarendon, 1985.
———. *Biblical Myth and Rabbinic Mythmaking*. Oxford: Oxford University Press, 2003.
———. "The Great Dragon Battle and Talmudic Redaction." In *The Exegetical Imagination: On Jewish Thought and Theology*, 41–55. Cambridge, MA: Harvard University Press, 1998.
———. "Rabbinic Mythmaking and Tradition: The Great Dragon Drama in b. Baba Batra 74b–75a." In *Tehillah le-Moshe: Biblical and Judaic Studies in Honor of Moshe Greenberg*, edited by Mordechai Cogan, Barry L.

Eichler, and Jeffrey H. Tigay, 273–83. Winona Lake, IN: Eisenbrauns, 1997.

Fisher, Philip. *Wonder, the Rainbow, and the Aesthetics of Rare Experiences.* Cambridge, MA: Harvard University Press, 1998.

Foley, John Miles. *How to Read an Oral Poem.* Urbana: University of Illinois Press, 2002.

Fonrobert, Charlotte Elisheva. *Menstrual Purity: Rabbinic and Christian Reconstructions of Biblical Gender.* Contraversions. Stanford, CA: Stanford University Press, 2000.

——. "On 'Carnal Israel' and the Consequences: Talmudic Studies since Foucault." *JQR* 95.3 (2005): 462–69.

——. "Plato in Rabbi Shimeon bar Yohai's Cave (B. Shabbat 33b–34a): The Talmudic Inversion of Plato's Politics of Philosophy." *AJSR* 31.2 (2007): 277–96.

Forster, E. M. *Aspects of the Novel.* Clark Lectures 1927. London: Harcourt, Brace, 1927.

Foulke, Robert. *The Sea Voyage Narrative.* Studies in Literary Themes and Genres 14. London: Routledge, 2002.

Fox, Harry. "A New Understanding of the Sobriquet דורשי החלקות: Why Qumranites Rejected Pharisaic Traditions." In *Law, Literature, and Society in Legal Texts from Qumran: Papers from the Ninth Meeting of the International Organization for Qumran Studies, Leuven 2016,* edited by Jutta Jokiranta and Molly Zahn, 65–98. STDJ 128. Leiden: Brill, 2019.

Fraade, Steven. *Multilingualism and Translation in Ancient Judaism: Before and after Babel* (Cambridge: Cambridge University Press, 2023).

Frank, Georgia. *The Memory of the Eyes: Pilgrims to Living Saints in Christian Late Antiquity.* Transformations of the Classical Heritage 30. Berkeley: University of California Press, 2000.

Fränkel, Jonah. *The Aggadic Narrative: Harmony of Form and Content* [Hebrew]. Tel-Aviv: Ha-qibbuts ha-meuhad, 2001.

——. "Chiasmus in Talmudic-Aggadic Narrative." In *Chiasmus in Antiquity: Structures, Analyses, Exegesis,* edited by John W. Welch, 183–97. 1981. Repr., Eugene, OR: Wipf & Stock, 2020.

——. *Darkhe ha-aggadah veha-midrash.* Masadah: Yad la-Talmud, 1991.

——. *Darko shel Rashi be-ferusho la-Talmud ha-bavli.* 2nd ed. Jerusalem: Magnes, 1980.

——. *'Iyyunim be'olamo ha-ruhani shel sippur ha-aggadah.* Tel-Aviv: Ha-qibbuts ha-meuhad, 1981.

——. "Paronomasia in Aggadic Narrative." In *Studies in Hebrew Narrative Art throughout the Ages,* edited by Joseph Heinemann and Shmuel Werses, 27–50. ScrHier 27. Jerusalem: Magnes, 1978.

Frankel, Zecharias. "Traditionelle Erklärung der Mischna und des Talmuds." *MGWJ* 11 (1862): 274–75.

Frazer, J. G., trans. *Pausanias's Description of Greece*. 6 vols. London: Macmillan, 1898.

Freeman-Grenville, G. S. P., ed. and trans. *The Book of the Wonders of India: Mainland, Sea, and Islands by Captain Buzurg ibn Shahriyār of Ramhormuz*. London: East-West, 1981.

Frendo, Joseph D. "Agathias' View of the Intellectual Attainments of Khusrau I: A Reconsideration of the Evidence." *Bulletin of the Asia Institute* 18 (2004): 97–110.

Friedlaender, Israel. *Die Chadhirlegende und der Alexanderroman: Eine Sagengeschichtliche und Literarhistorische Untersuchung*. Leipzig: Teubner, 1913.

Friedman, Shamma. Aristotle in the Babylonian Talmud?: A Scholastic Interpolation by the Talmud's Anonymous Glossator." *Maarav* 21.1–2 (2014): 311–17.

———. "The Further Adventures of Rav Kahana: Between Babylonia and Palestine." In *The Talmud Yerushalmi and Graeco-Roman Culture*, edited by Peter Schäfer et al., 3:247–71. 3 vols. Tübingen: Mohr Siebeck, 1998–2002.

———. "A Good Story Deserves Retelling: The Unfolding of the Akiva Legend." *Jewish Studies, an Internet Journal* 3 (2004): 55–93.

———. "Literary Structure in Bavli *Sugyot*" [Hebrew]. In *Talmudic Studies: Investigating the Sugya, Variant Readings, and Aggada*, 136–48. New York: Jewish Theological Seminary of America, 2010.

———. "*Nomen est Omen*: Dicta of the Talmudic Sages which Echo the Author's Name" [Hebrew]. In *These Are the Names: Studies in Jewish Onomastics*, edited by A. Demsky et al., 2:51–77. 2 vols. Raman-Gan: Bar-Ilan University Press, 1999.

———. "Now You See It, Now You Don't: Can Source-Criticism Perform Magic on Talmudic Passages about Sorcery?" In *Rabbinic Traditions between Palestine and Babylonia,* edited by Ronit Nikolsky and Tal Ilan, 32–83. Leiden: Brill, 2014.

———. "On the Historical Character of Dama ben Netinah: A Study in Talmudic *aggadah*" [Hebrew]. In *Talmudic Studies: Investigating the Sugya, Variant Readings, and Aggada*, 433–74. New York: Jewish Theological Seminary of America, 2010.

———. "On the Orthography of the Names 'Rabbah' and 'Rava'" [Hebrew]. *Sinai* 110 (1992): 140–64.

———. "Regarding Historical aggadah in the Babylonian Talmud" [Hebrew]. In *Talmudic Studies: Investigating the Sugya, Variant Readings, and Aggada*, 389–432. New York: Jewish Theological Seminary of America, 2010.

———. *Talmud Arukh: BT Bava Meẓi'a VI. Critical Edition with Comprehensive Commentary*. 2 vols. New York: JTS, 1996.

———. "Uncovering Literary Dependencies in the Talmudic Corpus."

In *The Synoptic Problem in Rabbinic Literature,* edited by Shaye J. D. Cohen, 35–57. BJS 326. Providence: Brown Judaic Studies, 2000.

———. "'Wonder Not at an Addition Recorded in the Name of an Amora': The Dicta of the Amoraim and the Anonymous Talmud in Bavli *Sugyot* Revisited" [Hebrew]. In *Talmudic Studies: Investigating the Sugya, Variant Readings, and Aggada,* 57–135. New York: Jewish Theological Seminary of America, 2010.

Frim, Daniel J. "'Those Who Descend upon the Sea Told Me …': Myth and Tall Tale in *Baba Batra* 73a–74b." *JQR* 107.1 (2017): 1–37.

Fuchs, Uzziel. "The Redaction and Objective of the Opening *Sugya* of Tractate *Baba Batra*" [Hebrew]. *Sidra* 23 (2008): 83–105.

———. "What?! Is there Thievery in the Firmament?!: On the Textual Correction of an Impiety" [Hebrew]. In *Ve-Hinneh Rivka Yotzet: Essays in Jewish Studies in Honor of Rivka Dagan,* edited by Leib Moscovitz, 205–7. Jerusalem: Tsur-Ot, 2017.

Furstenberg, Yair. "The Agon with Moses." In *Homer and the Bible in the Eyes of Ancient Interpreters,* edited by Maren R. Niehoff, 299–328. Jerusalem Studies in Religion and Culture 16. Leiden: Brill, 2012.

Gafni, Chanan. "Orthodoxy and Talmudic Criticism? On Misleading Attributions in the Talmud." *Zutot* 13 (2016): 70–80.

Gafni, Isaiah M. "Babylonian Rabbinic Culture." In *Jews and Judaism in the Rabbinic Era: Image and Reality—History and Historiography,* 219–45. TSAJ 173. Tübingen: Mohr Siebeck, 2019.

Garb, Jonathan. "From Fear to Awe in Luzzatto's *Mesillat Yesharim*." *European Journal of Jewish Studies* 14.2 (2020): 285–99.

García Martínez, Florentino, and Eibert J.C. Tigchelaar, eds. *The Dead Sea Scrolls Study Edition.* 2 vols. Leiden: Brill, 1997–1998.

Gasser, Julia Haig. "A Structural Analysis of the Digressions in the *Iliad* and the *Odyssey*." *HSCP* 73 (1969): 1–43.

Gaster, Moses, ed. and trans. *The Exempla of the Rabbis: Being a Collection of Exempla, Apologues and Tales Culled from Hebrew Manuscripts and Rare Hebrew Books.* 2nd ed. New York: Ktav, 1968 [1924].

Geertz, Clifford. *The Interpretation of Cultures.* New York: Basic Books, 1973.

Gennep, Arnold van. *The Rites of Passage.* Translated by Monika B. Vizedom and Gabrielle L. Caffee. Chicago: University of Chicago Press, 1960.

George, Andrew, trans. *Gilgamesh.* New York: Penguin, 1999.

Gerolemou, Maria, ed. *Recognizing Miracles in Antiquity and Beyond.* Berlin: de Gruyter, 2018.

Gershenson, Daniel E. "Understanding Puškanṣa (bB.B. 73:2)." *AcOr* 55 (1994): 23–36.

Getz, Elyaqum. *Sefer Even ha-Shoham u-Me'irat 'Enayim: She'elot u-Teshuvot ye-Ḥidushim u-Ve'urim.* Jerusalem: Zikhron Aharon, 2014.

Geus, Klaus. "Paradoxography and Geography in Antiquity: Some

Thoughts about the *Paradoxographus Vaticanus.*" In *La letra y la carta: Descripción verbal y representación gráfica en los diseños terrestres; Estudios en honor de Pietro Janni,* edited by Francisco J. González Ponce et al., 243–257. Seville: University of Seville Press, 2016.

Geus, Klaus, and Colin Guthrie King. "Paradoxography." In *Oxford Handbook of Science and Medicine in the Classical World,* edited by Paul T. Keyser and John Scarborough, 431–44. Oxford: Oxford University Press, 2018.

Giannini, Alexander, ed. *Paradoxographorum Graecorum reliquiae.* Milan: Istituto editoriale italiano, 1966.

Ginzberg, Louis. *Legends of the Jews* 2nd ed. 2 vols. JPS Classic Reissues. Philadelphia: Jewish Publication Society, 2003.

Goldberg, Abraham. "The Mishna: A Study Book of Halakhah." In *Literature of the Sages,* ed. Shmuel Safrai et al., 243–44. 2 vols. CRINT 2.3. Assen: Van Gorcum; Minneapolis: Fortress, 2006.

Gollancz, Hermann, trans. "The History of Sindban and the Seven Wise Masters." *Folklore* 8.2 (1897): 100–130.

Goshen-Gottstein, Alon. *The Sinner and the Amnesiac: The Rabbinic Invention of Elisha ben Abuya and Eleazer ben Arach.* Contraversions. Stanford, CA: Stanford University Press, 2000.

Gra (Elijah of Vilna). *Aderet Eliyahu,* in *Yonah: "Journey of the Soul"; An Allegorical Commentary Adapted from the Vilna Gaon's Aderes Eliyahu.* Edited by Moshe Schapiro. Rahway: Mesorah, 1997.

——— *Be'ure Aggadot: Kamah Aggadot.* Edited by Yosef Eliyahu Movshovitz. Jerusalem: Mossad ha-Rav Kook, 2020.

Gray, Alyssa M. "Intertextuality and Amoraic Literature." In *The Literature of the Sages: A Re-visioning,* edited by Christine Hayes, 217–71. CRINT 16. Leiden: Brill, 2022.

———. *A Talmud in Exile: The Influence of Yerushalmi Avodah Zarah on the Formation of Bavli Avodah Zarah.* BJS 342. Providence, RI: Brown Judaic Studies, 2005.

Green, W.S. "What's in a Name?: The Problematic of Rabbinic 'Biography.'" In *Approaches to Ancient Judaism,* vol. 1, edited by William Scott Green, 77–96. BJS 1. Missoula, MT: Scholars Press, 1978.

Greene, Robin J., ed. and trans. Entry 1680 in *Die Fragmente der Griechischen Historiker,* Part IV, ed. Stefan Schorn. Leiden: Brill, 2018.

Gribetz, Sarit Kattan. "Consuming Texts: Women as Recipients and Transmitters of Ancient Texts." In *Rethinking 'Authority' in Late Antiquity: Authorship, Law, and Transmission in Jewish and Christian Tradition,* edited by A. J. Berkovitz and Mark Letteny, 178–206. Routledge Monographs in Classical Studies. New York: Routledge, 2018.

———. "'Lead Me Forth in Peace': The Origins of the Wayfarer's Prayer and Rabbinic Rituals of Travel in the Roman World." In *Journeys in the Roman East: Imagined and Real,* edited by Maren Niehoff, 297–327.

Culture, Religion, and Politics in the Greco-Roman World 1. Tübingen: Mohr Siebeck, 2017.
Gross, Simcha. "Editorial Material in the Babylonian Talmud and Its Sasanian Context." *AJSR* 47.1 (2023): 51–76.
———. "Rethinking Babylonian Rabbinic Acculturation in the Sasanian Empire." *JAJ* 9 (2018): 280–310.
Grossman, Avraham. *Rashi*. Oxford: Littman Library, 2012.
Grossmark, Tziona. *Travel Narratives in Rabbinic Literature: Voyages to Imaginary Realms*. Lewiston: Mellen, 2010.
Halevi, Yosef Amar, ed. *Talmud Bavli Menuqad 'al pi Masoret Yehudei Teiman*. Vol. 14 of 20. Jerusalem, 1980.
Halevy, E. E.. *Aggadot ha-Amoraim* [Hebrew]. Tel-Aviv: Dvir, 1979.
Halivni, David Weiss. *The Formation of the Babylonian Talmud*. Edited and translated by Jeffrey L. Rubenstein. Oxford: Oxford University Press, 2013.
———. "The Reception Accorded to Rabbi Judah's Mishnah." In *Jewish and Christian Self-Definition*, edited by E. P. Sanders et al., 2:204–212, 379–382. 3 vols. Philadelphia: Fortress, 1981.
———. "Reflections on Classical Jewish Hermeneutics." *PAAJR* 62 (1996): 21–127.
Hamilton, J. R. "The Date of Quintus Curtius Rufus." *Historia* 37.4 (1988): 445–56.
Harkavy, Avraham, ed. *Zikaron la-rishonim ve-gam la-aharonim*. Berlin: Itzkowski, 1886.
Härter, Andreas. *Digressionen: Studien zur Verhältnis von Ordnung und Abweichung in Rhetorik und Poetik*. Munich: Fink, 2000.
Hartman, Joshua, and Helen Kaufmann eds. *A Late Antique Poetics? The Jeweled Style Revisited*. Sera tela. London: Bloomsbury Academic, 2023.
Hasan-Rokem, Galit. "Did Rabbinic Culture Conceive of the Category of Folk Narrative?" *European Journal of Jewish Studies* 3.1 (2009): 19–55.
———. *Tales of the Neighborhood: Jewish Narrative Dialogues in Late Antiquity*. Taubman Lectures in Jewish Studies 4. Berkeley: University of California Press, 2005.
Hasan-Rokem, Galit, and David Shulman. "Afterword." In *Untying the Knot: On Riddles and Other Enigmatic Modes*, edited by Galit Hasan-Rokem and David Shulman, 316–19. New York: Oxford University Press, 2006.
Hauptman, Judith. *The Stories They Tell: Halakhic Anecdotes in the Babylonian Talmud*. Judaism in Context 32. Piscataway, NJ: Gorgias, 2022.
Hayes, Christine Elizabeth. *Between the Babylonian and Palestinian Talmuds: Accounting for Halakhic Difference in Selected Sugyot from Tractate Avodah Zarah*. Oxford: Oxford University Press, 1997.
———. "Intertextuality and Tannaic Literature: A History." In *The Liter-

ature of the Sages: A Re-visioning, edited by Christine Hayes, 95–216. CRINT 16. Leiden: Brill, 2022.

Heinemann, Isaak. *The Methods of Aggadah* [Hebrew]. 2nd ed. Jerusalem: Magnes, 1954.

———. "Die wissenschaftliche Allegoristik des jüdischen Mittelalters." *HUCA* 23.1 (1950–1951): 611–43.

Heinemann, Joseph. "The Messiah of Ephraim and the Premature Exodus of the Tribe of Ephraim." *HTR* 68.1 (1975): 1–15.

Hellner-Eshed, Melila. *A River Flows from Eden: The Language of Mystical Experience in the Zohar.* Translated by Nathan Wolski. Stanford, CA: Stanford University Press, 2009.

Herman, Geoffrey. "'One Day David Went Out for the Hunt of the Falconers': Persian Themes in the Babylonian Talmud." In *Shoshannat Yaakov: Jewish and Iranian Studies in Honor of Yaakov Elman*, edited by Shai Secunda and Steven Fine, 111–36. Brill Reference Library of Judaism 35. Leiden: Brill, 2012.

Herman, Geoffrey, and Jeffrey L. Rubenstein, eds. *The Aggada of the Bavli and Its Cultural World.* BJS 362. Providence, RI: Brown Judaic Studies, 2018.

Hesiod. *Theogony, Works and Days, Testimonia.* Translated by Glenn W. Most. Loeb Classical Library. Cambridge, MA: Harvard University Press, 2006.

Hezser, Catherine. "The (In)significance of Jerusalem in the Talmud Yerushalmi." In *The Talmud Yerushalmi and Graeco-Roman Culture*, vol. 2, edited by Catherine Hezser and Peter Schäfer, 11–49. TSAJ 79. Tübingen: Mohr Siebeck, 2000.

Hidary, Richard. *Rabbis and Classical Rhetoric: Sophistic Education and Oratory in the Talmud and Midrash.* Cambridge: Cambridge University Press, 2018.

Hirshman, Menahem (Marc). "Aggadic Midrash." In *The Literature of the Sages*, edited by Shmuel Safrai et al., 1:107–32. 2 vols., CRINT 2.3 Assen: Van Gorcum; Minneapolis: Fortress, 2006.

———, ed. *Midrash Kohelet Rabbah I–VI.* Jerusalem: Schechter Institute, 2016.

———. "Pesiqta deRav Kahana and Paideia." In *Higayon L'Yonah: New Aspects in the Study of Midrash, Aggadah and Piyyut in Honor of Professor Yona Fraenkel* [Hebrew], edited by Joshua Levinson et al., 165–78. Jerusalem: Magnes, 2006.

———. "Yearning for Intimacy: Pesikta d'Rav Kahana and the Temple." In *Scriptual Exegesis: The Shapes of Culture and the Religious Imagination; Essays in Honour of Michael Fishbane*, edited by Deborah Green and Laura S. Lieber, 135–45. Oxford: Oxford University Press, 2009.

Hoff, Jean Connell, trans. "The Christian Evidence." In *The Trial of the Talmud: Paris, 1240.* Toronto: Pontifical Institute of Medieval Studies, 2012, 102–21.

Holub, Robert. "Reception Theory: School of Constance." In *The Cam-*

bridge History of Literary Criticism, vol. 8: From Formalism to Poststructuralism, edited by Raman Selden, 319–46. Cambridge: Cambridge University Press, 1995.

Honey, Linda Ann. "Thekla: Text and Context." PhD diss., University of Calgary, 2011.

Horovitz, H. S., with I. A. Rabin, eds. Mechilta D'Rabbi Ismael cum variis lectionibus et adnotationibus [Hebrew]. Jerusalem: Wahrmann, 1970.

Humbach, Helmut, and Pallan R. Ichaporian. Zamyād Yasht: Yasht 19 of the Younger Avesta; Text, Translation, Commentary. Wiesbaden: Harrassowitz, 1998.

Hundert, Gershon David. Jews in Poland-Lithuania in the Eighteenth Century: A Genealogy of Modernity. Berkeley: University of California Press, 2004.

Hunter, Richard. Hesiodic Voices: Studies in the Ancient Reception of Hesiod's Works and Days. Cambridge Classical Studies. Cambridge: Cambridge University Press, 2014.

ibn Adoniya, Jacob ben Hayim, ed. Biblia Rabbinica: A Reprint of the 1525 Venice Edition. Jerusalem: Makor, 1972.

ibn Chaviv, Yaakov. Ein Yaakov. Translated by Avraham Yaakov Finkel. Jerusalem: Aronson, 1999.

ibn Verga, Solomon. Liber Schevet Yehudah [Hebrew]. Edited by M. Wiener. Hannover: Lafaire, 1924.

Idel, Moshe. Absorbing Perfections: Kabbalah and Interpretation. New Haven: Yale University Press, 2002.

———. Kabbalah: New Perspectives. New Haven: Yale University Press, 1988.

Ilan, Yaaqov David, ed. Hiddushe ha-Ritva 'al Massekhet Baba Batra. Jerusalem: Mossad Ha-Rav Kook, 2005.

Ilan, Tal. Lexicon of Jewish Names in Late Antiquity. 4 vols. Tübingen: Mohr Siebeck, 2002–2009.

Irshai, Oded. "The Christian Appropriation of Jerusalem in the Fourth Century: The Case of the Bordeaux Pilgrim." JQR 99 (2009): 465-484.

Ish-Shalom, Meir, ed. Pesiqta Rabbati [Hebrew]. Vienna: Self-Published, 1880.

Iser, Wolfgang. "The Reading Process: A Phenomenological Approach." New Literary History 3.2 (1972): 279–99.

Jacob, Christian. "De l'art de compiler à la fabrication du merveilleux: sur la paradoxographie grecque." Lalies 2 (1983): 121-140.

Jacobs, Irving. The Midrashic Process: Tradition and Interpretation in Rabbinic Judaism. Cambridge: Cambridge University Press, 1995.

Jacobs, Jonathan. "Rashbam's Major Principles of Interpretation as Deduced from a Manuscript Fragment Discovered in 1984," REJ 170.3–4 (2011): 443–63.

Jaffee, Irma B., and Gernando Colombardo. "The Flying Gallop: East and West." Art Bulletin 65.2 (1983): 183–201. Accessed 16 July 2024.

Jaffee, Martin S. *Torah in the Mouth: Writing and Oral Tradition in Palestinian Judaism 200 BCE–400 CE*. Oxford: Oxford University Press, 2001.

———. "What Difference Does the 'Orality' of Rabbinic Writings Make for the Interpretation of Rabbinic Writings?" In *How Should Rabbinic Literature Be Read in the Modern World?*, edited by Matthew Kraus, 11–34. Judaism in Context 4. Piscataway, NJ: Gorgias, 2006.

Jakobson, Roman, and Claude Lévi-Strauss. "'Les Chats' de Charles Baudelaire." *L'homme* 2.1 (1962): 5–21.

James, Elaine T. *Landscapes of the Song of Songs: Poetry and Place*. Oxford: Oxford University Press, 2017.

Janni, Pietro. *La mappa e il periplo: Cartografia antica e spazio odologico*. Pubblicazioni della Facoltà di lettere e filosofia 19. Marcerata: Bretschneider, 1984.

Japhet, Sara. *Commentary of Rabbi Samuel ben Meir (Rashbam) on the Song of Songs* [Hebrew]. Jerusalem: ha-'iggud ha-'olami le-mada'ei ha-yahadut, 2008.

Jauss, Hans Robert. "Literary History as a Challenge to Literary Theory," *New Literary History* 2.1 (1970): 7–37.

Johnson, Scott Fitzgerald. *The Life and Miracles of Thekla: A Literary Study*. Hellenic Studies 13. Washington, DC: Center for Hellenic Studies, 2006.

Josephus, Flavius. *Judean Antiquities 1–4*. Translation and commentary by Louis H. Feldman. Flavius Josephus, Translation and Commentary 3. Leiden: Brill, 2000.

———. *Judean Antiquities 5–7*. Translation and commentary by Christopher T. Begg. Flavius Josephus, Translation and Commentary 4. Leiden: Brill, 2005.

Kahan, Kalman, ed. and trans. *Seder Tannaim veAmoraim*. Frankfurt: Hermon, 1935.

Kahana, Menahem. "The Arrangement of the Orders of the Mishnah" [Hebrew]. *Tarbiz* 76.1–2 (2006): 29–40.

———, ed. *Sifre on Numbers: An Annotated Edition*. [Hebrew]. Jerusalem: Magnes, 2011.

Kaldellis, Anthony. "The Historical and Religious Views of Agathias: A Reinterpretation." *Byzantion* 69.1 (1999): 206–52.

Kalmin, Richard. *Jewish Babylonia between Persia and Roman Palestine*. Oxford: Oxford University Press, 2006.

———. *Migrating Tales: The Talmud's Narratives and Their Historical Context*. Oakland: University of California Press, 2014.

———. "The Modern Study of Ancient Rabbinic Literature: Yonah Fraenkel's Darkhei ha'aggada vehamidrash." *Prooftexts* 14.1 (1994): 189–204.

———. "Quotation Forms in the Babylonian Talmud: Authentically Amoraic, or a Later Editorial Construct?" *HUCA* 59 (1988): 167–81.

Kaplan, Jonathan. *My Perfect One: Typology and Early Rabbinic Interpretation of Song of Songs*. Oxford: Oxford University Press, 2015.

Katzoff, Binyamin. "A Story in Three Contexts: The Redaction of a Toseftan Pericope." *AJSR* 38 (2014): 109–27.

Kaufman, Stephen A. *The Akkadian Influences on Aramaic*. Assyriological Studies 19. Chicago: Oriental Institute of the University of Chicago, 1974.

Kermode, Frank. *The Sense of an Ending: Studies in the Theory of Fiction, with a New Epilogue*. 2nd ed. Oxford: Oxford University Press, 2000.

Kessler, Gwynn. *Conceiving Israel: The Fetus in Rabbinic Narratives*. Divinations. Philadelphia: University of Pennsylvania Press, 2009.

Kiel, Yishai. "Redesigning Tzitzit in the Babylonian Talmud in Light of Literary Depictions of the Zoroastrian Kustīg*." In *Shoshannat Yaakov: Jewish and Iranian Studies in Honor of Yaakov Elman*, edited by Shai Secunda and Steven Fine, 185–202. Brill Reference Library of Judaism 35. Leiden: Brill, 2012.

Kiperwasser, Reuven. "Facing Omnipotence and Shaping the Sceptical Topos." In *Expression of Sceptical Topoi in (Late) Antique Judaism*, edited by Reuven Kiperwasser and Geoffrey Herman, 101–23. Studies and Texts in Scepticism 12. Berlin: de Gruyter, 2021.

———. *Going West: Migrating Personae and Construction of the Self in Rabbinic Culture*. BJS 369. Providence: Brown Judaic Studies, 2021.

———. "Narrative Bricolage and Cultural Hybrids in Rabbinic Babylonia: On the Narratives of Seduction and the Topos of Light." In *The Aggada of the Bavli and Its Cultural World*, edited by Geoffrey Herman and Jeffrey L. Rubenstein, 23–45. BJS 362. Providence, RI: Brown Judaic Studies, 2018.

———. "The Travels of Rabbah bar bar Hanah" [Hebrew]. *Jerusalem Studies in Hebrew Folklore* 20 (2008): 215–41.

———. "Sea Voyage Tales in Conversation with the Jonah Story: Intertextuality and the Art of Narrative Bricolage." *Journeys* 20, no. 2 (2019): 39–57.

Kiperwasser, Reuven, and Serge Ruzer. "Aramaic Stories of Wandering in the High Seas of Late Antiquity." In *The Past through Narratology: New Approaches to Late Antiquity and the Early Middle Ages*, edited by Mateusz Fafinski and Jakob Riemenschneider, 161–77. Heidelberg: Heidelberg University Publishing, 2022.

———. "Nautical Fiction of Late Antiquity: Jews and Christians Traveling by Sea." In *Jewish, Christian, and Muslim Travel Experiences: 3rd Century BCE–8th Century CE*, edited by Suzanne Luther, Pieter B. Hartog, and Clare E. Wilde, 295–311. Judaism, Christianity, and Islam – Tension, Transmission, Transformation 16. Berlin: de Gruyter, 2023.

Kiperwasser, Reuven, and Dan D. Y. Shapira. "Encounters between Iranian Myth and Rabbinic Mythmakers in the Babylonian Talmud."

In *Encounters by the Rivers of Babylon: Scholarly Conversations between Jews, Iranians, and Babylonians in Antiquity*, edited by Uri Gabbay and Shai Secunda, 285–304. TSAJ 160. Tübingen: Mohr Siebeck, 2014.

―――― "Irano-Talmudica I: The Three-Legged Ass and Ridyā in B. Ta'anith: Some Observations about Mythic Hydrology in the Babylonian Talmud and in Ancient Iran." *AJSR* 32.1 (2008): 101–16.

――――. "Irano-Talmudica II: Leviathan, Behemoth, and the 'Domestication' of Iranian Mythological Creatures in Eschatological Narratives in the Babylonian Talmud." In *Shoshannat Yaakov: Jewish and Iranian Studies in Honor of Yaakov Elman*, edited by Shai Secunda and Steven Fine, 203–36. Brill Reference Library of Judaism 35. Leiden: Brill, 2012.

――――. "Irano-Talmudica III: Giant Mythological Creatures in Transition from the Avesta to the Babylonian Talmud." In *Orality and Textuality in the Iranian World: Patterns of Interaction across the Centuries*, edited by Julia Rubanovich, 65–92. Jerusalem Studies I Religion and Culture. Leiden: Brill, 2015.

Kirk, David Morrison. *"The Digression : Its Use in Prose Fiction from the Greek Romance through the Eighteenth Century."* PhD diss., Stanford University, 1960.

Kitchen, Robert. "Jonah's Oar: Christian Typology in Jacob of Serug's Mēmrā 122 on Jonah." *Hugoye* 11.1 (2011): 29–62.

Kjær, Sigrid K. "'Rahman' Before Muhammad: A Pre-history of the First Peace (*Sulh*) in Islam." *Modern Asian Studies* 56 (2022): 775–96.

Kohut, Alexander, ed. *Arukh Completum* [Hebrew]. 9 vols. Vienna: Brog, 1878–1937.

Kortekaas, G. A. A., ed. *The Story of Apollonius, King of Tyre: A Study of Its Greek Origin and an Edition of the Two Oldest Latin Recensions*. Mnemosyne 253. Leiden: Brill, 2004.

Kosman, Admiel. "The Story of a Giant Story: The Winding Way of Og King of Bashan in the Jewish Haggadic Tradition." *HUCA* 73 (2002): 157–90.

Kovelman, Arkady. *Between Alexandria and Jerusalem: The Dynamic of Jewish and Hellenistic Culture*. Brill Reference Library of Judaism 21. Leiden: Brill, 2005.

Kraemer, David. "The Intended Reader as a Key to Interpreting the Bavli." *Prooftexts* 13.2 (1993): 125–40.

――――. *Reading the Rabbis: The Talmud as Literature*. Oxford: Oxford University Press, 1996.

Krauss, Samuel, and Immanuel Löw. *Griechische und lateinische Lehnwörter im Talmud, Midrasch und Targum*. 2 vols. Berlin: S. Calvary, 1898–1899.

Kristianpoller, Alexander, ed. and trans. *Traum und Traumdeutung im Talmud*. Wiesbaden: Matrix, 2006.

Kuhn, Peter. *Offenbarungsstimmen im antiken Judentum: Untersuchungen zu Bat Qol und verwandten Phänomenen*. TSAJ 20. Tübingen: Mohr Siebeck, 1989.

Labendz, Jenny R. "The Book of Ben Sira in Rabbinic Literature." *AJSR* 30.2 (2006): 347–92.

Lampurlanés Farré, Isaac. *Excerptum de Talmud: Study and Edition of a Thirteenth-Century Latin Translation*. Turnhout: Brepols, 2020.

Lawee, Eric. *Rashi's Commentary on the Torah: Canonization and Resistance in the Reception of a Jewish Classic*. Oxford: Oxford University Press, 2019.

Lehman, Marjorie. *The En Yaaqov: Jacob ibn Ḥabib's Search for Faith in the Talmudic Corpus*. Detroit: Wayne State University Press, 2012.

Lewin, Benjamin, ed. *Iggeret Rav Sherira Gaon*. Haifa: Itzkowski, 1921.

Lerner, M. B., ed. *Perush Qadum Le-midrash Vayyiqra' Rabbah*. Jersualem: Meqitse nirdamim, 1995.

Lev, Sarra. *And the Sages Did Not Know: Early Rabbinic Approaches to Intersex*. Philadelphia: University of Pennsylvania Press, 2024.

Levine, Lee I. *The Ancient Synagogue: The First Thousand Years*. 2nd ed. New Haven: Yale University Press, 2005.

Levinson, Joshua. "Dialogic Reading in the Rabbinic Exegetical Narrative." *Poetics Today* 25.3 (2004): 497–528.

———. "From Parable to Invention: The Rise of Fiction as a Cultural Category" [Hebrew]. In *Higayon L'Yonah: New Aspects in the Study of Midrash, Aggadah and Piyyut in Honor of Professor Yona Fraenkel*, edited by Joshua Levinson, 1–32. Jerusalem: Magnes, 2006.

———. "The Rabbinic Anti-Hero in the Exegetical Narrative" [Hebrew]. In *Studies in Talmudic and Midrashic Literature*, edited by Mosheh Bar-Asher, Joshua Levinson, and Berachyahu Lifshitz, 217–30. Jerusalem: Mossad Bialik, 2005.

———. "There Is No Place Like Home: Rabbinic Responses to the Christianization of Palestine." In *Jews, Christians, and the Roman Empire: The Poetics of Power in Late Antiquity*, edited by Natalie B. Dohrmann and Annette Yoshiko Reed, 99–120. Jewish Culture and Contexts. Philadelphia: University of Pennsylvania Press, 2013.

———. *The Twice Told Tale: A Poetics of the Exegetical Narrative in Rabbinic Midrash* [Hebrew]. Jerusalem: Magnes, 2005.

Levinson, Joshua, et al., eds. *Higayon L'Yonah: New Aspects in the Study of Midrash, Aggadah and Piyyut in Honor of Professor Yona Fraenkel* [Hebrew]. Jerusalem: Magnes, 2006.

Levy, Jacob, and Heinrich Fleischer. *Neuhebräisches und Chaldäisches Wörterbuch über die Talmudim und Midraschim*. 4 vols. Leipzig: Brockhaus, 1876–1889.

Leyra, Irene Pajón. "Paradoxografía Griega: Estudio de un género litterario." PhD diss., Universidad Complutense Madrid, 2009.

Lieber, Laura. "Theater of the Holy: Performative Elements of Late Ancient Hymnography." *HTR* 108.3 (2015): 327–55.

Lieberman, Saul. *Hellenism in Jewish Palestine: Studies in the Literary Transmission, Belieft and Manners of Palestine in the I century B.C.E.– IV Century C.E.* 2nd ed. Texts and Studies of the Jewish Theological Seminary of America 18. New York: Jewish Theological Seminary, 1962.

———. "How Much Greek in Jewish Palestine?" In *Biblical and Other Studies*. Edited by Alexander Altmann. Cambridge: Harvard University Press, 1963, 123–41.

———. *Shkiin* [Hebrew]. 2nd ed. Jerusalem: Wahrmann, 1970.

———. "Torah Shelemah." *JQR* 36.3 (1946): 317–24.

———. *Tosefta Ki-feshutah: A Comprehensive Commentary on the Tosefta* [Hebrew]. 10 vols. New York: Jewish Theological Seminary, 1955–2001.

Lincoln, Bruce. *Theorizing Myth: Narrative, Ideology, and Scholarship.* Chicago: University of Chicago Press, 1999.

Lindbeck, Kristen. *Elijah and the Rabbis: Story and Theology.* New York: Columbia University Press, 2010.

Lightfoot, Jessica. *Wonder and the Marvellous from Homer to the Hellenistic World.* Cambridge Classical Studies. Cambridge: Cambridge University Press, 2021.

Löw, Immanuel. *Fauna und Mineralien der Juden.* Hildesheim: Olms, 1969.

Lubian, Francesco. "Jeweled Sea Storm Descriptions in Zeno of Verona (and Juvencus)." In *A Late Antique Poetics? The Jeweled Style Revisited,* edited by Joshua Hartmann and Helen Kaufmann, 173–85. Sera tela. London: Bloomsbury Academic, 2023.

Lucian. *A True Story.* Translated by B. P. Reardon. In *Collected Ancient Greek Novels,* edited by B. P. Reardon, 619-49. 2nd ed. Berkeley: University of California Press, 2008.

Lytle, Ephraim. "The Red Sea Aristotle." *JHS* 142 (2022): 100–143.

Maharal. *Hiddushe Aggadot*, 4 vols. Jerusalem: 1972-77

Maharsha. *Sefer hidushe aggadot Maharsha ha-shalem: 'al masekhet Baba kama, Baba Metzi'a, Baba batra.* Jerusalem, 2008.

Maharshal. *Hokhmat Shlomo,* Brno: Neumann, 1796.

Marienberg-Milikowsky, Itay. "'Beyond the Matter': Stories and their Contexts in the Babylonian Talmud: Repeated Stories as a Test Case" [Hebrew]. PhD diss., Ben-Gurion University of the Negev, 2015.

Marincola, John. "Herodotean Narrative and the Narrator's Presence." *Arethusa* 20.1/2 (1987): 121–37.

Matt, Daniel C., ed. and trans. *The Zohar: Pritzker Edition.* 12 vols. Stanford, CA: Stanford University Press, 2004–2018.

Merchavia, Ch. *The Church versus Talmudic and Midrashic Literature* [Hebrew]. Jerusalem: Mossad Bialik, 1970.

Migash, Joseph ibn. *Hiddushe Ha-R. Y. Migash 'Al Massekhet Baba Batra.* Jerusalem: Or Yisrael, n.d.

Mikalson, Jon D. *Herodotus and Religion in the Persian Wars*. Chapel Hill: University of North Carolina Press, 2003.

Miller, Patricia Cox. *Dreams in Late Antiquity: Studies in the Imagination of a Culture*. Princeton, NJ: Princeton University Press, 1999.

Mingana, Alphonse, trans. "The Vision of Theophilus, Or the Book of the Flight of the Holy Family Into Egypt." In *1. Vision of Theophilus, 2. Apocalypse of Peter. Woodbrooke Studies* 3. Cambridge: Heffer & Sons, 1931.

Morgan, Jennifer L. "'Some Could Suckle over Their Shoulder': Male Travelers, Female Bodies, and the Gendering of Racial Ideology, 1500–1770." *William & Mary Quarterly* 54.1 (1997): 167–92.

Moscovitz, Leib. "'Ata' R' Peloni." In *Talmudic Studies III*, edited by Yaakov Sussmann and David Rosenthal, 2:505–18. Jerusalem: Magnes, 2006.

———. *The Terminology of the Yerushalmi: The Principal Terms* [Hebrew]. Jerusalem: Magnes, 2009.

Mowinckel, Sigmund. *He That Cometh: The Messiah Concept in the Old Testament and Later Judaism*. Translated by G. W. Anderson. Grand Rapids: Eerdmans, 2005 [1956].

Mullins, Sylvia Elizabeth. "Myroblytes: Miraculous Oil in Medieval Europe." PhD diss., Georgetown University, 2017.

Naeh, Shlomo. "ποτήριον ἐνχειρὶ κυρίου: Philo and the Rabbis on the Powers of God and the Mixture in the Cup." *Scripta Classica Israelica* 16 (1997): 91–101.

Nagy, Gregory. *The Best of the Achaeans: Concepts of the Hero in Archaic Greek Poetry*. 2nd ed. Baltimore: Johns Hopkins University Press, 1999.

Nahman of Bratslav. *Liqqute Moharan* Translated by Moshe Mykoff and Symcha Bergman. 8 vols. Jerusalem: Breslov Research Institute, 1990–2012.

Naiweld, Ron. *Les antiphilosophes: Pratiques de soi et rapport à la loi dans la littérature rabbinique classique*. Le temps des idées. Paris: Colin, 2011.

———. "There Is Only One Other: The Fabrication of Antoninus in a Multilayered Talmudic Dialogue." *JQR* 104.1 (2014): 81–104.

Naor, Bezalel. *Rabbi Abraham Isaac Hakohen Kook: Commentary to the Legends of Rabbah bar bar Ḥannah*. New York: Kodesh, 2019.

Naveh, Joseph, and Shaul Shaked, eds. *Magical Spells and Formulae: Aramaic Incantations of Late Antiquity*. Jerusalem: Magnes, 1993.

Neuman (Noy), Dov. *Motif-Index of Talmudic-Midrashic Literature*. PhD diss., Indiana University, 1954.

Neusner, Jacob. *Development of a Legend: Studies in the Traditions Concerning Yoḥanan ben Zakkai*. StPB 16. Leiden: Brill, 1970.

———. "How Much Iranian in Talmudic Babylonia?" *History of Religions* 9, no. 3 (1970): 274–305.

Newman, Hillel. "Closing the Circle: Yonah Fraenkel, The Talmudic Story, and Rabbinic History." In *How Should Rabbinic Literature Be Read in*

the Modern World?, edited by Matthew Kraus, 105–35. Judaism in Context 4. Piscataway, NJ: Gorgias, 2006.
Nichols, Andrew, trans. *Ctesias On India and Fragments of His Minor Works.* London: Bristol Classical, 2011.
Nicklas, Tobias, and Janet E. Spittler, eds. *Credible, Incredible: The Miraculous in the Ancient Mediterranean.* WUNT 321. Tübingen: Mohr Siebeck, 2013.
Nikolsky, Ronit, and Tal Ilan, eds. *Rabbinic Traditions between Palestine and Babylonia.* Leiden: Brill, 2014
Ní Mheallaigh, Karen. *The Moon in the Greek and Roman Imagination: Myth, Literature, Science, and Philosophy.* Greek Culture in the Roman World. Cambridge: Cambridge University Press, 2000.
Noam, Vered. "Why Did the Heavenly Voice Speak Aramaic?: Ancient Layers in Rabbinic Literature." In *The Faces of Torah: Studies in the Texts and Contexts of Ancient Judaism in Honor of Steven Fraade*, edited by Michal Bar-Asher Siegal, Tzvi Novick, and Christine Hayes, 157–68. JAJSup 11. Göttingen: Vandenhoeck & Ruprecht, 2017.
Noegel, Scott. "Jonah and Leviathan: Inner-Biblical Allusions and the Problem with Dragons." *Henoch* 37.2 (2015): 236–60.
Oldach, David W., M.D., et al. "A Mysterious Death." *New England Journal of Medicine* 338.24 (1996): 1764–69.
Oppenheimer, Aharon. *Babylonia Judaica in the Talmudic Period.* Beihefte zum Tübinger Atlas des Vorderen Orients B.47. Wiesbaden: Reichert, 1983.
Orlov, Andrei. *Supernal Serpent: Mysteries of Leviathan in Judaism and Christianity.* Oxford: Oxford University Press, 2023.
Ortega Villaro, Begoña. "Some Characteristics of the Works of Agathias: Morality and Satire." *Acta Antiqua* 50.2–3 (2010): 257–87.
Palaephatus. *On Unbelievable Tales.* Translated by Jacob Stern. Wauconda, IL: Bolchazy-Carducci, 1996.
Patai, Raphael. "Lilith." *Journal of American Folklore* 77.306 (1964): 295–314.
Paz, Yakir. "The Torah of the Gospel: A Rabbinic Polemic against the Syro-Roman Lawbook." *HTR* 112.4 (2017): 517–40.
Peters, Rik. "Beyond *ira* and *studium*: Tacitus and the Hellenistic Anxiety about Wonder." In *Tacitus' Wonders: Empire and Paradox in Ancient Rome*, edited by James McNamara and Victoria Emma Pagán, 52–76. London: Bloomsbury Academic, 2022.
Picus, Daniel Max. "Ink Sea, Parchment Sky: Rabbinic Reading Practices in Late Antiquity." PhD diss., Brown University, 2017.
Pomeranz, Jonathan Aaron. "Ordinary Jews in the Babylonian Talmud: Rabbinic Representations and Historical Interpretation." PhD diss., Yale University, 2016.
Poorthuis, Marcel. "Eve's Demonic Offspring: A Jewish Motif in German Literature." In *Eve's Children: The Biblical Stories Retold and Interpreted*

in Jewish and Christian Traditions, edited by Gerard P. Luttikhuizen, 57–74. TBN 5.Leiden: Brill, 2003.
Porter, James I. "Erich Auerbach and the Judaizing of Philology." *Critical Inquiry* 35.1 (2008): 115–47.
———. "Old Testament Realism in the Writings of Erich Auerbach." In *Jews and the Ends of Theory*, edited by Shai Ginsburg, Martin Land, and Jonathan Boyarin, 187–224. New York: Fordham University Press, 2018.
Priscian. *Answers to King Khosroes of Persia*. Translated by Pamela Huby et al. London: Bloomsbury Academic, 2016.
Raabe, Richard. *Die armenische übersetzung der sagenhaften Alexander-biographie*. Leipzig: Hinrichs, 1896.
Rabinovitz, Zvi Meir, ed. *The Liturgical Poems of Rabbi Yannai according to the Triennial Cycle of the Pentateuch and the Holidays* [Hebrew]. Jerusalem: Mossad Bialik, 1985.
Ramban (Nahmanides). *Kitve Rabbenu Moshe ben Nahman*. 2 vols. Edited by Charles Ber Chavel. Jerusalem: Mossad ha-Rav Kook, 1963.
Rappel, Dov. *The Debate over the Pilpul* [Hebrew]. Tel-Aviv: Dvir, 1979.
Rashba. *Commentary on the Legends in the Talmud* [Hebrew]. Edited by Leon A. Feldman. Jerusalem: Mossad Ha-Rav Kook, 1991.
Ravitsky, Aviram. *Aristotelian Logic and Talmudic Methodology: The Application of Aristotelian Logic to the Interpretation of the Thirteen Hermeneutic Principles* [Hebrew]. Jerusalem: Magnes, 2009..
Redfield, James Adam. https://jamesadamredfield.omeka.net (all author's cited work here; accessed September 24, 2024).
———. "Crossing Border Lines: Daniel Boyarin's Life/Work." In *Talmudic Transgressions: Engaging the Work of Daniel Boyarin*, edited by Charlotte Elisheva Fonrobert et al., 541–65. JSJSup 181. Leiden: Brill, 2017.
Redfield, James Adam, and Simcha Gross. "The Making of Rabbinic Pasts: Introduction." *JSQ* 30.4 (2023): 355–66.
Reeg, Gottfried. *Die Ortsnamen Israels nach der rabbinischen Literatur*. Beihefte zum Tübinger Atlas des Vorderen Orients B.51. Wiesbaden: Reichert, 1989.
Reiner, Elhanan. "Temurot bi-yeshivot Polin ve-Ashkenaz be-me'ot ha-טו–ha-י׳ veha-viquah ‚al ha-pilpul." In *Minhag Ashkenaz u-folin*, edited by Yisrael Bartal et al., 9–80. Jerusalem: Shazar Center, 1993.
Ricoeur, Paul. *Freud and Philosophy: An Essay on Interpretation*. Translated by Denis Savage. New Haven: Yale University Press, 1997.
Roberts, Michael. "Epilogue: The Jeweled Style in Context." In *A Late Antique Poetics? The Jeweled Style Revisited*, edited by Joshua Hartmann and Helen Kaufmann, 259–68. Sera tela. London: Bloomsbury Academic, 2023.
Robin, Christian. "The Judaism of the Ancient Kingdom of Himyar in Arabia: A Discreet Conversion." In *Diversity and Rabbinization: Jewish*

Texts and Societies between 400 and 1,000 CE, edited by G. McDowell et al., 165-269. Cambridge Semitic Languages and Cultures 8. Cambridge: Open Book, 2022.

Rollston, Christopher. "Ad Nomen Argumenta: Personal Names as Pejorative Puns in Ancient Texts." In *In the Shadow of Bezalel: Ancient, Biblical, and Near Eastern Studies in Honor of Bezalel Porten*, edited by Alejandro F. Botta, 367-86. CHANE 60. Leiden: Brill, 2013.

Romm, James S. *The Edges of the Earth in Ancient Thought: Geography, Exploration, and Fiction*. Princeton, NJ: Princeton University Press, 1992.

Ronis, Sara. "Imagining the Other: The Magical Arab in Rabbinic Literature." *Prooftexts* 39.1 (2021): 1–28.

Rosen, Ralph M. "The Death of Thersites and the Sympotic Performance of Iambic Mockery." *Pallas* 61 (2003): 121–36.

———. "Poetry and Sailing in Hesiod's *Works and Days*." *ClAnt* 9.1 (1990): 99–113.

Rosen-Zvi, Ishay. "Can the Homilists Cross the Sea Again? Revelation in *Mekilta Shirata*." In *The Significance of Sinai: Traditions about Sinai and Divine Revelation in Judaism and Christianity*, edited by George J. Brooke, Hindy Najman, and Loren T. Stuckenbruck, 217–45. TBN 12. Leiden: Brill Academic, 2008.

———. *Demonic Desires: "Yetzer Hara" and the Problem of Evil in Late Antiquity*. Divinations. Philadelphia: University of Pennsylvania Press, 2011.

———. "Introduction to the Mishnah" [Hebrew]. In *Palestinian Rabbinic Literature: Introductions and Studies*, edited by Menahem Kahana et al., 1–64. Jerusalem: Yad Ben-Zvi, 2018.

———. "Midrash and/as Allegory: The Case of 'Ella.'" *Oqimta* 10 (2024): 187–209.

———. "What Else Is Left to Interpret?: Reflections on Boyarin and What Comes Next." In *Midrash Tannaim: Intertextuality and the Reading of Mekhilta* [Hebrew], edited by Elhanan Reiner, trans. David Louvish and Ruthi Bar-Ilan, 273–86. Jerusalem: Hartman Institute, 2011.

Rosenthal, David. "'Al ha-qitsur ve-hashlamato: Pereq be-'arikhat ha-talmud ha-bavli." In *Talmudic Studies*, edited by Yaakov Sussmann and David Rosenthal, 3.2:791–863. Jerusalem: Magnes, 2005.

Rosenthal, Judah M. "The Talmud on Trial: The Disputation at Paris in the Year 1240." *JQR* 47.2 (1956): 145–69.

Rosenthal, Yoav. "Transpositions: Text and Reality." *AJSR* 41.2 (2017): 333–73.

Roubekas, Nickolas P. *An Ancient Theory of Religion: Euhemerism from Antiquity to the Present*. New York: Routledge, 2017.

Royal, Jeffrey G. "Iconographic Elements on the Warship Rams." In *The Site of the Battle of the Aegates Islands at the End of the First Punic War: Fieldwork, Analyses and Perspectives 2005–2015*, edited by Jeffrey G.

Royal and Sebastiano Tusa, 137–46. Bibliotheca archaeologica 60. Rome: "L'Erma" di Bretschneider, 2020.

Rubenstein, Jeffrey L. "Context and Genre: Elements of a Literary Approach to the Rabbinic Narrative." In *How Should Rabbinic Literature Be Read in the Modern World?*, edited by Matthew Kraus, 137–65. Judaism in Context 4. Piscataway, NJ: Gorgias, 2006.

———. "Coping with the Virtues of the Land of Israel: An Analysis of Bavli Ketubbot 110a–112b" [Hebrew]. In *Center and Diaspora: The Land of Israel and the Diaspora in the Second Temple, Mishna, and Talmud Periods*, edited by Isaiah Gafni, 159–89. Jerusalem: Shazar Center, 2004.

———, ed. *Creation and Composition: The Contribution of the Talmud Redactors (Stammaim) to the Aggadah.* Tübingen: Mohr Siebeck, 2011.

———. "Criteria of Stammaitic Intervention in Aggada." In *Creation and Composition: The Contribution of the Talmud Redactors (Stammaim) to the Aggadah,* edited by Jeffrey L. Rubenstein, 417–40. Tübingen: Mohr Siebeck, 2011.

———. *The Culture of the Babylonian Talmud.* Baltimore: Johns Hopkins University Press, 2003.

———. "An Eschatological Drama: Talmud Avodah Zarah 2a–3b." *AJSR* 21 (1996): 1–37.

———. "From Mythic Motifs to Sustained Myth: The Revision of Rabbinic Traditions in Medieval Midrashim." *HTR* 89 (1996): 131–59.

———. *Rabbinic Stories.* Classics of Western Spirituality. New York: Paulist, 2002.

———. "The Story-Cycles of the Bavli: Part 1." In *Studies in Rabbinic Narratives,* edited by Jeffrey L. Rubenstein, 227–80. BJS 367. Providence: Brown Judaic Studies, 2021.

———. *Talmudic Stories: Narrative Art, Composition, and Culture.* Baltimore: Johns Hopkins University Press, 1999.

Rufus, Quintus Curtius. *History of Alexander* Translated by John C. Rolfe. 2 vols. Loeb Classical Library. Cambridge, MA: Harvard University Press, 1946.

Russell, James R. "Sasanian Yarns: The Problem of the Centaurs Reconsidered." In *La Persia e Bizanzio,* 411–38. Rome: Lincei Academy, 2004.

Sabar, Shalom. "Childbirth and Magic: Jewish Folklore and Material Culture." In *Cultures of the Jews,* edited by David Biale, 671–722. New York: Schocken, 2002.

Salzer, Dorothea M. *Die Magie der Anspielung: Form und Funktion der biblischen Anspielung in den magischen Texten der Kairoer Geniza.* TSAJ 134. Tübingen: Mohr Siebeck, 2010.

Samely, Alexander. *Forms of Rabbinic Literature and Thought: An Introduction.* Oxford: Oxford University Press, 2007.

Saperstein, Marc. *Decoding the Rabbis: A Thirteenth-Century Commentary on the Aggadah*. Harvard Judaic Monographs 3. Cambridge, MA: Harvard University Press, 1980.

Satlow, Michael. *Tasting the Dish: Rabbinic Rhetorics of Sexuality*. 2nd ed. BJS 303. Providence, RI: Brown Judaic Studies, 2020 [1995].

Satlow, Michael, and Michael Sperling. "The Rabbinic Citation Network." *AJSR* 46.2 (2022): 291–319.

Schäfer, Peter. "Handschriften zur Hekhalot-Literatur." In *Hekhalot-Studien*, 154–232. TSAJ 19. Tübingen: Mohr Siebeck, 1988.

Schepens, Guido, and Kris Delcroix. "Ancient Paradoxography: Origin, Production, Evolution, and Reception." In *La letteratura di consumo nel mondo greco-latino: Atti del convegno internazionale*, edited by Oronzo Pecere and Antonio Stramaglia, 373–460. Cassino: Università degli studi di Cassino, 1994.

Schick, Shana Strauch. *Intention in Talmudic Law: Between Thought and Deed*. Brill Reference Library of Judaism 65. Leiden: Brill, 2021.

Schirmann, Jefim, ed. *The Battle between Behemoth and Leviathan according to an Ancient Hebrew Piyyut* [Hebrew]. Jerusalem: Israel Academy of Sciences and Humanities, 1970.

Schneider, Pierre. *L'Éthiopie et l'Inde. Interférences et confusions aux extrémités du monde antique*. Rome: École française de Rome, 2004.

Schofer, Jonathan Wyn. *The Making of a Sage: A Study in Rabbinic Ethics*. Madison: University of Wisconsin Press, 2005.

Scholem, Gershom. *On the Kabbalah and Its Symbolism* Translated by Ralph Manheim. New York: Schocken, 1965.

Schwartz, Marcus Mordecai. *Rewriting the Talmud: The Fourth Century Origins of Bavli Rosh Hashanah*. TSAJ 175. Tübingen: Mohr Siebeck, 2019.

Schwartz, Seth. *Were the Jews a Mediterranean Society?: Reciprocity and Solidarity in Ancient Judaism*. Princeton, NJ: Princeton University Press, 2010.

Secunda, Shai. "Gaze and Counter-Gaze: Textuality and Contextuality in the Anecdote of Rav Assi and the Roman (b. Baba Meṣi'a 28b)," in *The Aggada of the Bavli and Its Cultural World*, edited by Geoffrey Herman and Jeffrey L. Rubenstein, 149–71. BJS 362. Providence, RI: Brown Judaic Studies, 2018.

———. "Reading the Talmud in Iran," *JQR* 100.2 (2010): 310–42

———. "The Talmud of Babylonia," *Oqimta* 10 (2024): 347–77.

———. "Talmudic Text and Iranian Context: On the Development of Two Talmudic Narratives." *AJSR* 35.2 (2011): 193–216.

Sefer 'Aggadata' de-ve Rav: ma'amre R.b.B.H. Bava batra 73–74: 'im be 'ure gedole ha-dorot. Ashdod: Makhon Limmud Aggadah, 2008–2009).

Septimus, Bernard. "Iterated Quotation Formulae in Talmudic Narrative and Exegesis." In *The Idea of Biblical Interpretation: Essays in Honor of James L. Kugel*, edited by Hindy Najman and Judith H. Newman, 371–98. JSJSup 83. Leiden: Brill, 2004.

Septimus, Zvi. "The Poetic Superstructure of the Babylonian Talmud and the Reader It Fashions." PhD diss., University of California, Berkeley, 2011.

———. "Revisiting the Fat Rabbis." In *Talmudic Transgressions: Engaging the Work of Daniel Boyarin*, edited by Charlotte Elisheva Fonrobert et al., 421–56. JSJSup 181. Leiden: Brill, 2017.

———. "Trigger Words and Simultexts: The Experience of Reading the Bavli." In *Wisdom of Bat Sheva: In Memory of Beth Samuels*, edited by Barry S. Wimpfheimer, 163–86. Jersey City, NJ: Ktav, 2009.

Shaked, Gershon. "Ha-yesodot ha-mitiyim be-'Mete Midbar'" [Hebrew]. In *On 'The Dead of the Wilderness' (Metey Midbar): Essays on Bialik's Poem*, edited by Zvi Luz, 43–54. Ramat-Gan: Bar-Ilan University Press, 1988.

Sharon, Ossnat. "Elephant, Leviathan, and Nineveh the Great City: *Sibbuv Rabbi Petahiah* and *Midrash Yonah*, Printed Side by Side" [Hebrew]. In *Jerusalem Studies in Jewish Folklore: In honorem Tamar Alexander*, edited by Galit Hasan-Rokem et al., 30 (2016): 37–73. [Hebrew]

Sharvit, Shimon. *Language and Style of Tractate Avoth through the Ages* [Hebrew]. Beer-Sheva: Ben-Gurion University of the Negev Press, 2006.

Sheq, Yosef, ed. *Siaḥ ha-talmud: 'Otsar ha-miqra, ha-derashah, veha-lashon be-Talmud Bavli*. Bene Beraq: Morashah Qehillat Ya'aqov, 1999–2000.

Sherwin, Byron L. *Mystical Theology and Social Dissent: The Life and Works of Judah Loew of Prague*. Oxford: Littman Library, 2006 [1982].

Shinan, Avigdor, and Yair Zakovitch. *From Gods to God: How the Bible Debunked, Suppressed, or Changed Ancient Myths and Legends*. Translated by Valerie Zakovitch. Lincoln: University of Nebraska Press, 2012 [2004].

Simon-Shoshan, Moshe. *Stories of the Law: Narrative Discourse and the Construction of Authority in the Mishnah*. Oxford: Oxford University Press, 2012.

———. "Talmud as Novel: Dialogic Discourse and the Feminine Voice in the Babylonian Talmud." *Poetics Today* 40.1 (2019): 105–34.

Simpson, St. John. "The Land Behind Ctesiphon: The Archaeology of Babylonia during the Period of the Babylonian Talmud." In *The Archaeology and Material Culture of the Babylonian Talmud*, edited by Markham J. Geller, 6–38. IJS Studies in Judaica 16. Leiden: Brill, 2015.

Slatkin, Laura M. "Measuring Authority, Authoritative Measures: Hesiod's *Works and Days*." In *The Moral Authority of Nature*, edited by Lorraine Daston and Fernando Vidal, 25–49. Chicago: University of Chicago Press, 2004.

Slifkin, Natan. *Sacred Monsters*. Brooklyn, NY: Zoo Torah, 2007.

Smelik, Willem F. "Code-Switching: The Public Reading of the Bible in Hebrew, Aramaic, and Greek." In *Was ist ein Text? Alttestamentliche,* ägyptologische und altorientalistische Perspektiven, edited by Ludwig Morenz and Stefan Schorch, 123–54. BZAW 362. Berlin: de Gruyter, 2007.

———. *Rabbis, Language, and Translation in Late Antiquity.* Cambridge: Cambridge University Press, 2013.

Smith, Jonathan Z. *Drudgery Divine: On the Comparison of Early Christianities and the Religions of Late Antiquity.* Jordan Lectures in Comparative Religion 14. Chicago: University of Chicago Press, 1990.

———. "Earth and Gods." In *Map Is Not Territory: Studies in the History of Religions,* 104–28. SJLA 23. Leiden: Brill, 1978.

Socher, Abe. "The History of Nonsense." *AJSR Perspectives.* Fall 2006: 32–33.

Sokoloff, Michael. *A Syriac Lexicon: A Translation from the Latin; Correction, Expansion, and Update of C. Brockelmann's Lexicon Syriacum.* Winona Lake, IN: Eisenbrauns, 1999.

Sperber, Daniel. "On the Unfortunate Adventures of Rav Kahana: A Passage of Saboraic Polemic from Sasanian Persia." In *Irano-Judaica: Studies Relating to Jewish Contacts with Persian Culture throughout the Ages,* edited by Shaul Shaked, 83–110. Jerusalem: Yad Ben-Zvi, 1982.

Stanislawski, Michael. "The 'Vilna Shas' and East European Jewry." In *Printing the Talmud: From Bomberg to Schottenstein,* edited by Sharon Lieberman Mintz and Gabriel M. Goldstein, 97–102. New York: Yeshiva University Press, 2005.

Stefaniw, Blossom. "Knowledge in Late Antiquity: What Is It Made Of and What Does It Make?" *Studies in Late Antiquity* 2.3 (2018): 266–93.

Stein, Dina. "Believing Is Seeing: A Reading of Baba Batra 73a-75b" [Hebrew]. *Jerusalem Studies in Hebrew Literature* 17 (1999): 1–24.

———. "Let the 'People' Go? The 'Folk' and Their 'Lore' as Tropes in the Reconstruction of Rabbinic Culture." *Prooftexts* 29.2 (2009): 206–41.

———. *Textual Mirrors: Reflexivity, Midrash, and the Rabbinic Self.* Divinations. Philadelphia: University of Pennsylvania Press, 2012.

Stein, Edmund. "Die homiletische Peroratio im Midrasch." *HUCA* 8–9 (1931–1932): 353–71.

Steiner, Deborah. "Nautical Matters: Hesiod's Nautilia and Ibycus Fragment 282 PMG." *CP* 100.4 (2005): 347–55.

Steinmetz, Devora. "Agada Unbound: Inter-Agadic Characterization of Sages in the Talmud and Implications for Reading Agada." In *Creation and Composition: The Contribution of the Bavli Redactors (Stammaim) to the Aggadah,* edited by Jeffrey L. Rubentein, 293–337. TSAJ 114. Tübingen: Mohr Siebeck 2005.

———. "A Portrait of Miriam in Rabbinic Midrash." *Prooftexts* 8.1 (1988): 35–65.

Steinmetz, Mushka. "To Strengthen the Words of the Sages: An Analysis of Rav Elyakum Getz's *Rappeduni Ba-Tappuḥim* and Its Consonance with Seventeenth-Century Polish Rabbinic Thought." M.A. thesis, Touro University Graduate School of Jewish Studies, 2024.

Stemberger, Günter. "Dating Rabbinic Traditions." In *The New Testament and Rabbinic Literature*, edited by Reimund Bieringer et al., 79–96. JSJSup 136. Leiden: Brill, 2010.

———. "Münchhausen und die Apokalyptik: Baba Batra 73a-75b als literarische Einheit." *JSJ* 20.1 (1989): 61–83.

Stern, David. *Jewish Literary Cultures*. 2 vols. University Park: Pennsylvania State University Press, 2015–.

———. *Parables in Midrash: Narrative and Exegesis in Rabbinic Literature*. Cambridge, MA: Harvard University Press, 1994.

Stern, Eliyahu. "The Mitnagdim and the Rabbinic Era as the Age of Reason." In *Time and Eternity in Jewish Mysticism*, edited by Brian Ogren, 136–147. Studies in Jewish History and Culture 48. Leiden: Brill, 2015.

Stern, Gregg. "Philosophic Allegory in Medieval Jewish Culture: The Crisis in Languedoc." In *Interpretation and Allegory: Antiquity to the Modern Period*, edited by Jon Whitman, 189–209. Brill's Studies in Intellectual History 101. Brill: Leiden, 2000.

Sternberg, Meir. *Hebrews between Cultures: Group Portraits and National Literature*. ISBL. Bloomington: Indiana University Press, 1988.

———. *The Poetics of Biblical Narrative: Ideological Literature and the Drama of Reading*. ISBL. Bloomington: Indiana University Press, 1985.

Stoneman, Richard. "The *Alexander Romance* and the Rise of Paradoxography." In *The Alexander Romance: History and Literature*, edited by Richard Stoneman, Krzysztof Nawotka, and Agnieszka Wojciechowska, 49–62. Groningen: Barkhuis, 2018.

———. "Oriental Motifs in the Alexander Romance." *Antichthon* 26 (1992): 95–113.

Stoneman, Richard, Kyle Erickson, and Ian Netton, eds. *The Alexander Romance in Persia and the East*. Ancient Narrative: Supplement 15. Eelde: Barkhuis, 2012.

Stoneman, Richard, and Tristano Gargiulo, eds. *Il Romanzo di Alessandro*. 2 vols. Milan: Mondadori, 2007–2012. (Vol. 3 forthcoming.)

Strack, Hermann L., and Paul Billerbeck. *Kommentar zum Neuen Testament aus Talmud und Midrasch*. 3 vols. Munich: Beck, 1922–1928.

Strassfeld, Max K. *Trans Talmud: Androgynes and Eunuchs in Rabbinic Literature*. Oakland: University of California Press, 2022.

Strassler, Robert B., ed. *The Landmark Herodotus: The Histories*. Translated by Andrea L. Purvis. New York: Pantheon, 2007.

Sussmann, Yaakov. "'Torah shebe-'al peh' peshutah ke-mashma'ah – koho shel qotso shel yod." In *Talmudic Studies*, edited by Yaakov Sussmann and David Rosenthal, 3.1:209–384. Jerusalem: Magnes, 2006.

———. "Ve-shuv li-yerushalmi neziqin." In *Talmudic Studies I* [Hebrew], edited by Yaakov Sussmann and David Rosenthal, 55–133. Jerusalem: Magnes, 1990.

Svedlund, Gerhard. *The Aramaic Portions of the Pesiqta de Rab Kahana: According to MS Marshall Or. 24, the Oldest Known Manuscript of the Pesiqta de Rab Kahana, with English Translation, Commentary and Introduction. Acta Universitatis Upsaliensis: Studia Semitica Upsaliensia 2*. Stockholm: Almqvinst & wiksell, 1974

Ta-Shma, Israel. "Day and Night." In *Encyclopedia Judaica*, edited by Michael Berenbaum et al., 5:486–88. Detroit: Macmillan, 2007.

Tekin, Oğuz. "River-Gods in Cilicia in the Light of Numismatic Evidence." *Varia Anatolica* 13 (1999): 519–51.

Thomas, Rosalind. *Herodotus in Context: Ethnography, Science, and the Art of Persuasion*. Cambridge: Cambridge University Press, 2000.

Thrope, Samuel. "The Alarming Lunch: Judaism, Zoroastrianism and Colonialism in Sassanian Iran." *Journal of the Associated Graduates in Near Eastern Studies* 12.1 (2006): 23–44.

Tishby, Isaiah. *The Wisdom of the Zohar: An Anthology of Texts, trans.* David Goldstein. 3 vols. Littman Library of Jewish Civilization. Oxford: Oxford University Press, 1949.

Touati, Charles. *La pensée philosophique et théologique de Gersonide*. Paris: Gallimard, 1992.

Tov, Emanuel. *Textual Criticism of the Hebrew Bible*. 2nd ed. Minneapolis: Fortress, 2001.

Trachtenberg, Joshua. *Jewish Magic and Superstition: A Study in Folk Religion*. New York: Behrman's, 1939.

Trattner, Kathrin. "Von Lamastu zu Lilith: Personifikationen des weiblichen Bösen in der mesopotamischen und jüdischen Mythologie." *Disputatio Philosophica*, 109–18.

Tropper, Amram. *Like Clay in the Hands of the Potter: Sage Stories in Rabbinic Literature* [Hebrew]. Jerusalem: Shazar Center, 2011.

Turan, Sinai (Tamas). "'Wherever the Sages Set Their Eyes, There Is Either Death or Poverty': On the History, Terminology, and Imagery of the Talmudic Traditions about the Devastating Gaze of the Sages" [Hebrew]. *Sidra* 23 (2008): 137–205.

Twersky, Isadore Isaac. "Yeda'ya Ha-Penini's Commentary on the 'Aggadah" [Hebrew]. In *Studies in Jewish Religious and Intellectual History Presented to Alexander Altmann*, edited by Siegfried Stein and Raphael Loewe, סג-פב. Cambridge, MA: Harvard University Press, 1979.

Tyrell, Eva. *Strategies of Persuasion in Herodotus' Histories and Genesis-Kings: Evoking Reality in Ancient Narratives of a Past*. JSJSup 195. Leiden: Brill, 2020.

Ulrich, Eugene, et al., eds. *Qumran Cave 4.XI: Psalms to Chronicles*. DJD XVI. Oxford: Clarendon, 2000.

Ungar, Eli. "When 'Another Matter' Is the Same Matter: The Case of Davar-Aher in Pesiqta DeRab Kahana." In *Approaches to Ancient Judaism*, edited by Jacob Neusner. 2:1–43. BJS 9. Gainesville: University of South Florida Press, 1978.

Urbach, E. E. *The Sages: Their Concepts and Beliefs*. Translated by I. Abrahams. 2nd ed. Jerusalem: Magnes, 1979.

———, ed. *Sefer Pitron Torah: A Collection of Midrashim and Interpretations* [Hebrew]. Jerusalem: Magnes, 1978.

———. *The World of the Sages: Collected Studies* [Hebrew]. Jerusalem: Magnes, 1988.

———. "Yerushalayim shel matah veyerushalayim shel ma'alah." In *The World of the Sages: Collected Studies*. Jerusalem: Magnes, 1988, 376-91, at 390-91.

Ulmer, Rivka, ed. *A Bilingual Edition of Pesiqta Rabbati. Vol. 1: Chapters 1–22*. Berlin: de Gruyter, 2017.

———. *Egyptian Cultural Icons in Midrash*. SJ 52. Berlin: de Gruyter, 2009.

———, ed. *A Synoptic Edition of Pesiqta Rabbati Based upon All Extant Manuscripts and the Editio Princeps*. 2 vols. Atlanta: Scholars Press, 1999.

Veyne, Paul. *Did the Greeks Believe in Their Myths? An Essay on the Constitutive Imagination*. Translated by Paula Wissig. Chicago: University of Chicago Press, 1988.

Vidas, Moulie. "Greek Wisdom in Babylonia." In *Envisioning Judaism: Studies in Honor of Peter Schäfer on the Occasion of His Seventieth Birthday*, edited by Ra'anan S. Boustan et al., 1:287–305. 2 vols. Tübingen: Mohr Siebeck, 2013.

———. *Tradition and the Formation of the Talmud*. Princeton, NJ: Princeton University Press, 2014.

Vidas, Moulie, and Mira Balberg. "Impure Scholasticism: The Study of Purity Laws and Rabbinic Self-criticism in the Babylonian Talmud." *Prooftexts* 32.3 (2012): 312–56.

Visotzky, Burton L. "The Misnomers 'Petihah' and 'Homiletic Midrash' as Descriptions for Leviticus Rabbah and Pesikta De-Rav Kahana." *JSQ* 18.1 (2011): 19–31.

Vondrovec, Klaus. "Numismatic Evidence of the Alchon Huns Reconsidered." *BUFM* 50 (2008): 25–56.

Wacholder, Ben Zion. *Nicolaus of Damascus*. University of California Publications in History 75. Berkeley: University of California Press, 1962.

Walker, Joel. "The Limits of Late Antiquity: Philosophy between Rome and Iran." *Ancient World* 33.1 (2002): 45–69.

Waller, James Daniel, and Dorota Molin. *The Bible in the Bowls: A Catalogue of Biblical Quotations in Published Jewish Babylonian Aramaic Magic Bowls*. Cambridge Semitic Languages and Cultures. Cambridge: Open Book, 2022.

Wasserman, Mira Beth. *Jews, Gentiles, and Other Animals: The Talmud after the Humanities*. Divinations. Philadelphia: University of Pennsylvania Press, 2017.
Weiss, Avraham. *Studies in the Literature of the Amoraim* [Hebrew]. New York: Yeshiva University Press, 1962.
Weiss, Dov. *Pious Irreverence: Confronting God in Rabbinic Judaism*. Divinations. Philadelphia: University of Pennsylvania Press, 2017.
Weiss, Haim. *All Dreams Follow the Mouth: A Reading in the Talmudic Dreams Tractate* [Hebrew]. Kinneret, Zmora-Bitan: Dvir, 2011. [Hebrew].
———. "Ha-tsitsit shel Rabbah bar bar Hanah: ben ha-Talmud le-Sefer ha-aggadah," *'Odot*, 9/4/17.
Weiss, Haim, and Shira Stav. *The Return of the Absent Father: A New Reading of a Chain of Stories from the Babylonian Talmud*. Translated by Batya Stein. Divinations. Philadelphia: University of Pennsylvania Press, 2022.
West, Martin L. *The East Face of Helicon: West Asiatic Elements in Greek Poetry and Myth*. Oxford: Clarendon, 1997.
Whitman, Jon. *Allegory: The Dynamics of an Ancient and Medieval Technique*. Cambridge: Harvard University Press, 1987.
Wilfand, Yael. "Alexander the Great in the Jerusalem Talmud and Genesis Rabbah: A Critique of Roman Power, Greed, and Cruelty." In *Reconsidering Roman Power*, edited by Katell Berthelot, 337–60. Rome: L'École française de Rome, 2020.
Williams, A. V., trans. *The Pahlavi Rivāyat Accompanying the Dādestān ī Dēnīg*. 2 vols. Historisk-filosofiske meddelelser 60:1–60:2. Copenhagen: Royal Danish Academy, 1990.
Wimmers, Inge Crosman. *Poetics of Reading: Approaches to the Novel*. Princeton, NJ: Princeton University Press, 1988.
Wimpfheimer, Barry Scott. "The Mishnah's Reader: Reconsidering Literary Meaning." *JQR* 113.3 (2023): 335–67.
———. *Narrating the Law: A Poetics of Talmudic Legal Stories*. Diviniations. Philadelphia: University of Pennsylvania Press, 2011.
———. *The Talmud: A Biography*. Princeton, NJ: Princeton University Press, 2018.
Wineman, Aryeh. "The Zohar on Jonah: Radical Retelling or Tradition?" *Hebrew Studies* 31 (1990): 57–69.
Wolfson, Elliot. "The Face of Jacob in the Moon: Mystical Transformations of an Aggadic Myth." In *The Seductiveness of Jewish Myth: Challenge or Response?*, edited by Daniel S. Breslauer, 235–70. Albany: State University of New York Press, 1997.
———. "Images of God's Feet: Some Reflections on the Divine Body in Judaism." In *People of the Body: Jews and Judaism from an Embodied Perspective*, edited by Howard Eilberg-Schwartz, 143–82. SUNY Series,

The Body in Culture, History, and Religion. Albany: State University of New York Press, 1992.

Wollenberg, Rebecca Scharbach. *The Closed Book: How the Rabbis Taught the Jews (Not) to Read the Bible*. Princeton, NJ: Princeton University Press, 2023.

———. "The Dangers of Reading As We Know It: Sight Reading As a Source of Heresy in Early Rabbinic Traditions." *JAAR* 85.3 (2017): 709–45.

Wolohojian, Albert Mugrdich. *The Romance of Alexander the Great by Pseudo-Callisthenes*. Records of Civilization, Sources and Studies 82. New York: Columbia University Press, 1969.

Woytek, Bernhard. "Heads and Busts on Roman Coins: Some Remarks on the Morphology of Numismatic Portraiture." *Revue numismatique* 171.6 (2014): 45–71.

Wünsche, August. "Die Zahlensprüche im Talmud und Midrasch." *ZDMG* 65.1 (1911): 57–100, 395–421; vol. 66.3 (1912): 414–59.

Wynkoop, J. D. "A Peculiar Kind of Paronomasia in the Talmud and Midrash." *The Jewish Quarterly Review* 2, no. 1 (1911): 1–23.

Yadin, Azzan. *Scripture as Logos: Rabbi Ishmael and the Origins of Midrash*. Divinations. Philadelphia: University of Pennsylvania Press, 2004.

———. *Scripture and Tradition: Rabbi Akiva and the Triumph of Midrash*. Divinations. Philadelphia: University of Pennsylvania Press, 2015.

Yahalom, Joseph. "Angels Do Not Understand Aramaic: On the Literary Use of Jewish Palestinian Aramaic in Late Antiquity." *JJS* 47.1 (1996): 33–44.

Yassif, Eli. *The Hebrew Folktale: History, Genre, Meaning*. Translated by Jacqueline S. Teitelbaum. Bloomington: Indiana University Press, 1999.

———. "Humorous Stories in Aggadah: Typology, Theme, Meaning" [Hebrew]. In *Talmudic Studies*, edited by Yaakov Sussmann and David Rosenthal, 403–37. Jerusalem: Magnes, 2005.

Yu, Kenneth W. "Textualizing Wonders: Ancient Greek Paradoxography in Comparative Perspective." In *After Wisdom: Sapiential Traditions and Ancient Scholarship in Comparative Perspective*, edited by Glenn W. Most and Michael Puett, 251–83. Philological Encounters Monographs 4. Leiden: Brill, 2023.

Zank, Michael. "The Rabbinic Epithet *Gevurah*." In *Approaches to Ancient Judaism*, edited by Jacob Neusner, 14:83–169. Atlanta: Scholars Press, 1998.

Zeligman, Israel. *The Treasury of Numbers* [Hebrew]. Baltimore, MS: Schulsinger, 1942.

Zellentin, Holger. "Jewish Dreams between Roman Palestine and Sasanian Babylonia: Cultural and Geographic Borders in Rabbinic Discourse." In *Borders: Terminologies, Identities, Performances*, edited by Annette Weissenrieder, 419–57. WUNT 366. Tübingen: Mohr Siebeck, 2016.

———. "Typology and the Transfiguration of Rabbi Aqiva (*Pesiqta de Rav Kahana* 4:7 and BT Menahot 29b)." *JSQ* 25.3 (2018): 239–68.

Zakeri, Mohsen. "Translations from Greek into Middle Persian as Repatriated Knowledge." In *Why Translate Science? Documents from Antiquity to the 16th Century in the Historical West (Bactria to the Atlantic)*, edited by Dimitri Gutas, 52–169. Leiden: Brill, 2022.

Index of Sources

Genesis		14:20	115	26:13	335n60
1	74n218, 87	14:21	113, 114n347	26:44	384n14
1:6	111n339	14:21–22	108n323		
1:21	60, 74n217,	14:22	111n339	Numbers	
	131n382, 330n1	14:23	111n339	5:21	102n306
5:2	330	14:25	98n293	11	280
6–9	118	14:26–27	108n323	11:1	199n589
9:11	118n358	14:27	111n339	11:31–34	275–76, 279
22:3	292n838	14:29	111n339	11:34	280n801
32:26	326n321	14:29–30	108n323	13:33	67n186
32:33	326n321	15:3	105, 106n318	14:32–37	67
38:9	293n844, 378n8,	15:8	386n29	14:35	64n176
	379n18	15:14	107n321	15:39	379n16
41:1–4	142n428	15:18	304n866, 385n21	16:30–34	331n15
49:9	101n303	15:26	109n329	18:15	91n266
		16:15–16:31	115n350	23:24	100–101
Exodus		17:16	384n18	26:11	29
3	87, 112n345	24:10	108	27:20	336n67
3:2	96n283, 109,	24:10–11	108	31:6	100
	110, 110n336	25:7	335n54	31:8	100, 101n304
3:5	372	28:9	335n54, 335n54		
3:14	95, 97, 107,	28:20	335nn54–55	Deuteronomy	
	108n326, 384n16	28:36	100n299	1:28	67n186
7:17	327n341	28:38	101n302	12:26	91n266
7:20	327n341	33:23	116n353	25:17	380n22
10:17	91n266	34:6	106n318	28:29	91n266
12:39	384n12	34:29	336n69	28:33	91n266
13:17	64n179	35:9	335n54	29:18	379n16
14	111n339, 112n341,	35:27	335n54	32:15	271n780
	116–17	39:6	335n54	32:39	108
14:8	108n323	39:12	335n55	33:21	259n740
14:10	102n309, 112n341	39:13	335n54	34:7	336n69
14:15	112				
14:15–16	102n309	Leviticus		Joshua	
14:16	108n323, 111n339	10:2	110n337	1:8	273n786
14:19	115–16	10:5	110n337	13:2	101n304

421

422 Sources

Joshua (cont.)
24:3   95n280
Judges
5:10   380n23
2 Samuel
21:19   67n186
1 Kings
4:30 (5:10)   31n95
2 Kings
6:1–7   192
6:23   334n41
Isaiah
4:3   232n656,
                    246, 338n83
4:5   231, 232n656,
                    234n664, 246,
                    336n64, 337n76
4:6   233, 334n48,
                    367n1
5:24   97n284
10:12   330n6
11:1   338n80
11:9   331n18
19:17   92n270
23:8   231, 234,
                    334n46, 368n9
24:23   336n69, 385n24
26:2   386n33
27:1   60, 74n213, 77,
                    209n621,
                    330nn4–7
28:1   64
28:3   64
30:10   44n133
30:26   75n221, 336n68
34:4   385n24
41:4   108
43:7   232, 337n79
47:4   385n23
51:9–16   112n340
51:15   112, 113n346
54:9   118n358
54:11   238n676, 337n71
54:12   231, 236,
                    238n676, 335n52,
                    335n56, 368n10,
                    369

60:3   334n51
60:8   247n706,
                    253n728, 254n733
                    338n85, 338n87
Jeremiah
5   87, 104n313,
                    117
5:22   64n175, 95,
                    95nn278–80,
                    117, 120,
                    253n729, 314n24,
                    342n42
12:5   380n23
23:5   338n80
23:6   338n80
31   104n313
31:34 (31:33)   274, 276
31:35 (31:34)   112n344,
                    113n346
Ezekiel
7:16   254n733
20   274, 280
20:35   275, 279
20:35–38   272, 276, 278
20:38   275, 279
28:13   236n668, 337n71,
                    337n73
33:11   379n17
37   65n180
37:16   65n180
38:12   135n402
41:6   339n95
42:15–18   247n708
47:1–6   192
48:35   338n81
Hosea
7:4   384n13
11:9   107n320
12:7 (12:8)   234, 334n45
Amos
8:2   277n793
Obadiah
1:18   110n337
Jonah
1:4   383n9
1:15   106n319

2:1   94n276
2:4   383n3
4:5   253n730
Micah
3:3   31n93, 199,
                    214, 324n272
3:4   215
Zechariah
2:2 (2:6)   338n88
2:4 (2:8)   339n90
2:5 (2:9)   75n219
4   283n810
9:9   378n6
9:14   98
14:10   131n381,
                    246n705, 249n715,
                    252n727, 338n84
Psalms
18:14 (18:15)   98n293
24:2   332n26
38:2 (38:3)   98n291
41:13 (41:14)   386n32
42:7 (42:8)   298n852
                    383n3
42:8   94n276
49:4 (49:5)   261
50:10   67n188, 330n8
50:11   67, 67n188,
                    208, 319n145
65:7 (65:8)   106n319,
74:15–16   112n339
77:18–19   98
91:15   384n15
91:7   382
104   87n258
104:24   265
104:25–26   80n235
104:26   80n237, 331n12
107   87–93, 87n258,
                    92n272, 102,
                    102n309, 112,
                    112n341, 225,
                    302, 304
107:8   102n309
107:15   102n309
107:16   102n309
107:21   90n263, 102n309
107:21–31   89

107:22–30	90n263	40:16	331n10	**OLD TESTAMENT**	
107:23	90, 298, 298n852	40:19	333n34	**PSEUDEPIGRAPHA/**	
107:23–26	298–300,	40:23	332n22, 332n24	**APOCRYPHA AND**	
	299n856, 304	41:1 (40:25)	333n33	**SEPTUAGINT**	
107:23–30	88	41:5 (40:29)	334n50		
107:24	94n276, 298	41:6a (40:30a)	230, 233,	1 Enoch	
107:25	102n309, 299,		333n40, 367n5	20:7	76n223
	299n856	41:6b (40:30b)	230,		
107:25–27	90		334n43, 368n7	Septuagint	
107:26	88, 299n856, 381	41:7a (40:30a)	233	*Exodus*	
107:27	92nn271–72,	41:7a (40:31a)	74n215,	28:9	335n54
	94n275, 95n279,		231, 334n47,	28:20	335nn54–55
	262n752		337n71, 367n2		
107:28	90–91, 91n268	41:7b (40:30)	334n48	*Isaiah*	
107:29	90n263	41:7b (40:31b)	231, 233,	54:12	236n669
107:30	87n258		233n661,		
107:31	90, 102n309		367n3	*Ezekiel*	
107:40	102n309	41:15a (41:7a)	74	28:13	337n71
107:43	102n309	41:18 (41:10)	79, 328n368		
109:24	153n458	41:31 (41:23)	95n278	*Zechariah*	
114	114, 117	41:31a (41:23a)	333n35	14:10	246n705
114:3	114	41:31b (41:23b)	326n32,		
114:5	114		333n36	**TALMUDIC SOURCES**	
114:7–8	114	41:32a (41:24a)	333n37		
144:12	336n62	41:32b (41:24b)	333n38	Mishnah	
149:6–7	378	42:5	75n218	m. Berakhot	
150:6	385n20			1:5	337n72
		Song of Songs			
Proverbs		2:4	92n270	m. Demai	
1:9	334n49	8:13	334n42	1:1	33n104
1:20	273, 280, 282				
5:3–4	383nn8–9	Lamentations		m. Terumot	
5:5	383n10	2:1	254n733	1:8	153n458
23:5	258n738				
		Ecclesiastes		m. Shabbat	
Job		8:1	236n668	2:6	293n842
1:15	187n542				
3:13	98n290	Esther		m. Yoma	
5:13	92n272	1:42	298n852	3:10	102n306
7:5	331n16			5:6	251n725
10:22	386n30	Daniel			
26:12	331n17	7:9–10	108	m. Rosh Hashanah	
34:11	294n846, 378,	11:40	377n3	2:8	102n309
	381			3:8	101n304
38:4	74n218	Nehemiah			
38:8	115n352	9:11	94n276	m. Bava Batra	
38:8–11	95n278			5:1	128
38:10	95n281	1 Chronicles			
39:9	61n163	7:22	65n180	m. Sanhedrin	
40–41	77, 77n226	20:5	67n186	10:1	109n329
		29:1	339n92		

Sources 423

424   Sources

m. Avot		52b	109n333	54b	380n23
1:17	275–76, 279, 279n800	53b	30n91, 35nn116–17, 174n498, 217n636	55b	32n100, 33n106, 250n721
2:8	291n835, 294n844, 378n12	54b	33n106	63a	246n703, 252n726
		55a–57b	276, 277n792		
2:10	235	56a	277n792	b. Pesahim	
3:1	302n860	56b	291n832, 378n6	50a	248n711
3:4	293n843	56b–57a	378n7	51a	33n102
5:4–5	196n574	57a	273, 276, 291n832	53b	250n722
5:6	196n574	57b	150n448	54a	196n574
5:21	333n39	60a	337n74	68a	385n24
		75a	337n74	94a	5n7
m. Middot				94b	31n93, 135n402, 266n763
3:2	251n725f	b. Shabbat		115a	245n700
		12a	379, 380n21	117a	66n185
Tosefta		21a	34n109, 36n122		
t. Eruvin		22a	250n719	b. Yoma	
2:3	334n48	30b	66n185, 129	7b	100n297
		31b–32a	293n842	9b	30n90, 32n97
t. Pisha		32a	270n776, 291n834, 294n846, 381, 381n26	20a	250n721
3:20	234n665			20b	32n100, 33n105
		33b	247n707, 251n723	21b	109n329, 110, 110n337
t. Sotah		45b	248n711		
11:16	246n705	51b	198n585	38a	106n319
		60b	32n99, 33n102	39b	32n100, 33n105, 250n721
t. Qiddushin		67a	96n283		
5:17	31n93	82a	250n720	57a	143n432
		85a	31n95	75a	261n747
t. Avodah Zarah		90b	150n448	75b	33n106, 250n721, 274, 274n787, 276, 282, 282n806
7:7	271n776	105b	95n280		
		109a	380n21		
t. Hullin		109b	100n296	84a	96n283, 319n149
4:13	74	115b–116a	90n263	86b	282, 377n4
		116a	90n263		
Babylonian Talmud		119b	386n33	b. Sukkah	
b. Berakhot		127b	380n22	21b	265
3a	63n173, 235, 235nn666–67	141b	248n711	26b–27a	48n140
		145b	36n122	53a	83n243
5a	291n836, 378n9	147a	258n738		
8b	66n185	147a–148a	32n98	b. Betzah	
9b	108n326, 384n17	148a	32n98, 258n738	32b	290n830, 379n15
17a	384n11	151b	288n820		
24b	337n74			b. Rosh Hashanah	
28b	173n496	b. Eruvin		16a	90, 102n309
30b	143n432	6b	143n432	16a–17b	90
39a	243n693	10b	334n48	16b	90
40b	33n104	18b	288n820, 385n20	17a	379n15, 380n20
43a	248n711	21b	243n693	17b	90–91, 90n264, 91n268
44a	34n110	30a	34n110, 235n666		
44b	133n392				

Sources   425

18a	90, 102n309
26a	172n491
26b	30n89, 36n119

b. Ta'anit

10a	150n448
20b	270n776
22b	30n88, 199n588
23b	143n432
24b	228n642
25a	98, 274, 282n806, 284, 302n859
25b	174n498

b. Megillah

2a–2b	338n89
6a	32n100, 33n108, 250n721
18a	30n89, 36n119, 172n491
28b	120n360, 143n431

b. Hagigah

11b	198n583
25b	248n711

b. Yevamot

60b	101n302
120b	30n87, 81n239, 153n458, 250n720
121a	383n2

b. Ketubbot

5b	261n748
72b	30n86, 37n123
75a	29n85
111a	34n109
111b	33n108, 250n719, 250n721
111b–112a	36n121
112a	33–34n108

b. Nedarim

20a–b	382n31
20b	379n13, 379n16, 382
81a	28n77

b. Sotah

13a	192n560

47b	63n173
48a	273
49a	385n26
58a	250n719

b. Gittin

4a	33n107, 33n108, 36n121
17a	32n101, 33n103
21b	35n116
57a	143n436, 250n719
68a	142n428, 199n589
68b–70a	127n373
79a	246n703

b. Qiddushin

12a	134n399
13a	61n163
71a	248n711
81a	291n834, 383n7
82a	291n832, 299n854, 378n5

b. Bava Qamma

17b	66n185
21a	250n719
84b	274n787
92b	28n77, 162n472
114a	248n711
117a	250n722

b. Bava Metzi'a

36b	378n11
42a	378n11
59b	106n319, 173n494, 192n557
68a	170n479
84b	150n448
85b	250n719
86a	106n319, 142n428, 291n834
110a	248n711

b. Bava Batra

6a	372n3, 324–25n278
9b	66n185
16a	298n852, 383n6
16b	31n93
32b	153n458

52a	33n103
65b	128n376
67b	128n376
73a	100n297, 313n1
73a–74b	103n312
74b	131n381, 173n493
74b–75a	130n379
74b–75b	330–39
75a	130n379, 131n381
75a–b	251n723
75b	131n381, 251n723
77b	128n375
78a	128n376
78b	127, 128n375
78b–79a	127
88b	127
88b–89a	127
90b	126n370
90b–91b	126n370

b. Sanhedrin

11a	143n436
12b	100n297
17b	239n681
24a	283n810
29b	66n185
38b	110n337
39a	83n241, 195n572, 286n815, 289n825
65b	334n42
67b	30n87, 250n719, 262n752
91b	385n24
92b	65n180
93b	109n330
95a	162n472
96a	380n23
100a	229n647, 231, 251n723, 252n726, 257n736, 335n57
110a–b	29n82
100b	28n77
106a	100n300
108b	288n820
109b	36n120
110a	323n250
110b	64n176

b. Makkot

11a	248n711

Sources

b. Avodah Zarah	
17a	385n24
19b	265
20b	383n9
26a	143n436

b. Horayot	
12a	133n392

b. Zevahim	
12b	248n711
113b	29n81, 61n163

b. Menahot	
29b	91n265
41a	244n697
41b	217n636, 244n697

b. Hullin	
18a	246n703
22b	319n150
28b	248n711
49a	273
55b	31n94
60b	333n32
105a	28n79
106a	34n110
106b	258n738
122a	143n432
126a	143n432

b. Bekhorot	
8b	66n185
55a	332n20
57b	193n562, 263n756

b. Tamid	
32a	198
32b	198n584

b. Niddah	
14a	291n832, 378nn6–7
20b	143n432
24b	83n242, 288n820
27a	34n111
27b	248n711
30b	98n292
61b	246n703
71a	293n841

Palestinian Talmud

y. Berakhot	
1:1 2c	150n448
2:3 4d	239n681
4:2 7d	384n11
8:5 12b	35n113
9:5 14b	239n681
9:5 14c	273n786

y. Pe'ah	
1:1 15c	239n681
1:1 16a	36n118

y. Kil'ayim	
9:4 32c	229n648

y. Ma'aserot	
3:8 50d	28n79

y. Ma'aser Sheni	
3:6 54b	248, 248n712

y. Shabbat	
8:1 11a	239n681

y. Eruvin	
2:1 20a	115n35

y. Pesahim	
10:1 37c	239n681

y. Sheqalim	
6:2 49d	109n332

y. Yoma	
3:8 40d	102n305
3:10 41a	102n306

y. Sukkah	
5:5 55c	334n48

y. Ta'anit	
4:3 68b	111n339

y. Megillah	
2:1 73a	239n681
2:2 73a	30n89

y. Hagigah	
1:8 76d	239n681

y. Yevamot	
16:6 15d	35n115

y. Sotah	
5:5 20c	239n681
8:1 22d	109n332

y. Gittin	
3:3 44d	35n115

y. Qiddushin	
1:7 61b	239n681
4:4 65d	248n710

y. Bava Metzi'a	
2:4 8c	198n581

y. Sanhedrin	
10:2 29a	101n304

MEDIEVAL AND EARLY MODERN COMMENTATORS

Sherira and Hayya (Hai) Gaon
b. Bava Batra
74a s.v. אמר לי תא אחוי לך היכא דנשקי ארעא ורקיעא אהדדי (ed. Brody, *Otsar ha-Geonim he-Hadash* 290–91)   371nn2–3, 372n5

Rif
b. Bava Batra
73b, s.v. עתידין ישראל ליתן עליהם את הדין   31n92

Responsa
§314   135n402

Rashi (Bible commentary)
Genesis
21:16   92n270

Exodus
14:15   112n341
15:8   95n278

Sources

15:10	94n276	49a s.v. סדרים	386n31	73a s.v. שמעין בי מלכא	
17:16	384n19			וקטלוהו	290n826
Numbers		*b. Qiddushin*		73a s.v. הורמיז	269n772,
31:8	101n304	82a s.v. הספנין רובן חסידים			286n815
			299n854	73a s.v. ונחרביה	118n358
Isaiah		*b. Bava Metzi'a*		73a s.v. וניח	106n319,
19:17	92n270	32b s.v. משום צערא דישראל			253n730
27:1	330nn4–5		271n777	73a s.v. ורמא ליה גלא	
					298n852
Job		*b. Sanhedrin*		73a s.v. סריגן	291n833
26:12	331n16	39a s.v. דהורמיז	286n815	73a s.v. צוציתא דנורא חיורתא	
		100a s.v. שמשותיך	369n15		269n772,
Song of Songs		110a s.v. בלועי	323n250		298n852
2:4	92n270			73a s.v. שנאמר האותי	
		b. Avodah Zarah			143n433
Rashi (Talmud		32b s.v. א"ל גמרא גמור זמורתא		73b s.v. איהו בזקיפא	4n4
commentary)		תהא	281n803	73b s.v. באוסיה	80n235
b. Berakhot				73b s.v. ואקרא דהגרוניא	
44a, s.v. זיונא	34n110	*b. Zevahim*			167n473
44a, s.v. מזונא	34n110	113b, s.v. אורזילא	61n163,	73b s.v. פשקנצא	260n742
			330n3	74a s.v. דבחישא	153n458
b. Shabbat		113b, s.v. בר יומא	61n163	74a s.v. היכא דנשקי ארעא	
12a s.v. בני מחוזא				ורקיעא	9n17, 135n402
	290n831, 379n14	*b. Hullin*		74a s.v. למאי הלכתא	
32a s.v. כעין גשר	293n843	90b, s.v. גוזמא	266n763		244n697
77b s.v. כילבית	80n235	90b, s.v. שלוש מאות כהנים		75a s.v. כדין וכדין	236n670
90b s.v. שיתין	150n448		266n763	75a s.v. סוכה	334n48
109a s.v. מפנקי	290n831,				
	379n14	*b. Niddah*		ibn Ezra	
		14a s.v. דמכף	290n832,	*Exodus*	
b. Pesahim			378n7, 380n25	14:15	112n341
50a s.v. ואיתנגיד	98n290	24b s.v. דמות לילית			
			289n825	Tosafot	
b. Yoma				*b. Megillah*	
75b s.v. ותחתונה אינה נאכלת		Rabbenu Hananel		21a s.v. אלמלא	77n228
	274n787	*b. Rosh Hashanah*			
		17b	91n266	*b. Bava Qamma*	
b. Rosh Hashanah				92b, s.v. שיתין רהוטי רהוט	
17a s.v. בני מחוזא	290n831,	Rashbam			150n448
	379n14	*b. Bava Batra*			
		73a s.v. אמר רבא אשתעי		*b. Bava Batra*	
b. Ketubbot			77n226, 265	8a s.v. איפרא	286n815
62a s.v. מפנקי דמערבא			265n761	73b s.v. הכי גרסי' אורזילא בר	
	290n831, 379n15	73a s.v. אקופי דשורא		ראימא דהוי כי הר תבור	
111a s.v. דבירם בגו			269n772, 293n843		61n163, 62n165
	275n788	73a s.v. ביזרא	120n360	73b s.v. ודמו כמאן דמיבסמי	
		73a s.v. דכוכבא זוטא			64n176
b. Sotah			160n466	74a s.v. ועכשיו	260n745
49a s.v. אקדושא דסדרא		73a s.v. דלינן גלא		74a s.v. פסקי חדא קרנא דתכלתא	
	386n29		266n763, 341n13		244n697

Sources

b. Sanhedrin
5a s.v. רבה בר חנה   28n78
39a s.v. דהורמיז   286n815

b. Avodah Zarah
17a s.v. עד   298n852

b. Hullin
6a s.v. אשכחי ההוא סבא   247n707

Ritva
b. Bava Batra
73a s.v. אמר רבה אשתעו לי נחותי ימא   277n792
73a s.v. בין גלא לגלא ארבע מאה פרסי   5n8
73a s.v. הורמיז בר ליליתא   290n826
73a s.v. הורמין   286n815
73b s.v. אווזי דשמטי גדפייהו משומנייהו   272n781
74a–b s.v. אבן טבא   277n793
74a–b s.v. עובדא דקרטליתא   277n793

Gersonides (Ralbag)
Milhamot ha-shem
209a–212b   259n740

Maharshal
b. Bava Batra
73a s.v. כל אבא חמרא   28n79

Maharal
Netsah Yisrael
VI.6   150n448

Hiddushe Aggadot
3:101   372n3

Maharsha
b. Sotah
48a s.v. בטיל   273n785

b. Bava Metzi'a
85a s.v. דלשתכח תלמוד בבלאה מיניה   283n809

b. Bava Batra
73a s.v. אישתעו לי נחותי ימא האי גלא   275n788, 383n2
73a s.v. הורמיז   269n772
73a s.v. לדידי   291n834
73a s.v. לדידי חזי לי הורמין בר לילותא   377n3

Gra (Vilna Gaon)
Aderet Eliyahu
86, s.v. וימצא אניה   299n856, 383n5
87, s.v. הטיל רוח גדולה   383n6, 383n9

Be'ure Aggadot
1   297–98, 297n849, 298n850, 298n852
1–3   383n1
2–3   299n853
3   384n19, 385n25
5   298n852
8   299n856
11–14   298n850
17   299n856
18   274n786
23   299n856
25   372n3
87   383n2
317   98n852

Joel ben Samuel Sirkis (BaH)
Isaiah
4:5   246n704

KABBALISTIC WORKS

Zohar

Va-yeshev
1:181b   385n27

Va-yehi
1:216b   382n34
1:244a   303n861

Yitro
2:84b   111n33

Pequdei
2:242b   382n33

Ra'aya Mehemna
Pinhas
216a   263n756

OTHER RABBINIC WORKS

Pesiqta of Rab Kahana
1:3   109n333, 236n669
1:7   109n333
3:11   384n13
3:16   384–85n19
4:3   245n700
4:4   236n668
8:2   102n309
9:1   198n581
11:19   28n79
11:10   64n179
11:12   102n307
11:22   247n707, 251n723
16:11   384n13
18:5   231, 236n671, 237n673, 247n707, 251n723
19:6   112, 112n344sha
20:7   246n705
Supplement 2   74n213, 75n220

Pesiqta Rabbati
14:33–36   236n668
21   236n669
32:8–10   369n14

Kallah Rabbati
2:7   288n820, 378n8

Sifre Deuteronomy
306   95n281

Soferim
6:1   90n263

MIDRASHIM

Mekhilta of Rabbi Ishmael
§*Pisha*
14   116n356

§*Beshallah*
1   102n307, 108n327, 116n356, 232n654

Sources

3	98n293, 102n309	II:5.8 (ed. Shinan)		§Balaq	
4	104n313, 112n341,		110, 110n335	23	100, 100n298
	116n355, 343n42	21:6	115n352		
5	95n278, 113–14,			§Mattot	
	114n347, 343n42	Vayyiqra (Leviticus) Rabbah		4	100n300, 100n304
6	98n293, 254n733	13:3	74n216		
7	98n293, 111n339	19:5	298n852	§Ki Tetse'	
		22:10	36n118, 67n188,	18	385n19
§Shirata			236n670		
4	106–8, 106nn317–18,	25:5	239n681	§Nitsavim	
	107n320, 108n324,	27:1	198n581	4	74n213
	384n17	32:4	112n343		
5	94n276	35:4	92n270	Tanhuma-Yelammedenu	
		32:8	385n23	§Bereshit	
§Vayassa				1:1	109n332
4	283n807	Bamidbar (Numbers) Rabbah		26	288n820
		18:20	29n82, 36n120		
§Amalek		20:20	100, 100n298	§Vayyishlah	
2	385n19			2:7	199n589
		Shir Hashirim (Song of			
§Bahodesh		Songs) Rabbah		§Shemot	
4	109n332	1:4	77n226	15:1	110n337
		1:6	77n226		
Mekhilta of Rabbi Shimon				§Terumah	
ben Yochai		Ruth (Ruth) Rabbah		11	110n337
XXV.3 (to Ex. 14:25)		6:1	288n820		
	98n293			Pirqe de-Rabbi Eliezer	
		Eikhah (Lamentations)		3	385n22
Midrash Rabbah		Rabbah		4	94n275
Bereshit (Genesis) Rabbah		33	64n176	9	80n237, 209n621
5:2	95n278			10	80nn236–37
7:1	245n700	Qoheleth (Ecclesiastes)			
7:4	74n217	Rabbah		Midrash Psalms	
19:4	36n118, 67n188	3:11	102n305	9:10	385n19
20:11	288n820	10.1.2	36n118	87:2	369n14
24:5	288n820			93:6	191n556
26:4	288n820	Tanhuma		120:4	36n118
33:1	198n581	§Bereshit			
36:1	37n124	26	288n820	**BIBLICAL VERSIONS**	
59:4	97n284			**(TARGUMIC TEXTS)**	
64:10	242n691	§Shemot			
74:3	208n619	18	98n293	Targum Onqelos	
77:2	110n337			Genesis	
79:7	30n89, 36n119,	§Tsav		28:12	318n130
	172n491	7	386n32		
80:8	93n274			Exodus	
87:1	37n124	§'Emor		15:8	95n278
98:19	36n118	9	198n581		
				Targum Pseudo Jonathan	
Shemot (Exodus) Rabbah		§Qorah		Genesis	
I.34.1 (ed. Shinan)		27	29n82, 36n120	1:21	74n217, 131n381
	298n852				

Sources

Exodus
15:8   95n278

Leviticus
19:17   44n133

Numbers
21:35   33n106

*Targum Jonathan
Jeremiah*
5:22   95n278

Jonah
1:15   173n494, 253n730
2:1   80n236
2:4   298n852

*Targum Neofiti
Exodus*
15:4   98n293
15:18   95n282
19:13   98n293

Targum Psalms
33:7   95n278
50:11   193n562
78:13   95n278
107:23   88, 313n3
104:25–27   95n279

Targum Proverbs
5:3   44n133
6:24   44n133
7:5   44n133

Targum Job
39:13   193n562

Targum 2 Chronicles
23:11   101n301

DEAD SEA SCROLLS

4QPs^f (4Q88)   90n263

4Q554
col. III:20–21   247n708

4Q554a
Frag. 2 II:16   247n708

CD
I:18   44n133

CLASSICAL SOURCES

Homer
Odyssey
9.410   164

Hesiod
Works and Days (Op.)
646   125

Herodotus
Historiae (Histories)
1.78   142n428
2.2–5   192n559
2.28–29   189–90
3.23   204n605
3.106   33n108
7.34   97n284
7.54   201n592

Aristotle
Poetics
39n129   7.1450b
39n129   10.1452a
39n129   13.1453a
18.1455b   39n129

Pseudo-Aristotle
Of Marvelous Things Heard
29   204n609
12   203n602

Cicero
De Oratore
2.253, 28n80

Diodorus Siculus
Library of History
17.31.4   202n598
17.17.2   201n592

Strabo
Geography
14.5   203n601
15.1.28   212n624

Philo
Life of Moses
2.36   102n308

Valerius Maximus
Memorable Doings and Sayings
3.8 ext. 6   202n596

Pliny the Elder
Naturalis historia
13.8   203n601

Quintus Curtius Rufus
History of Alexander
I:93–95   202, 202n600

Josephus
Antiquities
2.347–48   201n592
7.12.2   67n186

Valerius Flaccus
Argonautica
8.67   97n288

Plutarch
Life of Alexander
19   202n595
46   212n625

Arrian
Anabasis
1.11.6   201n592
2.4.7–8   202n595
2.4.7–11   202n599

Lucian
De Domo
1   202n595

Vera historia (A True Story)
2.31   214, 214n629

Aulus Gellius
Attic Nights
9.4.1–5   213n626

Oppian
Halieutica
I.180–190.   4n4

Justin
Epitome of the Philippic History of Pompeius Trogus
11.8.3–4   202n595

Sources 431

Solinus
Polyhistor
30.11   204, 204n608
56.14   195n572

Iulius Valerius
Res Gestae Alexandri Macedonis
                 201, 201n594

Anonymous
The Story of Apollonius, King of Tyre
XI.16   137n407

Alexander Romance
I.42.11 (β/γ)   201n593
II.8.1–2 (α/Pseudo-
Callisthenes)   200

Photius
Bibliothēkē
72   203n603

Anonymous
Paradoxographus Florentinus
5–   , 204n604

Paradoxographus Vaticanus
3   203n602

ANCIENT NEAR EASTERN SOURCES

Bundahišn
24.II.8–9   39n127

Gilgamesh
IX.38–45   199n588

NEW TESTAMENT

Matthew
13:1–32   120n360

Mark
4:30–32   120n360

Luke
13:18–19   120n360

John
20:29   241n688

Revelation
13:1   130n379
16:4   327n341
21:16   247n708
21:19   236n669
21:21   237n672

Index of Subjects

Acts of Thomas, 72
adze, 191–92, 206
Agathias, 177–78
aggadah, 66, 126–27, 129, 257, 261–63, 304–5, 386
Ahriman, 104
Alexander Romance. *See under* Greek wonder writing
Alexander the Great, 197–205
allegory, 8, 10, 12–13, 209, 259–305, 309
Amoraim, 19, 24, 55, 59–62, 90, 125, 143, 171–75, 211, 226, 236, 247–48
angels, 74, 76, 115–16, 120, 192, 221, 236, 238, 240, 249, 335, 338, 382–83
Arabs, 29–31, 35–36, 148, 160–64, 187–88, 214–15, 320–21, 372, 374
Aramaic, 44, 62, 74, 130–31, 173, 239–41
  use of vs. Hebrew, 130n380, 130–31n381, 240, 346n125, 350n224, 360n469, 363n521
Ari (Isaac Luria), 288–89, 378, 382. *See also* kabbalah; Zohar
Aristoboulos, 202
ass:
  jackass: 28, 127, 169, 200, 217–18, 235, 244, 322–23
  Libyan/white: 198–99
attributions, 26, 51, 88, 123, 138–48, 166
audience, 7–8, 16–17, 20, 86, 125, 149, 160, 165, 168–70, 189, 210–12
Auerbach, Erich, 193, 213
Aulus Gellius, 213
authority:
  scholastic vs. visionary, 63, 176, 223, 226, 228–30, 243–44, 249–50, 252, 255. *See also* "Come See!";

"If I hadn't been there/seen it, I wouldn't have believed it"; "I myself have seen"
  sources of, 163, 189–90, 211, 213–19, 221–23, 308
  See also teller, authority of
autopsy (claim of firsthand knowledge), 189–90, 194, 196, 213, 215–16, 228

Behemoth, 61, 77, 233, 266, 330–32
Ben-Amos, Dan, 65–67
Bible, 50, 54–55, 86, 90, 208–9, 278, 280–81
bird, giant, 67–68, 72, 79, 137, 142, 169–70, 190, 192–93, 206–9, 267–68, 316, 318, 327, 374. See also ziz
bones, 221, 238, 240, 308, 335, 369
  finger, 98–99, 110
  fish, 78, 146–47, 317
  giant, 63–65, 185, 217–18
Boyarin, Daniel, 17, 96, 104, 209
bridges, 92, 136, 150, 201, 291–94, 296, 315, 377, 381
Bundahišn, 38, 71. *See also* Zoroastrianism
Burning Bush, 88, 95, 104, 109–11, 120, 138. *See also* Red Sea, parting of

canon, 14, 17, 47–56, 82, 164, 222, 225–27, 256–58, 259–305, 308–10. *See also* plural canonicity
Cassuto, Umberto, 73
catchphrases, 78, 220–21, 226–27, 229–30, 241–58
chiastic structure, 77, 207

Subjects

Christianity, 8, 181, 212, 260, 263
   Syriac, 72, 182
chronological layers of the tales, 166–76
collection, 24, 38–56, 124–26, 164–66, 225–26, 307–8. *See also* recollecting
   role of reader(s) in, 40–42
"Come see!" 85, 113, 117–18, 120, 142–45, 152, 169–70, 188, 244, 253, 268, 316. *See also* authority: scholastic vs. visionary
contextual interpretation *(peshat)*, 264–80, 283–90, 292, 294–96, 309
cosmology, 6, 55, 71–76
Cydnus, 205

Daniel (biblical book), 62, 131
Delattre, Charles, 207
demons, 72, 286–94, 377–82. *See also* Lilith
digressions, 55, 60–61, 82, 125–27, 129, 164–65, 187, 280–81
Diodorus Siculus, 202
dreams, 131, 273, 276–79, 284, 309, 379
dung, 62, 152, 154, 157–58, 160, 251, 316, 374

exile, 63, 218, 235, 301–3, 384–86

Feldman, Louis, 180
Fire (primordial/cosmological element), 71, 75, 96–98, 108–11, 120, 138, 185. *See also* white shoot of flame
fish, giant, 4–7, 78, 80–81, 133, 137, 140–41, 146–47, 150–51, 163–64, 267–68, 316–18
Fishbane, Michael, 55, 76–77
folklore, 24, 50, 60, 65–70, 78, 180, 210
Fort of Hagrunya, 68, 142, 167–69, 188, 316
Fränkel, Jonah, 15–17, 132, 149, 257
Friedman, Shamma, 18, 19–20n47, 142, 256
Frim, Daniel, 69–70
frog, giant, 68, 142, 151, 167–69, 259, 261–62, 267, 316
Fuchs, Uzziel, 134, 371–75

Gabriel (angel), 74, 78, 236, 333, 335
gaps, interpretive, 43, 60, 77, 275–76, 280, 285–86, 291, 294–96, 307
gazelle, giant, 61–62, 130n379, 152, 157, 167, 251, 316
Geertz, Clifford, 182
geese, 153, 269–84, 319–20
Gehinnom, 148, 198–99, 214, 290
genre, 13, 55–82, 121, 186, 210–11, 307–8
   role of in creating meaning, 57–58, 61–62, 65, 69–70, 81–82
genres of the tales:
   Adventure, 9, 41, 132–33, 141, 144, 194
   Apocalyptic, 62–65, 131
   Exegesis, 13, 55, 57–58, 76–81, 120
   Maritime/Nautical, 69
   Myth, 13, 55, 57–58, 70–76, 120
   Parody, 72
   Satire, 72
   Tall Tale, 65–70
   Tractate *(massekhet)*, 59
   Visions, 59–62, 132–33, 141, 144
   Wonders, 13, 59–62
Gershom (Rabbenu), 118, 171, 375
Getz, Elyaqum, 264, 285–96, 377–82
Glory, divine, 74–76, 78, 114, 116, 120, 232
glosses, 10, 59–61, 77, 79, 81, 128, 134, 205–9, 219–20, 234, 237, 286–87
Gra (Vilna Gaon), 264, 296–300, 302–5, 309, 383–86
Greek culture, Jewish appropriation of, 180–86, 210
Greek wonder writing, 56, 184–223
   Alexander Romance, 186, 197–212, 219, 222, 308, 371, 375
   history and ethnography, 186–93, 210, 222, 308
   paradoxography, 185–86, 193–97, 203–5, 207, 210, 213, 222, 308
Gribetz, Sarit Kattan, 20

halakhah, 126–27, 257, 261
Halivni, David Weiss, 18
Hall, Jonathan, 183

Hebrew, 62, 74, 130–31, 173, 239–41
  use of vs. Aramaic, 130n380, 130–31n381, 240, 346n125, 350n224, 360n469, 363n521
Heinemann, Isaak, 17–18
Herodotus, 189–93, 204–6, 210–11, 213–14
Hesiod, 125–26, 129
Homer 25, 126, 177, 217
Hormiz, 72, 83–85, 91–95, 105, 119, 136–37, 150, 152–53, 286, 288–89, 291, 295, 302, 315, 377, 379
horseman, 5–6, 78, 85, 94, 137, 141, 290, 315, 377, 380–81
humor, 67–68, 210
hyperbole, 5, 34, 67, 84, 150–51, 168, 178–79, 265, 308

idolatry (*'avodah zarah*), 181
"If I hadn't been there/seen it, I wouldn't have believed it," 68, 134, 142–43, 170, 216, 221, 242–43, 249, 369. *See also* authority: scholastic vs. visionary
"I myself have seen," 29, 68, 84, 132, 139–40, 142, 152, 167, 169, 187–89, 243–44, 247, 249–52, 315–16, 338, 379. *See also* authority: scholastic vs. visionary
inertia, role of in collection and canon, 47–50, 52–53, 225–26, 256
interpolations, 39, 125, 127n373, 164, 175
interpretive community, 18, 52
intertexts, 45–47, 54, 81–82, 104, 112, 225–30, 263–64, 275–76, 280–88, 294–96, 307
intertextuality, 16–18, 42–43, 53, 59
introductory formulae, 31, 33n108, 41, 44, 123, 138–49, 166, 171–75, 187
inverted/separated *nun*, 89–90n263
Iulius Valerius, 201, 204, 207

Jacob of Serugh, 8n13, 219
Jacobs, Irving, 73–76
Jerusalem, 75–76, 78, 221, 248–49
  Heavenly, 228–29, 231–37, 242, 246–47, 251–52, 254, 334–39

Jordan River, 62, 152, 157, 188, 196, 251, 316, 331–32, 374

kabbalah, 56, 289, 294, 298, 300, 302–3, 309, 379. *See also* Ari; Zohar
keywords, 78, 227, 229–30, 234–36, 241–58, 264, 278–79, 303–4
Khusro, 177–79
Kiperwasser, Reuven, 71–72
Ktēsiphōn, 177–78

Land, Dry (primordial/cosmological element), 6–7, 95, 117–18, 137, 297, 300. *See also* Sea (primordial/cosmological element)
law *(halakhah)*, 126–27, 257, 261
Leviathan, 60–61, 70, 74, 77–80, 130n379, 137, 173, 208–9, 228, 266, 326, 328, 330-33
  flesh of, 230, 234, 333, 367
  skin of, 75, 228, 231–33, 246, 266, 334, 367
Lieberman, Saul, 1, 180
Lilith, 288n820, 289, 291, 293–94, 378–79. *See also* demons
literary language, 43, 46–47, 50–52, 124–25, 154, 165, 192, 209–10, 266–67, 300
literary theory, 3, 13, 21
Lucian, 200, 213–15, 217–18

magic, 69, 97–98, 101, 105–6, 109, 113, 116, 231, 238
Maharsha, 50, 264, 269, 272–73, 275–85, 287, 292, 294–95
Mahoza, 136, 188, 286, 290, 315, 377, 379–80
manuscripts, variations of the tales among, 132, 137n408, 140–46, 149, 151, 153–54
Marincola, John, 189
Messiah, 270–71
metamorphic poetics, 137–38, 172n488, 196, 268
Michael (angel), 236, 335
midrash, 53–56, 82, 86–93, 96, 101–7, 109, 113–17, 119–21, 228–29, 239, 264, 275–84, 292, 294–300, 307–9

Subjects

Mishnah, 11, 35, 47–48, 59–60, 127–28, 262
moral lessons, 15, 265, 269, 275–78, 280, 285–86, 288–90, 295
Moses, 100–102, 109, 112–17, 148, 199, 214–15, 235, 324, 336]
   staff of, 96–97, 99, 111–16
mules, 92, 150, 287, 291–92, 315, 377, 318

Name(s), divine, 94–95, 97, 99–102, 105–7, 112–14, 120, 297, 300, 303–5, 314, 385
narrator, 5–7, 9, 15–16, 22, 139, 146, 161, 189, 211, 223. *See also* teller
   reliability of, 4–6, 9, 28, 68, 187, 218, 307
Neusner, Jacob, 180
New Criticism, 16
Nile, 102, 105, 189–90
novel (classical Greek), 186, 211–13, 215, 218, 308

oral-literary traditions, 13, 24–26, 46, 76, 87, 132, 140, 144–45, 149, 163–64, 166, 169–70, 175–76, 188, 226–27
oral performance, 41, 124–25, 160, 163–64. *See also* poetry: soundplay
Oral Torah, 221, 228–29, 239, 243–44, 247, 250
oral transmission, 22, 25, 145

Palaiphatus, 207
parable (*mashal*), 10, 51, 113–17, 187, 261, 291
paradoxography. *See under* Greek wonder writing
parasang (mile), 5, 129–30n379, 151–52, 157–62, 167, 246–47, 251–54, 267, 313, 316, 318, 321, 326, 338
parody, 63–65, 71, 83n241, 131, 213–15, 217
Pausanias, 191n556, 200, 205–6
pearls, 72, 221–22, 237–38, 326, 335, 369
peroration (*hatimah*), 228, 252
peshat, 264–80, 283–90, 292, 294–96, 309

Pesiqta de Rab Kahana, 227, 229, 233, 236–43, 245
pilpul, 273n786, 281–83, 299n856
plural canonicity, 50, 54, 225–26, 281, 305. *See also* canon
Plutarch, 212
poetry, 17, 56, 92, 94–96, 101–2, 105, 117–18, 120–21, 125–26, 132, 137–38, 149, 151, 153–66, 196, 266
   connections between tales formed by, 159–63
   meter/rhythm, 41, 157–58, 162–63
   repetition, 5, 22, 41, 46, 77, 148–57, 159, 164–66, 170, 249
   rhyme, 155–58
   scalar use of, 157–61, 163
   soundplay, 149, 151, 154–65, 238n675, 369n17
   stress, 125, 155–59, 162–65
   wordplay, 127, 165, 238n675
post-structuralism, 17
prayer shawl (*tekhelet*), 73, 167, 217–18, 244n697, 322, 327
priestly crown (*tsits*), 100–102

Qedusha desidra, 301–2, 304, 386
Qorah, 29, 148, 198–99, 214–15, 219, 323
Quintus Curtius Rufus, 202–3

Rashbam, 60, 264–72, 280, 286–87, 289–90, 295, 375, 377
Rashi, 265, 278, 293, 304, 379, 381
Ravnag River, 92, 150, 188, 315
reader, 11–24, 42–43, 50–56
   creativity of, 3, 13, 17, 23–24, 42, 50, 60, 62, 65, 76, 78, 82, 226, 230, 292
   hypothetical, 5
   idealized, 65
   impact of genre on, 57–58
   implied, 11, 21–22, 61, 86, 123, 257n736, 278, 295
   named, 11
   rabbinic, 20–21, 25, 37, 61–62, 64, 68–69, 86, 103–5, 207
reading tradition, 45–47, 50–53, 60, 67, 121, 123–24
recollecting, 14, 38–43, 47–48, 50, 52–53, 56, 124, 127, 164, 186–87,

222, 225, 244, 263–65, 285, 308. *See also* collection
"recounts"/"recounted", 44, 80, 133, 139–40, 172, 187, 253, 297, 313–14, 325–28
Red Sea, parting of, 88, 96–99, 104–5, 111–17, 302. *See also* Burning Bush
religion, 17–18, 62, 62–63n170, 103–4
remarks, 133–35, 139–46, 164–71, 174–76
　anonymous, 133–34, 142–43, 166–70
　attributed, 133–35, 139, 141, 143, 146, 165–66, 168, 171
　re-revelation, 103–5, 107, 111, 113, 116–21, 124, 303–4
responsa, 371–75
Rosen-Zvi, Ishay, 104
Rubenstein, Jeffery, 173
Ruzer, Serge, 72

Saperstein, Marc, 262
Sasanian empire, 70, 83–85, 177–80, 182
satire, 72, 158, 165
Schwartz, Seth, 182
scorpions, 63, 199, 235, 323, 374
scribes, 3, 5n8, 27n74, 89–91, 89–90n263, 125, 132, 137n408, 144–45, 149, 164, 166, 167n473
Sea (primordial/cosmological element), 6–7, 94–95, 99, 105, 109, 113–16, 297, 300, 302. *See also* Land, Dry (primordial/cosmological element); settings, Sea
　YHWH's battle with, 86–87, 96, 100–112, 119–20, 124, 228, 297, 300, 302–3. *See also* Leviathan; sea-serpents
sea-serpents, 60–62, 72, 137, 327, 330
seminal emissions, 288–91, 293–94, 378–82
Septimus, Bernard, 167n473
Septimus, Zvi, 256, 257n736
settings, 9, 135–38, 164, 166, 171, 174, 188
　Air, 137, 152–53, 164–65
　cosmological extremes, 135–36, 151–52, 185, 188, 194–96, 208, 212, 215, 253

Desert, 41, 135–37, 148, 151–52, 164–65, 196, 270, 272, 276, 278–80
　Sea, 41, 135–37, 152–53, 164, 171–72, 196, 208
Shapira, Dan, 72
Shema, 291, 378–80, 382
Shevet Yehudah, 259
Shinan, Avigdor, 110
Sinai, Mount, 63, 107, 119, 188, 199, 235, 322, 374
Solinus, 204–6, 214
Song at the Sea, 107, 304
source criticism, 19, 58, 65
Stammaim, 18–20, 22, 54, 59, 145, 167–68, 175
Stein, Dina, 55, 63, 82
Stein, Edmund, 228
Stemberger, Günter, 62–64, 67, 129–31, 135–36, 171
Sternberg, Meir, 193, 213
Strabo, 212
strangeness ("nonsense"), 1, 6, 18, 37–38, 41–43, 49–50, 52, 59, 79, 82, 123–24, 186, 194, 220, 263–64, 266, 297, 308–9
structuralism, 23, 73
syntax, 12, 133, 154, 265, 287, 294, 309
Syriac, 44, 44n134, 66n185, 99n295, 238n675, 242, 242n692. *See also* Christianity, Syriac

Tabor, Mount, 136, 152, 157–58, 167, 251, 316
tale, 24–27, 50–56, 307–9
Talmudization, 48–50, 54, 59n153, 76, 79, 186, 193, 207–9, 211, 220, 222–23, 256
teller, 27–38, 43–47, 50–52, 54, 86, 139, 141, 144–46, 186–93, 210–11, 307. *See also* narrator
　authority of, 189–91, 211, 215–18, 223
telling, 3, 43–47, 50–55, 124–25, 307–8
Tetragrammaton. *See* Name(s), divine
text, 11, 13–15
Thorpe, Samuel, 70–71
Tiamat, 87. *See also* Sea (primordial/cosmological element)

Torah, 109, 148, 181, 199, 214–15, 219, 223, 228, 239, 281, 305, 324, 369, 382
   Oral, 221, 228–29, 239, 243–44, 247, 250
transmission, textual, 19, 36, 48–49, 52–53, 159, 166, 176, 215, 260
   oral, 22, 25, 145
tree, giant, 68, 136, 142–43, 145, 169–70, 188, 267–69, 316

understory, 87–94, 96, 102–4, 112–13, 119–21, 264, 297–304
unreliable narrator. *See* narrator, reliability of
Uranius (Byzantine diplomat), 177–79

vows, 63–64, 218

Weiss, Avraham, 59–61
white shoot of flame, 96–100, 102, 105, 109–11, 120, 297, 300, 302, 314, 383. *See also* Fire (primordial/cosmological element)
Wisdom, 273–84
wobbly binaries, 138, 154, 165–66, 196
Wollenberg, Rebecca, 21

Yassif, Eli, 67–68

ziz, 36n118, 67, 130n379, 191, 209, 319. *See also* bird, giant
Zohar, 69, 288–89, 300, 378, 381–82. *See also* Ari; kabbalah
Zoroastrianism, 38, 70–72, 83, 103–4, 121, 289. See also *Bundahišn*

www.ingramcontent.com/pod-product-compliance
Lightning Source LLC
Chambersburg PA
CBHW021927290426
44108CB00012B/745